DATE DUE			
Apr 3 7			

GAYLORD M-2   PRINTED IN U.S.A.

INDIA

This volume forms part of a series on industry and trade in some developing countries edited by Ian Little, Tibor Scitovsky, and Maurice Scott. The others in the series are on Brazil, Mexico, Pakistan, the Philippines, and Taiwan (the last two in one volume). There is also a comparative volume by the editors.

INDUSTRY AND TRADE
IN SOME DEVELOPING COUNTRIES

INDIA
Planning for Industrialization
Industrialization and Trade Policies since 1951

JAGDISH N. BHAGWATI
Professor of Economics, Massachusetts Institute of Technology

and

PADMA DESAI
Research Associate, M.I.T. Center for International Studies
and Harvard Russian Research Center

Published on behalf of the
Development Centre of the
ORGANIZATION FOR ECONOMIC
CO-OPERATION AND DEVELOPMENT
PARIS
by
OXFORD UNIVERSITY PRESS
LONDON   NEW YORK   BOMBAY
1970

Oxford University Press, Ely House, London W. I

GLASGOW NEW YORK TORONTO MELBOURNE WELLINGTON
CAPE TOWN SALISBURY IBADAN NAIROBI DAR ES SALAAM LUSAKA ADDIS ABABA
BOMBAY CALCUTTA MADRAS KARACHI LAHORE DACCA
KUALA LUMPUR SINGAPORE HONG KONG TOKYO

Hardback edition SBN 19 215326 9
Paperback edition SBN 19 215334 X

338.9
B46i
73901
march, 1971

*Printed in Great Britain
by Richard Clay (The Chaucer Press), Ltd.,
Bungay, Suffolk*

For
Pitambar Pant
I. G. Patel
K. N. Raj
V. K. Ramaswami

Contents

List of Tables

Preface

IN writing a scholarly book, on a major subject such as India's experience with industrialization, we expected to run into several difficulties: and we did, in ample measure.

Much of the problem arises from the difficulty of getting information in a usable form. This reflects, in turn, the still inadequate character of empirical research in India: data improve when there is a demand for them. We have thus had to spend an enormous amount of time getting together quite elementary data, requiring adjustments in classifications, etc. An excellent example of these problems is Chapter 5, where we decided to put together data on imports, production, exports, taxes, etc., on a comparable commodity classification for four years: 1951, 1957, 1961, and 1963 (the last year for which we could do this). The purpose was to provide some solid statistical basis for our policy discussions. The astonishing thing was that, while several input–output tables had been constructed in India in the past few years, for different years, they were not on a comparable basis and we just had to carry through our work as if from scratch. This work alone took four months of our time, despite a conscientious research assistant and access to statistician friends who knew the sources well.

But the substantial part of our problems must be traced to the general paucity of analytical–empirical research in India. We just do not have the tradition of young research students and research workers in official and other institutions, steadily turning up analytical information on the working of the economy. We have had our version of institutionalists; and now we have a growing number of high-powered theorists whose interest in the Indian economy is largely casual (and, in some cases where public attention and prominence are sought by making policy pronouncements without even cursory analysis, even counter-productive).

Anyone writing a book on the large subject that we have picked is thus handicapped seriously: for it is not possible, in the Indian context, to draw freely on the research of other economists. Hence we have often felt the need to come to judgements on issues where the existing work was not fully decisive, even as economic analysis goes.

On the other hand, we have felt it easier to write on this broad scale because we have lived through, and discussed over the years, several of the issues that are raised in this volume. It has been possible for us, in consequence, to go to the important and relevant sources quickly; and to arrive at judgements in which we have greater confidence than would have been possible if our interest in Indian economic performance and policies had been contemporaneous with the actual work on the book over an eighteen-month period.

We have also been fortunate in having a number of economist and planner friends whose insights, and willingness to share them with us, have helped us to improve our analysis considerably. In particular, we have decided to dedicate this book to four friends, whose involvement in Indian economic policy, planning, and evaluation, has been notable through the last decade. They are: K. N. Raj, our eminent colleague at the Delhi School of Economics; I. G. Patel, who has been Chief Economic Adviser to the Ministry of Finance and is now Special Secretary in that Ministry; the late V. K. Ramaswami, who was Chief Economic Adviser; and Pitambar Pant, former chief of the Perspective Planning Division (Planning Commission) and present Member of the Planning Commission. We have also learnt a great deal from other friends: T. N. Srinivasan, B. S. Minhas, S. Guhan, P. N. Dhar, Sukhamoy Chakravarty, Manu Shroff, Daniel Thorner, K. G. Vaidya, Ashish Chakravarty, Vinod Parkash, K. Sundaram, J. Krishnamurty, Sharad Marathe, A. M. Khusro, D. T. Lakdawala, Dharm Narain, Manmohan Singh, R. K. Hazari, A. Vaidyanathan, R. Honavar, and Alan Manne. The comments of Maurice Scott and Ian Little, on successive drafts of the manuscript, have also been extremely valuable. We profited from general discussion at the Bellagio Conference, in March 1968, when the participants in the O.E.C.D. project presented their work-in-progress. We recall, in particular, the comments of Max Corden, Albert Hirschman, Paul Streeten, and Tibor Scitovsky.

We would like to thank especially V. R. Panchamukhi who has shared in the writing of Chapter 17 on effective rates of protection: without his unstinting interest, this chapter could not have been completed on time. We have also been assisted immeasurably by our former student, Jamuna Krishnaswami, who was an extremely conscientious, willing, and imaginative research assistant to us throughout the eighteen-month period. Our thanks are also due to a number of officials in the different Ministries of the Government of India, especially in the Ministries of Finance (Department of Economic Affairs), Commerce and Industry, and International Trade, who were helpful in getting at relevant data sources and, at times, even compiled the necessary information themselves at our request.

We would also like to record our thanks, for financing research time spent partly on this book, to the International Economics Workshop at Columbia University, New York, and the M.I.T. Center for International Studies.

Finally, we wish to thank C. Devarajan, Louise Woodland, and Katherine LaPerche, who have cheerfully typed different parts of this book.

Cambridge, Massachusetts　　　　Jagdish N. Bhagwati
December 1968　　　　　　　　　　Padma Desai

Selected important dates

I. *Constitutional events*

(*a*) Independence Day, 15 August, 1947
(*b*) Republic Day, 26 January, 1950

II. *India's Prime Ministers*

(*a*) Nehru, 15 August, 1947–27 May, 1964
(*b*) Interim (Nanda), 27 May 1964–9 June 1964
(*c*) Shastri, 9 June 1964–11 January 1966
(*d*) Interim (Nanda), 11 January 1966–24 January 1966
(*e*) Mrs. Gandhi, 24 January 1966–

III. *Wars*

(*a*) Indo-Chinese Conflict, 20 October 1962–21 November 1962
(*b*) Indo-Pakistan Conflict, 5 August 1965–23 September 1965

IV. *General Elections* [1]

(*a*) First General Election, October 1951
(*b*) Second General Election, 24 February 1957
(*c*) Third General Election, 16 February 1962
(*d*) Fourth General Election, 15 February 1967

---

[1] Opening dates are stated here. The first election ended in February 1952.
B

ECONOMIC

V. *Plans* [2]

(*a*) First Five-Year Plan, (1 April 1951 to 31 March 1956), December 1952

(*b*) Second Five-Year Plan (1 April 1956 to 31 March 1961), 15 May 1956

(*c*) Third Five-Year Plan (1 April 1961 to 31 March 1966), August 1961

(*d*) Interim–Annual Plans (1 April 1966 to 31 March 1969)

(*e*) Fourth Five-Year Plan, (1 April 1969 to 31 March 1974), not yet released

VI. *Industrial Policy*

(*a*) First Industrial Policy Resolution, 6 April 1948

(*b*) Second Industrial Policy Resolution, 30 April 1956

VII. *Devaluations* [3]

(*a*) 1949 Devaluation (Approx. 31 per cent), 20 September 1949

(*b*) 1966 Devaluation (Approx. 37 per cent), 5 June 1966

VIII. *Aid*

(*a*) Formation of the Aid-India Consortium, 1958

IX. *Planning: Miscellaneous*

(*a*) Formation of the Planning Commission, March 1950

(*b*) Publication of:

(i) Professor Mahalanobis' Second Plan Frame, March 1955

(ii) Draft Outline of Second Five-Year Plan, February 1956

(iii) Draft Outline of Third Five-Year Plan, June 1960

(iv) First Draft Outline of Fourth Plan (abortive), August 1966

---

[2] The dates listed relate to the formal adoption of the Plans.

[3] The magnitudes of the devaluations are calculated as changes in rupees per U.S. dollar as a percentage of the new rate.

Indian Terms and Units

Lok Sabha: Indian Parliament
1 crore: 10 million
1 lakh: 100,000

Abbreviations Frequently Used

A.S.I.	Annual Survey of Industry
A.U.	Actual User (Import) Licences
C.C.I. & E.	Chief Controller of Imports and Exports
C.G.	Capital Goods (Import) Licences
C.G.C.	Capital Goods (Import) Control
C.M.I.	Census of Manufacturing Industry
D.A.C.	Development Assistance Committee
D.G.T.D.	Directorate General of Technical Development
D.L.F.	Development Loan Fund
E.I.	Established Importer Licences
E.P.	Export Promotion (Import) Licences
E.P.C.	Export Promotion Council
G.A.T.T.	General Agreement of Tariffs and Trade
G.O.I.	Government of India
I.B.R.D.	International Bank for Reconstruction and Development (World Bank)
I.C.T.	Indian Customs Tariff
I. & S.C.	Iron and Steel Controller
I.T.C.	Indian Trade Classification
J.C.C.I.E.	Joint Chief Controller of Imports and Exports
N.D.C.	National Development Council
N.D.R.	National Defence Remittance

P.L. 480	Public Law 480
R.B.I.	Reserve Bank of India
P.P.D.	Perspective Planning Division, Planning Commission
S.I.T.C.	Standard International Trade Classification
S.S.M.I.	Sample Survey of Manufacturing Industries
S.T.C.	State Trading Corporation
T.C.A.	Technical Cooperation Agency
U.S.A.I.D.	United States Agency for International Development

Note. Full bibliographical details of all publications referred to in the notes are given in the Bibliography at the end of the book.

I

Introduction

THE Indian experience with industrialization in the two decades since Independence in 1947 has evoked reactions which appear to have regressed from great optimism to exaggerated despair. The turning-point seems to have come around the end of India's Third Plan (1961–6), the gloom deepening during two years of devastating droughts (1965 and 1966) and leaving its impact on overall assessments of Indian economic performance.[1]

The reasons for this change in evaluations are complex. They are to be traced to essentially three different types of factors:

(1) The performance of the Indian economy, judged by the familiar and traditional indices (such as rate of growth of national income) has undoubtedly decelerated in the years since 1963/4, thus raising inevitable doubts as to the capacity of the economy and the planners to push the performance levels back to their more satisfactory, if not impressive, levels in the years between 1951 and 1964.

(2) These objective facts have further been overlaid by political overtones which have never been far removed from the (foreign) evaluation of Indian economic growth. Just as the early growth was judged with an enthusiasm somewhat disproportionate to reality, because the reference point chosen was Communist

---

[1] Among the optimistic assessments, must be counted John P. Lewis's *Quiet Crisis in India*, which was written during 1961–2 after a field-trip to India. The title is deceptive, the book being aimed at the American public and designed to warn them of the numerous difficulties, political and sociological, which could overwhelm a remarkable experiment in democratic acceleration of economic development if U.S. foreign aid and support for India's Third Plan was not forthcoming. For the later assessments, which are more critical of Indian policies, we must turn primarily to unpublished documents of the donor agencies and the I.B.R.D. (World Bank) which has technically serviced the Aid-India Consortium of the major donor countries.

China,[1] the later deceleration has tended to be judged too harshly because the reference point chosen has been Pakistan. Whereas, in the earlier case, (Indian) 'democracy' was being weighed against (Chinese) 'totalitarian' techniques, the later years have been characterized by the weighing of (Indian) 'socialism' against (Pakistani) 'pragmatism' in the sense of reliance on the market and the ability to eschew issues such as land reform.[2] Here is undoubtedly part of the explanation of the frequent inability to distinguish between the temporary disasters (such as two severe agricultural droughts in 1965 and 1966) and long-term decelerative factors, if any.[3]

(3) Finally, there has been a change in the standards by which economic performance itself has come to be measured. In a situation where the traditional indices have been doing tolerably well, it is customary for economists to be somewhat complacent. However, when these indices show deceleration and a possibly impending disaster, economists have a tendency to look closer and see if the economic *policies* pursued look sensible. It has turned out that, when the Indian policies (in industrial, foreign exchange, and other sectors) have been examined in depth, the results have been seriously disturbing. The frequently extreme

[1] This comes through even in a perceptive book such as John Lewis, op. cit. (especially pp. 6 and 7), and in the explicit comparisons between Chinese and Indian performances in W. Malenbaum, 'India and China: Development Contrasts', *Journal of Political Economy*, Vol. 64, February 1956, pp. 1–24, and 'India and China: Contrasts in Development Performance', *American Economic Review*, Vol. 49, June 1959, pp. 284–309.

[2] The relative assessments of the performances of India and Pakistan have also been biased, in part, by the fact that a readier acceptance of advice inevitably influences the assessments of the advisers. Precisely because Pakistan has had a 'basic' democracy, with President Ayub Khan's powers (until very recently) *de facto* paramount, and because the local expertise has been fairly limited, it has been easier for the foreign technocrats to get their advice accepted in Pakistan than in India where there are several local economists of better quality than the technocrats sent by official agencies, whether bilateral or multilateral, and where the possibility of getting acceptance of economic policy changes is often constrained in any case by the complexities of the political situation which have freer play in India's democratic system.

[3] The recent experience in India has also been affected significantly by two wars: with China, over the northern border in late 1962, and with Pakistan, on the western sector in late 1965. These have played a major role in Indian economic performance by (for example) raising the percentage of resources allocated to defence. A proper evaluation of these later years would, therefore, require us to separate out the enduring effects of these wars from the transitory ones: the future may thus not be as bad as the present.

character of the disenchantment with India's planners is thus to be attributed partly to the fact that the shift of attention to these policies has come about somewhat abruptly. It is not that these policies have changed significantly over time, but just that the economists have suddenly realized their importance for performance, now that performance appears to have been lagging.

In fact, India's performance has been both remarkable and disappointing. Among her notable achievements, India can point to an impressive and reasonably steady rate of growth of G.N.P. at nearly 4 per cent per annum over practically three Five-Year Plans. As Max Millikan has aptly observed:

> The Indian performance was slightly below the average for the non-communist underdeveloped world, which for the decade 1955–1965 was around 4·5 per cent, and it was significantly below the performance of such outstanding successes as Mexico, Taiwan, Israel and, more recently, South Korea. But the Indian growth rate of nearly 4 per cent in this period represents a notable acceleration over the annual growth rate of British India for the first half of the twentieth century, which has been estimated at no more than 1 per cent, and compares very favorably with the growth rates of the presently advanced countries during their earlier development history.[1]

At the same time, governmental efforts have succeeded in steadily raising the proportion of taxes and domestic savings to G.N.P., thereby contributing to the programmes of accelerated development.

By such indices, India compares favourably with most other developing countries. Admittedly it has had the good fortune of inheriting an efficient civil service from the British (Chapter 8), a historically evolved entrepreneurial class and industrial structure (Chapters 2 and 3), and a fair supply of educated citizens (Chapter 3): all of which factors placed India at a special advantage compared to many other developing countries, especially of Africa.

On the other hand, India has been handicapped in its economic performance by other factors.

(1) Its vast size, with the attendant federal structure, has imposed inefficiencies resulting from Centre-State and inter-State

---

[1] 'India in Transition: Economic Development: Performance and Prospects', *Foreign Affairs*, April 1968, p. 532. This view has been expressed by other observers as well: for detailed treatment, see Chapter 4.

conflicts of interests (Chapter 7). These inefficiencies have been further accentuated by the democratic framework within which India has operated since its independence in 1947.[1] (2) The Indian Government's focus on political questions, relating to concentration of economic power for example (contributing to the deliberate expansion of the public sector, as described by us in Chapter 9, and the pattern of industrial licensing as described by us in Chapter 13), has occasionally resulted in conflicts with requirements of economic efficiency. (3) Further, the size of the country has meant that the considerable sums of foreign aid that India has received have none the less amounted to a significantly lower proportion of her G.N.P. than in the case of several developing countries (such as Taiwan and Israel) which have registered superior performance (Chapter 10). A similar observation applies also to private foreign investment where, even though the Indian Government's policy was not entirely an open-door variety (Chapter 11), it is impossible to conceive of private foreign investment entering the economy at anywhere close to the percentage-of-G.N.P. level it has been in some of the 'star' developing countries (such as South Korea, Taiwan, and Israel).

On balance, when some judgement is reached on the relative weights of these different, favourable and adverse, factors on the Indian scene, it appears to us that the Indian economic performance has been fairly impressive indeed.

Yet it has its disappointing facets: and it is on these that much of our study concentrates. For, while India grew at a fairly steady rate, and its performance in raising domestic savings is remarkable indeed, the mix of economic policies which governed the productivity of the increasing investments appears to have been quite unfortunate.

As we shall discuss in Chapter 6, the overall approach to economic development involved a planning framework within which certain basic decisions were taken. These related to the

[1] Millikan, op. cit., has made the following interesting comment, concerning the relationship of size to performance: 'Turning to characteristics of the Indian economy . . . the first is the sheer size and diversity of the country. In population it is equivalent to about six Brazils, nine Nigerias, fifteen Egypts or more than fifty Kenyas, and there is added to the population each year the equivalent of an Australia or a Peru. If it were broken into twenty good-sized normal countries, we would expect a fairly wide range of performance among them. To hope for an average equal to that of one of the small star performers is quite unrealistic.'

level of foreign aid, domestic savings, and taxation; and the level of investment expenditure, and its breakdown by major sectors (including agriculture and industry, and by 'heavy' and other industry in turn).

There is room to argue, and economists notoriously find it difficult to achieve consensus, whether (i) India planned unrealistically in terms of its overall investment, leaning continually towards bigger plans than could be carried out, (ii) the proportion of investment and current (developmental) expenditure in agriculture was on the low side, and (iii) the investment allotted, within industry, to 'heavy' industry (other than steel) could not have been reduced. Our judgements on these issues are that these were indeed the weaknesses of the overall planning decisions (Chapter 6).

But the major weaknesses lay rather in the economic policies which attended upon the planned targets and objectives. Planning in India was to grow sophisticated over time, in its techniques of putting targets together and its extension to 'perspective planning'.[1] But while the in-depth planning improved, in the sense of the (Leontief-type) models including larger numbers of sectors and being fed with improving data, the impact of this was to be seen nowhere in matching improvements in economic policies designed to accelerate the planned development.

More specifically, Indian economic policy suffered from a paradox of inadequate *and* excessive attention to detail. The inadequacy related to failure to work out in-depth programmes: major irrigation projects would yield low returns because the feeder-channels to take water to the fields had not been thought about; extension workers did not have adequate training to handle the complex task of initiating and guiding the agricultural revolution implicit in the planned rates of agricultural growth; and so on. This type of weakness in Indian planning has been variously described as 'lack of organization' and 'inadequate implementation'. In part, it is merely a symptom of the attitudes and habits which contribute to underdevelopment or, at any rate, accompany it. To some degree, however, it reflects a certain lack of empiricism

---

[1] For a detailed, critical review of the evolution of planning techniques in India, see J. Bhagwati and S. Chakravarty, *Contributions to Indian Economic Analysis: A Survey*, American Economic Association, Supplement to *American Economic Review*, September 1969, Section I.

in the Indian make-up: which typically leads to intentions being confused with action.[1]

But there were also failures arising from excessive attention to detail: and these were to be embodied mainly in the proliferation of ill-conceived direct and physical controls over industrial investments (down to product level) and foreign trade. The result, as we seek to document and demonstrate in Chapters 12–21, was the operation of the economy within a wholly inefficient framework, characterized by a plethora of restrictions and regulations which had little economic rationale. The adverse impact of such an economic régime on the productivity of the private sector was to be matched by the physical and non-economic character of the planning and running of the public sector industrial investments (Chapter 9) which were to absorb a major share of the investment in the (organized) industrial sector during 1951–66.

In this study, we restrict our detailed analysis to India's trade and industrial policies, while eschewing equally systematic analysis of areas such as population control and agricultural development.[2] As the reader will appreciate, the resulting canvas is still very large: and we do not expect our study to be the last word on this topic, although it does represent the first in-depth study of the major issues in this area.

Our thesis is, in essence, that Indian planning, in the area of trade and industrial policies, fell into the trap of excessively detailed, physical-targets-oriented planning, especially since 1956/7 when the Second Five-Year Plan began.

We can conceive of 'pre-take-off' countries, particularly in parts of Africa, where the problems of initiating and promoting economic development are almost outside the traditional, economic framework of analysis: there are neither the agents (entrepreneurs, either in the private or in the public sector) to make rational decisions from among alternative projects, or to respond to a

---

[1] V. S. Naipaul, in his vitriolic record of an Indian visit, *An Area of Darkness*, has described his impatience with 'symbolic action' as when the sweeper at his Delhi hotel leaves the floor dirtier after sweeping than before.

[2] A valuable reference for brief reviews of these areas is Paul Streeten and Michael Lipton (eds.) *The Crisis of Indian Planning*. For an excellent example of the model-building approach to the broader questions of balances between sectors such as 'agriculture' and 'industry', see R. S. Eckaus and Kirit Parikh, *Planning for Growth:* this study contains empirical experiments, using a multi-sector dynamic model, relating to India's Third and Fourth Plans.

framework of 'correct' economic policies, nor are there the facts to make choices from. In these areas it would make little sense to argue for an economic régime aimed at making non-existent (economic) agents take socially productive decisions or to suggest that the public sector projects be chosen only after careful cost–benefit analysis of blueprints (which are not available) by officials (who have no education or expertise).

Fortunately, when Indian planning efforts began in 1950/1 and especially by 1956/7, India had already experienced nearly a century of industrial expansion, growth of industrial entrepreneurship, social overheads, and financial institutions (Chapters 2 and 3). While this had made little impact on the occupational and output structure, the sheer growth in the size of the modern, factory sector was significant. At the same time, India had inherited from the British an efficient civil service and traditions of responsible administration. There was thus a remarkable endowment of agents and institutions for making rational economic decisions in response to a set of economic policies.

India could thus have planned for its further industrialization by exploiting these advantages, and was not constrained in quite the way that several developing countries (only beginning to embark on their industrialization) happen to be. Indian planners could thus have concentrated their planning efforts to taking certain major allocational decisions: between agriculture and industry, and between 'heavy' industry and the rest, on broad developmental-strategy grounds (of the sort we explore in Chapter 12, for example). These should then have been accompanied by the systematic devising of in-depth policies to implement these decisions efficiently: e.g. the building-up of the 'heavy industry' sector should have been attended by systematic cost–benefit analysis and choice from alternative designs, projects, and products, thus ruling out as far as possible the inefficiencies which we record in Chapter 9. The allocations of foreign exchange and 'basic' materials (such as steel) to the sectors, industries, firms, and plants *within* these broad sectors could then have been left to the market mechanism, instead of being controlled (with severely adverse impact on efficiency) rigidly and without any economic rationale. As it turned out, Indian economic policies in the industrial sector degenerated into an extravagant display of bureaucratic controls and restrictions, with these means turning into *de facto* ends. A shift towards more efficient policies was to become apparent towards the end of our period of study (1951–66), as we discuss in Chapter 23: but these delayed changes were themselves to run into difficulties which were generated in the main by the inefficient economic régime of the earlier, formative period of planning, thus underlining the moral that it is best to start from an efficient régime.

We document our thesis at length in this study. Since a major role is played in our thesis by the contention that India already had a tradition of industrialization, entrepreneurship, and financial institutions, we present these facts in Chapters 2 and 3 (Part I) with a brief review of such historical trends as are relevant to our analysis.[1] We present in Part II the major outlines of India's economic growth since Independence in 1947. Chapter 4 contains a broad analysis of indices such as G.N.P., income *per capita*, and savings rates. Chapter 5 presents the first, systematic, statistical analysis of import substitution in India during our period: this provides the statistical backdrop to our discussion of economic policies later. Part III, Chapter 6, outlines the planning framework within which the developmental process was promoted by the Government, and the policy instruments which were deployed to regulate this process.

Part IV sets out the institutional constraints and objectives which influenced the developmental process. Chapter 7 sketches the political structure which has obtained in India and interacted with her economic progress. Chapter 8 similarly discusses the state and role of the administrative structure. Chapter 9, which is a crucial element in our account of the inefficiency of the Indian economic experiment, is addressed to a full-length review of the working of the massive public sector investments in industry which India made during our period. Part V treats the important question of the role played by external resources in India's economic performance: Chapter 10 deals with foreign aid, whereas Chapter 11 considers private foreign investment.

Against this background, we then proceed to a detailed analysis of the domestic and foreign policy instruments deployed by the

[1] The tradition of economic–historical studies in India is relatively recent and this has constrained our review. Our confidence in the review, however, has been bolstered by the fact that Daniel Thorner and Tapan Raychaudhuri, two eminent Indian economic historians, have looked through our earlier drafts.

Government to regulate the economy: this, in fact, is the heart of the study. Part VI discusses the domestic policy instruments: industrial strategy in Chapter 12, industrial licensing in Chapter 13 and other industrial controls in Chapter 14. The foreign trade sector is considered in Part VII: import policy in Chapters 15 and 16; and export policy in Chapters 18, 19, and 20. Effective rates of protection are calculated and presented in Chapter 17; and the overall effective exchange rate system, resulting from the operation of the trade régime, is reviewed in Chapter 21.

This virtually completes the analysis in the volume. But we have added (Part VIII) Chapter 22 to indicate, in main outline, the shift of the Indian economy towards a 'new economic policy' near the end of our period and beyond. Part IX, Chapter 23, concludes the study with a brief restatement of our principal conclusions.[1]

---

[1] The reader should, therefore, be forewarned that we have examined India's development functionally, rather than on a Plan-by-Plan basis. For a most useful Plan-by-Plan account of the major economic developments over the three Plans, and an informed account of the major changes in the Plans as they unfolded and the processes by which these changes were formally accepted, A. H. Hanson's *The Process of Planning*, is a valuable reference.

PART I
Historical Trends

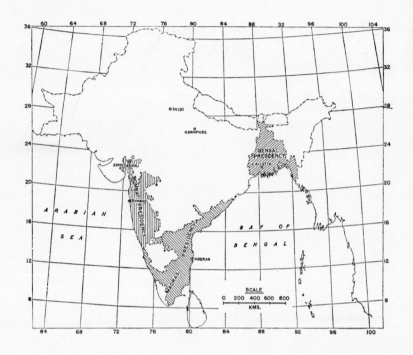

The Three Presidencies of British India: Bombay, Bengal, and Madras.

2

Industrialization and Entrepreneurship since the Eighteenth Century

THE growth and industrialization of India, in the modern period after her independence in 1947, need to be placed into a historical perspective. While, in terms of practically all conceivable economic indices, India has performed remarkably better than in the period before it (including the entire period of British rule from the eighteenth century), we need to remember that the tradition of economic growth, entrepreneurship, and industrialization, which modern India inherited, was quite impressive by contemporary standards, and this tradition certainly made the task of Indian planners considerably easier, enabling them to start building on a base of a 'semi-industrialized' system already endowed with entrepreneurial activity.[1]

In this chapter, therefore, we review sketchily the growth of indigenous enterprise and industrialization since the eighteenth century, when British political power began to consolidate itself in the Indian sub-continent.[2] In the next chapter, we detail the state of industrialization and related economic characteristics that India had attained in consequence on the eve of her independence.

I. MANUFACTURES AND ENTERPRISE BEFORE 1800

There is a widespread historical view that, prior to the nineteenth century, India was a 'great manufacturing country'.[3] During the seventeenth and eighteenth centuries, it is held that:

---

[1] Among the other advantages were the long history of educational facilities and a network of efficient administration, developed under British rule (but pre-dating it).

[2] Our review is based on currently available historical research which is not entirely satisfactory at a considerable number of points. However, the general outline that emerges seems reasonably accurate.

[3] T. Raychaudhuri, 'A Re-interpretation of Nineteenth Century Indian Eco-

C

'It would be a matter for some surprise if . . . productivity in manufacturing in a number of East European countries which have since
industrialized or in Tokugawa Japan, which had very limited foreign
trade, was higher than in the Coromandel Coast or Bengal, regions
supplying manufactured goods to an extensive overseas market . . .
India was *the* major supplier of textiles,—not just fine clothes, but every-
day wear for the masses,—to the whole of South East Asia, Iran, the
Arab Countries and East Africa. The European companies' trade
opened up fresh markets for the same commodity in Europe, West
Africa, the New World, Philippines and Japan . . . cotton textiles constituted the overwhelming bulk of India's exports . . . Raw silk, sugar
and even saltpetre,—three other major items of exports,—also do not
fit the description of primary agricultural products. The only primary
agricultural product exported in quantities was indigo,—even this
involved a certain amount of processing,—besides some rice sent to
Ceylon and, occasionally, Batavia . . . Except for an insignificant amount
of luxury goods, like richly carved swords, and occasionally, cannon,
India imported *no* manufactured metal products before the nineteenth
century. In her foreign trade, India was very much an exporter of
manufactured products and an importer of primary or intermediary
goods.[1]

Correspondingly, indigenous private entrepreneurship in India
had a historic origin:

In the 17th and 18th centuries India and China were about the only
Asian countries with a very rich merchant class trading in its own ships
with distant markets. Even in Europe, only a few countries had merchants so well provided with liquid capital and with such a wide area of
operation. Traders from [India's coastal] regions competed with the
powerful European companies in the markets of South East Asia and
towards the end of the seventeenth century reached out for new markets
in the Philippines . . . The Coromandel merchants showed a capacity for
imitative innovation by organising 'limited liability companies' to
supply the staples of export to the European factories.[2]

nomic History', *The Indian Economic and Social History Review*, V, 1, March
1968. This is a critical review of the earlier paper of Morris D. Morris in *The
Journal of Economic History*, XXIII, 4, December 1963, which attempted to
argue, among other theses, that nineteenth-century Indian growth was
'substantial' in view of the low base of the economy in 1800. Also see the
recent contributions of T. Raychaudhuri and Irfan Habib in papers read at
the 1968 International Economic History Congress held at Bloomington,
Indiana, U.S.A.

[1] Raychaudhuri, op. cit., pp. 84–5.
[2] Ibid., pp. 86–7.

II. INDIGENOUS ENTERPRISE IN THE EARLY EIGHTEENTH CENTURY

Indigenous private entrepreneurship in India thus had a historic origin, pre-dating the British period. Engaged in trade and lending activities, different business communities flourished at the time of the spread of British power in the eighteenth century.

The Shroffs and Poddars—money-changers and bill-brokers—were conspicuous through most of the century, not merely in banking but also in law, and had acquired considerable power even over currency circulation in Bengal.[1] It is noteworthy that the remarkable House of the Jagat Seths had branches in all the import trading centres of Northern India, ranging from Dacca in the east to Delhi in the west. It had been founded by a native of Marwar—from where many of the most enterprising entrepreneurs of British India were to come in the late nineteenth century.

While some of the Shroffs, notably the Jagat Seths, engaged in trade, native trade was primarily in the hands of merchants from various regions and communities. Witness the graphic description by Bolts of Bengal's trade in mid-eighteenth century:

A variety of merchants of different nations and religions, such as Cashmeerians, Multanys, Patans, Sheiks, Sunnaiasys, Poggayaks, Betteas and many others used to resort to Bengal in Caffeelahs or large parties of many thousands together with troops of oxen for the transport of goods from different parts of Hindustan.[2]

The raw silk trade, for example, was conducted by several Gujarati merchants who traded extensively with vastly distant places such as Surat, Bombay, Mirzapore, Nagpore, Poona, Multan, and Lahore. Armenian merchants, settlers in Bengal, handled trade in raw silk, cotton piecegoods, rose water, emeralds, dry fruits, salt, ginger, and spices to Surat, Bussorah, Cochin, and other places both inland and abroad.[3]

---

[1] 'The Shroffs held in their hands the bulk of the specie of the country. They had a network of houses in almost every part of the country. As they followed this trade from generation to generation, they were very subtle from long and early habit. Theirs was a close caste and their connections were very widespread.' N. K. Sinha, *The Economic History of Bengal*, Vol. I, p. 144.

[2] Quoted in Sinha, op. cit., p. 110.

[3] Sinha, op. cit., pp. 68–9 and 111–12.

III. THE EMERGENCE OF BRITISH POLITICAL POWER

The growth of British political power, concurrent with the rapid disintegration of the Mughal Empire since Clive's triumphs at Plassey in 1757, introduced a new epoch. The interplay between British and indigenous entrepreneurship, often competitive and (in the later period of British rule) at times complementary, was to dominate the scene thereafter.

British 'entrepreneurship', essentially that of the East India Company and its servants, penetrated the inland and foreign trade of the Bengal Presidency[1] under the aegis of the Company's political power, supplanting many native houses and reducing the indigenous entrepreneurs to essentially an intermediary role.

The East India Company itself engaged initially in purchases mainly through the so-called *dadni* system, under which advances were paid to merchants to enable them to relend to the weavers. The merchants were thus essentially contractors, with their contacts in different manufacturing and supplying centres. The most notable *dadni* merchants in 1751–2 in Calcutta were natives.[2] This policy was to be replaced by the agency system in 1753, under which '*Gomastas* or paid Indian agents of the Company now made their purchases under the direct supervision of the European servants of the Company'.[3] The agency system turned out to be extremely lucrative for the Company's servants who became the agents or contractors under the new arrangements. All the silk factories and several of the chief cloth centres had moreover been placed under the agency system. The effective commissions made by the agents were occasionally 'unscrupulously high'.[4] At the same time, the system permitted a remarkable

[1] The Bengal Presidency, embracing considerably more territory then than today, and representing an expanding frontier, was the focus of British expansion at that time.

[2] Sinha, op. cit., p. 6.   [3] Sinha, op. cit., p. 8.

[4] Indeed, the Directors of the East India Company were so exasperated as to write in April 1786: 'The Company's goods produced but 1s. 10d. per current rupee (in the English market) whilst private goods (handled by the Company's servants in their *private* capacity, as permitted by the Company's rules) after deducting 15 per cent netted upon an average 2s. 6d. per current rupee although our Investment was procured under every advantage that influence could give it and goods for captains and officers by an unsupported individual.' The Directors even filed suits in England against some of their employees who had been contractors! Cf. Sinha, op. cit., pp. 21–2. In this connection, Holden Furber's *John Company at Law*, dealing with the late eighteenth-century European expansion in India, is a valuable and classic source.

blending of the Company's trade and the private trade of the Company's servants, thus illegally extending to the latter the free-transit privileges which had been exacted from the native rulers by the Company for its own trade.

Both the side-stepping of native merchant houses by the agency system and the (illegally acquired) privileged position of the private trade by the Company's numerous servants *vis-à-vis* that of the native merchants encumbered by heavy transit duties spelled a setback for native enterprise after 1753. Simultaneously it heralded the emergence of a continuing involvement, outside of the East India Company, by British enterprise and entrepreneurship initially in trade and finance, and later (in the nineteenth century) in manufacture, in India. It also provided a foretaste of the attitudes of suspicion, distrust, and hostility with which indigenous enterprise was to regard the presence and expansion of British entrepreneurship in India in the nineteenth century.

IV. THE GROWTH OF AGENCY HOUSES

Concurrently with the growth of private trade by the Company's servants, there was a considerable amount of complementary as also competitive trade by the Dutch, Danish, and French traders.[1] There also was a growing number of British 'Free Merchants', who were attempting to gain a foothold in this lucrative trade. It was not uncommon for the interests of the Company's servants and of the Free Merchants to clash occasionally and, at times, to take the form of petitions by the latter to the Company.

Steadily, however, the Free Merchants entrenched themselves and were often joined by ex-servants of the Company who brought their past gains with them into their enterprise.

'Agency Houses' emerged, 'mostly run by the ex-servants of the Company who enjoyed the confidence of their successors in office and drew on their savings'. Already by 1790

There were fifteen agency houses in Calcutta, a majority of whom were British. The most prominent among them were Messrs. Fergusson, Fairlie and Company, Paxton, Cockerell and Delisle, Lambert and Ross, Colvins and Bazett, and Joseph Barretto. They controlled the country trade, financed indigo and sugar manufacture, cornered the

[1] For details, see Sinha, op. cit., Chapters III and IV. Also see A. Tripathi, *Trade and Finance in the Bengal Presidency: 1793–1833*, Chapter I.

Government contracts, ran the three banks and the four insurance companies at Calcutta and speculated in public securities. They also dealt in the homeward private trade of the commanders and officers of the Company's ships and negotiated bills and *respondentia* on the foreign companies. They had corresponding houses in London who collected their remittances and supplied them with funds. Agency was their least important business.[1]

The growth of the agency houses synchronized with the increase in abuses of the Company's servants in their private trade to a level so gross as to prompt Cornwallis to push through several reforms which dealt a death blow to their trade:

'The Collectors were forbidden to engage in private trade in 1787 and the prohibition was extended to the Revenue and the Judicial departments by 1789.' Thus, by 1788, when 'thirteen hundred Company servants in Bengal ceased their private trading following the regulation which prohibited it to all but the servants under the Board of Trade, the only competitors of the agency houses were laid low. Henceforth they dominated the scene, though still working on capital derived from the Company's servants or sometimes borrowed from the Indigenous bankers.'[2]

By the 1820s, the agency houses had already invested considerable capital in indigo cultivation, cotton, screws, and clocks. They had acquired shipping interests. They were now even lending to the Company's servants in distress. Their commercial interests had extended to 'establishments in Penang, Malacca, Java, Sumatra, China, Manila, New South Wales, the Cape of Good Hope, Mauritius etc. . . .'[3]

By 1826, however, a financial crisis had overwhelmed the prominent agency houses. The failure of the indigo crop in 1826 and decline of indigo prices in London led to the bankruptcy of six agency houses who had invested heavily in Bengal indigo. This exposed the precarious nature of the emerging British investments in India, not backed by anything like a lender of last resort, still centred on the fortunes of a very limited number of exports and agriculture-based commodities and founded on a form of organization which permitted panicky partners to withdraw capital and accelerate a collapse. The second indigo crisis of 1830,

[1] Tripathi, op. cit., p. 11.
[2] Tripathi, op. cit., p. 12. Also see Sinha, op. cit., Chapter VI.
[3] Tripathi, op. cit., p. 201.

tided over by assistance from Bentinck, was followed by the final crisis of 1832 which led to the closure of four of the six major houses; the remaining two were swept away by 1834.

V. THE EMERGENCE OF THE MANAGING AGENCY SYSTEM

'On the ruins of these agency houses a new organization of British capitalist enterprise arose—the managing agency system— which ushered in the industrial development of India and with it a new age'.[1]

Throughout the negotiations from 1828 for the East India Company's Charter Act of 1833, the growing desire of the English manufacturing classes to engage more actively in the Indian trade, and so harness with invested capital the raw materials available in India, had been actively brought to bear upon the British Parliament. The import of Indian cotton interested Manchester and was considered to be 'possible only through the introduction of European skill and capital'. The Liverpool East India Committee asked for better communication in India to 'facilitate movement of raw materials'. The introduction of a uniform currency and substantial banking houses was demanded. 'Most interesting of all, Dr. Wallich tried to rouse the Board (of Trade) to the possibility of cultivation of tea in the foothills of the Himalayas.'[2]

The ensuing charter of 1833, while it fell short of the manufacturing interests' demands, ushered in a new era. The end of the China Monopoly of the East India Company, the grant to Europeans of the right to own land in India, the reform of the monetary system implicit in the abolition of the so-called 'remittance trade', led to an unprecedented expansion of (private) British trade and investments in India:

Recognition of the Europeans' right to own land led to the introduction of the plantation system, when the tea plant was discovered in Assam and the Himalayan foothills by Lt. Charlton and Captain Jenkins in 1833. The mining of Bengal coals, already started by

[1] Tripathi, op. cit., p. 240. Blair Kling, in 'The Origin of the Managing Agency System', *Journal of Asian Studies*, XXVI, November 1966, pp. 37–48, has traced the origin of the managing agency system to 1836 when Carr, Tagore & Company promoted and then assumed management of the Calcutta Steam Tug Association.

[2] Tripathi, op. cit., p. 244.

Alexander and Co., could be further extended with the development of industry and transport. The establishment of cotton, twist, rice and flour mills near Calcutta had led to the erection of foundries which could be enlarged into a metallurgical industry. Industrial development necessitated a new system of communication. Steam navigation, introduced under the Government auspices in the mid-twenties,[1] was put on a sound basis by the creation of the New Bengal Steam Fund (on 22nd June, 1833) and the River Indus Steam Navigation Company. Though the first railway would be laid in the time of Dalhousie (in 1853, connecting Bombay and Thana, a distance of twenty-one miles) the Government was deliberating as early as 1828 on its comparative advantages over inland navigation. . . . The agency house, which had played such a chequered role in the early history of British capitalism in India gave way to a new type of organization—the managing agency system. It depended no more on the savings of the Company's servants or on loans from the native shroffs, on the limited accommodation offered by a single Chartered bank or an occasional charity of a sympathetic Government. It could rely on free import of surplus capital of Britain and on larger and cheaper banking facilities symbolised in the Union Bank, which got a Charter in 1835. It was as culmination of this process that the Bengal Chamber of Commerce was founded on 31st March, 1834 . . . This Chamber would be the spearhead of European capital in India in the coming age of enterprise.[2]

VI. THE EMERGING PATTERN OF INVESTMENTS AND ROLE OF INDIGENOUS ENTREPRENEURSHIP

Thus, by the late 1830s, British enterprise and capital had already extended to sugar manufacture, rice and flour mills, indigo and tea plantations, shipyards, mining, foreign trade, banking, and insurance. Traditional, indigenous enterprise had not played any role of significance in these developments in the Bengal Presidency; if anything, it was reduced to a rather subsidiary role in the process. There were, indeed, signs of a new entrepreneurial class emerging in Bengal at the time, from the class of *zamindars* created by the Permanent Settlement in Bengal.[3] Thus, for example:

[1] 'The *Diana*, the first steam vessel built in Calcutta, left Kyd's Yard in 1823.' Tripathi, op. cit., p. 249, n. 4.

[2] Tripathi, op. cit., pp. 249–50.

[3] The Permanent Settlement in the Bengal Presidency has been discussed by R. Guha, *A Rule of Property for Bengal: An Essay on the Idea of Permanent Settlement*.

Among the subscribers of the Chamber [of Commerce, Bengal] were three Indians—Dwarkanath Tagore, Prasanna Kumar Tagore and Rustomjee Cowasjee. Dwarkanath was also a director of the Union Bank, the founder of Carr, Tagore and Co. and a director of the Calcutta Steam Tug Association . . . he was a zemindar . . . he held out for the new spirit of enterprise. With justifiable pride he wrote about Carr, Tagore and Company to Lord Bentinck, '. . . it is so far a remarkable one in the commercial history of Bengal, as it is the first instance in which an open and avowed partnership has been established between the European and the Bengal merchant with the capital of the latter . . . instead of being left dependent upon those resources, which the melancholy experience of late years has proved but too precarious.' He seemed to be conscious of the role of his kind and to articulate the first positive assertion of the Indian capitalist that 'it will be our endeavour to merit the most extended confidence and to take up that position in supporting or unfolding the productive energies of the country which may hereafter connect our establishment and name, in some degree with the general prosperity of India and encourage others to base themselves upon the same principle of combining, as much as possible, the advantages, at present too seldom attained, of European and native integrity, wealth and experience'. Tagore, in fact, was responding to the challenge of the Industrial Revolution by way of an economic synthesis. . .[1]

There appeared briefly to be emerging a middle-class entrepreneurship with a constructive ideology. But British capital and enterprise were to dominate the Bengal scene for a long time to come and the promise of a new extrepreneurial class in Bengal was to be belied. Jute manufacture, for example, beginning with the first factory in 1854, resulted entirely from Scottish initiative (much like coal-mining earlier).

However, it is a remarkable contrast that the first cotton textile mill to be established, in 1854 in Bombay city, was the venture of a local Parsi cotton merchant then engaged in overseas and internal trade. And, indeed, as we shall see later, the vast majority of the early mills were the handiwork of Parsi merchants engaged in yarn and cloth trade at home and in Chinese and African markets. The growth of indigenous enterprise had in fact been the distinguishing characteristic of the growth of economic activity in Bombay since earlier decades.

After 1800 the port of Bombay had expanded business rapidly

---

[1] Tripathi, op. cit., pp. 250–1.

especially in view of its being the nearest port of call for the traffic of the Indian ocean. This had resulted in an unprecedented expansion of the commercial and banking facilities in the city.

And as early as 1836 the Bombay Chamber of Commerce was organised by a group of British and Indian merchants . . . one interesting characteristic of nineteenth-century Bombay enterprise suggested by the formation of the Chamber of Commerce is the extent to which economic activity was not dominated by Europeans but was shared by local merchants . . . moreover, the response in Bombay was quite different from that which characterised Calcutta at the same time.[1]

Apart from the growth of banking, insurance, and export trade, Bombay witnessed, as early as up to the 1830s, a steady expansion of port facilities, construction, and shipbuilding in the Bombay dockyard—the first steamship being built in 1829—and 'the East India Company ordnance factory . . . as early as 1823 employed nearly a thousand permanent and temporary workers in its gun-carriage section'.[2] By the 1840s, the expansion had gone yet further: by 1847, the Bombay dockyard already had two thousand workers. The substantial growth of the coastal trade was indicated by the operation, that year, of nine steamers out of Bombay, sailing as far as Colombo and Karachi among other ports, and largely carrying the raw cotton trade which, in turn, had led to an expansion in the number of steam cotton presses in the Bombay Presidency.

Less is known, for certain, of the third centre, the Madras Presidency. But it is indicative that the Madras Chamber of Commerce was founded in 1836. It is interesting, however, that: 'The Governor Sir Frederick Adam, while giving the new Chamber his blessing, expressed dissatisfaction at the absence of the "principal native merchants"; the Chamber was able to reply that only two of these gentlemen had expressed a wish to be admitted and these had been admitted.'[3]

---

[1] Morris D. Morris, *The Emergence of an Industrial Labour Force in India*, pp. 15–16. In this general connection, also see Daniel Thorner's classic work, *Investment in Empire*.

[2] Morris, op. cit., p. 17.

[3] Hilton Brown, *Parry's of Madras. A Story of British Enterprise in India*, p. 66. Quoted in M. Kidron, *Foreign Investments in India*, p. 8.

VII. GROWTH OF MODERN INDUSTRY, INDIGENOUS AND BRITISH ENTREPRENEURSHIP FROM 1850s UP TO THE FIRST WORLD WAR

Up to the 1840s, the major economic and commercial developments in India had thus been centred upon the growth of principally British private enterprise in banking, insurance, indigo plantations, steamships, cotton presses, early tea plantations, and coal mines, and similar activities geared almost exclusively to the growing external trade with Britain.

The ensuing period, beginning with the decade 1850–60 and ending with the first world war, saw an extended involvement of British capital and enterprise in these activities. There was also a simultaneous growth of jute manufactures, State-initiated railways expansion and associated growth of foundries and metallurgical industry, and significant expansion of coal-mining and tea plantations. Jute manufacture, beginning in 1854, already had four factories operating by 1862. By 1900 there were 15,000 looms installed in the industry. Coal production had increased, since the linking of the Raniganj coalfields to Calcutta by rail in 1854, to over a million tons by 1880 and 20 million tons by 1914.

The typical form of commercial organization that the British employed during this period was the managing agency (which was to survive into the period since independence, though with several governmental controls). The managing agency houses characteristically secured control over the management of concerns in which capital-wise they sometimes had even no controlling interest. They appointed their nominee as the chairman of the Board of Directors, often provided finance and, on top of the return on their capital investment, earned a commission on sales and also 'management fees'. These managing agency houses were thus to become the suppliers of capital, know-how, and management, and constitute a form of business organization most adapted to a country with practically negligible banking facilities (especially for long-term finance), an apathetic government, and lack of institutions for supply of know-how in modern industry.

The managing agencies, predominantly British (though, later in the century, there were to be a growing number of Indian houses), proceeded to build up vast interests by a process of diversification as external trade and domestic manufactures expanded through the nineteenth century.

From the start the lack of modern industry encouraged the agencies to seek self-sufficiency, each developing its own sources of raw materials, its own services, and a substantial market within its own operations. Martin Burn's steel output went largely into their railway engineering workshop which served their large railway interests, alternatively into their constructional engineering activities which found further support in their cement interests, and so on. Andrew Yule's jute mills required electricity and coal supplies which in turn required engineering facilities, transport, and the host of ancillary materials and services to be found within that complex. Parry's went from bonemeal to phosphates, and then through sulphuric acid to superphosphates; to plain jars to hold the acid and from there to pottery, sanitaryware, and crockery.[1]

But in two major respects, this period was important and qualitatively different from that ending towards 1850. On the one hand, 'import-substituting' investment in cotton textiles from the 1850s, and most noticeably in steel at the turn of the century, marked a significant shift from investments which until then had been almost exclusively geared to external trade. On the other hand, strikingly enough, indigenous entrepreneurship, centred in the Bombay Presidency, now led the way, whereas hitherto British capital and enterprise had initiated activity in nearly all the significant sectors such as indigo and tea plantations. Qualitatively, these contrasts with the earlier period are most significant; quantitatively, it is impossible to say, for example, whether indigenous enterprise in the aggregate invested a higher proportion of the total investment than British entrepreneurship.

Morris has recorded vividly the initiatory role played by purely indigenous merchants, many (but by no means all) of them Parsis, in the growth of the cotton textile industry in Bombay and later in Cawnpore and Ahmedabad. We quote him at length:

The industry had its real beginnings in western India in the 1850's, when we get a cluster of attempts at Broach, Ahmedabad, and Bombay. It was the activity in Bombay, particularly the efforts of C. N. Davar (1814–1873), which led directly to the development of the modern industry.

C. N. Davar's father, a wealthy Parsi merchant, was a broker for

English commercial firms engaged in the India and China trade. In 1830 the young Davar entered the family business, and after the death of the father in 1837 he and his elder brother opened a brokerage firm which also operated as agent for English firms in the Asian trade. Widening experience and the encouragement of success led Davar to extend the sweep of his activities. In 1846–47 he cooperated with some English partners in the formation of the Commercial Bank of Bombay. Success here led to a number of further banking ventures and into other types of enterprises. Davar was an active figure in the establishment of the Bombay Steam Navigation Company, and in 1853 to 1855 he helped organize the Bombay Hydraulic Press Company and a large cotton-cleaning enterprise.

His activities were not untypical of the bigger Indian businessmen of Bombay at the time. Involved in the export financing of raw cotton and the import of cotton textiles, it was inevitable that the notion of importing machinery and starting a textile mill would strike Davar or one of his contemporaries. Nevertheless, the boldness of Davar's conception in the face of considerable difficulties is impressive. Plant and machinery had to be imported. Skilled mechanics to guide the erection of the mill and equipment also had to be brought from Britain, as did the managerial talent. Coal and wood for fuel had to be brought by sea to Bombay. The only certain advantages were the availability of raw cotton and the existence of markets for yarn and cloth.

The Bombay textile industry was initially conceived and financed by Indians. Lacking details, it is impossible to establish the extent to which non-Indians participated in the early ventures, but it was not until 1874, after seventeen Indian-dominated mills had gone into operation, that the first English sponsored and financed company was established. In 1875 a report prepared for British textile interests pointed out that Indian mills 'are almost exclusively owned by natives, and are under native supervision'. Although other British financed mills were started after 1874, foreign capital never amounted to more than a few per cent of total investment in the industry.[1]

Why did Indian entrepreneurship in the field of manufactures focus on cotton textiles and play such an important and initiatory role in their development while letting British entrepreneurship exploit and develop other areas of investment?

Perhaps the answer to this question lies in the following facts:

(1) cotton textiles was perhaps the one single prominent industry in which Indian traders-cum-entrepreneurs could rely completely on the domestic market;

[1] Morris, op. cit., pp. 22–7. All footnotes have been omitted.

(2) there was certainty that this market consisted of private Indian consumers so that the purchase policy of the British Government could not be used discriminatorily against them—as was alleged and feared with the purchase of railway stores, etc.;

(3) there was competitive advantage in the local manufacture of coarser varieties of textiles—so that no protection had to be sought from a colonial government generally seized of British manufacturing interests;

(4) the necessary technology could be purchased abroad with comparative ease; and

(5) there was extremely limited requirement for skilled labour, coupled with the abundant supply (in the early decades) of the unskilled labour required to tend the machinery. The capital undoubtedly came from the savings made in the years spent in the cotton trade prior to the industrial ventures; so did the acquaintance with the trade and the necessary confidence.

This unique constellation of favourable circumstances apparently did not arise in any other industry during the nineteenth century. Indian enterprise and capital, where any, were largely to follow in the wake of the industrial ventures of the British in other fields. British investments and enterprise were, overwhelmingly, the outgrowth of other external trading interests; investments (and not merely the Flag) followed trade. The investments in such 'domestic'-type areas as foundries, metallurgical industry, and coal-mining were essentially geared to railway expansion and hence to a vertical diversification process supporting export and import trade at the end of the line.[1]

---

[1] The truly puzzling aspect of the pattern of indigenous and foreign enterprise in industrial activity during this period appears to us to have been not why indigenous enterprise did not pioneer in a larger number of areas than cotton textiles and (later) steel, but why foreign enterprise generally followed, rather than led, indigenous activity in these industries. It is tempting to argue that British investment must have been deterred from these industries by the thought of the damage it could have inflicted on British exporting interests: and there is little doubt that governmental policies and industrial pressure groups in Britain must have been swayed by these considerations to an important, but hitherto only casually studied, degree. But it is clear that this line of argument in itself cannot carry us very far. After all, there is no reason why such social concern for the industry's welfare (at the British end) should have prevented individual investments by British enterprise in these activities, if profitable. Moreover, we do know that it was never difficult

The most spectacular and far-sighted initiative and enterprise, however, were to be shown by indigenous entrepreneurship towards the turn of the century—when, against tremendous odds and with great tenacity of purpose, the Parsi, Jamshedjee Tata, was to realize his grandiose dream of erecting India's first steel plant at Jamshedpur in 1911.

Tata's were not, in fact, the first to have attempted the construction of a steel mill in India. There had been at least two major unsuccessful attempts, both failing owing to inadequate planning and insufficient initiative, in an industry which required both in enormous magnitude at the time.[1] In 1830 Josiah Marshal Heath, a retired civil-service employee, had secured a grant from the East India Company and started iron-works at Porto Novo, on the Madras coast, with foundries capable of turning out about 50 tons of iron a week. His blowing engine was driven by bullocks! Several factors appear to have contributed to the failure of the Heath company: chief among them were lack of adequate planning and exploration resulting in insufficient expertise, ore of uneven quality, and reliance on an exhaustible and expensive supply of charcoal as fuel. The subsequent attempt, the Barakar Iron Works, starting operations in 1875, was also to result in failure owing to poor quality ore. The works were shut down in four years. The comment of Keenan, who was Tata's first General Manager, a robust and radical man who shared Tata's vision and helped to translate it into reality, is interesting:

Those same works [the Barakar Iron Works] were reopened later by the Indian Government as the Bengal Iron and Steel Company, and prospered until Martin and Company, Calcutta engineers in charge of the plant, went into steel production in 1905. After eight months they had to shut down. They had a good excuse. The pig iron was found to have a high phosphorus content and the wear and tear on the furnaces in removing the phosphorus came high. I never understood, however,

---

for the pioneering Indian entrepreneurs in the textile industry to buy textile machinery from the British suppliers. Unless, therefore, a thorough analysis of the relative profitabilities of different activities in India, and the possible imperfections in the British capital market in its operation in India, is carried out, we are left here with yet another intriguing question in India's early industrial history.

[1] An excellent account of these and other minor attempts preceding Tata's can be found in D. H. Buchanan, *The Development of Capitalistic Enterprise in India*, Frank Cass & Co. Ltd., 1966, Chapter XIII.

why they didn't look around for some ore with lower phosphorus percentage. If they had, they'd have found it less than a hundred miles from Jherria, or about fifteen miles from our Noamundi fields. Now, after thirty-five years or so, having seen Tata's make a success of steel, they are back in production.[1]

It is indeed difficult to imagine the Tata venture, which was to prove a roaring success eventually, as anything but a happy historical accident. Two early failures, the enormous task of organization (of both technical know-how and finance), and prospecting for a suitable site—all these would have ruled out any entrepreneurial attempt except the visionary. Indeed, it is true that by 1914 British steel exports were already over a million tons a year; but it was difficult to imagine that Indians could build a modern steel plant and compete with British steel, especially when the techniques and skills required were complex and the prospect of tariff protection by a British imperial government, if required when operations began, extremely dim. But Jamshedjee Tata had the tenacity which was to be eventually crowned with success.

Aside from the Schumpeterian, innovative role of indigenous enterprise in cotton textiles and steelmaking, both of them further 'import-substituting' activities, indigenous enterprise did flourish on a larger scale during this period, entering new fields and extending their commercial and trading interests further. Indeed, through the nineteenth century, as industrialization proceeded at its slow pace, British and indigenous enterprise came to interpenetrate many common fields. Indian enterprise followed into coal-mining, and tea and jute manufactures, for example; British houses entered the cotton textiles industry. However, the mutual relations between the British and indigenous entrepreneurs seem to have reflected, by and large, the colonial situation; and indigenous entrepreneurship seems to have generally found it easier to organize itself into *separate* pressure groups:

While not debarred from membership in so many words, the workings and atmosphere of the foreign business organisations were such as to encourage them to set up bodies of their own. Ultimately, almost every foreign organisation in shared industries had an Indian mirror image. The Indian Tea Association, founded by British planters in 1881,

---

[1] J. Keenan, *A Steel Man in India*, p. 25.

was followed by the Indian Tea Planters' Association; The Indian Mining Association (1892) by the Indian Mining Federation (1913) and the Indian Colliery Owners' Association (1933) representing Indian interests large and small; the Indian Paper Makers' Association by the Indian Paper Mills Association. The Indian Jute Mills Association (1884), the Indian Central Cotton Committee, and the Exchange Banks' Association, all originally British, had each an Indian counterpart. Even the smallest were paired: for example, the (British) Cycle Manufacturers' Association with the (Indian) All-India Cycle Manufacturers' Association.

Commercial organisations were no different. The 1830's generation of British Chambers which followed the demise of the East India Company as a trader was matched in the 1880's by an Indian generation. The provincial organisations which came later continued the segregation and finally the national organisations—the (British) Associated Chambers of Commerce and Industry (1920) and the (Indian) Federation of Indian Chambers of Commerce and Industry (1927)—did the same.[1]

The growth in industrial entrepreneurship came essentially from three communities: the Parsis, Gujeratis, and Marwaris. The earliest entrepreneurs appear to have been mainly Parsis: they certainly initiated cotton textiles and later steel-making. But other communities participated in the expansion and financing of cotton textiles, from the very beginning.[2] Thus the spread of the industry to Ahmedabad, which was eventually to emerge as a rival centre to Bombay, was largely by the Gujerati trading classes. Both these communities came essentially from trade to manufacture: the classic pattern of transformation and emergence of an industrial, entrepreneurial class. However, the later emergence, and phenomenal growth, of the Marwari entrepreneurs was substantially from the moneylending groups. These groups were eventually to dominate centres such as Calcutta, initiate new industries such as bicycles and automobiles, and throw up industrial empires such as that of the Birlas and Sahu Jains.

Andrew Brimmer's study of a sample drawn from Bombay firms, classifying the firms by the community affiliation of their

---

[1] Kidron, op. cit., p. 8. Also see pp. 9-10 for similar contrasts, and the practices of foreign banks, with respect to banking.

[2] See, for example, the papers by Mrs. D. P. Pandit, 'Creative Response in Indian Economy: A Regional Analysis', *Economic Weekly*, 23 February and 2 March 1957.

D

managing agents or the chairman, depending on what was relevant
for identification, has underlined the continuing dominance of
these three business communities right into the modern period,
as is shown in Table 2.1.[1]

TABLE 2.1
PERCENT OF PAID-UP CAPITAL AND OF GROSS ASSETS CONTROLLED BY
VARIOUS COMMUNITIES IN BOMBAY PROVINCE (1912, 1935, 1948)

| | 1912 | | 1935 | | 1948 | |
| | Paid-up | Gross | Paid-up | Gross | Paid-up | Gross |
Community	capital	assets[a]	capital	assets	capital	assets
British	30·8	43·0	21·6	10·0	8·9	3·6
Parsis	49·7	31·4	47·6	41·3	36·0	46·5
Gujeratis	11·5	21·8	12·5	18·3	24·5	18·5
Marwaris	0	0	0·8	2·4	14·3	7·3
All others	8·0	3·8	17·2	27·9	16·3	24·6

[a] For approximately 40 per cent of the companies in the 1912 sample, the gross
assets are for 1913.

Source: Table 8, p. 22, in C. Myers, *Labour Problems in the Industrialization
of India*; Andrew Brimmer, 'Some Aspects of the Rise and Behaviour of the
Business Communities in Bombay', unpublished research paper, Massachusetts
Institute of Technology, Center for International Studies (August 1953),
adapted from Appendix II, Table I. Brimmer used a sampling technique. For
each year analysed, the sample contains from 4 to 10 per cent of public registered
companies in Bombay representing over 50 per cent of total paid-up capital.

By the end of the nineteenth century and on the eve of the first
world war, this continual expansion and endeavour by British
and indigenous capital and enterprise had expanded India's
industrial base considerably. But it was still narrow, and the
impact on the overall economic growth of the country could not
put India into the rank of the newly industrialized countries.

The industrial pattern was based largely on coal-mining, cotton
textiles, jute textiles, railways, and allied workshops, some foundries and metallurgical plants, and ordnance factories. There was
also an impressive growth of tea plantations, shipping and dock-
yards, insurance and banking facilities. The Tatas had, just on
the eve of the war, finally erected their steel mill at Jamshedpur.

A measure, however inadequate, of the narrow industrial base
during this period is seen in the distribution of her industrial

[1] The emergence of Marwari strength, even though understated by exclusion
of Calcutta from the sample, is also evident from these figures.

work force. Table 2.2, based on estimates of Myers, reveals the essential picture.

This shows the overwhelming predominance, from 1892 to 1919, of railways and workshops, mining, cotton, and jute textiles

TABLE 2.2
THE GROWTH OF INDUSTRIAL EMPLOYMENT IN INDIA*
(Thousands of employees)

	1892	1899	1909	1919	1929	1939	1949	1954b
Railways	259	309	510	713	818c	709c	901c	966
Coal minesa	33d	83e	129f	190	180	227g	345	341
All mininga				249	364	413g	519	594
Factory employment								
Cotton textiles	121c	163c	237	280	338	499	653	661
Jute textiles	66c	102c	204c	276	347	299	322	272
General and electrical engineering				30	53	58	136	150
Railway workshops		52h	93	134	136	104	108	118
Ordnance		13h	15	24	22	31	84	67
Iron and steel	12i	17i	24i	21	32	41	60	77
Chemicals				2·8	3·5	4·8	18	23
Total factory employment	254	452	786	1,171	1,553	1,751	2,434	2,590

* Because the definition of 'factory' and the degree of coverage (both in detail and geographic area) have changed over time, the figures are only generally comparable. Figures for 1939 and before are for British India, excluding native states; 1949 and 1955 are for the Indian Union (thus excluding Pakistan). Data, unless otherwise noted, are taken from the annual *Statistical Abstracts Relating to British India* (pre-1947), and the *Statistical Abstract, India* (post-1947): No. 35, 1890–1 to 1899–1900, pub. 1901; No. 52, 1907–8 to 1916–17, pub. 1919; No. 56, 1911–12 to 1920–1, pub. 1924; No. 65, 1930, 1931, pub. 1933; No. 72, 1939–40, pub. 1943; New Series, No. 1, 1949, Vol. II, pub. 1950; New Series, No. 2, 1950, pub. 1952.

a Employment in Mines: For 1890, see D. R. Gadgil, *Industrial Evolution of India*; for 1899 and 1909, see *Report of the Royal Commission on Labour in India* (June, 1931), pp. 7, 8, 9, 514; for 1919, see *Indian Year Book*, 1921, Stanley Reed (ed.), Bombay, Bennet Coleman & Co., 1929, pp. 354, 187.

b Employment statistics for 1954 are published on a different basis from that used for years up to 1949, and in certain cases, particularly engineering and chemicals, the comparability of figures provided is open to doubt. Factory employment statistics are from the *Indian Labour Gazette*, 616–646, No. 8 (February 1956); railway and mining employment from the *Indian Labour Year Book*, 1953–4, pp. 5, 8; mining employment statistics are for the year 1953.

c Accounting year.
d 1890.
e 1901–5 annual average.
f 1911–15 annual average.
g 1938.
h 1905.
i Includes brass foundries.

Source: Myers, op. cit., Table 6, p. 17.

in the overall employment in the 'modern sector' in India. It is also notable that, by 1919, the total employment in this modern, factory sector had grown to only 1·17 million, absorbing less than 1 per cent of the then working force.

Indeed, it is dubious whether, despite the undoubted growth and diversification (however limited) of enterprise and industrial investment through the nineteenth century, and the indisputable prosperity of burgeoning centres such as Bombay and Calcutta, the overall impact on the Indian economy was not anything more than perfunctory. Unfortunately little is known, but much conjectured, about the performance of the Indian economy during the nineteenth century: there are so few facts about the growth of income, *per capita* income, agricultural productivity, and agricultural output, among other important aspects of the subject, that it is impossible to draw reasonably firm conclusions. Systematic evidence for the later decades of the century suggests, however, a continuing sluggishness and a relatively unchanging character of the occupational structure.[1]

VIII. ENTREPRENEURSHIP AND INDUSTRIALIZATION BETWEEN THE FIRST WORLD WAR AND INDEPENDENCE (1947)

The preceding Table 2.2 shows that, between 1909 and 1940, the operation, maintenance, and construction of railroads continued to dominate employment in the modern sector. Within the area of manufactures, factory employment again was heavily concentrated on jute and cotton yarn and textiles, which continued to employ over a third of the factory labour.

The first world war seems to have merely highlighted the inadequacy of India's industrial base, bringing home to the British Government both the key role of the Empire in defence and the limitations of its contributions to the war effort in the absence of significantly greater industrial expansion. The personal account of John Keenan, retired from being Tata's General Manager, of their infant steel mill's contribution to the war effort is revealing:

Back in 1916, the roaring, pulsating, pounding, hissing organism that is a steel mill, and that in India was the booming Tata works, was, as it is now, running full out for war. And the war had brought its own set of special problems.

Warships and U-boats of the Central Powers lay in around the volcanic islands in the Straits of Messina and picked off at their convenience the Allied cargo boats as fast as they came along. Nothing could get through. The English and the French desperately needed steel for use in the East and needed it, so to speak, on the spot. That

---

[1] This, for example, is the conclusion of J. Krishnamurti's thorough work on the Census data since 1871: 'Secular Changes in Occupational Structure', *Indian Economic and Social History Review*, Vol. II, No. 2, June 1965.

meant Tata's. They vitally needed shells, and that meant Tata's, too. But we had no electric or other special furnaces to make steel shells with.

Old Tut got that look in his eye that we all knew. He took a deep breath and went to work. We made steel shells on open-hearth furnaces, something like 8,000 tons of them. As far as I know, that was the only time that such a thing was ever done, and we did it well.

But then we had no way to press them. Old Tut arranged with every railway or shipbuilding workshop that had a lathe to *bore* out those five-inch grounds into shells. And, by God, it worked. Most of them went to Maud and Allenby in Mesopotamia, across the Persian Gulf by way of Karachi and Basra.

Still, on a twenty-four-hour schedule, Tata's couldn't keep up with the need for iron and steel. We were even turning out hames for the horses that pulled field guns. Our total output had reached 150,000 tons of steel a year.[1]

A number of industries expanded, along with steel, through the war and beyond. Cotton textiles shot ahead under the impetus provided by the absence of traditional imports as the war diverted transport to other uses. Jute and coal-mining, like steel, fed the war machine. Among the other industries to benefit were leather, soap, fish-canning, ship-building (principally in Madras), and wool.

Within a decade after the war, factory industries had expanded and already diversified into minerals and metals; food, drink, and tobacco; chemicals and dyes; paper and printing; processes relating to wood, stone, glass, skins, and hides; and other miscellaneous activities.[2] By the beginning of the second world war, despite the effects of the great depression, the Indian industrial structure already sported a considerable production of cement (at 1·2 million tons per annum), paper (at 60,000 tons annually), cotton piecegoods (at 4·3 billion yards per year), sugar (at over a million tons already), pig iron (at 1·6 million tons), and steel ingots (at over a million tons), and industries such as cycles and textile machinery had already emerged.[3]

The diversification and expansion of industries during the inter-war period was, for once, encouraged by a tariff policy (however tempered by British exporting interests) which broke

Keenan, op. cit., Chapter IV.   [2] Buchanan, op. cit., pp. 136–40.
[3] Kidron, op. cit., pp. 20–1.

with the then tradition of free trade. The war had underlined the critical importance of Indian industries in case of further wars and thus helped in this change of policy. But the change was also dictated, to some extent, by the growing pressure of Indian public opinion as also the articulate expression of similar ideas by several Englishmen of repute.[1] The Montagu–Chelmsford Report on Indian Constitutional Reforms in 1918 thus included an excellent statement of Indian public opinion on this matter:

The theoretical free-trader, we believe, hardly exists in India at present. . . . Educated Indian opinion ardently desires a tariff. . . . Whatever economic fallacy underlies his reasoning, these are his firm beliefs; and though he may be willing to concede the possibility that he is wrong, he will not readily concede that it is our business to decide the matter for him. He believes that as long as we continue to decide for him we shall decide in the interests of England and not according to his wishes; . . . so long as the people who refuse India protection are interested in manufactures with which India might compete, Indian opinion cannot bring itself to believe that the refusal is disinterested or dictated by care for the best interests of India.[2]

The appointment in October 1921 of the First Indian Fiscal Commission, which reported in favour of a protectionist policy and led to its subsequent adoption by India, is one of the landmarks of Indian industrialization. The Tariff Boards, in the ensuing period, were to examine applications from numerous industries and grant protection to a fair number of them. During 1923–39, the Indian Tariff Boards made fifty-one inquiries, resulting in varying degrees of protection to the iron and steel, cotton textiles, sugar, paper and paper pulp, matches, salt, sericulture, magnesium chloride, and gold thread industries.[3] For industries such as iron and steel and cotton textiles, tariff protection was invaluable in getting over the depression following the vast expansion during the first world war. The Jamshedpur works would almost certainly have suffered a severe jolt, and even

---

[1] The precise interplay of different interests and political and economic philosophies in bringing this change about, as also in the free trade policies implemented earlier, is an important but relatively neglected field of Indian economic history.

[2] Quoted in Buchanan, op. cit., p. 469.

[3] Padma Desai, *Tariff Protection in India*, 1970. This monograph also examines the criteria employed by the Tariff Boards in their decisions to recommend or reject applications for protection.

bankruptcy, if protection had not been granted to bale it out of the expensive and considerable expansion during the war and the accentuation of the difficulties following continental dumping on the international market during these years.

The second world war, in turn, was to provide a yet greater (though short-lived) stimulus to the growth of Indian industries. As with the first world war, the increased demand could not *pro rata* be translated into investment and capacity: again, transportation bottlenecks on imports of capital goods were to be important in preventing fuller exploitation of this 'opportunity'.

Datar and Patel have argued that the major impetus to war-time expansion of employment and output came from the direct increase in defence outlays.[1] They estimate that total public outlay increased by over 400 per cent between 1939-40 and 1944-5; this was a phenomenal rise even when deflated for rising prices and thus reduced to a figure of around 200 per cent. The *additional* public outlay in 1944/5 over the 1939/40 level, expressed as a percentage of the national income for 1944/5, was as much as 10 per cent.

Employment was to increase, in consequence, by 103 per cent during the war.[2] Industrial production, however, increased by only 20 per cent between 1939 and 1946, largely owing to the inelasticity of supply caused by inability to translate investment intentions into plant and machinery during the war.

The incremental production, outdistanced by price rises except where price controls were effective, occurred in a variety of industries. Furthermore, it occurred principally through fuller utilization of idle capacity, through additional shifts, and through more efficient utilization of capacity in other ways. New plants were also added in the numerous newer industries: ferro-alloys such as ferro-silicon and ferro-manganese; non-ferrous metals and metal fabricating industries such as copper, copper sheets, wires, and cables; mechanical industries such as diesel engines, pumps, sewing machines, machine tools, and cutting tools; some items of textile, tea, and oil pressing machinery; and chemicals, which

---

[1] B. N. Datar and I. G. Patel, 'Employment during the Second World War', *Indian Economic Review*, February 1956.

[2] Datar and Patel, op. cit. This figure refers to British India, and to armed forces, factories, mines, and railways, and excludes princely states.

grew from minute proportions to include caustic soda, chlorine, superphosphates, photographic chemicals, and bichromates.[1]

Among the older industries to expand during the second world war, the most prominent were cement, paper, cotton textiles, iron and steel, and sugar.[2] Between 1937 and 1946, the cement industry's capacity increased from 1·5 to 2·6 million tons, with actual production nearly doubling to 2·0 million tons and employment rising to over 21,800 employees. Cement being a basic material for construction, the war generated a considerable increase in demand for it, which was directly responsible for the industry's rapid growth. The paper industry also registered a doubling of its output to 106,000 tons between 1937 and 1946, and a near-doubling of its capacity and of its employment to over 18,800 employees. As with cement, the industry had already grown sizeably before the war, a protective tariff since 1925 having assisted in this growth; and governmental demand in wartime provided a further spurt. The iron and steel industry was also to grow during the war, but less strikingly. By 1942 Tata's had expanded steel ingot capacity to a million tons and the Steel Corporation of Bengal (later merged with the Indian Iron and Steel Company), having entered steel production only in 1940, had built up a capacity of 270,000 tons by 1942. The cotton textile industry had also registered a boom which had lifted it out of the difficulties since the Depression. The 1938–9 situation of 'competitive price-reducing pressures', following the spread of the industry to cheaper producing centres outside Bombay state, was replaced by a burgeoning demand, both direct (with the Government taking a fourth of the output by 1943) and indirect (thanks to the increment in public outlays resulting in incremental consumer expenditure). Output was to increase by nearly 20 per cent and employment by nearly 30 per cent during the war. Protected by tariffs, the sugar industry had already grown sizeably by 1938–9, annual production having reached almost a million tons and employment exceeding 750,000 workers. Reduction in imports and rising domestic demand during the war raised domestic production to 1·2 million tons by 1943–4.

[1] Cf. *Report of the Indian Fiscal Commission* (*1949–50*), Vol. I, Government of India, 1951, pp. 20–1.
[2] These have been studied in depth by G. Rosen, *Industrial Change in India*, Illinois, Free Press, 1961. We concentrate only on the broad outlines.

By the time the second world war ended, India had thus completed nearly a century of industrialization and growth of indigenous (as also influx of foreign) entrepreneurship. In 1947 India was to be partitioned (into Pakistan and present-day India) and gain independence.

Where exactly had India been left by this long history of industrialization? The pattern and size of her industries, her production and occupational structure, indigenous entrepreneurship, financial structure, *per capita* income, transport and communications, educational levels, political structure and administration were among the important economic and other variables which had changed and evolved through this century and were to shape the future pattern of her growth under a planned framework. We now turn to a description of many of these variables, focussing primarily on industrialization, from the beginning of the period starting with independence.

3

State of Industrialization at Independence

In this chapter we will first discuss the state of industrialization and other related characteristics of the Indian economy as they were in the pre-partition period and then only briefly describe the major respects in which the 1947 partition was to affect this picture. An analysis of the principal aspects of India's economic and industrial growth during the three Five-Year Plans (starting with 1951) in the ensuing two chapters will provide a more detailed description of the relevant variables for (divided) India at the beginning of the period of her planned industrialization.

I. INDUSTRIALIZATION AT 1947

(a) Industrial structure

By 1946, when the first Census of Manufacturing Industries (C.M.I.) was undertaken, the industrial structure revealed the dominance of the following industries: sugar; vegetable oils; cotton textiles; jute textiles; iron and steel smelting, rolling and rerolling; and general engineering.[1] Table 3.1 summarizes the prinicipal findings of the 1946 C.M.I. with respect to value added, production, salaries, and wages, employment and productive capital employed, relating to twenty-nine industrial sectors distinguished in the Census.[2]

---

[1] Since mining and railways were excluded from the scope of this Census, we ought to note them as well as among the dominant economic activities in the industrial sector construed in a broader sense. Table 2 in Chapter 2 gives an approximate idea of their importance, in terms of employment, at this time. Moreover, the Census was confined to establishments employing twenty or more workers in any manufacturing process which was being carried on with the aid of power.

[2] These are wheat flour; rice-milling; biscuit making; fruit and vegetable processing; sugar; distilleries and breweries; starch, vegetable oils; paints

TABLE 3.

INDIA'S MANUFACTURING INDUSTRIES IN 1946: VALUE ADDED, PRODUCTION, SALARIES AND WAGES, EMPLOYMENT AND PRODUCTIVE CAPITAL EMPLOYED

Item	All industries	Wheat flour		Rice-milling		Biscuit making	
(1)	(2)	(3)	(4)	(5)	(6)	(7)	(8)
1. Number of factories							
(a) Registered	5,013	66	1·32%	1,554	31·00%	33	0·66%
(b) Percentage covered	80	92		76		88	
2. Productive capital employed (Rs.)							
(a) Fixed	1,63,35,93,501	1,52,21,456	0·93%	4,70,15,129	2·88%	32,26,437	0·20%
(b) Total	3,66,83,37,440	2,39,34,942	0·65%	18,14,98,127	4·95%	66,48,162	0·18%
3. Number of persons employed							
(a) Workers	13,87,010	5,068	0·37%	41,958	3·03%	3,018	0·22%
(b) Total	15,14,382	6,199	0·41%	49,818	3·29%	3,345	0·22%
4. Salaries and wages (Rs.)	1,01,80,48,701	43,01,095	0·42%	1,30,92,346	1·29%	21,50,495	0·21%
5. Production (Value) (Rs.)	6,00,84,51,346	12,27,00,673	2·04%	34,92,75,924	5·81%	1,92,46,873	0·32%
6. Value added by manufacture (Rs.)	2,11,41,31,393	72,10,821	0·34%	1,46,78,620	0·69%	76,68,512	0·36%

Item	Fruit and vegetable processing		Sugar		Distilleries and Breweries[a]		Starch	
(1)	(9)	(10)	(11)	(12)	(13)	(14)	(15)	(16)
1. Number of factories								
(a) Registered	19	0·38%	166	3·31%	46	0·92%	5	0·10%
(b) Percentage covered	68		73		85		100	
2. Productive capital employed (Rs.)								
(a) Fixed capital	17,57,342	0·11%	13,18,89,879	8·07%	1,67,44,088	1·03%	18,78,268	0·11%
(b) Total	36,33,263	0·10%	30,52,87,457	8·32%	2,51,79,890	0·69%	39,29,719	0·11%
3. Number of persons employed								
(a) Workers	1,070	0·08%	73,088	5·27%	3,781	0·27%	882	0·06%
(b) Total	1,328	0·09%	93,836	6·20%	4,832	0·32%	1,022	0·07%
4. Salaries and wages (Rs.)	4,47,616	0·04%	3,82,87,053	3·76%	28,43,599	0·28%	6,75,357	0·07%
5. Production (Value) (Rs.)	31,19,337	0·05%	37,99,76,438	6·32%	2,67,50,517	0·45%	47,29,856	0·08%
6. Value added by manufacture (Rs.)	11,14,880	0·05%	7,91,26,680	3·74%	1,21,01,774	0·57%	17,20,452	0·08%

a Including power alcohol manufacturing.

TABLE 3.1—continued

Item	Vegetable oils, oil-seed crushing and extraction and processing of vegetable oils		Paints and varnishes		Soap		Tanning	
	(17)	(18)	(19)	(20)	(21)	(22)	(23)	(24)
1. Number of factories								
(a) Registered	569	11·35%	28	0·56%	37	0·74%	65	1·30%
(b) Percentage covered	77		89		100		58	
2. Productive capital employed (Rs.)								
(a) Fixed capital	6,50,63,429	3·98%	53,41,851	0·33%	1,13,06,046	0·69%	47,73,298	0·29%
(b) Total	23,00,08,408	6·27%	1,57,93,190	0·43%	3,99,07,908	1·06%	2,18,24,366	0·59%
3. Number of persons employed								
(a) Workers	30,419	2·19%	3,194	0·23%	5,370	0·39%	5,192	0·37%
(b) Tota	35,917	2·37%	3,968	0·26%	6,083	0·40%	5,794	0·38%
4. Salaries and wages (Rs.)	1,90,39,715	1·87%	30,57,530	0·30%	45,46,012	0·45%	34,42,021	0·34%
5. Production (value) (Rs.)	59,93,73,160	9·97%	3,83,18,717	0·64%	9,13,29,208	1·52%	3,27,21,895	0·54%
6. Value added by manufacture (Rs.)	7,46,02,851	3·53%	1,34,67,482	0·64%	1,91,86,583	0·91%	56,96,179	0·27%

Item	Cement		Glass and glassware		Ceramics		Plywood and tea-chests	
	(25)	(26)	(27)	(28)	(29)	(30)	(31)	(32)
1. Number of factories								
(a) Registered	11	0·22%	126	2·51%	44	0·88%	36	0·72%
(b) Percentage covered	82		73		95		78	
2. Productive capital employed (Rs.)								
(a) Fixed capital	2,93,35,450	1·80%	1,23,85,974	0·76%	92,47,097	0·57%	64,86,666	0·40%
(b) Total	4,86,40,068	1·33%	1,96,35,726	0·54%	1,48,32,549	0·40%	1,03,14,210	0·28%
3. Number of persons employed								
(a) Workers	9,266	0·67%	18,132	1·31%	10,858	0·78%	2,354	0·17%
(b) Total	10,231	0·68%	19,660	1·29%	11,865	0·78%	2,884	0·19%
4. Salaries and wages (Rs.)	50,15,967	0·49%	1,01,02,920	0·99%	60,32,688	0·59%	16,10,444	0·16%
5. Production (value) (Rs.)	3,85,02,841	0·64%	2,69,29,308	0·45%	1,68,27,042	0·28%	77,84,031	0·13%
6. Value added by manufacture (Rs.)	1,49,54,020	0·71%	1,23,65,176	0·58%	1,07,66,158	0·51%	33,98,763	0·16%

Top table

Item	Paper and paperboardᵇ		Matches		Cotton textiles—spinning and weaving		Woollen textiles	
	(33)	(34)	(35)	(36)	(37)	(38)	(39)	(40)
1. Number of factories								
(a) Registered	36	0·72%	31	0·62%	482	9·62%	43	0·86%
(b) Percentage covered	86		84		88		70	
2. Productive capital employed (Rs.)								
(a) Fixed capital	3,13,20,625	1·92%	55,36,591	0·34%	55,39,98,126	33·91%	1,00,61,680	0·62%
(b) Total	5,37,16,130	1·46%	1,19,05,224	0·32%	1,30,60,70,364	35·60%	3,94,18,524	1·07%
3. Number of persons employed								
(a) Workers	18,759	1·35%	9,379	0·68%	6,15,593	44·38%	15,658	1·13%
(b) Total	21,405	1·42%	10,355	0·68%	650,067	42·97%	16,750	1·11%
4. Salaries and wages (Rs.)	1,41,18,988	1·39%	71,49,610	0·70%	51,23,73,242	50·33%	1,30,78,743	1·29%
5. Production (value) (Rs.)	8,86,74,716	1·48%	4,76,02,568	0·79%	11,34,606 lb.	n.a.	6,91,47,043	1·15%
6. Value added by manufacture (Rs.)	3,26,70,464	1·55%	2,69,92,879	1·28%	97,27,34,378	46·01%	3,08,55,353	1·46%

ᵇ Including strawboard.

Bottom table

Item	Jute textiles		Chemicalsᶜ		Aluminium, copper, and brass		Iron and steel smelting, rolling and re-rolling	
	(41)	(42)	(43)	(44)	(45)	(46)	(47)	(48)
1. Number of factories								
(a) Registered	95	1·90%	174	3·47%	133	2·65%	107	2·13%
(b) Percentage covered	95		87		84		90	
2. Productive capital employed (Rs.)								
(a) Fixed capital	19,98,58,748	12·23%	5,31,55,283	3·25%	5,13,04,440	3·14%	23,49,13,395	14·38%
(b) Total	50,05,72,288	13·65%	11,91,59,001	3·25%	11,69,76,354	3·19%	31,49,66,562	8·59%
3. Number of persons employed								
(a) Workers	308,172	22·22%	20,994	1·51%	17,425	1·26%	59,083	4·26%
(b) Total	319,850	21·12%	25,176	1·66%	19,379	1·31%	72,389	4·78%
4. Salaries and wages (Rs.)	16,06,80,326	15·78%	2,08,49,330	2·05%	1,88,93,391	1·86%	6,84,99,612	6·73%
5. Production (value) (Rs.)	88,29,32,026	14·69%	14,63,85,911	2·44%	13,11,48,043	2·18%	33,90,22,155	5·64%
6. Value added by manufacture (Rs.)	36,97,76,660	17·49%	9,94,24,629	3·28%	4,78,36,590	2·26%	16,01,75,736	7·58%

ᶜ Including drugs and pharmaceuticals.

TABLE 3.1—continued

Item	Bicycles		Sewing machines		Producer gas plants	
	(49)	(50)	(51)	(52)	(53)	(54)
1. Number of factories						
(a) Registered	5		3		5	
(b) Percentage covered	100	0·10%	100	0·06%	80	0·10%
2. Productive capital employed (Rs.)						
(a) Fixed capital	25,02,527	0·15%	21,63,905	0·13%	2,93,197	0·02%
(b) Total	44,34,260	0·12%	33,16,325	0·09%	4,79,697	0·01%
3. Number of persons employed						
(a) Workers	1,551	0·11%	679	0·05%	346	0·02%
(b) Total	1,747	0·12%	717	0·05%	414	0·03%
4. Salaries and wages (Rs.)	13,38,885	0·13%	4,69,663	0·05%	3,29,406	0·03%
5. Production (value) (Rs.)	44,37,061	0·07%	10,41,138	0·02%	9,56,225	0·02%
6. Value added by manufacture (Rs.)	23,44,440	0·11%	5,32,251	0·03%	5,99,353	0·83%

Item	Electric lamps		Electric fans		General engineering and electrical engineering[a]	
	(55)	(56)	(57)	(58)	(59)	(60)
1. Number of factories						
(a) Registered	6		34		1,053	
(b) Percentage covered	100	0·12%	88	0·68%	82	21·01%
2. Productive capital employed (Rs.)						
(a) Fixed capital	10,73,522	0·07%	48,04,192	0·29%	12,09,34,020	7·40%
(b) Total	32,16,203	0·09%	1,20,09,733	0·33%	23,19,40,789	6·32%
3. Number of persons employed						
(a) Workers	646	0·05%	4,470	0·32%	1,00,605	7·25%
(b) Total	811	0·05%	5,167	0·34%	1,12,243	7·41%
4. Salaries and wages (Rs.)	7,52,608	0·07%	42,01,815	0·42%	8,66,67,934	7·92%
5. Production (value) (Rs.)	34,77,006	0·06%	1,55,78,932	0·26%	27,05,43,469	4·50%
6. Value added by manufacture (Rs.)	8,56,006	0·04%	79,36,590	0·38%	11,32,37,113	5·36%

[a] Excluding generation and transformation of electrical energy.

Notes: (1) The percentage figures refer to the share of the industry in all industries.

(2) The production and value added figures are at factor cost.

Source: Calculated from *Ten Years of Indian Manufactures (1946–55),* Directorate of Industrial Statistics, Cabinet Secretariat, Calcutta. This is a summary

In terms of both value added and value of production, the important industries were cotton textiles (46·01 per cent of value added), jute textiles (17·49 per cent of value added and 14·69 per cent of production), sugar, vegetable oils, iron and steel, and general engineering. Rice-milling was significant only in value of production. In terms of employment, the same industries were prominent: with cotton textiles providing 44·38 per cent of total employment and jute textiles 22·22 per cent. The same pattern was evident for the other indices such as salaries and wages and the (dubious) productive capital employed. Between them, these industries (excluding rice) covered 83·71 per cent of total value added and 85·57 per cent of total employment estimated by the Census.

(b) Occupational structure and share of manufacturing

If, however, we examine the changes in occupational structure, it is clear that, while industrialization proceeded vigorously through the period, the impact on the occupational structure was negligible. The share of agriculture in the work force between 1901 and 1951, as recorded by the Censuses, shows little change; and manufacturing even declined slightly from 1911 to 1931, to be restored to the 1901 level by 1951, as is evident from Table 3.2. On the other hand, regional statistics reveal that the share of manufacturing did go up in the states of Kerala, Madras, Maharashtra, and West Bengal, while declining in Orissa and Rajasthan (Table 3.3).[1]

---

and varnishes; soap; tanning; cement; glass and glassware; ceramics; plywood and tea-chests; paper and paperboard; matches; cotton textiles (spinning and weaving); woollen textiles; jute textiles; chemicals (including drugs and pharmaceuticals); aluminium, copper, and brass; iron and steel smelting, rolling and rerolling; bicycles; sewing machines; producer gas plants; electric lamps; electric fans; and the two omnibus categories for miscellaneous engineering industries, each not yet grown to significant size: general engineering and electrical engineering.

[1] Table 3.2 is based on the detailed work of J. Krishnamurty. He has also supplied us with unpublished estimates of the distribution of males only, as this distribution is reputedly more reliably recorded. Note that variations among individual states within India have been present in all periods and for most indices of economic performance. Also see the paper by Alice Thorner, 'Secular Trend of the Indian Economy: 1881–1951', *Economic Weekly*, July 1962, Special Number.

TABLE 3.2
CHANGES IN THE INDUSTRIAL DISTRIBUTION OF THE WORKING FORCE (PERSONS) IN INDIA 1901–1961

Category	Years					
	1901	*1911*	*1921*	*1931*	*1951*	*1961*
1. Cultivators	46·92 (49·9)	48·20	52·32	47·79	50·02	53·80 (51·9)
2. Agricultural Labour	20·66 (15·9)	22·44	19·79	22·47	21·99	19·40 (17·4)
3. Live-stock, forestry, fishing, etc.	3·89 (4·5)	4·32	4·01	4·58	2·39	3·24 (2·4)
4. Mining and quarrying	0·09 (0·1)	0·24	0·26	0·25	0·42	0·48 (0·5)
5. Manufacturing	10·63 (10·4)	9·48	8·72	8·23	9·09	9·23 (9·7)
6. Construction	1·06 (1·1)	1·05	0·98	1·17	1·06	1·26 (1·3)
7. Electricity, gas, water, sanitary services	0·58 (0·5)	0·55	0·52	0·49	0·43	0·34 (0·4)
8. Trade and commerce	5·57 (5·7)	5·29	5·38	5·13	5·24	4·00 (6·2)
9. Transport, storage, communications	1·03 (1·5)	1·07	0·86	0·95	1·53	1·56 (2·0)
10. Services	9·65 (10·7)	7·36	7·16	8·94	7·84	6·70 (8·2)
TOTAL	100·00	100·00	100·00	100·00	100·00	100·00

Notes: These estimates exclude Jammu and Kashmir in 1951, Kerala in 1961, parts of Andaman and Nicobar Islands in 1901, 1911, and 1921, 60,991 persons in Kashmir in 1921, and 75,735 persons in Bombay in 1931. Otherwise they refer to all territories included in present-day India. The figures in brackets refer to *male* workers only. All estimates are derived from Census results.

Source: J. Krishnamurty, 'Secular Changes in Occupational Structure', *Indian Economic and Social History Review*, January 1965, Table 1; the bracketed figures were supplied from unpublished work by J. Krishnamurty.

TABLE 3.3
CHANGES IN THE INDUSTRIAL DISTRIBUTION OF THE WORKING FORCE
(MALES) IN STATES SHOWING SHIFTS BETWEEN AGRICULTURE AND
MANUFACTURING

State		Agriculture, %	Manufacturing (including construction), %	Services, %
Kerala	1911	65·7	13·5	20·6
	1961	55·0	16·2	26·5
Madras	1911	73·6	12·0	14·2
	1961	64·5	16·0	18·5
Maharashtra	1911	70·7	11·7	17·2
	1961	63·4	16·2	19·5
West Bengal	1911	68·7	11·6	17·9
	1961	59·5	16·9	21·9
Orissa	1911	81·1	7·3	11·4
	1961	84·2	6·5	8·9
Rajasthan	1911	63·3	13·5	22·2
	1961	78·4	8·3	12·8

Notes: 'Services' include trade and commerce, transport, storage and communications, and other services.
Source: Unpublished estimates by J. Krishnamurty.

(c) National income and share of manufacturing

The national income estimates show a clear trend in absolute
terms. Over the period 1900–47, *per capita* income also rose,
from an estimated Rs. 52.2 to Rs. 62.2: but this was an increment
of barely 20 per cent in nearly five decades, again indicating a
negligible impact of the century of industrialization on the overall
growth of the economy (Table 3.4).

The share of the 'secondary sector', comprising mainly industries and mining, in the national product was, however, to grow
from 12·7 per cent in 1900–5 to nearly 17 per cent by 1942–7,
reflecting the growth of industrialization and also a rising productivity in this sector (if we recall the relative stagnation in the share
of manufacturing in the occupational structure during this
period).[1]

[1] Cf., J. Krishnamurty, 'Changes in the Composition of the Working Force in
Manufacturing, 1901–1951: A Theoretical and Empirical Analysis', *Indian
Economic and Social History Review*, March 1967, for discussion of this rising
productivity in manufacturing. We may also mention a recent monograph
by K. Mukerji, *Levels of Economic Activity and Public Expenditure in India:
A Historical and Quantitative Study*, Gokhale Institute Studies Number 45,
Poona, 1965; this work gives broadly comparable estimates of national

E

TABLE 3.4
(UNDIVIDED) INDIA'S ABSOLUTE AND PER CAPITA NATIONAL INCOME: 1900/1–1946/47

	National income (Rs. million)	Per capita Rs.	Percentage arising in the primary sector	Percentage arising in the secondary sector	Percentage arising in the tertiary sector
1900/1–1904/5	15,022	52·2	63·6	12·7	23·7
1905/6–1909/10	15,753	53·0	61·7	13·5	24·8
1910/11–1914/15	17,300	57·0	60·1	13·9	26·0
1915/16–1919/20	17,662	57·9	59·6	13·7	26·7
1920/1–1924/5	18,442	59·3	57·4	13·4	29·2
1925/6–1929/30	20,498	62·9	52·1	14·9	33·0
1930/1–1934/5	21,306	61·6	51·4	15·8	32·8
1935/6–1939/40	22,498	60·6	49·9	16·4	33·7
1940/1–1944/5	24,407	61·6	47·5	16·7	35·8
1942/3–1946/7	25,243	62·2	46·0	16·9	37·1

Notes: The primary sector includes agriculture, animal husbandry, forestry, and fishing.

Source: S. Sivasubramonian, *National Income of India 1900/1–1946/47*, unpublished Ph.D. Thesis submitted to Delhi University, 1965, pp. 340 and 352.

(d) Indigenous enterprise

The share of Indian capital and control in the industrial framework had steadily grown through the inter-war period and the second world war. By independence, this control had become significant; by mid-1950s, after nearly a decade of independence, it was to become dominant. Kidron has noted that:

Strict comparison between the two is impossible, but where a list of companies founded by Indian managing agencies shows a heavy concentration of incorporations during the late thirties and the war, and then, after a hiatus, during the modern planning period, a group of thirty-two of the largest foreign houses shows a steep decline in the number of newly incorporated managed companies from 79 in the 1910–19 decade, to 55 in the twenties, 28 in the thirties, 13 in the forties, and 5 between 1950 and 1956. Between 1936–7 and 1942–3 non-Indian companies increased their paid-up capital by 1 per cent compared with 17 per cent for Indian companies.

Studies of individual industries reveal the same picture. The inquiry into the paper industry already quoted [Eddison, *op. cit.*] found 'initiative and leadership passing more and more into the hands of Indian-controlled companies' from 1936 onwards, despite the fact that the industry has been 'overwhelmingly dominated by British-managed firms for the first three-quarters of a century of its existence'. Although the British firms maintained higher and more consistent standards of quality, Indian management was found to be 'more energetic, aggressive, and willing to take financial risks . . . [They] were prepared to gamble on the growing demand for paper both in the late 1930s and in the early 1950s to a much greater extent than were their Western-managed counterparts. They did not limit themselves to the expansion they could achieve out of their own resources but made much of their growth on borrowed money.' After the war it was the Indian manufacturers that toured paper-making plants in North America; and it was the Birla group, today the largest producers, that first undertook a major expansion at the end of the decade, by doubling capacity at their Orient Mills. Subsequent expansion has made this group the best equipped technically and the cheapest producer in the country. Where British firms did grow—as has F. W. Heilger in Orissa—

income and its sectoral composition, as also estimates of public expenditure. We have preferred, however, to use Sivasubramonian's estimates of absolute and *per capita* national income in Table 3.4.

they did so piece-meal and reluctantly, in response to government pressure.[1]

The trend was similar in most other industries. The share of foreign-controlled enterprise in employment and output controlled by them fell in 'traditional' industries such as coal and tea as also in sugar, cement, and paper. Further, Indian business was to dominate, from the start, the growing new activities such as bicycles and textile machinery. Banking followed the same pattern, with the share of the foreign 'Exchange Banks' falling sharply to 17 per cent in 1947 from 70 per cent in 1914.[2]

Furthermore, towards the end of the period culminating in independence, Indian enterprise had already demonstrated its tendency to congeal into large groups or 'empires' which straddled several industries.[3] This foreshadowed the immense concentration of industrial investments in a few industrial 'houses' or groups which was to characterize even the period of planned growth from 1951 to 1966. The growth of none of these empires has been studied in depth from social and economic viewpoints, and this represents an important lacuna in Indian economic history. However, such a development appears to have been inherent in the tendency for entrepreneurial classes to spring from certain business communities and the close caste and kinship network which characterizes these classes, as is evident even today. It was also reinforced by the managing agency system's historical dominance on the Indian scene: this facilitated vertical integration. Thus, for example, the Birla group which had under their management, in 1939, six cotton mills, a rayon mill, and two jute mills, set up then the Textile Machinery Corporation which was to manufacture various machinery parts of all kinds with specializa-

---

[1] Kidron, op. cit., pp. 41–2. He draws upon several sources: Gokhale Institute of Politics and Economics, *Notes on the Rise of Business Communities in India*, 1951; J. Eddison, *Industrial Development in the Growth of the Pulp and Paper Industry in India*, Center for International Studies (M.I.T.), February 1955; Buchanan, op. cit.; and D. L. Spencer, *India, Mixed Enterprise and Western Business*.

[2] Pardiwala, 'Exchange Banks in India', *Economic Weekly*, 10 February 1951, p. 154; quoted by Kidron, op. cit., p. 42.

[3] For details, especially on the dominance of the Birla, Tata, Dalmia-Jain, Bangurs, and Thapar groups in overall investment, see R. K. Hazari's pioneering study, *The Structure of the Corporate Sector*, Bombay, Asia Publishing House, 1966.

tion in textile machinery.[1] Cases of extension into transportation were also to be found: Martin Burn, for example, set up and managed the Indian Standard Wagon Co. which was to manufacture railway carriages and other equipment for railways.

How 'production-minded' were these entrepreneurial classes? Their primary origin from trading and moneylending classes is likely to have imparted a strong tendency towards sales and financial, rather than production, acumen and, in some Marwari instances, even a tendency towards quick gain rather than long-term profit maximization. Parsis, in the main, appear to have been the exception. This reputation, however, seems to have been acquired largely through the traditions set by the house of Tata's who have been noted for their meticulous attention to product quality, design, and notions of consumer service which are in contrast to the traditions of many other industrial groups.[2] In fact, the stereotype of private, indigenous enterprise which India was to inherit with independence was very much the opposite of Tata's record: and it was eventually to be reinforced by the revelations of sharp practices by managing agencies and industrial groups such as Dalmia-Sahu-Jain which came to light in the 1950s,[3] and the strengthening of the economic and political power of these industrial groups through the period of planning despite the apparatus of industrial licensing and public sector investments.[4]

It is also noteworthy that, again with the exception of Tata's, few of the industrial groups appear to have been interested in providing for systematic research. In this respect, the Indian experience has been contrary to the Japanese and this lacuna, to be traced historically perhaps to the dominance of trading and

---

[1] S. K. Basu, *The Managing Agency System: In Prospect and Retrospect*, op. cit., pp. 33-5.

[2] Again, whether these widespread notions are justified by the actual performance of the other industrial groups, and indeed whether other Parsi entrepreneurs have followed practices similar to those of the Tata's are questions which have not yet been investigated throughly by Indian economic historians.

[3] See, in particular, the *Report of the Commission of Enquiry on the Administration of Dalmia-Jain Companies*, Government of India, New Delhi, 1963, which indicts a major industrial group for a variety of financial malpractices, constituting fraud on the shareholders and on the Government. These malpractices are widely held to characterize other Marwari groups as well.

[4] Cf. R. K. Hazari, *Industrial Planning and Licensing Policy*, Planning Commission, Government of India, 1967.

moneylending communities in industrial entrepreneurship in India and an explicit state policy for import-substitution in know-how in Japan, has continued in an attenuated form through the planning period for different reasons arising primarily from the operation of industrial and trade policies.

(e) Industrial skills

The lack of development of local technology and research establishments on any significant scale in the industries that were established by 1947 was matched by inadequate creation of opportunities for Indians to qualify for higher-skilled and executive jobs. Part of the problem was, of course, the difficulty of getting Indians employed in foreign-controlled concerns, at higher levels. But, even in indigenous concerns, Indians with technical skills were to grow in number in most cases unaided by governmental initiative in providing technical education or private-industrial programmes to train skilled, indigenous technicians.[1]

Again, among the leading exceptions were Tata's at Jamshedpur. Tata's in fact had started operations on the strength of a cosmopolitan foreign force of high-skilled technicians. The management had been American, the coke-oven installations had been carried out by the Welsh, the Germans were producing open-hearth steel and the British were in the rolling-mill. Jamshedjee Tata had chosen the best for each job. But this was soon to give way during the 1920s. John Keenan's account of this Indianization of Tata's is extremely vivid:

During the first World War the company's directors had not thought much about training Indians to take the place of imported nationals of other countries. But during its course many of them went to Japan on business; they met Japanese steel men and saw how their plants were run. The mills were operated entirely by Japanese, although Americans had been used to establish the industry and get it running. Returning to India, the directors recalled that when the original small steel plant came into operation Tata's had employed only two Europeans in the boiler plant and power house, and only two in the electrical department, the chief engineer and his assistant. All the operators were Indians and dozens of those under the chief engineer held university degrees. . . .

---

[1] Cf. Aparna Basu, *Indian Education and Politics, 1898–1920*, unpublished Ph.D. dissertation, Cambridge University, 1966; Chapter IV in particular.

The Tatas had always intended that the Company should be entirely Indian. After the various directors had returned from their very instructive trips to Japan there was a general agreement that the Indianization of the company was not only desirable but altogether possible as soon as the war should be won. The directors had before their eyes many concrete examples of Indian ability. . . .

In 1919 Sir Dorab Tata, reviewing what these young Indians had accomplished, pointed out to the company directors that if Indians could be educated and trained abroad to take over from foreigners highly technical jobs successfully, they could also be educated and trained at home. He proposed an Institute of Metallurgical Technology in Jamshedpur. The directors were so enthusiastic that within a year a large building with laboratories, lecture halls, classrooms, and a library was built and equipped. Three excellent Britishers and a number of ranking Indian instructors formed the nucleus of the teaching staff. The students were to receive enough pay for each month to cover living and incidental expenses. We advertised for students, stipulating that they must be Bachelors of Science from accredited Indian or foreign universities, and offering rail and travelling costs to the men we wanted to interview.

Out of the one thousand applications which poured in on us, we selected two hundred from whom to pick the final twenty students we could enroll in the school. Out of that first group of twenty, one is now superintendent of open-hearth furnaces, one is superintendent of the duplex plant, a third is superintendent of the older department controlling the rolling program, a fourth is head of the Institute itself. . . .[1]

While the experience at Tata's was by and large exceptional for indigenous (and British-controlled) enterprise, the private initiative of enterprising Indians ensured a steady though small growth in the supply of skilled, technical manpower. Turned out first by the country's primarily humanistic system,[2] geared to the bureaucracy and its own internal feedback, young men went abroad to get the training to qualify for technical positions at home. By 1947 the Indian educational system had also been modified, in response to the growing industrialization, to admit

[1] Keenan, op. cit., pp. 133–41.
[2] This began substantively in the early nineteenth century; and the famous Presidency Colleges of Madras, Calcutta, and Bombay were to initiate the steady growth of educational facilities imparting Western-type education through the rest of the century. On the role of Macaulay in this crucial development in India, as also more detailed discussion of the growth of education, Vincent Smith, *A History of India*, is an excellent source.

technical colleges. For example,[1] in the area that was to constitute India after the partition, the facilities for technical education and training had developed considerably, in the form of training schools and higher-education Colleges and Institutes embracing several different forms of engineering (but with primary emphasis on civil engineering, reflecting the relatively semi-industrialized character of the economy). By 1947, as many as 6,600 students were being admitted to such technical and professional courses and over 2,700 graduates with degrees and diplomas were being turned out per annum. Over 45,000 students were already enrolled in these courses at University level and over 92,000 were enrolled at lower levels.

(f) Industrial labour

By 1947 the labour force in the modern factory sector amounted to over 2 million workers, though this was only around 2 per cent of the working population. That this emergence of industrial labour had been painful, inefficient, slow, and halting because of continuing involvement with the countryside which resulted in excessive labour turnover, absenteeism, and insufficient commitment to factory discipline was a view largely current in the traditional literature in this area.[2] But it has been undermined by the recent, thorough work of Morris on the labour supply to the cotton textile industry during the long period of its growth from the 1850s to recent times. He has found that the industry was never faced by labour shortage and 'generally could recruit all the new raw labour it required to meet its needs for expansion'. Furthermore, the labour came from distances as far as United Provinces to seek employment in the industry: this clearly indicated that the costs of migration to the countryside, except occasionally, would be somewhat prohibitive. Moreover, an increasing proportion of the work force appears to have originated in Bombay itself—a fact which casts doubts on the importance of rural involvement. The commitment of the labour force to industry for its livelihood appears to have been fairly significant and the absenteeism and rural migration considerably exaggerated.

[1] Cf. *Progress of Education in India: 1947–1952*, Ministry of Education, Government of India, 1953; especially Chapter VI.
[2] Cf. C. A. Myers, *Labor Problems in the Industrialization of India*, op. cit.

The loose forms of labour discipline and utilization in cotton textiles were dictated by profit maximization considerations: it was generally cheaper to keep unskilled labour idle instead of expensive machines which, to be economic, had to be kept running continuously. The apparent inefficiency of labour was thus not *inherent* but dictated by the state of technology in textiles and the relative factor costs of labour and capital. In the steel industry, Morris persuasively argues, where such loose labour organization would have been inimical to efficiency and where a stable labour force was also a *sine qua non* of high productivity, the employers had no difficulty at all in achieving both:

The Jamshedpur enterprise, established in a very lightly populated district in 1908, built up a labor force which by 1957 amounted to 40,000 workers. The entirely new city which grew up around the steel plant claimed a population of nearly a quarter of a million in 1951. As in the Bombay [textiles] situation, the evidence suggests that at no time during the first half-century did TISCO suffer from an inadequate supply of raw labor which it could train to its needs. . . .

Within a decade of the production of the first iron ingots there is evidence of substantial stability in the labor force. In fact, by the 1950's, the firm found itself actually embarrassed by the lack of labor turnover.

The relative work-force stability in Jamshedpur as compared with Bombay certainly did not arise from any fundamental differences in the cultural characteristics of the workers recruited. What are involved are dissimilarities in the technical necessities of the two industries and the consequent variations in policies demanded of the employers.

For the bulk of its career the Bombay textile industry required workers who needed only very casual training and the most limited sort of supervision. The stability of individual workers was of no fundamental concern to employers; recruitment and administration of labor therefore could be turned over to jobbers. By contrast, the steel operation required a much broader range of skills and more elaborate investment in training. On the whole, TISCO could not tolerate a free-floating, near-casual work force if efficient and profitable operation was to be maintained. As a consequence, recruitment and administration of the labor force was always a matter of strong concern to the Company. Although the labor recruited was certainly as cosmopolitan and the cultural and linguistic distinctions as complex as in Bombay, the management never found itself forced to give to its low-level jobber equivalents the basic responsibilities for the administration of its work force. The ramshackle discipline appropriate in Bombay mills until the 1920's was never feasible in Jamshedpur, and it never appeared.

The evidence from Bombay and Jamshedpur suggests that the creation of a disciplined industrial labor force in a newly developing society is not particularly difficult. A comparison of the cotton textile and the steel industries makes it clear that the difference in worker stability cannot be accounted for by any substantial difference in the psychology of the raw labor recruited. Nor can it be attributed to dissimilarities in the traditional environment from which the workers came. If there were differences in work-force behavior, these flowed from employer policy. The necessities imposed by industrial technology and markets required employers to select different systems of discipline, and these determined the way labor would work.[1]

The fact that workers in India have come to factories from varying distances and yet managed to constitute a reasonably stable industrial work force, with 'commitment' to industrial employment, has been established by other analyses as well. Thus Lambert, in a recent study of five factories in Poona (in the State of Maharashtra) found that as many as 73·4 per cent of the workers in the textile factory, 64·7 per cent in the paper factory, 89·8 per cent in the engine factory, 77·5 per cent in the biscuit and chocolate factory and 76·2 per cent in the rubber factory expressed commitment to factory employment by answering affirmatively when asked whether they would seek other factory employment in event of a hypothetical lay-off.[2]

(g) Industrial finance

The finance to support the growth in industrialization up to 1947 came from: (i) the own wealth of the indigenous business communities, who had made their fortunes in trade and money-lending and who were now ploughing these funds directly into

[1] Morris, op. cit., pp. 209–10.
[2] Lambert, *Workers, Factories and Social Change in India*, Princeton University Press, New Jersey, 1963, pp. 84–5. Lambert also considers other sociological questions such as the tendency to use employment exchanges to secure factory jobs and attitudes with respect thereto. An important sociological contribution to these problems is N. R. Sheth, 'An Indian Factory—Aspects of Its Social Framework', *Journal of M. S. University of Baroda*, IX, March 1960. Among the economic contributions to this question, we found the following particularly helpful: Daniel Thorner, 'Casual Employment of a Factory Labour Force, 1851–1939', *The Economic Weekly*, January 1957, Annual Number; and Ralph C. James, 'The Casual Labor Problem in Indian Manufacturing', *The Quarterly Journal of Economics*, February 1960.

their new industrial ventures; (ii) the nascent but growing capital market in the country on which for example (as we saw) the Tata's drew quite successfully for their Jamshedpur works; and (iii) the system of 'direct deposits' under which the textile mills in particular invited direct investment, on a loan basis, from individual savers at favourable rates of interest. The steady growth of modern, commercial banks through the twentieth century was to provide working capital: however, in the English (as distinct from the continental) tradition, they were to keep away from industrial, long-term finance.[1] Moreover, there were few such banks, anyway: as late as the mid-1920s, India had only around 400 joint-stock banks or branches as against nearly 2,500 towns of 5,000 or more people.

(h) Urbanization

The urbanized nature of the Indian economy was traditionally conspicuous in India: and, at the time of the introduction of British power in India, north India and Bengal already contained 'many big and populous cities'.[2] When India's first Census was taken, the percentage of Indian urban population in 1872 turned out to be as much as 8·7 per cent. As Gadgil has noted, 'In Western countries the percentages of the urban population towards the beginning of the nineteenth century were: England and Wales 21·3, Scotland 17·0, France 9·5, Prussia 7·25, Russia 3·7, U.S.A. 3·8. We might then conclude that urban development in India had progressed at the beginning of this century at least as far as it had in France.'[3]

The industrialization which India experienced during the century prior to independence cannot definitely be described as

---

[1] 'Modern industrial banking has developed practically not at all. The principal institution was started in 1917 with the backing of the powerful house of Tata whose name it bore. But it fell a victim of the slump, lost half its capital, and was taken over by the Imperial Bank.' Buchanan, op. cit., p. 162.

[2] D. R. Gadgil, *The Industrial Evolution of India in Recent Times*, Oxford University Press, 4th edition, 1954, p. 134. Professor Gadgil also records 'that in Clive's opinion the city of Murshidabad was in his day more populous than London'.

[3] Ibid., p. 134. Gadgil does not, however, explicitly state that the definitions of urban population used in these different countries are comparable. By and large, places with population in excess of 5,000 were classified as towns in the Indian Census of 1872.

the source of the continuing spread of urbanization in India, until after 1911. Until then, several of the older cities declined, in particular the capital towns of Dacca, Lucknow, and Murshidabad, partly reflecting the decline of certain traditional handicrafts through this early period. At the same time, the new towns such as Bombay and Calcutta turned into burgeoning cities: reflecting the growth in new industries, foreign trade, and the linking up of the hinterland by railways. The influx of rural population into the cities was also prompted, it has been suggested by Gadgil, by recurrent famine conditions and the growth of the landless labouring class. After 1911, the urbanization was to proceed fairly distinctly: from 9·42 per cent of the population in 1911 to 10·2 in 1921, nearly 11 per cent in 1931, and over 11·7 per cent in 1941. The cities which grew rapidly were Bombay, Calcutta, Delhi, Ahmedabad, Nagpur, Salem, Sholapur, Lahore and Karachi (which went to Pakistan), and the steel town of Jamshedpur.

(i) Transport and communications

By 1947, the growth of inland transport, both by road and rail, as also coastal and foreign shipping had been considerable. So also were the communication facilities.[1]

The road mileage was already as much as nearly 300,000 miles, of which nearly a third was metalled. While this mileage fell short of the *per capita* or per square mile of area levels in the industrialized countries of the West at the time, it was impressive by the standards of developing countries.[2] At the same time, rail transport had reached an advanced stage. The total length of

---

[1] The British had started extending the road transportation facilities as early as the 1820s: 'Lord Bentinck, viceroy from 1828 to 1835, secured the building of the "Grand Trunk Road" between Calcutta and the Northwest Provinces, which was later extended to Peshwar near the present northwest frontier .... About 60 feet wide, lined with trees over much of its length, it is kept in fair repair and is now a passably good motor road stretching for 1,500 miles over the most fascinating plain in the world. A few other long distance roads were built by the British, the most important of which was the "Great Deccan Road" from Mirzapur on the Grand Trunk to Nagpur.' Buchanan, op. cit., p. 177.

[2] According to C. N. Vakil, *Economic Consequences of Divided India*, Vora and Co. Publishers Ltd., 1950, India had around 0·18 miles of roads per square mile of area, just prior to partition, as against 1 mile in the United States and 1·90 miles in France.

lines, including metre and narrow gauges, was over 41,000 miles by 1947, spanned by nine major railway systems straddling the entire country. Shipping had not developed to corresponding proportions; but India already had a modest tonnage of 327,000 tons. Besides, port facilities had assumed significant dimensions: there were already large ports, handling India's foreign trade, at Bombay, Calcutta, Madras, Cochin, Vizagapatam, and the ports of Chittagong and Karachi (which were to go to Pakistan with the partition). Air transport was at a stage of relative infancy: but there already were sixty-four airports, of which three handled international traffic, at Bombay, Calcutta, and Delhi, and the ten air transport companies then in existence had one hundred and seventy aircraft in service and thirty-nine Indian cities were connected by air.[1]

II. PARTITION

This picture, of a country still at a strikingly low level of *per capita* income but making substantial progress in the different dimensions of a modernized state, was to remain intact despite partition of the country into India and Pakistan in 1947.

Partition, which accompanied the grant of independence, essentially involved two major provinces: Bengal and Panjab. Measured as in 1948, partitioned India had a little over 77 per cent of the territory of undivided India and over 80 per cent of the population. India obtained a relatively larger share of the urban population and a disproportionately larger share of the manufacturing industries, such as jute and cotton textile mills. On the other hand, Pakistan was to get a lion's share of the raw materials fed into these industries: important producing centres for raw jute and raw cotton were to be found in East and West Pakistan respectively. India also was to lose her best irrigated areas in the state of Panjab to Pakistan.

Other facilities such as transportation were also to be divided. For example, India retained a little over four-fifths of the rail mileage and a somewhat larger share of roads. While Pakistan, mainly in the East, inherited a vast network of inland waterways, India was to enjoy a much larger share of civil aviation and ocean shipping. The major trading communities were essentially in

[1] *Economic Consequences of Divided India*, pp. 402–30.

India, although a few Parsis in Karachi represented a windfall to Pakistan. The major financial markets such as Bombay and Calcutta came to India as well. In the main, India appears to have emerged from partition no worse off, on the average, than undivided India, thinking purely in terms of the kinds of indices we have looked at in this chapter.[1]

On the other hand, the upheavals such as riots and massive transfers of population that followed upon partition were to dislocate both countries, politically and economically, during the period immediately after partition. This period of dislocation, coming close upon the termination of the second world war, was to leave the Indian economy in a state of continuing abnormality, characterized by frequent resort to controls over prices in the face of shortages and generally rising prices. By the time, however, the country formally went over to planned development in 1951, the economy was substantially on the way to normalization.[2]

The period since 1951 was to witness a new phase in Indian economic development, with the Government undertaking to regulate and accelerate the country's progress in a planned framework. The main focus of our study is precisely this period, which was to see three successive Five-Year Plans running through 1951–66. We shall now review the principal aspects of India's economic growth during this period, and then discuss in depth her industrial performance and import-substitution (by different industrial groups) in the subsequent chapter.

---

[1] Vakil, op. cit., Introduction, gives a useful, broad survey of the principal effects of partition on India's economic characteristics. Further details can be found in the rest of the volume.

[2] The Korean War, however, was already disrupting the economic situation: its beneficial effects to the economy being accompanied by serious price increases which were to prompt resort to extensive price controls again (via the 'Supply and Prices of Goods Ordinance', 1950). Cf. Vakil, op. cit., pp. 521–2.

PART II

Growth Since Independence

4
Economic Growth During 1951-66

In many respects, India's overall economic performance in the modern period has been impressive, even if inadequate to its needs. The rate of growth of its national income has *significantly* increased over its historical trend. Literacy, education, and health services have moved upward on a continuing basis. The distinct economic and social progress has further taken place in a framework of monetary stability through most of the period as also in the context of democratic institutions. Overall there is little doubt that the Indian experience has been notable in both economic and political terms. Although throughout this work we detail the many respects in which India's economic performance in the industrial (and trade) sectors could have been improved, and we draw important policy lessons therefrom, it is necessary to remember the significant acceleration in economic progress that has indisputably occurred.

I. PRINCIPAL FEATURES

(a) National income

Tables 4.1 and 4.2 show that, at constant prices, national income grew at an annual rate of 3·5 per cent during the First Five-Year Plan, 4·0 per cent during the Second Plan, and 2·9 per cent during the Third Plan.[1] We must add, however, that the picture of reduced level of performance in the Third Plan is exaggerated and gives a misleading impression of relative performance over the three Plans because the last year of the Third Plan was

---

[1] However, the revised estimates of net national income at 1960–1 prices indicate a growth of 2·8 per cent during the Third Plan. This corresponds to a growth of 0·3 per cent *per capita* during the period. *Economic Survey, 1967–68*, Government of India, p. A-5.

F

TABLE 4.1
NATIONAL INCOME, ABSOLUTE AND PER CAPITA, AT CONSTANT PRICES:
1948–67

	Conventional estimates of net national product (at 1948/9 prices) (Rs. crores = ten million)	Conventional estimates per capita net national product (at 1948/9 Prices) (Rs.)
1948/9	8,650	249·6
1949/50	8,820	250·6
1950/1	8,850	247·5
1951/2	9,100	250·3
1952/3	9,460	255·7
1953/4	10,030	266·2
1954/5	10,280	267·8
1955/6	10,480	267·8
1956/7	11,000	275·6
1957/8	10,890	267·3
1958/9	11,650	280·1
1959/60	11,860	279·2
1960/1	12,730	293·3
1961/2	13,060	294·0
1962/3	13,310	291·9
1963/4	13,970	299·2
1964/5[a]	15,000	313·7
1965/6[a]	14,660	299·4
1966/7[b]	14,950	298·8

[a] Preliminary.
[b] Quick estimate.
Source: *Economic Survey, 1967–68*, Government of India, p. A-4.

TABLE 4.2
ANNUAL GROWTH RATES OF NATIONAL INCOME, ABSOLUTE AND PER
CAPITA, BY EACH PLAN

	Net national product	Per capita net national product
First Plan	3·5	1·6
Second Plan	4·0	1·8
Third Plan	2·9	0·4

Source: *Economic Survey, 1967–68*, p. A-4.

characterized by an unprecedented drought and by the aftermath
of the Indo-Pakistan hostilities during late 1965 which included
temporary suspension of foreign aid from Western countries. If
we were to exclude the last year of this Plan and consider only the
first four years, the growth rate for the Third Plan turns out to
have been 4·2 per cent per annum at constant (1960/1) prices.[1]

[1] *Fourth Five-Year Plan (A Draft Outline)*, Planning Commission, Government
of India, p. 7.

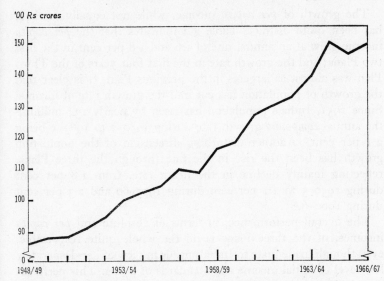

Figure 4.1 Net national product (at 1948/9 prices) 1948/9–1966/7.

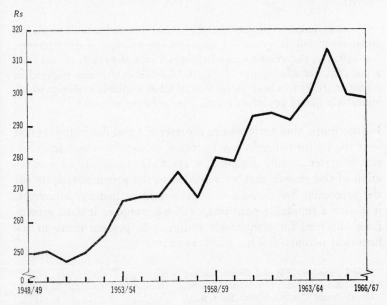

Figure 4.2. *Per capita* net national product (at 1948/9 prices) 1948/9–1966/7.
Source: Table 4.1

The growth of *per capita* income, while not equally marked, has been quite distinct. Table 4.2 indicates that the *per capita* income grew at an annual rate of 1·6 and 1·8 per cent in the first two Plans; and the growth rate in the first four years of the Third Plan was almost as large as in the previous Plan. It is clear that the growth of population has cut into the growth rate of income. Since 1951, India's population has risen by nearly 134 million,[1] the annual *compound* growth rate during 1950–2 to 1963–5 being 2·1 per cent.[2] Another disturbing dimension of the population growth has been the rise in the rate through the three Plans, reflecting mainly decline in the death rate, from 1·8 per cent during 1950–5 to 2·1 per cent during 1955–60 and 2·3 per cent during 1960–6.[3]

The overall performance, in terms of absolute and *per capita* incomes, of the three Plans is on the whole quite respectable, even though inadequate to India's needs in view of her desperately low level of initial income and standards of living. This performance looks yet better if we note that the official statistics that we have cited are almost certainly on the low side. As K. N. Raj has noted:

There is reason to suspect that the official national income series has under-estimated the growth of output in some sectors of the economy. For instance, the official series indicates a rate of growth of less than 1 per cent per annum in the output of small enterprises engaged in manufacturing; this is at variance with other available evidence which indicates a rate of growth of nearer 5 per cent per annum.[4]

Furthermore, this performance represents a distinct improvement over the performance in any historical period for which information is systematically available; it certainly represents an acceleration of the growth that we recorded in the previous chapter for the preceding five decades of India's modern history. Moreover, it is also a reputable performance if we compare it with growth rates observed for comparable countries in present times or for historical periods. Raj has noted again:

[1] *Fourth Five-Year Plan (A Draft Outline)*, p. 8.
[2] *Population of Less Developed Countries*, (Research Division), O.E.C.D. Development Centre, August 1967, p. 12.
[3] Ibid., p. 12.
[4] K. N. Raj, *Indian Economic Growth: Performance and Prospects*, p. 2.

The rate of economic growth that has been achieved in India since 1950–51 is 2 to 3 times as high as the rate recorded earlier under British administration. As a result, the percentage increase in national income in the last thirteen years has been higher than the percentage increase realized in India over the entire preceding half a century. Japan is generally believed to be a country which grew rapidly in the latter part of the 19th and the first quarter of the 20th century; yet the rate of growth of national income in Japan was slightly less than 3 per cent per annum in the period 1893–1912 and did not go up to more than 4 per cent per annum even in the following decade. Judged by criteria such as these the growth rate achieved in India in the last decade and a half is certainly a matter for some satisfaction.[1]

(b) Production and occupational structure

Has this process of expansion of national income been accompanied by marked shifts in the production and occupational structure? Table 4.3 records the available data on the absolute and relative distribution of net national income by sector of origin, at constant prices for the period 1950–65. It shows that, while the contribution of net income from agriculture, animal husbandry, and ancillary activities has declined visibly, that of net income from mining, manufacturing, and small enterprises has remained virtually stagnant at around 16·7 per cent. This conclusion, however, would be slightly modified if the contribution of small industries was revised upwards, as indicated in the preceding section.

At the same time, examination of the distribution of active population by sector of employment, as recorded in Table 4.4, indicates that the percentage of population engaged in agriculture has, if anything, increased slightly: thus indicating, while not conclusively establishing (in view of the statistical difficulties of occupational censuses and the changing concepts used in classifying multi-occupational workers by single occupational classifications), that the agricultural sector has had to absorb part of the growing population despite the acceleration in the growth of income. The occupational structure has, by and large, remained unchanged despite the growth and industrialization: much as in the century of industrialization preceding the modern period.

[1] K. N. Raj, *Indian Economic Growth: Performance and Prospects*, p. 2.

TABLE 4.3

CONVENTIONAL ESTIMATES OF NET DOMESTIC PRODUCT BY SECTOR OF ORIGIN (AT 1948-9 PRICES)

(RS. 100 CRORES)

	1950/1	1951/2	1952/3	1953/4	1954/5	1955/6	1956/7	1957/8	1958/9
1. Agriculture, animal husbandry, and ancillary activities (including forestry and fishery)	43·4 (48·9)	44·4 (48·8)	46·0	49·8	50·3	50·2	52·5	50·1	55·6
2. Mining, manufacturing, and small enterprises	14·8 (16·7)	15·2 (16·7)	15·8	16·5	17·0	17·6	18·4	18·6	18·8
3. Commerce, transport, and communications	16·6 (18·7)	17·3 (18·9)	17·9	18·3	19·1	19·7	20·8	21·1	21·9
4. Other services—including professional and liberal arts, government services, etc.	13·9 (15·7)	14·3 (15·7)	15·0	15·7	16·4	17·3	18·2	19·2	20·4
5. Net domestic product at factor cost	88·7 (100·0)	91·2 (100·0)	94·7	100·3	102·8	104·8	109·0	190·0	116·7
Net national output	88·5	91·0	94·6	100·3	102·8	104·8	110·0	108·9	116·5

	1959/60	1960/1	1961/2	1962/3	1963/4	1964/5a	1965/6a	1966/7b
1. Agriculture, animal husbandry, and ancillary activities (including forestry and fishery)	55·0	59·0	59·1	57·9	59·7	65·1 (43·1)	57·2 (38·6)	57·3
2. Mining, manufacturing, and small enterprises	19·7	21·1	22·1	23·0	24·4	25·3 (16·7)	26·6 (18·0)	27·2
3. Commerce, transport, and communications	22·7	24·6	25·4	26·4	27·8	29·5 (19·5)	29·8 (20·2)	30·2
4. Other services—including professional and liberal arts, government services, etc.	21·4	23·1	24·7	26·6	28·7	31·2 (20·7)	34·2 (23·1)	36·5
5. Net domestic product at factor cost	118·8	127·8	131·8	133·9	140·6	151·1 (100·0)	147·8 (100·0)	151·2
Net national output	118·5	126·9						

a Preliminary estimate.
b Quick estimate.

Notes: Figures in brackets give percentage distribution. These are derived by using net domestic product at factor cost as the divisor, and have been rounded to the first decimal.

Source: *Estimates of National Income*, October 1967, Central Statistical Organization.

TABLE 4.4
PERCENTAGE DISTRIBUTION OF ACTIVE POPULATION BY SECTOR OF EMPLOYMENT IN INDIA, 1951-61

Year	Total active population (thousands)	Agriculture	Mining and quarrying	Manufacturing	Construction	Electricity, gas, water, and sanitary services	Commerce, Banking, insurance, real estate, etc.	Transport, storage, and Communications	Services	Un-allocated	Total
1951	101,775	70·6	0·5	9·0	1·1	0·5	5·8	1·9	10·6		100·0
1961	188,676	72·9	0·5	9·5	1·1	0·3	4·1	1·6	8·8	1·2	100·0

Source: *Population of Less Developed Countries*, op. cit., Table 3.

TABLE 4.5
INDEX NUMBERS OF AGRICULTURAL PRODUCTION (AGRICULTURAL YEAR 1949-50 = 100)

Item	1950/1	1955/6	1956/7	1957/8	1958/9	1959/60	1960/1	1961/2	1962/3	1963/4	1964/5[a]	1965/6[a]	1966/7[a]
1. Foodgrains	90·5	115·3	120·8	109·2	130·6	127·9	137·1	140·3	133·6	136·5	150·2	120·9	124·6
2. Non-foodgrains	105·9	119·9	131·5	129·5	139·4	135·0	152·6	153·9	151·6	156·5	175·4	156·4	148·2
3. All commodities	95·6	116·8	124·3	115·9	133·5	130·3	142·2	144·8	139·6	143·1	158·5	132·7	132·4

[a] Provisional estimates.

Source: *Economic Survey: 1967-68*, adapted from p. A-8.

(c) Agricultural production

In view of the weight of agriculture in India's economy, the growing national income has also reflected a sizeable expansion of Indian agricultural output. If we leave out the last year of the Third Plan, which was characterized by an unprecedented drought, the annual compound rate of agricultural growth turns out to have been in excess of 3 per cent (see Table 4.5) during the period of the three Plans.[1] Furthermore, this growth has not been confined to area extension but has also reflected growth in yields per acre, particularly since the Second Plan (see Table 4.6).

TABLE 4.6
INDEX NUMBERS OF AGRICULTURAL AREA AND YIELD [a]
(Base 1950/1 = 100)

Crop year	Area	Yield per acre
1950/1	100·0	100·0
1951/2	101·8	99·0
1952/3	105·6	101·3
1953/4	109·1	104·2
1954/5	112·2	105·9
1955/6	113·8	107·3
1956/7	114·6	106·3
1957/8	116·1	109·8
1958/9	117·7	110·0
1959/60	119·7	115·7
1960/1	121·2	117·5
1961/2	122·4	119·0
1962/3	123·4	118·2
1963/4	123·7	121·7
1964/5	122·4	121·0
1965/6	122·0	118·3

[a] Three-year moving averages.
Source: *Economic Survey, 1967–68*, adapted from p. A-7.

This overall performance of Indian agriculture, over a sustained period of fifteen years, is remarkable by international standards, even though it has been inadequate to match the demand arising from growth in population and incomes, thus leading to food

[1] The next year, 1966/7, was also a bad drought year. However, 1967/8 has (at the time of writing) turned out to be a remarkably good year from the viewpoint of agricultural performance, lending credence to the views of many observers who consider that Indian agriculture is on the verge of, if it has not already entered, its take-off. See, in particular, M. L. Dantwala's excellent article: 'Incentives and Disincentives in Indian Agriculture', *Indian Journal of Agricultural Economics*, April–June 1967.

imports under the Public Law 480 programme of the United States Government:

These rates of growth are no doubt inadequate to sustain the overall rates of economic growth which the Indian economy needs to achieve now for making a visible dent on poverty and unemployment in the country; there is certainly no room for complacency. But it is important to recognize that the rates already realized do not compare very un- favourably with rates recorded in other countries placed in broadly comparable situations. For instance, in Japan, gross agricultural output increased by only about 120 per cent between 1878 and 1912, i.e., at a compound rate of growth of less than 2½ per cent per annum. The growth rate was even lower in the following three decades and pro- duction rose, therefore, only by 40 per cent between 1908–1912 and 1933–37. It required the land reform of the 'fifties and rapid in- dustrial growth (which took population away from agriculture at a fast rate) to bring about a more spectacular growth rate in agriculture in Japan.

Even in China such evidence as is available suggests that the rate of growth of agricultural production since 1952 has not been very much higher than in India.[1]

(d) Savings and investment

India's performance in raising her average rate of domestic saving appears to have been perhaps the most impressive aspect of her economic progress. Although the estimates of savings and investment in India are not altogether reliable, they strongly indicate a steady rise in the rate of domestic saving through the three Plans. The Draft Outline of the Fourth Plan has neatly summarized the Indian record on this important question:

In 1950–51, total investment in the economy is estimated to have been of the order of 5½ per cent of the national income; this was financed wholly from domestic savings, which are also estimated to have been around 5½ per cent of national income. In the years since, both these proportions have increased but at different rates. The ratio of invest- ment to national income had, at the end of the Third Plan Period, risen to about 14 per cent, while the ratio of domestic savings to national income rose at a somewhat slower rate—to around 9 per cent in 1960–61 and about 10·5 per cent in 1965–66. These disparate trends in the

[1] Raj, op. cit., pp. 9–10.

TABLE 4.7
REVENUE RECEIPTS AS A PERCENTAGE OF NET NATIONAL PRODUCT AT FACTOR COST

Item	1950/1	1951/2	1952/3	1953/4	1954/5	1955/6	1956/7	1957/8	1958/9	1959/60	1960/1	1961/2	1962/3	1963/4	1964/5	1965/6	1966/7
							Revenue receipts as a percentage of net national product (at factor cost)										
Tax revenue (total)	6·58	7·41	6·88	6·47	7·51	7·69	7·87	9·17	8·65	9·40	9·55 (10·04)	10·40 (10·78)	12·11 (12·20)	13·51 (13·24)	12·56 (12·72)	14·36 (13·87)	14·03 (13·43)
Direct taxes (total)	2·42	2·44	2·54	2·33	2·50	2·60	2·63	2·87	2·73	2·92	2·84 (2·99)	3·04 (3·14)	3·64 (3·69)	4·02 (3·94)	3·63 (3·63)	3·61 (3·49)	3·28 (3·13)
Land revenue and agricultural income tax	0·58	0·55	0·65	0·65	0·81	0·87	0·81	0·83	0·80	0·80	0·76 (0·80)	0·74 (0·77)	0·87 (0·88)	0·81 (0·80)	0·68 (0·68)	0·64 (0·62)	0·46 (0·44)
Indirect taxes (total)	4·16	4·97	4·33	4·14	5·00	5·10	5·24	6·30	5·92	6·47	6·71 (7·05)	7·39 (7·64)	8·47 (8·59)	9·48 (9·20)	9·09 (9·09)	10·75 (10·38)	10·76 (10·20)
Customs	1·65	2·34	1·77	1·51	1·92	1·67	1·53	1·58	1·10	1·21	1·20 (1·26)	1·43 (1·48)	1·60 (1·62)	1·95 (1·91)	1·96 (1·95)	2·65 (2·56)	2·58 (2·47)

Notes: The figures in brackets are derived from the *revised* C.S.O. estimates of net national product, available from 1960.

Source: Calculated from *Indian Economic Statistics, Part II (Public Finance)*, Ministry of Finance, Government of India; and from *Supplement to Monetary and Banking Statistics (1950–1960), Part II*, and *Reports on Currency and Finance* of the Reserve Bank of India, Bombay.

TABLE 4.8
PERCENTAGE SHARE OF DIFFERENT TAXES IN TOTAL REVENUE: 1950/1 TO 1967/8

	1950/1	1951/2	1952/3	1953/4	1954/5	1955/6	1956/7	1957/8	1958/9	1959/60	1960/1	1961/2	1962/3	1963/4	1964/5	1965/6	1966/7	1967/8
I. Direct taxes	36·79	32·95	37·00	35·55	33·30	33·75	33·46	31·30	31·55	31·10	29·77	29·11	30·03	29·80	28·56	25·13	23·36	21·51
(a) Corporate tax	6·27	5·51	6·34	5·98	5·06	4·75	5·66	5·32	4·98	8·76	8·12	10·14	11·88	11·81	12·08	10·43	10·63	9·71
(b) Land revenue and agricultural income tax	8·80	7·36	9·48	11·19	10·80	11·27	10·34	9·09	9·28	7·69	7·96	8·00	7·19	6·02	5·36	4·48	3·26	2·94
II. Indirect taxes	63·20	67·04	63·00	64·45	66·70	66·24	66·53	68·69	68·44	68·90	70·23	70·89	67·97	70·20	71·44	74·87	76·64	78·49
(a) Customs	25·07	31·53	25·63	23·56	25·66	21·71	19·45	17·22	12·69	12·83	12·59	13·76	13·19	14·40	15·30	18·45	18·37	17·83

Source: *Calculated from Indian Economic Statistics, Part II (Public Finance)*.

investment and savings ratios arise from the fact that, in subsequent years, a part of the investment within the country had been financed by means of a drawal upon the foreign exchange reserves accumulated in the war and post-war years, as well as utilization of credits secured from abroad.[1]

(e) Taxation

An important role in raising domestic savings has been played by the steady tax effort of the Government. As Table 4.7 shows, total revenue as a proportion of national product, at either market price or factor cost, has steadily gone up through the period. As a proportion of factor cost, tax revenue fell between $6\frac{1}{2}$ and 7 per cent in the early fifties but had climbed up to around 14 per cent by the end of the Third Plan. The average proportion for the First Plan was 7·18 per cent, for the Second, 8·93 per cent, and for the Third, 12·59 per cent.

If we examine the composition of the revenues we find that there has been no marked shift in favour of direct taxes, for example; if anything, their share in total tax revenue has declined over the period (see Table 4.8). This trend reflects, in a significant degree, the stagnation in the revenue from agricultural taxation (and even its falling ratio to national income). A favourable aspect of the situation, however, has been the decline in customs revenue as a proportion of the total tax bill, and even more as a proportion of the total of indirect taxes, indicating a switch from trade taxes to taxes on domestic supply. It is interesting that this decline in the importance of customs revenue as a source of taxation has remained fairly impressive even though it was arrested and mildly reversed through the reliance on import duties during much of the Third Plan in lieu of the formal devaluation of the rupee in June 1966 (see Part VII for a fuller analysis of this).

[1] *Fourth Five-Year Plan*, op. cit., p. 14. Apparently the procedure is first to estimate total investment as consisting of total public sector investment plus private investment in the organized industries and the component in the unorganized sector consisting of private investment in agriculture, small-scale industries, and housing. While the former two estimates are reliable, the last is not so. Savings are then derived by subtracting foreign resources from total investment. Thus, there are no *independent* estimates of savings generated in the economy.

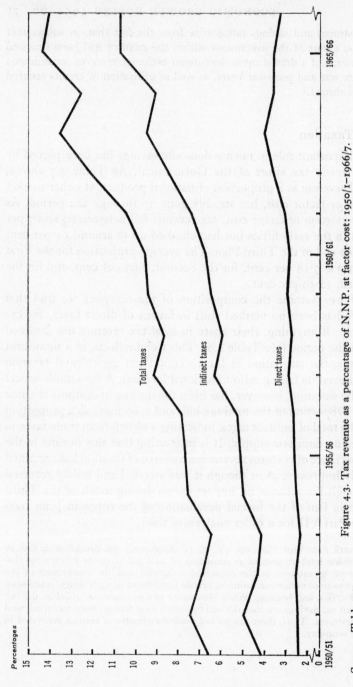

Figure 4.3. Tax revenue as a percentage of N.N.P. at factor cost: 1950/1–1966/7.

Source: Table 4.7.

Percentages

15
14
13
12
11
10
9
8
7
6
5
4
3
2
0

Total taxes

Indirect taxes

Direct taxes

1950/51   1955/56   1960/61   1965/66

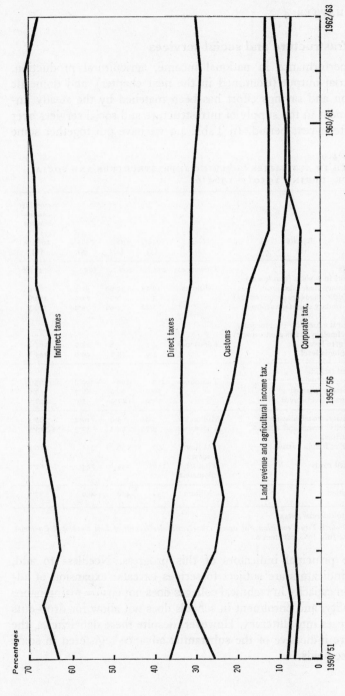

Figure 4.4. Percentage share of different taxes in total revenue: 1950/1–1962/3.

Source: Table 4.8.

(f) Infrastructure and social services

The performance in national income, agricultural production, industrial output (examined in the next chapter), and domestic taxation and savings effort has been matched by the steady improvement in the supply of infrastructure and social services over the fifteen-year period. In Table 4.9 we have put together some

TABLE 4.9
GROWTH IN ACTIVITIES COVERING INFRASTRUCTURE AND SOCIAL
SERVICES DURING 1950/1–1965/6

Activity (1)	Unit (2)	1950/1 (3)	1960/1 (4)	1965/6 (5)	Percentage change between 1950/1– 1965/6 (6)
1. Schools	Thousands	231	400	505	11·86
2. Students in schools (enrolment)					
(a) Primary stage (age group 6–11)	Millions	19·15	34·99	51·5	168·9
(b) Middle stage (age groups 11–14)		3·12	6·7	11·0	252·6
(c) Secondary stage (age group 14–17)		1·22	2·96	5·24	329·5
3. Technical education—engineering and technology: admission capacity					
(a) Degree level	Thousands	4·1	13·8	24·7	502·4
(b) Diploma level		5·9	25·8	49·9	745·8
4. Medical facilities:					
(a) Hospital beds	Thousands	113	186	300	165·5
(b) Doctors (practising)		56·0	70·0	86·0	53·6
(c) Nurses (registered)		15·0	27·0	45·0	200·0
5. Electricity: installed capacity	Million kw.	2·3ᵃ	5·6	10·2	393·5
6. Electricity: towns and villages electrified	Thousands	3·7	24·2	52·3	1,313·5
7. Railways: freight carried	Million tonnes	93	156	205	120·4
8. Surfaced roads	Thousand kilometers	156	235	284	82·0
9. Populationᵃ	Million	357	430	490	37·3

ᵃ Refers to calendar years.

Source: *Fourth Five-Year Plan*, for items 1–8; *National Accounts of Less Developed Countries* O.E.C.D., July 1968, for item 9.

of the principal indicators of this progress. Needless to add, these indicators are subject to serious caveats: expansion of admission capacity in technical colleges does not ensure maintenance of quality, and enrolment in schools does not allow for drop-outs and lapses into illiteracy. However, despite these deficiencies, the data are indicative of the substantial advance registered in some of these fields.

The educational system has expanded considerably. Technical colleges have multiplied their capacity nearly eightfold during the three Plans and take in over 70,000 students at degree and diploma levels. Over 51 million students in the 6–11 years age group are now in primary schools, representing 78·5 per cent of the eligible students as against only 42·6 per cent in 1950–1.

Medical facilities have also expanded, including the growth of doctors and the expansion of hospital bed facilities. Despite the doubling of the number of practising doctors, however, the doctor/population ratio has not improved, and a shortage of nurses has continued.

The quality of village life has clearly improved: the number of towns and villages electrified has gone up from 3,700 to as many as 52,300. Surfaced roads have nearly doubled, and the rail freight carried has increased by over 100 per cent to 205 million *tonnes*.

(g) Price behaviour

The economic progress reviewed by us so far was further distinguished by a period of remarkable stability in the price level during the major part of the period. Until after 1963–4 the rate of growth of prices, on the average, was not more than 2 per cent per annum: an extraordinary performance by Latin American

TABLE 4.10
INDEX NUMBERS OF WHOLESALE PRICES[a]
(1952/3 = 100)

Year	Agricultural commodities	Foodgrains	Total manufactures	All commodities
1955/6	88	73	100	92·5
1956/7	104	94	106	105·3
1957/8	107	98	108	108·4
1958/9	114	106	108	112·9
1959/60	116	102	112	117·1
1960/1	124	102	124	125·9
1961/2	123	100	127	125·1
1962/3	123	106	129	127·9
1963/4	132	116	131	135·3
1964/5	156	144	137	152·7
1965/6	169	150	149	165·1
1966/7	199	178	163	191·3

[a] Average of weeks.

Source: *Economic Survey, 1967–68*, adapted from p. A-42.

standards. Thus, as Table 4.10 shows, the index number of wholesale prices stood at 135·3 in 1963–4, with the base-year 1952–3.[1]

This impressive record, however, was to give way to a sharp series of price increases which resulted in an annual increase of nearly 12 per cent in the three years ending in 1966–7. This was a result largely of the two severe droughts which led to a sharp fall in agricultural output (see Table 4.5) and must also be attributed to the sharply increased defence spending that followed upon the Sino-Indian border war of late 1962, unmatched by corresponding net cuts in the Third Plan outlays.[2] Since 1967–8, when the agricultural performance was to reverse itself in a dramatic manner, the price situation seems to have begun to revert to its trend pattern: the year witnessing a price increase of under 6·0 per cent on the whole.[3]

II. FACTOR SUPPLIES

To conclude this chapter we review Indian experience with respect to factor supplies, in the classical sense, in the modern period of planning, focusing briefly on entrepreneurship, finance, and labour supply.

Entrepreneurship

During the period of planning the dominance of the traditional entrepreneurial communities was to continue in Indian manufacturing, although the relative share of the private sector in industrial investments was to decline during and after the Second Five-Year Plan.

It appears, furthermore, that the Marwari community provided the major thrust of industrial entrepreneurship: a role which they

---

[1] This index, it must be added, tends to understate price increases in so far as the prices of controlled commodities are usually taken at the controlled rather than their 'true market' level. On this issue, see Dantwala, op. cit., p. 4: '... for some commodities like cotton, there has been a statutory ceiling on prices, and though in reality the ceiling has never been operative, the Office of the Economic Adviser which prepares the index series records only the ceiling prices.' Note that the index of consumer prices, which has followed a similar pattern, is reproduced for 1951–61 in Table 4.11.

[2] For details, see Raj, op. cit., pp. 3–5.

[3] Cf. *Economic Survey*, op. cit., pp. 18–20.

were already beginning to assume towards the end of the inter-war period. Gujarati industrialists followed in importance, with entrepreneurs from Panjab, the South, and the Parsis following in that order.[1]

As in the past, however, investments tended to be concentrated in a few industrial houses, despite the declared policy to prevent concentration of economic power. The top twenty-eight industrial houses were to make over 20 per cent of the total number of industrial applications during the period from 1959 to June 1966, involving an investment in fixed equipment of Rs. 16,270 million representing 59 per cent of the total.[2] Furthermore, within these houses, the four top houses—Birlas, J. K., Tata's, and Shri Ram —claimed a large share amounting to over 20 per cent of fixed capital expenditure in all applications, whether successful or otherwise. The Government sought to encourage newer entre-preneurs by policy extending to import allocations and promotion of smaller industries (see Chapter 10) via industrial estates and technical advice; and an encouraging development was the entry of *professional* groups, such as engineers and scientists, into entrepreneurial activity in areas of traditional enterprise such as Gujerat and Panjab. In general, it is impossible to argue that lack of entrepreneurial activity or ability in India has been a bottleneck to more rapid development of the economy.

Industrial finance

The traditional forms of financing, which we have described in Chapter 3, were to prove inadequate to the needs of the industrial-ization which characterized the three Plans. The bulk of the financing, therefore, had to be provided by State-sponsored institutions.

After independence the Government directly assisted in putting

---

[1] This was the finding of R. K. Hazari, *Industrial Planning and Licensing Policy*, Planning Commission, Government of India, 1967 with respect to his exam-ination of the share of these major trading communities in approved industrial licensing applications during the period 1959/60–1965/6. It must be admitted, however, that these data exclude the applications which were rejected as also a fair number of applications for which no data were recorded; hence the rela-tive ranking of the different communities in entrepreneurial activity, in a wider sense, may be vitiated if the impact of these omissions on any one community is skewed.

[2] Hazari, op.cit., p.6.

G

up essentially four major institutions for this purpose: (i) the Industrial Finance Corporation of India; (ii) the National Industrial Development Corporation; (iii) the Industrial Credit and Investment Corporation of India; and (iv) the Refinance Corporation for Industry Private, Ltd. In addition, the Government helped to channel part of the (nationalized) Life Insurance Corporation funds into industrial investments in the private sector.

The Industrial Finance Corporation (I.F.C.), and its state-level counterparts (S.F.C.s), were built up from governmental contributions and subject to governmental direction. Their direct contribution to long-term financing (via loans of up to twenty years, but mainly ten to fifteen years, at a uniform 7 per cent rate of interest) was in the range of 12 per cent of estimated long-term industrial finance from external sources, and over 5 per cent of estimated gross fixed investment in the private organized industrial sector during 1950–8.[1]

The National Industrial Development Corporation was started at the beginning of the Second Plan, also with a range of development tasks in the industrial sector, but was eventually utilized primarily for credits to the jute and cotton textile industries for modernization. The Refinance Corporation (R.F.C.), beginning operations in 1958, was set up mainly 'to provide refinancing for the normal commercial banks for medium-term (3–7 years) loans of moderate size (up to Rs. 5 million) for medium- and large-size industrial firms (whose paid-up capital and own reserves do not total less than Rs. 500,000 or exceed Rs. 25 million) for directly productive purposes in accordance with the various plans'.[2]

The Industrial Credit and Investments Corporation (I.C.I.C.I.), begun as a private institution with governmental and World Bank support, was to provide foreign exchange financing in addition to rupee finance and it reached operational levels similar to the I.F.C. fairly rapidly. Its operations extended to numerous industries, including paper, engineering, sugar, plastics and chemicals, automobiles, cycles, shipping, and other miscellaneous industries, in that order of importance. The impact of these

---

[1] See George Rosen, *Some Aspects of Industrial Finance in India*, whence much of the information in this section has been derived. Further details can be found in this valuable work.

[2] Ibid., p. 102.

institutions on the availability of industrial finance in the country, for the private sector's investments, has been aptly summed up by Rosen:

The sum total of direct assistance or loans disbursed by the various special financial institutions in a year—such as 1956/57 or 1957/58—is approximately Rs. 100 million. They have also underwritten or guaranteed about another Rs. 20 million worth of financing per year. Their financing amounts to 13–20 per cent of the total long-term finance from external sources to privately owned public limited companies in each year and represents about 9 per cent of the gross fixed investment of the organized private industrial sector in the same year. It is estimated that the direct assistance of these institutions has made it possible to invest a total amount of funds approximately double the actual institutional financing, so that the total role of these institutions is closer to one-third of the external long-term finance supplied and 15–20 per cent of the gross fixed investment. The two leading institutions—the I.F.C. and the I.C.I.C.I.—through 1958 had financed 212 privately owned firms (excluding cooperatives), of which 78 were new. Of the total sanctioned loans and other assistance given by these two institutions of Rs. 680 million to firms exclusive of cooperatives, the engineering industry (including automotive and non-ferrous metals) received Rs. 144 million; textiles other than chemical fibers, Rs. 113 million; chemical Rs. 111 million; paper, Rs. 88 million; sugar, Rs. 76 million; cement, Rs. 69 million; ceramics and glass, Rs. 19 million; shipping, Rs. 10 million; and miscellaneous smaller industries, Rs. 50 million. Of the sixteen industries ranked by either gross profit rate or annual rate of growth for the period from 1955/56 through 1957/58, the engineering, cement, paper, and shipping industries tend to rank high while the sugar and textile industries rank relatively low—although high ranking in terms of size. These institutions probably do somewhat better than the normal commercial banks in making finance available to rapidly growing industries. All the major recipient industries of special institutional finance were also major industries within the context of the First and Second Five-Year Plans. Thus one can conclude that on the whole the special financial institutions have made major contributions to industrial finance and that without their assistance the rate of industrial growth would have been lower.[1]

Labour

The experience with labour supply, during the modern period of planned industrialization, was surprisingly similar to that described

[1] *Some Aspects of Industrial Finance in India*, pp. 104–5.

by Morris for the cotton textile industry for the earlier century. One of the notable aspects of the labour situation, which seems to be a fairly obvious consequence of the generally sluggish expansion of job opportunities in relation to the initial backlog of underemployed labour and a rising population, was the tendency of real wages of factory labour to remain stagnant throughout the period.

This trend was interrupted by fluctuations which appear to have been the consequence of stickiness in the response of average money wages to price changes. Thus Table 4.11 shows, for the period 1951–61, the behaviour of real wages. These estimates indicate that the trend has been relatively stagnant. However, the

TABLE 4.11

ALL-INDIA INDEX NUMBERS OF CONSUMER PRICES, EMPLOYMENT, AVERAGE ANNUAL MONEY WAGES, AND REAL WAGES PER WORKER IN FACTORIES

(1951 = 100)

Year	Prices	Money wage per worker	Real wage per worker	Employment
1952	98	107	109	n.a.
1953	101	108	107	n.a.
1954	96	108	112	n.a.
1955	91	113	124	n.a.
1956	100	115	115	106
1957	106	121	114	110
1958	111	122	110	111
1959	115	126	110	113
1960	118	134	114	117
1961	120	139	116	121
1962	124	144	116	128
1963	128	145	113	135
1964	145	151	104	144

Notes: (1) 'Worker' here covers employees earning less than Rs. 200 per month.

(2) The Index of Employment relates to annual average daily employment in factories and has been computed from Index Numbers with 1956 = 100 by shifting the base to 1951. The Index Number for 1951 (1956 = 100) was 93·9.

Source: Computed by K. Sundaram from *Indian Labour Statistics*, 1968. Data are presented in this form, for 1951–61, by H. Shivmaggi, 'Trends in Money and Real Wages in India: 1951–1961', *Reserve Bank of India Bulletin*, April 1964, p. 422. However, we are thankful to K. Sundaram for detecting that: (1) his money wages for 1958, 1959, and 1960 are not comparable with those for other years in omitting Madhya Pradesh and Madras (including Andhra Pradesh), and (2) his employment figures for 1951–5 (which indicate a steady rise in employment) are not comparable with those for later years. Tables 4.11 and 4.12 are divided in their different definititons of 'workers'.

real wage per worker rose during the last two years of the First Plan (when prices fell in consequence of excellent harvests) and fell thereafter as prices rose again.[1] Furthermore, it has been shown that, during this period, the rise in real wages in seven

TABLE 4.12
ALL-INDIA INDEX NUMBERS OF CONSUMER PRICES, EMPLOYMENT, AVERAGE ANNUAL MONEY WAGES AND REAL WAGES PER WORKER IN FACTORIES
(1961 = 100)

Year	Prices	Money wages per worker	Real wages per worker	Employment
1962	103	106	103	105
1963	106	109	103	111
1964	121	131	108	119
1965	132	128	97	121
1966	146	133	91	121

Notes: (1) 'Worker' here refers to employees earning less than Rs. 400 per month, thus differing from the definition in Table 4.11. Data are not available on the Table 4.11 definition for 1962–6.

(2) Index Numbers for Employment computed from the Index Numbers with 1956 = 100, by shifting the base to 1961. The Index Number for 1961 (1956 = 100) was 114·4.

Source: Same as for Table 4.11.

major industries (cotton textiles, jute textiles, iron and steel, cement, paper and paper boards, chemicals, and sugar), lagged behind the improvement in labour productivity.[2] All these indicators suggest therefore that the supply of labour to the industrial economy, despite a steady rise in factory employment (Tables 4.11 and 4.12) was not characterized by an upward slope, at least within the relevant ranges. The considerable elasticity of supply of (unskilled) labour was further consistent with growing unionization in several industries as also the spread of welfare legislation (relating, for example, to minimum wages and industrial arbitration).

But while industrialization was not impeded by scarcity of labour, in the sense of its growing real cost to entrepreneurs, the reverse implication of this phenomenon was the growth in open

[1] The real wage was to fall more dramatically towards the end of the Third Plan, when the price rises turned out, as we have seen, to be unprecedented in India's recent history. Cf. Datar, *Labour Economics*, Delhi, Allied Publishers, Ltd., 1966.

[2] Cf. Shivamaggi, N. Rajagopalan, and T. R. Venkatachalam, 'Wages, Labour Productivity and Costs of Production, 1951–1961', *Economic and Political Weekly*, 4 May 1968; especially Table 1, columns 3–5.

urban unemployment during the bulk of the period and presumed disguised unemployment in the rural areas. Although it had no clear focus on employment as an objective, the First Plan had been substantially stepped up in the middle of its course in order to create more employment than originally envisaged.[1] By 1953 unemployment in the urban areas had become fairly large, the major (even though inadequate) indicator being the numbers carried on the registers of the Employment Exchanges. The Second Plan was clearly cognizant of this problem; it was largely this factor which led the shift in favour of heavy industry to be combined with reliance on labour-intensive cottage industries in other areas (as we shall see later in the chapter on industrial strategy). Emphasis was also placed on rural works to absorb the 'surplus' labour at grass roots.[2] Nonetheless open unemployment by 1961, at the end of the Second Plan, was estimated as having gone up over the 1951 level by 4–5 million workers, not to take into account under-employment in the rural (and, to some extent, in the urban) areas. The Third Plan surprisingly did not attempt to come to grips with the problem of unemployment, presumably expecting to surmount the problem in the long run, after industrialization had led to self-sustained growth of income and employment opportunities at a faster rate than growth in working population.[3]

---

[1] In fact, it is interesting that, as in many other countries, the Labour Investigation Committee, reporting in 1946, had predicted that the post-war situation would be characterized by 'mass unemployment', which did not materialize. It was perhaps the mood of immediate relief inspired by this happy outcome which took the attention of the authors of the First Plan away from the problems that were to be created by the steady growth of population and the working force.

[2] This programme had been prompted also by the revelation by the Second Agricultural Labour Inquiry (1956/7) that the economic condition of landless labourers had failed to improve since 1950/1, and that measures such as legislative minimum wages had made hardly any impact, and that direct employment programmes were called for. In making this observation, we fully recognize the fact that the Second Agricultural Labour Inquiry used a different concept of 'landless labourers', which was more restrictive and confined more strictly to the virtually landless labouring classes, so that there would have been a downward bias in the comparison between the two inquiries. On this issue, see the important set of essays in V. K. R. V. Rao (ed.), *Agricultural Labour in India*, Studies in Economic Growth, No. 3, Institute of Economic Growth, New Delhi, Asia Publishing House, 1962.

[3] See, for example: *Second Five-Year Plan*, pp. 26–8 and 109; *Third Five-Year Plan*, p. 154; and *Draft Fourth Five-Year Plan*, (1966), pp. 106–7.

The growth of open unemployment through the bulk of the period was further accentuated, in political terms, by the unemployment of the educated. Partly, of course, this reflected the fact that education was being demanded by larger numbers of candidates purely as a means of 'beating the next man to the job', with educational requirements for many jobs thus being upgraded in consequence. An apocryphal story, with a double twist, runs: in response to an advertisement for the job of a floor-sweeper, the applicant with higher secondary school education was dismayed to find a rival with a B.A. degree, who in turn faced a rival with an M.A., to be capped by an applicant with a Ph.D. (in the art of sweeping), only to find that the job ultimately went to the son-in-law of the advertiser.

The experience of the *technically* educated was often the opposite, however. Right through the First and Second Plans, there were shortages of many kinds of technical personnel, despite efforts at manpower planning and a rapid expansion of training institutes and university facilities. As we shall argue later, this problem affected the public sector even more acutely than the private sector, with the latter being in a position to attract away personnel from the former by freer use of the mechanism of increased incentives. None the less, it must be admitted that the governmental efforts at planning ahead (with, for example, the Planning Commission's Working Group for the Third Plan on the subject looking ahead as far as 1976 to plan for expansion of educational and training institutes) were, in this area, of considerable value and undoubtedly helped in reducing shortages below the levels they would have reached if the earlier orientation towards liberal arts education and civil engineering had continued.

It is clear therefore that, thanks partly to historical traditions and partly to governmental planning and intervention in order to set up new institutions, the Indian effort at accelerated industrialization in the modern period did not run into significant bottlenecks from lack of entrepreneurship or financial institutions and skilled labour.[1] What the precise nature of the industrialization which characterized the modern period was will be discussed in the next chapter.

[1] See Part V for an examination of the role of external resources, financial and technological, through foreign aid and via private investment.

5
Industrial Performance and Import-Substitution during 1951–66

THIS chapter consists of an empirical analysis of the growth and structural change, with special emphasis on import-substitution, in the Organized Industrial Sector in India during the period of this study.[1]

Growth and changing composition

Current assessments of the performance of this sector in India during 1950–65 emphasize two principal aspects.

First, it is stressed that the Organized Industrial Sector during the period has grown fairly rapidly. Note the following statement:

The revised index numbers of industrial production (with 1956 as the base year) show a compound rate of growth of 5¾ per cent per

---

[1] The bulk of this chapter is based on two studies of import substitution in the Indian manufacturing sector undertaken by Padma Desai: 'Growth and Structural Change in the Indian Manufacturing Sector, 1951–1963', *Indian Economic Journal*, 1970, and 'Alternative Measures of Import Substitution', *Oxford Economic Papers*, November 1969. The term 'Organized Industrial Sector' needs some clarification. For the period of our study, two sources, namely the Sample Survey of Manufacturing Industries (S.S.M.I.) and the Annual Survey of Industry (A.S.I.) are available for the required data. The S.S.M.I. covering sixty-three groups of industries was begun in 1950. It covers, on a sample basis, two sets of establishments, namely (i) those employing ten to forty-nine workers with the aid of power and twenty to ninety-nine workers without the aid of power and (ii) those employing fifty or more workers with the aid of power and a hundred or more workers without the aid of power. The A.S.I. reports are available from 1959 and replace the S.S.M.I. In the A.S.I., factories under set (ii) are completely enumerated (the Census sector) and those under set (i) are covered on a sample basis (the sample sector). Thus the S.S.M.I. and A.S.I. sources, on which our empirical analysis is based, include all establishments except those employing less than ten workers using power and less than twenty workers without power. Therefore, the 'Organized Industrial Sector' in our analysis coincides with the coverage of the S.S.M.I. and the A.S.I.

annum in the period 1951–55 and of nearly 7½ per cent since the beginning of the Second Five-Year Plan. In the first three years of the Third Plan period, the rate of growth has been close to 8 per cent per annum.[1]

The second but related descriptive feature lays stress, through various indices, on the changing structure of the Organized Industrial Sector, especially since the beginning of the Second Five-Year Plan in April 1956. These indices emphasize the shift, since 1957, towards the production of the metal machinery and chemical industries.[2] For example, the following two statements from the Draft Outline of the Fourth Five-Year Plan suggest this shift in terms of investment and growth capacity:

A special feature of industrial development, especially since the commencement of the Second Plan in 1956–57 has been the growth of capacities in steel, aluminium, engineering, chemicals, fertilisers and petroleum products.

Apart from these large investments have been made in industries producing heavy electrical equipment, heavy foundry forge, heavy engineering machinery, heavy plates and vessels etc.—all of which will become available in increasing quantities from now on.[3]

More concretely, the allocations as a proportion of planned expenditures in industry, to the metal, machinery, and chemical industries were 70 per cent for the Second Plan and 80 per cent for the Third Plan.

As would be expected, this shift in investment strategy has resulted in striking growth of output and value added in these 'basic' industries leading to a marked shift in the output composition of the organized industrial sector. Thus in Table 5.1 (at the end of this chapter) among the activities with impressive growth during 1951–66 and with growth rates decidedly above the general growth rate are chemicals and petroleum (9 and 10), non-metallic mineral products and basic metals (11 and 12), and manufacture of metal products and machinery (except electrical machinery) (13 and 14). Again, a comparison of relative shares at

[1] K. N. Raj, *Indian Economic Growth: Performance and Prospects*, Allied Publishers, 1965, p. 15. The First Five-Year Plan started in April 1951, and was succeeded without break by the Second Plan (1956–61) and the Third Plan (1961–6).

[2] Machinery includes machine tools, electrical and non-electrical machinery and equipment, and transport equipment. Chemicals include oil refining and the manufacture of fertilizers.

[3] Ibid., pp. 10–11.

1960–1 prices in total value added in 1965–6 indicates that the relative shares in the latter year increased in categories such as chemicals and chemical products, basic metals and other primary products, electrical engineering and equipment, transport equipment and machinery.[1]

Detailed evidence indicative of the shift of the Organized Industrial Sector in terms of gross value added, gross output at factor cost, and gross output at market price, towards the 'basic' industries is presented in Tables 5.2 and 5.3 (at end of chapter). Again, the following conclusions emerge unambiguously from an examination of the data presented in these Tables:[2]

(a) The relative shares in terms of gross value added, gross output at factor cost and gross output at market price, of consumer goods industries decline steadily over the period 1951–63 whereas those of investment goods industries rise sharply, with the raw materials and intermediates category maintaining shares around 35–40 per cent.

(b) The average annual rates of growth given in Table 5.2 are consistently higher in raw materials and intermediates and in investment goods than in consumer goods irrespective of the index used and the period under consideration. One noticeable feature of the average annual growth rates is that the extension of the period from 1951 to 1963 as compared to 1951–61, yields distinctly higher growth rates in these categories (raw materials

---

[1] K. N. Raj, *India, Pakistan and China: Economic Growth and Outlook*, Lecture II, 1966, Table 6.

[2] However, these conclusions are subject to the following qualifications: (i) All the data are at current prices and we have not been able to eliminate the influence of price changes in the absence of the required price deflators. (ii) Output at market price does not include sales taxes and export taxes which, for reasons mentioned in the Appendix, we were not able to allocate to various items in an acceptable manner. (iii) Indirect taxes on production appear excessively large in relation to gross output at factor cost in the case of a small number of items marked with asterisks in Table 5.2. The product composition of these industries suggests that the discrepancies must be due to the tax figures including the collections on the output of the small-scale industries which are not included in our output figures. These discrepancies, which are, however, not very serious, imply that for the affected items gross output at market prices is somewhat overestimated. (iv) Despite careful cross-classification, intertemporal comparability of the data may be imperfect owing to the fact that the sources of production data for 1961 and 1963 are different from those for the years 1951 and 1957. In view of these qualifications, and especially of (iii) and (iv), it may be unwise to attach undue significance to industry-wise figures as distinct from group-wise estimates.

and investment goods), thereby implying an acceleration of performance in these groups in the last two years.

(c) The breakdown of the period 1951–63 into two sub-periods 1951–7 and 1957–63 introduces a sharp rise in the latter half of the period in the average rate of growth of raw materials and intermediates in terms of *all* the three indices. On the other hand, for investment goods, this sharp kink is noticeable, in the second sub-period, only in terms of gross value added. In this connection it must be stressed that the metals and chemicals group, where large investments during 1957–63 had already started yielding outputs, are included in the intermediate and raw material group and not in the investment group.

Thus it is clear that the growth of the Organized Industrial Sector accelerated through the three Plans and that the shares in investment, outputs, and value added shifted decidedly in favour of metals, machinery, and chemicals.

However, there is no detailed and systematic analysis relating these developments to the pattern of imports, by sector-of-origin, through the period. Such an analysis is necessary not merely from the point of view of understanding an important feature of the changing structure of the Indian economy but also for putting the growth of output in different industries in relation to the growth of competing imports so as to evaluate the role played by import-substitution policies in promoting the growth of different industries.[1]

We shall, therefore, evaluate the performance and changing structure of the Organized Industrial Sector in India in relation to imports by sector-of-origin. The import-substitution pattern and performance will be analysed in terms of three major groups of industries, namely, consumer goods, intermediates, and investment goods over the periods 1951–61 and 1951–63, and the two sub-periods 1951–7 and 1957–63.

In the next section we shall briefly describe the measures in terms of which we subsequently carry out an empirical analysis of import-substitution. In the concluding section we shall present our findings and also consider if, in terms of *these* findings, the structure of the Organized Industrial Sector has shifted towards

[1] For example, a relatively large growth rate of output at 10 per cent per annum would acquire a different perspective if it could be shown that the competing imports grew at 25 per cent, rather than 2 per cent, per annum.

metal, machinery, and chemicals, and against the consumer goods sector from 1951 to 1963.

Proposed measures of import substitution

The following four measures of import substitution will be employed:

Measure 1

According to the first measure we shall compute the difference between the ratios of imports to availabilities during the different periods and say that there is import substitution over the period, indicated by the difference, if the change is positive. Thus if M_1 and M_2 are the imports during Periods 1 and 2 and if S_1 and S_2 are total availabilities during Periods 1 and 2, then if $\dfrac{M_1}{S_1} - \dfrac{M_2}{S_2} > 0$ there is import-substitution to the extent of the change in the value of the ratio.

Measure 2

In the second measure, the magnitude of import-substitution yielded by Measure 1 is expressed as a proportion; i.e. if

$$\left(\frac{M_1}{S_2} - \frac{M_2}{S_2}\right) \Big/ \frac{M_1}{S_1} > 0,$$

there is import-substitution to the extent of the relative change in the ratio.

Measure 3

An indirect way in which the departure from the initial period's import availability ratio is taken to measure import-substitution has been introduced by Hollis Chenery[1] and adapted by Lewis and Soligo.[2] Thus according to this measure, import-substitution is defined as the 'difference between growth in output with no change in the import ratio and the actual growth'.[3] Symbolically,

[1] Hollis Chenery, 'Patterns of Industrial Growth', *American Economic Review*, 1960, p. 640.
[2] S. R. Lewis and R. Soligo, 'Growth and Structural Change in Pakistan Manufacturing Industry, 1954–1964', *Pakistan Development Review*, Spring, 1965.
[3] Chenery, op. cit.

the measure of import-substitution is given by $(u_2 - u_1)S_2$ where u_2 is the ratio Q_2/S_2 of output (Q_2) to availabilities (S_2) in Period 2 and u_1 is the ratio Q_1/S_1 of output to availabilities in Period 1. This measure can be expressed in relative terms by dividing $(u_2 - u_1)S_2$ with ΔQ or the change in output over the period. More specifically we can say that if

$$\frac{\dfrac{\sum\limits_{i=1}^{n} Q_2{}^i}{\sum\limits_{i=1}^{n} S_2{}^i} - \dfrac{\sum\limits_{i=1}^{n} Q_1{}^i}{\sum\limits_{i=1}^{n} S_2{}^i}}{\sum\limits_{i=1}^{n} \Delta Q_i} \cdot \sum_{i=1}^{n} S_2{}^i > 0,$$

there is import-substitution. In order for import-substitution to take place, the value of the difference in the ratios has to be positive because the numerators in the ratios, unlike in the previous two measures, are outputs rather than imports.

Measure 4

According to Measure 4, import substitution arises if

$$\frac{\sum\limits_{i=1}^{n} \left\{ (u_2{}^i - u_1{}^i)S_2{}^i \right\}}{\sum\limits_{i=1}^{n} \Delta Q_i} > 0$$

Measures 3 and 4 give different magnitudes of import-substitution, arising out of the different aggregation procedure adopted in each, for broad groups of industries such as 'consumer goods', 'investment goods', and 'intermediates'. It is clear that Measure 3 works directly with the (aggregated) totals of imports, supplies, and production for a given group as a whole whereas Measure 4 first computes the import-substitution component for each industry and then aggregates these components into total import-substitution for the group as a whole. This total is finally divided by the incremental output for the group as a whole, resulting in the group import-substitution measure.[1]

---

[1] For a detailed discussion of the logical relationships among these four Measures, see Padma Desai, 'Alternative Measures of Import-Substitution'. It is also stressed in the same article that all these measures deal with actual situations without any reference to optimality considerations.

It is clear that the results given by Measures 3 and 4 can diverge. More important, the ranking of different groups can be reversed by the choice of a different method of aggregation. In principle such a possibility of reversed rankings can arise with all the four measures.[1] In view of this possibility, we have used all the four measures in our computations of import-substitution for the Indian economy and based our conclusions on the results in terms of all the four measures rather than rely on the indications given by a single measure.

Import-substitution during 1951–63

The observations made in the preceding section are illustrated strikingly by our estimates of import-substitution incorporating Indian data for the period 1951–63. The period could not be extended further, owing to lack of availability of suitable production data (as explained in the Appendix).

Table 5.4 (at end of chapter) summarizes the final results of our calculations. We have computed all the four measures of import-substitution defined in the preceding section.[2]

Before we get to the substantive conclusions concerning import-substitution, we would like to emphasize that the relative rankings of the three groups of industries according to the four measures of import-substitution are, in general, inconsistent. For example, a comparison of Measures 3 and 4 (columns 4 and 5) indicates that the 1951–61 rankings are inconsistent: although the investment-group remains at the top, the other two groups reverse their ranks. Furthermore, it is worth noting that the direction of import-substitution itself changes in some cases. For example, this is the case in 1951–61 and in 1951–63 for all industries taken together.

[1] The choice of an 'appropriate' method of aggregation would appear to be arbitrary as these measures are 'descriptive'. However, it should be noted that Measure 3 is appropriate if we expect the implicit premise of the constancy of the ratio of output to availabilities to make sense *directly* at the group-level, whereas Measure 4 is appropriate if we expect that this premise would hold instead at the level of *individual* industries. Apropos of this, we should also note that Measure 4 will yield estimates of group-level import-substitution which will vary, in general, with the industrial classification employed: this arbitrariness is absent from Measure 3.

[2] For detailed discussion of the problems relating to the choice of the period under consideration, the source of data, the coverage of industries and the statistical operations and qualifications underlying these, see the Appendix at the end of the chapter.

Now if we compare Measure 2 with Measure 3 (columns 3 and 4), the divergent rankings are noticeable in all periods except in 1951-7. The results thus fully illustrate the possibilities of inconsistent rankings arising from the sensitivity of the ranking to the measure employed.[1]

As for the substantive conclusions, relating to the Indian economy, the following three seem to stand out:

(1) For the entire decade 1951-61 or 1951-63, import-substitution in the investment group seems to predominate.

(2) For 1951-7, broadly overlapping with the First Plan period, all the measures underline the relatively substantial import-substitution in consumer goods followed by the investment and intermediates group in that order.

(3) All measures show that for 1957-63, approximately with the beginning of the Second Plan and its emphasis on heavy industries, import-substitution in the consumer goods industries was the lowest and in investment and intermediates group considerably higher with investment goods generally dominating.

While we shall examine the *rationale* of this shift in investments and import-substitution towards capital goods and intermediates in Chapter 13, we proceed immediately to a discussion of the broad planning framework and policy instruments which were deployed during the three Plans to engineer and regulate the economic and industrial expansion which we have so far reviewed.

APPENDIX

(a) Choice of the years under consideration

The Indian data used for the computations underlying Table 5.1 relate to four benchmark years: 1951, 1957, 1961, and 1963. 1951 is practically the beginning of the planning period in India, and 1963 is the last year for which production figures were available in the required detail. 1957 is the year witnessing a major

---

[1] No such contradictions are to be found in comparisons between columns 2 and 4 even though, as we have seen in the text, the possibility of such inconsistent rankings arising cannot be ruled out. Note, however, that such a contradiction does arise in 1951-61 if one compares column 2 instead with column 5.

shift in industrial investment towards investment-goods industries under the Second Five-Year Plan. 1961 is also considered because 1963 is a slightly abnormal year in having followed immediately upon the Sino-Indian border war in November 1962. All the years are calendar years.

(b) Sources of data

As is indicated in footnote 1 on page 84 the production and value added data underlying our computations were collected from the Sample Survey of Manufacturing Industries (S.S.M.I.) for 1951 and 1957 and the Annual Survey of Industries (A.S.I.) for 1961 and 1963. The advantages of using these sources over the *Monthly Statistics of Production* available from the Ministry of Industry are that their coverage is more systematic and the value added statistics, apart from being available only from these sources, are in terms of the same industrial classification as the production figures.

The 1957, 1961, and 1963 exports (f.o.b.) and imports (c.i.f.) estimates were collected, on a calendar year basis, from the *Monthly Statistics of Foreign Trade in India*. However, the 1951 data had to be accepted from the *Annual Statistics of Foreign Air and Sea-Borne Trade*, on a fiscal year (April 1951–March 1952) basis, as monthly or quarterly breakdowns were not available. The comparability of the foreign trade classifications with the A.S.I. and S.S.M.I. classification of production and value added had to be resolved for two separate classifications as the trade data classification was changed to S.I.T.C. only in 1957 and in consequence our period spanned both the trade classifications. The keys to the cross-classifications are available from us and have not been reproduced here.

The Export and Import Duties were obtained from the *Customs and Excise Revenue Statements of the Indian Union*, for the years 1957, 1961, and 1963, and the Foreign Air and Sea-Borne Trade of India (1954) for the fiscal year 1951.[1]

Indirect taxes on production include both Union and State excise duties on commodities. The Union excise duties have been

[1] Export subsidies did not begin significantly until around 1962 and are ignored here. Omitting them introduces negligible error in the analysis for 1963.

obtained from the *Customs and Excise Revenue Statement of the Indian Union* for the years 1957, 1961, and 1963 and could be adjusted to calendar year basis. But the 1951 estimates of Union excise duties had to be accepted, from the *Explanatory Memorandum to the Central Government Budget*, on a fiscal year basis. The State excise duties had to be accepted entirely on a fiscal year basis and were obtained from *Financial Accounts*.[1]

(c) Coverage of industries

We have included all the industries listed in the S.S.M.I., with the exclusion only of a negligible miscellaneous item. Since the A.S.I. data are available by two different establishment sizes, namely the Census and the Sample sectors, these two had to be added up, for each industry, so as to secure comparability with the S.S.M.I. estimates for 1951 and 1957.

Note that the estimates cover manufacturing industries in the Organized Industrial Sector and (as is already indicated in footnote 1 on page 84) they exclude establishments (a) employing less than ten workers using power, and (b) employing less than twenty workers without power. This sector is also sometimes described as the 'factory sector'.

No adjustments have been attempted for the excluded, small-scale sector establishments: in any case, this is a notoriously difficult sector, the estimation of whose contribution to national income has proved to be a major headache.[2]

The industries covered are listed below in the three groups of consumer goods, raw materials and intermediates, and investment goods.

[1] The error introduced by the fiscal year basis, however, is not important as the state excise duties affecting our study are insignificant. Under the constitution, the states are authorized to levy excise duties 'on the following goods manufactured or produced in the state and countervailing duties at the same or lower rates on similar goods manufactured or produced elsewhere in India: (a) alcoholic liquors for human consumption, (b) opium, Indian hemp and other narcotic drugs and narcotics . . . ' (Item No. 51 of List II of the Seventh Schedule). In addition, the taxes on medicinal and toilet preparations containing alcohol are collected for the Union and retained, by the states. Of relevance to us, therefore, as state excise taxes are only the taxes on alcoholic liquors and on medicinal and toilet preparations.

[2] See, for example, the chapter on 'Income from Small Enterprises' in *National Income Statistics, Proposals for a Revised Series*, Central Statistical Organization, Government of India, May 1961.

H

The following explanation, however, is necessary regarding the intertemporal comparability of the production data. The industrial classifications in the two sources, S.S.M.I. and A.S.I., were substantially similar, although adjustments were called for in some cases. For example, in the case of the bicycle industry, which was not separately classified in the A.S.I., adjustments were made on the basis of the ratio of bicycle output to total output in the group in 1951. Note especially that, for the A.S.I. data in 1961 and 1963:

Consumer goods

(1) Flour-milling	includes wheat, rice, and dal mills
(2) Biscuit-making	includes confectionery (chocolate and sugar)
(3) Soap	includes glycerine
(4) Vegetable oils	includes hydrogenated oil
(5) Bicycles	figures derived from total of bicycles and motor-cycles on the basis of output of bicycles to total output in S.S.M.I. for 1951
(6) Sewing machines	figures derived from total of sewing and knitting machines on the basis of output of sewing machines to total output in S.S.M.I. for 1951
(7) Footwear and leather manufactures	includes all footwear except rubber footwear
(8) Rubber and rubber manufactures	includes rubber footwear

Raw materials and intermediates

(1) Ceramics	includes refractories, furnace-lining bricks, pottery, sanitary-ware, and insulations
(2) Paper and paperboard	excludes hardboard
(3) Bricks, tiles, etc.	includes only tiles
(4) Turpentine and rosin	figure for (1963) derived from total of turpentine, rosin, and other products of power-alcohol on the basis of output of turpentine and rosin to total output in S.S.M.I. for 1951
(5) Plastics	excludes gramophone records
(6) Electricity generation and transmission	figure derived from total of electricity generation and gas manufacture on the basis of output of electricity generation of total output in S.S.M.I. for 1951

Investment goods

(1) Railways and automobiles	includes railway rolling stock, automobiles, and motor-cycles
(2) General and electrical engineering	includes metal furniture, electrical apparatus n.e.s., machinery n.e.s., scientific instruments and transport equipment n.e.s.

It must again be emphasized that problems of a classificatory nature arise in dividing the total list of fifty-seven industries into the three groups of consumer goods, raw materials, and intermediates and investment goods. In particular, note that (1) S.S.M.I. Code Numbers 54, 56, and 57 (in particular, air-conditioners, radios, refrigerators, etc.) contain several durable consumer goods as well; (2) Code Numbers 14, 17, 32, and 40, listed under consumer goods, contain some intermediates; and (3) Code Numbers 6, 29, 33, 35, 47, and 49, listed in intermediates, conceal some consumption.

I. Consumer goods industries

S.S.M.I.

Code No.	Industry
1	Flour-milling
2	Fruit and vegetable processing
3	Biscuit-making
4	Sugar
5	Distilleries and breweries
7	Vegetable oils
8	Soap
9	Matches
10	Cotton textiles
11	Woollen textiles
26	Clothing and tailoring
28	Silk and art silk fabrics
12	Bicycles
13	Sewing machines
14	Electric lamps
15	Electric fans
16	Footwear and leather manufactures
17	Furniture and woodware
18	Printing and bookbinding
19	Tobacco
20	Tea
32	Glass and glassware
40	Rubber and rubber manufactures

II. Raw materials and intermediates

S.S.M.I.

Code No.	Industry
6	Starch
21	Webbing and narrow fabrics
22	Hosiery and knitted goods
23	Thread- and threadball-making
24	Cotton ginning and processing
27	Rope-making
29	Paints and varnishes
30	Tanning
31	Cement
33	Ceramics
34	Plywood
35	Paper and paperboard
36	Jute textiles
37	Chemicals
38	Aluminium, copper and brass
39	Iron and steel
41	Enamelware
42	Hume pipes and other products of cement concrete
43	Asbestos cement
44	Bricks, tiles, etc.
45	Lac
46	Turpentine and rosin
47	Plastics
48	Jute-pressing
49	Electricity generation and transmission
50	Petroleum-refining
51	Saw-milling
52	Groundnut decorticating

III. Investment goods

S.S.M.I.

Code No.	Industry
53	Textile machinery
54	Railway and automobiles
55	Aircraft
56	Shipbuilding
57	General and electrical engineering

(d) Statistical operations and qualifications underlying the calculations

For the statistical computations, involving Measures III and IV, we needed values of total supplies for the years under consideration. In estimating these values, we have taken domestic production at market prices. Indirect taxes were added to gross output at factor cost obtained for 1951 and 1957 from the S.S.M.I. and for 1961 and 1963 from the A.S.I.[1] As is already indicated in the previous section, the indirect taxes include Union and state excise duties on commodities. We were, however, compelled to omit sales taxes from these estimates of domestic production at market prices despite their growing quantitative significance over time. These vary considerably by states: in rates, selectivity, and point of levy. In addition, there is a Central Sales Tax for inter-state movements.[2]

The value of imports was taken at c.i.f. plus import duties. No

[1] Gross output at factor cost refers to the total value of products and by-products of the industry and includes also work done for consumers. Gross value added is the gross output at factor cost *minus* the inputs but gross of depreciation.

[2] Thus, 'The work of dealers has increased. They have to seek registration under the two Acts, namely, the State Sales Tax Act and the Central Sales Tax Act. . . . Inter State sales have to be classified under different categories, namely, (i) those that are taxed at one per cent, (ii) those that are taxed at seven per cent, (iii) those that are taxed at less than one per cent because the tax on such sales within the State is less than one per cent, (iv) those that are exempt from tax because there is no tax on such sales within the State, (v) those that relate to the sale of "declared goods" to unregistered dealers or consumers in the States, which are taxed at the same rate at which such sales or purchases within the State are taxed' (R. N. Bhargava, *Indian Public Finances*, p. 137). There are similar variations on the intra-state sales taxes as well. The result is that the rates applicable tend to vary considerably, depending not merely on the commodity sold but also on the nature of the sale with respect to who buys it and where. It has been thus found impossible to allocate these sales tax revenues, whether state or central, by manufacturing sector. Rather than allocate these sales revenues among the sectors on an arbitrary basis, we have decided to omit them altogether.

Then there are also taxes on motor vehicles which vary between states. The vehicles taxed include scooters, motor-cycles, auto-rickshaws, private cars, taxis, buses, and lorries. However, since these taxes arise principally from the use of the vehicles and are not levied on the act of purchasing them they are more appropriately treated as indirect taxes on road transportation and are hence omitted from our table.

Moreover, electricity duties are levied on electricity consumption by several states. Since electricity generation is treated as a manufacturing sector in our tables, this is included by us in the estimate of indirect taxation.

TABLE 5.1

INDEX NUMBERS OF INDUSTRIAL PRODUCTION: 1951–66

(Base 1956 = 100)

Industry	Weights	1951	1952	1953	1954	1955	1956	1957	1958
1. Food manufacturing	13·99	79·0	83·3	81·8	91·6	93·5	100	100·3	106·8
2. Beverage and tobacco industries	1·48	81·6	76·5	70·0	75·4	86·8	100	110·7	113·4
3. Manufacture of textiles	41·76	78·5	81·5	87·2	90·3	93·4	100	99·9	98·5
4. Manufacture of footwear	0·28	91·5	86·3	87·4	84·2	86·3	100	115·6	114·3
5. Manufacture of wood and woodware	0·24	55·3	70·4	48·8	61·4	87·7	100	104·1	105·4
6. Manufacture of paper and paper products	1·39	66·5	69·2	72·1	81·4	95·9	100	109·5	127·3
7. Manufacture of leather	0·18	109·5	87·7	87·1	89·0	93·1	100	93·2	94·7
8. Manufacture of rubber products	3·04	75·4	68·1	71·3	83·9	92·0	100	104·1	108·1
9. Chemicals (all)	3·58	72·8	78·4	83·6	84·4	96·2	100	100·4	116·3
10. Petroleum	3·79	6·4	6·0	6·3	16·5	77·7	100	114·3	122·7
11. Non-metallic mineral products (all)	2·47	64·4	69·1	70·2	80·0	87·5	100	114·6	128·7
12. Basic metals	9·25	83·1	85·3	80·5	94·5	96·1	100	99·0	106·2
13. Manufacture of metal products	0·99	54·3	54·3	58·2	86·6	96·5	100	97·8	102·5
14. Manufacture of machinery except electrical machinery	1·10	45·2	35·7	37·7	57·5	83·3	100	129·5	148·3
15. Manufacture of electrical machinery	2·41	43·6	49·4	52·2	58·4	71·9	100	118·6	124·6
16. Manufacture of transport equipment	2·86	46·1	39·7	41·6	49·5	80·0	100	105·4	95·5
17. Electricity and gas generation	3·68	60·9	63·7	69·0	77·4	88·1	100	112·8	127·4
18. All manufacturing	88·85	72·8	74·8	77·0	82·4	91·6	100	103·2	106·0
GENERAL INDEX (including mining and quarrying)	100·00	73·4	75·6	77·7	83·0	91·9	100	104·1	107·5

TABLE 5.1—continued

Industry	Weights	Year							
		1959	1960	1961	1962	1963	1964	1965	1966
1. Food manufacturing	13·99	108·8	117·1	128·3	126·4	121·8	132·8	142·7	147·8
2. Beverage and tobacco industries	1·48	122·9	140·6	150·0	156·3	152·3	175·6	205·8	220·5
3. Manufacture of textiles	41·76	102·4	105·1	108·7	113·8	123·1	130·2	130·6	124·9
4. Manufacture of footwear	0·28	120·2	144·0	166·0	180·4	214·4	212·2	246·1	265·8
5. Manufacture of wood and woodware	1·39	137·2	147·8	150·2	169·0	200·2	206·3	236·1	226·7
6. Manufacture of paper and paper products	0·18	145·4	173·4	181·9	190·9	226·8	237·8	255·4	281·7
7. Manufacture of leather	3·04	101·6	115·3	115·6	125·2	149·0	138·6	140·2	136·3
8. Manufacture of rubber products	3·58	118·1	141·3	157·4	169·5	187·0	198·0	218·0	218·0
9. Chemicals (all)	3·79	131·0	149·9	172·2	190·5	219·7	238·8	253·1	262·3
10. Petroleum	2·47	132·4	147·7	156·5	192·2	196·6	216·6	231·0	285·9
11. Non-metallic mineral products (all)	9·25	146·0	168·1	180·8	220·2	204·7	213·9	232·5	230·1
12. Basic metals	0·99	137·8	182·5	209·9	256·1	294·4	292·4	300·9	318·0
13. Manufacture of metal products	1·10	98·3	105·9	152·3	179·1	201·0	218·9	239·8	221·5
14. Manufacture of machinery except electrical machinery		185·8	236·7	268·7	293·2	367·2	414·9	489·7	530·1
15. Manufacture of electrical machinery	2·41	133·4	175·9	183·2	211·1	239·1	276·1	313·2	340·6
16. Manufacture of transport equipment	2·86	101·4	119·4	130·8	150·8	150·6	190·2	206·6	187·5
17. Electricity and gas generation	3·68	151·4	171·0	198·8	223·4	257·9	296·8	326·5	355·3
18. All manufacturing	88·85	114·9	127·9	137·9	149·2	162·9	173·6	182·3	186·0
GENERAL INDEX (including mining and quarrying)	100·00	116·8	130·2	141·0	152·9	167·3	177·8	177·7	192·6

Source: Monthly Statistics of Production of Selected Industries of India, for July and August 1967, (Central Statistical Organization, Industrial Statistics Wing.)

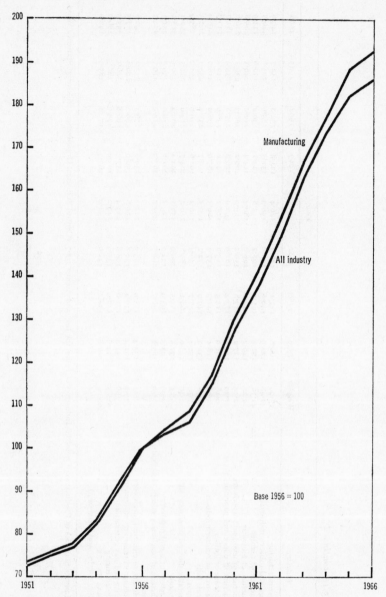

Figure 5.1. Index numbers of industrial production, 1951–66
Source: Table 5.1.

TABLE 5.2

RATES OF GROWTH OF MANUFACTURING INDUSTRIES, AT CURRENT PRICES, FOR 1951–61, 1951–63, 1951–7, AND 1957–63 BY GROSS VALUE ADDED, GROSS OUTPUT AT FACTOR COST AND GROSS OUTPUT AT MARKET PRICES

(A) Consumer goods industries

	1951–61			1951–63		
	Gross value added	Gross output at factor cost	Gross output at market price	Gross value added	Gross output at factor cost	Gross output at market price
	(1)	(2)	(3)	(4)	(5)	(6)
Flour-milling[a]	2·31	1·37	1·37	0·37	0·38	0·38
Fruit and vegetable processing	2·33	3·17	0·64	1·52	2·37	0·32
Biscuit-making[a]	0·32	0·69	0·69	0·62	1·31	1·31
Sugar[a]	0·64	1·17	1·52	0·41	0·66	1·14
Distilleries and breweries[a]	0·14	0·29	0·53	0·30	0·66	0·90
Vegetable oils	−0·38	−0·23	−0·19	−0·34	−0·46	−0·44
Soap	0·90	0·62	0·73	0·95	0·84	1·06
Matches[a]	0·26	0·31	0·68	0·19	0·14	0·75
Cotton textiles	14·05	0·34	0·42	14·21	0·47	0·58
Woollen textiles	1·47	0·98	1·08	2·67	2·32	2·59
Clothing and tailoring	0·12	1·03	1·03	5·00	2·00	2·00
Silk and art silk fabrics	1·36	1·43	1·58	3·77	3·09	3·20
Bicycles	4·65	8·78	9·57	6·74	11·88	12·84
Sewing machines	1·91	2·23	2·23	2·76	3·04	3·04
Electric lamps	3·36	4·00	5·00	5·47	6·93	8·89
Electric fans	2·00	3·10	3·50	2·75	4·54	5·09
Footwear and leather manufactures[a]	−0·78	−0·59	−0·40	−0·48	−0·07	0·19
Furniture and woodware[a]	1·66	9·98	9·98	11·50	16·91	16·81
Printing and book-binding	1·23	1·54	1·54	1·62	2·25	2·25
Tobacco	1·59	0·59	0·63	1·20	0·71	0·59
Tea[a]	0·38	0·31	0·35	0·27	0·41	0·48
Glass and glassware	1·33	1·85	2·10	2·23	2·71	3·16
Rubber and rubber manufactures	6·09	3·49	2·97	6·39	5·03	4·52
TOTAL	0·68	0·55	0·64	0·76	0·55	0·66

	1951-57			1957-63		
	Gross value added	Gross output at factor cost	Gross output at market price	Gross value added	Gross output at factor cost	Gross output at market price
	(7)	(8)	(9)	(10)	(11)	(12)
Flour-milling	1·27	0·99	0·99	-0·40	-0·31	-0·31
Fruit and vegetable processing	-0·18	0·39	-0·46	2·09	1·43	1·43
Biscuit-making	-0·08	0·20	0·20	0·76	0·93	0·93
Sugar	0·05	0·31	0·50	0·34	0·27	0·43
Distilleries and breweries	-0·17	-0·17	0·03	0·56	1·01	0·85
Vegetable oils	-0·29	-0·09	-0·06	-0·08	-0·40	-0·41
Soap	0·28	0·50	0·58	0·53	0·23	0·30
Matches	0·03	0·06	0·28	0·15	0·08	0·36
Cotton textiles	8·09	0·002	0·08	0·67	0·47	0·46
Woollen textiles	-0·15	0·31	0·36	3·33	1·54	1·65
Clothing and tailoring	-0·26	0·31	0·31	7·08	1·29	1·29
Silk and art silk fabrics	1·56	1·40	1·44	0·86	0·71	0·72
Bicycles	4·05	6·21	6·21	0·53	0·79	0·92
Sewing machines	2·48	3·17	3·17	0·08	-0·03	-0·03
Electric lamps	1·46	1·71	2·05	1·63	1·93	2·24
Electric fans	0·44	0·93	0·97	1·59	1·87	2·09
Footwear and leather manufactures	-0·77	-0·59	0·34	1·32	1·28	-0·12
Furniture and woodware	3·07	2·90	2·90	2·07	3·56	3·56
Printing and book-binding	0·35	0·64	0·64	0·94	0·98	0·98
Tobacco	0·58	0·23	0·22	0·39	0·39	0·31
Tea	1·99	0·63	0·62	-0·58	-0·14	-0·08
Glass and glassware	0·56	0·61	0·61	1·08	1·30	1·59
Rubber and rubber manufactures	2·63	1·74	1·32	1·04	1·20	1·38
TOTAL	0·25	0·23	0·29	0·41	0·25	0·28

	1951–61			1951–63		
	(1)	(2)	(3)	(4)	(5)	(6)
Starch	20·76	8·13	8·13	28·63	10·52	10·52
Webbing and narrow fabrics	−0·32	−0·19	−0·19	0·05	0·38	0·38
Hosiery and knitted goods[a]	3·98	1·19	1·19	6·34	2·53	2·53
Thread- and threadball-making	7·45	5·51	5·51	15·25	8·64	8·64
Textile dyeing and bleaching	−0·03	0·69	0·69	0·30	1·41	1·41
Cotton ginning and pressing	0·23	0·30	0·30	0·42	−0·18	−0·18
Jute pressing	−0·92	−0·95	−0·95	−0·89	−0·93	−0·93
Saw-milling	−0·71	−0·49	−0·49	−0·63	−0·21	−0·21
Groundnut decorticating	—	—	—	—	—	—
Rope-making	0·13	0·66	0·66	0·98	2·02	2·02
Paints and varnishes[a]	0·07	0·52	0·73	0·90	1·29	1·70
Tanning	0·22	0·28	0·28	0·01	0·01	−0·01
Cement	0·86	1·92	2·79	1·34	2·60	3·64
Ceramics	2·24	3·03	3·17	2·99	4·15	4·43
Plywood	0·41	0·63	0·63	1·57	2·07	2·46
Paper and paperboard	1·46	2·28	2·76	2·37	3·50	4·26
Jute textiles[a]	−0·31	−0·18	−0·18	0·20	−0·09	−0·07
Chemicals	3·30	3·48	3·60	4·54	4·99	5·20
Aluminium, copper, and brass	2·32	1·67	1·77	4·85	3·04	3·24
Iron and steel	1·04	1·95	2·11	2·58	4·27	4·62
Enamelware	4·04	5·51	5·51	5·05	6·00	6·00
Hume pipes and other products of cement concrete	1·84	3·18	3·18	3·26	6·62	6·62
Asbestos cement[a]	5·57	3·37	3·37	9·16	5·59	6·25
Bricks, tiles, etc.[a]	−0·28	−0·30	−0·30	−0·15	−0·16	−0·16
Lac[a]	0·46	−0·32	−0·32	0·65	−0·55	−0·55
Turpentine and rosin	4·81	1·92	1·92	0·44	1·47	1·47
Plastics	0·51	0·17	0·35	2·28	1·90	2·33
Electricity generation and transmission	2·56	3·65	3·65	5·37	6·95	6·95
Petroleum refining	3·78	5·65	5·66	3·91	7·16	7·16
TOTAL	0·97	0·97	1·06	1·99	1·77	1·93

	1951-7			1957-63		
	(7)	(8)	(9)	(10)	(11)	(12)
Starch	11·83	4·26	4·26	1·31	1·19	1·19
Webbing and narrow fabrics	0·20	0·33	0·33	—0·12	—0·04	—0·04
Hosiery and knitted goods	3·37	0·97	0·97	0·76	0·79	0·79
Thread- and threadball-making	4·78	2·88	2·88	1·46	1·48	1·48
Textile dyeing and bleaching	0·13	0·72	0·72	0·49	0·40	0·40
Cotton ginning and pressing	0·81	0·97	0·97	—0·22	—0·58	—0·58
Jute pressing	0·49	—0·19	—0·19	—0·92	—0·91	—0·91
Saw-milling	0·66	1·88	1·88	—0·78	—0·72	—0·72
Groundnut decorticating	0·68	0·23	0·31	—	—	—
Rope-making	—0·23	—0·15	—0·15	1·57	2·57	2·57
Paints and varnishes	0·29	0·61	0·73	0·47	0·43	0·56
Tanning	—0·01	—0·19	—0·19	0·02	0·22	0·22
Cement	0·06	0·56	0·93	1·22	1·30	1·40
Ceramics	0·50	0·70	0·70	1·66	2·02	2·19
Plywood	0·57	0·69	0·69	0·64	0·82	1·05
Paper and paperboard	0·35	0·64	0·84	1·49	1·74	1·86
Jute textiles	—0·32	—0·40	—0·40	0·77	0·51	0·56
Chemicals	0·81	0·84	0·84	2·06	2·26	2·37
Aluminium, copper, and brass	1·34	1·32	1·32	1·50	0·74	0·82
Iron and steel	0·87	1·15	1·14	0·92	1·45	1·62
Enamelware	2·56	2·26	2·26	0·70	1·15	1·15
Hume pipes and other products of cement concrete	4·46	5·85	5·85	—0·22	0·11	0·11
Asbestos cement	4·50	2·23	2·23	0·85	1·04	1·24
Bricks, tiles, etc.	—0·27	—0·27	—0·27	0·17	0·16	0·16
Lac	1·51	0·30	0·30	—0·34	—0·65	—0·65
Turpentine and rosin	0·69	0·37	0·37	—0·15	0·81	0·81
Plastics	0·24	0·21	0·21	1·64	1·40	1·75
Electricity generation and transmission	0·31	1·13	1·13	3·87	2·73	2·73
Petroleum refining	1·12	3·30	3·30	1·32	0·90	0·90

(C) *Investment goods*

	1951-61				1951-63	
	(1)	(2)	(3)	(4)	(5)	(6)
Textile machinery	3·16	3·24	3·24	6·24	6·29	6·29
Railways and automobiles	7·16	6·34	6·64	11·73	8·83	9·19
Aircraft	2·29	1·83	1·83	2·42	1·84	1·84
Shipbuilding	0·18	0·50	0·50	0·53	0·83	0·83
General and electrical engineering	4·94	7·78	7·78	8·03	12·89	12·89
TOTAL	4·64	6·15	6·27	7·62	9·59	9·72
GRAND TOTAL	1·04	0·92	1·00	1·65	1·32	1·42

	1951-7			1957-63		
	(7)	(8)	(9)	(10)	(11)	(12)
Textile machinery	2·03	1·79	1·79	1·39	1·62	1·62
Railways and automobiles	2·97	2·96	2·98	2·21	1·48	1·56
Aircraft	1·15	1·16	1·16	0·59	0·31	0·31
Shipbuilding	0·57	1·16	1·16	−0·02	−0·15	−0·15
General and electrical engineering	0·03	2·53	2·33	5·81	3·18	3·18
TOTAL	1·11	2·40	2·40	3·08	2·12	2·15
GRAND TOTAL	0·35	0·39	0·43	0·96	0·67	0·69

ᵃ In the case of these items, the figures either of indirect taxes on production or of import taxes are, in general, excessively large in relation to the corresponding estimates of production and imports.

Source of Table 5·2: Calculated from primary tables referred to in the text and Appendix; primary tables have been printed in Padma Desai, *Indian Economic Journal*, 1970, op. cit.

adjustments were made for import premia because reliable information on these was not available. The sum of domestic production and imports thus estimated represents the value of total supplies at market prices, net of trading profits and transport margins.

It must, however, be emphasized that supply at market prices has been taken *net* of export duties for the calculations. Since the

TABLE 5·3
GROSS VALUE ADDED, GROSS OUTPUT AT FACTOR COST, AND
GROSS OUTPUT AT CURRENT MARKET PRICES BY INDUSTRY GROUPS

	Gross value added		Gross output at factor cost		Gross output at market price[a]	
	Value, Rs.	%	Value, Rs.	%	Value, Rs.	%
	1951					
Consumer goods	34,08,085	57·74	1,34,29,522	64·01	1,42,48,322	65·35
Raw materials and intermediates	21,07,345	35·70	66,53,676	31·72	66,59,176	30·54
Investment goods	3,87,043	6·56	8,95,913	4·27	8,95,913	4·11
TOTAL	59,02,473	100.00	2,09,79,111	100·00	2,18,03,411	100·00
	1957					
Consumer goods	42,46,044	53·12	1,65,71,640	56·81	1,83,98,257	59·08
Raw materials and intermediates	29,29,480	36·66	95,56,853	32·76	96,93,845	31·14
Investment goods	8,17,052	10·22	30,42,866	10·43	30,46,542	9·78
TOTAL	79,92,576	100·00	2,91,71,379	100·00	3,11,38,644	100·00
	1961					
Consumer goods	57,24,188	47·50	2,07,72,313	51·52	2,33,34,411	53·53
Raw materials and intermediates	41,43,643	34·38	1,31,38,707	32·59	1,37,46,949	31·54
Investment goods	21,83,872	18·12	64,09,854	15·89	65,10,259	14·93
TOTAL	1,20,51,703	100·00	4,03,20,874	100·00	4,35,91,619	100·00
	1963					
Consumer goods	59,99,829	38·37	2,07,85,854	42·70	2,36,35,314	44·81
Raw materials and intermediates	63,02,434	40·30	1,84,03,560	37·81	1,95,03,569	36·98
Investment goods	33,36,490	21·33	94,87,928	19·49	96,06,933	18·21
TOTAL	1,56,38,753	100·00	4,86,77,342	100·00	5,27,45,816	1 00·00

[a] We have used the estimates net of export duties as throughout the paper and as explained in the Appendix.

Source: Calculated from primary tables, referred to in the text and Appendix. These primary tables have been printed in Padma Desai, *Indian Economic Journal*, 1970, op. cit.

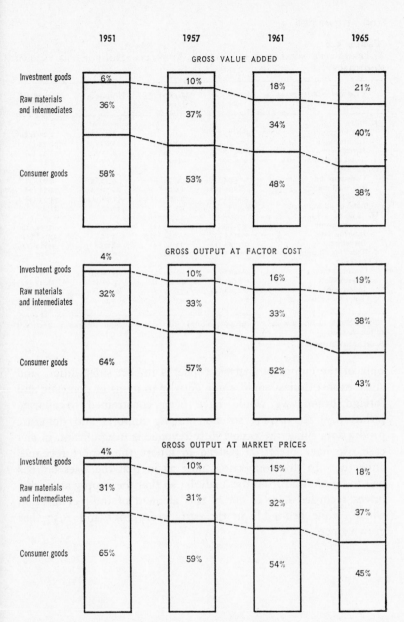

Figure 5.2. Industry group shares in gross value added, gross output at factor cost and gross output at market prices.

Source: Table 5.3.

TABLE 5.4

ALTERNATIVE MEASURES OF IMPORT SUBSTITUTION FOR THE INDIAN
ECONOMY

Period and industry-group (1)	Measure 1 (2)	Measure 2 (3)	Measure 3 (4)	Measure 4 (5)
I. *1951–7*				
Consumption	0·0173 (1)	41·09 (1)	7·73 (1)	7·21 (1)
Intermediate	−0·0850 (3)	−48·82 (3)	−36·65 (3)	−30·15 (3)
Investment	−0·0220 (2)	−3·89 (2)	−8·25 (2)	−3·11 (2)
Total of all industries	−0·0809	−63·41	−33·71	−5·11
II. *1957–63*				
Consumption	0·0094 (3)	3·79 (3)	4·58 (3)	4·63 (3)
Intermediate	0·1251 (2)	44·03 (1)	28·70 (2)	32·70 (2)
Investment	0·2203 (1)	37·78 (2)	51·28 (1)	54·75 (1)
Total of all industries	0·0638	30·59	17·98	31·47
III. *1951–61*				
Consumption	0·0278 (2)	66·03 (1)	7·29 (2)	7·59 (3)
Intermediate	−0·0131 (3)	−7·52 (3)	−3·10 (3)	12·48 (2)
Investment	0·1388 (1)	24·59 (2)	28·05 (1)	31·89 (1)
Total for all industries	−0·0328	−25·62	−7·65	15·56
IV. *1951–63*				
Consumption	0·0267 (3)	61·05 (1)	6·90 (3)	9·17 (3)
Intermediate	0·0401 (2)	23·03 (3)	7·01 (2)	18·11 (2)
Investment	0·1983 (1)	35·14 (2)	34·44 (1)	38·41 (1)
Total for all industries	−0·0171	−13·40	−3·29	21·13

Note: Figures in brackets indicate group rankings. All the measures are defined in Section I
of the chapter.

Source: See Appendix.

bulk of the empirical analysis concerns import substitution, and
since export duties would apply equally to items of domestic and
foreign origin, we would have been constrained to allocate
(arbitrarily) the export revenue among imports and domestic
production. Since the export duty revenue is insignificant, in any
case, we have preferred instead to ignore the export revenues
altogether. In this connection, note again that the sales tax has
had to be omitted from the analysis; so that the supply at market
prices recorded here is net of this element of indirect taxation
which, while negligible in the early years 1951 and 1957, has
grown since.

PART III

The Overall Policy Framework

6

Planning, Strategy and Policy Instruments

THE growth and industrialization of the Indian economy, which
has been reviewed in some detail in Part II, was promoted and
regulated within a planning framework which will now be described in its main elements.

The planning commission

The notion that the country's economic growth must be planned
systematically, by an enlightened government, had been inherited
by India from the time of the Independence Movement. And,
indeed, there had been many precursors of the Five-Year Plans
on which India was to embark in 1951.[1]

The Indian Planning Commission, which was to take the formal
responsibility for formulating and following the implementation
of the Five-Year Plans, thus grew out of the ferment of ideas
which had been implanted deeply in Indian élite thinking. Its
immediate establishment, however, followed the recommendations
made by the officially appointed Advisory Planning Board (1946)
and their endorsement by the Economic Programme Committee
of the Congress (1948).[2]

The Planning Commission was established on 15 March 1950.
Although its role was envisaged as advisory, and it was conceived
as an adjunct to the Cabinet, its initial distinguished membership
with Prime Minister Nehru as its Chairman and a prominent

---

[1] For an excellent review of these earlier 'Plans', put together by groups such
as prominent industrialists (who formulated the well-known 'Bombay Plan' of
1944), engineers, and intellectuals, as also the numerous resolutions of the
Indian National Congress on the role and nature of economic planning after
Independence, see A. H. Hanson, *The Process of Planning*, op. cit., Chapter II.

[2] For details of the evolution, and the further changes over time in the composition and powers, of the Planning Commission, see Hanson, op. cit., Chapters
II and III.

Congressman (Nanda)[1] as its Deputy Chairman, assured it an informal status and *de facto* powers considerably beyond those actually defined.[2]

In the subsequent period, the Planning Commission was to formulate the three successive Five-Year Plans, spanning the period (1951–66) which we study in this volume. In this task it was occasionally assisted by 'outside' institutions such as the Indian Statistical Institute which, under the leadership of its distinguished Director, Professor Mahalanobis, took a prominent part in providing the intellectual basis for the Second Plan.[3] Among the Planning Commission's further efforts at getting intellectual expertise associated with the planning exercises was its Panel of Economists whose contribution to the Second Plan debate, while ineffective, was the most significant activity of its career.[4]

But, distinct from these intellectual associations,[5] the Planning Commission's role was set within a complex political framework and set of institutions. Chief among the latter was the National Developmental Council (N.D.C.). Established in August 1952, and consisting of the Prime Minister, the Chief Ministers of the States, and the members of the Planning Commission, the N.D.C. was originally designed

[1] Gulzarilal Nanda was later to become the Acting Prime Minister on two occasions, when India lost Nehru and Shastri.
[2] Nehru's deep, personal interest in planning was also to play a significant role in creating for the Planning Commission its key role in Indian development.
[3] Bhagwati and Chakravarty, op. cit. (Part I), have dealt at length with the precise nature of the contribution of Mahalanobis's ideas to Indian planning.
[4] On details, see Hanson, op. cit., pp. 128–30 in particular.
[5] The association of foreign economists with Indian planning was also very much visible from the Second Plan onwards. Oskar Lange, Ragnar Frisch, Richard Goodwin, and Jan Tinbergen were among the prominent visitors to the Indian Statistical Institute at the time of the Second Plan discussions. The M.I.T. Center for International Studies was also the vehicle for the visit of many economists, especially at the time of the Third Plan discussions: Ian Little, Trevor Swan, Brian Reddaway, Sir Donald MacDougall, Paul Rosenstein-Rodan, Arnold Harberger, Richard Eckaus, Louis Lefeber, Jim Mirrlees, and Alan Manne being among the most notable contributors to the Indian policy debates. Furthermore, distinguished Indian economists such as D. R. Gadgil, V. K. R. V. Rao, M. L. Dantwala, and C. N. Vakil among the older generation, and V. N. Dandekar, K. N. Raj, P. Brahmananda, P. N. Dhar, A. M. Khusro, and D. T. Lakdawala in the younger generation, provided continuing commentary on the Plans and economic policies during this period.

(1) to review the working of the National Plan from time to time;

(2) to consider important questions of social and economic policy affecting national development; and

(3) to recommend measures for the achievement of the aims and targets set out in the National Plan, including measures to secure the active participation and co-operation of the people, improve the efficiency of the administrative services, ensure the fullest development of the less advanced regions and sections of the community and through sacrifices borne equally by all citizens, build up resources for national development.[1]

In effect, the N.D.C. meetings were to become important occasions for confronting the politicians with major, proposed economic and planning decisions. With the different states represented through their Chief Ministers, often assisted by *their* civil servants, experts, and Ministers, the N.D.C. was to prove an excellent sounding-board for exploring the political feasibility of tricky items such as the raising of resources (taxation). Hanson has aptly summed up the N.D.C.'s role, *vis-à-vis* the Planning Commission, as follows:

From its creation to June 1962 the N.D.C. held eighteen meetings. To these should be added the six meetings of a Standing Committee of the Council, established in 1955 and discontinued in 1958. The printed —and largely verbatim—minutes of these gatherings record a steady increase in its influence. During the period when the Third Five-Year Plan was being formulated and the Second Five-Year Plan repeatedly 'adjusted', the Commission presented the Council with lengthy and carefully drafted memoranda, which usually asked it to decide between alternative lines of policy. Admittedly, the Commission had on these occasions come to its own conclusions, which it pressed vigorously and for the most part successfully. But the show of respect with which it approached the Council was more than a façade; for the Commission realized that in the Council it had the most important of its many sounding-boards. Discussions might be disorderly and inconclusive, but they did reveal just how much, when it came to the crunch, the states were prepared to stand for, and how far they were prepared to go in carrying out centrally-determined priorities. . . . The N.D.C. is, *de facto*, more than an advisory body; but it is also less than an executive one. It may best be described, rather lengthily, as the most important organized gathering where plans undergo adjustment in the light of the needs, pressures, prejudices, and capacities of the states.[2]

[1] V. T. Krishnamachari, *Fundamentals of Planning in India*, pp. 65–6; quoted in Hanson, op. cit., p. 61.

[2] Op. cit., pp. 61–2.

Strategy: the 'major' decisions

Fundamentally, the Planning Commission was to engage in making two basic decisions for the Indian economy: (1) what was to be the size of the investment (savings), and (2) how was the investment to be allocated among alternative uses?

The first question, in turn, raised the thorny problems of how much foreign aid could be expected and should be accepted,[1] and what marginal rate of saving would be politically acceptable and economically desirable. The second question, on the other hand, led in particular to important controversies relating to the shares of investment going to agriculture as distinct from industry, and to 'heavy' as against 'light' industry.[2]

The planners were increasingly conscious of the limitation of considering investment outlays as the only productive element in the economy; and 'current' outlays on agricultural extension service and education, for example, came to be regarded in policy debates as equally important despite the general tendency to consider the (investment) 'size' of the Plan as the index of its productivity and boldness. Clearly, a very wide range of such current outlays would, in a country with India's poverty, have investment-aspects to them. It is indeed arguable, and empirical observation frequently corroborates this, that direct consumption itself will improve the efficiency of labour and have productive effects: a point of view which underlay, among other things, the view that Indian planning ought to be more biased towards consumer (wage) goods output than investment (machinery) production.[3]

The First Plan was largely a collection of projects, with the allocation of outlays in the public sector taking the brunt of the analysis, (while a modified Harrod–Domar analysis was provided to give a picture of the growth in the Indian economy over a twenty-five-year period with increasing marginal and average rates of saving). Table 6.1 shows the major divisions into which the public sector outlays were to be divided during the three

---

[1] These issues are discussed at length in Chapter 10.

[2] This latter problem is discussed in depth in Chapter 12.

[3] Thus, see the interesting work of P. R. Brahmananda and C. N. Vakil, *Planning for An Expanding Economy*, and the discussion of their general approach to planning in India in Bhagwati and Chakravarty, op. cit.

Plans. Such a breakdown relates, of course, to total governmental outlays and has a very limited value except in so far as the analyst is concerned with the relative magnitudes of governmental expenditures within each Planning period. In terms of such a limited index, however, it is clear that the attention of the Government was evenly divided among sectors such as power and transport (in so far as we can trace them consistently through the Plans) during the fifteen-year period. But there were major changes in the overall strategy, as exemplified in three major areas: agriculture (together with irrigation) declined from 33 per cent in the First Plan to 20 per cent in the Second Plan (achievement) and 23 per cent in the Third Plan; expenditures on social services, education, etc., (categories 7 and 8) declined from 25 per cent in the First Plan to 18 per cent in the Second Plan (achievement) and 17 per cent in the Third Plan; whereas organized industry and minerals grew rapidly from (a maximum of) 7 per cent in the First Plan to 20 per cent in the Second Plan (achievement) and in the Third Plan.

From the Second Plan, economic analysis was addressed explicitly to *national* investments, as distinct from *public sector* investments and developmental outlays. We thus have (rough) estimates of the overall investments in the Second and Third Plans, by different sectors, as included in Table 6.2. In the absence of reliable estimates for investments in the First Plan, but noting the public sector's disbursements at the time from Table 6.1, we can infer that the decline in the share of agricultural investments from the First Plan level must have paralleled the decline in the share of agriculture in governmental outlays. While there was no major difference in the investment pattern, planned and actual, in the Second and Third Plans, indicating a broad continuation of policies in this regard, the Second Plan differed from the First in two major respects: in the reduced share of agricultural investments; and in the shift, within the enlarged share of the organized industrial sector, towards 'heavy' industry.[1]

Altogether, these two major decisions were to prove controversial: with economists and politicians generally divided on the

[1] In terms of *output* growth and import substitution, we have already given statistical measures of such a shift in Chapter 5. For qualitative discussion of the shift, *The Second Five-Year Plan*, op. cit., is an excellent source. As for the rationale underlying this shift, and a critical analysis thereof, Chapter 12 contains the relevant discussion. Also refer to Bhagwati and Chakravarty, op. cit.

TABLE 6.1

PERCENTAGE OF PUBLIC SECTOR OUTLAYS UNDER DIFFERENT HEADS IN THE FIVE-YEAR PLANS

Head	First Plan (revised)	Second Plan (draft outline)	Second Plan (original)	Second Plan (first revision)	Second Plan (second revision)	Second Plan (achieve-ment)	Third Plan (draft outline)	Third Plan
1. Agriculture and community development	16	12	11·8	11·8	11·3	11	23·1	14
2. Irrigation	17	9	10·1	17·9	18·2	9		9
3. Power	11	9	8·9			10	12·8	13
4. Industries and minerals	7	19	18·5	18·4	17·5	20	20·7	20
5. Village and small-scale industries				4·2	3·6	4	3·4	4
6. Transport and communications	24	29	28·9	28·0	29·8	28	20·0	20
7. Social services, housing, and rehabilitation	23	20	19·7	18·0	18·0	18	17·2	17
8. Miscellaneous	2	2	2·1	1·7	1·6	—	2·8	3
9. Inventories	—	—	—	—	—	—		
10. Total	100	100	100	100	100	100	100	100

Source: Plan documents, Government of India, New Delhi.

advisability of the extent to which these shifts had been envisaged and implemented. In retrospect, it appears that the critics were right, even though their arguments had not been cogently put.[1] The *relative* neglect of agriculture, and hence of the 'wage-goods constraint', with its attendant, somewhat exaggerated concern with the building up of the investment sector to break eventually the 'capital-goods constraint', were to be shown by the subsequent turn of events to have been unfortunate and harmful to the process of economic development in the country.[2]

But, equally with the questions of investment allocations among these major sectors, the Planning Commission and the public debates were seized continually with the question of the overall 'size' (rate of investment) of each Plan. This was particularly the case from the Second Plan onwards, when in fact the focus shifted (as we have noted) from public sector outlays to the question of overall, national investments. The debate, within the Planning Commission, the Government, and in public forums, was between the 'big planners', who wanted larger investments, and the 'small planners', who were willing to settle for smaller investments. In essence, since the two groups were equally intent on equating *ex-ante* savings and investment in the interest of planning without inflation, and since (until the later, Fourth Plan discussions) the expectations about the aid flow and its desirability were not matters of contention between these groups, the dividing point between the groups was nothing more than their divergent views about the political feasibility of the marginal rates of saving implicit in their respective investment-targets.

The 'big planners' in the Planning Commission were typically

---

[1] Thus, for example, the critique of B. R. Shenoy against investments in heavy industry, as typified in his collection of essays: *Indian Economic Policy*, Part I, lacked comprehension of the structural models which justified a shift towards heavy-industrial investments; on the other hand, events were to show that this shift had been somewhat excessive.

[2] Even consistent with the same share of industrial investments going to heavy industry in the Second Plan, the construction of plants to produce fertilizer plants, rather than the erection of the gigantic Heavy Engineering Plant at Bhopal, for example, would have eased some of the later constraints on agricultural expansion which were to prove very critical in the mid-sixties. On the question of the *relative* neglect of the agricultural sector, a thesis which we broadly agree with but do not explore in detail, we have found the following two analyses of considerable interest: Michael Lipton, 'Strategy for Agriculture: Urban Bias and Rural Planning', in Streeten and Lipton, op. cit., and Richard Eckaus and Kirit Parikh, *Planning for Growth*, op. cit.

the 'physical' planners, such as Mahalanobis and Pitambar Pant (the Chief of the Perspective Planning Division), who considered that, provided the investments were technically feasible, savings ought to be forthcoming somehow. The naïve view, among these so-called 'physical planners', was that if you produced capital goods and steel, thus increasing the share of investment goods in G.N.P., that would automatically mean a higher savings rate since 'one cannot eat steel'. This view was, of course, false since a gap between *ex-ante* savings and the savings required to support the planned share of investment in G.N.P. could mean a number of alternative outcomes: excess capacity in capital goods industries, for example, or excess demand for consumer goods resulting in a reduction of exports and hence in imports of capital goods, implying an *ex-post* reduction in the savings/investment share in G.N.P. after all. But the more sophisticated view among the 'physical', 'big' planners was that the Finance Ministry *ought* to tax sufficiently in order to get the savings up to the required level; and since the Finance Ministry had to raise the necessary taxes, often the internal, governmental debate turned out to be between the 'reactionary' Finance Ministry which wanted a 'smaller', politically feasible Plan, and the 'progressive' Planning Commission which wanted the more ambitious, 'bigger' Plan.

The ultimate 'size' of the planned savings and investments inevitably represented a compromise between these opposing points of view. The big planners, however, found their targets less seriously compromised, thanks to the fact that, given India's poverty and the pressing urgency to grow rapidly, the boldness of their targets made more idealistic sense and appealed to Nehru's vision and leadership; whereas the Finance Ministry's conservative, 'lower-sights' approach seemed unsuited to the times, even though more realistic given the political constraints within which development was being planned in the economy.

Furthermore, it is interesting to note that the 'big' planners frequently managed to smuggle in more ambitious plans of investment than, in fact, the compromise exercises in the Plan documents indicated. Since the overall investment-savings exercise (aimed at equalizing planned savings and investment) involved the estimation of (relatively uncontrolled) private investment in agriculture and small industries, the big planners typically conceded 'cuts' in these investments, when negotiating with the small planners, as a way of retaining larger public sector investment outlays consistent with a lower overall investment outlay. Of course, all that this meant was that the Plan then underestimated the private investments which would, in fact, be larger in reality: and thus the Plan was implicitly building into itself an excess of investment over planned savings and the overall investment outlay was actually larger than pretended. Similarly, investments in inventory holdings were systematically and grossly underestimated, despite repeated criticisms, in the Second and Third Plan exercises. Since these investments could not be wished away, and would occur irrespective of whether the planners took them into account or not, the result was again that the apparent size of the planned investments fell below the actual, and the apparent equality of planned savings and investment actually concealed an (inflationary) excess of investment over savings. Apart from these underestimates of (largely uncontrolled) investments, there appears to have been a tendency also to *overestimate* the private sector savings that would be forthcoming to 'finance' the planned investments. Finally, the big planners even left an open excess of planned investment over savings in the Second Plan document, to be filled in by unspecified resources!

What were the presumed advantages in planning 'big' in this built-in inflationary manner? Two major views appear to have provided the tactical basis for such planning. (1) The big estimates at the time of the Second Plan appear to have been motivated, in some quarters, by the notion that an ambitious Plan would, via the resulting foreign exchange crisis, precipitate a larger foreign aid inflow than would otherwise be forthcoming. As it happened, this reasoning was not altogether unjustified in view of the escalation of the aid programmes subsequent to the 1956/7 crisis in the balance of payments. (2) The predominant argument in support of the ambitious investment targets, however, appears to have been that a Stakhanovite approach would produce higher savings: the Finance Ministry, committed to price stability, would just have to impose the taxation necessary to finance the planned outlays, or remain reconciled to inflation. This tactical policy was not tested during the Second Plan because the massive aid inflow happened to swamp such built-in inflationary pressures.

However, during the Third Plan, the stochastic factors were unfavourable: the two border wars, increased defence spending, and the two severe droughts; and an inflationary rise in prices thus became inevitable. While, therefore, the issues were obscured by exogenous factors in each Plan, we sympathize with the view that the tendency to smuggle in larger investment outlays than *ex-ante* savings, behind the façade of a planned equality between them, did *not* induce a higher taxation effort, but may actually have been counter-productive in inhibiting tax effort (below what would have been the case) in so far as taxation is politically difficult in a situation of rising prices. Indeed, the net result might also have been partly a pulling-in of outlays to more realistic levels: with the result that, with a number of projects started on a basis of the larger-outlays Plan, the eventual slowing-down would involve cut-backs on most of them, leading to the observed phenomenon of too many starts and too few completions. Stakhanovite planning in this sector therefore may well have been very expensive.

Policy instruments

The major planning decisions just reviewed were taken in conjunction with other, equally important decisions in the matter of industrialization itself. Among these were decisions relating to the detailed topography of industrial development (see Part VI for a fuller discussion).

The policy instruments deployed to guide industrialization (which is the focus of study in this volume) into desired patterns included both domestic and foreign instruments. The domestic policy instruments consisted mainly of a powerful and comprehensive industrial licensing system (discussed intensively in Chapter 13), occasionally combined with price and distributional controls (briefly reviewed in Chapter 14). The rapid growth of the public sector, while considered an objective in itself (Chapter 9), also provided a significant means of influencing the pattern of new investments in targeted directions. These policies were further buttressed by the policies relating to trade and payments. As we analyse in Part VII, the industrial targets were supported by the quantitative restrictions (QRs) which shielded domestic production automatically from foreign competition; and the framework of import and export policies, in turn,

TABLE 6.2
SECOND AND THIRD PLANS: ANALYSIS OF PUBLIC AND PRIVATE SECTOR INVESTMENT

Head	Second Plan			Third Plan (Draft outline)			Third Plan		
	Public sector	Private sector	Total	Public sector	Private sector[b]	Total	Public sector	Private sector[b]	Total
Agriculture and community development	6	20	12	11	20	14	10	20	14
Major and minor irrigation	12	a	6	10	a	6	10	a	6
Power	12	1	7	15	1	10	16	1	10
Village and small industries	3	6	4	3	7	4	2	7	4
Organized industry and minerals	24	22	23	24	25	25	24	26	25
Transport and communications	35	4	21	23	5	16	24	6	17
Social services and miscellaneous	9	31	19	10	27	17	10	26	16
Inventories	—	16	8	3	15	8	3	15	8
TOTAL	100	100	100	100	100	100	100	100	100

[a] Included under agriculture and community development.
[b] Excludes transfers from public to private sector.
Note: The totals do not always add up to 100 because of rounding.
Sources: *Five-Year Plans.*

provided the incentives which affected the non-targeted industrialization.[1]

Before turning to an extended analysis of these policies, however, we proceed to a brief review of the political, administrative, and other institutional constraints and objectives subject to which these policies were designed.

[1] The reader will note therefore that we have not entered into a detailed examination of fiscal policy, other than to indicate its broad contours in our brief discussion of taxation in Chapter 4. An excellent treatment of this subject, however, can be found in I. M. D. Little's contribution in P. N. Rosenstein-Rodan (ed.), *Pricing and Fiscal Policies*. We have also not analysed the question of financial resources in the private sector's growth, except again in Chapter 4; for further details, Rosen, op. cit., is a valuable source.

PART IV
Institutional Constraints and Objectives

7

The Political Structure

DEVELOPMENTAL plans must be conceived and implemented within a framework whose major dimensions are political and sociological. A Poujadist party cannot be expected to raise the share of taxes in national income nor can a political party built on *junker* support be expected to implement land reform, no matter how crucial these policies may be from a strictly economic point of view. Similarly, a Plan which requires a sophisticated and streamlined administrative apparatus for its execution, or is premised on popular enthusiasm and willingness to work in a 'common cause', will founder if neither assumption is realistic.

Since some of the principal inefficiencies in Indian planning undoubtedly have their source in an inadequate appreciation of these elementary and elemental constraints, and some possibilities of improving the economic performance were ruled out by such 'non-economic' restrictions on the feasibility of superior economic policies, we must address ourselves to them before proceeding to discuss the governmental exercise of more traditional, economic policy instruments, both domestic and foreign, in Parts VI and VII. Since the primary focus of analysis in this volume is on industrialization policies, we will avoid more general discussion and confine ourselves to the manner in which both the political structure (Chapter 7) and the state of administration (Chapter 8) have provided the major institutional constraints directly on Indian industrialization policies.[1] In Chapter 9 we discuss, in depth, the major area where political, ideological, and administrative factors have particularly influenced economic policies relating

[1] For a thorough and exhaustive discussion of the more general issues, including the impact of these constraints on agricultural growth and on plan-formulation in general, A. H. Hanson's work, *The Process of Planning*, is an excellent reference. Also see, in this connection, Bhagwati's review of Hanson in *Public Administration*, Summer, 1967.

K

to industrialization: the relative importance of the public and private sectors.

Since political factors have influenced nearly every area of policy-making, in some degree or other,[1] we merely review briefly in this chapter the important facets of the Indian political scene which have had a bearing on industrialization policies and then outline the principal respects in which they have done so.

The overriding aspects of the Indian policy are its democratic political system, patterned after the British model, and its federal structure. Since independence in 1947 the basic political system has not been changed although numerous new political parties have emerged, some (like the Praja Socialist Party) having split from the Indian Congress, others like the Swatantra and Jana Sangh being of more recent origin, and the Communist Party having split into two warring factions since the Sino-Soviet dispute burst into an open sore.[2]

The Indian Union is further a federation which consists today, after several reorganizations, of sixteen states including Nagaland and the state of Jammu and Kashmir. In the course of time these states have come to exercise considerable power over the country's politics and thence on the economy: this power has increased significantly with the two Prime Ministerial elections, since Jawaharlal Nehru's death in 1964, during which the state Chief Ministers played a crucial role in 'kingmaking'.[3] The centripetal

---

[1] For example, two other areas where ideology has tended to intrude have been foreign aid and private foreign investment: we consider these questions separately in Part V addressed to the general problem of external resources utilized for and during Indian development. Needless to add, ideology and 'lesser' political considerations have affected also the classical, economic policy instruments which we discuss in Parts VI and VII.

[2] The Swatantra is the 'laissez-faire' party and Jana Sangh is reputed to be communalistic and somewhat 'feudal'. The Congress is 'ideologically confused', accused of being Leftist by the Swatantra and Jana Sangh and of being Rightist by both the Communist factions and other, minor 'radical' parties. Many of these stereotypes, borrowed from Western thought and practice, are however misleading and, in fact, the Indian parties and politics are swayed by religious, linguistic, regional, and caste considerations which cut across many of these traditional, Western distinctions. On this question, the eminent social anthropologist, M. N. Srinivas, *Caste in Modern India and Other Essays;* F. G. Bailey, 'Politics and Society in Contemporary Orissa', in C. H. Philips (ed.), *Politics and Society in India;* W. H. Morris-Jones, 'India's Political Idioms', in Philips (ed.), op. cit.; and A. H. Hanson, op. cit., Chapter VIII, are all extremely valuable.

[3] Cf. M. Brecher, *Succession in India: A Study in Decision-making.*

forces, which had begun to assert themselves even while the Indian Congress, which still rules at the Centre, ruled the states as well (with brief exceptions, as in the state of Kerala where the Communist Party ruled during 1957–9), have become rather more explicit since the 1966 elections when the Congress lost several states in major reverses.[1]

Among the principal areas in industrial policy where India's politics have had an impact of some kind are (1) the role of public sector investment, (2) the location of public and private sector industry, (3) the role of 'small', cottage industry, (4) industrial licensing, (5) exchange rate policy, and (6) foreign investment.

(1) As we shall discuss at length in Chapter 9, the phenomenal growth of the public sector in India during the three Plans is to be attributed largely to the 'socialist', ideological goals which the Indian National Congress embraced as early as the 1930s and to the leadership of Jawaharlal Nehru during the period of recent planning. The size and pattern of these investments in the public sector were to be determined, in the ultimate analysis, by the interplay of pragmatic, economic and political, ideological factors, with Nehru playing essentially the role of a moderate on the issue, balancing the opposed political forces by shelving nationalization but promising, in effect, the Marxist millennium by formally adopting policies which seemed progressively to raise the share of public sector investment in total investment and thus asymptotically approach the situation of dominant state ownership of the capital stock.

(2) Further, the federal set-up has directly affected the question of the efficient location of industry (see Chapter 13). It has been difficult to avoid a scramble by many states for a share in most investments, whether public or private, that are being considered at any time. This is inevitable and the resulting inefficiencies, typified by uneconomic plants allocated to many claimant states, perhaps unavoidable. On the other hand, planners have done little to evolve a coherent, economic policy on this issue. Formally, it should have been possible to consider the problem from the

---

[1] The political situation since then has been extremely fluid, with politicians 'defecting' from their parties in several states, repeatedly and cynically in search of office and leading to instability akin to that in France before the Fifth Republic and in Pakistan before the military takeover by Ayub Khan. Cf. Dilip Mukerjee, 'India in Transition: Politics of Manoeuvre', *Foreign Affairs*, April 1968.

viewpoint of second-best optimization, the additional constraints taking the form of regional or statewise industrial and/or employment and/or income levels. In point of fact, the planners have neglected spatial planning, the majority of the industrial targets having no space dimension at all, and the field has thus been left largely to the politicians and the relative strengths of different states *vis-à-vis* one another and the Centre.

(3) The role of 'small', cottage industries in industrial planning has also been prompted in part by ideological considerations, of the Gandhian variety. These ideological factors were to influence the Second Plan in particular towards the encouragement and protection of cottage industries in the traditional consumer goods industries, such as rice-milling, oil-crushing and cotton spinning and weaving, alongside the creation of a heavy industry complex in keeping with a Soviet-type ideology.

(4) The pattern of industrial licensing, quite apart from the political impact on locational and scale decisions which we have already touched upon, has been sensitive to political issues such as the concentration of economic power and wealth. The Left, and a fair number of economist intellectuals, have kept this important issue in the forefront of parliamentary debates and influenced, among other things, the industrial licensing system marginally towards applicants outside the larger and heavily concentrated business houses, and also provided an additional political rationale for breaking up plants into smaller and superficially more competitive units.

(5) A freer use of exchange rate policy has also been inhibited, among other causes, by its association with 'Rightist' elements, reinforced by the advocacy of devaluation over a long period by the *laissez-faire* economist, B. R. Shenoy, and by the World Bank (leading to the June 1966 devaluation). Furthermore, business groups have sensed that a freer use of the exchange rate could lead to a reduced reliance on (i) quantitative import restrictions (Q.R.s) and the automatic protection they have traditionally furnished to Indian industry, as we document in Part VII, and (ii) *ad hoc* export subsidies (which are necessary to correct the adverse effects on exports of an overvalued exchange rate) which also provide lucrative sources of profits to those who can exploit them (see Part VII). These groups therefore have also turned into powerful pressure groups opposed to parity changes.

(6) Finally, the area of private foreign investment (and, in a lesser degree, foreign aid) has also invited ideological controversies, especially from the 'Left' parties. Although private foreign investment has rarely been of a dimension large enough to undermine national interests, political or economic, in any dramatic manner, it has been the subject of extensive debate, as we shall record at somewhat greater length in Chapter 11.

8

Administration

COMPARED with most developing countries, India emerged into independent nationhood with an administrative structure that, at the élite level, was perhaps the equal of anything to be found in the developed countries. Although, through partition and repatriation of British civil servants, India was to lose as many as seven hundred members of the élite corps (the Indian Civil Service), the educational expansion since the early nineteenth century, beginning with the Presidency Colleges in Calcutta, Madras, and Bombay, had left India with an invaluable legacy of a large, educated middle class from which emergency recruitment was readily possible, without any significantly adverse impact on the quality of the service.

And yet this élite corps, wisely retained by the nationalist, Congress Government despite the distrust and antagonism built up against it during the decades of its 'collaboration' with the British Government during the independence struggle, was not to prove an unmitigated benefit. Geared to the efficient running of the British law-and-order machine, and occupying a position of unrivalled power in a political system which involved alien rule, the I.C.S. had inherited, by and large, work methods and an attitude of omnipotence which were to interfere seriously with the vastly different and complex administrative tasks of a modern, planned India where administration and implementation extended into fields as diverse as public sector investments in industries and agricultural extension and developmental programmes.

The paradoxical situation of a highly efficient, inherited administrative machine hindering the adaptation of the system to the needs of the new order, has been highlighted in several Reports and Plan documents.[1] The latest commentary, by

[1] See, in particular, the two celebrated reports by Paul Appleby: *Public Administration in India: Report of a Survey*, Cabinet Secretariat, Government of

Professor D. R. Gadgil, the present Deputy Chairman of the Planning Commission, sums up the situation admirably:

The 'generalist', i.e., the Indian civil servant and his successor, the I.A.S., still completely dominate the scene. There is an enormous concentration of power on top in this strata and new elements of specialists or managers of business still rank low in prestige and authority. The I.C.S. and the I.A.S. function as an exclusive club and it is openly alleged that you cannot function effectively in top positions in administration unless you belong to this group. The attitudes of the public towards officials and of the officials towards the public are still coloured largely by the older situation and this has special meaning in the context of the plan of development. . . .

. . . one has to consider the relevance and appropriateness of the present state of administrative arrangements in India to the specific requirements of the effort at planned economic development. Apart from the results of transition to self-rule after independence, it is planned economic development that has added enormously to the dimensions of Government effort. The activities of Government have increased tremendously both in width of coverage and in depth and intensity. The direct responsibilities that Government now undertakes cover large fields of social and economic life. Government takes upon itself the responsibility of erecting the structure of public services and utilities required for development of a modern industrial society and of continuously maintaining that structure. It undertakes in addition a large variety of welfare activities. Government owns and conducts a large number of industrial production businesses which are basic to building of the industrial structure. Government occupies large sections of trading and it tries to regulate many other aspects of social and economic life. The number of administrators at various levels required in Government service has increased enormously and the qualifications needed by them have become extremely varied. The contrast with the situation in, say, 1939 is extremely glaring. . . . It will be thus seen that very large ground had to be covered as between the highly limited Government activity of British times for which the particular

India, New Delhi, 1953; and *Re-examination of India's Administrative System with Special Reference to Administration of the Government's Industrial and Commercial Enterprises*, Government of India, New Delhi, 1956. Also, see V. T. Krishnamachari, *Report on Indian and State Administrative Services and Problems of District Administration*, Planning Commission, Government of India, New Delhi, August 1962; and chapters on Administration and Implementation in the successive Plan documents. For other references relating to public sector projects in particular, especially to the excellent work of H. K. Paranjape, see Chapter 9.

[administrative] structure was fashioned and the requirements of the administrative system of the planned development era.

It must, in the first instance be recognized that the Indian administrative system has grown rapidly, adapted itself partially to the changed situation and tried to meet the large and manifold new requirements. Inefficiency and corruption may have increased, but there has been no real breakdown of the system and this itself is creditworthy. However, huge problems remain unsolved and it is necessary to pay urgent attention to these. I shall deal with some indicated by the analysis above. Two major difficulties are related to the dominance and the changed attitude of the generalist I.C.S. and I.A.S. service personnel at the top. The first is the lack of a coordinated view and of a frame of considered policy. In fact this indicates a failure on the part of the Council of Ministers but it is also related to the short-term, departmental view that Secretaries and others take. This flows partly from their lack of specialization and partly from the absence of conjoint operations. Ad hocism in policy decisions is the result. The second and even more important difficulty is sheer incompetence resulting not only from the lack of expert knowledge of the generalist but also equally from the degradation and frustration of the experts and specialists in government service.[1]

While these problems were highlighted from the end of the First Plan, the successive efforts at evolving a different administrative system, more efficient in meeting the new challenges, have led to altogether inadequate results. As late as the Third Plan document, the Planning Commission was constrained to admit to a rather dismal picture:

The past decade has been a period of considerable change and adaptation in the field of administration. Innovations have been introduced and new institutions established, although perhaps many of them have yet to be integrated with one another and with the structure as a whole. With the increase in the range of Government's responsibilities and in the tempo of development, the volume and complexity of administrative work has also grown. The administrative machinery has been strained and, at many points in the structure, the available personnel are not adequate in quality and numbers.... In the recent past, certain aspects of administration have attracted pointed attention. These include the slow pace of execution in many fields, problems involved in the planning, construction and operation of large projects, especially increase in costs and non-adherence to time-schedules ... achieving

[1] 'Planning and Administration', Barve Memorial Lecture, delivered on 6 March 1968, New Delhi; to be published.

coordination in detail in related sectors of the economy. . . . As large
burdens are thrown on the administrative structure, it grows in size; as
its size increases, it becomes slower in its functioning. Delays occur and
affect operations at every stage and the expected outputs are further
deferred. New tasks become difficult to accomplish if the management
of those in hand is open to just criticism. In these circumstances, there
is need for far-reaching changes in procedures and approach and for
re-examination of prevalent methods and attitudes.[1]

The Fourth Plan (Draft Outline) further draws a picture
which, despite references to numerous studies (completed and in
progress), appears to have changed little in terms of *actual*
practices and procedures:

In *each* of the Five Year Plans, there has been a significant gap between
planning and implementation. The burdens thrown upon the political
system and the administrative structure have increased steadily. . . .
The Third Plan had stressed the need for far-reaching changes in
procedures and approach and had made a series of recommendations
for raising administrative standards, managing projects in the public
sector with efficiency, building up personnel, achieving economies in
construction and strengthening the machinery for planning. In several
directions, as a result of work during the Third Plan and the studies
undertaken, deficiencies in implementation are now more closely
identified, the use of improved methods and techniques has been more
fully *demonstrated* and the improvements to be made in the immediate
future and the conditions requisite for them are better *known*. *When
the recommendations of the Administrative Reforms Commission*, which is
engaged in a comprehensive study of all aspects of administrative
reform, *become available, it should be possible to go beyond the immediate
tasks* and to consider more basic changes in the structure and functioning of the administrative system as a whole.[2]

In short, after over a decade of realization of the many problems,
detailed Reports on the whole range of issues by foreign consultants and Indian scholars, the Fourth Plan document still reads
like an academic exercise in good intentions rather than a record
of concrete achievements on which further progress in reform
would be built.

[1] *Third Five Year Plan op. cit.*, p. 277; quoted by Hanson, *op. cit.*, whose Chapter
VIII contains an excellent, detailed account of the numerous Reports and
attempted measures at reform, in the field of administration in a wide sense,
up to the end of the Third Plan.
[2] Draft Outline, op. cit., pp. 154-5 [our italics].

The administrative machine, in brief, has failed to adapt itself so far to the needs of a State which aimed at planning in depth. As we shall discuss in detail in Chapter 9, the effect of this on the efficiency of the public sector industrial undertakings, which have absorbed an enormous amount of investment, has been seriously adverse.

Yet another serious consequence, for the industrial and trade sectors on which we concentrate in this volume, has been the tendency to impose *detailed regulation of the private sector* through an administration which was rapidly put together and was ill-equipped for the task, resulting in gross inefficiencies which were compounded by the fact that even the top-level civil servants and planners had extremely vague ideas in any case as to the principles which should be followed in respect to *detailed* licensing of capacities, imports, and scarce materials. '*Ad hocism* at the top and corruption at the bottom' might have been an apt description of the state that administrative machinery was to reach eventually as it increasingly concerned itself with detailed control of decisions in the private sector (this will be documented in depth when we discuss industrial and trade policies in Parts VI and VII). These failures have, however, been not merely of administration: they reflect a more basic factor, the then-current economic philosophy that the best form of planning is physical and involves detailed controls. The bureaucrats, especially at the top levels, have traditionally taken to this doctrine with some enthusiasm, for it has conferred on them great power and re-emphasized their inherited notions of omnipotence. For much the same reason, many politicians in power (and in search of patronage) have also embraced these policies of detailed regulation. With these two vested pressure groups thus deeply committed to the economic philosophy of detailed regulation of all industrial activity via controls, the eventual shift towards a new economic policy of greater 'liberalism', beginning with the June 1966 devaluation, has proved to be an uphill task (see Part VIII).

9
Public and Private Sectors

ECONOMIC policy with respect to the relative importance of the public and private sectors in industrial investments through the period of the three Plans has been directly affected by political, ideological considerations. We therefore discuss first of all the interplay between ideological and pragmatic economic considerations that has resulted in the public sector appropriating a significant share in the growth of industries in the country.

Furthermore, in view of the sizeable public sector investments in industry, we examine critically the policies governing this sector and determining its efficiency. These policies—relating to choice of projects, location, staffing, political and audit control, pricing, etc.—have been of central importance in reducing the economic efficiency of public sector investments. Apart from the overall framework of steadily growing and mainly distorting bureaucratic controls which, in the sphere of domestic and foreign policy instruments, contributed to the inefficiencies in the private sector (see Parts VI and VII for a detailed documentation) perhaps the next most important set of inefficiencies has related to the public sector. Between them, these inefficiencies have significantly reduced the productivity of investment in the economy.

Growth of the public sector investments

Public sector investments, taken in the aggregate for the Indian economy, have been considerable, not merely in absolute terms but as a proportion of overall investments. Table 9.1 shows that the First Plan (actuals) resulted in over 46 per cent of the aggregate investment in the public sector. During the Second Plan, this share was to be raised to over 61 per cent, but largely owing to buoyant investment by the private sector and shortfalls in public sector outlays (prompted again partly, though by no means predominantly, by the shortage of overall 'real' savings in view of 'overfulfilment' by the private sector), the share of the public sector was to turn out to be only 54 per cent.[1] Both the Third

TABLE 9.1
THE SHARE OF AGGREGATE PUBLIC SECTOR INVESTMENT IN
TOTAL INVESTMENT

	Proposed shares		Actual shares	
	Public sector	Private sector	Public sector	Private sector
First Plan	—	—	46·4% (1,560)	53·6% (1,800)
Second Plan	61·3% (3,800)	38·7% (2,400)	54·0% (3,650)	45·9% (3,100)
Third Plan	58·6% (6,100)	41·3% (4,300)*	n.a.	n.a.
Fourth Plan	63·7% (13,600)	36·4% (7,750)	—	—

Notes: (1) The figures in brackets give actual amounts of investments in Rs. crores (ten millions), at current prices.
(2) * Includes Rs. 200 crores of funds transferred from the public to the private sector.
(3) The percentage shares have been rounded to the first decimal place.
(4) The figures relate to gross investments.
Source: *The Second Five-Year Plan; The Third Five-Year Plan;* and *The Fourth Five-Year Plan: A Draft Outline.* The shares have been calculated by us.

Plan (proposed shares) and Fourth Plan (shares outlined in the Draft Frame) registered intentions to raise this overall share further: 58·6 per cent in the Third Plan and 63·7 per cent in the Fourth Plan. Table 9.2 shows further that, apart from a mild increase (in the public sector) of investments in the organized industrial sector, the important increments were in the investments in agriculture and irrigation as also in miscellaneous social services, partly reflecting, in turn, the growing importance of these sectors in the overall developmental strategy.[2]

[1] At this stage of our discussion, however, we should enter the *caveat* that these estimates must be taken as indicating only *rough* orders of magnitude. Investment and savings estimates for India are notoriously poor, particularly in view of the large, unorganized sector involving the genuinely small-scale industries and numerous small farms and businesses in the rural sector.

Again, we must enter the *caveat* that not too much should be read into the sectoral investments and shifts therein. Intersectoral classifications, as also the distinction between 'investment' and 'current outlays', have not always been consistently drawn in the different Plans. For example, public sector (additions to) inventories are not noted in the Second Plan, are put at an obviously low figure in the Third Plan and then again dropped in the Fourth Plan. Moreover, the likelihood of a careful economist's acceptance of these estimates as reliable is somewhat shaken by occasional confusions in the Plan documents between 'real' and 'financial' resources. For example, to the total investment in 'housing and construction' in the *Fourth Plan Draft Outline* (p. 41), which represents one part of an overall, *ex-ante* investment estimate

TABLE 9.2
THE COMPOSITION OF PUBLIC AND PRIVATE SECTOR INVESTMENTS DURING SECOND, THIRD, AND (DRAFT) FOURTH PLANS
(In Rs. crores)

Head	Second Plan (actuals)			Third Plan (proposed)			Fourth Plan (draft outline)		
	Public sector	Private sector	Share of public sector in total, %	Public sector	Private sector	Share of public sector in total, %	Public sector	Private sector	Share of public sector in total, %
Agriculture and community developm't	210	625 } a	50	660	800 } a	62	1,575	900 } a	74
Major and minor irrigat'n	420	a		650	a		964	a	
Power	445	40	92	1,012	50	95	2,030	50	98
Village and small industries	90	175	50	150	275	35	230	320	42
Organized industry and mining	870	675	56	1,520	1,050	59	3,936	2,350	63
Transport and communications	1,275	135	90	1,486	250	86	3,010	630	83
Misc. social services (including education)	340	950	26	622	1,075	37	1,855	1,600	54
Inventories	—	500	—	200	600	25	c	1,900	—
TOTAL	3,650	3,100 b	54	6,300	4,100 b	60	13,600	7,750	64

Notes: a Included under the head: Agriculture and Community Development.
b Excludes transfers from public to private sector. Hence the apparent discrepancy in the Second Plan shares of aggregate investment, in Tables 9.1 and 9.2.
c The Fourth Plan: Draft Outline claims that: 'Part of the inventories under public sector is covered in sectoral outlays [and] part will be financed through the banking system', op. cit., p. 41.
The percentage shares have been rounded off.

Sources: Third Five-Year Plan, and Fourth Five-Year Plan: A Draft Outline. The shares have been calculated by us.

TABLE 9.3

CUMULATED INVESTMENTS IN THE LARGE, PUBLIC SECTOR ENTERPRISES AS PERCENTAGES OF TOTAL, CUMULATED INVESTMENTS BY PUBLIC SECTOR ENTERPRISE: 1962–6

Enterprises	1962/3	1963/4	1964/5	1965/6
1. Hindustan Steel	52·77	45·17	43·45	39·75
2. Neyveli Lignite Corporation	6·92	6·35	6·33	6·00
3. Heavy Engineering Corporation	5·25	5·11	6·87	5·88
4. National Coal Development Corporation	5·10	4·94	5·15	5·30
5. Oil and Natural Gas Commission	4·52	4·83	6·38	5·51
6. Fertilizer Corporation of India	3·79	4·61	4·47	4·31
7. Heavy Electricals (India)	3·35	4·04	3·24	3·48
8. Indian Refineries	2·62	3·76	—	—
9. Air India	2·33	1·74	1·81	—
10. Shipping Corporation of India	1·89	1·74	1·67	1·66
11. Indian Oil Corporation	—	—	4·86	5·92
12. Bharat Heavy Electricals	—	—	—	2·61
13. Aggregate investment in these enterprises as proportion of investment in public sector enterprises (total of 1–12)	88·54	82·29	84·23	80·42
Total value of investment in all public sector enterprises (in Rs. crores)	1,372	1,705	2,037	2,145

Notes: (1) Public sector enterprises are only those under the Central Government.

(2) The dashes refer to non-availability of data in the required form, often due to legal reorganization of the enterprise as when Indian Refineries was amalgamated with Indian Oil Co. Ltd. in September 1964. The estimates of capital stock are as of the end of each year.

Source: *Annual Reports of the Working of Industrial and Commercial Undertakings of the Central Government: 1962–63, 1963–64, 1964–65 and 1965–66*, Finance Ministry, Government of India, New Delhi. Percentage shares have been calculated by us.

It is further clear that, not merely is the overall share of the public sector quite large and intended to be steadily increased, but the public sector has been investing, with practically the same

later to be balanced against the *ex-ante* savings, there is a startling footnote '*In addition*, funds are likely to be available from the Life Insurance Corporation and the Employee's Provident Fund for investment in housing programmes' [italics inserted]. Another example is the footnote, in the same table, explaining where public sector inventory (accumulation) has been assigned, in view of the blank entry in the relevant cell: 'Part of the inventories under public sector is covered in sectoral outlays [and] *part will be financed through the banking system*' [italics inserted].

share, in the field of organized industry and mining. Furthermore, such industrial investments have been about 25 per cent of overall public sector investments.

Moreover, while the precise composition of this industrial outlay in the public sector is not available, we can get a fairly shrewd idea of the industrial composition by examining the investment in public sector enterprises, under the Central Government, which constitute the bulk of this industrial investment. Table 9.3 gives the percentage share of the *major* enterprises in the total, cumulated investment outlays of all such public sector enterprises for each year during 1962–6, underlining the considerable dominance of steel, engineering, and chemicals enterprises, in that order. This conclusion is underlined by Table 9.4 which

TABLE 9.4

SECTORWISE DISTRIBUTION OF CUMULATED INVESTMENT IN PUBLIC SECTOR PROJECTS;

(In Rs. crores)

Industries	1963/4		1964/5		1965/6	
	Amount	%	Amount	%	Amount	%
Steel	804	47·16	890	43·69	981	40·62
Engineering	269	15·78	355	17·43	490	20·29
Chemicals	172	10·09	198	9·72	220	9·11
Petroleum	170	9·97	241	11·83	295	12·22
Mining and minerals	130	7·62	158	7·76	181	7·49
Sub-total	1,545	90·62	1,842	90·43	2,167	89·73
Aviation and shipping	92	5·40	101	4·96	120	4·97
Financial institutions	6	0·35	6	0·29	7	0·29
Building and repairing ships	9	0·53	10	0·49	11	0·46
Miscellaneous	53	3·11	78	3·83	110	4·55
TOTAL	1,705	100·00	2,037	100·00	2,415	100·00

Source: *Annual Reports*, op. cit. Percentage shares have been calculated by us; they do not necessarily add up to a hundred because of rounding.

gives the industrial classification of *all* cumulated investments by these enterprises and shows steel leading with 47·16 per cent in 1963/4, 43·69 per cent in 1964/5, and 40·62 per cent in 1965/6 and mining and minerals at the bottom of the scale with an average of about 7·62 per cent for the three-year period. Between them, steel, engineering, chemicals, petroleum, and mining and minerals, constituting the principal organized industrial investments, accounted for an average of over 90 per cent of aggregate public sector enterprise cumulated investments during this period.

Political and ideological factors

This phenomenal growth of public sector investments, in the aggregate as also in the heavy industries in particular, has taken place against a political and ideological background that is specific to Indian political history and the recent balance of political forces.

The Indian National Congress had traditionally couched its social and economic aspirations in radical, even Marxist, terms. The 1929 Lahore resolution, for example, had declared that 'in order to remove the poverty and misery of the Indian people and to ameliorate the conditions of the masses, it is essential to make revolutionary changes in the present economic and social structure of society and to remove gross inequalities'. The subsequent Karachi resolution was to include the rather more explicit objective of nationalization and social control in industry: 'The State shall own or control key industries and services, mineral resources, railways, waterways, shipping and other means of public transport.'[1] By the time, however, that the National Planning Committee was set up by the Congress in 1938, and the economic programme was being formulated in more action-oriented terms, the internal divisions in the Congress on these issues had become more explicit. The Gandhians, who distrusted centralized planning and had a totally different conception of the social order and economic reconstruction, as also the financial and industrial interests which were influential in the Congress movement, were opposed to the radical, socialist ideas of leaders such as Jawaharlal Nehru. Thus, while agreement was readily obtained in the N.P.C. for nationalization of defence industries and the ownership of public utilities, no such unanimity was forthcoming on the state ownership of other key industries, banking, and insurance.

This basic opposition of rival ideologies and political forces was to continue into the post-independence period. While sentiments continued to be expressed in favour of radical reconstruction of the social and economic order,[2] the actual programmes to be

[1] Hanson, op. cit., pp. 28–32. An important, original source is K. T. Shah, (ed.).

[2] Thus, for example, even the *Second Report on Reconstruction Planning* (*1945*), produced by the Reconstruction Committee under the then Viceroy's Chairmanship, talked radically about the elimination of 'the existing glaring anomaly of immense wealth side by side with abject poverty'. Cf. Hanson, op. cit., pp. 34–5.

recommended, and even more the attempts at implementing them, were to represent compromises between different ideological positions on these questions.

This compromise was obvious in the first Industrial Policy Resolution of 1948 which, until the second Industrial Policy Resolution of 1956, was to govern the framework within which industrial development was to proceed, including the respective roles of the public and private sectors.

Among the central features of the first Resolution was its explicit rejection of nationalization of existing private enterprises for a period of ten years. From an ideological, Left, viewpoint, this was a major concession to the reactionary elements in the Congress and in the country at large. But Nehru's pragmatic endorsement of the role that private enterprise could play in the forthcoming plans for industrialization had clearly won the day. In this context, Nehru's subsequent statement in the Indian Parliament (Lok Sabha), when the Second Resolution was being debated, is so lucid and cogent that it merits being quoted:

I have no shadow of doubt that, if we say 'lop off the private sector', we cannot replace it adequately. We have not got the resources to replace it, and the result would be that our productive apparatus will suffer. And why should we do it? I don't understand. We have our industries, there is a vast sector, and we have to work it. Let the State go on building up its plants and industries as far as its resources permit. Why should we fritter away our energy in pushing out somebody who is doing it in the private sector?

There is no reason except that the private sector might build up monopoly, might be building economic power to come in the way of our growth. I can understand 'Prevent that, control that, plan for that'; but where there is such a vast field to cover, it is foolish to take charge of the whole field when you are totally incapable of using that huge area yourself. Therefore, you must not only permit the private sector, but, I say, encourage it in its own field.[1]

Immediate nationalization having been ruled out, the Industrial Policy Resolution (I.P.R.) proceeded to assign industries between the two sectors. Monopoly by the state of atomic energy, arms,

---

[1] Statement in the Lok Sabha on 25 May 1956; quoted in John P. Lewis, *Quiet Crisis in India*, p. 207.

L

ammunitions, and railways was to continue. Furthermore, the state was to have exclusive access to the setting up of new establishments in iron and steel, shipbuilding, mineral oils, coal, aircraft production, and telecommunications equipment, with possible exceptions 'in the national interest'. The remaining area of industrial investments was left open for simultaneous establishment of new enterprises by both sectors, with the promise of progressive participation by the state especially in relation to several 'basic' industries such as fertilizers and essential drugs. While the I.P.R., therefore, seemed to take a position intermediate between ideological extremes, it also left considerable room for manoeuvre on the part of the planners in the *actual* allocations between the two sectors. It is interesting that the authors of the First Five-Year Plan (1951–56) did not lay down any specific targets for aggregate or industrial investments in either sector, as was to become the practice for the later Plans. Nor did they hesitate to express rather forcefully the pragmatic view, at variance with the spirit of the allocations in the I.P.R., that: 'The scope and need for development are so great that it is best for the public sector to develop those industries in which private enterprise is unable or unwilling to put up the resources required and run the risks involved, leaving the rest of the field free for private enterprise.'[1]

The second I.P.R., of April 1956, was in many ways a reiteration of the first. Its stress on the public sector's importance was only a shade more emphatic. However, it accompanied (i) a significant acceleration in public sector investments in industry during the Second Plan, and (ii) a surfacing of the notion that the share of public sector investments, in the national aggregate, ought not to be allowed to fall below that in earlier Plans and should instead increase: a direct consequence of the Avadi Congress resolution and the Lok Sabha adoption of a 'socialist pattern of society' in 1954. The ten-year guarantee against nationalization was not repeated; and the focus was again on the allocation of industries between the two sectors. Seventeen industries, including heavy electrical plant, heavy castings, and forgings of iron and steel, were grouped into one category where the state would either have total monopoly (as with arms, ammunition, atomic energy, railways, and now air transport) or have exclusive right to establish

---

[1] *First Five-Year Plan*, op. cit., p. 422.

new industrial establishments.[1] Twelve other industries (including machine tools, ferro-alloys and tool steels, fertilizers, synthetic rubber, and chemical pulp) were specified as the sector where the state would progressively establish new units: corresponding to the 'basic' industries of the first I.P.R. The remaining industries were to be left largely to the initiative of the private sector, although naturally the state retained the option to enter.

The second I.P.R., despite its close similarity to the first, appears to have been issued partly to re-emphasize the importance of the public sector and the necessity to regulate the growth of the private sector in the light of the shift to a more explicitly 'socialistic' stance by the Government. Nehru, despite his early pragmatic approach to the question, appears to have been enthusiastic about the role that such an I.P.R. could play in the evolution of a 'socialist' society, while equally registering pragmatism at other times.[2]

However, the shift to heavy industries, which came largely on economic grounds with the Second Plan (as we discuss in Chapter 13) also lent a sharper edge to the second I.P.R. in so far as the heavy industries generally involved projects in which private enterprise, even if offered a choice, would not have opted to invest its funds or have had the funds to do so. Thus, both the socialist declarations and the pragmatic imperatives of the new industrial strategy were to dictate the shift towards the public sector in industrial (and hence, *ceteris paribus*, in total) investment

---

[1] As with the first I.P.R., the second I.P.R. also left a loophole in this respect, allowing for the possibility of private enterprise setting up new units 'in the national interest'.

[2] On this issue, Hanson, op. cit., correctly records that the Union Cabinet itself was divided on the advisability of overly strong demarcation of industrial investments between the two sectors. The Finance Minister T. T. Krishnamachari's scepticism in this regard was dramatically expressed in the Lok Sabha: 'It is not possible to demarcate any sector in a planned economy as belonging either to the private sector or the public sector. If anybody attempts it, he will be attempting folly, because in an under-developed economy, where our resources are inadequate, where everything that we have has to be put to some kind of use which will generate more production and therefore more wealth, we cannot afford these nuances of demarcating spheres and saying, "I will have none of it: I won't enter that".' Hanson, op. cit., p. 124. Krishnamachari was clearly taking the pragmatic line, emphasizing purely economic aspects, while the ideologues would emphasize the importance of the public sector as such, and its necessity in 'key' industries, from sociological and political standpoints.

in the Second Plan.[1] Thus the Second Plan was to witness few major conflicts between economic efficiency and political objectives in so far as there was not much that was denied to the private sector *de facto*.

There were, however, some important respects in which socialist ideas and resolutions undoubtedly affected adversely investment decisions during the Second Plan. Hanson has noted, for example, that the fulfilment of the coal target, raising production by 22 million tons to 60 million tons by the end of the Second Plan, was seriously undermined by the Planning Commission having had to locate the bulk of the new production in the public sector: a decision undoubtedly prompted by having to pay greater attention to the I.P.R. directives in view of the adoption of the 'socialist pattern of society'. The eventual rise of public sector production by a mere 3·2 million tons by 1959, as against 6·8 million tons in the private sector, was to lead to a serious shortfall in the overall target fulfilment. The attempt was later made to explain these shortfalls in terms of the difficulties of setting up new units in the public sector *vis-à-vis* the ease with which private sector could expand production from its existing base. Hanson's comments on the whole episode are apt:

Of current production, the bulk was in the private sector, and the question was therefore whether to rely mainly on a well-established collection of private enterprises to effect the necessary increase, or to concentrate on expanding the comparatively embryonic state-owned collieries. Economic rationality demanded that the Commission should have . . . (*b*) compared the efficiency, actual and prospective, of public and private sector undertakings; and (*c*) divided responsibility between the two sectors on the basis of the estimated yields of the investment projects put up by each. There is no evidence in the plan report, however, that the Commission did any such thing. Instead, it referred to the Industrial Policy Resolution of 1948 . . .

[With respect to the eventual shortfalls in public sector production, the references of the Third Five-Year Plan] to building up an organ-

---

[1] This is probably the most effective argument in support of the view that, at least during the Second Plan, the 'socialist' slant of the I.P.R.s did not have any significant 'economic cost'. By contrast, many of Lewis's arguments (op. cit., Chapter 8) are special pleadings designed to make the average American reader feel that India's policies are not as 'ideological', and hence 'bad', as they appear!

ization 'practically from nothing' and to the 'serious shortage of experienced technical personnel' are at least thought-provoking. Could the private sector, by developing its existing organization and expanding its existing personnel, have brought these coalfields into production more rapidly and more economically? This is a possibility that neither the government nor the Commission appears to have seriously considered.[1]

Conflicts between economic and ideological factors were, however, to become more likely in the Third Plan. The public sector had 'learnt by doing' and some of the initial difficulties about starting from scratch in industry were not quite so important any longer. At the same time, it was no longer possible to say that the State, *in any case*, would have to invest massively in industries through the public sector because the private sector would not, or could not, undertake the 'socially necessary' investments. Investments in heavy industries were no longer considered, in the light of the investment and protective policies of the Government, to be unprofitable. And, thanks in turn to the financial institutions established by the Government itself, large-scale investments were not quite so impossible in the private sector as in the preceding decade. As the private sector therefore increasingly became interested in investing in the whole range of Schedule A industries, including steel (where the Birlas went so far as to discuss the matter seriously with Kaisers before being discouraged from the venture by the authorities), the possibilities of a divergence between pragmatic considerations of economic efficiency and ideological factors (as embodied in the second I.P.R.) became more frequent and acute. This conflict was further accentuated by the (relatively) reduced role of heavy industry in the Third Plan as against the Second and the consequent

[1] Op. cit., pp. 466–7. Hanson's detailed analysis of investment decisions with respect to oil, and the ideological factors affecting them, is also excellent and should be consulted. However, his account omits mention of the important, long-term role played by public sector refineries and related investments in increasing Indian bargaining power *vis-à-vis* the Western oil monopolies. Whether this advantage was decisive in giving the investment decisions in favour of the public sector an economic legitimacy is not altogether clear, however; and the policies of the relevant Minister K. D. Malaviya (who, with Krishna Menon, represented at the time the radical left in the Congress) were certainly motivated by ideological considerations, quite openly expressed and backed by reference to the second I.P.R. (which had explicitly included oil in the first, Schedule A, category).

narrowing, in any event, of the area where the private sector may have decided to opt out.[1]

Yet another significant implication of these developments was to be the jeopardizing of the asymptotic approach to the Marxist goal of state ownership of the means of production, which was one of the major, if largely implicit, premises of the second I.P.R. This millennium could no longer be reached by a progressively increasing share of the public sector in total *investments*, gradually leading to an overwhelming share of it in the total *stock* of capital, without the private sector being told, on straightforward, ideological grounds, that it could not expand beyond a certain amount. The opposed ideological forces were thus to come very much to the forefront since the Third Plan and, as was to be expected, the results show inevitable compromise in the shape of a slackening of the public sector's share in investments combined with numerous restrictions (as with the example of coal in the Second Plan) on the growth of the private sector.

The compromise not merely represents the triumph, in some degree, of economic pragmatism over ideological imperatives but also reflects the inherent political contradiction in this typically Indian 'gradualist' approach to the Marxist state. It is naïve to expect that the state, in a mixed economy, where the private sector and industrial empires therein continue to play a major economic (and hence political) role and keep on growing, will be able gradually to subordinate the strength of this sector: a 'democratic liquidation of capitalism' is a utopian programme. It could even be argued that the private sector will take over the public sector increasingly in such a situation. As many ideologues have complained in the Indian context, the boards of management of public sector enterprises have often been manned by private sector potentates: e.g. the appointment of Bharat Ram, an important northern industrialist, to the Chairmanship of the Indian Airlines Corporation.[2]

---

[1] On these questions, see J. Bhagwati, 'Uneasy Co-existence', *Seminar*, February 1960, New Delhi, pp. 24–7. This entire issue of *Seminar*, a monthly magazine devoted to topical questions with contributions on a selected subject by writers of different points of view, is worth reading for the range of economic and ideological questions relating to the public *v.* private sector debate at the time.

[2] Such appointments have been made in order to improve the efficiency of these enterprises. But their *political* interpretation, which we discuss in the text, is a different matter.

In any event, faced with these ideological conflicts, the Government have tended to follow somewhat schizophrenic, apparently 'neutral' policies at times: appointing, for example, K. D. Malaviya (on the Left of the Congress) to the Chairmanship of the Heavy Engineering Corporation.[1] Ideological factors have thus intruded, beyond the field of mere investment allocations, into operational policies as well. And, as we shall see shortly, purely *political* considerations have affected the working of the public enterprises leading to overstaffing and other inefficiencies.

Economic efficiency of the public sector

How efficient has been the enormous expansion of public sector investments in Indian industry? This question is not merely of intellectual interest. It has also become critically relevant to India's economic performance and prospects in view of the heavy investments in the public sector so far and the prospects of continuing such investments in the future. Two major sources of worry, which might be ideologically motivated but are none the less quite real and should concern any objective observer of the Indian scene, relate to: (i) the apparent, gross, economic inefficiencies of the public sector, as reflected in its productivity; and (ii) the growing infiltration of (non-ideological) politics into the sector, making the prospects of improved productivity seem even more remote.

A typical example of disillusionment with the economic returns produced by the public sector, containing pertinent facts and stark conclusions though not compelling in its economic logic, is the following recent statement in the economic weekly, *Commerce*:

As for the performance of the public sector, most of the enterprises are standing examples of incompetence and inefficiency. . . . The Third Plan report recognised that the enlargement and ploughing back of the profits of public undertakings had an important contribution to make to the financing of development. But what did they actually contribute? From the Draft Outline of the Fourth Plan, it is evident that the only public enterprises which have made some contribution to additional

---

[1] Among other concessions to the socialist ideology has been the recent decision to extend 'social control' to the banking sector. This again represents a compromise solution, the socialist demand being for nationalization and since social control involves certain measures (such as appointments of governmental representatives on Boards of Directors) which go beyond normal central banking control.

resource mobilisation during the Third Plan were the Railways and the postal services of the Centre and the electric and transport undertakings of the States. It is well known that a majority of public sector projects have taken a longer time to complete than was initially estimated, the benefits from them have come much later than expected, their capital costs have been higher than originally planned and consequently the returns from them have been smaller than anticipated.

The Audit Report (Commercial) for 1967 reveals that sixty-eight Government companies with a total investment of Rs. 2,225·88 crores gave a return of only Rs. 53·03 crores or 2·4 per cent in 1965–66. Purely on the basis of profits and dividends, these companies with a total paid-up capital of Rs. 1,187·90 crores made a net profit of Rs. 9·92 crores. ... The Report discloses the grant of an interest holiday to the Hindustan Steel Limited loans amounting to Rs. 357·10 crores up to March 31, 1962; the recovery so waived amounted to Rs. 39·71 crores. The Government also granted to a number of companies moratorium on repayment of loans for periods ranging from two to ten years.

This is a distressing state of affairs. What is more disconcerting is that in spite of substantial concessions such as supply of capital on easy terms, interest holidays and moratorium on loan repayments, the performance of industrial enterprises in the public sector has deteriorated perceptibly over the years. As the bulk of the investible resources available during the Second and Third Plans had been appropriated for expansion of the public sector, it would not be wrong to conclude that the declining trend in the rate of growth of the economy is, in no small measure, due to the poor performance of the public enterprises.[1]

The political factors have further begun to intrude in some quite unforeseen ways. That the state governments would seek to interfere with the selection of skilled staff and prompt overstaffing of unskilled labour (in the interest of local employment), for example, was not entirely unforeseen; and we shall discuss these problems later in this chapter. The role played by Parliament, and by some of the opposition parties, in undermining morale in the public sector and in the administrative services generally, has, however, been almost unique to the Indian scene.

The widespread nature of bureaucratic controls, leading to an inevitable corruption of some sections of the bureaucracy and politicians in power, has made for innumerable attacks on the integrity of politicians and civil servants at the Centre, by

[1] 9 March 1968; p. 645. This is a well-established journal, which could be described as mildly on the Right in its general approach to political and economic questions.

self-appointed watchdogs in Parliament. These personal attacks have ironically come from the minor socialist parties (such as the Samyukta Socialist Party), and almost never from the right-wing parties such as the Swatantra. And, almost invariably, they have focused on ministers and civil servants who are, by all accounts, among the more reputed for efficiency and integrity.[1] Since the infinite range of bureaucratic rules inevitably make the exercise of initiative in cutting through red tape frequently appear like an act of corruption, the Government have usually been weak in meeting allegations and have let the unfortunate Minister or civil servant ride out the situation as he best can.[2] The inevitable result, which many civil servants in the traditional tasks or in the public sector enterprises readily testify to, has been the atrophy of initiative and the tendency to make *absolutely certain* that no conceivable rule is infringed in taking any action: the consequences of which are inflexibility, routine-mindedness, and endless red tape, results which are not quite so disastrous for post-office socialism but which can be fatal to industrial socialism.[3]

These political factors have brought the question of the future of public sector industrial enterprises to a head. If the political preconditions, in the form of faith in the integrity and honesty of purpose among the politicians and civil servants, including those involved directly in public sector enterprises, are lacking (contrary

---

[1] The latest such 'scandal' involved the dynamic Steel Minister C. Subramaniam from Madras, and his top civil servant Bhoothalingam, who were both eventually to be cleared after detailed inquiries but after considerable personal embarrassment and wild charges levelled at them under the cloak of parliamentary immunity to prosecution for libel. It is noteworthy that both Subramaniam and Bhoothalingam were extremely influential and yet shown to be vulnerable on the floor of the Lok Sabha to unsubstantiated allegations. The earlier 'Mundhra scandal', which toppled the Finance Minister T. T. Krishnamachari and another brilliant and influential civil servant, H. M. Patel, was perhaps the forerunner of such events in the Lok Sabha.

[2] Another factor of importance in explaining the Government's weak behaviour has been the fact that some of Jawaharlal Nehru's spirited defences of his political colleagues against such allegations turned out to be notoriously ill-advised. For example, Panjab's Chief Minister, Kairon, was vigorously defended by Nehru over a long period, even in the teeth of strictures passed by the Supreme Court, and was later indicted, for gross corruption, without hesitation by the one-man investigating Commission on which the ex-Chief Justice of India, S. R. Das, served.

[3] In consequence, the cultivation of Ministers and Members of Parliament by heads of public sector enterprises has also become quite common: independent action 'for the good of the cause' (to borrow from Solzhenitsyn's recent story) no longer seems possible without courting personal disaster.

to what has obtained in countries such as Great Britain), then it becomes all the more important to ask whether the resulting inefficiencies—quite apart from other, more traditionally alleged defects of the public sector—do not make the whole programme for *expanding* the public sector on purely ideological grounds, so expensive that a *poor* country needs must re-examine and possibly shelve it.

But let us return to the more traditional aspects of the question of the economic efficiency of public sector enterprises, dealing with the following questions in turn: (*a*) private rates of return; (*b*) social rates of return and choice of projects; (*c*) delays in execution; and (*d*) personnel staffing and management policies.

(a) Private rates of return.

Several critics have focused on the comparison of the rates of return actually exhibited by public sector enterprises to argue that both the absolute rates, and their relative comparison with the average return in the private sector, imply that these enterprises are socially wasteful.

The facts are indeed as such criticism implies. Table 9.5 gives the rate of return, measured as the percentage ratio of gross profit to employed capital, in private sector limited companies in twenty-nine industries, based on the Reserve Bank of India's annual sample analysis of 1,333 public limited companies.[1] Table 9.6 gives similar calculations for the Central Government's industrial and commercial undertakings (leaving out the purely trading enterprises such as the State Trading Corporation). Table 9.6 further divides the enterprises into Group I and three others, where Group I consists of enterprises whose cumulated, employed capital had exceeded Rs. 10 crores by 1964. Between them, these enterprises had something of the order of Rs. 1,100 crores invested in them at the time. It is interesting that nearly all of them, with the exception of Hindustan Machine Tools and Indian Telephone Industries, exhibit dismal returns. As for the remainder, Group II consists of enterprises whose performance compares favourably with the average return in the private sector

---

[1] The definition of the rate of return, employed by the R.B.I. and adopted here, is not ideal from many points of view. For example, 'gross profits' include interest payments. We bring up this question later: for the time being, since we are largely summarizing the usual mode of criticism of public sector enterprises, this definition is adequate to our purpose.

TABLE 9.5
GROSS PROFITS AS PERCENTAGE OF CAPITAL EMPLOYED IN PRIVATE
SECTOR COMPANIES BY TWENTY-EIGHT INDUSTRY GROUPS: 1960–4

Industry	1960	1961	1962	1963	1964
Tea	12·0	9·4	10·9	8·8	9·5
Coffee	10·4	6·4	12·3	17·9	16·9
Rubber	17·1	14·2	13·4	14·4	12·9
Coal	8·9	8·3	9·6	8·3	5·7
Edible vegetable and hydro-genated oil	8·6	7·3	7·3	6·8	10·4
Sugar	8·6	7·3	7·4	11·1	10·7
Tobacco	13·4	11·7	14·5	11·4	15·5
Cotton textiles	12·2	13·1	8·1	8·9	8·7
Jute textiles	8·0	3·8	17·0	11·1	5·5
Silk and rayon	15·8	13·2	9·7	10·5	12·6
Woollen textiles	19·4	20·1	17·4	16·4	13·1
Iron and steel	7·3	8·3	10·1	12·5	11·7
Non-ferrous metals	12·8	10·9	10·0	9·9	12·3
Transport equipment	9·8	10·1	10·6	10·2	11·3
Electrical, mechanical, appliances, etc.	12·5	11·5	13·9	15·5	15·0
Mechanical (other than transport and electrical)	11·6	10·5	10·9	12·1	11·7
Foundries and engineering workshops	8·5	9·4	10·5	10·9	11·1
Ferrous and non-ferrous metal products	11·2	10·9	10·9	12·4	13·9
Basic industrial chemicals	13·6	12·4	10·5	10·3	11·7
Medicinal and pharmaceutical preparations	14·6	13·6	13·7	15·6	17·2
Other chemical products	11·6	11·3	13·6	12·3	10·1
Matches	16·1	16·2	17·6	15·0	10·8
Mineral oils	12·8	14·1	14·3	14·5	12·1
Cement	8·3	8·7	11·4	10·2	10·0
Paper and paper products	9·5	8·4	8·4	7·9	6·6
Electricity generation and sub-stations	7·6	8·1	7·8	9·9	10·1
Trading	8·3	8·8	8·5	9·3	8·8
Shipping	−0·1	0·8	3·8	3·9	4·2
TOTAL (including others)	10·2	10·1	10·2	10·6	10·3

Note: For definitions of 'gross profit' and 'total capital employed', see the
notes to Table 9.6.

Source: *Reserve Bank of India Bulletins*, Reserve Bank of India, Bombay,
1960–5; Sample Survey of 1,333 Public Limited Companies, from published
balanced sheets.

TABLE 9.6
PERCENTAGE OF GROSS PROFIT TO CAPITAL EMPLOYED IN PUBLIC SECTOR UNDERTAKINGS OF THE GOVERNMENT OF INDIA: 1960/1–1966/7

Public sector concerns	Year of commencement of construction (when unambiguously identifiable)a	Capital employed,b,d (Rs. crores)		Percentage of gross profit to capital employed,b,d						
(1)	(2)	1964 (3)	1966 (4)	1960/1 (5)	1961/2 (6)	1962/3 (7)	1963/4 (8)	1964/5 (9)	1965/6 (10)	1966/7 (11)
GROUP I										
Engineering										
1. Hindustan Steel	n.a.	664	693	Loss	Loss	Loss	2·1	3·3	3·0	0·1
2. Hindustan Aeronautics	n.a.	23	26	3·4	3·7	5·2	5·8	5·8	5·3	8·1
3. Heavy Engineering Corporation	n.a.	101	n.a.	n.p.	n.p.	n.p.	n.p.	n.p.	n.p.	Loss
4. Heavy Electricals	n.a.	40	53	n.p.	Loss	Loss	Loss	Loss	Loss	Loss
5. Hindustan Machine Tools	1953	15	31	9·9	14·0	21·4	21·2	20·1	7·9	7·3
6. Indian Telephone Industries	1948 (1950)	10·5	15	9·0	10·7	13·8	16·3	16·0	19·3	18·9
Chemicals										
7. Fertilizers and Chemicals (Travancore)	n.a.	10	9	n.p.	n.p.	n.p.	3·7	Loss	Loss	4·6
8. Fertilizer Corporation of India	n.a.	64	79	2·6e	1·2	3·7	4·5	4·4	1·9	1·6
9. Indian Refineriesf	n.a.	23	n.a.	n.p.	n.p.	Loss	3·2	Amalgamated with Indian Oil Co. Ltd., September 1964		
Mining and minerals										
10. National Coal Development Corporation	n.a.	78	50	3·2	0·8	3·3	1·4	Loss	3·5	0·1
11. Neyveli Lignite Corporation	n.a.	113	120	n.p.	n.p.	n.p.	n.p.	n.p.	1·0	Loss
GROUP II										
Engineering										
1. National Newsprint and Paper Mills	1947 (1958)	5·54	5·28	6·2	9·1	10·0	13·7	12·6	11·4	7·2
2. Hindustan Cables	1952	3·91	7·31	11·4	8·9	12·9	10·2	12·9	1·7	7·4
3. National Instruments	1957	1·19	1·20	6·7	2·0	11·1	15·9	12·2	4·4	Loss
Chemicals										
4. Hindustan Antibiotics	1954	6·51	7·8	27·1	27·8	22·5	22·2	12·0	21·3	26·7
5. Hindustan Insecticides	1954	2·11	2·6	14·7	15·6	23·2	19·9	20·6	16·3	18·3
6. Hindustan Salts	1958	1·81	1·4	n.a.	9·9	9·9	17·3	9·9	Loss	Loss
7. Indian Rare Earths	1959	1·22	1·6	4·8	4·5	11·2	17·7	16·7	10·5	23·8

	Year	(1)	(2)	(3)	(4)	(5)	(6)	(7)	(8)	(9)
8. Travancore Minerals	1950	0·75	n.a.	18·7	18·8	24·2	Indian Rare Earths took over the assets and liabilities and the Company went into voluntary liquidation, January 1965			
Transport, hotels, etc.										
9. Ashoka Hotels	1955	1·7	2·03	13·3	14·8	17·5	19·8	21·5	12·8	14·1 Loss
10. Janpath Hotels	1963	n.a.	0·3	n.e.	n.e.	n.p.	26·0	21·9	2·7	Loss
11. Central Road Transport Corporation	1964	Was incorporated as a Company on 6 March 1964	0·9	n.e.	n.e.	n.e.	n.p.	10·9	6·0	Loss
12. Mogul Line	1938	1·51	3·15	n.a.	17·9	17·5	20·5	42·1	20·3	5·7
GROUP III										
Engineering										
1. Bharat Earth Movers	1964	The Company was incorporated on 11 May 1964	6·6	n.e.	n.e.	n.e.	n.p.	2·0	5·0	5·8
2. Hindustan Teleprinters	1960	Under construction	3·0	n.p.	n.p.	n.p.	n.p.	n.p.	11·6	19·4 Loss
3. Praga Tools	1943 (1959)	2·3	3·4	1·8	n.a.	1·9	4·6	7·8	3·3	Loss
4. Nahan Foundry	1952	Transferred to H.P. State Government on 24 September 1964		9·4	3·5	Loss	Loss	n.a.	n.a.	n.a.
Building and repairing ships										
5. Garden Reach Workshops	1934 (1960)	2·5	3·5	n.a.	3·4	7·0	9·1	5·9	12·4	14·0
6. Hindustan Shipyard	1952 (1961)	6·0	7·8	0·3	0·5	0·1	0·2	0·4	2·2	Loss
Transport, construction, etc.										
7. Shipping Corporation of India	(Merger of 10 and 11 in 1961)	33·0	41·7	n.a.	5·3	6·3	5·4	6·1	6·3	10·5
8. Hindustan Housing Factory	1953	1·0	1·1	7·6	14·2	6·2	7·2	8·0	17·0	9·2
9. National Buildings Construction Corporation	1960	1·9	2·0	Loss	Loss	Loss	Loss	Loss	Loss	Loss
10. Eastern Shipping Corporation	n.a.	n.a.	n.a.	0·9	Merged into Shipping Corporation of India 7					
11. Western Shipping Corporation	n.a.	n.a.	n.a.	3·3	Merged into Shipping Corporation of India 7					
GROUP IV										
Engineering										
1. Bharat Electronics	1954	9·0	11·5	2·5	4·7	7·2	8·1	12·6	15·9	21·1
Building and repairing ships										
2. Mazagaon Dock	n.a.	2·73	3·4	n.a.	7·9	11·8	11·9	8·6	8·0	9·1
Transport, construction, etc.										
3. Air India	n.a.	37·3	40·1	4·3	3·0	8·3	11·6	9·4	3·1	3·1
4. Indian Airlines Corporation	1953	22·0	23·3	0·6	0·6	3·6	5·2	10·3	1·3	8·1 Loss

TABLE 9.6—continued

Public sector concerns	Year of commencement of construction (when unambiguously identifiable)[a]	Capital employed,[b][a] (Rs. crores)		Percentage of gross profit to capital employed,[b][d]						
(1)	(2)	(3) 1964	(4) 1966	(5) 1960/1	(6) 1961/2	(7) 1962/3	(8) 1963/4	(9) 1964/5	(10) 1965/6	(11) 1966/7
5. Indian Oil Corporation	n.a.	n.a.	110·10	Loss		11·8	8·1	7·9	8·5	8·8
6. National Projects Construction Corporation	1957	4·24	7·40	1·7	13·4	8·2	11·3	6·8	5·5	5·4
Undertakings with Central Government Investment without direct responsibility for management.										
GROUP II										
1. Oil India	1959	58·7	63·7	n.a.	1·6	13·4	7·8	11·2	11·3	13·1
2. Singareni Collieries	1920 (1959)	12·1	18·7	n.a.	12·3	14·0	10·0	6·7	6·2	3·8
3. British India Corporation	1920	8·0	9·4	n.a.	19·6	20·9	31·1	14·8	5·7	2·6
4. Indian Explosives	n.a.	6·0	5·5	n.a.	23·8	24·9	21·1	24·1	37·8	38·4
5. Bolani Ores	n.a.	1·8	1·7	n.a.	n.a.	9·4	21·6	10·7	12·2	1·2
6. Machinery Manufacturers Corporation	n.a.	1·9	3·2	n.a.	17·9	26·0	29·6	27·7	12·0	4·9
GROUP III										
1. Damodar Valley Corporation	n.a.	166·4	179·7	(No profit and loss account was prepared)				2·8	3·8	4·3
2. Sindhu Resettlement Corporation	1948	1·3	1·4	n.a.	1·6	2·3	1·5	12·4	2·3	0·1
GROUP IV										
1. Manganese Ore (India)	1962	1·9	2·2	n.e.	n.e.	n.p.	6·3	27·3	27·2	42·9

Notes:
[a] The figures in brackets relate to the year of incorporation, where significantly different.
[b] Capital employed represents gross fixed assets minus depreciation plus working capital.
[c] Gross profit is gross of taxes and also interest payments.
[d] Work-in-progress is not included in the capital estimates.
[e] The 1960/1 figures relate only to the Sindri plant.

The estimates relate only to the Gauhati refinery. The rate of return at 3·2 is an underestimate in so far as excise duties have been netted out from gross profits.

The notation n.p. refers to the plant not being in production; n.e. refers to the concern being not in existence; and n.a. refers to data not being available. Where the plant is not in production, 'losses' are clearly being incurred but have not been explicitly indicated here. Where the loss is incurred *after* production has started, it has been specified as such.

Further, the concerns have been classified into four groups. Group I consists of eleven concerns, among the largest investments in the public sector, each of whose employed capital was in excess of Rs. 10 crores halfway through the Third Plan, by 1964. Groups II, III, and IV constitute the 'smaller' investments. Group II consists of those concerns which generally appear to have reached a position where their rate of gross profit on employed capital tends to equal or exceed the average return of around 10·5 per cent in the private sector (and recorded in Table 9.5). Group III consists of those concerns whose rates of return appear distinctly to fall below the average private sector Return. Group IV consists of concerns which seem to fluctuate between the preceding two types of behaviour and therefore are not readily classified into II or III.

Source: *Annual Reports of Industrial and Commercial Undertakings of the Central Government.*

[at around 10·5 per cent in Table 9.5], Group III of those enterprises whose performance is poorer than in the private sector, and Group IV of those enterprises whose performance in this respect has been variable.

The striking result to emerge from this empirical evidence is the overwhelming weight attached to the overall performance of the public sector enterprises by the 'top' concerns, especially Hindustan Steel and Heavy Engineering (Ranchi). A fair number of others, in Group II and in Group IV, show performance which is certainly not discouraging. The majority of those in Group III further belong to shipping which is notoriously low-yielding in both private and public sectors (and may be justified on 'defence' grounds).

It is also clear that the performance even among the top concerns is substantially affected by the operation of the Heavy Engineering Corporation and the Neyveli Lignite Corporation (which had not come into production at *any* level until 1964/5), Heavy Electricals, Indian Refineries, and (most important) Hindustan Steel which were still building up steadily to fuller capacity utilization.[1]

There are also two other, important qualifications to be borne in mind. (1) In cases such as steel, there has been explicit price control by the Government. Furthermore, in other cases such as Hindustan Machine Tools and Hindustan Shipyard, it has been the policy of the Board of Directors to fix domestic prices close to the landed cost of similar products. In either case the consequence is to keep monetary rates of profit below what they could otherwise have been. This underlines the fact that the observed rates of return cannot be accepted, without further analysis, as evidence of wasteful investment. This is indeed a more general point: in a situation where domestic prices are distorted by a variety of endogenous and policy-imposed factors, the observed rates of return cannot be taken to give a proper ranking of the social profitability of alternative investments. (2) In fact, such a

---

[1] Cf. J. Bhagwati, 'Monopoly in Public Enterprise', in V. V. Ramanadham (ed.), *The Working of the Public Sector*, Papers and Proceedings of the Third All-India Seminar on Public Enterprise at Osmania University, Hyderabad, December 1963, for an early discussion of these and related issues in interpreting the profit rates in the public sector. The comment of A. K. Kelkar, Managing Director, Praga Tools Ltd., a participant in this Conference, is also of some interest.

distortion may be imposed by the creation of monopoly, as is indeed the case with many Indian industries (in both the public and private sectors) thanks to strict controls on imports and domestic entry.[1] In such cases, there is a likelihood that, even if the observed profit rates are high, the presence of effective monopoly power may lead to inefficiency in production in the basic sense of average cost per unit output, at any given scale of output, being higher than it would be were competitive conditions to prevail. Such inefficiencies would not be detected by mere observations of the rates of return actually recorded by the enterprises.[2]

While, however, the observed rates of return are an extremely poor index of the social profitability of public sector enterprises or of whether these enterprises manage to minimize the average cost of production at any scale of output, they do have other implications of economic significance. Firstly, a policy of under-pricing may result in distortion of choice of technique by the user industries. Thus, for example, under-priced steel can result in excessive, and sub-optimal, use of it as against other materials wherever choice is available (e.g. with office furniture). Secondly, even where no such choice is available, the fact that, in many cases, there is no *de jure* (or *de facto*) regulation of the prices of the end-products of the user industries (e.g. the prices of textile machinery), implies that the profits foregone by the public sector enterprises wind up with the users, who *eventually* tend to be in the private sector.[3] The effect of under-pricing by public sector

---

[1] Cf. Bhagwati, ibid., pp. 91–2 and 96–7; and also Chapters 13, 15, and 16.

[2] In fact, if profitability is reduced through such inefficiencies, attributed mainly to the monopolistic structure of the industries in which these enterprises operate, then we should expect it to be similarly reduced also in the private sector (which is reduced also to a monopolistic structure, in general) so that the *relative* rankings of the two sectors also would not be affected in general. In so far, however, as the public sector is subject to *additional* inefficiencies, that is a different matter.

[3] This argument assumes, of course, that cost-plus pricing combined with informal rationing of sales at the cost-plus price by the final suppliers (e.g. of textile machinery), is not the case for the bulk of the Indian industry and that instead prices to final consumers tend to be determined on the principle of market-clearance at what the market will bear. Although no *systematic* study of industrial pricing behaviour has been undertaken in India by economists, it is pertinent to note that whatever studies of control of price and distribution of scarce materials, including foreign exchange, have been attempted seem to indicate that the prices which consumers end up paying, *de facto*, reflect the scarcity value. Cf. *Report of the [Raj] Committee of Steel Control*, Ministry of Steel and Heavy Industries, Government of India, October 1963.

enterprises is thus substantially to redistribute revenue in favour of the private sector: which, in turn, compromises the effort of the Government at raising real savings in so far as this leads to additional consumption in the private sector.[1]

The effect on overall savings, resulting from the low returns exhibited by public sector enterprises, has attracted considerable attention in India. Take, for example, a typical pronouncement on the subject by V. K. R. V. Rao, one of India's prominent economists:

... the [price] policy should be such as to promote the growth of national income and the rate of this growth. This involves in turn the abandonment of the popularly accepted principle of no-profit, no-loss as the supreme criterion for pricing of the products of public enterprise. Looked at from this angle, it is obvious that public enterprise must make profits and the larger the share of public enterprises in all enterprise, the greater is the need for their making profits. Profits constitute the surplus available for savings and investment. . . .[2]

The impact of this type of thinking is to be seen in the increasing number of policy statements aimed at getting the public sector enterprises to earn some minimum rate of return. The thinking on this question, which crystallized during the progress of the Third Plan, focused on 10 per cent as the minimum, target rate of return (obviously by reference to the private sector's average return)[3] but has now reached the figure of 'not less than 11 to 12 per cent'.[4]

---

[1] To quantify this effect, we would need a matrix of inter-industrial transactions, with each row and column divided into public and private sectors, as suggested by J. Bhagwati, 'More on Devaluation', *Economic Weekly*, 6 October, 1962. Unfortunately, despite its importance in planning in a mixed economy with a sizeable public sector, such a transaction matrix is not yet available for any year.

[2] 'The Public Sector in India', *Applied Economic Papers* (Osmania University), March 1961, p. 3. Rao is careful to argue that even loss-making enterprises may be beneficial in social terms. However, he argues against public sector enterprises exercising monopoly power in setting prices (ibid., p. 4), which is dubious in so far as there may be, and in fact often is, monopoly power being exercised by the private sector. On this last issue, see Bhagwati, 'Monopoly in Public Enterprise', op. cit.

[3] Cf. *Notes on Perspective of Development: 1960–61 to 1975–76*, P.P.D., Planning Commission, 1964. Pitambar Pant, then Chief of the P.P.D., and Arnold Harberger of the M.I.T. Center for International Studies (India Programme) were among the articulate advocates of such a target.

[4] *Fourth Five-Year Plan: A Draft Outline*, p. 83.

M

(b) Social rates of return and choice of projects.

How far have the public sector enterprises been *socially* productive? We can take a view on this question at a general level, by examining how these projects have been selected and whether they show, in any case, evidence of contributing significant value added when we have evaluated them in a framework that distinguishes between private and social returns. Other detailed dimensions of efficiency such as management, staffing, labour, implementation, and locational policies can be analysed *directly* to examine whether they exhibit inefficiencies, distinguishing between those endemic to the Indian sociological and economic scene and those which pertain only to the public sector.

The actual choice of projects involves two basic, and fundamentally interdependent, decisions: (1) whether to produce the item at all, and (2) the design of the project, involving decisions with respect to technology.[1] The question of the actual decision to produce an item or group of items (e.g. heavy engineering products or machine tools) is part of the general policy relating to industrial targeting, which is discussed in depth in Chapters 13 and 14; hence we consider here only questions relating to the choice of design.

A careful scrutiny of the methods adopted to plan for the projects, as revealed by the reports of several governmental committees appointed for this purpose as also to evaluate the reasons for subsequent increasing costs, underlines the extremely poor quality in general of the work, both from a technical viewpoint and even more so from the point of view of economic, cost and benefit analysis. These reports have not followed any uniform format, varying in their coverage and inquiry, underlining that no systematic thought was given to questions of project appraisal and that rough, sketchy, and haphazardly incomplete reports were often considered adequate for embarking upon quite expensive investments. In fact both the Government of India *and* the donor countries financing these projects, through most of our period, appear to have considered that the mere fact of these projects producing outputs considered to be 'within the Plan targets' was adequate guarantee of their utility, regardless of costs

---

[1] In its widest sense, technological choice extends also to questions of location, scale, and time-phasing of expansions.

and efficiency of design.[1] This also meant that political factors were to dominate questions such as site selection, as with the Fertilizer Technical Committee, in 1959, whose terms of reference involved the constraint that a fertilizer plant be located within *each* state and led to corresponding decisions to initiate construction at places which were unsuitable from the viewpoint of either demand or raw materials.

It would be enough to refer to one example in detail, to illustrate some of these critical remarks. We choose Heavy Electricals Limited, at Bhopal, which is a major investment of the Indian Government with British aid. The history of this project indicates that the site selection was made without any explicit calculation of the cost of alternative locations and later was changed when found unsuitable. No attempt appears to have been made to estimate any rates of return on capital. These deficiencies in the Report of the Consultants, Associated Electricals Incorporated (A.E.I.), sprang from the fact that no demands for such calculations were made by their clients, the Government of India. Furthermore, Ian Little (who had the opportunity to study this project in detail) found that the actual figures of costs included in the blueprints showed immediately that, even if all expectations about capacity utilization and efficiency of operations were to be fulfilled, the project would yield very poor returns.[2] (In fact, the Government had even demanded that the plant be designed to yield the required output only with *one-shift* working—a clearly uneconomic demand in view of capital scarcity.) At one-shift, the blueprints showed a yield (including profits and interest) of only 2·7 per cent. The net value added (at domestic prices) *minus* capital outgoings and repayments worked out to 7 and 8·5 per cent respectively on one- and two-shift working, implying capital–output ratios of 14·0 and 12·0 respectively! While these figures were startling, and might have prompted questions relating to

---

[1] This general lack of interest in cost–benefit analysis was evident also in other areas of governmental investment such as the immense irrigation works of the type of Bhakra–Nangal in Panjab. K. N. Raj, examining the Bhakra–Nangal project *post facto* was to find, for example, that the dam was unduly capital-intensive, many labour-using techniques having been ignored. Cf. *Some Economic Aspects of the Bhakra–Nangal Project*. On this general issue, see J. Bhagwati and S. Chakravarty, 'Contributions to Indian Economic Analysis: A Survey', *Supplement* to the *American Economic Review*, September 1969, a Survey commissioned by the American Economic Association.

[2] Unpublished Memorandum, prepared for the I.B.R.D. in 1965.

the design, and even the advisability, of any such project, no such examination was to follow.

The subsequent estimates by Little of the return on the Bhopal project by evaluating inputs and outputs at *international* prices, showed that the real return (leaving out possible, but unspecified, externalities) on the blueprint project was still dismal.[1] In point of fact, of course, the results have been even more depressing because the project construction to capacity levels has proved more expensive per unit of output than anticipated, and the efficiency of production has also been considerably below blueprint levels. A rough application of a similar technique, evaluating the returns at international prices, to the four component projects in the Heavy Engineering Corporation at Ranchi, has also shown the internal rate of return, at c.i.f. prices, to be around only 1·00 per cent in the Heavy Machine Building, Coal Mining Machinery, and Foundry Forge projects.

While, however, we cannot generalize from these analyses to argue that the social returns to most projects in the public sector have been low, the facts that no systematic analysis of costs of alternative designs and technologies was undertaken and that the all-too-few studies of important projects reveal rather low returns (in a sophisticated, economic sense) are disturbing. These wasteful planning methods are yet persistent, though greater awareness of

[1] Basically the idea behind the evaluation at *international* prices is to take into account correct opportunity costs, rather than to make the evaluations at domestic prices which reflect a variety of policy-imposed distortions. This idea, reflecting the policy implications of the static gains-from-trade theory, is undoubtedly an important improvement over the more traditional methods of cost–benefit analysis at domestic prices and was also independently arrived at by Tinbergen who would like an *entire* macro-plan to be *built up* from choice among alternative projects. Tinbergen's method has been explained systematically, and developed with insight, by Bent Hansen in his 1966 de Vries Lectures, *Long- and Short-term Planning in Underdeveloped Countries*, North-Holland Series, Amsterdam, 1967. The technique is elegantly analysed also in a forthcoming work of I. M. D. Little and J. Mirrlees, (to be published by the O.E.C.D. Development Centre, Paris). While the technique is an improvement over earlier methods, it runs into difficulties (recognized and discussed by the authors) over questions such as the treatment of non-traded goods and the associated question of whether to take c.i.f. or f.o.b. prices for any goods: questions which would be eliminated in a world free from transport costs. On the other hand, as a method of *practical* analysis, it appears superior to techniques where the 'shadow' exchange rate is derived to deal with these questions: we know of no satisfactory manner in which this can be done *in practice*.

the need for cost–benefit analysis has lately crept into governmental decisions and is part of the general departure from the hitherto mere 'physical planning' of outputs and inputs with negligible regard for costs and returns or for a proper framework of economic policies to induce such a regard in the economy by decision-takers. There is also greater awareness of the role of cost–benefit analysis in approving projects for aid-finance by donor countries, although the increasing resort to devices to make source-tying of aid more effective is, as we shall discuss in Chapter 11, a step away from this newly emergent trend.

(c) Delays in implementation and inflation of costs

In fact, many of the delays in implementation and rises in costs are attributable to the problem of getting aid-finance. Projects occasionally tend to get 'shunted around' among possible donors until some source 'bites'. Then, the source-tying gets into the picture, often involving redesigning of plant and technology, adding directly to the cost of project designing and leading frequently to increased procurement costs from the tied source. There are numerous examples of such projects: the Ranchi project which was financed and procured from the Soviet Union rather than the United Kingdom (as originally considered optimal) because of the availability of Soviet, rather than United Kingdom aid, and the Bokaro Steel plant which was shunted again to the Soviet Union because U.S. assistance was not forthcoming in the end.

But domestic factors have also played a considerable role in contributing to delays in implementation and bringing plants to efficient capacity utilization. Inadequate project preparation has its impact on the speed of implementation. As late as 10 August 1961 a governmental statement in the Lok Sabha admitted: 'Arrangements for technical preparation of projects and scheduling of work relating to them require to be strengthened, particularly as information relating to a large proportion of projects included in the Third Plan is still unsatisfactory.'[1] Dilatory bureaucratic procedures have made their own contribution.[2] Examples of both these types of inefficiencies are easy to find. The Estimates

[1] Quoted in Hanson, op. cit., p. 277.
[2] We shall have occasion to examine this aspect of Indian bureaucratic procedures when we discuss import policy in Chapter 18.

Committee has pointed for example to the delays in the Heavy Electricals (Bhopal) project, arising from changes in project phasing and the decision to introduce steam turbines as a possible product.[1] As for bureaucratic red tape, the policy of requiring 'indigenous clearance' before imports are permitted, to ensure that domestic production automatically gets first and overriding priority, has been known to create considerable delays for many projects, with permission to import eventually being given in any case.[2] The construction procedures have also been criticized by the Planning Commission's Committee on Plan Projects (C.O.P.P.).[3] In all these respects, as with the question of design and social productivity, there is a growing consciousness of the need to remove these inefficiencies: but changes in organization and procedures are inevitably slow to come.

The increasing costs of many projects have also reflected aid-finance problems and the domestic inefficiencies we have described.[4] But the tendency to 'overbuild' the social overheads has also been noticed by many observers. The following comments on the record of the Fertilizer Corporation of India (F.C.I.), which controlled six undertakings in 1965 (Sindri, Nangal, Trombay, Namrup, Gorakhpur, and Korba, the last three still being planned) are worth reproducing:

Evidently, all the projects have been lavish with the use of land (p. 85). At Sindri there is one house constructed per acre of land, the argument being that land is cheap. Even at Trombay, FCI thinks it

---

[1] *Report of the Estimates Committee*, Lok Sabha, 1962–3, Thirty-fifth Report, New Delhi. Similar examples can be found for other projects, including the Heavy Engineering Corporation (Ranchi) and Neyveli Lignite Corporation. See also the *Sixth Report of the Committee on Public Undertakings*, 1965, New Delhi, on the Fertilizer Corporation of India, especially on the Nangal and Trombay plants.

[2] As we shall see in Chapter 18, this problem of *unnecessary and inefficient* delays has plagued the private sector as well.

[3] Cf. several studies of C.O.P.P., including that on *Heavy Electricals (India) Limited*, November 1964, New Delhi. The Sixth Report of the Committee on Public Undertakings, op. cit., mentions that the construction period for Trombay, Namrup, and Gorakhpur plants would be about five and a half years, citing that the estimate of the U.N. Fertilizer Team for such construction was only thirty-five to forty-seven months for India.

[4] Few project reports seem to take fully into account prospects of rising prices due both to the overall inflationary increase and to additional indirect taxation. The delays also make for increased underestimation on this count in so far as the price increases are a positive function of time.

necessary to provide housing to 96·9 per cent of its workers. The cost of township formed 12·6 per cent of the total cost of project at Sindri, and 12 per cent at Nangal. Surely this must be a civil contractors' paradise. . . .

The capital cost of all the projects has been high, higher than original estimates (pp. 44, 45) and higher than the recent estimates submitted by Bechtel Corporation. The costs have been inflated by the large element of township costs and by administrative delays and consequent rise in overheads. . . . This waste of capital is most clearly noticeable in staffing and in inventory holding practices. The number of personnel employed at Sindri was 8,103 and at Nangal 3,429; even Trombay which is still to go into production has already on its roll 1,543 persons against a total strength of 1,803. In this, of course, FCI is not unique. Visiting the Heavy Engineering Corporation, one can see people sitting idle or loafing about. This not only increases the running cost of the projects, but, when one relates it to the housing policy of FCI also the capital cost—and the real resources which go to constitute this capital cost.[1]

(d) Labour, personnel, and management

Indeed, the problems relating to labour, skilled personnel, and management have been the focal point of many inefficiencies in the public sector set-up.

The *political* involvement in public sector enterprises has helped in contributing to its overstaffing of unskilled labour (e.g. Bhopal) and payment of higher average unskilled wages than in the private sector (e.g. Ranchi). It is widely held to have also affected adversely the efficiency of the labour and handling of industrial relations:

Talking of industrial relations the Government should pause to think why State-owned plants are beset by more problems than comparable private sector units. Bhopal has had strikes and lock-outs every year since it started production in 1962. The loss on this account is estimated at Rs. 4 crores. In HSL the loss in a single year—1967–68— came to over Rs. 6 crores. The main cause, as a document claims, is the multiplicity of trade unions. This problem is by no means confined to the public sector. If the private sector is better able to cope with it, the explanation probably is that its managements are less vulnerable to political pressure.

[1] Arthagnani, 'How Not to Set Up and Run a Project', *Economic Weekly*, 15 May 1965. This is a commentary on the Sixth Report of the Committee on Public Undertakings, op. cit.

In the case of public sector undertakings the Minister with whom the final decision rests in major disputes has to look after the interests of the enterprise as well as his political career. The conflict between the two can be awkward in the extreme, especially where State Governments become involved in the dispute because of affiliations between the ruling party and the union concerned. A political lightweight Minister prefers to buy peace rather than offend a State Government, whether run by the Congress or other parties.[1]

The problems relating to skilled technical personnel have been even more acute. They have largely revolved around the flight from public sector undertakings, which became sufficiently alarming for the Government in 1961 to commission H. K. Paranjape, of the Institute of Public Administration, to examine the question and suggest remedies. Among the major causes of this flight were (i) the relatively low scales of pay in relation to the private sector, (ii) the tendency, on the part of many enterprises, to indulge in restrictive practices with respect to permission to apply for other jobs, and (iii) the absence, in most undertakings, of a good system of personnel appraisal, which made reliance on promotions by seniority more likely in practice and encouraged the younger and talented people to leave.[2] The intrusion of ideological beliefs about the proper salaries to pay in the public sector, as also the alleged influence of the top I.C.S. and I.A.S. civil servants in ensuring, as much as possible, that no comparable public sector employee would get more than they, have been among the principal factors in making for these inefficiencies.

The heavy hand of the traditional administrative services has also been evident in management policies in general. Numerous studies have shown that the task of management was seriously underestimated by the traditional civil service, who proceeded to assume most of the managerial functions in these complex, industrial enterprises in the assured belief that their general, non-specialized expertise would be adequate to the job.[3] The effect

[1] Dilip Mukerjee, 'Heavy Hand of Politics on Public Sector', *Statesman*, 3 May 1968.

[2] H. K. Paranjape, *The Flight of Technical Personnel in Public Undertakings.* Chapters VII, VIII and XI are of particular interest.

[3] Thus, for example, R. K. Nigam's examination of the composition of the Chairmanship and Managing Directorships of several public sector, industrial enterprises, as on 30 September 1961, reproduced in Table 9.7, reveals a very high proportion of 'officials' in these jobs; this proportion has, however, declined later. On this general issue, there are several competent discussions,

of this was not merely general incompetence but also rapid turnover of people in important roles such as chairmanships, managing directorships, and general managerships.[1] At the same time it has meant that, with their civil service background and continuing involvement in that career, these officials have inevitably tended to act with bureaucratic caution and unimaginativeness rather than in bold and inventive ways. While efforts to move towards more efficient and stable management, as via the Industrial Management Pool, have been made, they have proved only a little better than abortive.[2]

Furthermore, the actual management has been hemmed in by traditional audit procedures which extend beyond mere certification of expenditures to an evaluation by the Auditor-General's office of whether these expenditures were properly incurred within the framework of the authorizations. Since this scrutiny is intensive and any departure from its exacting standards can lead to censure and disgrace, the scope for imaginative and quick action in the interest of better economic performance is inevitably jeopardized.[3]

The overall dissatisfaction with the public sector's performance so far is therefore not entirely unjustified;[4] and the prospects of

prominent among them being H. K. Paranjape, *The Industrial Management Pool, An Administrative Experiment*, Indian Institute of Public Administration, New Delhi, 2963; Paul Appleby, *Reexamination of India's Administrative System with Special Reference to Administration of the Government's Industrial and Commercial Enterprises*, op. cit.; and A. H. Hanson, op. cit., Chapter VIII.

[1] See, for example, the statistics on this question in the Fifty-second *Report* of the Estimates Committee, 1963–4, on *Personal Policies of Public Undertakings*, New Delhi.

[2] See Paranjape, *The Industrial Management Pool . . .* , op. cit.; and Hanson, op. cit., Chapter VIII on Administration.

[3] It is a moot point, however, whether these procedures can really be revised in view of the general suspicion with which politicians and civil servants have come to be treated in the Lok Sabha: a matter which we discussed at length earlier in this chapter.

[4] Among the manifestations of incompetent management, we might note the contention that there is inadequate inventory control and that public sector inventories are excessive. Table 9.8 shows that, for some major projects such as the Hindustan Aeronautics and Hindustan Shipyard, inventories run up to significantly over a year's stocks. However, there is not enough evidence available to argue conclusively that there is any *greater* inefficiency in inventory control in the public than in the private sector, on the average. Better management practices, in this respect, appear by most accounts to be called for in *both* sectors. A related point of some substance, however, is that the low interest rates charged by the Government, the certainty of losses being made up by subsidies, and the tendency to judge results by physical performance

TABLE 9.7

COMPOSITION OF THE BOARDS OF DIRECTORS OF INDUSTRIAL GOVERN-
MENT COMPANIES ON 30 SEPTEMBER 1961

Company	Chairman: whether Secretary/Joint Secretary or other official	Managing Director: whether official or non-official
1. Bharat Electronics	Secretary	Official
2. Eastern Shipping Corporation	Joint Secretary	Official
3. Fertilizer Corporation of India	Secretary	Official
4. Heavy Electricals	Retired Official	Official
5. Heavy Engineering Corporation	Official	
6. Hindustan Cables	Joint Secretary	Official
7. Hindustan Antibiotics	Non-official	—
8. Hindustan Housing Factory	Joint Secretary	—
9. Hindustan Insecticides	Non-official	Official
10. Hindustan Machine Tools	Official	Official (same as Chairman)
11. Hindustan Organic Chemicals	—	Official
12. Hindustan Salt	Retired Official	Official
13. Hindustan Steel	Official	—
14. Hindustan Teleprinters	—	Official
15. Indian Oil	Non-official	Official
16. Indian Refineries	Non-official	Official
17. Nahan Foundry	Joint Secretary	—
18. National Buildings Construction Corporation	Secretary	Official
19. National Coal Development Corporation	Non-official	Official
20. National Instruments	Joint Secretary	—
21. Neyveli Lignite	Official	Official (same as Chairman)
22. Western Shipping Corporation	Joint Secretary	Official
23. Hindustan Aircraft	Secretary	—
24. Indian Rare Earths	Non-official	—
25. National Projects Construction Corporation	Secretary	Official
26. Ashoka Hotels	Secretary	—
27. Hindustan Shipyard	Non-official	Official
28. Indian Telephone Industries	Secretary	Official
29. National Newsprint and Paper Mills	Non-official	—
30. Praga Tools Corporation	Non-official	—
31. Mughal Lines	Joint Secretary	—
32. Pyntes and Chemicals Development Co.	Joint Secretary	—
33. Orissa Mining Corporation	Joint Secretary	Joint Secretary

Source: Adapted from Statement in R. K. Nigam, 'Composition of Boards of
Directors of Government Companies', in V. V. Ramanadham (ed.), *Efficacy of
Public Enterprise*, Proceedings of the Second Seminar on Public Enterprise,
1962, pp. 155–6.

TABLE 9.8

INVENTORIES HELD BY (RUNNING) PUBLIC SECTOR, INDUSTRIAL CONCERNS, MEASURED AS NUMBER OF MONTHS OF VALUE OF PRODUCTION HELD

Concerns	1960/1	1961/2	1962/3	1963/4	1964/5[a]	1965/6[a]
1. Hindustan Aircraft	24	34	38	34[a]	37[a]	36[a]
2. Hindustan Shipyard	55	35	21	37	31	24
3. Travancore Minerals	3	4	6	27	n.a.	n.a.
4. Bharat Electronics	16	11	20	23	26	22
5. Indian Telephone Industries	14	17	14	14	13	17
6. Praga Tools	19	15	16	14	14	17
7. National Coal Development Corporation	11	13	12	13	12	6
8. Fertilizers and chemicals, Travancore Ltd.			7	10	8	8
9. Hindustan Salts	13	23	14	10	13	24
10. Hindustan Antibiotics	11	12	11	10	10	9
11. National Instruments	7	7	8	9	8	8
12. Hindustan Steel	12	11	10	9	8	8
13. Nahan Foundry	5	4	7	8	n.a.	n.a.
14. Hindustan Machine Tools	17	15	11	8	9	10
15. Garden Reach Workshops	4	7	11	8	6	7
16. Fertilizer Corporation of India	10	8	8	7	6	8
17. Hindustan Insecticides	6	6	5	6	5	5
18. Mazagon Dock	5	6	6	6	6	6
19. Hindustan Cables	6	6	8	6	8	9
20. Hindustan Housing Factory	6	4	6	5	5	5
21. National Newsprint and Paper Mills	4	4	4	4	4	6
22. Indian Rare Earths	5	5	4	4	7	8
23. Hindustan Teleprinters	n.a.	n.a.	n.a.	35	39	15
24. Bharat Earthmovers	n.a.	n.a.	n.a.	n.a.	28	9
25. Heavy Electricals	n.a.	n.a.	n.a.	n.a.	n.a.	21
26. Sambhar Salts	n.a.	n.a.	n.a.	n.a.	n.a.	11
27. Neyveli Lignite Corporation	n.a.	n.a.	n.a.	n.a.	n.a.	9
28. Natural Mineral Development Corporation	n.a.	n.a.	n.a.	n.a.	n.a.	8
TOTAL	13	12	12	11	11	10

[a] Refers to cost, rather than value, of production.

Source: *Annual Reports of the Working of Industrial and Commercial Undertakings of the Central Government.*

its future performance are fairly dim, unless the political intrusions into its efficient working are removed. The question is, will the political system in the end prove flexible enough to adapt to the demands of economic efficiency (as it failed to do in Menderes' Turkey, where public enterprises succumbed to political infiltration). The answer will decide whether the 'socialist pattern of society' is going to retain its tempo in the shape of a continuing, if not expanding, share of the public sector in total investments in future Plans.

(which depends on inventories being available) are all factors likely to make the public sector more inefficient in inventory holdings, from a *social* point of view, than the private sector.

Foreign Aid

WHILE much of India's planning strategy has been conceived by influential planners in terms of closed-economy theoretical frameworks, a significant contribution to her economic development has been made in practice by the influx of external resources, both financial and technological. Furthermore, these resources have come on both private and official account. However, the dominant position has been taken by *official* transfers, with private foreign investment and technical collaboration playing a relatively minor role.

We begin therefore by analysing, in this chapter, the foreign aid programmes which have been designed to assist in India's planned development, examining both their importance and their efficiency in achieving this objective. Our analysis of the role of external resources in Indian economic performance will be completed with a brief examination, in the next chapter, of the *private* foreign transfers of resources during the recent period of Indian planning.

I. PRINCIPAL FEATURES

We review initially the magnitude, sources, terms, and conditions of aid, as also its composition by grants and loans, and the pattern of aid utilization by sectors. We later review the questions of aid-tying and the pace of aid utilization, in relation to questions about the efficiency of aid.

(a) Magnitude

The magnitude of aid received by India, taken at both its absolute value and as a proportion of world aid flow, appears very substantial. The proportion of D.A.C. aid, for example, that came to

TABLE 10.1

AUTHORIZED EXTERNAL ASSISTANCE TO INDIA BY SOURCE: 1951–68

(In Rs. crores at pre-devaluation rate of exchange)

(1)	Up to end First Plan	During Second Plan	1961/2	1962/3	1963/4	1964/5	1965/6	Total Third Plan	1966/7	(Apr.–Sept.) 1967–8
	(2)	(3)	(4)	(5)	(6)	(7)	(8)	(9)	(10)	(11)
Loans										
(a) Repayable in foreign currency	212·26	1,050·63	342·94	596·40	455·42	492·91	412·73	2,300·40	686·71	15·94
(i) United States	90·31	108·53	33·11	330·36	197·22	81·65	147·05	789·39	150·06	72·81
(ii) United Kingdom		122·66	60·00	66·66	40·00	39·98	35·33	241·97	47·33	25·33
(iii) Japan		26·81	38·09	4·76	38·09	28·57	28·57	138·08	21·43	24·76
(iv) I.B.R.D.	57·21	260·79	50·17	82·37	14·29	88·09	63·81	144·43	14·28	10·86
(v) I.D.A.					9·52		47·62	277·77	145·71	
(vi) Other Western countries										
Total (Consortium members)	147·52	668·57	342·94	575·45	452·15	338·32	401·73	2,110·59	464·41	148·80
(vii) U.S.S.R.	64·74	319·07				100·50		100·50	164·05	
(viii) Other East European countries										
Total (Soviet bloc)	64·74	375·52		15·50		151·00	3·38	169·88	218·02	
(ix) Others		6·54		5·45	3·27	3·59	7·62	19·93	4·28	7·14
(b) Repayable in Rupees	14·63	230·15	48·56		1·03			49·59	15·71	
(i) United States	14·63	230·15	48·56					48·56	15·71	
(ii) Others					1·03			1·03		
Grants										
(i) United States	137·96	125·47	22·47	14·74	15·69	25·66	59·31	137·87	39·41	0·96
(ii) United Kingdom	91·77	54·57	7·46	3·87	1·54	4·11	4·81	21·79	2·76	
(iii) Japan	0·39	0·42	0·05	0·05	0·54	0·05	0·35	0·99		
(iv) Other Western countries		0·35			0·05		0·03	0·13		
(v) U.S.S.R.	124·50	114·53	19·64	12·92	10·56	20·22	46·35	109·69	39·41	0·96
(vi) Other East European countries		1·15		0·40	2·00	0·98	0·83	4·21		
(vii) Others	13·46	9·79	2·83	1·42	3·13	4·46	12·13	23·97	0·96	
Commodity assistance	16·92	1,130·73		43·33	4·91	225·20	177·19	450·63	249·30	101·26
(i) United States	16·92	1,130·73		43·33	4·91	225·20	177·19	450·63	249·30	101·26

Source: Economic Survey 1967–68, Government of India.

N

TABLE 10.2

UTILIZATION OF EXTERNAL ASSISTANCE TO INDIA BY SOURCE: 1951–68

(In Rs. crores at pre-devaluation rate of exchange)

(1)	Up to end of First Plan	During Second Plan	1961/2	1962/3	1963/4	1964/5	1965/6	Total Third Plan	1966/7	(Apr.–Sept. 1967/8)
	(2)	(3)	(4)	(5)	(6)	(7)	(8)	(9)	(10)	(11)
Loans										
(a) Repayable in foreign currency	124·13	607·93	190·41	247·90	359·26	468·41	486·11	1,752·09	420·39	241·84
(i) United States	90·31	36·84	32·45	107·36	165·73	164·43	169·54	639·51	143·39	84·96
(ii) United Kingdom		121·85	22·98	29·76	34·74	39·96	43·08	170·52	57·47	28·31
(iii) Japan		16·01	7·23	7·68	17·90	24·56	30·85	88·22	19·16	14·87
(iv) I.B.R.D.	33·82	222·80	35·91	33·59	14·94	17·59	21·34	123·37	16·38	7·29
(v) I.D.A.			1·23	9·04	42·00	58·40	89·89	200·56	85·52	55·57
(vi) Other Western countries										
Total (Consortium members)	124·13	533·08	65·81	214·67	307·30	388·44	428·94	1,505·16	377·78	223·67
(vii) U.S.S.R.		74·85	24·57	32·43	47·29	64·97	37·97	207·23	22·97	12·04
(viii) Other East European countries				0·23	1·61	0·13	4·07	6·04	7·17	2·84
(ix) Total (Soviet bloc)		74·85	24·60	33·00	50·35	79·84	53·10	240·89	35·45	15·33
(b) Repayable in Rupees	2·29	116·82	38·51	58·83	29·41	17·07	12·57	156·39	6·67	1·49
(i) United States	2·29	116·82	38·51	58·83	29·41	16·66	12·38	155·79	6·27	1·49
(ii) Others						0·41	0·19	0·60	0·40	
Grants										
(i) United States	70·18	160·64	21·74	14·85	16·32	20·02	34·22	107·15	46·44	25·11
(i) United States	44·26	85·59	10·01	8·36	2·94	4·30	5·47	31·08	3·04	0·35
(ii) United Kingdom	0·03	0·43	0·10		0·10	0·19	0·41	0·80	0·04	
(iii) Japan		0·35			0·05	0·05	0·03	0·13		
(iv) Other Western countries										
Total (Consortium members)	63·99	147·28	19·67	14·25	12·82	16·78	24·76	88·28	46·44	21·69
(v) U.S.S.R.		1·15			2·00	0·98	0·83	3·81		
(vi) Other East European countries										
Total (Soviet bloc)		1·15			2·17	1·10	0·94	4·21		
(vii) Others	6·19	12·21	2·07	0·60	1·33	2·14	8·52	14·66	3·42	
Commodity assistance	5·07	544·81	88·01	122·72	185·19	218·12	239·18	853·22	228·40	93·40
(i) United States	5·07	544·81	88·01	122·72	185·19	218·12	239·18	853·22	228·40	93·40

Source: Economic Survey 1967–68, Government of India.

TABLE 10.3
UTILIZATION OF EXTERNAL ASSISTANCE BY INDIA, AS PERCENTAGE OF NET NATIONAL PRODUCT AT FACTOR COST: 1951/2–1966/7

	1951/2	1952/3	1953/4	1954/5	1955/6	1956/7	1957/8	1958/9	1959/60	1960/1	1961/2	1962/3	1963/4	1964/5	1965/6	1966/7
1. Loans	0·81	0·34	0·02	0·02	0·08	0·25	1·06	1·78	1·27	1·33 (1·39)	1·55 (1·60)	1·99 (2·02)	2·26 (2·21)	2·38 (2·38)	2·45 (2·37)	1·85 (1·77)
2. Grants	0·04	0·12	0·16	0·10	0·28	0·35	0·30	0·19	0·26	0·21 (0·22)	0·15 (0·15)	0·10 (0·10)	0·09 (0·09)	0·10 (0·10)	0·17 (0·16)	0·20 (0·19)
3. Assistance under P.L. 480/665, etc.	—	—	—	—	0·05	0·45	1·01	0·74	0·75	1·32 (1·39)	0·59 (0·61)	0·80 (0·81)	1·08 (1·05)	1·07 (1·07)	1·18 (1·14)	0·99 (0·95)
4. Total Aid	0·86	0·47	0·19	0·11	0·40	1·05	2·37	2·71	2·28	2·86 (3·01)	2·29 (2·37)	2·89 (2·93)	3·34 (3·35)	3·54 (3·55)	3·80 (3·67)	3·04 (2·91)

Note: The bracketed figures refer to the revised national income estimator. Blanks mean zero assistance.
Source: Calculated from Table 10.2 and Table 4.1(a).

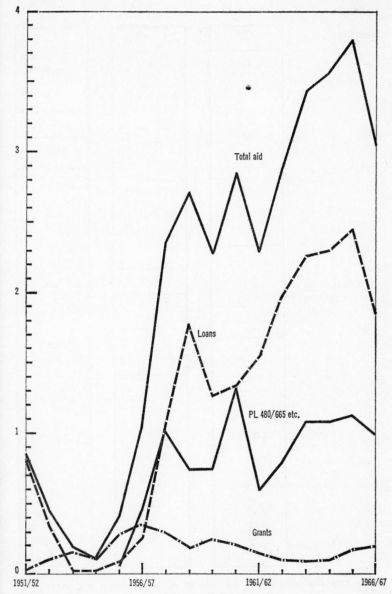

Figure 10.1. External assistance as a percentage of net national product (at factor cost).

Source: Table 10.3.

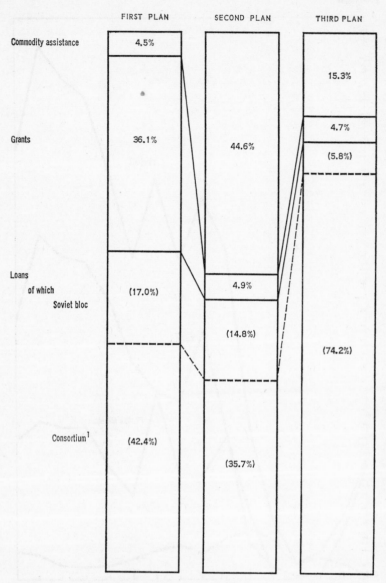

Figure 10.2. Authorization of aid: shares of loans, grants and commodity assistance by each five-year plan.

[1] Includes very small amounts of non-consortium loans.

Source: Table 10.1.

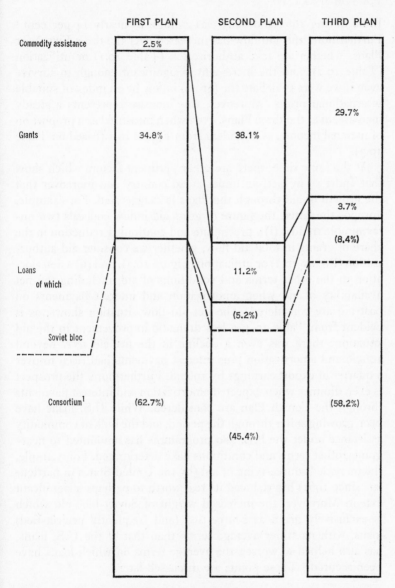

Figure 10.3. Utilization of aid: shares of loans, grants, and commodity assistance, by each five-year plan.

[1] Includes very small amounts of non-consortium loans.

Source: Table 10.2.

India during 1962 and 1963 was as high as nearly 14 per cent.[1] Furthermore, this aid flow has increased over the three Five-Year Plans, whether we take authorization (Table 10.1) or utilization (Table 10.2); and the increment is significant enough to survive even if we were to deflate the (gross) inflow by an index of suitable international prices. Moreover, this increase represents a steady increase, over the three Plans, even when measured as a proportion of national income, as is evident from Figure 10.1 (based on Table 10.3).

At the same time, there are other pertinent factors which show that India is, in fact, an under-aided country and moreover that the growth of aid through the Plans is exaggerated. For example, apropos the latter, the figure of gross aid inflow conceals two unfavourable trends: (i) a precipitate and continuing reduction in the share of grants in total aid flow, whether we consider aid authorization (Figure 10.2) or utilization (Figure 10.3); and (ii) a deterioration in the other terms and conditions of aid, including the net availability of aid when amortization and interest payments on past aid are considered. The net aid flow situation shows, as is evident from Table 10.4, a less dramatic improvement in the aid situation: there was even a decline in the net aid *level* beyond 1965/6 and amortization plus interest payments had risen to over a quarter of export earnings by 1967/8. Furthermore, the prospect is even dimmer when expected amortization and interest payments through the Fourth Plan are considered. While U.S. loans have been growing softer through the period, and the bulk of commodity assistance under the P.L. 480 programme has amounted to near-grants, other terms and conditions have deteriorated. For example, the increased source-tying of aid (by the United States in particular, since 1961) has reduced its real worth to perhaps a significant extent. Moreover, the increased weight of Soviet-bloc aid which is exclusively given as source-tied (and frequently project-tied) loans, with its stiffer average terms than that of the U.S. loans, has also helped to worsen the average terms on which loans have been secured.[2] These points are discussed later.

---

[1] This represents India's share of 'net lending' plus 'grants and grant-like contributions' to all developing countries, in these two years. Cf. I. M. D. Little and J. M. Clifford, *International Aid*, Table 3, p. 66.

[2] On the other hand, the fact that the Soviet-bloc accepts repayments in kind has been a plus factor (which has been publicized to the neglect of unfavourable

TABLE 10.4

NET AID UTILIZATION BY INDIA: 1951–68
(In U.S. $ million)

	Up to end of First Plan	During Second Plan	During Third Plan	1961/2	1962/3	1963/4	1964/5	1965/6	1966/7	1967/8
1. Gross aid utilization	413	1,860	4,232	526	675	850	1,062	1,120	1,026	1,150
2. Amortization and interest payments	50	251	1,141	214	186	224	254	263	318	444
3. 2 as per cent of 1	12·1	13·5	27·0	40·7	27·6	26·4	23·9	23·5	31·0	38·6
4. Net aid inflow, 1–2	363	1,609	3,091	312	489	626	808	857	708	706
5. Amortization and interest payments as per cent of exports	0·8	3·9	14·3	15·0	12·4	13·4	14·8	15·5	20·6	27·8

Notes: 1. Aid utilization figures exclude U.S. Commodity assistance under P.L. 480/665.

2. Export figures relate to customs figures as recorded by D.G.C.I. & S. Calcutta.

3. While aid figures 'up to end of First Plan' include some utilization prior to the First Plan, export figures relate to those during the First Plan.

4. The constituent items may not always add up to total due to rounding.

Source: Compiled by Messrs. Gopal Behari and V. K. S. Nair of the Department of Economic Affairs, Ministry of Finance, at the authors' request.

As for the general question whether India has been over-aided in relation to developing countries on the average, it is clear that India's sheer size, both of population and overall income, creates this misleading impression. As many proponents of greater aid to India[1] have repeatedly noted, India is in fact a grossly under-aided country if one takes suitably 'deflated' measures such as aid per head. Streeten and Hill have noted that

India received in 1961 $1·5, in 1962 $1·7, and in 1963 $2·1 from O.E.C.D. countries and multilateral agencies, compared with Pakistan's massive doses: $2·8 excluding Indus Waters Scheme, $4·0 including it (some of this should, however, be credited to India) in 1962; $4·2 excluding, $4·9 including it (1963), and a further rise to about $6·0 in 1964.[2]

Comparisons with countries other than Pakistan also put India near the bottom of the list (Figure 10.4), when we take gross aid flows as measured by D.A.C.[3]

(b) Sources

Perhaps no single developing country has received aid from sources so varied and under terms and conditions so diffuse as India. The donor countries are, from the point of view of political philosophy and practice, as disparate as the United States and the Soviet Union. The diffusion of sources is also reflected in the wide spectrum of techniques and methods adopted in metal and machinery production in chemicals and fertilizers, in oil exploration and in the simple devices which raise agricultural productivity. The development effort and more particularly the strains imposed by the deteriorating balance of payments have resulted in the tapping of aid sources of such a wide variety that in a single activity

---

aspects of Soviet-bloc aid already noted). Whether, *on balance*, the Soviet-bloc aid compares favourably with D.A.C. aid is an issue which has not been systematically explored in the Indian literature and one to which we have been unable to allocate our limited research time on this volume.

[1] Cf. I. M. D. Little and J. M. Clifford, *International Aid*, op. cit.; and Paul Streeten and R. Hill, 'Aid to India', in P. Streeten and M. Lipton (eds.), *The Crisis of Indian Planning*, op. cit.

[2] Ibid., p. 332.

[3] These measures do not adjust for the differences among recipients, relating to the terms and conditions of the aid received. However, there is no reason to believe that these are less onerous for India than for other countries on the average.

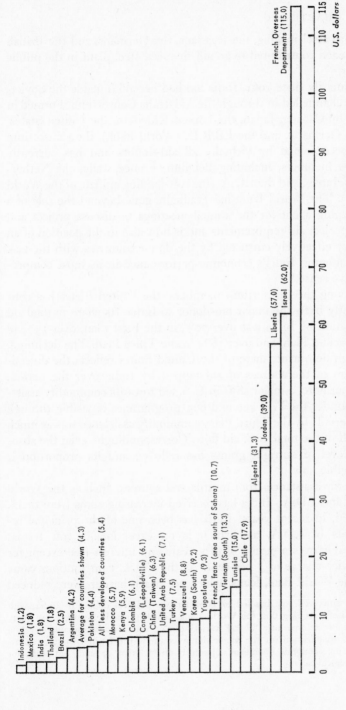

Figure 10.4. Receipt of O.E.C.D. and multilateral aid (loans and grants) per head of population: average of 1962 and 1963.

Source: *International Aid*, I. M. D. Little and J. M. Clifford, p. 66.

such as steel-making, the Russians, the Germans, and the British have each contributed to an aid-financed steel plant in the public sector.

Primarily since 1961, India has had her aid (outside the Soviet-bloc) channelled in through the Aid-India Consortium. Formed in 1958 by Canada, Japan, the United Kingdom, the United States, West Germany, and the I.B.R.D. (World Bank), the Consortium has been joined by virtually all aid-donors and has currently twelve members, including Belgium, France, Italy, the Netherlands, Japan, and the I.D.A. (the soft-lending affiliate of the World Bank). The World Bank has gradually gone beyond the role of a convening agent for the annual meetings to discuss project and non-project aid requirements and is now also in the position of an agency effectively entrusted by the donor countries with the task of evaluating India's economic performance in its most comprehensive sense.[1]

Among the Consortium members, the United States has consistently been the major aid-donor to India. Its share in total aid utilization by India was over 70% in the First Plan, over 55% in the Second Plan, and over 58% in the Third Plan. The declining, though dominant, share of the United States reflects the diversification in the sources of aid tapped by India over the period. Furthermore, a major shift in U.S. aid towards commodity assistance under the P.L. 480 and 665 programmes is visible through the period: by the Third Plan, commodity assistance was as much as half of the total U.S. aid flow. Correspondingly, even the absolute level of outright grants has reduced and its proportion is negligible now.

As for assistance from multilateral sources, such as the World Bank and I.D.A., India has received increasing sums from them. Indeed, in recent years, India has been one of the principal recipients of I.D.A. aid which is on exceptionally soft terms: repayable over a period of fifty years and interest-free except for a service charge of $\frac{3}{4}$ per cent. As the I.D.A. contributions came in, the World Bank loans, which are much harder, were reduced

---

[1] This enhanced role has led to considerable political debate in India, with the 'Left' arguing that the World Bank, which pushed effectively for many economic reforms of a 'liberal' variety during 1966, has become effectively a front organization for the major donor country, the United States, recommending economic liberalism apparently on technical grounds but really for ideological reasons.

during the Third Plan; the total increase in aid from multilateral sources thus did not keep up during the Third Plan with the general growth of aid—although its *average* terms and conditions were considerably softened thanks to the I.D.A. credits. In any case, as a proportion of total aid flow into India, aid from the multilateral agencies has not exceeded 12–13 per cent of the total aid received by India since Independence.

The proportion of Soviet-bloc aid in total aid to India grew steadily from practically zero during the First Plan to under 6 per cent during the Second Plan and under 12 per cent during the Third Plan. Furthermore, the bulk of this aid was concentrated on the Soviet Union, which supplied over 90 per cent of the total aid from this source through the entire period.

While the relationship of Soviet-bloc aid to Consortium aid is generally complementary, Soviet-bloc aid has occasionally made for greater manoeuvrability on the part of India by allowing for a competitive edge through offers of aid-finance and know-how for projects which the West could not, or would not, help to implement: a phenomenon of particular importance in oil refining and steel. As it turns out, Soviet-bloc aid has been used almost exclusively for projects in the 'heavy' industrial sector, including power, coal, drugs, steel, and oil.

The terms of the Soviet loans have almost invariably involved an interest rate of $2\frac{1}{2}$ per cent per annum, with the principal repayable over a period of twelve years (except in the case of a drugs project where the repayment period was shortened to as little as seven years), repayment beginning one year after the completion of deliveries of the (source-tied) equipment for the project. By contrast, both the rate of interest (at $\frac{3}{4}$–1 per cent for the first ten years and $2\frac{1}{2}$ per cent thereafter) and the period of repayment (starting with a ten-years' grace period and extending to forty years) on the thirty-six AID loans extended from November 1961 to 31 March 1966 compare extremely favourably with Soviet-bloc terms.[1]

Furthermore, the Soviet loans have been made part of trade-cum-aid arrangements and therefore result in repayments in kind. This has definitely eased the burden of repayments in so far as

---

[1] We produce, in Table 10.5, the estimated average maturities and interest rates for major donor countries, for the Third Plan period, underlining the fact of the United States being the softest lender among the bilateral donors.

TABLE 10.5
AVERAGE MATURITY AND INTEREST RATES ON FRESH LOANS
AUTHORIZED DURING THE THIRD PLAN BY MAJOR DONORS

Donor	Grace period for repayment	Total maturity including grace period	Interest rate
	Number of years	Number of years	Per cent per annum
1. United States	8·7	35·5	1·86
2. United Kingdom	6·9	25·0	4·43
3. West Germany	4·8	17·3	4·82
4. Japan	5·0	15·2	5·84
5. U.S.S.R.	1·0	12·0	2·50
6. I.B.R.D.	4·4	21·2	5·64
7. I.D.A.	10·0	50·0	0·75
Total: all countries/ institutions	5·8	25·8	3·20

Notes: 1. The estimates include credits meant for use in the Third Plan, though actual agreements were signed in the Second Plan period.

2. The averages have been compiled by weighting the loans by size.

Source: Compiled by Messrs. Gopal Behan and V. K. S. Nair of the Department of Economic Affairs, Ministry of Finance, at the author's request.

such provisions have led to net additions to Indian exports.[1] By contrast the Consortium loans, despite their softer terms, have not been subjected to similar 'reverse-tying' of repayments, although Western aid itself has progressively been source-tied in the past few years (as we shall see).[2]

Among other contrasts between Soviet-bloc and Consortium aid is the almost exclusive grant of Soviet-bloc aid to public sector projects as contrasted with the mixed nature of Consortium aid. The ideological desire of the Soviet Union to support the public sector, rather than the private sector, has matched the Indian Government's preference for having heavy industrial projects, for which Soviet aid has predominantly been used, substantially in the public sector: hence it is not entirely clear that the Soviet policy has resulted in the expansion of the Indian public sector

[1] On this issue, we have more to say in the later chapters on Export Policy.

[2] This asymmetry in Western aid practice underlines the rather perverse rule that the rich can, but the poor cannot, behave as they wish to: that somehow the payments difficulties of the rich are 'exogenous' and justify aid-tying but those of the poor are 'government-made' and do not.

beyond what domestic policy would anyway have wanted it to be. The United States, with its matching ideological passion but opposed ideology, has had more catholic disbursements. Its preference for the private sector has shown through, however, in provisions such as the Cooley Amendment Loans from P.L. 480 counterpart funds which are exclusively made to private sector firms: again, however, it is almost impossible to argue that this has resulted in anything more than the wiping out of these counterpart funds in a manner agreeable to average American opinion.

(c) Pattern of utilization

Before we examine the actual pattern of utilization of foreign aid, we should enter the obvious *caveat* that the apparent utilization of aid for certain projects or commodities need not coincide with the projects and commodities which the recipient country finds it feasible to implement and import thanks to the inflow of aid. Aid utilized for a project may well have made it possible for another quite different project, otherwise marginal, to be included in the Plan.

None the less, we must content ourselves with the observable data. Which projects and programmes would have dropped out if aid had not been forthcoming at all or at the recorded level is an interesting question which it is impossible to answer meaningfully without making a host of speculative and untestable assumptions.[1] In any case, the pattern of actual utilization is interesting in itself, and it is indicative of the preferences of the donor countries, if not altogether of the recipient country.

Table 10.6 records the available information on the actual pattern of aid utilization during each Plan. The data are not in an ideal form: 'maintenance' imports are not distinguished from 'project' imports and furthermore P.L. 480 proceeds are shown, not against commodities but assigned to the sectors to which the counterpart funds are allocated.

These factors affect primarily the category 'Industrial Development', which received the bulk of maintenance aid (which has

---

[1] We shall, however, have to concern ourselves with such broad questions when reviewing the critiques of the foreign aid programme from both the extreme 'Left' and the extreme 'Right' in the country.

TABLE 10.6

DISTRIBUTION OF FOREIGN LOANS/CREDITS BY PURPOSE (FIGURES IN BRACKETS SHOW PERCENTAGE OF DISTRIBUTION)
(In Rs. million)

Loans/credits	Authorized				Utilized			
	Up to end of First Plan (1)	During Second Plan (2)	During Third Plan (3)	Total 1 to 3	Up to end of First Plan (1)	During Second Plan (2)	During Third Plan (3)	Total 1 to 3
1. Railway development	156 (6·9)	1,952 (15·1)	1,392 (6·1)	3,500 (9·2)	156 (12·3)	1,432 (20·1)	1,850 (10·1)	3,438 (12·8)
2. Power projects	196 (8·6)	623 (4·8)	2,414 (10·5)	3,233 (8·5)	121 (9·6)	293 (4·1)	1,529 (8·3)	1,943 (7·2)
3. Iron and steel projects^a	786 (34·7)	2,242 (17·4)	2,078 (9·1)	5,106 (13·4)	27 (2·1)	2,541 (35·6)	1,049 (5·7)	3,617 (13·5)
4. Ports and development	—	205 (1·6)	186 (0·8)	391 (1·0)	—	68 (0·9)	180 (1·0)	248 (0·9)
5. Transport and communications	—	148 (1·2)	930 (4·1)	1,078 (2·9)	—	90 (1·3)	759 (4·1)	849 (3·2)
6. Industrial development	193 (8·5)	7,555 (58·7)	15,266 (66·7)	23,104 (60·5)	23 (1·8)	2,554 (35·8)	12,836 (69·6)	15,413 (57·5)
7. Agricultural development	34 (1·5)	—	621 (2·7)	655 (1·7)	34 (2·7)	—	225 (1·2)	259 (1·0)
8. Wheat loans	903 (39·8)	157 (1·2)	—	1,060 (2·8)	903 (71·5)	157 (2·2)	—	1,060 (3·9)
TOTAL	2,268 (100)	12,882 (100)	22,887 (100)	38,037 (100)	1,264 (100)	7,135 (100)	18,428 (100)	26,827 (100)

^a Includes Orissa Iron Ore Project.

Source: Reserve Bank of India, *Report on Currency and Finance*, 1965–6 (1966), Statement 83. Also quoted in Streeten and Hill, op. cit., p. 334.

been of importance, as we shall see, mainly since 1964) and where also P.L. 480 counterpart funds are largely assigned. It is clear from Table 10.6 that, apart from commodity assistance, the overwhelming proportion of aid to India has gone directly into overheads (including harbours, power, and railways) and industrial projects (including iron and steel projects which have taken a sizeable share of total aid for industries). This is in keeping with, and indeed sharply underlines, the general Indian strategy for development as also the economic philosophies of the time which under-emphasized the *productive* significance of expenditure on education and other social services as also the role of agriculture.

II EFFICIENCY OF THE AID FLOW

While the composition of aid, principally between loans and grants, as also the terms (relating to grace period, maturity, and interest rates charged) of the loans determine the relevant magnitude of the aid flow, as contrasted with the unadjusted dollar values, the real worth or efficiency of this aid flow will also depend on the conditions imposed with respect to its utilization. These relate primarily to different forms of aid-tying: by project, by commodity, and by source. In point of fact, we should also subtract the cost associated with political strings, of which much has been made in India recently: this is an issue to which we turn in the next section where we treat the wider question as to whether India should have developed on the basis of aid programmes quite so large as she sought and accepted, especially during the Second and Third Plans.

(d) Lag between authorization and disbursement

Before, however, we discuss the alternative forms of aid-tying in this section, we should note the fact that the Indian aid programme has been characterized by a rather long lag between the authorization and the utilization of foreign aid. This lag, with its obvious implications for the efficiency of the aid programme, is also partly linked to the tying of aid by source and by project: hence it is best considered at this stage of our analysis.

If we refer back to Tables 10.1 and 10.2, and examine the

TABLE 10.7

UTILIZATION OF EXTERNAL ASSISTANCE
(In $ million)

	Loans	Grants	P.L. 480/665 third country currency assistance	Total
	(1)	(2)	(3)	(4)
1. Amount undisbursed as at the end of March 1961	1,375	60	1,256	2,691
2. Fresh authorization during				
1961/2	828	46	—	874
1962/3	1,250	30	91	1,371
1963/4	952	29	10	991
1964/5	1,035	52	473	1,560
1965/6	877	121	372	1,370
Total for Third Plan	4,943	278	947	6,168
3. Total available for utilization (1+2)	6,318	338	2,203	8,859
4. Utilization during				
1961/2	480	46	185	711
1962/3	644	31	258	933
1963/4	816	34	389	1,239
1964/5	1,019	43	458	1,520
1965/6	1,050	69	502	1,621
Total for Third Plan	4,009	223	1,792	6,024
5. Amount undisbursed at the end of March 1966 (3−4)	2,309	115	226[a]	2,651[a]
6. Fresh authorizations during				
1966/7	1,491	104	524	2,119
1967/8	615	21	324	960
Total (6)	2,106	125	848	3,079
7. Total (5+6)	4,415	240	1,074	5,730
8. Utilization during				
1966/7	900	126	480	1,506
1967/8	1,078	71	414	1,564
Total (8)	1,978	197	894	3,070
9. Balance at the end of March 1968 (7−8)	2,437	43	180 ·	2,660

[a] Outstanding balance excludes a sum of $184 million against which further imports of food under P.L. 480 are not expected.

(1) The constituent items may not always add up to the total due to rounding.
(2) P.L. 480/665 assistance represents rupee deposits effected against imports.

Source: Reserve Bank of India, *Reports on Currency and Finance;* compiled by Messrs. Gopal Behari and V. K. S. Nair at our request.

proportion of aid utilization to aid authorization during each Plan, the percentage rates are approximately 53, 56, and 98 per cent respectively. These figures, however, are treacherous and must be interpreted carefully. Thus, for example, the low rate of utilization in the Second Plan conceals the fact that authorizations for commodity assistance, to be utilized in the Third Plan, happened to be bunched at the end of the Second Plan: a fact which brings out the misleading character of rates of utilization based on Plan periods.[1] An alternative, though again not fully satisfactory, way of quantifying the lag leads to Table 10.8 where

TABLE 10.8
UTILIZATION OF LOANS: 1961–8

End of	Authorized and undisbursed (1)	Used in following year (2)	(2)/(1): Percentage (3)
March 1961	2,691	711	26·4
March 1962	2,854	933	32·7
March 1963	3,292	1,239	37·6
March 1964	3,044	1,520	49·3
March 1965	3,084	1,621	52·6
March 1966	2,833	1,506	53·2
March 1967	3,446	1,564	45·3
March 1968	2,842	—	—

Source: Calculated from Table 10.7.

the rate of utilization, defined as the percentage of the authorized but undisbursed aid at the end of the *preceding* year, is given for the Third Plan (with more detailed data in Table 10.7). It is interesting that this rate is in the range of only 26–53 per cent, while showing an improvement in the later years. Although no fully satisfactory measure of this lag is to be found in the released statistics, it is thus clear enough that there is indeed such a lag, and of significant dimensions.

The following quotes from the *Eleventh Report of the Estimates Committee* (1967–8) of the Fourth Lok Sabha, giving individual examples, are quite instructive (pp. 119–51):

[1] Adjusting for this factor, which would reduce the utilization figure for the Third Plan by Rs. 500 crores, would bring the percentage rate down from 98 per cent to below 80 per cent.

O

Agreement for a 'General line of credit' for $25 million was signed with the U.S. Ex-Im Bank on 21st August, 1964. The repayments in regard to the loan are to commence from 1st June, 1967, It is, however, noticed that as on 31st March, 1966 only $7·00 million were drawn against the credit.

Agreement for Ex-Im Bank credit of $27·00 million to Coromondel Fertilizers Ltd., was signed on 16th April, 1964 for the construction of a Fertilizer Plant at Vishakhapatnam. The repayment of loan is to commence from 30th June, 1968. By 31st March, 1966, however, only $8·15 million were drawn against the credit.

Large balances have been indicated as remaining undrawn on 31st March, 1966 against U.S. DLF/AID credit granted in 1963 for power projects as follows:

(In $ millions)

Project	Date of loan	Amount of loans	Amount drawn as on 31-3-1966
(a) Delhi 'C'—Thermal Power Extension Station	8-3-63	16·00	5·97
(b) Satpura Thermal Power Project	8-3-63	25·10	11·52
(c) Ramagundum Thermal Power	21-5-63	8·40	1·62

[The] Soviet Government had extended three credits for industrial projects during the Second and Third Plan periods. The credit for the Second Plan amounting to Rs. 59·53 crores was agreed to on 1–11–1957 while the two credits for the Third Plan aggregating Rs. 238·11 crores were extended at the beginning of the Plan: the first about 1½ years prior to the beginning of the Plan in September 1959 and the second at the beginning of the Plan period in February 1961. Till 31–3–1966, against the industrial credit authorised for the Second Plan, orders were placed with the Soviet authorities for 77 per cent of the value authorised while the actual drawals constituted only 73 per cent thereof. In the use of the industrial credits for the Third Plan, the value of orders placed and actual drawals till 31–3–1966 constituted only 65 per cent and 54 per cent respectively of the value authorised.

For German assistance for the Third Five-Year Plan (1961–6) amounting to Rs. 306·69 crores, including Rs. 1·43 crores for the import of fertilizers for which agreement was signed on 14 March 1966, the situation was as follows:

(In Rs. crores)

Item (1)	Amount authorized up to 31-3-66 (2)	Amount disbursed up to 31-3-66 (3)	Unutilized balances (2)–(3) (4)
1. Rourkela Refinancing	66·66	66·66	—
2. Rourkela Steel Plant Services and Maintenance Requirements	6·67	4·46	2·21
3. Rourkela Expansion	49·28	33·13	16·15
4. Cash Credits	28·58	28·58	—
5. Maintenance requirements including commodity assistance	42·08	25·61	16·47
6. Project financing	51·06	27·95	23·11
7. Direct loans to IFC, ICICI and NSIC	20·20	8·10	12·10
8. Balance of payment support for making downpayments for ships	3·35	3·35	
9. Suppliers' credits for ships and other purposes	38·81	8·62	30·19
	306·69	206·46	100·23

It was, in fact, concern at this lag that led the Indian Government to appoint the V. K. R. V. Rao Committee to investigate the causes of the slow utilization of aid and suggest remedies. As a result of the Rao Committee Report in 1964, and other investigations into individual aid-financed projects, it is possible to make certain observations on the efficiency implications of this lag although it is not possible to reach any quantitative assessment in this regard.

To begin with, we should note that the lag we are discussing is between authorization and disbursement. In addition, there is the lag, not always negligible and frequently afflicting many aid transactions, between *pledging* (usually done at the Consortium) and authorization. The Rao Committee has listed several examples of such lags ranging from four to twenty months, for aid from practically all sources.[1] It should be emphasized, however, that the responsibility for this lag is not to be attributed entirely to the donor countries. For instance, a telling example of delays in negotiations, resulting from tardiness at the Indian end, is provided

[1] *Report of the Committee on Utilization of External Assistance*, Ministry of Finance, Government of India, New Delhi, 1964; p. 8, in particular.

by the time taken in finalizing, in June 1966, the USAID credit for one of the units of the Durgapur Thermal Power Station. The Indian Government took more than six months to file the Draft Consultation Agreement with AID and more than three months to reply to AID queries. After the draft loan agreement was received from AID, four more months were allowed to lapse before the loan agreement was signed.[1] The problem of tardy execution, which is not exclusive to Indian bureaucracy, is particularly acute in India where the opportunity cost of time has long been negligible and social institutions, including the bureaucracy, appear to have adapted themselves to this situation over a period.

If we revert to the lag between authorization and utilization, the causes may again be allocated to both sides. The donors have made their contribution to the delays through their frequent insistence on source- and project-tying, whereas the Indian lack of planning at the project level and the heavy hand of bureaucratic restrictions on all economic activity in the organized sector appear to have contributed equally to this area of inefficiency in the aid process.

(1) The principal reason at the Indian end, and perhaps in overall delays, has been the lack of proper project planning during this period. This is reflected in the frequent absence of project blueprints or in availability of blueprints based on inaccurate data, at times leading to the adoption of defective designs and subsequently of alterations in these. In this connection, the Rao Committee remarks:

We have been impressed by the fact that the projects included in lists put forward to the Consortium are often not ready for immediate implementation in the event of funds being made available. In fact, there is a dearth of well conceived projects for which all the necessary preparations have been made for the placing of orders as soon as foreign exchange becomes available.[2]

Instances of slow utilization of aid resulting from inadequate project planning have been numerous. Thus the utilization of USAID credits of March and May 1963 for several power projects was delayed because of reasons such as delays in the finalization of

---

[1] Rao Committee Report, op. cit.   [2] Ibid., p. 13.

specifications and of procurement orders and contracts for want of drawings.[1]

Yet another example of lack of proper and advanced project planning resulting in the non-utilization of external assistance of the magnitude of Rs. 33 crores is provided by the bungling of loan agreements with the Ente Naxionale Indrocarburi (E.N.I.) signed on 29 August 1961, for meeting the foreign exchange costs of certain projects in the petroleum and petro-chemical industries. A sum of about Rs. 3·04 crores lapsed because additional projects could not be proposed for financing within the time limit of two years. The earlier proposals for financing thirteen projects amounting in aggregate to Rs. 42·67 crores were, on reassessment, revised and the requirements of these projects were put at Rs. 13·21 crores only. Some of the projects were dropped altogether because they were not considered economical. As the terms or the original (1961) agreement with the E.N.I. specified that no new projects, excepting those included in the agreement and its supplementary list, could be financed out of the credit, much of the credit had to be allowed to lapse.[2]

Again the utilization of the second I.D.A. loan for the Koyna Power Scheme, authorized in August 1962, was delayed because the basic decisions on the location of the dam and the proposed aluminium factory to which power was proposed to be supplied, were not taken.[3]

An interesting example in this genre, which illustrates a different type of possibility, relates to the disbursements from the I.D.A. credit of Rs. 3·81 crores, authorized in November 1961 for the Salanadi Irrigation Project in Orissa. The disbursements were stopped in May 1963 because the I.D.A. team which came to review the progress of the project noticed that considerable changes were made in the scope and design of the project by the project authorities (without prior intimation or clearance). These changes were necessitated because the data, on the basis of which the original design was adopted, were found to be inaccurate. While this example points to the need to have more flexible arrangements to handle unforeseen difficulties, it is nonetheless a reflection on

[1] *Eleventh Report of the Estimates Committee*, Fourth Lok Sabha, Ministry of Finance, 1967–8, p. 124. (This is hereafter referred to as *Eleventh Report of the Estimates Committee*.) One of the reasons mentioned here is also delay in clearance of goods at Indian ports.

[2] Ibid., pp. 179–80.   [3] Ibid., pp. 87–8.

the nature of the planning as also execution of an aid-financed project by India.

These instances of inadequate planning are all too common and reflect a weakness in Indian planning techniques which has frequently been noted by earlier observers;[1] and we shall have occasion to revert to this question later when we discuss industrial targeting and licensing. At this stage, however, we should make some qualifying observations. (i) While Indian planning of projects is certainly weaker, by all accounts, than it need be, the fact of the backwardness of the economy and 'learning by doing' in this area, as in others, needs to be remembered in evaluating the system. While this cannot condone the inefficiency we have noted, it would certainly put it into some perspective. (ii) Further, some delays must be regarded as inevitable in an aid process where the cost of investment in getting a project ready with blue prints for execution as soon as aid is authorized must be set against the cost of the probability that the necessary aid may not be forthcoming after all, or may be from a different source (and hence with different design) than planned for. This proposition also qualifies the recommendation of the Rao Committee that no project should be proposed for aid unless the feasibility report, both from the technological and financial aspects, has been completed.[2] (iii) Finally, we should note that some of the defects in designing have been the direct responsibility of *foreign* consultants, chosen either by India or by the donor countries. Thus, for example, the defective designing of the coking unit of the Barauni Oil Refinery, and the difficulties encountered in completing other units there, were responsible for delaying the full utilization of capacity by eighteen months. Similarly, the expensive 'over-building' (from a structural

---

[1] Cf. P. Streeten and M. Lipton, 'Two Types of Planning', in Streeten and Lipton, *The Crisis of Indian Planning*, who point to the tendency in Indian planning practice, during this period, to focus on 'the big aggregates of physical investment'. Several Indian economists, such as Professor D. R. Gadgil, have also long pointed to the related phenomenon of having detailed targets of exports, agricultural output etc. without any supporting set of economic policies *spelled out* to attain them.

[2] It is an interesting commentary on the bureaucratic tendency to delay matters that, while this recommendation of the Rao Committee was accepted by the Government as early as April 1964, the expert group set up by the Planning Commission to report on the *pro forma* which should be used for making the necessary evaluation was not submitted until May 1966 and it is not clear if any systematic action thereon has been taken yet.

point of view) of the Bokaro Steel Plant by the Soviet Union, since the Third Plan, pointed out by the Indian engineering firm M. N. Dastur & Co., was largely responsible for delays in the initiation of the work even though the aid pledge had come much earlier. Inadequate or inefficient project planning has thus not been characteristic exclusively of the Indian planners.

(2) The other variety of domestic factors accounting for the delays in utilization of aid has its roots in India's planning procedures which have relied, as we shall analyse at length in later chapters, on comprehensive controls in virtually all important spheres of economic activity during this period.

The most obvious illustration in this category is the delay imposed by the industrial and import licensing procedures of the Government. One of the relevant details here is the indigenous clearance requirement according to which permission to import the required item is given only if evidence is produced that the item is not produced domestically.[1] Illustrating the inefficiency in aid utilization that results from this requirement, the Rao Committee has referred to an extreme case of a dairy development scheme aided by the United Nations International Children Emergency Fund (UNICEF): the required cheese plant was not allowed to be imported as some components of cheese plants were made in India. Ultimately the Government, having lost the opportunity of getting it free from the aiding agency, ended up by *buying* it from abroad!

Delays in aid utilization have also resulted from the restrictions imposed by the Finance Ministry on public sector project authorities before they are allowed to place orders for equipment from abroad. Then there have been instances of delays arising from lack of co-ordination among various government agencies. For example, one of the blast furnaces of the Bhilai Steel Plant was completed in May 1966 but electric power was not made available to it from the Korba Power Station till the middle of November 1966 because there was a dispute about the price of coal to be supplied by the National Coal Development Corporation to the Korba Power Station managed by the Madhya Pradesh State Electricity Board: similar instances are not difficult to find in the case of delays in aid utilization.

These causes of delays, detailed by us so far, are almost certainly

[1] This cornerstone of Indian import policy is discussed at length in Chapter 16.

due to lack of efficiency, and have therefore an economic cost in so far as aid has positive social value and hence any delay in its utilization has a social cost. In assessing the magnitude of this loss, however, it is relevant to remember that the level of authorizations may well have an inverse relationship, at the margin, to the pace of aid utilization: it is easier to authorize aid when it is anticipated that all of it will not be utilized anyway.

In any event, it is an interesting question whether we should attach any such economic cost to delays in utilization which occur thanks to shortages in the economy, rather than directly due to governmental red-tape and bureaucratic inefficiencies. There are numerous instances, of course, of aid utilization being slowed down because of the shortage of complementary factors or inputs. A host of such factors was responsible, for example, for the late commissioning of the Security Paper Mill at Hoshangabad—a public sector concern financed with aid from the United Kingdom. The reasons ranged from shortages of building and other materials such as cement, steel, and copper to the difficulties encountered in getting suitable contractors and qualified personnel for senior appointments. Such shortages are endemic to any planned or unplanned system, although they could be accentuated by red tape and comprehensive, but ill-informed, restrictions. In so far as aid utilization was delayed owing to such factors, it reflected only the waste inherent in the operation of an economic system under uncertainty. However, in so far as this utilization could have been stepped up if only the aid had not been assigned to the projects which were experiencing delays and could have been utilized for other purposes, there *was* an avoidable element of waste. This assignment was, either by domestic policy or because of the donor's aid procedure itself, a result of the commodity- or project-tying of aid. The latter possibility takes us directly into the question of aid-tying.

(3) Delays arising from aid-tying by source and by project are not difficult to find in Indian practice. A particularly extreme example is provided by the slow utilization of the credits from Canada, extended through the Export and Credit Insurance Corporation during 1964 and 1965. The Canadian authorities insisted that (*a*) the goods be bought in Canada, (*b*) the goods should have a certain prearranged minimum percentage of Canadian-content, and (*c*) the contract between the Indian importer and the Canadian sup-

plier must precede the credit agreement with the Export Credit Insurance Corporation. Explaining the reasons for the slow utilization of these credits, the representative of the Ministry of Finance reasoned thus with some exasperation before the Lok Sabha Estimates Committee:

It is the reverse of what happens elsewhere. Therefore, with having to locate what Canada produces that we want and also considering the price factor therein, then having to check up whether it has the appropriate Canadian-content—otherwise to look about for something else—having to enter into supply contracts between the local importer and the Canadian exporter before we go in for the Government financing agreement, I should say that—after all these operations—it is a surprise that we have got the agreements signed so quickly.[1]

Clearly, source-tying in particular imposes difficulties in the nature of delays involved in finding suitable, low-cost, and reliable suppliers, frequently from unfamiliar sources.

In addition, the Rao Committee indicated a rather different kind of way in which aid-tying *by project* may have slowed down the pace of aid utilization in India. It argued that, since project aid is less valuable, in view of excess capacity, than maintenance aid, the slow utilization of overall aid is due to a presumably reluctant governmental response to the available aid which is biased towards projects. However, this argument seems inconsistent with the fact that few loans remain *totally* unutilized while nearly all are utilized but at a slow pace. It is more likely that the slower utilization of project, as distinct from maintenance, aid is due to the inadequate and sloppy project planning which we have discussed earlier and which the Rao Committee itself noted. The argument for shifting to more maintenance aid would thus have to turn on other grounds than the fact of its greater pace of utilization.[2] Indeed, this leads us directly into the questions relating to the costs of different forms of aid-tying and their incidence in India.

---

[1] *Eleventh Report of the Estimates Committee*, p. 169.

[2] Indeed, if (i) inadequate project planning is the cause of delayed utilization of aid, (ii) this planning will improve as the delayed utilization of aid is seen to be socially expensive, (iii) the rate of investment in India is directly related to the implementation of these projects, and (iv) the rate of investment is regarded as the objective, then there might even be a 'second-best' case for tying aid, at least at the margin, to projects rather than giving it for maintenance imports.

(e) Aid-tying

We can distinguish between three forms of aid-tying. Aid may be tied by source; it may be tied as between projects and non-project uses; and it may be tied to specific commodities, including the extreme case of the so-called commodity assistance under P.L. 480 programmes. Naturally, there can be *double*-tying: both by project and source, for example.

In analysing the costs of aid-tying, in each of these ways, we generally assume that aid given without any such restrictions has no corresponding inefficiency. However, even when aid is totally untied in these ways, it is perfectly possible that, for purposes of aid administration, the donor may require that it be assigned to any specific form of utilization, left entirely to the recipient country's convenience. In a world of perfect foresight, or full flexibility of reassignment in case the unfolding economic situation requires it, there should be no cost to such assignment. However, in the absence of full flexibility for reassignment, the effects will be to reduce the efficiency, and/or utilization, of the aid flow, once earmarked for certain uses. A good example of what can happen is provided by the I.B.R.D. loan of $35 million to the Government of India for the maintenance and expansion of coal production in the private sector during the Third Plan. The utilization of this loan was inordinately slow: the private sector offtake was unenthusiastic even though the Government extended credit for raising rupee resources, there being an unforeseen general lack of demand for coal.[1]

In point of fact, of course, donors impose restrictions directly with respect to source, project, and commodity tying, instead of giving general-purpose aid which can be *freely* assigned, either with or without the flexibility of reassignment, to any source or use by the recipient country. What are the costs of such aid-tying and how important has such aid-tying been, in practice, for India? To these questions, we now turn.

---

[1] Of course, this specific example relates to project-tied aid by the I.B.R.D However, even if the I.B.R.D. had given general-purpose aid, requiring that *India* should assign it to some use optimally and then India had assigned it to coal production, not to be reassigned thereafter, the results would have been identical as far as utilization is concerned.

(1) *Source-tying of aid.*

The tying of aid by source is notoriously difficult to detect, as it operates in a variety of ways.[1] (i) There are *formal* restrictions which contractually require the recipient country to spend the aid funds for importing goods and services only from the designated source(s). In order to implement such tying, the aid has to be disbursed in such a way as to give rise to directly identifiable imports, whose source or origin can be ascertained to ensure that the formal restrictions on procurement by source are not violated. Where, however, such direct identification is impossible, this has led to secondary, formal restrictions or informal and indirect restrictions. The secondary, formal restrictions, which are deployed when there is local cost component of project aid or a straight-forward budgetary grant, generally take the form of restricted account arrangements under which the recipient country is re-quired to spend the aid received on specified source(s). The United States has operated such arrangements, particularly in order to ensure that, although the aid recipients are allowed to use aid funds to procure from eight specified developing countries (including India), the receipts from such procurements are *even-tually* spent by these eight countries on U.S. goods and services. (ii) Among the class of formally restricted aid, we may also include *official* credits such as U.S. Export–Import Bank Credits which are automatically linked to exports from the donor source, as also commodity assistance under programmes such as P.L. 480. (iii) Tying of aid by informal methods is also quite important. The most common such practice is to impress on the recipient that any departure from *de facto* tying by source in procurement would be short-sighted and would cause difficulties in continuing or even granting aid. (iv) Finally, the subtlest form of tying, not infrequent in its incidence, is best described as indirect and takes essentially two forms:

23. One method is to treat the aid flow as part of an over-all trade arrangement, as is done by the socialist countries. An alternative method,

---

[1] Part of the analysis that follows has been developed further in J. Bhagwati, 'The Tying of Aid', UNCTAD Secretariat, New York, TD/7/Supp. 4; Item 126(ii) of the agenda of the New Delhi Second UNCTAD Conference, February 1968; reprinted in J. Bhagwati and R. S. Eckaus (eds.), *Foreign Aid*.

practised by the French authorities, is to couple the aid flow with provisions under which the aid is to be spent on French goods and services while France 'reciprocally' purchases from the former French-African territories on a preferential basis. In fact, the entire Franc Zone arrangements, with their monetary and trading implications, are generally recognized as making the question of informal or formal tying somewhat academic. It is interesting to note, in addition, that France has nevertheless resorted to formal tying restrictions in cases where these *de facto* tying arrangements were considered to be inadequate. Thus, for example, the policy of the *Fonds d'Aide et de Cooperation* (FAC) has been to tie aid disbursements explicitly via financing conventions signed with local governments: nearly 20 per cent of total French bilateral and multilateral aid was estimated as being informally and formally tied in 1961.

24. Another method, which seems to have gained ground whenever formal and informal restrictions have been considered undiplomatic, is to finance only those commodities and/or projects where the donor country is considered to have a decided advantage in tendering or supplying the specified items. This policy, widely believed to be now practised by the Federal Republic of Germany (and we shall have more to say about this later), can be implemented by letting it be known generally and informally that the chance of securing aid would improve if the project or commodities required were 'suitably chosen' so as to result in directly identifiable imports from the donor country despite competitive tendering.

25. Variations of the preceding policy may also be mentioned. Thus, a donor country wishing to avoid formal and informal tying may reduce the amount of 'local cost' financing or purely budgetary-support grants that it will make. Also, it may deliberately direct projects towards using materials imported from the donor country even though they could have been devised to use cheaper domestic materials that would have necessitated 'local cost' financing.[1]

It is clearly difficult therefore to quantify meaningfully the extent of source-tying of aid. At minimum, we can argue that the multilateral-agency loans, from I.B.R.D. and I.D.A., have always been free from source-tying of aid wherever they have been made, including India. These agencies not merely permit but require global tendering—which is, however, restricted to member countries—and the contracts are awarded on the basis of the bids.[2]

[1] Bhagwati, 'The Tying of Aid', op. cit., pp. 6–7.
[2] Hence non-tying of aid is not the same as arguing that the recipient country has full *autonomy* in making purchases. This distinction between non-tying

When it comes to loans and grants from bilateral sources, however, the degree of source-tying is almost impossible to assess. However, there is little doubt that it has increased, during the Third Plan, to a fairly comprehensive proportion, thanks to the growing measures for source-tying taken since 1959 by the major donor country, the United States (as can be seen from Table 10.9).

TABLE 10.9
BREAKDOWN OF EXTERNAL ASSISTANCE (EXCLUDING U.S. COMMODITY ASSISTANCE) INTO SOURCE-TIED AND UNTIED CATEGORIES
(In Rs. million)

Period	Total assistance	Source-tied		Untied	
		Value	%	Value	%
(1)	(2)	(3)	(4)	(5)	(6)
I. During the Second Five-Year Plan (i.e. from 1.4.56 to 31.3.61)					
(i) Authorized	14,004	10,356	73·9	3,648	26·1
(ii) Utilized	8,854	5,868	66·3	2,986	33·7
II. During the Third Five-Year Plan (i.e. from 1.4.61 to 31.3.66)					
(i) Authorized	24,853	20,675	83·2	4,178	16·8
(ii) Utilized	20,143	16,610	82·5	3,533	17·5

Note: These estimates include (untied) assistance from I.B.R.D. and I.D.A.
Source: Compiled by Messrs. Gopat Behari and V. K. S. Nair at the authors' request.

Thus while, during the Second Plan, some of the D.L.F. loans were partly untied, the Third Plan witnessed a steady and complete elimination of this practice, under the growing pressure of the U.S. payments deficit.[1] In the matter of grant financing, the trend has been parallel. Since 1960 procurement under U.S. grants has been restricted to the United States and less developed countries

by source associated with global tendering and recipient's autonomy comes up whenever the recipient would prefer to buy from *indigenous* sources, even though they are not competitive: a question that crops up often in India whose entire import policy is based, as we shall see, on the principle of automatic preference for indigenous products. The World Bank has also been recently seized by this problem and discussions have been held on what cost-wise preference, if any, should be given to indigenous bidders.

[1] Among the rare exceptions, permitted at discretion by waiver on reference to inter-agency committees and the A.I.D. Administrator, is the D.L.F. loan for the Birsingpur Thermal Power Project during the Third Plan.

(in the 'free world'). In March 1966 the restrictions were further stepped up and procurement has since been restricted to the United States and only eight developing countries (Taiwan, India, Morocco, Pakistan, Philippines, South Korea, Singapore, and Thailand) where, again, payments for procurement have been tied to the United States through special letter of credit arrangements.[1]

At the same time, the weight of P.L. 480 assistance in the overall U.S. aid programme has increased to very high levels in the Second and Third Plans: and this is automatically source-tied. The same is true for Ex-Im Bank loans.

Further, both the United Kingdom and Germany have also increased their tying over this period, the former owing to payments deficits and the latter (*via* indirect restrictions) because competitive aid-tying has been difficult to rule out in the face of export pressure groups and domestic public opinion. Moreover, the growing Soviet-bloc aid has been entirely source-tied. The conclusion is thus inescapable that the degree of source-tying in aid to India has, for the bilateral aid flows, become nearly comprehensive through the Third Plan period.

How expensive has this source-tying of aid been? This is a notoriously difficult question to answer. It is clear, for example, that *de jure* tying is consistent with *de facto* untying, via exploitation of substitution possibilities. Furthermore, we must distinguish between the irreducible, minimum cost of aid-tying by source (assuming that India had maximized the use of available opportunities to untie aid *de facto* and to minimize the costs of tying in general) and the additional costs accruing from the failure to exploit such opportunities.[2]

While, however, a close look at this problem has been attempted for Pakistan by Haq, there has been no similar attempt in India to put a quantitative estimate on the excess-costs imposed by source-tying of aid.[3] On the other hand, we can make a number of observations of some importance in this area.

---

[1] J. Bhagwati, 'The Tying of Aid', op. cit.

[2] J. Bhagwati, op. cit., pp. 20–32, for an extended treatment of these questions.

[3] Cf. Mahbub ul Haq, 'Tied Credits: A Quantitative Analysis'. Indian spokesmen have been articulate in making assertions of 30–35 per cent excess cost from source-tying. In fact, however, they have no empirical basis, except stray project 'estimates', for making such claims. Attempts by us to get proper estimates made, via UNCTAD, failed to elicit response from the Indian Government.

It is well understood that double-tying, by source and by commodity or project, increases the cost of aid-procurement and also creates the prospect of monopolistic pricing by the aid-financed suppliers. In this connection it is pertinent to note that, as far as maintenance imports are concerned, the Indian import licensing system (which we discuss at length in Chapters 15 and 16) itself has actively contributed to such double-tying. Indian import licences have specified both source (to satisfy the source-tying) and commodity (to satisfy its own priority criteria), thereby bringing about *de facto* double-tying. It is perfectly possible for the authorities to get around such double-tying, while satisfying both source-tying and priorities, by merely making it possible for the licensees to source-swap licences in the market.

Thus, for example, there is no reason why, consistent with both source-tying and priorities being satisfied, a recipient of a licence to import tractors from the United Kingdom should not be allowed to swap his licence, for an equal value, with the licensee of imports of lathes from Germany so that the former can import tractors from Germany and the latter can import lathes from the United Kingdom. Making such swaps possible would enable the licensees to import from the cheapest possible sources, subject to the *overall* source and commodity-specification constraints, while also preventing the grant of monopoly power to suppliers (e.g. to United Kingdom tractor suppliers and German lathe suppliers in our example). We cannot help concluding, therefore, that the Indian import régime itself made the costs of aid-tying greater than they need have been.

Where, however, the choice of projects and commodities was required from the donor's side, how expensive was this? It is impossible to determine quantitatively how far the choice of projects and commodities has been determined by India's convenience and needs. Interviews suggest, however, that the Indian experience in this regard has been generally favourable, both with the Soviet bloc and with the Consortium donors. John Lewis's detailed account of the manner in which the AID traditionally 'ticks off' projects, against which the P.L. 480 counterpart funds are assigned, from a list whose compilation is left virtually to the Indian Government is considered to be more or less typical of the general situation in this regard.[1] Furthermore, 'switching' has generally been

---

[1] Cf. John P. Lewis, *Quiet Crisis in India*, op. cit., Chapter 11. On the other hand, recently there have been contractual restrictions, requiring that a

permissible, essentially via the Consortium meetings and between Consortium and the Soviet bloc in turn.

On the other hand, there is little doubt that excess costs have persisted. While the Government have not so far made necessary estimates of the *observable* cost of aid-tying, as we have already noted, in the sense of the excess cost of the actual bundle of aid-financed goods bought from different sources as has been done by Haq for Pakistan,[1] there is much scattered evidence that aid-financed goods could have been purchased considerably more cheaply from alternative sources. This evidence comes mainly from industry. Thus Deepak Lal, who has examined in depth the excess prices paid by the chemicals sector, using data supplied by Imperial Chemical Industries in India, finds significant loss levels.[2] Similarly, the market quotations for Soviet-bloc licences to import dyes and chemicals have been sold at a discount, in relation to convertible-currency-area licences, indicating a margin of loss around 30–40 per cent. Furthermore, Honavar, who has examined the 'non-price' aspects of the aid programme to India, notes in particular the loss of economies of scale in maintenance and inventories which follows from many plants having managed to acquire bits and pieces from different sources, thus giving the appearance of 'international exhibitions' of machinery.[3] In particular, this has been the consequence of tied credits coming from sources such as Ex-Im Bank, Japanese Yen Credits, and other credits offered by export-group-prompted official agencies.

(2) *Project-tying of aid.*

In the Indian context, it has often been argued that the costs imposed by source-tying have been matched by the fact that aid has

---

large fraction of the counterpart funds be used for agricultural development: although, even here, this requirement matches Indian objectives and is not considered a binding constraint.

[1] This observed cost would include, of course, the avoidable costs arising from the recipient's own failure to maximize switching and minimize procurement prices despite tying. Moreover, it is clear that excess cost measured thus will generally overestimate or underestimate the *compensating* flow of aid that would make the recipient country as well off under tied aid policy as it would be if the aid flow were untied instead: the so-called Hicksian compensating variation. Cf. Bhagwati, 'The Tying of Aid', op. cit., Annex III.

[2] D. Lal, 'The Costs of Aid Tying: A Study of India's Chemical Industry' UNCTAD Secretariat, New York, 1968.

[3] R. M. Honavar, 'Industrial Efficiency and Aid Tying', Economic Development Institute, I.B.R.D., Washington, Mimeographed, 1967.

overwhelmingly been available for projects rather than non-project purposes. Whether this thesis is valid or not (and it certainly seems likely in view of the considerable shortage of imported inputs and spares, through the Third Plan, associated with excess capacity in several import-using industries)[1] it is indeed true that non-project, non-commodity-assistance aid to India has enjoyed a significantly large share in the total aid flow only since 1963/4. As Table 10.10 further shows,[2] non-project aid moved up sharply during 1965/6 to over half the pledged aid flow from the Consortium, increasing yet further in 1967 (when, in fact, some influential Indian economists began to complain reversely that India was getting too much maintenance and too little project aid). It may be noted that non-project aid during the Third Plan has come exclusively from the Consortium members.

Non-project aid, apart from commodity assistance, falls into two categories: (i) that which is given as general balance of payments support, including financing the repayment of earlier debt; and (ii) that which is given for imports of raw materials, components, and spares. The former includes loans such as that received from West Germany in 1961/2 for balance of payments assistance and again from 1961 onwards, for almost every year, to finance repayments of credit for the Rourkela Steel Plant. In fact, the *net* amount of non-project aid available for maintenance purposes is exaggerated, especially as aid repayments and interest have begun to reach sizeable dimensions beginning with the Third Plan.

Why this preference on the part of the donors, for project aid? Among the most obvious reasons have been:

(i) The greater political impact of projects as against general balance of payments aid: Indians talk of the British Durgapur Steel Plant, not of the Kipping Loans.

(ii) The desire to make certain that particular projects, considered

---

[1] We have deliberately refrained from reproducing the excess capacity *figures* published from the Ministry of Commerce and Industry. These are extremely unreliable, thanks to bad methodology, unclear concepts, and poor maintenance.

[2] Since a way in which more aid can be made to finance 'maintenance' is to redefine projects so as to include the supply of such items over a period and since this has undoubtedly been done lately by some aid donors for India, the estimates of maintenance aid in Table 10.10 must be regarded as slightly on the low side.

P

NON-PROJECT ELEMENT IN LOANS AUTHORIZED FOR INDIA UP TO THE END OF THIRD PLAN

(In Rs. million)

	Up to end of First Plan, i.e. up to 1955/6	During Second Plan, 1956/7–1960/1	During Third Plan					Total
			1961/2	1962/3	1963/4	1964/5	1965/6	
1. Total loans authorized	2,269	12,789	3,941	5,952	4,553	4,929	4,175	23,530
2. Of which non-project allocations	Nil	2,471	1,169	2,748	1,833	1,434	2,512	9,696
3. 2 as percentage of 1	Nil	19·3	29·7	46·2	40·4	29·1	60·2	41·2

Note: Adjustments have been made to eliminate the cancelled fractions of original loans.

Source: Compiled by Messrs. Gopal Behari and V. K. S. Nair, Department of Economic Affairs, Ministry of Finance, at the authors' request.

beneficial, are *definitely* implemented; and this aid-linkage would ensure at some stage.[1]

(iii) The desire to finance only priority projects: which constitutes, in general, the fallacy of misplaced concreteness;

(iv) The exigencies of aid administrations; as John Lewis has argued with respect to the project-tying of U.S. aid:

> Quite plainly the strongest factor . . . is simply the desire of the United States government, in the interests of adhering to its own procedural standards, to retain substantial accountability and control over United States expenditures. Such retention is constitutionally and politically required—the United States Congress being unwilling to make a larger delegation of its spending power to the government of India than it is to the government of the United States. Moreover, regardless of the legalities and politics of the matter, most conscientious United States aid officials are unwilling to make the . . . blanket assumption that Indian planning is uniformly sound or, even less, that the planned development scheme will be faithfully executed in all its particulars. They insist on retaining some right to participate in decisions made as to Indian uses of American funds and some right to review the results. And these impulses, combined with the mixture of American diffidence and Indian aloofness that has kept the United States government at arm's length from general development planning in India, have strongly inclined United States officials toward discrete, manageable, and measurable projects in which they can satisfy their own requirements for program and administrative review with a minimum of intergovernmental embarrassment.[2]

And finally, but perhaps least important:

(v) The expectation that additionality from source-tying would follow more easily with suitable project-tying; and, in some cases, the fact that suitable project-tying combined with source-tying,

---

[1] In this connection, we may also note Lewis's, op. cit. (p. 276), argument that an important reason for preferring project-tied assistance in India would be the fact that 'it is far easier to package together extensive, meaningful technical assistance with project-oriented commodity assistance than with general balance-of-payments support, and second, . . . that the Indians are inclined to underestimate their needs for technical assistance. To the extent that the United States can effectively staff such arrangements, it would be greatly to the Indians' advantage for us to follow the Soviet example and press them into more such capital-cum-technical assistance package deals.' This argument does not *explain* U.S. project-tying but constitutes a *recommendation* for it by Lewis, writing in 1962. As such it ignores the possibility that there might be alternative ways of getting the Indians to accept more technical assistance than project-tying; and that these alternatives may be cheaper to the Indians.

[2] Lewis, op. cit., p. 276.

could get contracts for the export pressure groups actively interested in the grant in aid.

(3) *Commodity assistance to India.*

Among the most controversial forms of aid to India has been commodity assistance, which has almost entirely come to India under the U.S. aid programme.

TABLE 10.11
IMPORTS UNDER TITLE I, P.L. 480
(Since the beginning of the programme in India)

	Agreements signed to December 1967		Commodity arrivals to September 30 1967
	Programmed quantity in thousand metric tons[a]	Value in million dollars	Approximate quantity in thousand metric tons[a]
Wheat	45,912·2	2,816·4	40,262·4
Feed grains	5,242·3	264·4	4,142·0
Rice	1,748·1	208·1	1,760·6
Cotton	3,258·0[b]	374·7	2,283·7[b, c]
Tallow	80·0	15·4	74·1
Tobacco	7·2	16·6	6·6[d]
Non-fat dry milk	20·9	3·6	21·0
Soybean/vegetable oil	296·7	74·6	154·2[e]
Evaporated milk	13·0	4·1	14·99
Whole milk powder	0·23	0·3	0·23
Cheese (processed)	0·08	0·1	0·10
Canned fruit	0·40	0·1	0·42
Total market value	—	3,778·4	
Ocean transportation	—	443·5[f]	
Total, including ocean transportation	—	4,221·9	

Notes:
[a] Programmed quantities are based on prices at time of agreement. Arrivals are based on actual quantities purchased, shipped, and received, and vary from the programmed amounts with price fluctuations.
[b] Cotton is reported in thousand Indian Bales (392 lb. each).
[c] Arrivals through 31 August 1967.
[d] Arrivals through 31 July 1967.
[e] 146·1 soybean oil and 8·1 cottonseed oil.
[f] This figure also included ocean transportation differentials for which the Commodities Credit Corporation is not reimbursed.
Source: U.S. Information Service, *Fact Sheet on United States Economic Assistance to India*, New Delhi, 22 July 1968; reproduced in Sundaram, op. cit.

Since the first Indo-U.S. agreement was signed in August 1956, under Title I of Public Law 480 (the U.S. Agricultural Development and Assistance Act enacted in 1954), thirteen agreements were signed up to December 1967 for the import of diverse commodities to the value of $4,221·2 million. As Table 10.11 shows, wheat has been the dominant imported commodity under these agreements.[1] In addition, there have been imports worth $443·6 million (up to July 1968) under Title II which authorizes famine relief and donations of food. The imports under these (Title I) P.L. 480 agreements involve payment in non-convertible Indian rupees for the f.o.b. value[2] and 50 per cent of the ocean freight incurred for transporting the commodities from the United States to India.

The considerable magnitude of commodity aid to India has inevitably led to controversy in India as to its impact on the Indian economy. Two major questions have been discussed in this context: the effect of the accumulating counterpart funds; and the impact of food supplies on the growth of Indian agriculture.

The former question has raised serious doubts at the political level. Although, as we have already noted, the bulk (over 80 per cent) of the counterpart funds were given away as grants and long-term loans to the Indian Government (Table 10.12), the remaining counterpart funds have been accumulating rapidly (in view of the massive size of the P.L. 480 programme) and are, in principle, expendable by the U.S. Government within India. It is felt by radical opinion in India that the desire to prevent excessive accumulation leads the Indian Government to sanction U.S. expenditure (from these funds) on sensitive areas such as education which would otherwise be closely guarded from penetration by ideologically oriented foreign powers.[3]

---

[1] The details of these agreements have been stated succinctly in K. Sundaram, *Some Economic Aspects of P.L. 480 Imports in Indian Economic Development*, Ph.D. Thesis, University of Delhi, September 1968, Chapter I.

[2] There was always a provision, however, for conversion of a small fraction of these counterpart funds for specified purposes. This portion was 3 per cent for agreements prior to June 1967 (although only 0·7 per cent was so converted) and was changed to 20 per cent thereafter. Cf. Sundaram, op. cit., p. 2, for more details.

[3] This question surfaced prominently when the intention to start an Indo-U.S. Education Foundation, with a vast sum of P.L. 480 counterpart funds as its capital and with interest thereon to be spent annually on Indian education, was announced by President Johnson during Prime Minister Mrs. Gandhi's

TABLE 10.12
PROGRAMMED USE OF P.L. 480 (TITLE I) COUNTERPART FUNDS
(In $ 1,000)

Agreement dates (as supplemented and amended)	Grants to Government of India	Loans to private enterprises	Loans to Government of India	U.S. Government uses	Total
29.8.1956	54,000 (15·23)	—	226,256 (63·81)	74,300 (20·96)	354,556 (100·00)
23.6.1958	—	13,819 (25·00)	33,377 (60·38)	8,081 (14·62)	55,277 (100·00)
26.9.1958	37,500 (14·44)	65,000 (25·02)	129,700 (49·92)	27,600 (10·62)	259,800 (100·00)
13.11.1959	119,110 (39·99)	14,910 (5·00)	119,110 (39·99)	44,740 (15·02)	297,870 (100·00)
4.5.1960	577,565 (42·16)	68,555 (5·01)	577,565 (42·16)	146,115 (10·67)	1,369,800 (100·00)
1.5.1962	—	393 (1·00)	34,977 (89·00)	3,930 (10·00)	39,300 (100·00)
20.11.1962	—	5,155 (5·00)	87,635 (85·00)	10,310 (10·00)	103,100 (100·00)
30.11.1962	—	255 (5·00)	4,338 (85·00)	510 (10·00)	5,103 (100·00)
30.9.1964	—	80,740 (6·80)	911,893 (76·80)	194,727 (16·40)	1,187,360 (100·00)
20.2.1967	29,700 (22·00)	6,750 (5·00)	87,750 (65·00)	10,800 (8·00)	135,000 (100·00)
24.6.1967	—	4,390 (5·00)	76,386 (87·00)	7,027 (8·00)	87,800 (100·00)
12.9.1967	—	3,375 (5·00)	58,725 (87·00)	5,400 (8·00)	67,500 (100·00)
30.12.1967	—	8,430 (5·00)	146,682 (87·00)	13,488 (8·00)	168,600 (100·00)
TOTAL	817,875	271,772	2,494,394	547,028	4,131,066
PER CENT	19·8	6·6	60·4	13·2	100·00

Note: Figures in brackets represent percentages of the respective row-totals.
Source: *Fact-Sheet on United States Economic Assistance to India*, 22 July 1968; reproduced in Sundaram, op. cit.

The latter question, concerning the impact on Indian agriculture, has been more widely debated in India. There are basically two possible criticisms of the P.L. 480 programme: firstly, that India was given more P.L. 480 aid than she wanted; and secondly, that India wanted (and obtained) more P.L. 480 aid than was good for her.

It is plausible that, in the early years of the P.L. 480 programme,

---

visit to the United States in 1966. Several Indian intellectuals, quite aware that the primary intention was to immobilize the bulk of the P.L. 480 funds, nonetheless objected strenuously to this project which would have annually spent more funds on Indian education than the Indian Government itself, thus lending itself to the possibility of unprecedented ideological penetration of the educational system; and the project was eventually shelved.

the ready availability of surplus agricultural commodities from the United States, by way of aid, prompted recipient countries such as Pakistan and India to plan the absorption of more such food imports than they would have cared to if the same value of foreign aid were forthcoming in an untied form. A lower growth of domestic agriculture and a correspondingly larger absorption of agricultural commodities from abroad, via P.L. 480 programmes, may have led to a larger net availability and absorption of foreign aid than otherwise. This argument has some degree of plausibility in view of the large surpluses in the United States at the time of India's Second Plan. The domestic counterpart of this argument has been the occasional criticism levelled against the Government, alleging that it has disposed of P.L. 480 stocks on the domestic market, even when there was no sharp rise in food prices to worry about, merely in order to raise resources: thus depressing the incentive to invest in agriculture.[1] In either case, however, we are not persuaded by the available evidence as to the validity, at least at a significant level, of these critiques.

Indian absorption (and release on the domestic market) of increasing amounts of P.L. 480 surpluses was promoted, in the ultimate analysis, by the desire to keep the market prices of foodgrains from rising with politically uncomfortable consequences especially in urban areas. The really meaningful and important question therefore seems to us to be whether this level of absorption was desirable.[2]

Those critics who have answered this question in the negative have focused on two different kinds of questions. On the one hand, it has been argued that the growth of Indian agriculture was impeded by the very fact of the aid-financed imports of surplus commodities; and that Indian agricultural growth would have been more adequate to her needs in the absence of the imports. On the other hand, it has been claimed that, even if there had been a continuing shortage (at some acceptable price), this should have been met by procurement of foodgrains and distribution thereof on an equitable basis: that there was enough food in the country

---

[1] This has been alleged, for example, by K. N. Raj, *Indian Economic Growth: Performance and Prospects*, op. cit.

[2] In answering this omnibus question, we would have to reach some judgement on the issue as to the relationship between P.L. 480 aid and *total* aid. We suspect that more P.L. 480 aid was not at the expense of other U.S. aid, within relevant margins for most of our period.

to go round without having to accept more food aid from abroad.[1]

We are persuaded that the former view is broadly correct, although there are qualifications to be noted. A policy providing better terms of trade for agriculture *in toto* is unlikely to have produced very significant production response, in so far as the evidence showing high response relates generally to acreage and output shifts between crops rather than to acreage and output response of agriculture as a whole.[2] Furthermore, a policy of providing higher price incentives to farmers would have involved raising food prices (among other things) for the urban consumers: hence, given the political constraints which clearly weighed in policy-making, the policy would have involved the implementation of a suitable subsidization programme to safeguard the real incomes of the low-income, urban consumers. Finally, we may note that, as a supplement to seeking an increment in agricultural output via direct price incentives, the Government could have increased financial and organizational allocations to agriculture.[3] While there has been considerable scepticism in India with respect to the productivity of such increases in expenditures, there is little doubt that increased resource allocations to agriculture would have yielded returns commensurate with returns in alternative investments. It seems to us that P.L. 480 aid was indeed carried too far, in practice, and that shifts in resource allocation to agriculture, involving both increased governmental outlays and also augmented private outlays following upon better agricultural terms of trade (with insulation of low-income urban groups through appropriate subsidization programmes), would have been in the economic interest of the country.[4]

[1] For a more detailed review of these questions, we refer the reader to Bhagwati and Chakravarty, op. cit., Part II. We make here only a few, pertinent comments.

[2] Professor M. L. Dantwala has made this point with cogency in 'Incentives and Disincentives in Indian Agriculture', *Indian Journal of Agricultural Economics*, April–June 1957, 22, pp. 1–25.

[3] For an excellent discussion of the possibility of such a policy shift, see Lipton's paper in Streeten and Lipton, op. cit.

[4] Lipton, op. cit., has provided an excellent case for such a shift in investments and governmental expenditures towards agriculture. Also refer again to Bhagwati and Chakravarty, op. cit., for further analysis of the policy issues in this area, including the tricky questions relating to zonal arrangements in food distribution and governmental procurement of food in the interest of a price stabilization and distributional policy: questions which also bear upon the issue whether P.L. 480 imports could have been avoided by making food 'go around' by suitable distributional and procurement arrangements.

III. TECHNICAL ASSISTANCE

While the question of P.L. 480 aid has been controversial in India, there has been little reaction to the programmes for technical assistance from abroad. In fact, the scale of such assistance has not had to be large because India's educational facilities have reduced the need to absorb large amounts of technical assistance from abroad. There has thus been no influx of foreign civil servants, for example, as in the countries of French Africa. On the other hand, the acceleration in her industrial growth and the shift

TABLE 10.13
TECHNICAL ASSISTANCE TO INDIA

	Number of experts who came to India			Number of Indians trained abroad		
	Colombo Plan	T.C.A. (U.S.A.)	Total	Colombo Plan	T.C.A. (U.S.A.)	Total
I. Up to the end of the First Plan	107	589	696	765	644	1,409
II. During Second Plan	296	838	1,134	3,275	2,312	5,587
III. During the Third Plan						
1961/2	76	160	236	830	443	1,273
1962/3	96	190	286	742	343	1,085
1963/4	157	190	347	693	336	1,029
1964/5	88	191	279	828	293	1,121
1965/6	78	155	233	605	245	850
Total Third Plan	495	886	1,381	3,698	1,660	5,358

Notes: 1. In the course of extending assistance for projects, India secures technical assistance as a part of the project complex. This is included in the normal aid disbursement figures; segregation of this component is difficult.

2. Besides Colombo Plan and T.C.A., India received technical assistance in the form of experts, training facilities, etc., from some countries like France under bilateral agreements, and from institutions like United Nations, Rockefeller Foundation, Ford Foundation, etc.

Source: Calculated by Messrs. Gopal Behari and V. K. S. Nair, Department of Economic Affairs, Ministry of Finance, at the authors' request.

therein towards heavy industry, have prompted significant reliance on technical assistance programmes designed to provide the immediate personnel as also to train Indian nationals in unfamiliar, technical jobs.[1]

Such technical assistance has come from both bilateral and multilateral sources. The United Nations, through its numerous agen-

[1] In addition, India has absorbed (on a lesser scale), technical assistance for sectors such as education, medical health, and agriculture. Cf. Dharm Narain and V. K. R. V. Rao, *Foreign Aid and India's Economic Development*, pp. 48–9.

cies such as F.A.O. and W.H.O., provided as many as 1,600 experts to India between July 1950 and June 1961, and fellowships (for foreign training) to 1,421 Indian nationals. While it is impossible, with the current availability of data, to make meaningful comparisons (which would require realistic weighting for quality differences, for example, among alternative programmes), it is interesting that this multilateral assistance compares favourably with the estimates of technical assistance under two other major programmes: the Colombo Plan (involving the countries of the British Commonwealth) and the United States Technical Assistance Programme (as shown in Table 10.13).[1]

IV. ATTITUDES TOWARDS FOREIGN AID

It is appropriate to conclude our review of the role of foreign aid in India's developmental effort with a sketch of the broad political spectrum of opinion within which Indian planners have had to operate their aid programmes.

Predictably enough, the reliance on aid has been assailed by the ultra-left parties: the large share of Western, and in particular United States aid has given cause for alarm at the possible ideological influence towards *laissez faire* and private enterprise that may follow.

Left-wing public opinion has been concerned also about the retarding effects of aid on the pursuit of determined policies of self-help and progressive reform. This has been true especially with respect to policies relating to agriculture: the availability of P.L. 480 aid has frequently been attacked, as we have just seen, as an important contributory cause of lack of concerted attention to (productivity-increasing) land reform and to agricultural policies for rapid growth in general.[2] The fears that Western pressures may be exercised to influence Indian policies, once the Indian economy became 'aid-dependent', while confined originally to only a limited

---

[1] It is necessary to stress, however, that the figures in Table 10.13 exclude the technical assistance which has often come in *together* with project-aid, so that the bilateral extension of technical know-how is significantly underestimated. Unfortunately, we have not been able to make a reliable estimate of such 'integrated' technical assistance.

[2] This view is particularly manifest in the writings of radical economists such as D. R. Gadgil, V. N. Dandekar, and K. N. Raj. Cf. Bhagwati and Chakravarty, op. cit., Section II.

segment of radical Indian opinion, have also become fairly wide-spread, thanks to (i) the suspension of Western aid during and immediately after the Indo-Pakistan War of 1965, (ii) the apparent willingness of President Lyndon Johnson to hold up P.L. 480 shipments during near-famine conditions in India in 1966 for political reasons, and (iii) the pressures (which were tantamount to the withholding of aid until the changes were effected) brought to change economic policies, including those relating to private foreign investment, towards greater use of the private sector and the price mechanism, during early 1966 through the World Bank.[1] 'Nationalists' have thus increasingly combined with radicals to view foreign aid with caution and criticism.[2]

At the same time, criticisms of foreign aid have been heard from conservative intellectuals. Reflecting the Friedman-type viewpoint, Professor B. R. Shenoy has assailed foreign aid as the major factor which has permitted India to indulge in public sector expansion and inefficient, bureaucratic policies, since aid withdrawal would have chastised the planners into pursuing more efficient policies (defined as those involving greater reliance on the private sector and the price mechanism).[3]

[1] We discuss these events at somewhat greater length in Chapter 22.

[2] The slashing down of foreign aid in the revised Draft of the Fourth Plan, put out in late 1968, is thus to be explained not mainly as a realistic recognition of dim aid prospects but as a reflection of the growing sentiment against aid in many influential quarters.

[3] Cf. B. R. Shenoy, *Indian Economic Policy*. For a similar position, see P. T. Bauer, *Indian Economic Policy and Development*, 1961, which has been heavily, and very justly, criticized.

II

Private Foreign Investment

WHILE the role of foreign aid in Indian industrialization attracted considerable attention only after the initiation of large-scale inflows of official assistance in the Second Plan, the debate over private foreign investment pre-dates independence in 1947.

This contrast is to be attributed to the fact that post-war foreign aid programmes on the massive scale that they assumed in the two decades since the termination of the second world war had not been foreseen, while there had been long experience with the influx of private investments from the colonial powers (in the main) leading to the natural expectation that (despite the assumption of independent political status) these inflows could continue into the future, and that, at minimum, the problems resulting from the existing *stock* of such investments would have to be confronted. Hence, although official aid played a significantly greater role in India's industrialization,[1] private foreign investment has attracted disproportionately greater attention in political and economic debate.

Business attitudes and governmental policies

The attitudes of Indian business, in particular, had been conspicuously expressed on the question of private foreign capital, since almost the beginning of the twentieth century. Furthermore, these views had grown steadily more hostile until Independence: to the point of eliciting demands that once independence was secured, the sterling balances accumulated during the war should

[1] Thus Michael Kidron, in *Foreign Investment in India*, estimates that, on a gross basis, the Indian absorption of foreign aid and private foreign investment during 1948–61, was in a ratio of 4·6:1; and on a net (of amortization and interest/dividends) basis, was in the proportion 6:1.

be used to buy out existing foreign investments.[1] Latent in these views was also the fear of competition with more powerful and resourceful foreign firms: a fear which was to dominate business attitudes and demands well into the mid-fifties.[2]

These views were paralleled by the National Planning Committee of the Indian National Congress which adopted a critical resolution on the subject in November 1945, proposing (among other things) that even existing foreign capital should be eliminated from 'key industries' and declaring that foreign capital had 'warped and retarded the nation's development'.[3] They were furthermore to be carried over, in spirit, into the First Industrial Policy Resolution (I.P.R.) of the Government in 1948.[4] While the I.P.R. did concede the value of private foreign investment in specific circumstances, it also promised to constrain such investment, and avoid its deleterious effects, by legislation. In particular, stress was laid on Indian majority ownership and effective control, and on the training of Indian personnel.

In the event, such legislation was not to be enacted; and governmental policy was to be far more favourable than could have been forecast in 1948 and was desired by the indigenous entrepreneurs until the mid-fifties.

In April 1949 Prime Minister Nehru formally announced the Government's liberalized policy towards private foreign investment. Its major points were:

1. Existing foreign interests would be accorded 'national treatment': 'Government do not intend to place any restrictions or impose any conditions which are not applicable to similar Indian enterprise.'

2. New foreign capital would be encouraged: 'Government would so frame their policy as to enable further foreign capital to be invested in India on terms and conditions that are mutually advantageous.'

3. Profits and remittances abroad would be allowed, as would capital remittances of concerns 'compulsorily acquired'.

4. Fair compensation would be paid 'if and when foreign enterprises are compulsorily acquired'.

---

[1] For details, Kidron, op. cit., Chapter 3 is an excellent reference, which we draw on for the brief review in this chapter.

[2] These fears were similar to those to be found in Latin America, for example, vis-à-vis foreign investment by U.S. firms. Cf. Sidney Dell, *A Latin American Common Market?*

[3] Kidron, op. cit., pp. 71–2.

[4] We discuss the other important dimensions of the I.P.R. in Chapter 13.

5. Although majority ownership by Indians was preferred, 'Government will not object to foreign capital having control of a concern for a limited period, if it is found to be in the national interest, and each individual case will be dealt with on its own merits.'

6. 'Vital importance' was still attached to rapid Indianization of personnel, but 'Government would not object to the employment of non-Indians in posts requiring technical skill and experience, when Indians of requisite qualifications are not available. . . .'[1]

Altogether, domestic entrepreneurs were unsympathetic to such liberalization, in the absence of a number of explicit safeguards to eliminate the threat of resulting foreign competition, and they were joined in these attitudes by their natural foes: the Communists and the Socialists in the Lok Sabha.[2]

Despite such opposition, the policy of liberalization was to stay and indeed be accentuated in the early years of planning. In particular, the Government relaxed the policy concerning majority ownership on a number of occasions, on an *ad hoc* basis, and provisions concerning double taxation relief and tax exemptions for salaries of foreign personnel were negotiated successfully. These relaxations were prompted by the assessment that the industrial development of the country required the influx of technical know-how and capital, and that private foreign investment was an appropriate and, in fact, a possibly major source for these scarce resources. This view was reinforced by the foreign exchange crisis in 1956-7, with the initiation of the Second Plan: the shortage of foreign exchange, and the continued reliance on exchange and import controls which ensued (and which we analyse in Part VII), weakened the objections within the Government to absorbing private foreign capital. Indeed, the sheltered markets which then followed were to play a major role in prompting the indigenous business interests to revise their hostile attitudes to foreign capital: they began to see the influx of foreign capital as essentially a method by which they could get the know-how to produce in the profitable domestic market and a technique by which they could persuade the Government that the foreign exchange cost of the project was being met by the capital inflow itself.

While, however, the liberalization of the regulations concerning foreign investment followed from this conjunction of changing

---

[1] Kidron, op. cit., p. 101.   [2] Cf. Hanson, op. cit., pp. 457-9.

business and Governmental attitudes, these changes also led to a simultaneous stiffening of other aspects of governmental policy in this area. Since the long-run balance-of-payments implications of the influx of foreign investment, consisting in the outflow of profits and dividends as also the royalty payments on sales of know-how, were equally in the minds of the policy-makers, governmental regulations required detailed (but by no means informed or effective) scrutiny and approval of each such act of foreign investment and/or sale of technical know-how *per se*. This also prompted the Government to regulate the industrial pattern of the private investment inflow: while, on political grounds, certain 'key' industries such as steel continued to be out of bounds,[1] there was also a definite tendency to exclude foreign investment, on economic grounds, from 'inessential' industries such as certain consumer goods, 'services', and 'trade'. Provided these criteria were met, and the terms and conditions approved by the licensing authorities (discussed later in Chapter 13), however, governmental policy was generally to encourage the inflow of private capital from abroad. And, towards this end, the Government occasionally made conciliatory gestures, through ministerial statements, parliamentary speeches, assurances by officials on foreign tours, and by eventually establishing an Indian Investment Centre in 1961, with offices in the major sources of private foreign capital, to disseminate information and advice concerning the profitability of investing in India to potential investors.

Magnitude and composition

What were the quantitative results of these policies, in terms of overall levels of capital inflow and its composition by industry and origin? Before we discuss these questions, it is useful to distinguish between the two distinct types of private foreign operations that have characterized Indian experience during the period since Independence. The two conceptual types are equity investment and (purely) technical collaboration agreements. Under the latter, the local firm would be buying know-how, ranging from

---

[1] However, even here there were distinct elements of liberalization in practice. As Kidron, op. cit., has noted: during 1957–8, 'foreign firms were invited to take up the more profitable parts of state-reserved industries, notably in drugs, aluminium, heavy electrical equipment, fertilizers, and synthetic rubber' (pp. 158–9).

patents to personnel required to work with the patented techniques. In practice, of course, there were many hybrids: equity
participation, whether majority or minority interest, would be
coupled with agreements to sell know-how; and technical collaboration agreements might carry options to buy equity later. India
witnessed both hybrids and (to a lesser extent) the pure types.
Thus, witness the results of an R.B.I. census survey of all public
and private limited companies with foreign capital participation
as on 31 March 1964; and of all companies having foreign technical collaboration agreements (in force) on 1 April 1961, plus
agreements subsequently approved and come into force until
31 March 1964.[1] This survey covered all together 827 companies
in the private sector: 591 involved equity participation (with 367
having only minority, foreign holdings) and 236 were pure technical collaboration companies. Of the 591 companies with equity
participation, as many as 351 also had entered into technical collaboration agreements to purchase know-how from either the
'parent' investor or (in infrequent cases) from other foreign sources.
Furthermore, the survey revealed that there was a greater tendency
for the minority-holding companies than for the majority-holding
subsidiaries to enter into technical collaboration agreements: as
would indeed be expected since the majority-holding would
generally ensure eventual sale of know-how from the parent,
holding company without formal technical collaboration agreements.

While we revert to the question of technical collaboration agreements later, we turn now to the question of *financial* investments.
Table 11.1 presents the available estimates for the period mid-1948
to end of 1961, on the pattern of foreign business investment by
industry. It is notable that the bulk of the investment seems to
have been in petroleum (25·6 per cent) with manufacturing as a
group taking 37·8 per cent. Within the manufacturing sector,
further, the pattern of investment appears to have shifted towards
metals and metal products, capital goods of different kinds, and
chemicals.[2]

---

[1] See 'Foreign Collaboration in Indian Industry', *Reserve Bank of India Bulletin*,
January 1969, pp. 20–4.
[2] Although systematic information, on a comparable basis to that in Table 11.1,
is not available, the trend towards investments in capital goods industries of
various kinds and in chemicals has continued well into the Third Plan.

TABLE 11.1
INDIA: DISTRIBUTION OF FOREIGN BUSINESS INVESTMENT FROM PRI-
VATE SOURCES BY INDUSTRY, MID-1948 TO END OF 1961
(In Rs. crores)

	Mid-1948		End 1961		Per-centage growth 1948–61
	Invest-ment	%	Invest-ment	%	
Plantations (mostly tea)	52·3	20·4	103·8	17·9	198
Mining	11·5	4·5	12·4	2·1	108
Petroleum	22·3	8·7	148·6	25·6	666
Manufacturing	71·0	27·8	219·4	37·8	309
Foods, beverages, etc.	10·1	14·2	36·1	16·0	357
Textile products	28·0	39·4	20·7	9·4	74
Transport equipment	1·0	1·4	13·0	5·9	1,300
Machinery and machine tools	1·2	1·7	11·4	5·2	950
Metals and metal products	8·0	11·3	32·1	14·6	401
Electrical goods and machinery	4·8	6·8	14·7	6·7	306
Chemicals and allied products	8·0	11·3	50·5	23·0	631
Others	9·9	13·9	40·9	18·6	415
Trading	43·1	16·8	29·3	5·1	68
Construction, utilities, transport	31·2	12·2	41·3	7·1	132
Financial (excluding banks)	6·8	2·7	6·3	1·1	93
Miscellaneous	17·7	6·9	19·3	3·3	109
TOTAL	255·9	100·0	580·4	100·0	227

Sources: R.B.I. Surveys: reproduced from Table 11 in Kidron, op. cit., pp. 243–4.

Note: It is possible to give a more detailed breakdown for the year ending 31 December 1960. The changes since mid-1948 for selected industries would read as follows:

Within manufacturing	Rs. crores	%
Cigarettes and tobacco	24·3	13·2
Medicines and pharmaceuticals	17·0	9·2
Building and building materials	6·8	3·7
Rubber goods	12·2	6·6
Total (including others)	184·3	100·0
Other than manufacturing		
Managing Agencies	23·3	4·1
Total business investment (including others)	566·3	100·0

Q

TABLE 11.2
NUMBER OF FOREIGN TECHNICAL COLLABORATIONS—BY INDUSTRY
(Cases approved by Government)

Industry	1957	1958	1959	1960	1961	1962	1963	1964	1965	Total 1957–65
1. Plantations	3	6	4							13
2. Sugar	4	2	2				1			9
3. Cotton textiles	9	4	3	2			4			22
4. Jute textiles	1	1		1						3
5. Silk and woollen		1	5	2	3	1		1	2	15
6. Iron and steel	2	1	1	1	3	1		38	6	53
7. Transport equipment	4	4	11	20	6	9	14	9	4	81
8. Electrical machinery, apparatus, appliances, etc.	11	11	12	72	73	44	54	43	33	353
9. Machinery other than transport and electrical	8	11	26	107	143	81	88	107	82	653
10. Aluminium	1	1	2	1	1	1				7
11. Basic industrial chemicals	5	4	4	2	3	3	4	15	7	43
12. Medicines and pharmaceuticals	4	10	9	6	3	9	2	4	5	52
13. Other chemical products	6	9	14	21	29	18	11	15	12	135
14. Cement	3	3	4	3	1		4	3	1	22
15. Rubber and rubber manufactures	2	3	3	5	3			6		22
16. Paper and paper products	2	2	1	9	8	8	1	6	1	38
17. Electricity generation and supply			3				1			4
18. Trading	4	1	4	2	1		2			14
19. Shipping		2	1							3
20. Banks and insurance	3	4	3							10
21. Others	9	28	38	126	129	123	108	156	89	806
TOTAL	81	103	150	380	403	298	298	403	242	2,358

Source: *Journal of Industry and Trade*, different issues.

TABLE 11.3

FOREIGN TECHNICAL COLLABORATION IN INDIAN INDUSTRIES—BY COUNTRY OF ORIGIN

(Cases approved by Government)

Country	1957	1958	1959	1960	1961	1962	1963	1964	1965	Total 1957-65
1. United States	6	4	10	61	77	57	67	78	48	408
2. United Kingdom	17	34	52	120	126	79	70	105	60	663
3. West Germany	2	6	13	58	67	42	48	68	44	348
4. East Germany			1	5	4	5	10	24	6	55
5. France	2	1	2	9	16	14	16	11	12	83
6. Italy	4	4	4	9	13	11	6	8	7	66
7. Japan	1	3	8	39	30	24	32	35	26	198
8. Sweden	1		1	13		6	1	6	3	31
9. Canada		1		1	3	6		3	1	15
10. Pakistan		2								2
11. Austria			1	3	5	4	2	5	1	21
12. Czechoslovakia				6	5	1	5	4	3	24
13. Holland				6	10	7	4	5	2	35
14. Switzerland	1	2	1	13	19	19	19	19	18	110
15. Belgium			2	4	2	4	3	5		20
16. Yugoslavia					1	1	3	2	1	8
17. Denmark			2	6	4	2	3	9	1	27
18. Finland				2	1	1				4
19. Panama		2	1							3
20. Poland				1	6		3	4	2	16
21. Hungary				1	2	2		3	1	9
22. Others	47	44	52	23	12	13	6	9	6	212
TOTAL	81	103	150	380	403	298	298	403	242	2,358

Source: *Journal of Industry and Trade*, different issues.

The statistics on technical collaboration agreements, on the other hand, are available only from 1957 and are presented, on an industry basis in Table 11.2 and on a country-of-origin basis in Table 11.3, for the period 1957-65. It is clear that the capital goods and chemical industries (serial numbers 7-13) were the major absorbers of such technical know-how, if we take the numbers of (unweighted) agreements as an index; however, the share of these groups in the total does not appear to have moved up over the period. As for the source of origin, the clearest trend seems to have been the growth of the United States, West Germany, Japan, Italy, and Switzerland as suppliers of technical know-how to Indian industry.[1]

Costs and benefits

The entire process of absorption of private foreign investment and know-how has been accompanied, as we have seen, by continual debate. From an economic viewpoint, the central questions in this area have been: (1) whether the nature of the regulation practised was well-conceived; and (2) whether the process has been beneficial to Indian development on the whole.

On the former question, it is difficult not to agree with the Government's preoccupation with issues such as the hiring and training of Indian personnel. While admittedly there is a conflict here between short-run efficiency and long-run advantage, there is also an argument for intervention in so far as the hiring policies reflect inertia and convenience rather than profitability. However, a puzzling phenomenon has been the Indian Government's desire to regulate the industrial composition of capital and technological inflow. The desire to prevent capital inflow from entering 'inessential' industries appears to have been almost certainly a case of misplaced concreteness. Thus, if a foreign investor buys up a restaurant, this will bring into the economy foreign exchange which can be used to import 'essential' machinery: to argue, therefore, that foreign investment should be excluded from the restaurant industry is just a simple and widespread fallacy. However, in the

---

[1] The continuance of the United Kingdom as an important source for know-how may also be noted. We must also repeat the *caveat* that we are constrained to use (unweighted) numbers of agreements in our analysis; unfortunately, the availability of statistics in this field is extremely limited and independent researchers have no access to primary information.

Indian case, there *were* some complicating factors which could have made the unrestricted entry of foreign investment into all activities economically undesirable. Thus, for example, as we shall argue in depth in Parts VI and VII, the combination of industrial and import controls led to a strongly sheltered market which implied the existence of widespread monopoly rents in the system. In this situation, it made sense to exclude the foreign investor from entering an industry where the monopoly rents were considerable, so as to prevent the foreign investor from appropriating a larger return than his social contribution to the economy. Similarly, if there were unrestricted entry in an activity with a number of small, indigenous entrepreneurs, the unrestricted entry of a large and resourceful multinational corporation could well result in the elimination of domestic entrepreneurship and thus discourage the growth of domestic entrepreneurship in the interest of development. Furthermore, in areas (such as oil) where the country faces world monopolies, the country may well get better terms on foreign investments by governmental intervention than by unrestricted entry. Thus, while it is certainly not clear that well-conceived reasons were behind the actual operations of the restrictions on foreign investments, there was an undoubted rationale for controlling the industrial composition of private foreign capital.

Regulation of both investment and technical collaborations again seemed justified in view of the frequent tendency to impose export-restriction clauses by foreign firms. Such restrictions, forbidding sales in third markets (which are pre-empted by the foreign firm) inhibited India's export drive; and, in so far as governmental policy could affect their inclusion in private contracts, such regulation was justified. In practice, a number of such restrictionist clauses did get through in the early years. Thus the R.B.I. survey found that almost half of the technical collaboration agreements in the survey had such clauses: of these, '52 per cent related to demarcation of countries to which exports were permitted and about 33 per cent to stipulations requiring "permission of collaborators for exports". Clauses enforcing a total ban on exports figured in only 8 per cent of the agreements with export restrictions.'[1] Predictably, the minority-ownership foreign investors had a larger proportion of such clauses than subsidiaries (which did

[1] R.B.I. Bulletin, op. cit., p. 22. For industrywise and source details, see p. 23.

not generally need contractual restrictions); and the highest proportion was to be found in the case of pure technical agreements.
How far these clauses have been restrictive, in fact, has not yet
been studied: although the fact that several foreign firms felt it
necessary to include such clauses indicates that, at least in some
cases, the restriction was imposed to eliminate feasible exports
from India.

It is impossible to judge whether India imported too much
technology and of the wrong kind. There is indeed room to
argue the former point: Indian industry, unlike Japanese, is not
distinguished by its expenditure on R. & D. (research and development) and the record of repeated purchases of technology from
abroad in a number of industries has been disappointing. It is
difficult to see, however, what governmental policy could have
achieved in this respect, by regulation. In some degree, the failure
to innovate and imitate in technology is itself a symptom of the
inefficient, totally sheltered-markets approach to industrial
development in the country since the Second Plan (as discussed
in Parts VI and VII). As for the latter question, whether India
imported wrong kinds of technology, two different criticisms can
be distinguished. (1) On the one hand, governmental policy has
been criticized for permitting the influx of foreign patents and
know-how in 'inessential' industries: cosmetics, lingerie, ink,
toothpaste, etc. This argument is, however, better made against
the very establishment of these industries; and, even then, we
would have to face up to the facts that (i) the basic problem is
skewed income distribution rather than the expenditure pattern,
and that (ii) the emphasis on the import-intensiveness of certain
forms of consumption requires correction through an appropriate
exchange rate (which should be applicable to all other choices in
the system as well). (2) The other criticism has been against the
tendency of foreign firms to smuggle in plants, obsolete and/or unsuited to Indian conditions. In a perfect market this could not
happen: the Indian firm which bought inefficient technology
would lose out to the firm which was smarter. In practice, of course,
the market for technology is not perfect, and information is typically not readily available to local entrepreneurs. Furthermore,
Indian industrial and import policies (Parts VI and VII) themselves prevented the competitive process from penalizing the inefficient Indian firms, thus making inefficiency in importation of

know-how both feasible and likely. In these conditions it is again difficult to see what a committee of bureaucrats, overseeing the technical collaboration agreements, but with no practical knowledge of techniques and indeed generally possessing no more information than supplied by the applicants, could have done to get economically superior know-how for India. In practice, therefore, the licensing committee was to be guided by nothing more effective than a 'consideration of each case on its merits' rule: a practice which could not adequately substitute for a more efficient framework of overall policies.

Finally, we may end our brief review of foreign investment and sales of technology by touching upon the question of the net benefits from *private* investment. Were the terms too high to yield net benefit to India? Leaving aside the imponderables such as spread effects concerning, for example, the influx of new management standards in the economy, was the effective rate of return to foreign investment higher than its contribution to India? Qualitatively, the distribution of monopoly rents in the economy makes it theoretically possible that, despite the private return to foreign capital being reduced approximately by half from its social contribution thanks to the corporation tax, certain foreign investments may yet have been harmful on balance—leaving out the imponderables. Unfortunately, no *rigorous* evaluation of this question, with its complex ramifications, is yet available for us to come to any strong conclusion.

Surprisingly, however, this important question has not been seriously attacked in Indian economic debate. Instead, much of the controversy has related to the question of the relative merits of private foreign investment and official aid.[1] In practice, however, this has hardly been a relevant choice from the Indian point of view: the effective choice has been whether, given the aid flow and other parameters of the developmental programmes, private foreign investment should be encouraged and accepted.[2]

[1] Cf. K. N. Raj, *Indian Economic Growth*, op. cit., Part II.
[2] This is, of course, a simplification. The willingness to accept foreign investment on liberal terms has certainly been related, to some extent, to the availability of aid flow itself. For example, the World Bank has put pressure on the Indian Government lately to accept private investment in fertilizer plants, indicating that such a 'sensible' policy would make it easier to have the required aid programme approved by the Consortium.

Domestic Policy Instruments

PART VI
Domestic Policy Instruments

12

Industrial Strategy and Target-Setting

THE industrial development of the country has been intensively
regulated since the beginning of the planning period. Investments
in public sector enterprises have naturally been subject to *direct*
planning in both choice and implementation, and have taken (as
we have already seen in Chapter 9) a very substantial part of the
planned and estimated industrial investment in the organized
manufacturing sector.

But even the private sector's industrial investments have been
directed by the state, by physical controls operated primarily
through an exhaustive licensing system combined with a detailed
setting of 'targets' by the Planning Commission in the course of
the formulation of the successive Five-Year Plans.

The system was operated in a manner calculated to influence,
and determine, (i) the pattern of investment down to *product*-level,
and (ii) the choice of technology, extending to scale, expansion,
location, direct import-content, and the terms of foreign collaboration in finance and know-how. Thus if the economic régime
had worked as intended in the designing of the control mechanism,
the degree of state determination of the pattern of industrial growth
in the private sector would have been as complete as in the case
of the public sector. However, theory and practice often diverged
in this area, as in others, and any sophisticated analysis of industrial
planning in India must also consider these divergences carefully.

In this chapter, we discuss the theoretical rationale underlying
the setting of industrial targets and the practical procedures by
which they were apparently defined, thus evaluating the *economic*
efficiency of such targets. We also offer some analysis of the relationship, in broad terms, between these targets and industrial
policy. In the following chapter, we proceed to analyse the principal instrument of industrial policy, industrial licensing, and

examine how far its use was in fact informed by the targets set and its actual efficacy for purposes of efficient planning of the industrial sector. In either case, our conclusions are depressing. The economic evaluation of the industrial planning techniques and procedures, right up to the end of the Third Plan, exhibits the tendency to work within a framework of detailed physical targets, derived without reference to notions of costs and benefits in a systematic manner, supported in turn by industrial licensing and trade policies[1] designed to make the corresponding investments (privately) profitable. Industrial licensing further is revealed: (i) to have been operated without any obvious economic criteria to choose between alternative projects, even within targeted capacities, indeed to have had procedures which often made such evaluations impossible; (ii) to have been ill-designed and concerned with excessive detail, contributing to significant delays without any *quid pro quo* in terms of improved economics of the licensed capacities; and (iii) to have even led perhaps to an accentuation of some of the undesired features of an unplanned expansion of industries, such as undue concentration of ownership of industries in a few hands, which it was intended to remove. The undue reliance on industrial licensing, which is essentially an instrument for *control*, also led to a neglect of instruments for *encouraging* investments in priority areas to reach the targeted levels.

I. Target-setting

The analytical methods used in target-setting in the industrial sector, for both private and public sectors, changed through the three Plans, largely because the planning techniques used for drawing up the overall Plans also were to undergo radical transformation during the period of our study.

The industrial targets were relatively few in the First Plan and were little more than projections of industrial capacities, based on rough estimates of what was likely to be demanded and produced in the system. The looseness with which these targets were gener-

---

[1] Trade policies, especially import control policies, which we refer to here are discussed in depth in Chapters 14 and 15. There we particularly highlight the use of quantitative restrictions to provide 'automatic' protection to domestic industries.

ally derived reflected, in turn, the fact that the First Plan itself was very much a collection of many *overhead* projects; and notions of planning for consistency, at an inter-industrial level, let alone optimality considerations, were still not present on the planning scene.[1] In the absence of any firm notions about what kind of industrial pattern (e.g. heavy industries) was desirable, and also in view of there being no attempts at matching supplies and demands at industry level except in a rudimentary and micro-level fashion, it is surprising that the estimates-cum-targets in the official documents, including the First Plan, were to serve as the basis for the operation of the comprehensive industrial licensing system introduced with the Industries (Development and Regulation) Act, 1951.

The situation in the Second Plan was, however, to change in an important respect. This Plan had, unlike its predecessor, an explicit *theoretical* frame and called for a marked shift in favour of capital goods industries. This frame was provided by the two-sector growth model developed by Professor P. C. Mahalanobis.[2] The same model had been independently developed by Feldman in the Soviet Union in the 1920s and later revived by Domar in an improved form.[3] The basic model, as stated by Mahalanobis, can be described briefly.

Current investment flow I_t is divided into two parts, $\lambda_k I_t$ and $\lambda_c I_t$, where λ_k indicates the proportion going to the capital goods sector and λ_c the corresponding proportion for the consumption sector. β_k and β_c are the marginal output–capital ratios in the capital and consumption goods sectors respectively.

[1] The First Plan merely incorporated a simple 'decision model' which was a variant of the Harrod–Domar model, the sole modification being the introduction of the distinction between the average and the marginal propensities to save. However, as J. Bhagwati and Sukhamoy Chakravarty have argued, in *Contributions to Indian Economic Analysis: A Survey*, op. cit.: 'The connection between the actual First Five-Year Plan and the Harrod–Domar type model contained in the document was left vague by the planners. It appears as though the selection of projects for governmental expenditure reflected essentially the "overhead capital" approach to developmental planning and the model was largely an intellectual appendage with little impact on actual Plan-formulation, although it did serve to give some kind of longrun perspective to the Plan.'

[2] 'Some Observations on the Process of Growth of National Income', *Sankhya*, September 1953.

[3] E. D. Domar, 'A Soviet Model of Growth', in *Essays in the Theory of Growth*, New York, 1957. Our discussion of the Mahalanobis model is taken from Bhagwati and Chakravarty, op. cit.

It is clear that

$$I_t - I_{t-1} = \lambda_k \beta_k I_{t-1}$$

and $$C_t - C_{t-1} = \lambda_c \beta_c I_{t-1}.$$

Now the first equation implies that

$$I_t = I_0(1 + \lambda_k \beta_k)^t.$$

Further, $C_t - C_0$ can be written as

$$\sum_{\tau=1}^{t} (C_\tau - C_{\tau-1}) = \sum_{\tau=1}^{t} \lambda_c \beta_c I_{\tau-1}$$

$$= \lambda_c \beta_c I_0 + \lambda_c \beta_c I_1 + \ldots + \lambda_c \beta_c I_{t-1}$$

$$= \lambda_c \beta_c I_0 + \lambda_c \beta_c I_0(1 + \lambda_k \beta_k) + \lambda_c \beta_c I_0(1 + \lambda_k \beta_k)^{t-1}$$

$$= \frac{\beta_c \lambda_c}{\beta_k \lambda_k} I_0[(1 + \lambda_k \beta_k)^t - 1]$$

Since $I_t - I_0 = I_0\{(1 + \lambda_k \beta_k)^t - 1\}$, we get by adding it to $C_t - C_0$ in the preceding equation:

$$C_t - C_0 = \frac{\beta_c \lambda_c}{\beta_k \lambda_k} I_0\{(1 + \lambda_k \beta_k)^t - 1\},$$

the complete solution for output at time t,

$$Y_t = Y_0 \left[1 + \alpha_0 \left(\frac{\beta_c \lambda_c + \beta_k \lambda_k}{\beta_k \lambda_k} \right) \{(1 + \lambda_k \beta_k)^t - 1\} \right]$$

where $\alpha_0 = I_0/Y_0$, the initial investment–income ratio.

Several things are quite clear from this equation. First we note that the relative rate of growth of consumption or output is changing over time. It is also clear that the asymptotic rate of growth of the system is given by $\lambda_k \beta_k$, where λ_k is the crucial allocation ratio which indicates the proportion of capital goods output which is devoted to the further production of capital goods. Thus a higher λ_k would always have a favourable effect on the asymptotic growth rate of the system, irrespective of whether it is consumption or output. But what about its immediate effect on consumption? If $\beta_c > \beta_k$, then a higher value of λ_k would imply a lower immediate increment in consumption. Thus, there is implicit in the choice of 'λ_k' a choice of alternative time-streams of consumption.

It may be further noted that, while the implicit assumption underlying the Harrod–Domar model is that the savings rate is a reflection of the behavioural characteristics of the decision-making units such as the household, the corporate sector or the Government, Mahalanobis effectively made it a rigid function of certain 'structural' features such as the capacity of the domestic capital goods industry and capital–output ratios of the capital goods sector and the consumer goods sector. By making the allocation ratio of current investment going into investment goods sector the policy variable, he showed that a higher allocation would mean a higher saving rate at the margin and hence a greater rate of growth of output or consumption.[1] This can be seen readily by noting that $\lambda_k \beta_k / (\lambda_c \beta_c + \lambda_k \beta_k)$ is none other than the share of incremental investment in incremental output. Macro-economic balancing for a closed economy would then imply that this is also the share of incremental savings in incremental income. If $\beta_k = \beta_c$, then this ratio of incremental savings to incremental income is exactly equal to λ_k. If $\beta_k \neq \beta_c$, then $\Delta I / \Delta Y$ is a more general function of λ_k, β_k, β_c, but the fundamental qualitative point remains unaltered.

Despite the fact that the Mahalanobis model is a severely rigid construct, it has one important virtue. This lies in its recognition of the fact that capital equipment once installed in any specific producing sector of the economy may not be shiftable.[2] An important consequence is that changes in the savings rate, and hence in the rate of investment, are not necessarily feasible and become conditional upon the composition of the existing capital stock; hence, optimal programmes of capital accumulation worked out under the assumption of non-shiftability differ crucially from those derived from models with complete shiftability in capital stock among alternative uses.

It needs to be stressed, of course, that foreign trade also can get the economy out of the problems raised by limited transformation possibilities domestically owing to non-shiftability of capital equipment: the assumption of a closed economy automatically rules out this important escape route from the problems raised by

[1] In deriving this proposition, Mahalanobis implicitly ignored the role of foreign trade altogether and assumed that the Government was in a position to control consumption completely.

[2] Whether, however, the Mahalanobis-assumed non-shiftability from consumer-goods to investment-goods capital equipment is greater than that within the former group, and how important it is anyway, are matters on which evidence is scant and, as we shall soon argue, was in any case not sought by the Indian planners before adopting Mahalanobis's ideas.

non-shiftability. Of course to escape these problems completely, we would have to assume the possibility of indefinite transformation at constant rates—the so-called 'small-country' assumption in trade theory. Therefore, the essential problems raised by non-shiftability will persist if the reciprocal foreign demands facing the planning country are less than perfectly elastic.

Mahalanobis, who assumed a closed economy and total non-shiftability of the capital stock from the consumption goods to the investment goods sector, appears to have used his model merely to provide the rationale for a shift in industrial investments towards building up a capital goods base. However, the *precise* choice of the proportion of investments in the capital goods sector, during the Second Plan and possibly thereafter, appears to have been arbitrary—at any rate, if there were specific economic considerations underlying it, these were not spelled out. In any case, an optimum choice would have required, at the very least, a quantification of the transformation constraints (both domestic and foreign)—and we know that neither was attempted.

Indeed, it appears quite plausible to argue that Mahalanobis (who had just then visited the socialist countries and with whose economists he had close contacts) was impressed with Soviet thinking on industrialization, with its emphasis on the building up of the capital goods base, without full recognition of the fact that such a strategy presupposes constraints on domestic and foreign transformation which need to be empirically verified. Further, it seems likely that, being a physicist by training and a statistician by practice, he directly identified increased investment with increased availability of capital goods, which in turn he identified with domestic production thereof, ignoring foreign trade in particular. It is interesting that the Second Plan did not explicitly state the rationale of the shift to heavy industries in terms of foreign trade constraints, so that the later justification of this strategy by alluding to 'stagnant world demand' for Indian exports comes somewhat close to *post facto* rationalization. Indeed, the Second Plan's examination of export earnings through the Plan is so cursory that it is difficult to believe that the 'stagnant world demand for Indian exports' assumption, by virtue of which the shift to heavy industries was later sought to be justified, was seriously made: such a crucial assumption, if made, would surely have been examined more intensively. Further, it is important to note that the preceding Five-Year Plan's experience with the balance of payments *and* exports was comfortable, so that it hardly seems likely that the export prospects could have been viewed with such pessimism as has later been imagined.

While, therefore, the Mahalanobis two-sector model was used to provide the rationale for a general shift in investments to building up a capital goods base, though the actual magnitude of this shift was otherwise determined, Mahalanobis provided yet another model, a four-sector model which broke down total investment among three further sectors, in addition to the capital goods sector: (1) factory production of consumer goods; (2) household production of consumer goods, including agriculture; and (3) the sector providing services such as health, education, etc.[1]

Mahalanobis assumed that all four sectors had independent output–capital and labour–output ratios. These were symbolized by β_1, β_2, β_3, β_4, θ_1, θ_2, θ_3, and θ_4 respectively. He assumed a given total of investment. The problem was to allocate the total between the sectors in such a way that specified increases in income (ΔY) and in employment (ΔN) were reached. The policy variables were the shares of investment going to each sector, denoted by λ_1, λ_2, λ_3, and λ_4.

The model was determined, of course, only if one of the three independent λs (the policy instruments) was exogenously determined, since there were only two objectives: ΔY and ΔN. With the λ for the capital goods sector given a preassigned value (the reason for which was never spelled out clearly) the system was solved by Mahalanobis to assign investments among the three remaining sectors. However, as Komiya pointedly noted, the Mahalanobis solution was inefficient, in that it was situated in the interior of the feasibility locus between incremental output and incremental employment.[2] Thus, greater employment and/or output could have been obtained by merely reallocating the given investments among the three sectors, although such a solution would not assign a positive fraction of investment to every sector.

The very fact that a simple linear-programming exercise by an

[1] The entire economy was supposed to be divided into these four sectors. Cf. Mahalanobis, 'The Approach of Operational Research to Planning in India', *Sankhya*, December 1955, Vol. 16, pp. 3–130.
[2] R. Komiya, 'A Note on Professor Mahalanobis' Model of Indian Economic Planning', *Review of Economics and Statistics*, February 1959, Vol. 41, pp. 29–35.

outsider could show the inefficiency of the Mahalanobis allocations, in conjunction with the fact that Mahalanobis did not use this technique even though the planners at his Indian Statistical Institute were certainly not lacking in knowledge of these elementary techniques,[1] indicates that the four-sector model was essentially produced to impart (unsuccessfully, as it turned out) intellectual respectability to investment allocations arrived at on other, unspecified, considerations. This conclusion seems also warranted by the fact that the statistical source of the parameters (relating to labour–output and capital–output ratios) was not spelled out. Nor was any attempt made to reconcile the model with the real facts of the situation, especially the presence of foreign trade.

Thus, from an economic-efficiency point of view, neither the order of shift to capital goods industries nor the overall levels of investment in consumer goods industries in the two aggregated sectors (factory and household) could be regarded as having a sound empirical basis. The breakdown of each such aggregate target into yet further targets—of sugar mill and cement machinery, bicycles, tyres, P.V.C., P.F. moulding powder, etc.—was still further removed from any notion of economic optimality. The choice from among alternative heavy industries, even within some *overall* target for such heavy industries, as also the problem of choosing the sequence of investments therein within a single Plan period—these are the kinds of issues for a discussion of which one may search in vain among the official documents.[2] Even attempts at inter-industrial consistency, in any systematic framework, were to come only with the Third Plan. In consequence, the massive investments in public sector enterprises for heavy industry were to be based on such (efficiencywise) 'weak' targets; and private sector investments in many targeted industries were to be constrained and regulated by a set of figures whose value was, at worst, worthless and, at best, no better than what the market forces left to themselves would produce.

[1] The Indian Statistical Institute is internationally renowned for its contributions to mathematical statistics and its distinguished Faculty which currently includes two Fellows of the Royal Society in this subject. Besides, they had the benefit of visits, at the time, by Richard Goodwin, Jan Tinbergen, Ragnar Frisch, and Oskar Lange.

[2] The only empirical discussion of choice on the Indian scene at the time related to the question of the choice of technique, especially in cotton textiles, which was part of the more general controversy about the role of small-scale industries. For more details, see Bhagwati and Chakravarty, op. cit.

The Third Plan, in whose formulation the dynamic and remarkable Chief of the Perspective Planning Division (P.P.D.) of the Planning Commission, Pitambar Pant, was to play a decisive role, was to continue basically the same strategy of sizeable investments in heavy industry. The notion of a foreign exchange bottleneck had become more explicit now, but the choices about the *magnitude* of investment in heavy industry as also the *pattern* of such investments and others were still to be without reference to notions of economic calculus. Improvements over the Second Plan consisted in the explicit search for inter-industrial balances and growing attention to the phasing of investments: but questions of choice were still absent from the scene. Reddaway, who was associated at the time with the P.P.D. as a Consultant on the staff of the India Project of the M.I.T. Center for International Studies, has lucidly explained the reason for this omission:

It is obvious, in broad terms, that a *cumulative* process of development, at a compound rate of 5 or 6 per cent per annum, will call for increasing quantities of machinery to be supplied each year, both for replacements and for expansion. If we take the concept of machinery broadly, to cover all types of capital goods other than construction (i.e. broadly to include such things as aeroplanes and railway rolling-stock and other 'engineering goods'), then we can make a somewhat over-simplified statement on these lines.

In 1960–61 the supply of these goods was worth about Rs. 500 crores, of which import of finished items accounted for about half; the remainder of the total value is made up partly of machines produced in India and partly of distribution transport and installation charges for all kinds of machinery incurred within India. The total supply probably 'ought' to have been about Rs. 600 crores rather than Rs. 500 crores; but it was held down by the fact that relatively few orders for machinery had been placed in the preceding years, owing to foreign exchange difficulties.

In 1965–66 the value of 'machinery' required for the process of development should probably rise to Rs. 1000 crores, and five years later should rise further to about Rs. 1500 crores. These figures do not pretend to be more than orders of magnitude, but especially if one remembers that the figure for 1960–61 should have been higher, there is no reason to doubt that they are broadly right on that basis. It is apparent that if the Indian contribution to the required value were left at roughly 50 per cent, as in 1960–61, then the value of imported machinery (still taken in the broad sense) would rise in a manner which would be disastrous for the balance of payments. Thus after ten years the *increase* in imports would be of the order of Rs. 500 crores per annum, which is not far short of the total present exports from India. It follows inevitably that if the balance of payments in 1970–71 is to be balanced, there must be an enormous expansion of the Indian engineering industry. If, for the sake of illustration, we assume that the imports of machinery both in 1965–66 and in 1970–71 were of the order of Rs. 400 crores, then the Indian element in the total would have to rise from 250 crores in 1960–61 to 600 crores in 1965–66 and 1100 crores in 1970–71. . .

This is not the place to discuss whether the job can in fact be done. I would only say that, on the assumption of technical co-operation with the more advanced countries, there is no *obvious* reason why an absolute increase of this size should not be achieved in the next ten years. If there were no time problem, so that the process could be spread out over many more years, there is no doubt that the expansion could be achieved. Once again, the essence of the problems of development is the matter of *time*.

Indeed, the true moral to deduce from this illustration is that a very big increase in the Indian output of machinery, etc., must be achieved in the next ten years, and that if this is to be done it is most important to get started on the job in as big a way as is reasonably possible on technical grounds *without delay*.[1]

While such reasoning appears cogent, and certainly at the time most economists in India were persuaded of its validity, its ultimate conclusion, which ignores choice *among* alternative 'machinery' investments, is obviously fallacious. It is just not correct to maintain that a foreign exchange bottleneck justified *all* import-substitution in heavy industry except for the most bizarre: the very fact, for example, that competing imports continued in most sectors, at some level or other, implies that the targets for certain activities could have been set at higher levels and for others at lower: and the choice required economic calculus and/or a suitable policy framework. In fact, as we have seen in Chapter 9, the later evaluation of massive public sector investments in projects such as the Heavy Electricals at Bhopal has shown that the Bhopal project, for example, was extremely low-yielding in terms of economic returns (duly adjusted to reflect social advantage) and thus

[1] W. B. Reddaway, *The Development of the Indian Economy*. The interchange between Padma Desai, 'The Development of the Indian Economy: An Exercise in Economic Planning', *Oxford Economic Papers*, November 1963, and Reddaway, 'The Development of the Indian Economy: The Objects of the Exercise Restated', *Oxford Economic Papers*, November 1963, is also of interest in judging the *consistency* of the Third Plan.

either better design should have been invented or the heavy industry chosen should have been other than heavy electricals altogether (if no better design was available).

We may finally note that, quite apart from the extensive resort to purely physical target-setting, with no procedures devised to examine the social profitability of alternative projects and targets, the targets generally lacked phasing, with no annual Plans worked out so as to give guidance, for example, to the Licensing Committee on the phasing of their licence-issuance to the (mainly private sector) applicants for industrial licences. At the same time, as we shall discuss at some length in the next chapter, the targets lacked a space-dimension despite the clear need to have this for efficient planning in a federal country such as India. There is little evidence, further, of the targets having been distinguished into 'core' and 'non-core' targets, to meet contingencies such as shortfalls in foreign exchange, or alternatively of their having been revised in any *systematic* fashion, using economic criteria, in light of such developments.[1]

How influential was this system of industrial targeting in shaping the actual industrial policies? We offer some general comments on this question before investigating it more thoroughly in the next chapter where we discuss industrial licensing in depth.

II. Relationship of targets to industrial policy

These targets were not merely indicative but were treated as full-scale targets with regard to which the Industrial Licensing Committee operated and lapses from which were considered by even governmental agencies and inquiry committees as 'failures of planning'.

A single example should suffice. The Estimates Committee (1967–8) of the Lok Sabha, in its Report on industrial licensing, has produced Table 12.1 which relates capacities licensed, and installed, as also production achieved, during each Plan period with the targets set in the Plans. Having done so, the Committee proceeds to highlight examples of shortfalls in production, the cases where licensed capacity itself falls short of production targets

---

[1] On the last point, see R. K. Hazari's trenchant critique in his Report on *Industrial Planning and Licensing Policy*, Planning Commission, Government of India, 1967.

and the cases where the installed capacity in turn is below the licensed capacity, for the Third Plan. Cases such as steel castings and dry batteries, where the licences issued exceeded significantly the Third Plan targets, are also noted by the Committee. It observes then that: 'All this would appear to indicate the deficiencies in planning and industrial licensing.'[1]

The notion that targets for non-priority industries should be considered indicative rather than as programmes to be fulfilled, has come only belatedly into the debate in this area. Thus the Estimates Committee (1967–8) has observed:

As regards industries, particularly those catering for non-essential consumer goods, the targets of capacity and production may be indicative so that these could be rolled forward or backward in the light of development and achievement.[2]

Similarly, R. K. Hazari in a report submitted to the Planning Commission in 1967 on the subject of industrial licensing has gone so far as to suggest that:

In a plan, only the targets of aggregate income, consumption and investment can be considered as relatively invariant. I am unable to uncover any sanctity or utility in treating each component target as a constant, though I readily concede that some targets should be less variable than others.[3]

Writing earlier in 1963, Bhagwati had also raised these and other questions relating to the relationship of targets to actual *and* efficient planning of industries. For example:

. . . is there any way in which we can say that some targets are 'more important' than others? Can we, for example, afford to ignore the non-fulfilment of some and not of others? Clearly targets embodying national *objectives* are of crucial importance. Among these can be counted: national income, level of employment, consumption. . . . With these must also be reckoned the objectives of raising the level of savings, improving the export performance and ensuring a steady investment in the capital goods industries, all of which buttress the

[1] Ninth Report, *Industrial Licensing*, Lok Sabha Secretariat, New Delhi, July 1967, p. 47. For other examples, see also *Third Five-Year Plan Progress Report 1961–62; Third Five-Year Plan—A Mid-Term Appraisal;* and *Third Five-Year Plan Progress Report: 1963–1965*, Government of India, New Delhi.

[2] Op. cit., p. 47.

[3] R. K. Hazari, *Industrial Planning and Licensing Policy*, op. cit., p. 18.

grand, forward-looking targets of an increased rate of investment and growth (and therewith employment creation and elimination of general poverty) in the stipulated 25-year perspective spanned by the entire planning process. *It need hardly be emphasised that all other targets, such as detailed industrial targets of investment, are only subsidiary to and instrumental in the fulfilment of these objective-targets.* This also means that *it is of little significance whether the stipulated target of aluminium falls short by some tons but of steel exceeds by others.* The shortfalls and leads are of negligible importance whether they occur within broad sectors like industry and services or between them, except in so far as they impinge upon the objective-targets. The analyst of the unfolding situation, therefore, has to examine whether this is so, before throwing up his hands at non-fulfilment of the *detailed* targets.

The analysis prompts two further observations of some interest. (1) Do we *need* to fulfil rigidly as many targets as we currently work with for there to be efficient planning?[1]

While we revert to some of these questions in the next chapter, we may note here that, although industrial targets undoubtedly influenced industrial growth significantly, they could not *determine* it. To begin with: (i) shortfalls in available inputs and foreign exchange, delayed executions, exigencies of the licensing procedure itself and similar factors often held up fulfilment of targets by holding up licensing or installation of licensed capacities or their utilization to achieve targeted levels of production; (ii) the reliance on licensing could restrict but *not* encourage investments by the private sector in fulfilment of the targets—a factor which, among others, explains shortfalls in cement and coal production during the Second and the Third Plans. But, quite apart from these inevitable and obvious factors, there were three *additional* reasons why the actual course of industrial developments could not have been expected to follow the 'targets'.

(iii) These targets, while specified in detail, were never exhaustive and the Licensing Committee, which processes applications for industrial investments and whose activities we examine in the next chapter, was expressly required under Rule 11 of the Registration and Licensing of Industrial Undertakings Rules (1952) to 'have regard to the approved plans, if any, of the Central Government for the development of the scheduled industry con-

[1] 'The Art and Science of Targetry', *Yojana* (Planning Commission *Journal*), 13 October 1963; p. 17 [italics inserted by us in the first two italicized sentences].

TABLE 12.1

SELECTED INDUSTRIAL TARGETS DURING THE THREE FIVE-YEAR PLANS AND THEIR FULFILMENT

Serial No.	Industry	Unit	Plan-period	Production target laid down during each Plan period	Production capacity in existence at the beginning of the Plan period	Production capacity licensed during each Plan period	Capacity actually set up during each Plan period	Production actually achieved during each Plan period
(1)	(2)	(3)	(4)	(5)	(6)	(7)	(8)	(9)
1.	Commercial vehicles, cars, and jeeps	Numbers	I	30,000	30,000	29,000	29,000	25,350
			II	57,000	29,000	28,000	27,700	52,675
			III	100,000	56,700	39,500	31,300	70,736
2.	Motor cycles/scooters, and 3-wheelers	Numbers	I	—	—	11,000	1,500	2,500
			II	11,000	1,500	36,000	24,500	25,490
			III	50,000	26,000	28,500	49,500	48,859
8.	Radios	Numbers	I	350,000	87,200	12,200	125,800	102,000
			II	300,000	213,000	113,725	66,180	280,123
			III	800,000	279,180	312,820	213,340	605,634
9.	Fans	Numbers	I	320,000 to 350,000	288,000	—	113,700	287,336
			II	900,000	401,700	1,177,150	470,050	1,058,151
			III	2,500,000	871,750	97,200	648,400	1,358,300
13.	Domestic refrigerators	Numbers	I		Not included in the First Plan			
			II		Not included in the Second Plan			
			III	50,000	13,600	17,000	11,400	30,800
14.	Room air conditioners	Numbers	I } II	Not included in the First and Second Plans				
			III	50,000	20,050		—	12,600
17.	Sugar mill machinery	Rs. in Lakhs	I	Not included	Negligible	213	160	32·06
			II	200	Negligible	1,407	1,000	466·55
			III	1,400	1,160	149	110	868·09
18.	Cement mill machinery	Rs. in Lakhs	I	Not included	Negligible	100	50	42·38
			II	250	Negligible	900	60	90·79
			III	450	110	1,300	1,790	490·88
19.	Boilers (in private sector)	Rs. in Lakhs	I	Not included	Negligible	120	30	6·84
			II	Not included	Negligible	691	340	101·18
			III	2,500	370	289	385	529·42

No. and item	Unit						
23. Steel castings	Tons	I	Not included	—	—	15,620	15,000
		II	Not included	15,620	139,130	39,000	29,000
		III	200,000	54,620	431,112	122,720	59,626
24. Steel forgings	Tons	I	Not included	41,340	126,320	41,340	—
		II	Not included	84,240	345,910	42,900	35,000
		III	200,000	120,000	833,000	71,910	67,800
27. Bicycles	Numbers	I	200,000		753,000	760,000	513,000
		II	530,000		—	1,117,500	1,307,000
		III	1,250,000		206,700	1,679,000	1,570,550
28. Sewing machines	Numbers	I	2,500,000	37,500	323,500	46,500	111,057
		II	91,500		85,500	267,400	297,300
		III	300,000		96,400	470,000	430,040
30. Typewriters	Numbers	I and II	850,000	45,000	—	66,400	—
		III	100,000	Not included	9,000	—	39,558
37. Agricultural tractors	Numbers	I	Not included	Negligible	—	Negligible	—
		II	—	6,320	21,000	11,000	92
		III	10,000	40,000	30,970	33,600	5,714
38. Diesel engines	Numbers	I	50,000	47,700	49,449	7,700	10,000
		II	20,500	33,000	8,546	52,500	43,448
		III	66,000	—	38,310	36,000	93,100
39. Power-driven pumps	Numbers	I	80,000 to 85,000	69,000	95,806	—	36,000
		II	86,000	128,000	48,420	59,000	94,689
		III	150,000	—	—	172,000	261,676
45. Cement	Million tonnes	I	n.a.	3·3	7·9	1·6	20·23
		II	n.a.	4·9	6·5	4·4	32·48
		III	15·0	9·3	4·3	2·7	47·16
49. Particle board	Million sq. ft.	I	Not included		195·55	6·0	0·7
		II	Not included		137·73	24·7	8·1
		III	n.a.		—	—	—
50. Sulphuric acid	Tons	I	200,000	150,000	390,092	92,000	166,910
		II	470,000	242,000	1,316,214	338,630	367,731
		III	1,500,000	580,630	2,152,360	501,690	663,622
52. Phosphatic fertilizers P2O5	Tons	I	30,000	21,000	55,666	14,000	11,864
		II	120,000	35,000	477,624	17,441	52,441
		III	400,000	52,441	493,820	115,502	121,666
55. Automobile tyres	Million numbers	I	Not included	0·96	0·03	0·03	0·957
		II	2·3	1·05	1·89	0·157	1·546
		III	3·85	1·46	1·74	2·0577	2·533
56. Bicycle tyres	Million numbers	I	Not included	4·87	3·54	—	5·80
		II	20·00	6·87	8·28	7·533	11·14
		III	20·00	15·11	3·78	7·174	18·45

TABLE 12.1—continued

Serial No.	Industry	Unit	Plan-period	Production target laid down during each Plan period	Production capacity in existence at the beginning of the Plan period	Production capacity licensed during each Plan period	Capacity actually set up during each Plan period	Production actually achieved during each Plan period
(1)	(2)	(3)	(4)	(5)	(6)	(7)	(8)	(9)
59. Acetic acid		Tonnes	I	—	n.a.	3,109	3,109	n.a.
			II	—	3,109	7,576	480	3,258
			III	28,000	3,589	5,137	8,146	8,231
60. Methanol		Tonnes	I and II	First and Second Plan not included.	—	—	—	—
			III	21,500		33,000		1,654
66. Synthetic detergent		Tonnes	Not included	20,000			2,100	8,408
72. Pesticides: B.H.C.		Tonnes	I	No target	—	7,200	7,200	n.a.
			II	2,500	7,200	16,200	3,600	3,891
			III	15,000	2,500	2,500	2,500	7,441
73. Pesticides: D.D.T.		Tonnes	I	No target	3,900	4,100	1,400	n.a.
			II	2,800	700	3,600	3,300	2,838
			III	2,800	2,800	2,640	700	2,745
87. Oxygen gas		Million cubic metres	I and II	Plan not included.	24·35	—	—	—
			III	38·24	n.a.	35·1	30·25	29·7
97. Refractories		Million tonnes	I	No target		0·57	n.a.	0·29
			II	0·8	0·44	1·60	0·38	0·55
			III	1·5	0·82	0·88	0·42	0·70
99. Biscuits		Million tonnes	I		n.a.	n.a.	n.a.	11,765
			II	15,000	33,750	n.a.	n.a.	23,700
			III	40,000	30,528			44,049
100. Confectionery		Million tonnes	I		n.a.	4,550	n.a.	7,840
			II	10,000	40,600	n.a.	n.a.	17,000
			III	25,000	51,840	600		25,889
105. Infant milk food		Million tonnes	II	No target	n.a.	4,898	—	—
			III	6,000	4,000	6,000	3,898	5,281

Source: Selected from *Ninth Report of Estimates Committee* (1967–8), on Industrial Licensing, Lok Sabha Secretariat, New Delhi, July 1967; Appendix IV, pp. 309–24. The data were supplied to the Estimates Committee by the Ministry of Industrial Development and Company Affairs.

cerned and, *where no such plans exist*, to the existing capacity of the scheduled industry, the demand and supply position, availability of raw materials and plant and machinery'.[1] Thus what was *not* targeted was *not* ruled out: the industrial targets, as published in the Plan documents and (in far greater detail) in the *Programmes for Industrial Development* did not convey the total picture of the intended industrial developments in the private sector.

The degree to which investment approvals were granted during the three Plans, for investments in areas not covered by Plan targets, cannot be ascertained from published statistics with any accuracy: but it is likely to have been in the range of 25–30 per cent of licensed private sector investments in the Organized industrial sector during the first two Plans and was less in the Third Plan. Table 12.1 which records the bulk of the industrial targets *and* their absence during each of the three Plans, shows for nearly half the listed industries that, while there were no targets fixed, apparently capacity was still licensed and/or set up during the corresponding Plan period.[2] Among such industries were, for example: (*a*) motor-cycles/scooters and three-wheelers in the First Plan; (*b*) steel forgings in the Second Plan; (*c*) particle board in the Second Plan; (*d*) acetic acid in the Second Plan; (*e*) automobile tyres in the Second Plan; (*f*) synthetic detergents in the Second Plan; and (*g*) biscuits and confectionery in the Second Plan.

(iv) Further, these targets referred generally to production in the Organized sector and whenever production could, technologically and with profit, take place outside the Organized sector, the targets were inadequate as a guide to *overall* industrial investment and production.

(v) In addition, as we shall see later, investments below a certain sum (which changed upwards over time) were exempt from the licensing procedure and hence could proceed without any effective control, thus again rendering the relevance of the targets as an upper limit somewhat dubious. We may also note that industrial licensing, as we shall see in the next chapter, was confined to the so-called 'scheduled' industries, whose coverage became very

[1] Quoted in Estimates Committee (1967–8), *Ninth Report on Industrial Licensing*, op. cit., p. 137 [italics have been inserted by us].

[2] Although the table does not appear to be fully accurate, like all governmental tables on this subject, it is adequate for our purpose.

large only since 1956 and even then could not be described as exhaustive.

Having thus examined the efficiency-wise weak basis on which industrial targets were in practice arrived at, and the manner in which they broadly interacted with industrial policy, we now proceed to explore in depth the pattern and efficiency of industrial licensing which operated since 1952 and was intended to be the principal instrument for regulating the industrial development of the country.

13
Industrial Licensing

THE Industries (Development and Regulation) Act of 1951, following closely upon the Industrial Policy Resolution of 1948, provided the framework for the licensing and regulation of industrial investments (and related questions such as pricing and distribution controls) in the country during the period of the three Five-Year Plans and thereafter. As the Minister of Industry and Supply correctly observed, when introducing the Bill to the Select Committee of Parliament on 6 April 1949:

. . . the object of this Bill is to create a suitable legislative framework by virtue of which the industrial policy can be implemented. This Bill, I would say, constitutes a landmark in the industrial legislation of India. It marks the beginning of planning for the industrial development of this country.[1]

This was indeed the case: but the precise form that this regulation and planning was to take was to be deficient and, from the viewpoint of both economic efficiency and the very objectives it aimed at, almost a contradiction of what rational governmental intervention would imply. In this chapter we undertake a detailed analysis of the actual working of this system of industrial licensing and planning, leading to the conclusion which we have just stated.

I. OBJECTIVES AND INSTRUMENTS OF INDUSTRIAL LICENSING

Among the principal objectives which the Industrial Policy Resolution listed, and which the Industries Act, 1951, was designed to implement, were:

[1] Quoted in the *Ninth Report of the Estimates Committee* (1967–8), op. cit.

(1) the development and regulation of industrial investments and production according to Plan priorities and targets;

(2) the protection and encouragement of 'small' industries;

(3) the prevention of concentration of ownership of industries; and

(4) balanced economic development of the different regions in the country, so as to reduce disparities in levels of development.[1]

In order to pursue these objectives, the Industries Act conferred powers upon the Government, among them that (i) all existing undertakings in the 'scheduled' industries had to be registered with the Government, and (ii) no 'new' industrial undertaking could be established, nor any 'substantial extension' effected to existing plants, without the prior procurement of a licence from the Central Government.[2] Although the initial list of scheduled industries covered only forty-two major industries, with the gaps left therein 'more by accident than design',[3] this was eventually expanded to include an additional twenty-eight industries in 1956: the schedule, as obtaining at the time of June 1966 devaluation, being nearly complete.

Although the detailed procedures occasionally varied through the period of our study, the principal organizational features were relatively constant and can be briefly described. In essence, with a few exceptions, the applications for industrial licences were cleared by an (Inter-Ministerial) Licensing Committee, set up in September 1952 to operate within the framework of the 1951 Industries Act.[4] The applications were generally placed before the

---

[1] Cf. Hazari, op. cit., p. (i); also *Ninth Report of the Estimates Committee*, pp. 11–12.

[2] There were also powers for regulating the supply, distribution, and prices of the products of the Scheduled Industries. And in 1953, extensive powers were conferred on the Government to order an investigation of any scheduled unit or industry on suspicion that output had been reduced or price had been increased or quality had deteriorated without 'justification', and thereafter to take over its management if necessary.

[3] *Ninth Report of the Estimates Committee*, p. 20.

[4] The exceptions were relatively unimportant.

'To obviate the necessity of all cases coming up to the Licensing Committee, some delegations have been made by the Committee to the administrative ministries. The following categories of applications are generally disposed of without reference to the Licensing Committee subject to the State Government

Licensing Committee for approval only when they had already been recommended by the administrative Ministry within whose general jurisdiction the specific, applicant industry would lie. Where such recommendation was withheld, the application went to the Rejection Committee, to be reconsidered for grant or rejection of the licence. The final decision on the issuance of the licence was taken, on the advice of these Committees, at the level of the Minister for Industrial Development.

A Directorate General of Technical Development (D.G.T.D.) was set up with the task (among others) of examining from a technical angle the applications under the Industries Act for establishing new units or undertaking substantial expansion. The Estimates Committee (1967–8) has described the functions of the D.G.T.D. in this connection:

> The D.G.T.D. makes a technoeconomic appreciation of the applications for industrial licensing, indicating *inter-alia*—
>
> (a) if there is need for more capacity for the item(s) of production proposed in the application, also keeping in view import substitution and export possibilities;
>
> (b) if the scheme of manufacture is technically sound;
>
> (c) whether the capacity asked for by the entrepreneur is commensurate with the capital goods to be installed, taking into consideration the capital goods which the party may already possess;
>
> (d) whether the scheme as submitted or as further modified in the light of discussion with D.G.T.D. will ensure reaching the maximum possible indigenous content within a reasonable time;
>
> (e) whether the plant to be installed and/or method of manufacture to be adopted is modern and economic;
>
> (f) whether the location lends it to economic viability and disposal of effluents.

---

or Governments concerned having no objection and provided the schemes are found satisfactory after technical scrutiny:

(a) Where it is necessary to regularize the manufacturing activities of existing industrial undertakings;

(b) Where a change of location within one State or from one State to another is proposed;

(c) Where the production of new articles is proposed and such production does not involve installations of any additional machinery or the use of imported raw material;

(d) Applications in respect of items which have been put on the rejection list. These are ordinarily rejected without submission to Licensing Committee.'

Ninth Report of the Estimates Committee, pp. 137–8.

Based on the aforesaid basic considerations D.G.T.D. recommends to the Licensing Committee either acceptance or rejection of the application.[1]

We may also note at this stage that, quite apart from the industrial Licensing Committee, there were numerous other physical controls to be cleared by the prospective investor. The C.G. (capital goods) licence had to be procured from the C.G. Licensing Committee which cleared allocations of import licences for the purpose: a procedure which could not be obviated if imports of capital goods were necessary. Furthermore, if there was foreign collaboration involved, the (inter-Ministerial) Foreign Agreements Committee got into the picture and its consent to the terms of the collaboration had to be secured as well. In many cases, where the local finance had to be procured from a State financial institution, such as the Industrial Finance Corporation (I.F.C.), the scrutinies exercised by these committees were repeated afresh.

II. ECONOMIC EFFICIENCY OF THE LICENSING SYSTEM FROM THE VIEWPOINT OF INDUSTRIAL PLANNING

In analysing the working of this system we shall begin by evaluating its economic efficiency for industrial planning: examining initially questions such as the economic criteria used, the information utilized for reaching judgements, possible delays without rational justification, phasing of licences and related matters. Only later, when we discuss objectives such as the prevention of concentration in industrial ownership and balanced regional development, we shall analyse other related aspects of efficiency, such as the contribution of the licensing system to monopolistic situations and uneconomic-scale plants.

Absence of criteria

The licensing system was supposed to operate within the framework of targets which had been worked out by other agencies such as the Planning Commission. Its function was therefore to ensure that, within this framework, the actual choice of plants, technologies, locations, etc., was carried out in a manner which would ensure social, as distinct from private, profitability. If this were

---

[1] *Ninth Report of the Estimates Committee*, pp. 200–1.

not the case, and private entrepreneurs could be expected to ensure social advantage as well, then suitable fiscal incentives and taxes designed to keep industrial investments within the defined targets would be an efficient and adequate policy and detailed licensing of literally thousands of applications for licences would be a highly wasteful procedure. Thus the important questions are: (*a*) what criteria were defined to deal with the applications; and (*b*) were they systematically deployed in practice? If our answers to these questions are negative, the situation through the three Plans appears to have been one in which not only were the targets themselves fixed (as we have seen) without any systematic attention to costs and benefits, but even the methods by which economic choices relating to their fulfilment were made were defective and could not be described as constituting 'rational' intervention.

(1) *Operation of Licensing Committee*

That the Licensing Committee operated essentially in an *ad hoc* manner, without explicit statement and weighting of different objectives and without explicit publication of any criteria in terms of which applicants could assess their chances of getting licences with reasonable firmness and hence plan more soundly, has long been known. Detailed *official* analyses of the licensing procedures and policies, which have recently been made, have only underlined this conclusion:

3.6. A Chemical Manufacturers' Association has represented to the Committee that 'So far it has not been possible to find out the underlying principles for either giving or rejecting the industrial licences for setting up new plants or for expansion by the Licensing Committee. The guidelines either for giving or rejecting the licence applications are changing, depending on the applications. Perhaps it would be desirable to clearly state the guidelines for considering the licence applications and in particular when an application is rejected the reasons for doing so should be made known, not only to the applicant but also for the benefit of the other entrepreneurs so that the whole process of making and considering applications for industrial licences may be streamlined and the least amount of time spent on this'.

3.7. Asked during evidence whether any general principles had been laid down for issuing licences for establishing new undertakings or substantial expansion of existing undertakings, the representative of the Ministry of Industrial Development and Company Affairs informed the Committee that '*Not in the sense of laying down principles*. But the things

S

are well-known, that the unit should be economical and so on and it is the normal principle that we prefer expansion of the existing unit to setting up a new one as it is less costly'.

3.8. Asked further whether any general principles have been formulated by Government on the advice of the Sub-Committee of the Central Advisory Council, as provided in Rule 18* of the Registration and Licensing of Industrial Undertakings Rules, 1952, the Secretary of the Ministry stated that *I don't think they have laid down any principles.* This Council meets, there is an exchange of information and matters are discussed' . . .

3.11. The Committee are concerned to note that since the inception of the licensing system under the Industries (Development and Regulation) Act, 1951, no general principles/guidelines have been laid down which are followed for the consideration of applications for grant of an industrial licence for establishing a new undertaking/expansion of existing undertaking under the Act although the Rules specifically provide for it. It is obvious that in the absence of such principles/guidelines, the merits of each application are apt to be judged on an *ad hoc* basis.[1]

In the absence of well ordered priorities and flexibility of inter-related programmes at various levels of performance, *there has been a tendency to rely upon various ad hoc criteria.* One of these has been the policy of licensing projects, the foreign exchange costs of which on capital and/or maintenance account are covered by available credits and/or foreign collaboration and/or export obligations. It can be said in defence of this policy that there has been no resulting distortion of planning or industrial development because the projects so approved are, in nearly all cases, included in the plan. That does not, however, answer the basic argument that this is a reversal or inversion of what is implied in planning. A project must first of all be intrinsically feasible and occupy a high place in the list of priorities before it can be considered for the allotment of scarce resources, especially foreign exchange. Just because a project is, or can be made, amenable to availability of foreign exchange should not qualify it for approval.[2]

---

*Rule 18 of the Registration and Licensing of Industrial Undertakings Rules 1952 lays down that 'A Sub-Committee of the Central Advisory Council shall be constituted which will review all licences issued, varied, amended or revoked from time to time and advise the Government on the general principles to be followed in the issue of licenses for establishing new undertakings or substantial expansion of the existing undertakings.'

[1] *Ninth Report of the Estimates Committee,* pp. 135–6 [italics have been inserted by us in paragraphs 3.7 and 3.8].

[2] Hazari, op. cit., pp. 19–20 [italics have been inserted by us].

In attempting to cover almost the whole range of large scale industrial development, licensing inevitably loses sight of the relative importance of different projects and/or products. The licensing authority and the departments which service it are loaded at any one time with hundreds or thousands of proposals, *without clear and definite criteria to appraise their worth* in terms of relative costs and the attainment of targets in related, particularly basic, industries/projects.[1]

The absence of explicit *economic* criteria as also the weighting of different objectives, in the grant or rejection of industrial licences was matched, through the period, by the generally poor quality of the 'techno-economic' examination of proposed industrial investments which the D.G.T.D. was supposed to carry out in each case. There is no evidence of any studies having been carried out by the D.G.T.D. of the optimal size, time-phasing, and location of industrial units, for example, in order to guide the Licensing Committee in its deliberations.[2] A detailed examination of the working of the D.G.T.D. by an American firm of consultants was to confirm what many observers and applicants for licensing already knew: that few systematic criteria, if any, existed in the D.G.T.D.'s decision-making process and that the D.G.T.D. was occasionally demanding duplicate information which, in any case, was not scrutinized for inconsistencies and often remained on a company basis and few data existed on an aggregated product basis as would be the case if only techno-economic decisions were being taken in a systematic and informed manner.[3]

---

[1] Hazari, op. cit., p. 20 [italics have been inserted by us]. Similar conclusions were reached by the first Industries Development Procedures Committee, the so-called Swaminathan Committee, appointed in September 1963 and reporting in March 1964 and by the second Swaminathan Committee, appointed in August 1965 and reporting in February 1966, even though these Committees mainly examined licensing procedures rather than the entire question of industrial planning and its efficiency.

[2] This was pointed out by Bhagwati, 'Economics of Scale, Distribution of Industry and Programming', *Economic Weekly*, 1 September 1962. Attempts at discovering whether the D.G.T.D. had any such studies for the aluminium industry, in which Bhagwati was interested, revealed the absence at the time of even comprehension of such problems, leave aside their systematic resolution. Later work by T. N. Srinivasan and Alan Manne, at the Indian Statistical Institute, was to develop techniques for such analysis: Alan Manne (ed.), *Investments for Capacity Expansion*.

[3] Cf. *Ninth Report of the Estimates Committee*, pp. 216–18. The shocking state of affairs in the D.G.T.D. with respect to allocations of the Actual User (A.U.) import licences for *raw materials and components* is dealt with separately by us in Chapter 17.

Not merely was the D.G.T.D. unable to evolve any traditions of 'techno-economic' work which would improve the efficiency of industrial planning and regulation,[1] and gear its informational system to such work, but even its *purely* technical work, devoid of any economic considerations, was of dubious quality, at best. The reports of both the Management Consultants from the United States and the local Mathur Team on the D.G.T.D.'s working, as also the examination by R. K. Hazari who reported on industrial planning to the Planning Commission, have agreed on the need to improve the technical strength of the D.G.T.D. and to prevent the organization from becoming technically obsolete. It is dubious how far such an organization, staffed generally with engineers whose technical qualifications and practical experience were limited (and commensurate only with the generally unattractive salaries they got, in relation to the private sector's pay scales), whose desks were loaded with an average of nearly two thousand fresh applications for 'technical advice' every year, and whose informational system was ill-organized for taking decisions in the light of

---

[1] The economic quality of the D.G.T.D.'s work can be judged also from the following quote from the *Ninth Report of the Estimates Committee*, p. 207:

'The Director General of Technical Development has issued instructions (on 29th December, 1965) that:

(*a*) The concept of indigenous content should be basically revised. The general object should be to start 100 per cent or near 100 per cent indigenous content, at least in the engineering industries.

(*b*) So far as the existing approvals are concerned, steps should be taken to improve upon the phased programmes earlier approved with a view to reaching 100 per cent indigenous content as early as practicable.

(*c*) So far as foreign collaborations are concerned, if a collaboration in a particular field has already been approved, fresh collaborations in the same field should be discouraged and the possibility of persuading the undertaking which has already come into existence, to part with their knowhow to new-comers, on the basis of some payments, should be explored.

4.14. The representative of D.G.T.D. has informed the Committee during evidence that "A much higher indigenous content is being insisted on in regard to all new licences. It may not be practicable in every industry to achieve 100 per cent indigenous content, but we are definitely insisting on a much higher percentage of indigenous content when new licences are being issued." He added that "The earlier units which were required to achieve an indigenous content of say 80 per cent, are now being pressurised to achieve a higher percentage themselves." '

Factors such as *indirect* import demands or the possibility of any particular process being uneconomic or the possibility of there being *better* know-how available than what has been obtained in the past are matters which don't seem to have bothered the D.G.T.D. at all.

explicit criteria, could operate efficiently. In view of these limitations, one wonders if the D.G.T.D. could take even the purely
technological decisions which might, in *some* sense, contribute
improvements in the growth of industrial capacities justifying the
bureaucratic apparatus and the delays which we shortly describe.
An impartial analysis of the reasons stated and the methods of
analysis used by the D.G.T.D. in declaring specific applications
as technically or techno-economically unsound would be revealing: unfortunately, only an officially constituted body would
be allowed to have access to the relevant files.

(2) *Inadequate and ill-organized information*

We have already referred briefly to the inefficient information
system obtaining in the D.G.T.D. concerning industrial (and
A.U.) licensing. The American Management Consultants showed
that:

(i) The quality of data received by the D.G.T.D. is neither consistent
nor is it audited.

(ii) The D.G.T.D.'s current information processing system is related
to but not fully compatible with the information needs of industry and
other government agencies. Many common needs exist which are not
now satisfied by common data. . . .

(iii) The D.G.T.D. most often request data from companies that is
very similar to data already received. Moreover, the D.G.T.D. is not
presently in a position to supply industry with desired statistical or
reference data.

(iv) The data storage is by company and little data exists on a total
product basis. . . .

(vi) Reliance is placed on manual checking and transferring of data to
ledgers and on mental computations. These techniques are slow, are a
source of inaccuracy, and are inappropriate to the large volume of data
to be handled. Development Officers, as a result, seldom have all the
data they desire available when making an allocation decision.[1]

Further, the Mathur Study Team and other analysts have
examined the 'G' return, which is required to be submitted by the
licensee twice annually so that the D.G.T.D. and other interested
authorities keep track of progress in implementation—a matter of
admitted importance if industrial planning is seriously taken and
is extended to ensuring that implementation of licensed capacities

---

[1] *Ninth Report of the Estimates Committee*, pp. 216–17.

proceeds on plan and if new capacities are to be licensed on the basis of reliable information on the progress in installation of earlier-licensed capacities. This has shown that: (i) the D.G.T.D. did not maintain this information with any degree of accuracy, with the G-returns coming in irregularly and sometimes with excessive delays if at all; (ii) the returns, in any case, received only *routine* and junior-level treatment in the vast majority of cases; and (iii) the copies of the return required to be sent to several other authorities such as the Planning Commission were merely filed and represented infructuous work on the part of the licensee.[1] That mere licensing of capacities, within some margin of the targets where available, was enough in practice and there was no need to have a systematic analysis of the follow-through, to examine whether the targets (which were presumably taken very seriously, as we have argued) would be fulfilled *and* whether any remedial action would be necessary (in the shape, for example, of facilitating finance availability, prodding the state governments involved, entry of the public sector if necessary), seems to have been the prevailing philosophy. The apparatus of 'returns' about the progress of the licensee was, in effect, a conspicuous substitute for actual analysis, evaluation, and rethinking of policies in the light of the progress of licensees in different industries.

(3) *Sequential choice among applicants*

So far we have discussed the absence of criteria and informed judgements on the question of rejecting or granting a *single* application for an industrial licence. However, we may well ask whether efficient industrial planning should not also be designed to choose, from among alternative applications for fulfilling a certain target, those which are socially most advantageous.

The procedure used by the Licensing Committee in general was to proceed on a first-come-first-served basis, reflecting to some extent the philosophy of 'fairness' in allocating a scarce resource (i.e. a profitable, industrial licence) that was also to characterize many other allocational decisions by the Indian bureaucracy.[2] This practice, combined with overall ceilings in many cases where

---

[1] *Ninth Report of the Estimates Committee*, pp. 218–22.

[2] See, for example, our extensive discussion of such practices in import allocations in Chapter 17. Evidence supporting the 'first-come-first-served' rule is found in the *Ninth Report of the Estimates Committee*, p. 152.

targets were laid down, further resulted in several other inefficiencies such as the foreclosing of capacity by better-organized and better-informed industrial houses who could often put up the applications more quickly than others (a question we discuss later in the chapter when we analyse the efficiency of the licensing system in achieving the stated objective of prevention of concentration in the ownership of industrial investments).

The effective elimination of efficient choice among different applicants that this procedure of licensing implied has been noted by several economists and committees.[1] The latest official discussion of this question, contained in the Report on Industrial Licensing by the Estimates Committee (1967–8) is revealing and may be quoted at length:

3.63. The Committee desired to know the views of Government regarding a suggestion made by a leading industrialist of the country that 'it is not uncommon that the application for expanding the existing plan facility or installing a new capacity has been granted to entrepreneur A, while an application from entrepreneur B for a similar licence has been rejected on the grounds that sufficient capacity has already been allowed though the investment cost and foreign exchange cost per annual tonne output of the project put up by the entrepreneur B is about one-third or one-fourth the cost per annual tonne of the project of entrepreneur A, merely because entrepreneur A applied for the licence earlier than the entrepreneur B. A more practical approach to this problem would be to invite from prospective entrepreneurs fairly firm statements regarding the current and capital cost per ton of the major products they wish to manufacture either anew or in the process of fresh expansion. The Government could then select that scheme which would, other things being equal, have the highest rate of return in terms of capital employed consistent with the lowest price chargeable to the consumer and the lowest foreign exchange content.'

3.64. The Secretary of the Ministry of Industrial Development and Company Affairs stated that 'This is an important suggestion. I would like to consider it before offering any views. It is an interesting suggestion which, I think, will have to be considered carefully.'

3.65. In a written note subsequently furnished to the Committee the position has been explained by the Ministry of Industrial Development and Company Affairs as under:

[1] Cf. Bhagwati, 'Economies of Scale, Distribution of Industry and Programming', *Economic Weekly*, op. cit.; and the Report of the [Mathur] Study Team on D.G.T.D., op. cit.

. . . The possibility of introducing a procedure of inviting applications in specified fields and considering them together periodically with a view to giving preference to entrepreneurs who require the minimum foreign exchange etc. was examined by the Industries Development Procedures Committee. The conclusion was that such a procedure is likely to present serious practical difficulties. This was likely to result in bunching of licences instead of their being spread appropriately throughout the Plan period and would result in delays or failures to utilise available foreign loans and credits to the overall detriment of the interests of the country. The Committee, therefore, recommended that there need be no change in the present procedure. Though the Government have accepted the recommendation, further thought is being given to this matter.[1]

Among the interesting aspects of this interchange between the Estimates Committee and the Ministry in overall charge of licensing procedures is the relative degree of surprise with which the proposal for simultaneous, as distinct from sequential, licensing of competing applications was received by the Ministry, as late as 1966.[2] Also, the reasons cited for the rejection of a revised procedure, aimed at introducing considerations of choice, appear to have been hastily drawn up: for example, while licences may have been bunched under this procedure, there was massive evidence of their bunching, in any case, under the existing procedures;[3] indeed the proposal made for simultaneous licensing at repeated intervals might have made it necessary for the licensing authorities to give more systematic thought to phasing than was evident through the period. Furthermore, it is equally likely that some form of simultaneous consideration of industrial licensing applications would have been an inducement to the licensing bodies to evolve

[1] Op. cit., pp. 152–4.

[2] We hasten to add that the notion that simultaneous consideration should result in choice of projects with 'minimum foreign exchange content' is of course absurd as it ignores *indirect* imports and also implicitly puts an infinite price on foreign exchange.

[3] Cf. R. K. Hazari, op. cit., p. 18:

'Licences are normally or, in most cases, issued for a capacity 10 to 25 per cent above the target for the end-Plan year and that, too, mostly around the beginning of a Plan period. An excessive—though quantitatively un-verifiable—pressure is thus exerted on the available foreign exchange and possible collaborators and also on domestic suppliers. This leads to bottle-necks and delays, apart from adversely affecting the terms of negotiations with foreign and domestic suppliers and creditors.

Also see the *Ninth Report of the Estimates Committee*, pp. 162–4.

some systematic criteria and compelled the D.G.T.D. to undertake supporting analysis. The sequential licensing procedures were, in fact, part of the general apathy to notions of efficient industrial planning and regulation.

(4) *Delays*

The two Swaminathan Committees, reporting in 1964 and 1966, as also the Mathur Study Team's Report on the D.G.T.D., revealed several inefficiencies in the administrative procedures, leading to delays without any corresponding *quid pro quo*. The lapse of time in acquiring information in order to take informed decisions on licensing applications would have a social justification (assuming, of course, that the criteria used were sensible and social and private profitabilities diverged so as to necessitate rational intervention). But where the delays are attributable to inefficient procedures and inadequate appreciation of the opportunity cost of time and the necessity to implement programmes on schedule, they represent a net loss to society.

The first Swaminathan Committee found, for example, that the requirement under Rule 15 of the Registration and Licensing Undertakings Rules (1952) that the applications must be decided upon in three months, had been flouted in most cases, and without justification: 'during the course of case studies it has been noticed that undue delays have often taken place *in the process of mere physical distribution of applications.*'[1] The revised procedures suggested by this Committee were sought to be implemented and disposals of applications were expected to take five weeks: however, the subsequent investigation of the 1965 Mathur Study Team on the D.G.T.D. showed that, on the basis of 122 case studies, six months was still the *average* time taken for case disposal. The Estimates Committee, reporting in 1967, was still to find the procedures dilatory and was constrained to comment:

While the Committee note that as a result of the implementation of the recommendations of the Industries Development Procedures Committee the time taken in the processing of applications for industrial licensing has come down from over 6 months i.e., 180 days to nearly 145 days; they, however, consider that even the period of 145 days is still on the high side. The Committee cannot but strongly urge that constant

[1] Cf. 'Speeding up Industrial Licensing', *Economic Weekly*, 18 January 1964 [italics have been inserted].

endeavours should be made to bring down the period at least to the level of the time table (70 days in the case of more simple cases and about 100 days in others) suggested by the Study Team on D.G.T.D. as a result of their case study. They have a feeling that if the records are kept properly up to date and the movement of the applications is closely watched, it should not be difficult to achieve the desired results.[1]

These delays were characteristic of the entire bureaucratic régime involved in industrial licensing. With respect to the Foreign Agreements Committee, for example, the situation was equally dismal. Thus, the Estimates Committee (1967–8) again observed:

. . . Government have furnished the following break-up of the time taken up to 6 months, between 6 months and one year and more than one year in deciding applications for foreign collaboration during the last 2 years:

	1965	*1966*
1. Total number of applications for foreign collaboration decided during the years 1965 and 1966	264	226
2. No. of applications out of (1) above which were decided within 6 months	153	138
3. No. of applications out of (1) above which were decided between 6 months and one year	79	51
4. No. of applications out of (1) above which were decided after more than a year	32	37

. . . The Committee regret to note that there is considerable delay in finalising applications for foreign collaborations. As many as 42 per cent applications in 1965 and 39 per cent in 1966 remained undecided after 6 months of their receipt. Out of these, over 12 per cent in 1965 and over 16 per cent in 1966 were decided after more than a year. It would appear that strict watch is not being kept over the time taken in the disposal of these applications.[2]

For capital goods import licensing, for which separate clearance again had to be obtained from the C.G.C. (the Capital Goods Committee), Hazari has noted that:

As of January 1964 (for which the latest data are available), 751 applications for foreign exchange equivalent to Rs. 231 crores (pre-devaluation) were pending with CGC for more than one year. Applications received in 1961 and earlier, i.e., pending for more than two years, were 182, and these indented foreign exchange of Rs. 173 crores.[3]

---

[1] *Ninth Report*, p. 172.   [2] Ibid., pp. 240–1.
[3] Op. cit., p. 33, para. 41.1.

(5) *Administrative exemptions and restrictions without economic rationale.*

Further, it is interesting that the operation of the licensing system was extended only to units over a certain size. The precise exemption limit was to vary over the period. From February 1960, all industrial undertakings in the scheduled industries employing less than one hundred workers and with fixed assets less than Rs. 10 lakhs, were exempted from licensing. From January 1964 this exemption limit was raised to fixed assets less than Rs. 25 lakhs—except for a few industries such as coal, textiles, leather, and matches.[1]

It is difficult to see any *economic* rationale in operating with such exemptions given the fact that the licensing system was aimed at operation of the industrial sector within the framework of targets. If capacities had to be licensed so as to approximate target fulfilment, then the procedures could not exempt units *merely* because their assets fell below a certain size. On this criterion: (i) capacities could end up diverging from targets in industries where such 'smaller', organized-sector units were possible (and could not be eliminated by competition from the larger units, whose capacities were controlled by the licensing bodies); and (ii) industries where such enterprises were readily feasible could end up being virtually delinked from regulation in terms of targets.[2]

---

[1] Economists such as Hazari have recently recommended raising this limit further to Rs. 1 crore for new undertakings, with a view to reducing the load of work for the licensing bodies: according to his examination of the licensing data, this would mean that 75 per cent of the investment would be covered and the number of applications to be considered would reduce to less than 100 (op. cit., p. 31). Such a suggestion, of course, seems welcome on *administrative* grounds and one may only wonder why the limit should be placed where it is. Furthermore, Hazari does not consider the possibility that the effect of raising the exemption limit to Rs. 1 crore may well be to induce some of the present more-than-one-crore applicants to redesign their plants downwards to escape the licensing botherations, so that the actual proportion of investments covered under his scheme may be less than his estimate.

[2] The same criticism would apply with respect to efficiency of location and regional balance, choice of technique, etc., which were presumably the objectives of the licensing mechanism and would need to apply equally to the units exempted by virtue merely of their size. However, we must qualify this extension of our argument on the ground that it may well be 'economic' to confine a control to a smaller number of projects if this ensures that the control is more efficiently operated (since each case can be given more careful attention) and if it still covers the bulk of investment. When administrative resources are scarce, this is obviously an important aspect to remember.

The fact that exemptions designed to reduce the administrative load could interfere with the efficiency of planning (*as conceived by the authorities*) does not appear to have bothered them into re-designing the exemptions so as to be consistent with efficiency.

But if the exemptions had little economic rationale[1] within the given system, this was even more so with respect to the *restrictions* which the licensing régime imposed upon the successful applicants. The licensing system, we may note, distinguished between three basic categories: applicants for: (i) new undertakings; (ii) substantial expansion; and (iii) manufacture of new articles.

In addition to applications for setting up new plants, Section 13(*d*) of the Industries Act also laid down that no 'substantial expansion' could be undertaken by any licensed or registered industrial undertaking without prior procurement of a licence. Similarly, Section 11-A of the same Act had even laid down the condition that the manufacture of a 'new article', not specified in the initial licence, also required a fresh authorization and licence.

In practice, the 'substantial expansion' restriction was not merely ambiguous because entrepreneurs were unsure what the bureau-crats would consider to be substantial rather than insubstantial increment in productive capacity,[2] but there were also several instances where improvements in *productivity*, arising from greater efficiency, would not be 'legitimated' by the authorities. The difficulty arose because, in view of the general practice of allocating A.U. import licences *pro rata* to capacity—as we discuss in Chapter 17—the authorities were suspicious of any claims that productivity had increased thanks to improvements in organization, etc. But this also meant that better methods of capital utilization (e.g.

[1] Other exemptions from licensing, which came with the general liberalization beginning in 1965 and accelerating with the June 1966 devaluation, were rather more radical in nature and are considered by us in Part VIII when we review all the major shifts towards the liberal, 'new economic policy'.

[2] Cf. *Ninth Report of the Estimates Committee*, p. 189:

> During the course of evidence in October 1966, the Secretary of the Ministry of Industrial Development and Company Affairs confirmed that 'the Industries Act does not define positively what is substantial expansion. It does not really lay down in terms of percentage.' About the percentage he stated that 'up to 10 per cent we do not really treat as in any way substantial, because if expansion of production takes place up to about 10 per cent, we recognize it automatically'. When asked to state after how many years the increase of 10 per cent was allowed, he stated that 'There was no fixed period but if the same entrepreneur comes along every alternate year for a 10 per cent increase that will be taken note of.'

through increased shifts or better management practices) were, in practice, difficult to adopt without much fuss and were occasionally frustrated.[1] A possible way to minimize such inefficiencies would have been to define substantial expansion in terms of *investments* rather than output: but clearly no thought was given to the matter.

In this connection, it is also worth noting a more novel criticism directed at the licensing bodies' general failure to approve of an industrial licence envisaging and approving expansion in different stages over a long period of time:

It has been represented to the Committee by a leading industrialist that 'Where expansion involves more than one stage, the practice of the Government has been to sanction only the first stage expansion without any assurance or guarantee that the subsequent expansion would follow automatically. The routes to two different stages of expansion, for technical reasons, cannot be identical though fundamentally the process is the same and unless the Government accord the company a letter of intent for entire expansion from first stage to last, it would be uneconomic to order out the equipment required for the expansion schemes in two different distinct stages.' It has been suggested that 'Where the expansion involves more than one stage, a letter of intent or licence should be issued for the entire expansion programme so that the industrial unit can take appropriate action to implement the entire expansion programme in an integrated and co-ordinated manner.'

3.160. Expressing his views on the above suggestion, the Secretary of the Ministry of Industrial Development and Company Affairs stated during evidence that 'This has to be very carefully considered in each case because otherwise a man may book a lot of capacity and create monopoly. We have to consider each case on merits and also consider what is the nature of the industry and the position of the industrialist.'

3.161. It is well recognized that goods can be produced more economically by expansion of the existing units rather than by setting up new

[1] Yet another effect of these occasional refusals to 'recognize' improved productive capacities was a tendency typically to understate the capacity figures which the D.G.T.D. compiled regularly for publication. These estimates, in any case, were notoriously bad, with no attempts made to define capacity systematically and with most of the estimates given on the basis of a single-shift only. Again, the 'techno-economic' inexpertise of the D.G.T.D., as revealed by their competence in dealing with the question of capacity estimation and evaluation of reasons for underutilization, was dismal. Cf. Bhagwati, 'Economies of Scale, Distribution of Industry and Programming', *Economic Weekly*, 1 September 1962.

undertakings. Keeping in view the public demand for supply of goods at competitive prices, the Committee suggest that Government should earnestly consider the suggestion that the expansion programme submitted by established units, may be expeditiously considered and where found acceptable, letters of intent covering the entire expansion programme may be issued provided this does not encourage and create monopolies. Import licences for implementing the expansion programme may be regulated keeping in view the stage of expansion and the availability of foreign exchange.[1]

The Ministry's raising of the standard difficulty about monopoly creation, in this instance as in others, is clearly unconvincing and a convenient substitute for revising a licensing procedure which was not worked out with reference to considerations of economic efficiency.

The *severe* restrictions on manufacture of 'new articles' had little economic rationale either. Although the diversification of production was to be permitted, with many restrictions including a ceiling of 25 per cent of the capacity, in 1965–6, the full-scale restrictions on diversification were to continue through practically the entire period of the three Plans. Since hardly any targets were specified at the level of detailed *products*, the restriction imposed was excessive even in relation to the stated objectives of planning; and relaxation permitting automatic diversification of output, within broader limits, would have been compatible with such objectives. In any case, for industries where *no* targets were specified, the possible diversification, in response to market forces, could have been allowed within yet *wider* limits.[2] The technological possibilities of product diversification, from the type of plant being sanctioned, could have also been readily considered, with the aid of the D.G.T.D., in such cases and, if necessary, certain products ruled out to begin with. Again, therefore, we have here an example of licensing procedures devised without reference to clear notions of efficient, industrial planning.

---

[1] *Ninth Report of the Estimates Committee*, pp. 190–1.
[2] Note that our criticisms so far have been based on the limiting assumption that the targeting system was desirable and the targets should be fulfilled. Our preference for a system with indicative planning in most industries, with a few priority areas regulated in depth, would lead to still stronger criticism of such restrictions as the one on diversification: we enter into this discussion later in the chapter.

III. LOCATIONAL POLICY

We now examine the efficiency with which the licensing and regulation system managed to achieve the objectives of balanced development and prevention of concentration in the ownership of industrial wealth.

On locational policy, the Industries Act (1951), the Industrial Policy Resolutions and the Five-Year Plan documents have been equally articulate in stressing the need for balanced development. Any policy relating to industrial planning in a federal country such as India would, in any case, have had to come to terms with the needs of regional claims. In fact, the Licensing Committee's operation was continually sought to be influenced by the states which wished to attract industrial investments within their borders. Thus, the Estimates Committee (1967–8) records that:

It has been stated by the official representative of the Ministry that 'Quite a number of States keep on representing that their areas have not received adequate share of licences. I have not got the figures of the number of representations, but it is a fact that from time to time, Chief Ministers of States and Industries Ministers of States do write to us pointing out that their States, in their opinion, have not received a fair share of the licences. As my colleague explained, we have no compulsive means of attracting people to particular areas. We consider the applications as we receive them and provided the location in a particular area is not too uneconomic, other things being reasonably equal, we do give preference to the more underdeveloped areas.'

2.46. In reply to another question, the representative of the Planning Commission has informed the Committee during evidence that besides the economic and technological considerations 'there may be other elements like regional considerations which may have to be introduced in the consideration of particular projects. But for major projects and for projects in the export industries particularly, the economic and technological considerations are considered paramount.[1]

As the foregoing quote also underlines, the intervention by the States was not exactly unsuccessful and, except when there were major or, of late 'export-intensive' projects, the remaining applications could be influenced by political pulls and pressures. The considerable proliferation of *uneconomic-scale* plants which attended

[1] *Ninth Report*, paras. 2.45 and 2.46.

the progress of industrialization in the country during the three Plans has been generally admitted to be a consequence of these pressures, with the Licensing Committee preferring, *de facto*, to satisfy as many claimant states as possible.[1]

In effect, the situation was similar to that obtaining at the international level, where the eagerness to industrialize has led many less developed countries (L.D.C.s) to industrialize behind high tariff walls, and quantitative restrictions, prompting economists to advocate greater, *mutual* reduction in barriers to trade expansion enabling exploitation of economies of scale and specialization, *consistent with each L.D.C. attaining the same degree of industrialization.*[2]

The failure of the Indian planners to work out the space-dimension of their industrial targets, on the basis of economic efficiency constrained by state targets of overall industrial investments designed to assure the states that they would get some minimum industrialization, in effect left the field almost entirely to political pressures. With no state assured of ultimately (at the end of the Plan) getting some minimum largesse, there was a scramble for most industrial licences, thus creating a great political pressure for dividing up each target among as many states as possible; with the Licensing Committee, aided in turn by no clues to optimal size, location, and phasing of expansion of plants by its 'techno-economic' counsel (the D.G.T.D.), these political pulls often ruled the day.[3]

---

[1] In this policy, they were also assisted by their reference to the fear that monopoly power may follow if there were a fewer number of units in an industry. We return to this contention, exposing its fallacy, when we turn to the discussion of monopoly power and concentration.

[2] Cf. C. A. Cooper and B. Massell, 'Toward a General Theory of Customs Unions for Developing Countries', *Journal of Political Economy*, October 1965; and J. Bhagwati, 'Trade Liberalization Among LDC's, Trade Theory and Gatt Rules' in J. N. Wolfe (ed.), *Value, Capital and Growth: Essays in Honour of J. R. Hicks.*

[3] Cf. the *Ninth Report of the Estimates Committee*, p. 195, quoting an eminent industrialist's evidence:

> [The] Government were proposing to have two units of an industry in U.P. in the public sector. Then pressure came from Madhya Pradesh. They said: You must have something for us also. Our State is also backward. The result was that the Government yielded and decided to have one Unit in U.P. and another in M.P. This is purely because of regional consideration. This should not be the criterion for putting up an industry or industrial unit. Factors such as land, water, power and transport facilities must be taken into consideration before we finally decide on the location.

The failure was thus again of industrial *planning*. Clearly, the level of real income that could be attained, subject to the political constraint that each state should have some pre-defined share of industrial investments, would be less than if there were no such constraints. But industrial planning in India failed to reduce the cost of such a constrained system to its minimum and, in fact, operated with a consistent bias in favour of plants being reduced to uneconomic scale most of the time.[1]

IV. CONCENTRATION AND MONOPOLY POWER

The success of the licensing and regulation system in checking the concentration of industrial ownership and in promoting a competitive system was no greater and, paradoxically, the system is almost certain to have even worked in the contrary direction in many respects.

(i) As many observers, including the Monopolies Inquiry Commission (1965), have noted, the bigger business houses could utilize the licensing-plus-targeting system to the detriment of smaller rivals.[2] They could put in for licences more readily, since they were better informed and organized, and thus jump ahead of others in the queue—a matter of some importance, as we have seen, in a *sequential* licensing system. Furthermore, they could get their successful applications moving more quickly towards implementation and hence suffer a smaller risk of the licence-revocation practised by the licensing authorities: the market mechanism would not have made the smaller rivals quicker but it would have permitted them entry.[3] Moreover, the implicit acceptance of the

---

To further elaborate this, I would point out to you that Government has been thinking of putting up steel plants in Salem and Andhra Pradesh. Tell me from raw-materials point of view or even power, whether these two sites are suitable?

[1] Cf. Bhagwati, 'Economies of Scale . . . ', *Economic Weekly*, September 1962, op. cit. Also see Hazari's 1967 Report on *Industrial Planning and Licensing Policy*, op. cit., pp. 24–5.

[2] 'The percentage of licenses issued to those applied for, works out at 71·6 per cent for big business and 65·1 per cent for the rest' according to the *Ninth Report*, p. 173, quoting the Monopolies Inquiry Commission. This, of course, is only indicative rather than decisive.

[3] The following quote from the Monopolies Inquiry Commission, in the *Ninth Report*, p. 176, is of interest:

Much more, we think, can be done, to make it easy for the comparatively smaller entrepreneur to get industrial and import licences without undue

T

availability of foreign collaboration and finance as a criterion for preferring an application, which Hazari has recorded, also put the smaller entrepreneur at a disadvantage in relation to bigger rivals with more international contacts.

(ii) More important, it appears likely from the available evidence that the bigger houses realized that they could corner a considerable amount of targeted capacity by putting in multiple and early applications for the *same* industry, and thus develop a fairly dominant place in the industries where this tactic worked.[1] Hazari, who has investigated this possibility at length, is inclined even to argue that the intention behind multiple applications was to 'foreclose capacity', the intention to implement the successful licence applications being sometimes not even serious, as in the case of some Birla trading concerns which secured licences but had practically no assets, could not pursue them and ended up seeking their transfer or resale.

These arguments are obviously not decisive. Just as Adam Smith pointed to the possibility of collusion among independent producers, the reverse possibility of different Birla concerns, part of a huge and diffused empire, being competitive in seeking expansion—particularly when *reinvestment* of profits in expansion was restricted by licensing and other outlets were therefore necessary—is not entirely implausible. Furthermore, in view of the political pressures for regional balances that we have already described, it is possible that, rather than submit one application for a large plant in a single location, the business houses found it shrewder to submit more applications for smaller plants in *different* states. Hazari's contention thus bears more careful investigation; nonetheless, it is quite suggestive.

(iii) Much more pertinent, however, is the criticism that the entire attempt at controlling the growth of industrial houses in

---

expenses and wasteful delay. Many of the leading industrialists, we understand, have found it necessary to maintain expensive establishments in the capital for facilitating the obtaining of licences. Those who cannot afford the expenses of running such establishments which include sometimes, it seems, large amounts required to employ high paid 'contactmen' and to give lavish parties—are at a disadvantage.

[1] Hazari has produced a considerable amount of evidence in support of his thesis that several industrial houses put in, often successfully, multiple applications for a single industry in a single Plan period. See Table 16, in op. cit., which is particularly exhaustive on the house of Birlas.

different industries by industrial licensing was likely to be ineffective as there were no provisions for preventing acquisition of existing undertakings by the large industrial houses.[1]

A belated awareness of this fundamental critique of the industrial policy, given its objective of reducing concentration, is evident in the statement of the Minister of Industrial Development and Company Affairs in the Rajya Sabha (the Upper House) on 31 May 1967:

it is possible that today the Licensing Committee may give a licence to 'A' who may have nothing to do with Birla, or Tata or any other company, but after that 'A' has implemented all the requirements of that licence or has set up a particular industry, what is there to prevent Birla or Tata from purchasing that industry? Therefore in many of the cases when you find that the companies multiply, it may not be because of the defect in the licensing system or because of any illegality committed by our officers in giving licences but because of *this inherent defect in our system* and because of our inability to control such kind of lapses on the part of those who are getting licences, who are not able to carry on and then ultimately they are purchased by other big persons. These are matters which we have to take into consideration.[2]

(iv) Finally, Bhagwati has pointed to another fundamental defect of the licensing-plus-targeting system, combined with strict Q.R.s on competing imports and non-transferability between firms of A.U. import licences for raw materials and components: namely, its elimination of the possibility of competition in any meaningful sense of the term:

The first major point that occurs to an economist, when discussing the question of monopoly and competition in the Indian economy, is that a very large segment of the economy . . . works under monopolistic

---

[1] Cf. J. Bhagwati and T. N. Srinivasan, 'Licensing and Control of Industry', Paper submitted to the *Prime Minister's Conference for Young Industrialists*, March 1966: 'Under the existing system, since there is no effective control on resale of enterprises once they are licensed, it is not clear how the first objective [of reduction in concentration of ownership] is served by investment licensing. Even if there is resale control or anti-merger regulations, there is nothing to prevent an entrepreneurial group getting licences through benami [i.e. use of different names] transactions. The same objectives could be more efficiently, though perhaps less dramatically, served by more positive action through easier access to credit and "know-how" to potential new comers.'

[2] Quoted in the *Ninth Report of the Estimates Committee*, p. 172 [italics have been inserted by us].

conditions. The creation of new capacity in the organized industrial sector is strictly controlled at various levels. Capital issues control, licensing and the permission to import machinery are the principal points at which the *entry* into an industry is controlled by the government. This is the concomitant of a system under which the government works with a set of *targets*. The net effect of this system is to make the entry of new competitors impossible—as the government will not allow creation of more capacity than current, estimated demand. It thus rules out the elimination of inefficient current producers by efficient, *new entrants*. It *also* rules out the possibility of the more efficient, *current* units expanding and eliminating the inefficient, current units: expansion by current units is as much subject to control within targets as expansion through new firms. (This elimination of competition is applicable even to the *utilisation* of existing capacity. Materials and exchange are frequently allocated on a *pro rata* basis rather than to efficient producers.) If, then, competition from efficient rivals at home is ruled out by our economic planners, what about foreign competition? Here again, competition has no chance! The use of import quotas rules out the possibility of competition from abroad. We are thus in an economic situation where the possibility of competition from potential entry by domestic or foreign rivals is minimised.[1]

This picture is clearly overdrawn for emphasis. And Bhagwati was careful to note that exceptions would arise in industries where small-scale entry was easy and viable and where capacity creation based on the targets happened to exceed the actual demand—a fairly uncommon situation in Indian industries until 1966. But basically the picture was correct.

Thus, not merely was the licensing-targeting system, with related policies, responsible for creating monopolies over much of the industrial scene but also the attempts at breaking up plants into a larger number of uneconomic plants to increase the number of 'competitors' ignored the important economic insight that it is the possibility of *entry* that makes a situation competitive and not just increasing the number of units (especially in a framework which itself fostered a monopolistic environment).

[1] Bhagwati, 'Monopoly in Public Enterprise', *The Working of the Public Sector* (Proceedings of the Third All-India Seminar on Public Enterprise at Hyderabad, 1963), op. cit., pp. 91–2. Also see Bhagwati, *Economic Weekly*, September 1962, op. cit.

V. THE OVERALL PICTURE

Thus the overall picture of industrial planning emerging from our analysis in this and the previous chapter is dismal. Through nearly all the period spanning the three Plans, target-setting had a weak economic basis, was overly detailed and comprehensive, and was taken too seriously in industrial licensing as far as *restraining* the growth of capacity was involved. At the same time the licensing procedures were not designed to ensure or encourage fulfilment of important targets, the follow-through was weak, the criteria of efficient choice among applicants were not defined, and the licensing procedures were designed so as even to rule out the consideration of such choices, and objectives such as balanced regional growth and prevention of concentration in ownership were reiterated, but no procedures were devised to achieve them at minimum economic cost. Indeed, in some cases the procedures even encouraged the frustration of these very objectives.

By 1965/6, when new economic policies in the direction of 'liberalism' were to be seriously debated and their implementation begun, several economists were to propose alternative ways in which industrial planning might be pursued with efficiency and the Government was to initiate some changes such as the delicensing of several industries. A critical discussion of these proposals and governmental measures will be found in Part VIII. We turn now to a brief consideration of the related control measures, on price and distribution, which also affected to some degree the course of industrialization in the country.

14
Other Industrial Controls:
Price and Distribution

RELIANCE on physical controls, rather than the price mechanism, was a characteristic of Indian policy on price and distribution of several manufactures and semi-manufactures and was not confined to industrial licensing.

Powers to control the distribution and prices of industrial products can be traced to the second world war, when they were systematically used under the Defence of India Rules. They were replaced by other statutory enactments in the immediate post-war period and finally culminated in the Essential Commodities Act of 1955. At the same time, under Section 18(G), the Industries Act of 1951 had already conferred such powers with respect to the Scheduled Industries (discussed by us in the two preceding chapters).

Thus, among the major statutory provisions under which the Government could operate controls during the period of our study were: (i) the Essential Commodities Act under which, for example, controls over iron and steel, coal, fertilizers, and cotton textiles were operated; and (ii) the Industries (Development and Regulation) Act under which, for example, cement, motor-cars, and commercial vehicles were controlled. In addition, the operation of 'informal' price controls was not uncommon.

The entire period of our study witnessed the operation of price and distribution controls over several manufactures: iron and steel, non-ferrous metals, coal, fertilizers, cinema carbons, cotton textiles, paper, sugar, motor-cars, scooters, commercial vehicles, ethyl alcohol, molasses, cement, drugs and medicines, kerosene and other petroleum products, bicycles, tyres and tubes, natural rubber, vanaspati, soap, and matches. Not all these items were controlled at all times. Nor were they all subjected to both price and distribution controls, many being subjected merely to price control.[1]

Among the motivating factors behind this direct regulation of distribution and prices, we find the following on detailed review of these controls:

(1) Several controls were motivated by a desire to ensure allocation of adequate amounts to 'priority' sectors, often at some 'reasonable' price. For example, the control over iron and steel embraced both price and distribution. But, as we will discuss at length when we come to our discussion of import policy, the Committee appointed by the Minister for Steel, C. Subramanian, under the Chairmanship of a well-known socialist (Professor K. N. Raj of Delhi University) to investigate the working of steel distribution, reported in 1963 the grossest abuses of the control mechanism that could be feared.[2] Priorities were not defined and allocations were chaotic and often prompted by graft. It also turned out that, quite apart from the Iron and Steel Controller's Office having little clue to priorities in making its distribution decisions, price control merely implied that (largely) public sector steel was being sold to (mainly) private sector users at controlled prices, whereas these users were under no obligation whatsoever to price their outputs on a cost-plus basis and hence priced what the market would bear. The effect of such price control, therefore, was merely to subsidize the user industries, enabling them to earn the profits which otherwise would have been earned by the producers of iron and steel (who were mostly in the public sector). This represented therefore a policy leading to loss of 'revenue' for the Government, without any real 'benefit' (in terms of lower prices) accruing to the *final* consumers of products using iron and steel.

Cement controls were also prompted by similar considerations. Originally, the control over price and distribution had been imposed in 1942, during the second world war, largely to ensure the supply of cement for defence purposes at controlled rates. But this control was to continue later and the system of pricing and distribution came to be directly controlled by the Government. In

---

[1] Sometimes there was merely price, rather than distribution, control as with bicycles; at times, there were distribution, but not price, controls as with scooters.

[2] *Report of Steel Control*, Ministry of Steel and Heavy Industries, Government of India, New Delhi, 1963.

July 1956 a uniform all-India selling price was fixed for packed cement and the distribution was handed over to the State Trading Corporation. However, the *retail* prices for users were allowed to be fixed by different state governments. Essentially, therefore, the scheme amounted to ensuring that the producers received no more than a preassigned price, the price to users was determined by different state governments, the shares of different regions in the country in the allocations were a function of direct allocational decisions implemented by the State Trading Corporation, and the industry-level priorities were determined by a variety of agencies on criteria which were left ill-defined (much as with import allocations which we discuss in depth in Part VII). The problems with cement control were similar to those with steel control: priorities were frequently unclear; the *final* prices paid by consumers of items produced by the users of cement did not reflect necessarily the fact that the cement price itself was controlled at a lower level than market forces required; and the distributive agencies were frequently known to demand graft which tended to offset the differential between controlled and market prices anyway.[1] In addition, it was soon realized that the price obtained by the producers was fixed at too low a level to permit the expansion of supplies in the long run; cement production was known for falling way behind the targets in the Plans.

(2) Some distribution and price controls were motivated by 'equity' considerations. For example, the distribution and sale of motor-cars was controlled from May 1959 under the Industries (Development and Regulation) Act and an informal, but effective, price control was exercised. An important part of the distributive system was the allocation of a quota for official allotment to civil servants and politicians in government on a 'priority' basis. Since the 'free' market rates on cars were frequently in considerable excess of the controlled prices, the system amounted to subsidizing

---

[1] The fact that several governmental 'priority' sectors were getting cement at controlled rates, whereas a large premium attached to cement in the black market, also led to considerable illegal evasion through the priority sectors leaking cement on to the market. Thus, private construction was frequently observed to flourish, despite lack of legal cement allocations, whenever there was a public sector project under construction nearby. Such a practice would not have arisen, with its consequences for the quality of public sector construction and public morality in general, if alternative means had been found for ensuring supplies to the 'priority' sectors (see Chapter 22).

the use of cars by civil servants: this being a subsidy designed by the civil servants and politicians in power for their own benefit.[1] Since the remaining car sales were made on a queuing system, this amounted also to conferring on those who were ahead in the queue the sale of a premium-fetching car when their turn came.[2] Since the Government could well have levied excise duties to pick up such premia as revenue, the entire system amounted to an implicit subsidy, of a regressive kind, to consumers who were sufficiently well off to be able to buy and maintain cars—an income class which would generally be in the top two deciles in India—and, in particular, to the politicians and civil servants themselves. If this subsidy had been paid *explicitly* from governmental revenues, we may well wonder whether it would not have provoked stiff opposition.

(3) Another major reason for price control was the desire to prevent 'inflationary' effects. This was undoubtedly one of the important motivations underlying the steel, cement, and coal controls. For example, coal prices were controlled continuously through our period, until 1960 when partial moves towards liberalization began. It was only by July 1967 that the prices of all coking and non-coking coals were to be decontrolled (with coal distribution also being decontrolled with minor exceptions). In this case, as also with steel and cement, the fear was that increased prices, reflecting scarcity, would spill over into an *overall* rise in the price level because these were 'basic' products with many forward linkages. As we shall see later in Part VII, this was an argument used also with respect to import policy, to discourage any move towards an exchange rate adjustment. On the other hand, this argument lacked an empirical basis. As the Raj Committee found, for example, in its investigation of steel controls, the final price paid by users of steel *products* rarely failed to reflect market scarcities. Furthermore, as many beneficiaries of allotments of quotas found, especially with respect to steel and cement controls, quotas just failed to come through speedily unless, in several cases, a part

---

[1] From a sociological point of view, it is interesting that controls (such as on cars), which redounded to the benefit of the groups recommending and implementing the controls, were more readily implemented than the controls (on foodgrains distribution, for example) which would have had far greater, and ethically more acceptable, impact on income distribution.

[2] There were occasional restrictions on resale of cars allotted under official quotas; but these were hardly effective.

of the premium were handed over as graft at various levels. Finally, the argument that such shifts in relative prices were necessarily inflationary, even if we were to rule out the preceding two empirical objections, presupposed that no adjustments in relative prices of these 'basic' goods were feasible: a proposition which seems to have no empirical basis at all.

In general, therefore, the bulk of the controls over prices and distribution which were exercised by the Government through our period of study were ill-advised and formed a part of the general economic philosophy of direct intervention without careful examination of direct efficiency *and* of efficiency *vis-à-vis* alternative ways of achieving given objectives. Controls over prices and distribution *can* be a rational form of policy, as we shall argue in Chapter 22 when we review the later moves towards economic liberalism in general, and decontrol of prices and distribution in particular. There is little evidence, however, that the actual choice and working of price and distributional controls conformed to such rationality.

Having thus reviewed the principal forms of industrial policy, relating to investments, pricing, and distribution, which were exercised by the Indian Government during the period of the three Five-Year Plans, we now proceed to examine at length the working of *foreign* trade policy instruments in Part VII.

Foreign Trade Policy Instruments

15
Import Policy: 1

In this chapter and the next, we describe and evaluate the methods of foreign exchange allocation among competing users which India came to acquire and maintain through the bulk of the period under examination.

These methods, which involved essentially the operation of a tight régime of import (and complementary exchange) restrictions, were perfected especially after the 1956/7 exchange crisis and were somewhat relaxed for a period after the devaluation in June 1966. Thus they applied, strictly speaking, in the form in which we shall now proceed to analyse them, for most of the decade: 1956–66.[1]

A few remarks will nonetheless be addressed to the evolution of the system prior to 1956/7. The period after June 1966, which initiated certain major changes which were not to survive for long, is discussed in a later chapter.

I. EVOLUTION OF THE IMPORT CONTROL RÉGIME

Import controls in India date back to the second world war and were imposed first in May 1940, starting mainly with consumer goods, and were gradually extended till they embraced practically all imports by January 1942. The specific stated aims of the policy were to conserve scarce foreign exchange and shipping for the war. The principle of 'essentiality' was evolved for regulating imports but the controls remained essentially qualitative and no ceilings were laid down for specific imports on a comprehensive basis. Imports from the Sterling Area were regulated mainly by reference

---

[1] Even this statement is a little strong. For example, already by 1965 many procedural improvements had been effected in import policy, which reduced delays in principle and attempted to remove a few other inefficiencies.

to shipping availability rather than by considerations of the balance of payments.

In the post-war years, extensive liberalization followed, with the scope of Open General Licences being considerably widened during 1945 and 1946 and extended comprehensively to the Sterling Area countries. This was soon to be followed by revival of restrictions from 1947 as India's balance of payments turned adverse. With formal restrictions on the rate at which the sterling balances (accumulated during the war by India) could be run down, exchange control was extended in July 1947 to the entire world including the Sterling Area and the main objective of import controls became the regulation of scarce foreign exchange. Thus began the changeover from 'qualitative' to 'quantitative' licensing on the basis of specified exchange ceilings allotted for specific commodities and groups, designated by currency areas.

During the subsequent years, there were occasional periods of 'liberalization' as in mid-May 1948 when a large number of 'non-essential' industrial and consumer goods were added to the list of articles which were freely licensable from sterling and other soft currency areas, and in November 1948 when the items under O.G.L.s were further expanded. These periods of liberalization alternated with periods of increasing restriction when the payments position became tight as in early 1949 and through the rest of that year. The period of the First Five-Year Plan (1951–5), however, was generally one of 'progressive liberalization', especially towards the end.

The machinery for import and exchange control remained intact right up to the beginning of the decade 1956–66, although it went through many administrative and structural changes.[1] It is of some importance and interest to note, further, that (in contrast to the experience during the subsequent period 1956–66) the Government sought occasionally to reduce reliance on the import control system by using the tariff mechanism. Thus, for example, the second half of 1954 saw substantial changes in the tariff structure, effected by the India Tariff (Second Amendment) Act, 1954. Import duties were stepped up in the case of thirty-two items, permitting the Government to experiment with some relaxation in import policy: as a result, quota percentages in many cases were

---

[1] It would be too tedious to trace all of these here. In any case, they have little relevance to the analysis we presently engage in.

increased, and in other cases provision was made for the issue of additional licences over and above normal entitlements.

The progressively liberal measures and the willingness to use tariff policy to ease the pressure on quantitative restrictions were both to be undermined by the exchange crisis which attended upon the beginning of the Second Five-Year Plan. As a result, the import control régime was to become much more tight. It was also, in consequence of the continuing difficulties with the balance of payments and plans for rapid industrialization through the ensuing decade, to become geared more directly *in principle* to the notion of 'priorities'.

II. ORGANIZATION AND PROCEDURES

We shall describe briefly here the principal organizational and procedural features of the import control régime, so as to provide the necessary background to the discussion that will follow, relating to the principles of allocation and the economic aspects thereof.

The import and exchange policy régime, throughout this period, aimed at comprehensive, direct control over foreign exchange utilization. Thus administrative decisions had to be made over the allocation of foreign exchange for practically all uses in the economy. For the overwhelming bulk of imports, further, the Government (except for a beginning in this direction after the budget in 1965) did not explicitly aim at using tariffs either to siphon off the resulting import premia or to regulate imports via the price-mechanism; the only well-known exceptions being crude rubber, pulp and waste paper, cotton, and kerosene.[1] Reliance on the direct allocative mechanism was thus almost complete during this period.

The allocation of permissible imports was broadly by two administrative categories: private sector and public sector. Further, there was an important, operational distinction between imports of raw materials, spares, and components as against imports of

---

[1] Furthermore, in the case of kerosene, imports were quite freely licensed with the import duty flexibly used to restrict imports to desired levels, the duty having risen threefold to 170 per cent *ad valorem* by 1965 from its 1960 level. For the other three commodities, however, the administrative controls were used as a supplement in times of acute shortage. On all this, see Lindblom, *Indian Import Controls*, U.S.A.I.D., New Delhi, July 1965, p. 3.

capital goods and equipment. The allocation of different permissible imports by these categories among industries, and further still by firms and plants, was carried out by an elaborate administrative machinery which evolved through the period. Since the details of this evolution are of little economic significance, we confine ourselves here to describing the system as it was at its peak, around 1965, when it began to be 'liberalized' gradually into the somewhat major changes that came with the devaluation of the rupee in June 1966.[1]

For every six months, 1 April to 30 September, and 1 October to 31 March, the Foreign Exchange Budget Branch of the Department of Economic Affairs in the Ministry of Finance would prepare its estimate of available foreign exchange for the six-month period.[2] When the first charge expenditures such as debt repayments and Embassy expenditures had been netted out, the residual estimate of available foreign exchange would have to be allocated among different users. Food, fertilizers, P.O.L., and defence would be normally pre-empted first.

The administrative allocation, at the next stage, was essentially at three points: (i) an allocation was earmarked for the different public sector undertakings, for both raw materials and equipment, and was assigned to the Ministries within whose domain they lay; (ii) the Iron and Steel Controller would get a bulk allocation; and (iii) the Economic Adviser, Ministry of Commerce, would get a bulk allocation for the private sector's imports of raw materials, spares, and components (excluding, among other things, iron and steel, newsprint, and P.O.L.).

The industry and unit-wise allocations, under each of these heads, involved a variety of bodies. For example, the Economic Adviser, Ministry of Commerce, would in turn make allocations by commodities (such as copra and caustic soda), by groups of industries (such as bulk allocations to the D.G.T.D. for chemical and engineering industries), by size of industrial sector (such as bulk allocations for the small-scale sector) and by schemes (such as the Export Promotion scheme under which exporters were given en-

---

[1] The details of the description that follows are derived from the *Mathur Report* Vol I, op. cit., and interviews with officials of the Government of India.

[2] This naturally involved consultations with the Reserve Bank of India and the Ministry of Commerce, in estimating the inflow of export earnings. Tied funds and rupee payments fell within the province of the Finance Ministry itself.

titlements to import licences). In most of these cases, different administrative agencies were involved (for example, the D.G.T.D. and the Textile Commissioner) in dividing up the bulk allocations among units. Frequently, the same unit would thus receive import allocations from different agencies: iron and steel from the Iron and Steel Controller, non-ferrous metals from the corresponding Ministry Department, other inputs from the D.G.T.D. bulk quota, and so on.

The licensing procedures, through which each unit had to process all imports, involved three licence-*issuing* authorities: (1) The Chief Controller of Imports and Exports (C.C.I. & E.); (2) The Iron and Steel Controller (I. & S.C.); and (3) The Development Officer (D.O.), Tools, Development Wing of the Ministry of Commerce and Industry.[1] Except for iron and steel (cleared by the I. & S.C.), and certain types of machine tools (licensed by the D.O.), the C.C.I. & E. controlled the issuance of all other licences.

The licences issued by the C.C.I. & E., which constituted the overwhelming bulk, were divided into the following categories: (1) *established importers* (E.I.); (2) *actual users* (A.U.), which were in turn broken down into various categories: for instance, different licences existed for new products, for small-scale industries, for consumers' co-operative societies, etc.; (3) *new-comers* (not covered by E.I. and A.U.); (4) *ad hoc* (covering items such as State Trading Corporation imports); (5) *capital goods* (C.G.); (6) *heavy electrical plant* (H.E.P.); (7) *export promotion*, given as import entitlements to exporters in specific schemes; and (8) *miscellaneous* categories: such as *Railway Contract* (relating to orders placed by the Railways), *Replacement Licences* (to replace defective or unsuitable imports) and *Blanket Licences* (mainly for P.O.L.). While the E.I. licences, granted to traders, took in the early years the major share in total licensing, their role declined through our period and A.U. licences (for materials, components and spares) and C.G. + H.E.P. licences (for investment) came to dominate the import licensing system.[2]

---

[1] The following description is taken from J. Bhagwati, 'Indian Balance of Payments Policy and Exchange Auctions', *Oxford Economic Papers*, February 1962.

[2] Cf. Bhagwati, op. cit. It was only the later years that saw growth of Export Promotion (E.P.) licences which gave to eligible exporters the entitlement to import licences at rates *pro rata* to the f.o.b. value of the exports effected. These licences are treated in detail when we come to the chapters on Export Policy

The procedures followed by each category of licences, and the authorities involved in the process, reflected two major criteria: (i) the principle of 'essentiality'; and (ii) the principle of 'indigenous non-availability'. Thus imports, in terms of *both* magnitude and composition, were only to be permitted under each category if some designated agency of the Government had certified that they were 'essential' (as inputs or equipment for production). At the same time, some agency had to clear the imports from the viewpoint of indigenous availability: if it could be shown that there was domestic production of the imports demanded, then the imports were not permitted (regardless of cost and quality considerations). Thus, in addition to the licence-*issuing* authority, there was a 'sponsoring' agency certifying 'essentiality' and a 'clearing' agency for 'indigenous clearance'.

The resulting procedures may be illustrated with reference to private sector A.U. applications (for raw materials, spares, and components). These were generally divided into three categories of applicants: (i) the small-scale sector; (ii) the organized (large-scale) sector, Scheduled Industries assigned to the Directorate General of Technical Development (D.G.T.D.); and (iii) Other Scheduled Industries (such as textiles and sugar) plus non-scheduled, large-scale industries (such as fisheries). Among these, the D.G.T.D. units had to look to the D.G.T.D. for *both* essentiality and indigenous non-availability certificates. The small-scale sector applications, on the other hand, required essentiality certificates from State Directors of Industries, whereas indigenous clearance came from other bodies such as the D.G.T.D. For the other scheduled industries there were different sponsoring authorities, such as the Central Silk Board (for the silk industry), the Coal Commissioner (for collieries), the Textile Commissioner and the Tea Board; for the non-scheduled, large-scale units there were similar bodies, such as the Coir Board and the State Directors of Fisheries. It was only when these respective bodies had certified both essentiality and indigenous non-availability that the C.C.I. & E. could issue the licence specifying the quantum and composition of imports in favour of the applicant.[1]

[1] For C.G. licensing, which was the other important category, the agencies were generally different, although essentiality certificates were invariably given by the same sponsoring authority as in the case of A.U. licences. For details of the actual procedures for both C.G. and E.I. licensing, the *Mathur*

For *public sector* applications, the procedures were basically similar. Paradoxically, the procedures were even more complex at times—as when the sanction of the Department of Economic Affairs had to be obtained, *in addition* to indigenous clearance and essentiality certification, for many applications for raw material imports. Besides, in certain cases, the project authorities themselves had the authority to grant indigenous clearance and essentiality certificates. But these and others were, by and large, differences of detail.

III. PRINCIPLES AND CRITERIA OF ALLOCATION

The allocation of foreign exchange among alternative claimants and uses in a direct control system such as that just described would presumably be with reference to a well-defined set of principles and criteria based on a system of priorities. In point of fact, however, there seem to have been few such criteria, if any, followed in practice. This is a rather strong, and important, conclusion and hence will be supported by us with detailed evidence in the rest of this section. We shall examine, in particular, the allocations arising from A.U. licensing.[1]

A.U. licensing

There are basically two questions of economic significance which need to be asked here: (i) how were industry-wise allocations decided? and (ii) how were these allocations further divided up among the constituent firms or units? We shall examine each of these questions in turn.

Industry-wise allocations.

As far as the industry-wise allocations were concerned, it is clear that the sheer weight of numbers made any meaningful listing of

---

Report, is an excellent source. The economic implications of industrial licensing, of which C.G. licensing has been a segment, are discussed in Chapter 13 on industrial licensing.

[1] E.P. licences, constituting import entitlement for eligible exporters, are considered at length in the later chapters on Export Policy. C.G. licensing is also more appropriately considered in relation to Industrial Licensing Policy as a whole. In this chapter and the next, therefore, we have concentrated in the main on A.U. licensing, which involves essentially 'maintenance' imports of inputs, components, and spares, while dealing with *explicit* policies concerning exports and industrial investments in separate chapters.

priorities extremely difficult. The problem was Orwellian: all industries had priority and how was each sponsoring authority to argue that some industries had more priority than others? The magnitude of the problem can be seen from the following list of industries within the generic 'engineering' industry under the D.G.T.D., none of which seemed to have any edge (on any possible criteria) over the rest:[1]

1. Machine tools and small tools
2. Paper machinery
3. Chemical machinery
4. Construction machinery
5. Mining machinery
6. Coal washeries
7. Weighing machinery
8. Rayon machinery
9. Tea machinery
10. Metallurgical machinery
11. Solvent extraction plants
12. Fibre and chipboard plant
13. Rice-, dal-, and flour-mill machinery
14. Boilers
15. Conveyors
16. Core drills
17. Reduction gears
18. Cement machinery
19. Electroplating machinery
20. Ceramics machinery
21. Printing machinery
22. Dairy machinery and other miscellaneous industrial machinery
23. Automobiles and ancillary industries including trailers
24. Motor-cycles, scooters, and three-wheelers
25. Diesel engines
26. Tractors
27. Power-driven pumps
28. Earth moving equipment
29. Air compressors
30. Road rollers
31. Fire-fighting equipment
32. Fans and blowers
33. Fork-lift trucks
34. Miscellaneous auto and allied industries
35. Electric motors
36. Radio receivers and radio components
37. Electric lamps
38. Switchgear and control gear
39. Cables and wires
40. Transformers
41. Generators
42. Refrigerators, etc.
43. Batteries
44. House service meters and electrical instruments
45. Power-factor capacitors
46. Permanent magnets
47. Electrical accessories
48. Domestic electrical appliances
49. Electric fans
50. Television sets
51. Scientific, surveying, and industrial instruments, including water meters
52. Welding electrodes
53. Wire ropes

---

[1] The list is taken from *Lindblom*, op. cit., pp. 43–7; it comes from D.G.T.D., *Annual Report* (1962–63), Government of India. A similar list could be reproduced also for the 'chemical' industry under the D.G.T.D.

54. Rolling stock
55. Structural fabrication
56. Bicycle parts
57. Woven wire screws
58. Ball- and roller-bearings
59. Typewriters and calculating machines
60. Sewing machines
61. Springs
62. Machine screws
63. Wood screws
64. Rubber conveyor belting
65. Drums
66. Gun-metal bushes
67. Hypodermic syringes
68. Tin containers
69. Sewing machine needles
70. Collapsible tubes
71. Steel balls
72. Furniture
73. Grinding media balls
74. Wire netting
75. Dental apparatus, etc.
76. Wire mesh
77. Sanitary fittings
78. Surgical and medical instruments
79. Oil pressure stoves
80. Miscellaneous light mechanical engineering
81. Non-ferrous metals, alloys, and semis
82. Steel castings
83. Steel forgings
84. Steel shots and grits
85. Chilled iron and cast steel rolls
86. Soda ash
87. Caustic soda
88. Calcium carbide

89. Sodium hydrosulphite
90. Other alkali and allied chemicals
91. Acids and fertilizers
92. Industrial gases
93. Carbon dioxide gas
94. Potassium permanganate
95. Manganese dioxide
96. Barium salts
97. Electroplating salts
98. Other miscellaneous chemicals
99. Power alcohol
100. Organic chemicals
101. Insecticides, plastics, plastic chemicals, and fine chemicals
102. Dyestuff
103. Industrial explosives
104. Drugs and pharmaceuticals
105. Cement, asbestos, and gypsum wall-board
106. Refractory and ceramics
107. Glass
108. Paper- and paper-board
109. Timber
110. Viscose rayon
111. Staple fibre
112. Cellophane
113. Synthetic fibres
114. Leather and leather goods
115. Rubber goods manufacturing industry
116. Oils and soaps
117. Paints
118. Zinc oxide
119. Synthetic resins
120. Titanium dioxide
121. Lead oxides
122. Shell liquid
123. Food

In turn, many of these were further divided by the D.G.T.D. into numerous other categories. Thus, for example, the first item, 'machine tools and small tools' was divided into:

1. Metal-cutting machines
2. Metal-forming machines
3. Wood-working machines
4. Glass industry machines
5. Plastic machines
6. Portable pneumatic tools
7. Portable electric tools
8. Hydraulic system and hydraulic equipment
9. Flexible shafts and machines
10. Machine-tool accessories
11. Cutting tools, such as reamers, twist drills, tap dies, etc.
12. Hand-tools, such as files, rasps, etc.
13. Forged tools, such as spanners, pliers, etc.
14. Other tools, such as diamond tools, tungsten carbide, etc.
15. Grinding wheels
16. Coated abrasives
17. Jigs, fixtures, and other tool-room activity
18. Metal moulds and metal patterns for foundry
19. Precision workshop instruments, like micro-meters, etc.

It is not surprising, therefore, that the agencies involved in determining industry-wise allocations, fell back on vague notions of 'fairness', implying *pro rata* allocations with reference to capacity installed or employment, or shares defined by past import allocations and similar other rules of thumb without any clear rationale. Thus, take the following telling examples.

1. When the Economic Adviser, Ministry of Commerce, had to divide up his bulk allocation from the D.E.A., the allocations were under more than thirty different heads many of which related to permitted imports (e.g. cashew nuts and raw cotton) whereas others referred to allocations to users (e.g. raw materials for D.G.T.D. industries). Thus, the Economic Adviser was implicitly required to determine the imports that industries would eventually be entitled to: for example, the D.G.T.D. allocation would virtually determine the imports of raw materials that broad groups of industries such as 'engineering' would expect to get, whereas the raw materials allocated for small industries would constrain what industries falling within this category could eventually get.[1]

Clearly, a single glance at the long list of these allocations, most of them amounting to bulk allocations to be later allocated among user-industries, will convince one that the most likely *modus*

---

[1] The methods of division of these bulk sub-allocations among yet further industries, by the D.G.T.D. and the Directors of Industries for the small-scale sector in the two specific cases cited in the text, will be treated shortly. Needless to say, they were no better.

operandi must have been to go by simple administrative rules, history, and 'pragmatism' at the decision level.

In fact, decisive evidence points in this precise direction. While the information on these allocations is, quite predictably, kept from public scrutiny, it has been shown[1] that a great number of the allocations under these different categories were repeated period after half-yearly period by the Economic Adviser's office, despite the changing payments situation, thus providing *prima facie* evidence of absence of clear, economic, criteria for determining import allocations. Interviews with officials engaged in these allocative decisions also confirm this negative finding.

2. The further allocations, from these bulk allocations, among different industries were equally without any clear rationale and remained essentially *ad hoc* and discretionary.

While the D.G.T.D. claimed to have a list of priorities and clear principles to govern allocations on this basis, in its submission to the Mathur Study Team, Shourie's comment on this claim is revealing:

> Extensive interviews with Development Officers, Industrial Advisers, the Deputy Director-General (Engineering) and the Director-General revealed that in fact no formal and detailed categorization of industries between high, medium and low priorities nor of the principles on which priorities should be assessed is in use. A list was compiled by the Deputy Director-General in 1962 but it was never used and it has never been brought up-to-date.[2]

In addition, Shourie has been able to show how, in the period October 1962 to March 1963, just subsequent to the Sino-Indian border war, when the notion of priorities might have been expected to be put into sharp focus, the cuts that were imposed in industry-wise allocations were overwhelmingly uniform:

> The Engineering Division [of the D.G.T.D.]—which later claimed that it uses a detailed categorization of industries between high, medium and low priority industries—instructed the CCI & E's office that when Actual User licenses issued for 1962–1963 are put up for

---

[1] A. Shourie, in an unpublished Ph.D. thesis for Syracuse University, September 1966, on the *Allocation of Foreign Exchange in India*. Shourie's dissertation is a most valuable source of detailed information on the allocational procedures adopted by the Indian authorities.

[2] Ibid., p. 68.

revalidation a general cut of 6 per cent should be imposed for all licenses covering imports of raw materials as well as spares. . . . However, for 7 industries heavier cuts were to be imposed: cars (33·3 per cent), scooters (33·3 per cent), bicycles (33·3 per cent), aluminium foil and container sheets (33·3 per cent), radios (10 per cent), refrigerators (50 per cent) and air-conditioners (50 per cent) . . . It should be obvious that ear-marking only seven industries for heavier cuts and all the others for an across the board cut of 6 per cent does not amount to any detailed assessment of relative inter-industry priorities. This becomes apparent when we note that the total foreign exchange allotted to these seven industries in April–September 1962 . . . was only about 8·8 per cent of the total foreign exchange available to the D.G.T.D. . . .[1]

3. The fact that the notion of 'fair sharing' was dominant, in one sense or another, in the case of most authorities in this control system is also underlined by the fact that the Mathur Team, which aimed at many procedural reforms, also found itself constrained by concepts such as historical allocations and installed capacity. Thus, witness its recommendations concerning how the bulk allocations, for the small-scale sector, should be divided up by State:

. . . it is stressing the obvious that an equitable basis will have to be found for operating the idea of State-wise allocations. . . . We consider that ultimately allocations will have to be based on the installed capacity to be assessed on a uniform basis on an all-India norm by the D.C., SSI, and the Directors of Industries jointly. So long as this is not done, an ad hoc formula is necessary which will take account of the need, on the one hand, to maintain the tempo of industrial production already attained in different States and, on the other, of the special development needs of backward areas.

We recommend that State-wise allocation of the available foreign exchange should in the first-year be made in proportion to the average of the licences issued to each State for the last 3 yearly licensing periods. Having got the State-wise inter se ratio, the total amount available to the SSI sector should be distributed in the following manner by taking, say, Rs. 12 crores as the 'core' allocation:

(a) If the allocation in 1965–66 is Rs. 12 crores or less, the State-wise allocation may be made on the basis of the ratio arrived at above.

(b) If the allocation is more than Rs. 12 crores, the first Rs. 12 crores should be allocated on the ratio mentioned above. Out of the balance,

[1] *Allocation of Foreign Exchange in India*, pp. 69–70.

50 per cent should again be allocated to the different States in the same ratio to meet the requirements of normal growth. The remaining 50 per cent should be allocated keeping in view the special development needs of the various States.

The allocation should be made by the D.C., SSI, who should take steps to equip himself with whatever information he may require to discharge this responsibility. Allocations for the subsequent years, i.e., 1966–67 onwards, should be made according to the same formula as indicated in (*a*) and (*b*) above, except that instead of Rs. 12 crores, the allocation of the preceding year should be taken as the 'core' figure. This inter-State ratio will be based on the preceding year's State-wise allocations.[1]

Unit-wise Allocations

The principles and criteria adopted for further subdividing industrial allocations among constituent firms/units were equally without any rationale other than the spreading-out evenly of a scarce resource on a 'fair' and 'equitable' basis.

The *Mathur Report* again provides excellent evidence on this issue, with respect to the D.G.T.D.:

. . . an attempt was also made to find out whether any norms were prescribed by the Directorates for allocation of foreign exchange among the various units in a particular industry. Since this information was not directly available from the files, it was separately called for. This has been received from a few Directorates only.

It appears that there is no single criterion for this allocation and the criteria also differ from Directorate to Directorate. In some cases the norm prescribed is utilisation of the foreign exchange in the past *periods* while in some others the criterion is the production in the *current* year. In some cases, consumption of indigenous raw material is the norm while in others, allocation may be justified on the grounds of the industry being a 'priority industry'. In some cases, it was found that the firms were given foreign exchange even without conforming to these norms. For example, in one Directorate, the firm was not sending the production returns but still it was allowed imports. In another Directorate, two similar cases of import of spares are given different treatment and the reason for discrimination is not given. In certain cases, the allocation of foreign exchange granted to the firm was more than the previous year's while in a few cases it was less than the last year's. No precise reasons for changing this are given on the files and it appears that

[1] *Mathur Report*, Vol. I, pp. 18–19.

this must have been done by the D.O. concerned in his decision. In one case, the Assistant and the J.T.O. had recommended import up to Rs. 7·5 lakhs on 'repeat' basis (which was perhaps the basis followed in similar other cases also) but the D.O. in his discretion reduced it to Rs. 7 lakhs without assigning any reason. In the absence of any clear indication on the files, it is difficult to say whether discretion used was arbitrary or based on valid grounds. In any case, the above instances would seem to suggest that there is ample scope for exercise of arbitrary discretion in the matter of recommending import of raw material and spares.[1]

Further, the Mathur Team also writes:

The allocation made in respect of each industry is then distributed among the various industrial units in that industry. The procedure for making this sub-allocation, however, varies from Directorate to Directorate. In some places, the foreign exchange allocation among the various industrial units is decided and communicated to the parties in advance, asking them to submit their import applications to cover their six months' requirements within the specified allocations. This sub-allocation is made on the basis of the past performance and past imports of the industrial units involved. This practice is in vogue in the Rubber, Leather and Ceramics Directorates. In some cases, the allocations are made after bulk of the applications have been received and their requirements tabulated. This however involves avoidable delay in as much as, in the ultimate analysis, the value of the imports of raw materials and spares recommended is mainly based on the past performance and past imports, figures of which should be available in the Directorates concerned.[2]

There was thus a great variety of norms used, with significant possibility and occasional exercise of discretion. But the overwhelming bias of the system was towards some form of 'equitable' allocations and cuts therein. This conclusion holds, not merely for the D.G.T.D. but also for small-scale sector allocations, the scheduled industries not on the books of the D.G.T.D. and the other classes of import applicants.

In this connection, it is also interesting to note the valuable work of Panchamukhi who, on tabulating laboriously the A.U. imports, by firm, for three industries (paper and paper products, non-ferrous metals and alloys, and machinery manufactures), found that few significant relationships could be discovered be-

---

[1] *Mathur Report*, Vol. I, p. 98. 　　　　　[2] Ibid., pp. 91–2.

IMPORT POLICY: I 295

tween important allocations and alternative indices of profitability and that, in any event, the less profitable (and, therefore, *prima facie*, the less efficient) firms had presumably been given relatively more import licences (the regression coefficients being often negative).[1] We have reproduced Panchamukhi's principal results in Table 15.1 (Group A). While the profitability indices used by Panchamukhi are not fully satisfactory, and his analysis extends to only three (rather broad groups of) industries, it is none the less significant that the general nature of the conclusions he reaches, with respect to the unit-wise (or firm-wise) allocations of A.U. imports is fully consistent with the more qualitative results of our analysis.[2]

IV. QUALITY OF INFORMATION ON BASIS OF WHICH PRIORITIES WERE APPARENTLY ENFORCED

As we have already noted, numerous authorities were involved in the licensing procedure: sponsoring bodies, authorities granting indigenous clearance and actual licence-issuing authorities. Each such authority presumed to act on some set of priorities, in principle, and therefore had to have reasonable information so as to enable it to exercise its functions meaningfully. We have already seen how difficult it is to talk of any well-defined set of priorities at any level in this bureaucratic machine, except in relation to overriding matters, such as defence. At the same time, however, no allocations were ever made without intensive scrutiny and examination of individual applications at each stage in the bureaucracy. The quality of the information on which these examinations and ensuing decisions were presumably based can be inferred from what is known about (1) the small-scale sector applications, and (2) the working of the D.G.T.D. concerning imports.

[1] V. R. Panchamukhi, *The Problem of Import Substitution*, Mimeographed, University of Bombay, 1965.
[2] Group B regressions in Table 15.1 are equally remarkable. Here, the import allocations become the independent variable and the results are again substantially 'perverse': but the results may be 'explained' quite simply by the fact that A.U.-import-availability may be only one of several factors determining profitability (as Panchamukhi himself notes).

TABLE 15.1

RELATIONS BETWEEN PROFITABILITY AND IMPORT-CONTENT FOR PAPER AND PAPER PRODUCTS, MACHINERY MANUFACTURES, AND NON-FERROUS METALS AND ALLOYS

Industry	Dependent variable Y	Independent variable X	Year	Regression equation	Correlation coefficient
(1)	(2)	(3)	(4)	(5)	(6)
(Group A) Regressions					
Paper and paper products	1. Import content to sales ratio	Final net profit to net sales ratio	1960/1	$Y = 0·0645 - 0·0767\ X$ (0·1707)	−0·148
			1962	$Y = 0·0583 - 0·7273\ X$ (1·256)	−0·180
	2. Import content to sales ratio	Final net profits to gross assets ratio	1960/1	$Y = 0·0796 - 0·5288\ X$ (0·4648)	−0·379
			1962	$Y = 0·0872 + 0·2559\ X$ (1·635)	0·049
Machinery manufactures	1. Import content to net sales ratio	Final net profit to net sales ratio (with one year's lag)	1957/8	$Y = 0·6512 - 1·0·2752\ X$	−0·6326
			1962	$Y = 0·1240 - 1·1064\ X$	−0·464
	2. Import content to net sales ratio	Final net profits to gross assets ratio (with one year's lag)	1957/8	$Y = 0·6512 - 1·0·2752\ X$	−0·3107
Non-ferrous metals and alloys	1. Import content to net sales ratio	Final net profits to net sales ratio (with one year's lag)	1962	$Y = 0·1261 - 1·3499\ X$	−0·4514
			1957/8	$Y = 0·3494 - 2·059\ X$	−0·403
			1960/1	$Y = 0·2553 - 1·5436\ X$	−0·26
	2. Import content to net sales ratio	Final net profits to gross assets ratio (with one year's lag)	1962	$Y = 0·1406 - 0·3410\ X$	−0·222
			1957/8	$Y = 0·2550 - 0·662\ X$	−0·887
			1960/1	$Y = 0·3954 - 4·226\ X$	−0·441
			1962	$Y = 0·2931 - 2·397\ X$	−0·784
(Group B) Regression					
Paper and paper products	1. Gross profit to net sales ratio	Import content to sales ratio	1957/8	$Y = 0·2450 - 0·0458\ X$ (0·34)	−0·14
			1960/1	$Y = 0·2638 - 0·7023\ X$ (0·43)	−0·46
			1962	$Y = 0·241 - 0·172\ X$ (0·924)	−0·06

		Year	Equation	
2. Operating net profit to net sales ratio	Import content to sales ratio	1957/8	$Y = 0.0463 + 0.0258\,X$ (0.924)	0.027
		1960/1	$Y = 0.0841 - 0.1526\,X$ (0.1327)	-0.176
		1962	$Y = 0.0757 - 0.0013\,X$	-0.003
3. Final net profit to net sales ratio	Import content to sales ratio	1957/8	$Y = 0.0155 + 0.0747\,X$ (0.187)	0.118
		1960/1	$Y = 0.0644 - 0.1297\,X$ (0.213)	-0.187
		1962	$Y = 0.0459 + 0.0333\,X$ (0.109)	0.0948
4. Final net profit to total assets ratio	Import content to sales ratio	1957/8	$Y = 0.0333 - 0.01326\,X$ (0.23)	-0.055
		1960/1	$Y = 0.0426 + 0.0114\,X$ (0.217)	0.000
		1962	$Y = 0.035 - 0.0846\,X$ (0.1294)	0.000
Machinery manufactures				-0.0636
1. Gross profit to net sales ratio (of the next year)	Import content to net sales ratio	1957/8	$Y_1 = 0.2823 - 0.2365\,X$	0.8615
2. Operating net profit to net sales ratio (of the next year)	Import content to net sales ratio	1962	$Y_1 = 0.2665 - 0.7977\,X$	-0.6452
		1957/8	$Y_2 = 0.0954 - 0.0915\,X$	-0.703
3. Final net profit to net sales ratio (of the next year)	Import content to net sales ratio	1962	$Y_2 = 0.0967 - 0.5789\,X$	0.588
		1957/8	$Y_3 = 0.0511 - 0.0438\,X$	0.671
4. Final net profit to total assets ratio (of the next year)	Import content to net sales ratio	1962	$Y_3 = 0.0468 - 0.2276\,X$	-0.606
		1957/8	$Y_4 = 0.0513 - 0.0387\,X$	-0.658
Non-ferrous metals and alloys				
1. Gross profit to net sales ratio (of the next year)	Import content to net sales ratio	1962	$Y_4 = 0.0442 - 0.2177\,X$	-0.606
		1957/8	$Y_1 = 0.2869 - 0.53\,X$	-0.162
2. Operating net profit to net sales ratio (of the next year)	Import content to net sales ratio	1960/1	$Y_1 = 0.2138 + 0.1485\,X$	0.38
		1962	$Y_2 = 0.2934 - 0.3259\,X$	0.33
		1951/8	$Y_2 = 0.0928 + 0.065\,X$	0.277
		1960/1	$Y_3 = 0.1200 + 0.0608\,X$	0.17
		1962	$Y_2 = 0.1929 - 0.4458\,X$	-0.57

TABLE 15.1—continued

Industry	Dependent variable Y	Independent variable X	Year	Regression equation	Correlation coefficient
(1)	(2)	(3)	(4)	(5)	(6)
3. Final net profit to net sales ratio (of the next year)	Import-content to net sales ratio	1957/8 1960/1 1962	$Y_3 = 0{\cdot}0714 - 0{\cdot}026\ X$ $Y_3 = 0{\cdot}0742 + 0{\cdot}0103\ X$ $Y_3 = 0{\cdot}0750 - 0{\cdot}0905\ X$	$-0{\cdot}183$ $0{\cdot}309$ $-0{\cdot}207$
4. Final net profits to total assets ratio (of the next year)	Import-content to net sales ratio	1957/8 1960/1 1962	$Y_4 = 0{\cdot}0536 + 0{\cdot}016\ X$ $Y_4 = 0{\cdot}0787 - 0{\cdot}0163\ X$ $Y_4 = 0{\cdot}0793 - 0{\cdot}1628\ X$	$0{\cdot}18$ $-0{\cdot}097$ $-0{\cdot}736$

Source: V. R. Panchamukhi, *The Problem of Import-Substitution*. Our table is adapted from Tables 7.3, 7.6, and 7.9. The original data are from balance sheets published in *The Stock Exchange Official Directory* (Bombay), Vol. I, The Stock Exchange, Bombay.

Definitions: The definitions of different concepts used are as follows:

(1) *Net sales:* Net sales is derived by deducting goods returned, allowances and discount from the gross amount received from sales. In the case of financial and investment companies, the gross operating revenue is given from interest and dividend income and service charges.

(2) *Gross profit:* Gross profit is gross of depreciation, as also of selling, administrative, and other indirect expenses, including debentures and other interest changes.

(3) *Operating net profit:* The operating net profit of a company is defined as the gross profit minus operating expenses such as administrative and general expenses, provision for depreciation and doubtful debts, and debenture and other interest charges.

(4) *Final net profit:* The final net profit is defined as the operating net profit minus the corporation and income tax liability.

(5) *Import content:* The import-content is defined as the estimated A.U. (Actual User Licence) imports by the industry.

(a) Small-scale sector

The State Directorates of Industries were the authorities which were supposed to process the import applications in the first instance and to attach Essentiality Certificates (E.C.s). While considerable time was indeed taken in granting these E.C.s, as we shall soon see, the quality of the information on which the relevant decisions had to be made can be inferred from the following excerpts from the Report of the International Perspective Planning Team on Small Industries (1963) concerning allocations of controlled materials in general:

[In one of the States] 26 per cent of all allocations went to non-operating or 'bogus' firms obviously for resale in the black market.

Some States do not assess capacities but depend completely on demand levels from some prior year (usually 1958). . . . Generally, assessed capacities (one shift) run below the capacity demands from enterprises.

The Raj Committee on Steel Control (1963) also had some telling examples relating to the allocations of iron and steel for the agricultural sector (small-scale):

Except in Mysore, no scientific or systematic method is followed in assessing the demand. No survey is made in the villages nor are all the fabricators of agricultural implements consulted.

In (one State) the number of fabricators of agricultural implements in the State is 25 according to the figures available in the Directorate of Agriculture but the Provincial Iron and Steel Controller who is not under the Agriculture Department issues supplies to around 500 supposed fabricators of agricultural implements.[1]

There is no reason to expect that the allocation of *import* licences by State Directorates was any more systematic or informed than the foregoing observations concerning the distribution of scarce materials indicate. There are clearly diverse reasons for this state of affairs:

(i) there was little incentive to attempt any systematic assessment of needs or essentialities of units in the small-scale sector

---

[1] All the four quotations are reproduced from *Report of Steel Control*, Ministry of Steel and Heavy Industries, Government of India, October 1963, pp. 41–3. The Chairman of the Committee was Professor K. N. Raj of Delhi University.

when the actual allocations had hardly any relation to the estimates sent up to the licensing authorities;

(ii) the considerable premia that have attached, through most of the period covered by our study, to imports also constituted considerable inducements to create illegal claims for imports, thereby complicating greatly the problem of ascertaining genuine demands; and

(iii) in the small-scale sector, there are far too many units, with diverse demands, for any run-of-the-mill departments to be able to handle efficiently, even on a scientific, sample basis.

(b) D.G.T.D.

The case of the D.G.T.D. was hardly any better, despite its obvious advantages over the Directorates in charge of the small-scale sector.

It is well known, for example, that the capacity as also the capacity utilization data, both of which were taken ostensibly into account in making unit-wise allocations, are bad.[1] Similarly, with respect to those units which must seek indigenous clearance from the D.G.T.D., it is known that the D.G.T.D. directorates frequently maintain incomplete records of the indigenous suppliers, do not have sufficient information in adequate detail on what these suppliers can produce and of what quality, do not distinguish adequately between the mere fact of the existence of an indigenous supplier and the availability of the supply to an individual purchaser, and thus end up withholding sanction even for critical imports.

Thus, note what the *Mathur Report* says:

. . . considerable time can be saved by firstly rationalising the indigenous formula itself, and secondly by keeping each Directorate up-to-date on indigenous demand and supply position. *In most of the cases, on further representation, the DGTD had to allow indigenous clearance.*[2]

The inevitable inefficiency of the indigenous-clearance formula, from the viewpoint of administrative implementation, is seen most glaringly in the occasional attempts to get round some of its worst

---

[1] See J. Bhagwati, in *Economic Weekly*, October 1962, op. cit.
[2] *Mathur Report*, p. 37 [italics inserted by us].

results, as revealed by the Redbook on *Import Control Policy*. Here is a telling example quoted from Appendix 27 of the April 1964 to March 1965 Redbook:

Representations have been received that scientific, photographic and other instruments are often rendered idle on account of the fact that they need special types of electric bulbs for use with them and normally speaking the importers of such equipment do not hold import licenses for electric bulbs.[1]

The D.G.T.D. not merely tried to secure indigenous clearance prior to permitting imports but even seemed to determine the quantitative mix of permissible imports in many cases! Note what the Mathur Report has to say about this:

The D.G.T.D. has to examine essentiality on a qualitative as well as on a quantitative basis, i.e., whether a particular item is required for a particular end-product and, if so, in what quantity. Sometimes matching of various items of raw materials with each other is also ensured.

Clearly, the D.G.T.D. had, in the nature of the case, no capacity to form reasonable judgements on this issue in the absence of very detailed information on plant conditions—something that was automatically ruled out when we see that the D.G.T.D. carried on its book (1965) about 4,500 licensed units and 650 registered units! It is not surprising therefore that even the bureaucracy-dominated Mathur Team argued that:

After careful consideration, we have come to the conclusion that, subject to the overall ceiling of a license being indicated, and subject to the scrutiny of the list of items of raw materials, spare parts and components asked for, there should not be any meticulous examination or restriction of quantities of each item to match with each other *inter se* as also to match with the total estimate of production. We feel that the optimum utilisation of foreign exchange within the specified items should best be left to the discretion of the manufacturer and *itemised restriction calculated on the basis of a theoretical production figure for a particular year without taking into account the itemised stock position, works in hand, etc.* is likely to create an unbalanced inventory position.

[1] We state in Chapter 16 the solution provided to this situation, and its arbitrariness, under the sub-section 'Inflexibility Arising from Restrictions'.
[2] Ibid., pp. 37–8 [italics inserted by us].

X

The same lack of any systematic information with respect to stock position, works in hand, capacity and capacity utilization at both unit and industry levels, affected also the allocation of *total* import quotas.

... administering agencies do not know at any given time just where they stand with respect to available and committed foreign exchange by major category. And officers responsible and officers in the Directorate General for Technical Development who prepare licenses for individual firms report that they do not generally have information on import inventories.[1]

V. PRIORITY IN FAVOUR OF THE SMALL-SCALE SECTOR

While, however, clear criteria for the allocation of imports among alternative uses were generally conspicuous by their absence and the informational basis for decision-making was exceptionally weak, it might be contended that certain broad priorities were pursued by the authorities:

(1) that the small-scale sector was supported; and
(2) that foreign exchange was saved for investment by curtailing its utilization for consumer goods.

We shall investigate these contentions in turn, starting with the small-scale sector.

A typical defence of the import control system was that it was the only way of ensuring that supplies went on a 'fair and equitable' basis to 'small' entrepreneurs. This is not an argument for economic efficiency; but it is a valid argument for income redistribution *if* alternative ways of subsidizing the smaller entrepreneurs are not feasible.

But it is extremely difficult to take this defence of the import control system seriously. In point of fact, there are a great many reasons to conclude that the control system discriminated against the small-scale sector. It does not follow, of course, that the small-scale sector would have either secured greater allocations or been more competitive if it had had to purchase imports in a free

---

[1] C. Lindblom, *Indian Import Controls*, op. cit., p. 38; based on interviews with G.O.I. officials.

market.[1] On the other hand, it does cast grave doubt on the usual claim that the import control system made the small-scale sector better off than under alternative import régimes. Let us examine the available evidence.

(1) The International Perspective Planning Team (1963),[2] in one of its sample investigations, found that large firms received 85 per cent of their one-shift requirements, whereas their smaller rivals received only 33–40 per cent of their one-shift requirements.

(2) The Estimates Committee (1963–4), *Forty-eighth Report* had the following to say on this issue:

It has been represented to the Committee that the small scale industries are being given a raw deal while allotting foreign exchange to the various sectors of industry. While the scheduled industries are given licenses for the import of raw materials on the basis of their capacity or as near to it as possible, the small industries sector, irrespective of its capacity, receives only an *ad hoc* allotment of foreign exchange which is thoroughly incommensurate with their requirements of raw materials and components. The starvation of legitimate supply of raw materials forces the small units to make up the deficiency by purchases from the so-called open market at very high prices which renders its physical cost of production higher than that of the scheduled units and therefore makes it face unfair competition from the latter ... It has been admitted by the representative of the Ministry of Industry that while the scheduled units are always assured of the necessary raw materials, the position regarding [the] allocation of foreign exchange for small scale industries has been really serious during the last 18 months, particularly after the emergency. . . .[3]

Such discrimination would make sense if the small-scale sector's industrial composition was of smaller priority than the organized, scheduled sector's industrial composition; there is little evidence, however, to this effect.

(3) The Mathur Report also established conclusively that the licensing procedures for actual-user imports were decidedly more onerous for the small-scale sector. It is worth quoting from it at some length on this issue:

---

[1] This seems to have been erroneously inferred by many observers, including Lindblom, op. cit., even though this inference is often only implicit in the conclusions reached.
[2] Cited in *Report of Steel Control*, op. cit.
[3] G.O.I., Lok Sabha Secretariat, op. cit., pp. 82–3; cited by Lindblom, op. cit.

In contradistinction to the procedure for large-scale sector . . . the units in the small-scale sector have to process two applications in parallel in two different organizations for their import. As soon as the import policy is declared, they have to apply to the respective Directors of Industries or other sponsoring authority concerned for the issue of what is known as an Essentiality Certificate. For example, in the case of Maharashtra, applications for essentiality certificates are required to be submitted in quadruplicate, the form being far more complicated than of the main application for the import license itself. E.C. applications are required to be submitted by the 31st of May. Import licence applications are required to come in to the licensing authorities by the 15th August. If an applicant gets his essentiality certificate before that date, he attaches that with his licence application, otherwise the licensing authority simply waits for the essentiality certificate from the sponsoring authority (Directors of Industries, etc.). This entails the trade following up both these applications in two different offices, some of which are hundreds of miles apart. (In the case of the large-scale sector, like the D.G.T.D.'s units, there is only one application for import licence which itself is routed through the sponsoring authority who gives the recommendation while forwarding the application to the licensing office.)

The licensing office, after receiving the Essentiality Certificate from the sponsoring authorities, which in some cases takes matters much beyond the licensing period, has to consult technical authorities on indigenous clearance, etc. This also entails a great deal of follow-up action on the part of the applicant. From the study of cases selected at random in the Bombay Port Office, it is found that on an average it takes 101 days for an import application to be disposed of even after the foreign exchange is allocated at end of June every year. On this basis, licences are issued some time in the middle of October, i.e., after the entire first half (April–September) of the licensing year has expired. *The holders of licences issued after the expiry of the first half of the licensing period are thus deprived of the benefit of using them during the first half. In certain cases, where such delays go beyond the closure of the half-yearly ceilings the entitlement of an applicant is automatically reduced for no fault of his.* Delayed licensing by forced non-utilization inflates the figures of stock in position and licences in hand and deprives the licensees further of their legitimate entitlement for the next licensing period, as the next entitlement is calculated by deducting the stocks in hand and expected arrivals against unutilised licences.

Under the existing scheme, if a licence is above Rs. 5,000 in value, the licensee can utilise only 50 per cent of the value in the first half of the validity period, and for the second half he has either to await a public notice or get his licence endorsed for a particular amount before he can enter into any commitment for the remaining part of the licence. This process, magnified by the large number of licences involved, seems to reproduce the same administrative problems again in the middle of the licensing period, entailing time and effort at all levels not commensurate with the results achieved. Further *the splitting of a licence into two halves and the uncertainty of the value of the second half restricts the licensee in the small-scale sector in a very unenviable manner. The total value of an individual licence itself being very small in most cases, its break-up into two halves accentuates the difficulty of negotiating deals with foreign suppliers. And, in any case, the 'juggernaut' of problems of negotiations, payment and consignment vis-à-vis the Reserve Bank of India, foreign supplier, Customs and other intermediaries has to be gone through twice over.*[1]

Take again the question of restrictive import lists and how smaller entrepreneurs found the procedures much more constrictive, in view of their limited resources and manoeuvrability:

Items to be imported fall into broadly three categories: those on the 'open' list can be freely imported, subject only to foreign exchange availability; those on the 'banned' list cannot normally be imported at all; and those on the 'restricted' list can be imported subject to what is called 'indigenous clearance'. This third category represents a sort of twilight area, and is the cause of the largest number of complaints from Actual Users generally. *Particularly for the SSI sector, the restricted list creates major inconveniences since the resources of the small industrialists do not permit their being able to follow up their cases in New Delhi.* Also, a feeling persists in the SSI sector that the D.G.T.D., who is the final authority for technical clearance in such cases, does not have time to spare for quick enough handling of references arising out of the SSI sector. The total value of SSI cases involving imports of restricted items is necessarily small, since the whole SSI ceiling itself is small. We have, therefore, considered whether much is gained by subjecting the SSI sector to the same rigorous drill for indigenous clearance as the scheduled sector. Our view, supported by officers of D.G.T.D., is that there is not much to be lost, and a great deal to be gained by doing away with the restricted list altogether so far as the SSI sector is concerned, and we recommend that this should be done, at least as a trial for one year.[2]

(4) Finally, as the Raj Committee on Steel Control has pointed out, even within the small-scale sector, the relatively larger enterprises managed to get a higher proportion of their assessed capacity covered by allocations than the smaller ones; and the smaller

[1] *Mathur Report*, Vol. I, pp. 14–15 [italics inserted by us].
[2] Ibid., Vol. I, pp. 24–5.

enterprises were therefore compelled to buy a larger proportion of their (steel) requirements in the black market.[1]

VI. FOREIGN EXCHANGE SAVED FROM BEING SPENT ON CONSUMPTION

It might be contended that the import policy régime was directed at preventing scarce foreign exchange from being 'frittered away' on consumer goods; and that this general priority was strictly maintained by the import-licensing authorities.

Now it is certainly true that, over the period of our study, the direct imports of consumer goods were slashed down. This was reflected in the steady reduction of E.I. licences and the growth of A.U. licences granted to producers. However, three important points need to be made on this question.

(1) While imports of manufactured consumer goods indeed went down, it is pertinent to note that these were frequently offset by growth in domestic production of the same and other consumer manufactures.[2] We had occasion elsewhere to comment on this phenomenon in the context of overall licensing policy for industrial investments. In the present context, where we are discussing rather the allocation of 'maintenance' imports, the following further points need to be noted.

(2) The maintenance imports necessary to support current production of domestic consumer goods industries were not negligible. Taking the following commodities as 'luxuries':

electric tubes	scooters
radio receivers	automobiles
domestic refrigerators	ancillaries
air conditioners and water coolers	vanaspati ghee
electrical household appliances	alcoholic beverages
dry cells	non-alcoholic beverages
storage batteries	biscuits
precious metals and jewellery	confectionery
steel furniture	fruits and vegetables preserved
cars	cashew nuts

---

[1] Op. cit., p. 41.
[2] This fact emerges clearly from the analysis of import-substitution using the measure of changes in import/availability ratios, in several consumer goods manufactures over the period 1950–64, by Padma Desai, *An Analysis of Import Substitution in India: 1961–1964*, Delhi School of Economics, 1970.

other fruits
other vegetables (excludes banana, papaya, sweet potatoes and potatoes)
motor spirit

car tyres
car tubes
scooter and motor-cycle tyres
tubes

and the following as 'necessities'.

electric fans
electric lamps
flashlight torches
sewing machine parts
clocks and watches
typewriters
thermos flasks
wood furniture and fixtures
bicycle complete
bicycle repair and auto repairs
bicycle parts
sugar
tea
coffee
vegetable oil
salt

cigarettes
cereals
cotton
cotton cloth
woollen yarn
woollen cloth
sugarcane
banana
papaya
sweet potatoes
potatoes
kerosene oil
bicycle tyres
bicycle tubes
paper
matches

Hazari has worked out estimates of the direct and indirect import requirements of consumption in India, divided by these two groups. He finds, for the years 1961–2 and 1963–4, that the proportion of *total* imports which went to support the level of consumption of 'luxuries' was 7·6 and 8·5 per cent, and of 'necessities' was 28·7 and 32·9 per cent respectively.[1]

(3) Further, as we have already noted, there is little evidence that at times of serious curtailment of foreign exchange availability more than a few consumer industries were deprived disproportionately of their import allocations. It will be recalled that only the quotas of six consumer goods industries were disproportionately cut by the D.G.T.D. in the aftermath of the Sino-Indian conflict: and the proportion of these to the total foreign exchange with D.G.T.D. was less than 8·8 per cent.[2]

[1] B. R. Hazari, 'The Import-Intensity of Consumption in India', *Indian Economic Review*, October 1967.
[2] See p. 292. The economics of such disproportionate cuts on the 'luxury' industries, and implications for industrial licensing policy have been discussed earlier.

In any event, it seems that, irrational as it may be to seek to prohibit imports of 'inessential' consumer goods while permitting their production domestically, even such an objective could have been as readily achieved, with none of the other detrimental effects of a full-fledged control system embracing all transactions, by a selective set of prohibitive tariffs or quotas on specific items sought to be excluded from imports.

VII. CORRUPTION AND FRUSTRATION OF APPARENT PRIORITIES

We have noted that the import control system worked on: (i) incomplete and unsystematic information; (ii) lack of any economic criteria; and (iii) a series of *ad hoc*, administrative rules of thumb operated by a time-consuming bureaucracy. Further, whatever limited allocational aims it may have had were frustrated, in varying degrees, by the corruption that inevitably arose from the large premia on imports under the control system.

There are essentially two different kinds of illegality which the control system generated: (i) since imports were remunerative in general, there were innumerable bogus claims to import licence entitlement under the existing rules of allocation; and (ii) since numerous restrictions obtained with respect to transferability of imports and import licences, black markets throve on such illegal traffic.

(*a*) The Estimates Committee of the Lok Sabha (Parliament) has prepared an interesting list of the malpractices resorted to by persons in Import and Export Trade:[1]

1. applying for licences on the basis of forged essentiality certificates of the Director of Industries or certificates obtained by mis-representation;

2. applying for licences on the basis of forged quota certificates of such certificates obtained by false or forged documents of past imports;

3. applying for licences on the basis of false turnover by producing certificates from the Chartered Accountant obtained by misrepresentation or in collusion with the Chartered Accountant;

4. applying for licences on the basis of other false or forged documents;

[1] *Forty-eighth Report* (1963–1964), Lok Sabha Secretariat, G.O.I., pp. 104–5; quoted also in Lindblom, op. cit., pp. 47–9.

5. applying for licences on the basis of wrong Income-tax verification number or such number having been obtained on production of false or forged Income-tax Clearance Certificate;

6. applying for licences on the basis of Imports or Exports which do not qualify for establishment of quota;

7. applying for more than one licence for the same goods during the same period on different basic years;

8. applying for licences both as established importers and as actual users for the same goods and for the same periods;

9. applying for licences separately in the name of different branches of the same firm and for the same goods on the basis of performance in different basic years;

10. applying for licences on the basis of forged or fabricated recommendation of the Directorate General of Technical Development;

11. applying for licences on the basis of forged or fabricated orders purported to have been placed by a Government department for the supply of goods sought to be imported;

12. applying for licences by concealing changes in the ownership or constitution of business;

13. obtaining clearance of goods from the customs by producing false or fabricated recommendation purported to have been issued by the Import and Export Trade Control authorities or by obtaining such recommendation by influencing the staff of the Import and Export Trade Control Organization;

14. selling of goods imported, against actual user licences by contravening the conditions of the licences;

15. trafficking in licences;

16. selling of goods before their clearance through the customs;

17. tampering with licences or any other documents;

18. over-invoicing and under-invoicing of goods at the time of import or export or applying for licences by misdeclaration of the value, quality, sort, quantity or description of goods.

19. applying for duplicate copy of licences by concealment of facts;

20. making unauthorised changes or interpolations in the licences by means of chemical washing of the original entries in the licences or in the lists attached to licences;

21. importing goods against a bogus licence;

22. applying for licences in the name of fictitious firm;

23. soliciting of licences;

24. smuggling of goods;

25. offering illegal gratification to the staff.

(*b*) The reverse side of some of these practices is the corruption of the bureaucracy itself. This ranged from the top-level contact

men—many of them retired bureaucrats with inside connections—
who establish personal relationships with the top bureaucracy and
politicians through numerous methods of concealed financial
transfers,[1] to the local employee who passes on an occasional suit-
case or watch to the lower-division clerk who must send the file up
for decision. The extent of such corruption, even though reputed
among some political-scientist observers to be less than that to be
found in some of the other less developed countries, increased
significantly with the proliferation of controls, undermining
honesty, and creating cynicism concerning planning within the
country. As a businessman, interviewed by us, put it: 'It is impossible to remain honest and yet survive in business in India
today. For scarce commodities and imports, contacts and bribery
have become essential. Things have come to a stage where we have
frequently to bribe officials not merely to do what they should
not do but in order to make them do what they are supposed to,
and paid to, do!'

(c) At the same time, the numerous restrictions on permissible
imports were evaded through smuggling past the customs by false
declaration and even by getting demands for imports suitably
specified (by misrepresentation to the sponsoring authority) of
commodities with greater premia, whereas the non-transferability
of imports and import licences was evaded systematically through
transactions in black markets. In this connection again, it is interesting to note what the Raj Committee on Steel Control had to say
about the manner in which such illegal demands were made and
transfers effected, with respect to (domestic plus imported) steel:

. . . sheets which can be sold at a premium in the open market are all
lifted by the permit-holders though it was difficult for the State Governments to assess whether in all cases these were actually used for agricultural purposes also.

Even though iron sheets are in great demand, and the producers

---

[1] Contact men (1) throw parties with abundant liquor, otherwise extremely
expensive, (2) help friends in the bureaucracy buy land which has excellent
prospects of appreciation—which is an effective bribe, as the land could have
been bought by the contact men or their employers themselves, (3) supply
cars for weddings and other social occasions, (4) help find jobs for wives, sons
and daughters, and so on. None of this involves any *obvious* income transfer;
nonetheless they are all effective investments in the bureaucracy, which
improve the financial position and standard of living of the bureaucrats and
the politicians and which, quite obviously, yield high returns to the employers
of the contact men.

have not been able to make supplies in respect of indents [by the Iron and Steel Controller's Office], some as old as 4 years, supplies in the open market at Calcutta, Lucknow, Kanpur, Bangalore and Delhi are plentiful. The price demanded is 60 to 80 per cent above the controlled price.

The stockists . . . charge high prices for (scarce) categories, either by not issuing cash memos or by slightly turning the ends of the rods and angles and calling them manufactured goods on the price of which there is no control.

. . . large quantities are moved from State to State by operators in the open market for the purpose of obtaining higher prices from pockets of scarcity in the country.

It is noteworthy that the state governments themselves were not exempt from the general attempts at diverting materials and imports allocated for specific uses to them: 'Some State Governments divert supplies meant for agricultural quota, for other purposes, sometimes even without consulting the Agriculture Department.'[1] Public-sector project officials are also occasionally known to have inflated demands for scarce imports and materials and off-loaded them in the black market: the availability of cement for domestic residential construction is supposed to ease whenever there is a public-sector project construction in the vicinity.

[1] Report of Steel Control, op. cit., pp. 42–3.

16

Import Policy: II

WE now proceed to note how the import régime had the following adverse economic effects: (1) delays; (2) administrative and other expenses; (3) inflexibility; (4) lack of co-ordination among different agencies; (5) absence of competition; (6) bias towards creation of capacity despite under-utilization; (7) inherent bias in favour, *ceteris paribus*, of industries with imported, as distinct from domestically produced, inputs; (8) anticipatory and automatic protection afforded to industries regardless of costs; (9) discrimination against exports; and (10) loss of revenue.

I. Delays

The working of any system of allocation will take a certain amount of time. Even if a free foreign exchange market were to operate, the participants in the market would have to expend time, for example, in acquiring information about availabilities of different kinds of foreign exchange. The administrative system of allocations need involve no significant increase in time, and hence in 'delays', than a price system under which scarce foreign exchange is rationed out in the market: the introduction of priorities would, in principle, be equally time-consuming in both cases, though the procedure would be different, since the price system would involve administrative decisions as to tax and subsidy incentives whereas the control system would involve administrative decisions as to quotas.

In practice, however, the exchange control system seems to degenerate into an inordinately time-consuming allocational device. There are essentially three reasons for this. (i) In a situation of general scarcity of foreign exchange, the definition of priorities becomes exceptionally difficult, as we have seen earlier, and the system ends up having to accommodate all conceivable demands on some 'equitable' basis, while making a pretence of administering priorities: this pretence frequently taking the form of collection of yet more information from applicants and time taken in 'scrutinizing' it and 'arriving at an informed decision'. Delays become, sociologically, the 'conspicuous' substitute for exercise of priorities by the bureaucracy. (ii) Equally important, the multiplication of the bureaucratic apparatus leads to plain inefficiency, with files failing to move quickly and decisions being delayed because procedures are time-wasting. As we shall see shortly, much of the delay to which the Indian import-control system was subject can be put down to the inefficiency of administrative procedures: for example, where indigenous clearance had to be obtained by the D.G.T.D. from two or more other Directorates, these were sought sequentially rather than simultaneously.[1] (iii) Finally, some significance must be attached, in explaining delays under the Indian allocation system, to the fact that, with files often moving from the bottom to the top in the Indian administrative system, they often fail to move until suitable graft is paid to the lower-level clerks. If all graft were paid promptly, there should be no delay on this account; but newcomers and honest applicants are unlikely to conform readily to this widespread practice and hence delays occur on this count in the system as well.

How serious were the resulting delays? Fortunately, we have some concrete information on this subject, thanks to the investigations carried out by the Mathur Committee during 1965. The report of this Study Team on Import and Export Trade Control Organization[2] contains sample studies on the time taken to process import applications of different varieties: (1) Small-scale Sector (S.S.I.) units, for import of raw materials and components; (2) Non-S.S.I. units, sponsored by the Textile Commissioner, for raw materials and components; (3) Scheduled Industry units carried on the books of D.G.T.D.; (4) Other Scheduled Industry

---

[1] It might be argued that these inefficiencies are endemic to the Indian scene and would hold equally if the price system of allocations were in force. This is not correct, however, as the price system, even with priorities being enforced among industries by tax-cum-subsidy schemes, would not involve a parallel bureaucratic machinery in the private sector. Besides, even if it did, competition among rival private interests would tend to produce greater efficiency, unless competition were ruled out, in turn, by government policies (as in fact it was over much of the Organized Industry Sector).

[2] Ministry of Commerce, Government of India; Part I, 1965; Part II, 1966.

TABLE 16.1
DELAYS ON APPLICATIONS FOR IMPORTS OF RAW MATERIALS

1. *Kind of applicant*	(A) *S.S.I. units*	(B) *Non-S.S.I. units*	(C) *Scheduled industries*	(D) *Scheduled industries on D.G.T.D.*
2. Number of applications studied	243	279	203	154
3. Nature of application	Application pertaining to raw mat./comp. studied by J.C.C.I.E., Bombay	pertaining to raw mat./comp. studied in J.C.C.I.E. office, Bombay	import of raw mat. and spares studied in the office of C.C.I.E.	
4. Average time taken by licensing office to make up deficiency	39 days	34 days	n.a.	n.a.
5. Average time taken by each authority:				
(a) Sponsoring authority for essential commodities	71 days (Dir. of Industries)	(Tex. Commr.) (i) 79·2 (ii) 147 } average 113·1 days	80 days (D.G.T.D.)	114·5 days
(b) Licensing office	30 days	16 days	21·5 days	n.a.
(c) Consulting bodies (e.g. D.G.T.D.) for indigenous clearance	10·6 days	55 days	10·64 days	34·5 days
6. Disposal of appeals—average time per application	11·1 days	n.a.	2·88 days	n.a.
7. Adjustments—average time taken per application	1·67 days	0·6 day	22·3 days	n.a.
8. Revalidation—average time in disposal of total applications	7 days		2·75 days	n.a.
9. Total time taken (4 + 5a, b, c, + 6 + 7 + 8)	163·4 days	218·7 days	140·1 days	149 days

Notes: *a* These figures are somewhat dubious: the source is unclear on whether they are part of the other figures or supplementary.

Source: The data on columns *A–C* are taken from Appendix IV, and on column *D* from Appendix V, of the Report of the Study Team on Import and Export Trade Control Organization, Part I, Ministry of Commerce, Government of India, 1965.

The average delays arising out of appeals, adjustments, and revalidation, where available, have been worked out by taking the total days consumed on the cases where such action was taken and then dividing through by the *total* number of applications.

units for raw materials and spares; (5) Public Sector Projects for free-foreign exchange licences for non-C.G. (capital goods) purposes; (6) Export Promotion Licensing, and (7) Applications for Capital Goods imports classified by four administrative categories: (i) applications passing through the (main) C.G. committee; (ii) applications passing through the (*ad hoc*) C.G. committee; (iii) applications involving foreign collaboration; and (iv) other cases.

In few of these cases was any scientific sampling procedure adopted; and therefore it is best to look upon the results of these studies as merely indicative of the kinds and nature of delays that were built into the trade control system in 1965. In point of fact, since the delays are recorded on an *average* basis, it is possible to imagine what the actual delays in the least-fortunate cases must be.

Tables 16.1 to 16.3 summarize the results of these investiga-

TABLE 16.2

APPLICATIONS FOR (I) PUBLIC SECTOR PROJECTS FOR FREE-FOREIGN EXCHANGE LICENCES FOR NON-C.G. PURPOSES AND (II) EXPORT PROMOTION LICENSING

Kind of applicant	Average time taken for issuing licence	Average time not accounted for in calculation
(A) Public Sector projects (50)	20·1 days (taken by licensing authority)	Excludes (i) time taken in appeals, (ii) time in getting foreign exchange from Ministry, and (iii) time in getting indigenous clearance from D.G.T.D.
(B) Export promotion licensing (408)	51 days (taken by sponsoring authority) 28 days (taken by licensing authority) 0·8 day (taken for revalidation and amendments) 79·8 days (Total)	Excludes time taken in appeals

Source: *Report* of the Study Team on Import and Export Trade Control Organization, Part II, Appendices II and V, Ministry of Commerce, Government of India, 1966.

tions, putting them in a form where the general pattern of delays, as also their magnitude, are easily discernible.[1] Table 16.1 lists the results in categories 1–4 above, with some detail. Table 16.2 is a summary statement of the delays in categories 5 and 6, whereas

[1] The original data are scattered in detailed Appendices to the *Mathur Report*. Sorting them out in a meaningful manner was quite difficult; and the reader should be warned against taking the precision of the figures too seriously. As a further *caveat*, note that the decimal points in the figures come from the necessity to work out averages.

TABLE 16.3

APPLICATIONS FOR CAPITAL GOODS IMPORTS

Decomposition of delays on (1)	I. Applications (30) through the (main) C.G. committee (2)	II. Applications (100) through the (ad hoc) C.G. committee (3)	III. Applications (13) involving foreign collaboration (4)	IV. Other cases (8) involving reference to neither C.G. committee (5)
(A) Common delays[a]				
(i) Average time (in days) taken between receipt of application and bringing deficiencies to notice	31·0	31·0	31·0	31·0
(ii) Average time (in days) taken between receipt of application in C.C.I. & E. Office and initial scrutiny in C.G. cell	12·5	12·5	12·5	12·5
(iii) Licensing authority's delay (in days) in respect of lists of permissible imports	34·7	34·7	34·7	34·7
(iv) Average time (in days) for clearing appeals	14·3	14·3	14·3	14·3
(v) Average time (in days) for clearing amendments	5·8	5·8	5·8	5·8
(vi) Average time (in days) for clearing revalidation	5·0	5·0	5·0	5·0
Total common-factor delays (in days)	103·3	103·3	103·3	103·3
(B) Other delays				
I: C.G. (Main) committee				
(i) C.C.I.E.'s delay (in days) in sending papers for necessary action to organizations concerned	27·0			
(ii) Average time (in days) taken by D.G.T.D. for furnishing comments	73·5			
(iii) Average time-lag (in days) between issue of	48·0			

comments by D.G.T.D. and date of circulation of brief to committee

(iv) Average time-lag (in days) between date of circulation of summary and date of meeting of committee — 23·0

(v) Average time-lag (in days) between date of meeting and date of communication of decision to party — 44·0

(vi) Average time-lag (in days) between date of communication of decision and receipt of papers in C.C.I.E.'s office for further action — 16·0

(vii) Average time lag (in days) between date of receipt of application in C.C.I.E.'s organization and its final disposal — 201·0

Total other delays (in days) — 432·5

II: *C.G.* (ad hoc) *committee*

(i) Average time (in days) taken by D.G.T.D. in sending application to C.C.I.E. along with comments on indigenous angle — 88·5

(ii) Average time-lag (in days) between date of receipt of applications in C.C.I.E.'s office and date of making reference to D.G.T.D. for comments — 30·5

(iii) Average time (in days) taken by D.G.T.D. in furnishing their comments — 36·0

(iv) Average time (in days) taken between date of receipt of applications in C.C.I.E.'s organization and its final disposal — 177·0

Total other delays — 332·0

Y

TABLE 16.3—continued

Decomposition of delays on	I. Applications (30) through the (main) C.G. committee	II. Applications (100) through the (ad hoc) C.G. committee	III. Applications (13) involving foreign collaboration	IV. Other cases (8) involving reference to neither C.G. committee
(1)	(2)	(3)	(4)	(5)
III: *Foreign collaboration*				
Average time-lag (in days) between date of receipt of applications in C.C.I.E.'s organization and its final disposal			87·6	
Total (in days)			87·6	
IV: *Other cases*				
(i) Average time (in days) taken by C.C.I.E. office in issuing rejection letters				33·0
(ii) Average time (in days) taken by C.C.I.E. office in dealing with applications				16·0
Total				49·0
GRAND TOTAL (A) + (B) (in days)	535·8	435·3	190·9	152·3

Note: For further details, see the *Report*, op. cit. Note that the information on other delays is frequently based only on a few case studies.

Source: *Report* of the Study Team on Import and Export Trade Control Organization, Part II, Appendix I, Ministry of Commerce, Government of India, 1966.

Table 16.3 is a detailed statement of the pattern and magnitude of delays in capital goods licensing, category 7.

These results show that the average delays in raw materials/ components licensing were quite large, ranging from five to seven months, whereas for capital goods licensing the time expended between initial application and final issuance of licence went up to nearly 1½ years (for the applications passing through C.G. main committee).

The Mathur Committee's comments on most of these delays are revealing. In their opinion, most of them could be cut down without any difficulty. (1) Lack of clarity of procedures, they found, often led to avoidable delays. Complicated patterns of import licensing, leading to numerous channels through which applications may pass, sometimes created difficulties of determining the exact channel through which any specific application should be routed. Thus, delays arose from having to re-route applications. (2) Applications also turned out to be deficient, in which case they had to be resubmitted. These deficiencies, in turn, could be traced in some cases to lack of clarity in instructions. (3) The action taken in remedying deficiencies could also be inefficient. For the S.S.I. units studied (Table 16.1), 'In 12 cases deficiencies were called for piecemeal'.[1] (4) When there was delay in submitting applications for a specific licensing period, there might be lack of co-ordination between different authorities. 'The delay was condoned by the D.G.T.D. in all these cases. However, in 8 such cases, the D.G.T.D. did not inform the Chief Controller of Imports and Exports about the condonation of delay with the result that the Chief Controller of Imports and Exports had to refer these cases back to the D.G.T.D. for advice. This process involved, on an average, a loss of 20 days.'[2] (5) There was also an occasional failure to take all relevant decisions at the same time, even though the authority involved was the same.

In 36 out of 162 cases, where licenses were issued, the D.G.T.D. either did not forward the list of items to be allowed for import or furnished a mutilated copy of the list and advised that the parties should be asked to submit revised lists through the D.G.T.D. for alteration. The D.G.T.D. took, on an average, 18 days in clearing the revised lists and the Chief Controller of Imports and Exports took 22 more days in attesting and issuing the lists. In 10 cases, the D.G.T.D. omitted to

---

[1] *Mathur Report*, Vol. I, p. 86.   [2] Ibid., p. 89.

attest the list of items recommended for import. These cases had, therefore, to be referred back to them for necessary attestation which, on an average, took 18 days.[1]

(6) Similarly, there might be sequential, rather than simultaneous, seeking of information from other authorities by the responsible authority.

In 23 (i.e. nearly 2/3rd) cases the indigenous clearance had to be obtained only from one Directorate. It was only in 8 cases that 3 or more Directorates had to be consulted for this purpose. In 6 out of these 36 cases, the clearance given by the Directorates concerned was partial, necessitating back reference to them. . . . It was observed that only rarely were the Directorates concerned consulted simultaneously by the Sponsoring Directorate, the common practice being to approach the Directorates for indigenous clearance one after the other.[2]

Numerous other such examples of inefficient procedures, adopted by the bureaucracy involved in import licensing, can be found in the Mathur Committee Report. As one more telling example of the supreme irrationality of the procedures, note the following comment by the committee on the allocation of foreign exchange by some D.G.T.D. Directorates among constituent units:

In some places, the foreign exchange allocation among the various industrial units is decided and communicated to the parties in advance, asking them to submit their import applications to cover their six months' requirements within the specified allocations. This sub-allocation is made on the basis of past performance and past imports of the industrial units involved. This practice is in vogue in the Rubber, Leather and Ceramics Directorates. *In some cases, the allocations are made after the bulk of the applications have been received and their requirements tabulated. This, however, involves avoidable delays in as much as in the ultimate analysis, the value of the imports of raw materials and spares recommended is mainly based on the past performance and past imports.* . . .[3]

And one final example, relating to the small-scale sector:

Case studies showed that out of an average 101 days spent in the actual processing of import applications, 71 days were taken by the Directors of Industries in processing the Essentiality Certificates (ECs).

---

[1] *Mathur Report*, Vol. I, p. 89. [2] Ibid., pp. 92–3.
[3] Ibid., pp. 91–2 [italics inserted by us].

In spite of this, in 85 per cent cases the licenses did not conform entirely to the recommendations made on the Essentiality Certificates. This shows firstly, that the EC applications take considerable time for disposal in the Directorates of Industries, and secondly that *recommendations made on the Essentiality Certificates cannot be given effect to and they represent infructuous work.*[1]

II. Administrative and other expenses

Apart from the delays and corruption, and the economic waste that attended the control system and which we analyse later,[2] the import control system analysed here inevitably imposed costs in three additional ways: (i) the large bureaucratic apparatus, whose personnel and paperwork must be supported at real cost to the economy; (ii) the costs of frequent travel and the opportunity cost of time in getting decisions made by the bureaucracy; and (iii) the social cost implicit in diverting entrepreneurial interests away from improvements in production and investment towards 'getting past controls' as a more efficient method of increasing profits.

III. Inflexibility

The twin principles of 'essentiality' and 'indigenous non-availability' also imparted considerable inflexibility to the pattern of utilization of imports. This occurred via a rigid itemization of permissible imports, frequently by specified value for different items, both for A.U. and E.I. licences.

At the same time, the theoretical premise that A.U. allocations were being made on the basis of well-defined priorities at detailed-industry-level, led the authorities to rule out legal transferability of the licences among the different industries; and bureaucratic logic took the inevitable next step and eliminated transferability even among units within the same industry, thus making A.U. licences *altogether* non-transferable by the licensee units. Needless to say, none of the imports under the A.U. licences were allowed to be sold either.

---

[1] *Mathur Report*, Vol. I, p. 16 [italics inserted by us].
[2] By these economic costs, we refer to the effects on unit-wise efficiency via effects on competitiveness of industry, inducements to create capacity in economically desirable areas and flexibility in procuring critical imports whose social return is correspondingly considerable.

As many specific instances of the itemized restrictions on licences can be obtained, for the E.I. licences, from the Import Policy Redbook as one may care to look up. Take, for example, the following instance from the April 1964 to March 1965 Redbook. For 'Chemicals for which licences will be granted on a quota based on imports of individual items', item 33 reads as follows:

33. Laboratory and reagent chemicals except those specified in List III: Remarks: (i) Not more than 15% of the face value quota licenses can be utilised for the import of any single item.[1]

The itemized restrictions on A.U. licences can, in turn, be inferred from the detailed lists of permissible (and impermissible) imports of specific categories of goods which were published in the Redbooks. For example, Appendix 30 of the April 1964 to March 1965 Redbook had a list of imports of tyres and tubes which were not permissible, extending to 143 specific types.

The rigid pattern of permissible imports (only occasionally adjusted through changing the contents of the lists by discretionary action) as also the non-transferability of the A.U. licences and imports thereunder were bound to create inflexibility leading to economic inefficiency because:

(1) the *total* A.U. allocations to individual units were neither by well-defined priorities nor based on assessment of reasonably accurate and analysed information, but were mostly based on notions of 'fair sharing' with occasional injection of 'pragmatism' and 'judgement of cases on merits';

(2) the *itemized* breakdowns were based on (i) indigenous non-availability which, as we have noted, was assessed with inaccuracy by the responsible bodies such as the D.G.T.D., and (ii) these bodies' assessment of the optimal mix of imported inputs, which again was more on an administrative and *ad hoc* basis than on any recognizable criterion of economic efficiency; and

(3) there is considerable uncertainty in the availability of foreign exchange, leaving aside the general unpredictability of the entire economic situation, so that no 'optimal mix' of inputs laid down in advance (even if worked out on the basis of well-defined criteria, accurately gathered available information and

[1] p. 443, Ministry of International Trade, Government of India, Delhi, 1964.

explicitly assumed future developments) can hope to be optimal *ex post*, thus requiring flexibility in the matter of the input-mix and transfers of inputs from one set of users to another.

That these restrictions were quite bizarre and productive of significant inefficiency can be inferred from the occasional notifications of relaxation (again hemmed in by numerous other restrictions) that can be found in the Redbooks (and which must represent a very small fraction of the number of similar cases where action failed to be taken). An impressive example is provided by Appendix 27, again from the April 1964 to March 1965 Redbook. In the preceding chapter, we had noted how this Appendix had recorded the receipt of representations that 'scientific photographic and other instruments are often rendered idle on account of the fact that they need special types of electric bulbs for use with them and normally speaking the importers of such equipment do not hold import licenses for electric bulbs.' The solution to this problem, provided in the same appendix, is of interest:

(*a*) In future, whenever a complete equipment is imported, in which an electric bulb having some peculiarity as to size, shape or filament is used, it will be permissible to import three spare bulbs of precisely the same type and make as is fitted to the equipment imported. If the number of bulbs fitted to the equipment exceeds one, the number of spare bulbs to be imported will be thrice the number of bulbs in the equipment. . . .

(*b*) In order to enable the supply of replacements to equipment already imported in the country in the past, importers holding licenses for equipment of a type for which such special non-G.L.S. type lamps are required will be permitted to apply for the endorsement of their existing licenses to cover the imports of special types of lamps. This concession will *only* be granted to established importers who have imported equipment needing such bulbs during the past three years and it will be necessary for them to produce documents (bill of entry and invoices) to show that they have made such imports during *each* of the last three years. On production of such documents, their *existing* licenses for the import of particular equipment will be made valid for the import of spare bulbs also up to a value not exceeding $2\frac{1}{2}$ per cent of the total c.i.f. value of the license.

(*c*) Where the equipment in question has been imported in the past under Open General License, established importers will be granted a special licence for the import of non-G.L.S. types of bulbs to fit such equipment equal in value to $2\frac{1}{2}$ per cent of the value of such equipment actually imported by them during any of the three years ending 31 March, 1952, *provided* they produce documents to show that they have been making imports during *each* of the last three years.[1]

Note that, even though 'liberalization' of imports was permitted in order to remove a typical bottleneck resulting from the rigid import-specification system, numerous restrictions on the magnitude, pattern (E.I. *v.* A.U.) and distribution (how much extra each licensee could import) were imposed, each of these reflecting purely administrative rules of thumb. Thus, for example, the grant of the licences only to importers who had imported the lamps before for a continuing and immediately preceding period of three years was just an administratively simple method of distributing the largesse (via import premia) to be earned by securing the licences.[2]

Instances of serious bottlenecks arising from the inability to secure minor import items, which could raise productivity considerably and which would therefore be successfully competed for (to social advantage) by the concerned entrepreneurs if there were any market for foreign exchange, have been observed independently by many analysts.[3]

Yet another implication of the inflexibility arising from the non-transferability of import licences might have been an excessive holding of inventories by Indian firms. Indian inventories, especially the raw materials and intermediates held, compare unfavourably with those of firms in similar industries elsewhere.[4] However, other factors on the Indian scene probably explain these large inventories. For example, interest rates in the organized industrial sector are quite low, thus making inventory-holding relatively inexpensive;[5] on the other hand, it is not clear that the relevant

[1] Italics inserted by us.

[2] Further, for example, there was no economic justification produced for determining the figure of $2\frac{1}{2}$ per cent.

[3] Thus, for example, a joint and unpublished study by the Ministry of Finance and the USAID in early 1966 of some engineering plants (among others) is reported to have revealed several such instances in this 'priority' industry.

[4] On this, see H. Mazumdar and M. J. Solomon, 'Inventory Holding by Manufactures in India and the United States', Indian Statistical Institute, 1960 (mimeographed), in particular.

[5] The recent, thorough work of K. Krishnamurthy and D. U. Sastry, *Inventories in the Organised Manufacturing Sector of the Indian Economy*, Institute of Economic Growth, Delhi, 1966 (in press), has shown that inventory holding in Indian industries responds to changes in the short-term interest rate.

Indian interest rates are lower than abroad. Lower efficiency in transport (and shortage thereof) would also make inventory-holding more valuable. Furthermore, inventory holdings, including raw materials and intermediates, appear to have declined (as a proportion of output) generally through the period of our study, for most industries.[1] Hence, while it makes *a priori* sense to argue that, *ceteris paribus*, an import control régime of the Indian type would tend to inflate inventory holdings, it would not be correct to argue that the empirical analyses currently available support this hypothesis.

IV. Lack of co-ordination among different agencies

The multiplicity of agencies dispensing imports further accentuated the improbability of itemized restrictions on permissible imports, as also bulk restrictions on value, being optimal and thus the probability of significant economic inefficiency following from such rigidities.

Recall, for example, the typical unit under D.G.T.D.'s jurisdiction would get its share in the bulk allocations by the Economic Adviser to the D.G.T.D., and would *also* get allocations of iron and steel from the I. & S.C.'s office as also non-ferrous allocations from decisions made by the corresponding Department (which, in turn, got bulk allocations for this purpose). Unfortunately, co-ordination of these allocations, either in initial allocations, or in cuts therein, does not appear to have been a routine matter. Thus, take the following telling example: 'In the current year (1964–1965) . . . steel licensing for DGTD-borne units has not taken place until the date of signing this report (11th June 1965) although licensing for other raw materials and components has been largely attended to.'[2]

V. Absence of competition

In addition, the import allocation system in force had virtually eliminated the possibility of competition, either foreign or domestic.

We have already noted how foreign competition was ruled out

[1] See Krishnamurthy and Sastri, op. cit., pp. 213–25, which summarizes these and related findings.
[2] *Report of the Study Team on Directorate General of Technical Development*, Part I (New Delhi: Ministry of Industry and Supply, 1965).

because of the principle of 'indigenous availability': every item of indigenous production, no matter how much its cost of production exceeded the landed c.i.f. price,[1] was automatically shielded from competition through imports, indeed the onus being put on the buyer to show conclusively that he could not procure the item from indigenous producers.

At the same time, the possibility of domestic competition was, in turn, minimized by the combination of C.G. licensing (concomitantly with other industrial licensing provisions) and the method of A.U. licensing on a 'fair-share' basis among rival firms in an industry. Strict C.G. and industrial licensing eliminated free entry by new firms as also efficiency-induced expansion by existing firms. And the fact that each firm was entitled to its 'share' of A.U. licences, and no more, ensured that the efficient firms could not even (legally) enlarge output from existing capacity by competing away the scarce imports from less efficient firms.

Thus, all forms of effective competition, potential and actual, were virtually eliminated from the industrial system. The effects, therefore, were (1) to eliminate incentives to reduce costs per unit output (as the penalty for sloppy operations was no longer incapacity to survive against more efficient rivals), and (2) to prevent production from being concentrated in the most efficient units (and industries).

VI. Bias towards creation of capacity despite under-utilization

The tendency to relate equity in allocations to installed capacity, as a simple guide in many cases, was noted by us earlier. This, in turn, led to the creation of an artificial and wasteful incentive to overbuild capacity by linking further entitlement to premia-fetching imports with creation of more capacity.

(1) An entrepreneur, with given capacity which was underutilized through lack of imported inputs, would not be able to expand output through additional utilization of capacity even if it were potentially profitable to do so. The only way he could respond

[1] We shall comment later on the economic waste implicit in this principle of 'anticipatory and automatic protection' by discussing how *investments* must have been (mis)guided wherever they were determined by market profitabilities as defined by such a policy. Here we confine ourselves to the effects via competition only.

to the profitability of the industry was by getting more capacity installed and having some import quota allotted to him on basis thereof. (2) But even if the entrepreneur could be allowed access to more imports at market prices,[1] so that he could expand utilization of existing capacity, the fact that he would have to purchase inputs at import-premia-inclusive market prices in order to do this whereas expansion of capacity would enable him to expand output by access to premia-exclusive import allocations, would certainly bias his choice between these two courses of action towards more capacity creation.[2]

Furthermore, it may be argued that the artificial cheapening of C.G. imports under an overvalued exchange rate system based on direct allocations could lead to suboptimally increased capital intensity in relation to the primary factor, labour.

VII. Bias in favour of industries using imported, as distinct from indigenous, inputs

Under the actual-user system of allocation of imports, combined with the principle of indigenous non-availability, it may be expected that the *quantum* of import allocations would, *ceteris paribus*, tend to be inversely related to the availability of indigenously produced inputs.

But this, in turn, would lead to a bias in the effective incentive provided to the processes using relatively more imported inputs: they would be able to get relatively greater allocations of imports under A.U. licences and hence obtain these inputs at import-*exclusive* prices (which would include only the explicit tariff duty) whereas the other industries would have to buy import-substitute, indigenous items at premium-*inclusive* prices (since these items would fetch a price equal to the c.i.f. price plus

---

[1] This could happen, to some extent, through illegal purchases in the black market. It also became possible when the import entitlements, under the Export Promotion Schemes, were made legally transferable, and a market developed for them around 1965. (We discuss these import entitlements in greater detail in a later chapter.)

[2] Needless to say, this incentive becomes relevant only if the gain from import-premia-exclusive access to materials exceeds the cost of installation of yet more capacity. Hence, the likelihood of the bias leading to installation of yet more capacity (despite current under-utilization) increases with the import premium and the proportion of imported inputs to value added and decreases with the cost of capacity installation.

the import premium). The effective incentive given to the former industries or processes would thus be greater, other things being equal. And, while it may fortuitously be the case that some of these industries may require relative subsidization on economic grounds, there is no gainsaying the fact that the import system in India gave rise to these differential incentives purely as an incidental side-effect.[1]

VIII. Anticipatory and automatic protection to industries

Another, far more significant, impact of the Indian import policy, under which the principle of indigenous availability was used to exclude or restrict imports in favour of purchase of domestic import-substitutes, was that protection was automatically extended to all industries regardless of cost, efficiency, and comparative advantage. This automatic protection was further fully to be anticipated by every producer, only as long as he was willing to make his capacity and production known to the relevant agencies (e.g. the D.G.T.D.) in charge of 'indigenous clearance'.

The influence of this policy on the pattern of industrial investments that emerged through the period must have been considerable. It is clear that the policy of anticipatory and automatic protection that inhered in the working of import policy served to divorce market-determined investment decisions from any guidelines that international opportunity costs (with suitable modifications) might have otherwise provided.

It is pertinent, in this connection, to note that the implicit, nominal tariff rates which were observed under the system could rise to as much as 300/400 per cent in some cases, and to yet higher levels sometimes (Table 16.4).[2] Further, even the effective tariffs

[1] We quantify this kind of effect, though with considerable reservations as to the conceptual and statistical basis of the estimates, in Chapter 17.

[2] As we note later, though, the import premia used in deriving such estimates reflect not merely quantitative import restrictions but also restrictions on domestic entry (enforced via industrial capacity licensing); hence it would be incorrect to infer from these implicit tariffs that the activity with the higher implicit tariff was doing better (in terms of resource-attraction) than the activity with the lower implicit tariff (as compared with the free-trade situation) leaving altogether out of account that, in a multi-commodity world, such a resource-allocational effect could be inferred only for the two commodities at each end of the chain. This qualification, which cannot be ignored in the context of the Indian economy, applies equally to the effective tariffs on value added, which we compute later.

TABLE 16.4

IMPORT PREMIA ON SELECTED PRODUCTS CARRYING HIGH PREMIA,
(DEFINED AS THE EXCESS OF DOMESTIC OVER THE C.I.F. PRICE DIVIDED
BY THE C.I.F. PRICE AND EXPRESSED AS PERCENTAGES)

Item	1961	1962	1963	1964	1965
Steel files					
1. 8 inch taper heavy	—	266·0	—	—	—
2. 6 inch taper slim	—	324·0	—	—	—
Electric motor starters					
3. Push-button automatic, 5–10 h.p.	504·0	—	—	—	—
4. Push-button automatic, 10–15 h.p.	392·0	—	—	—	—
5. *Saccharine powder*	312·0	—	—	—	—
Lead pencils					
6. Taj Mahal	602·0	620·0	—	—	—
7. Kohinoor (United Kingdom)	260·0	—	—	—	—
8. Kohinoor (Czech)	310·0	—	—	—	—
Steel pens					
9. Goldwing	380·0	—	—	—	—
10. Waverly	291·0	—	—	—	—
11. Hindoo	387·5	—	—	—	—
Coloured pencils					
12. Camel	671·0	—	—	—	—
Paste boards					
13. Holland	250·0	250·0	—	—	—
14. Sweden	321·5	330·0	—	—	—
15. *Camphor*	430·0	630·0	600·0	524·0	517·0
Menthol					
16. B.P.	462·0	302·0	231·0	244·0	275·0
17. *Crystal*	465·0	176·0	118·0	124·0	140·0
18. *Dextrose anhydrous*	53·0	301·0	363·0	288·0	650·0
19. *Thymol*	128·0	160·0	258·0	422·0	420·0
Writing paper					
20. Radio	270·0	162·0	—	—	—
21. Conqueror	610·0	516·0	—	—	—
22. *Printing paper* (Solex)	265·0	276·0	—	—	—
23. *Calcia*	410·0	624·0	632·0	—	—
24. *Cinnamon*	510·0	532·0	—	—	—
25. *Cloves*	740·0	634·0	497·0	—	712·0
26. *Mace*	484·0	400·0	339·0	550·0	398·0
Betelnuts					
27. Split	1,382·0	1,087·0	1,390·0	1,360·0	—
28. Whole (Thailand)	220·0	323·0	149·0	139·0	150·0

Notes: The items included in this table extend to producers' goods, consumer goods, and intermediates. The estimates should be taken to represent broad orders of magnitude only and have often been rounded off from recorded, monthly figures. Some figures relate to the financial, and others to the calendar year. The blanks represent non-availability of information.

Source: Data originally secured at different Ports; obtained by us through interviews with relevant authorities.

on value added could rise to high levels, as we shall see in Chapter 17. Moreover, there was a considerable variation in these tariffs, nominal and effective, as was to be expected from the fact that they were totally 'unplanned' and emerged entirely thanks to the policies of automatic protection and controlled distribution of A.U. licences among alternative industries.[1]

TABLE 16.5

IMPORT PREMIA (IN EXCESS OF TARIFF DUTY) ON CERTAIN CHEMICAL AND ENGINEERING ITEMS (MEASURED AS THE EXCESS OF DOMESTIC PRICE OVER TARIFF-INCLUSIVE C.I.F. PRICE, DIVIDED BY THE C.I.F. PRICE AND EXPRESSED AS PERCENTAGES)

Item	1961	1962	1963	1964	1965
Chemicals					
1. Hydrosulphate of soda	30	212	—	—	—
2. Sodium	129	155	—	—	90
3. Sulphadimidine b.p.	—	55	—	121	—
4. Calcium	60	74	—	—	—
5. Titanium dioxide (rectile)	36	117	138	—	—
Engineering					
6a. Shock absorbers: Jeep	75	146	—	—	—
6b. Shock absorbers: Landmaster	103	150	—	—	—
7a. Carbons (1): 12 x 300 mm.	54	42	40	—	—
7b. Carbons (2): 14 x 300 mm.	42	44	42	—	—
8a. House service meters (1): a.c. 10 amps	19	19	—	—	—
8b. House service meters (2): a.c. (20 x 40) amps	66	66	—	—	—
9a. Files: bastard, 12 inch	301	250	250	—	—
9b. Files: flat bastard, 12 inch	297	256	256	—	—
9c. Files: round bastard, 12 inch	282	166	175	—	—
10a. Electric motors a.c.: ¼ h.p.	19	19	19	—	—
10b. Electric motors a.c.: ⅓ h.p.	25	25	25	—	—
11a. Piston assembly: Land-Rover	139	139	—	—	—
11b. Piston assembly: Packard	184	228	—	—	—

Notes: The items included in this table are selected at random from a large list of items for which data were available for varying periods. Even when allowance is made for 'handling charges' and a 'normal' trading profit, these figures do indicate a net import premium which is, in a large number of cases, not negligible, thus underlining the general redundancy of tariffs as an instrument of potential or actual protection. Blanks in the table indicate non-availability of information.

Source: Data originally gathered at different ports; obtained by us through interviews with relevant authorities. Detailed data are available from authors on request.

We might restress finally that explicit tariffs had practically fallen into disuse through most of 1956–66, from the point of view of their protective effect, as is again indicated by the fact that the import premium (taken as wholesale market price minus the

[1] As we have noted, the industries which received rather larger allocations of A.U. licences, which gave access to import-premia-exclusive imports, enjoyed higher effective protection, *ceteris paribus*.

landed cost gross of import duty) as a percentage of the c.i.f. price tended to be quite significant for almost all of the commodities for which we managed to get information for the period 1961–6. We have reproduced here these estimates for some major items, including chemicals and engineering goods, for selected years (Table 16.5). This fact is also underlined by a detailed study of the Tariff Commission during the period, which reveals both the sudden decline in applications for tariff protection since 1956/7 and the impotence of the Commission in influencing the pattern of industrial development in the country thereafter.[1]

IX. Discrimination against exports

Our analysis of the import-control policy would be incomplete if we were not to mention the rather obvious fact that such a system discriminates against exports. The effective export rate, on the average, was inevitably less than the effective import rate; and this was the case at the level of each industry also, until (from around 1962) the initiation and later intensification of significant export subsidization schemes begin to redress, though not restore, the balance (and, in some cases, must have even led to a net subsidization rate in excess of the import rate).[2]

Again, one of the important side-effects of the principle of indigenous availability was that exportable items which therefore were forced to rely on inferior-quality domestically produced inputs and capital equipment were, in turn, faced with enhanced difficulties in the highly competitive international markets. This was particularly the case with the new exports, in the engineering industries, which in any case faced serious difficulties in cultivating foreign markets almost from scratch.

Further, since there was little flexibility for getting more inputs through bidding in the market, in view of the restrictive character of the import policy, and capacity also could not be expanded owing to equally stringent controls on entry, industries which needed flexibility in production in order to get hold of large foreign

[1] Padma Desai, *Tariff Protection in India: 1947–1965, (A Study of India's Tariff Commissions at Work)*, Delhi School of Economics (Advanced Center for Economics), 1970.

[2] We consider these export measures in greater detail in later chapters. Also, some (rough) quantification of the net export 'disincentive' prior to the export subsidization schemes emerges from our later study of effective rates of protection.

orders, whenever available, found themselves unnecessarily handicapped.

Clearly, until late 1964, the entire industrial licensing and import policy was unfavourable to manufacturing exports, largely because it was devised with a substantially inward-looking bias.

X. Loss of revenue

Another noteworthy and obvious effect of the import-control system was the inevitable loss of revenue that it involved, in passing the profits on scarce imports on to the private sector.

(1) Where the imports were channelled through traders, as with E.I. licences, there is little reason to doubt that the import premium fully reflected the scarcity value of the items. Thus, Tables 16.4 and 16.5 contain information on premia for several items, with particularly high values,[1] in order to underline our assertion. It may therefore be expected that, if the Government had channelled these imports through its own agencies *or* auctioned them off *or* levied suitable tariffs, the scarcity premium would have accrued to it as revenue.[2]

(2) For the A.U. imports, it may again be expected that the entrepreneurs who obtained them would nonetheless proceed to charge for their outputs the prices that the market would bear. Hence, the effect of raising tariffs by the 'implicit' premium on A.U. licences, for example, would not have been to affect the price of the outputs but merely to cut into the profits that accrued to the entrepreneurs purely as a result of access to scarce inputs. However, under cost-plus pricing, this result would not follow and it could not be argued that there was a simple loss-of-revenue effect thanks to the import-control system. In view of the fact, however, that the vast majority of the import premia got seriously reduced without there being a significant rise in final prices, subsequent to the devaluation of June 1967, we are inclined to assert that profit maximiza

---

[1] Table 16.5 is confined to items which had domestic production as well, and is by and large confined to items coming under C.G. + H.E.P. and A.U. licences. The commodities in Table 16.4, on the other hand, are mainly E.I. items.

[2] Indeed, this is what it sometimes, but all too infrequently, tried to do when it transferred the import trade in certain high-premium commodities to the State Trading Corporation, as with caustic soda.

tion, rather than cost-plus, seems to be a better approximation to the behaviour of Indian firms.[1]

We may finally touch on two important 'distributional' questions that have been raised in defence of the direct-allocational system of import regulation used in India.

(1) It has, for example, been argued that the method of A.U. allocations such that each unit gets *some* share of the scarce imports ensures that employment is not eliminated in inefficient units which would, under an alternative (market) system, fail to bid successfully for the imports. Concerning this argument, we may quote what one of us wrote elsewhere:

> This argument, however, assumes that the increase in employment in the efficient firms which get more imputs under the [market system] is less than the decrease that accompanies the failure of the inefficient to get exchange (which may be true if the inefficient firms are labour-intensive). It should also be remembered that a policy that creates extra real income will promote greater capital formation and employment in the longer run.[2]

(2) The other argument is superficially more difficult to dispute. It relates to the fact that *regional* constraints in a country such as India make it impossible to leave allocations of scarce imports (and materials) to the market. Since value is attached by each state to production and investment in themselves, it is not possible to take the position that allocations should be by economic criteria alone and that income transfers should be made as compensation to the states that do not attract inputs or investments. In short, the problem of allocating resources in a federal country such as India involves economic solutions similar to those that would have to be provided in customs unions or free-trade areas among sovereign countries where constraints have to be provided in the shape, for example, of the distribution of manufacturing investments as a whole among the constituent countries.

---

[1] Of course, the post-devaluation situation was also characterized by a significant increase in availability of imports for A.U. licensing, thanks to foreign aid, and soon thereafter large-scale recessionary tendencies developed in the economy's manufacturing sector: these two factors therefore make it difficult to arrive at our conclusion concerning profit-maximizing behaviour quite unambiguously. It may be noted further that the profit-maximizing assumption also underlies the analysis and recommendations of the Raj Committee's Report on steel distribution and control, op. cit.

[2] Bhagwati, *Oxford Economic Papers*, op. cit.

Z

But if this is indeed the case, and (while it may not have been as important a problem during the early part of our period of study) it certainly is of considerable importance today,[1] the question again is whether the 'subsidization' of the states that are likely to 'lose' in a system of market-ruled allocations of A.U. imports should be undertaken through an import-control régime with all the disadvantages we have discussed or whether it is not more sensible to achieve the politically required allocations *among* regions or states by direct subsidization policies, such as differential corporation taxes between regions, which would at the same time permit the import policy to be run on sounder lines. We have little doubt, in the light of our analysis, that this latter would be very much the better course.[2]

[1] Especially with the political changes in India at the last General Election in 1966 leading to *different* parties in power at the Centre and in many States.
[2] Similar considerations apply to industrial licensing for capacity creation, see Chapter 13.

17

Effective Rates of Protection[1]

OUR discussion of the Q.R. régime in India has so far been primarily qualitative. We now proceed to complement it with quantitative estimates of effective rates of protection in the Indian organized industrial sector, for eighteen industries covering consumer goods, raw materials and intermediates, and capital goods, for the years 1961 and 1962.

Although we shall emphasize numerous conceptual and statistical difficulties in attaching resource-allocational implications to these estimates, we think that certain important qualitative conclusions none the less emerge.

(1) The tariff structure which is implicit in the working of the Q.R. régime has been fairly bizarre. This is inevitable in so far as the premia resulting from the kinds of import policy described by us would tend to have no definite pattern as between different protected activities.

(2) This tariff structure further had no stability and, in fact, *shifted* with changes in premia resulting from changing interaction of domestic and foreign availabilities *vis-à-vis* demands.

(3) Thus there was *unpredictability* concerning what effective incentives would be provided to different industries under such a régime.[2]

---

[1] V. R. Panchamukhi of Bombay University has helped to write this chapter. As the book goes to press, we are engaged in extending the results to several other A.S.I. industries, and to 1963. We also expect to do additional sensitivity analyses, mainly by working with alternative estimates of premia. We may emphasize, however, that the qualitative conclusions that we have drawn in this chapter, from the estimates presented in the text, will not change but are only being reinforced by this further work.

[2] In addition, we also produce some order of magnitude on the *average* level of effective protection, and its dispersion, based on the eighteen-industry estimates.

THE CONCEPT OF THE EFFECTIVE RATE OF PROTECTION

The concept of the effective rate of protection refers to the protection of a process as distinct from the 'nominal' tariff on output. It is a notion which was occasionally used implicitly by tariff-making bodies, as in India where the protection of domestic leather manufactures has been sought to be implemented by imposing a tariff on the export of hides and skins.[1] It has also long been the cornerstone of demands by the less developed countries (L.D.C.s) at the G.A.T.T., the common complaint being that finished manufactures were typically over-protected in relation to the semi-finished manufactures and raw materials, and this discriminated against exports (and hence production) of finished manufactures from the L.D.C.s.[2]

The *precise* statement of the effective tariff on a process, defined as the incremental value-added (due to the tariffs) divided by the value-added at c.i.f. prices, seems to have been first made by Travis in 1962. Later, other authors such as Corden, Johnson, and Balassa appear to have rediscovered it independently.[3]

Although it is clear that such effective tariff rates, if accurately

[1] See, for example, the Report of the (First) *Indian Fiscal Commission, 1921–28.* 'In 1919, an export duty was imposed on raw hides and skins as a measure of protection to the Indian tanning industry. This was combined with a rebate of ⅔ of the duty on hides and skins exported to any part of the Empire with a view to maintaining the tanning industry within the Empire.' Also, for many recent policy decisions of this variety, for traditional exports in India, see Manmohan Singh, op. cit.

[2] For a statement of this precise notion, taken from the G.A.T.T. reports in 1963, but without formalizing it into a *rate* of effective protection, see J. Bhagwati, *The Economics of Underdeveloped Countries*, Chapter 25.

[3] Cf. C. L. Barber, 'Canadian Tariff Policy', *Canadian Journal of Economics and Political Science*, XXI (November 1955).

B. Balassa, 'Tariff Protection in Industrial Countries: An Evaluation', *Journal of Political Economy*, LXXIII (December 1965), 573–94.

W. M. Corden, 'The Tariff', in Alex Hunter (ed.), *The Economics of Australian Industry*, Melbourne University Press, 1963.

W. M. Corden, 'The Structure of a Tariff System and the Effective Protective Rate', *Journal of Political Economy*, LXXIV (June 1966), 221–37.

H. G. Johnson, 'The Theory of Tariff Structure with Special Reference to World Trade and Development', *Trade and Development* ('Études et Travaux de l'Institut Universitaire de Hautes Études Internationales'), Geneva: Librairie Droz, 1965.

W. P. Travis, 'On the Theory of Commercial Policy', Ph.D. dissertation, Harvard University, 1961.

For details of the actual formula, W. M. Corden is an excellent source. The formula is also stated in Section II where we set out the methodology.

measured, would be more relevant than nominal tariffs as guides to the effects on the allocation of domestic resources and the relative outputs of different commodities, there are well-known difficulties.

For example, while in a model with only two commodities we could rank the two commodities by their effective tariffs, and infer that resources would then move towards producing the commodity with the higher tariff, this is not true, in a multi-commodity model, for commodities in the middle of the chain (excluding the two at each extreme).

Furthermore, it turns out that, if factor substitution obtains, it is no longer possible to claim that an industry enjoying a higher effective rate of protection will necessarily attract (domestic) resources away from the other industry if we analyse the question in a general-equilibrium framework using primary domestic factors which, combined with imported factors, produce the commodities which are traded for the imported factors. Ramaswami and Srinivasan have recently produced such an analysis which demonstrates conclusively the impossibility of devising any measure of effective rates of protection, regardless of the coefficients at which the measure is taken, which would be able to predict correctly the resource-allocational pulls.[1]

Quite apart from these qualifications to the assertion that resource-allocational direction can be inferred from the ranking of activities by their effective tariffs, there are major conceptual difficulties of yet other varieties in this area. For example, how are we to treat non-traded goods? This phenomenon arises thanks to transport costs and similar cost-raising factors which make it necessary to distinguish between c.i.f. and f.o.b. prices and which make it possible for non-traded goods to arise, whose domestic prices lie within the range defined by these two international prices. Two alternatives have been suggested to deal with this range of goods: either to treat them as part of value added (i.e. as primary factors) or to treat them as zero-tariff inputs. Corden has argued for the former course on the strength of a simple model which shows that the latter procedure would bias the measures away from the correct resource-allocational predictions. On the

---

[1] See their fundamental paper on this subject in the *festschrift* volume for Charles P. Kindleberger (edited by J. Bhagwati, R. W. Jones, R. A. Mundell, and J. Vanek), forthcoming (1970).

other hand, in Corden's model, the non-traded input is just a proxy for a primary factor which is not traded itself; hence the analysis does not really come to grips with the problem in any essential way.[1] It must be admitted therefore that, at the moment, there is no relevant theoretical guideline for anyone who measures effective protection, relating to the treatment of non-traded goods. At another level, the measures are constructed on the assumption of infinite elasticities of international demand and supply; hence we have no manner of dealing yet with the important phenomenon of imperfection in foreign trade.

In view of these conceptual difficulties surrounding the effective-rate-of-protection concept from the viewpoint of predicting the results of resource-allocation between industries, we would have hesitated to use our measures of effective rates of protection for this purpose even if we had access to ideal information. In point of fact, even the data problems are enormous (as we shall soon see). To take only three examples at this stage: (i) there is the difficulty of converting specific into *ad valorem* tariffs in a meaningful manner; (ii) then there is the problem of how to get the 'correct', weighted tariff rate when there are preferential tariffs and imports from both preferential and non-preferential sources are aggregated; and (iii) how can one identify correctly weighted tariffs when the inputs are available only in a semi-disaggregated form such as 'Non-ferrous metals' without any clue to the relative composition of the different metals in this group? When, therefore, both the conceptual traps and the necessity to adjust and manipulate data at nearly all stages of the calculations are admitted frankly, there seems no way in which to attach resource-allocational, directional inferences to ranking of industries by their calculated effective rates of protection.

We have therefore decided to look upon our alternative measures as nothing more than relatively rough indicators of the *differential* nature of the incentives generated by the foreign trade régime. In opting for this 'weak' interpretation, we have been influenced by several further conceptual and statistical difficulties which arise when the foreign trade régime is characterized by Q.R.s. We have found that these raise fresh difficulties which have not

---

[1] W. M. Corden, op. cit. In consequence, we have proceeded to compute effective rates for Indian industries on *both* assumptions, treating the procedure as amounting to some form of sensitivity analysis.

been discussed in the available literature which has taken (explicit) tariffs as the effective form of protection. We therefore proceed to discuss these here at some length, before presenting our detailed analysis and results.

The standard practice, whenever the existence of Q.R.s is recognized in such calculations, is to regard the ratio of the premium on imports to c.i.f. value as the *implicit*, nominal tariff rate which is to be used *in lieu* of the (lower) explicit, nominal tariff rate in making the effective tariff rate calculations. But there are conceptual difficulties with this method, as also extremely difficult problems of data collection associated with it.

At a conceptual level, can we really treat the observed implicit tariff as equivalent to an identical, explicit tariff? To put it differently, if the Q.R.s on imports were to be removed and instead an explicit tariff imposed of the same magnitude as the implicit tariff defined by the premium on imports, would the real equilibrium (e.g. import and output levels) remain the same? For this equivalence is really what is asserted when we use the implicit tariff as the nominal tariff in making the effective rate calculations.

In point of fact, we cannot argue that this equivalence will necessarily obtain except when we assume universal competitiveness—in foreign supply, in quota-holding, and in domestic production. When the assumption of competition breaks down in either area, the possibility that equivalence may break down can be demonstrated. Thus Bhagwati has shown elsewhere that in the case when foreign supply is monopolistic, the implicit tariff rate is zero under the quota—but setting the actual tariff rate at zero and removing the quota restriction will not yield the same level of imports and domestic production; the truly equivalent tariff rate is higher.[1] Similarly, in the case where there is domestic import monopoly instead, the truly equivalent tariff is lower than the implicit tariff rate in the quota alternative. Similar conclusions apply to three other cases: (i) where there is monopolistic-holding

---

[1] J. Bhagwati, 'On the Equivalence of Tariffs and Quotas', in Caves, Kenen, and Johnson (eds.), *Trade, Growth and Balance of Payments* (Essays in Honor of Gottfried Haberler); and Bhagwati, 'More on the Equivalence of Tariffs and Quotas', *American Economic Review*, March 1968, pp. 142–6. These two papers have been rewritten together, with minor changes, for reprinting in Bhagwati, *Trade, Tariffs and Growth; Essays in the Theory of International Trade*.

of quotas, but competition elsewhere, again the implicit tariff rate will exceed the explicit tariff rate, thus overstating the truly equivalent tariff rate, when the quota is under-utilized; (ii) where there is monopoly in domestic production as well as in holding of quotas, again the under-utilization of the quota would imply an

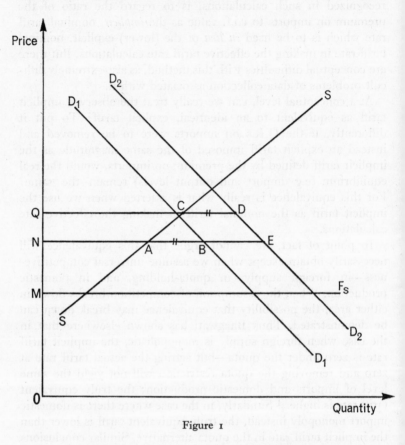

Figure 1

implicit tariff rate that exceeds the explicit tariff rate and hence overstates the truly equivalent, effective tariff; and (iii) where there is monopoly in domestic production but competition every-where else, the implicit tariff will exceed the explicit tariff, thus overstating again the truly equivalent, effective tariff that the quota represents.

Furthermore, contrary to the situation where (explicit) tariffs are effective, a Q.R. régime results in variable, implicit tariffs. This variability arises largely from the fact that the premium will vary, given the quota level, with changes in supply and demand conditions. Thus Figure 1 illustrates, using a partial-equilibrium Marshallian diagram, how a given quota level ($AB = CD$) leads to a higher implicit tariff level (QM/MO) than earlier (NM/MO) if domestic demand rises from D_1D_1 to D_2D_2, with foreign supply F_s and domestic supply SS remaining unchanged. On the other hand, if the earlier situation had been characterized by an equivalent tariff at rate (NM/MO), the tariff would have remained unchanged at the initial value (and imports would have increased by BE). This argument therefore underlies the importance of measuring Q.R.-determined protection over a period rather than at one point of time: the premia, in fact, move fairly significantly and frequently in practice, making one-shot calculations of implicit protection meaningless in themselves. The (expected) *average* of the implicit rates is clearly of greater relevance to allocational decisions than the implicit protection at a single point of time. To underline this point, we have calculated the effective rates of protection for two different years: 1961 and 1962.

We may next mention three complicating factors, largely endemic to the Indian scene, which are relevant to calculating and interpreting our measures of effective rates of protection.

(1) The Indian mixture of economic policies presents serious difficulty in regarding the effective rates of protection, calculated from implicit, nominal tariffs in a Q.R. régime, as indicators of the direction in which resources will have been pulled in relation to a situation of unified exchange rates. This difficulty arises from the fact that, as we have already seen, Indian policy involved the use of industrial investment licensing: this meant that there were controls on *domestic entry* as well. In so far as these are operative for any industry, a higher premium on output (and hence a higher calculated effective rate on the process), *ceteris paribus*, could indicate not merely that imports were scarce owing to Q.R.s but also that domestic entry had been restricted. Where, therefore, the premium is high, the resulting higher effective rate may imply, not that resources have been pulled towards this industry but just the opposite: namely, that resources have been prevented from going into the industry.

This significant qualification to the usual interpretation of effective rates is illustrated in Figure 2. DD and SS are the domestic demand and supply schedules; F_s is the foreign supply schedule. If an import quota of AB were allowed, the equilibrium domestic price would be AR and the implicit, nominal tariff rate

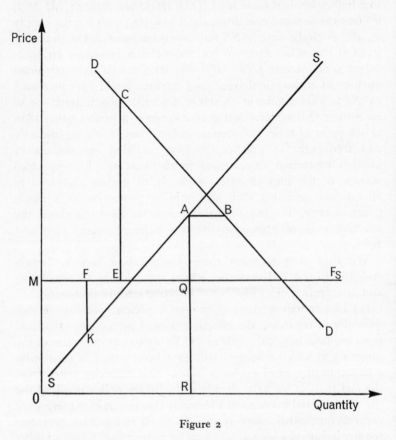

Figure 2

would be (AQ/QR). However, if this import quota were accompanied by investment/output licensing which restricts domestic output to MF, the equilibrium price would rise to $(QR + CE)$, the premium on imports from AQ to CE, and we would find that the implicit, nominal tariff (as normally measured) would now have increased to (CE/QR). But, far from this apparent increase in the implicit tariff implying that domestic output has increased, the fact is that the restriction of output to MF has led to the increased premium and the consequent rise in the measured, implicit tariff.

Ideally, it should be possible to decompose the premium into: (i) the amount that would accrue *if* domestic entry were unrestricted but imports were restricted at the specified level; and (ii) the amount that is to be attributed to the restriction of domestic output itself. To do this, however, we would have to guess at the domestic supply and demand elasticities (over the relevant range), assuming (with our theory) that the foreign supply is infinitely elastic.

In the estimates that we present later in this chapter, we have not ventured into this area of speculative econometrics. We therefore leave the reader with the caveat that, except in the case of industries with *de facto* free-entry through the small-scale sector which escaped investment licensing, as matches, bicycles, and sewing machines, the measures of effective rates of protection are likely to include varying biases arising from restrictions on domestic entry.

(2) Ideally, we should also have adjusted our measures for export subsidies, which are an element of protection to the process if paid on outputs and a disincentive to the process if given on inputs. The major difficulty in the Indian case would have been to arrive at reliable estimates of the *ad valorem* export incentives implicit in the import-entitlement (or exchange-retention) schemes of export promotion which we describe and analyse at length in Chapters 19 and 20. We therefore deliberately selected 1961 and 1962 when the export incentives were relatively minor and hence the bias from our procedure of omission probably negligible.

In the Indian context, furthermore, there was also a novel conceptual problem relating to export subsidization. We had the genuine possibility, certainly since 1964, that an industry which was itself being protected from imports was then being subsidized for exports. In such cases, how are we to measure the net 'protective' effect (from the viewpoint of resource allocation) of these policies? If there is a *unique* international price, there is no problem: the difference between the domestic price and the international price would yield the relevant, nominal export subsidy that would have to be taken into account in our calculation.

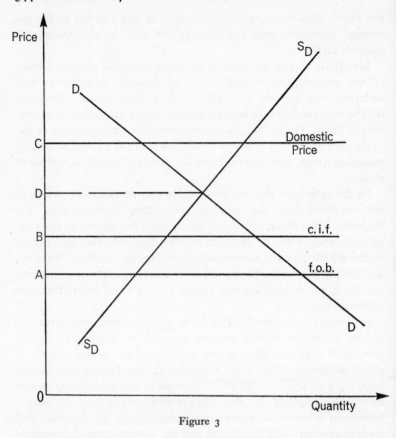

Figure 3

However, where the f.o.b. price differs from the c.i.f. price owing to transport costs, we would have to follow a more complex procedure.[1]

Thus, take Figure 3. If we write

w = import tariff rate which just suffices to cut out imports
s = export subsidy rate
q = excess of c.i.f. over f.o.b. price, divided by f.o.b. price,
z = operative, 'true' protective rate, which we seek,

then, in the Marshallian Figure 3 where S_D is the domestic supply curve, D the domestic demand curve, OA the f.o.b.

---

[1] We are grateful to Max Corden for the following analysis, worked out by him when the problem raised in the text was pointed out to him at the Bellagio meetings by the authors.

international price, and OB the c.i.f. international price, we have:

$$w = \frac{BD}{OB}$$

$$s = \frac{CA}{OA}$$

$$q = \frac{AB}{OA}$$

and

$$z = \frac{BC}{OB}$$

where z is the operative, 'true' protective rate that we want because it represents the proportionate amount by which the domestic price moves from the free-trade situation (at OB) to the actual domestic price (OC), which determines the shift in domestic *production* (i.e. the resource-allocation effect that we are after). We can then write:

$$z = \frac{s - q}{1 + q}$$

Thus, the 'true', operative tariff rate will lie between the export subsidy rate and the 'prohibitive', import tariff rate: $s > z > w$.[1]

In any event we have treated all our industries as basically import-substituting industries, abstracting from the problems just discussed.

(3) Finally, we should note that producers in India obtained A.U. licences, as we discussed in Chapter 15, under which they could import intermediates *directly*. Hence, practically all producers had two sources of imports: (i) A.U., which gave them import-premium-exclusive imports; and (ii) imports brought from the market at premium-inclusive prices.[2] Our analysis thus has treated A.U. imports and other *tradeable* inputs separately.[3]

---

[1] Where, of course, $w > \frac{s - q}{1 + q}$, w will be the 'true' operative protective rate that we want.

[2] Imports were available from the market through E.I.-licensed importation and through illegal sales. Later, the market expanded to include the sale of Export Promotion licences under the import entitlement schemes which we discuss in Chapters 19 and 20.

[3] The precise procedure is explained in the next section.

Methodology

The following procedure has been adopted by us in estimating the effective rates of protection due to Q.R.s on imports (and other restrictions) and tariffs. The notations used are described below:

X_{ij} = Total input-value of the ith item for the jth industry, in domestic market prices.

M_{ij} = Imported inputs of ith type through actual-user-import licences, in the jth industry.

D_{ij} = Rest of the inputs of the ith type, in the jth industry.

r_i = *Ad valorem* tariff rate on the ith import.

m_i = The rate of premium (difference between market price *in the ports* and the c.i.f. price) as a proportion of the c.i.f. price.

T_i = Transport margin as an *ad valorem* rate per unit value of the ith item.

V_j = Net value-added in the jth sector, at domestic prices.

S_j = Total non-traded inputs in sector j.

X_j = Output-value in domestic market prices for sector j.

The observed values refer to a situation when there are tariffs on inputs and outputs, and when there are Q.R.s on imports. We 'relax', by stages, the conditions of (i) Q.R.s on imports, and (ii) tariffs on inputs and outputs, and estimate the extent of value-added in these cases.

Suppose that there were no import quotas. Then, the domestic market prices would be the tariff-inclusive c.i.f. prices. In this situation, there would not be any premium on the tariff-inclusive c.i.f. prices. The value-added in the jth industry, when non-traded inputs are treated as inputs with zero tariffs would then be:[1]

$$V_j' = \frac{X_j(1 + r_j)}{(1 + T_j)(1 + m_j)} - \sum_{i=1}^{n} \frac{D_{ij}(1 + r_j)}{(1 + T_i)(1 + m_i)}$$
$$- \sum_{i=1}^{n} M_{ij}(1 + r_i) - S_i$$

[1] Since our premium rates refer to the *values in the ports*, they are presumed to exclude the domestic transport margin. Hence, in getting the values of outputs and inputs in terms of world prices, by using these premium rates, some adjustment for transport-mark-up was necessary. Hence the factor $(1 + T_j)$ is used to deflate the values in domestic market prices.

The value-added when the non-traded inputs are included alternatively in the value-added, as suggested by Corden, op. cit., will be $V_j' + S_j$. We have adopted this alternative procedure also in our computations, as already noted.

The difference, $V_j - V_j'$ is to be attributed to the imposition of Q.R.s on imports (ignoring domestic restrictions). Now consider a situation when there are no tariffs and no Q.R.s on imports, so that all the inputs and outputs are valued in c.i.f. prices. The value-added in the jth sector will then be:

$$V_j'' = \frac{X_j}{(1 + T_j)(1 + m_j)} - \sum_{i=1}^{n} \frac{D_{ij}}{(1 + T_i)(1 + m_i)}$$
$$- \sum_{i=1}^{n} M_{ij} - S_j$$

The difference, $V_j' - V_j''$, would indicate the effect of the imposition of tariffs (alone). The difference $(V_j - V_j'')$ is clearly the change in value-added in the jth sector on account of tariffs and Q.R.s on imports.

It is obvious that

$$(V_j - V_j'') = (V_j - V_j') + (V_j' - V_j'')$$

If we divide both the sides by the value added in world prices, viz. V_j'', we get

$$\frac{V_j - V_j''}{V_j''} = \frac{V_j - V_j'}{V_j''} + \frac{V_j' - V_j''}{V_j''}$$

or

$$\tau = \tau^{(1)} + \tau^{(2)}$$

where

$$\tau = \frac{V_j - V_j''}{V_j''}$$

$$\tau^{(1)} = \frac{V_j - V_j'}{V_j''}$$

and

$$\tau^{(2)} = \frac{V_j' - V_j''}{V_j''}$$

$\tau^{(2)}$ is the effective rate of protection due to the (explicit) tariffs; and $\tau^{(1)}$ is the (additional) effective rate of protection due to the Q.R.s. The measure τ is the *total* effective rate of protection.

Although we carried through a wider number of calculations, we have opted in favour of publishing four alternative sets of estimates:

(1) *Case I:* The standard (nominal) tariff rates are used for all the items.

(2) *Case II:* The preferential tariff rates (for the United Kingdom) are used where applicable.[1]

In each case, furthermore, we have made our calculations under two alternative assumptions relating to non-traded inputs: (*a*) that they are inputs with zero tariffs; and (*b*) that they are primary factors and hence part of value added.

We do not consider any of these alternative calculations as the 'best'. On the contrary, we regard them as defining some order of magnitudes within which the 'true' results could lie. Cases I(*a*), I(*b*), II(*a*), and II(*b*) are thus a form of 'sensitivity' analysis. Since, for reasons already set out by us at length earlier, we do not wish to attach any resource-allocational, *directional* significance to the tariff-structure estimates by us, clearly this form of analysis is more appropriate to our needs.[2]

We may finally note that our procedure consisted in operating with domestic value-added data, available from the industrial censuses, and then working backwards (*via* deflation with the import premium, etc.) to arrive at c.i.f. values and hence value added at international prices. We discarded the alternative procedure of taking average, unit values from foreign trade data, to arrive directly at estimates of c.i.f. prices, as relatively more unreliable.

---

[1] Ideally we might have tried to weight the preferential and standard tariff rates by, for example, the share of the two sources in total imports. However, in view of the problems of product differentiation being clearly at the heart of the matter—e.g. why should there be any imports from a higher-tariff source at all if products were homogeneous and if, as seems reasonable for India, the supply elasticities in the relevant range were infinite—we decided to make instead the two alternative estimates in the text, which assume alternatively that all imports came in at standard and at preferential tariff rates.

[2] We had also worked out yet four other estimates which we have not reproduced here. These had been arrived at by a different way of turning specific into *ad valorem* tariffs. In the cases we have included in the text, we did this conversion by reference to average values in the industrial censuses. These, however, may be taken to present possible overestimates in so far as these average values would be purchase-prices and hence would include the import premium (plus transport costs, etc.). In the unpublished estimates, therefore, we decided to deflate these average values by the premium data and then relate them to the *specific* duties to arrive at *ad valorem* rates. These alternative estimates are available in detail from the authors on request. However, we have reproduced in Table 17.3, which gives the *average* rates of effective protection, and the standard deviations, the results of these alternative estimates, listing them as III(*a*), III(*b*), IV(*a*), and IV(*b*): III(*a*) corresponds to I(*a*), III(*b*) to I(*b*), IV(*a*) to II(*a*), and IV(*b*) to II(*b*), the only difference in each case being the method of conversion of specific into *ad valorem* tariffs.

The list of industries for which we calculated the effective rates of protection is the following:

A. *Consumer goods industries*

1. Soap
2. Matches
3. Bicycles
4. Sewing machines
5. Electric lamps
6. Electric fans
7. Leather and leather manufactures
8. Glass and glassware
9. Rubber and rubber manufactures

B. *Raw materials and intermediates*

10. Paints and varnishes
11. Paper and paper products
12. Non-ferrous basic metals
13. Iron and steel
14. Turpentine and rosin
15. Plastics

C. *Capital goods industries*

16. Textile machinery
17. Automobiles
18. Shipbuilding

COLLECTION AND PROCESSING OF DATA

The data required for our work had an extensive range. We had to collect information on (1) value added; (2) inputs, classified by tradable and non-tradable categories and in sufficient detail for comparability with other information (such as tariff rates and premia on imports); (3) tariff rates on inputs and outputs; (4) import premia on inputs and outputs; and (5) breakdown of the inputs by Actual User imports and the remainder. At most stages there were considerable difficulties, which we proceed to record.

(*a*) The data on value added and inputs were taken from the *Annual Survey of Industries* for 1961 and 1962. The A.S.I. gives

AA

input data classified by detailed materials, broadly divided into: (i) water, power, fuels, etc.; (ii) basic materials; (iii) chemicals and auxiliary materials; and (iv) packing materials.

(b) These input data were then classified by the Indian Trade Classification (I.T.C.), so as to relate them to the Actual User (A.U.) imports by sector-of-use which Panchamukhi had earlier computed by detailed examination of the Daily Lists of imports from Customs houses for 1962.[1] Since Panchamukhi's earlier work was extremely laborious, we decided not to repeat it for 1961 and instead assumed that the 1962 A.U. values would be applicable in 1961 as well.

We set out here, schematically, how we derived the A.U. import-content of each of the eighteen industries we have reported on in this study.

Industry	1962	1961
1. Soap	Import-coefficients of the chemicals industry were used	Import-coefficients of 1962 of the chemicals industry were used
2. Matches	,,	,,
3. Paints and varnishes	,,	,,
4. Turpentine and rosin	,,	,,
5. Bicycles	Import-coefficients of the industrial machinery industry were used	Import-coefficients of 1962 of the industrial machinery industry were used
6. Sewing machines	,,	,,
7. Electric lamps	,,	,,
8. Electric fans	,,	,,
9. Textile machinery	,,	,,
10. Leather and leather manufactures	Actual collection of data from Daily Lists	Import-coefficients of 1962 were used
11. Glass and glassware	,,	,,
12. Rubber and rubber manufactures	,,	,,
13. Paper and paper products	,,	,,
14. Non-ferrous basic metals	,,	,,
15. Iron and steel	,,	,,
16. Plastics	,,	,,
17. Automobiles	,,	,,
18. Shipbuilding	,,	,,

[1] The exact procedure used by Panchamukhi in arriving at the final distribution of A.U. imports by sector-of-use has been described in an earlier, mimeographed study of Panchamukhi's, which is available from him on request.

(c) The actual breakdown of the input values into A.U. imports and the remainder involved, however, further adjustments. The A.U. import data were in c.i.f. values, while the A.S.I. input values represented the market-prices paid for inputs. The latter included (i) not merely the A.U. imports at c.i.f. value but also (ii) the value of domestically produced and other imported inputs at market price and (iii) the duty on A.U. imports. Thus, to get the breakdown between A.U. and the remaining inputs, we had to deduct the A.U. imports, duty on A.U. imports and transport margin on A.U. imports, from the total input-value of each item. The data on transport margins were obtained, for this purpose, from *The Supplement to the Report of the Railway Board on Indian Railways, 1961-2* which gave the unit transport cost, as incurred on the different commodities we were interested in.[1] These unit freights were, in turn, converted into *ad valorem* freight rates by taking the available, corresponding producers' prices from Mathur's earlier work on freight rates.[2] Clearly, this procedure gives only an approximation to the 'true' margins although we seriously doubt whether more reliable estimates can be obtained by alternative methods.

(d) The tariff rates were collected from the *Indian Customs Tariff*.[3] Four comments, in particular, need to be made in this regard: (i) The cross-classification of I.T.C. and I.C.T. items was sometimes difficult. In several cases, we had to use simple averages of tariffs on the categories into which the A.S.I. input appeared to fall. (ii) The *specific* duties had to be converted to some *ad valorem* equivalent. For this purpose, we took the average unit purchase-value of these items from A.S.I. input data and divided the specific duty through by this average value, treating this as a lower-bound estimate of the tariff rate. We also inflated this estimate by the import premium, thus arriving at the ratio of the specific duty to c.i.f. value and considered this as the higher, alternative estimate of the 'equivalent' tariff rate. (iii) When considering the preferential tariff rates, we decided to confine

---

[1] Cf. *Supplement to the Report of the Railway Board on Indian Railways, 1961-62*, Ministry of Railways, Government of India, New Delhi; Table 29.

[2] P. N. Mathur, (in collaboration with) A. R. Kulkarni, P. Venkataramaiah, and Narain Das, 'Notes on 32 x 32 Input-Output Table: 1963', Paper Presented at Second All-India Input-Output Seminar, Poona (India), 1967.

[3] *Indian Customs Tariff* (50th Issue), as on 30 June 1961, Department of Commercial Intelligence and Statistics, Calcutta.

ourselves to the preferential rates for the United Kingdom. Furthermore, we assumed in our calculations that this preferential rate would apply to all imports: thus defining merely a lower-bound estimate to put against the higher estimate derived from the non-preferential tariffs. While therefore we present alternative estimates based on both the United Kingdom-preferential and the non-preferential tariff rates, the precise estimates will lie somewhere in between. (iv) We have used tariff rates as of 30 June 1961 and applied these to our calculations of effective tariffs for both 1961 and 1962. Using averages of tariff rates through 1961 and 1962 respectively would have involved a considerable amount of work and no significant improvement in the reliability of our calculations of effective protection.

(e) The import premium data were collected from Bombay and Calcutta, by inquiry and interviews, for a large number of commodities, for 1961 and for 1962. Whenever the premia were available from both sources (Bombay and Calcutta), they were averaged. Next, they were classified by I.T.C. categories and entered against the corresponding inputs and outputs. Wherever the input or output categories had no observed premium, the premium of the 'closest', observed I.T.C. category was taken over. This was the case for I.T.C. Code Numbers 08, 21, 23, 24, 25, 26, 28, 29, 31, 41, 55, 62, 73, and 82, for some of which the following correspondence was assumed:

$$I.T.C. (25) = I.T.C. (64)$$
$$I.T.C. (24) = I.T.C. (63)$$
$$I.T.C. (21) = I.T.C. (61)$$
$$I.T.C. (28) = I.T.C. (68)$$
$$I.T.C. (26) = I.T.C. (65)$$

For the remaining code numbers, we used the *average* premium on other inputs in each industry (where inputs with these code numbers appeared). Fortunately, such cases were relatively few and affected only a small fraction of the industries covered by us.[1]

STATISTICAL RESULTS

The results of these elaborate statistical calculations have been collected into Tables 17.1 and 17.2, for the years 1961 and 1962

[1] Further details are available, on request, from any of the authors.

respectively. For convenience, the nominal tariffs (both standard and United Kingdom-preferential) have also been included.

We have reproduced the estimates exactly as they emerged from the procedures we described earlier, without further 'adjustments' or 'doctoring' to make them conform more to our *a priori* notions about any particular industry. In particular, note that our procedures result in negative value added at international prices during 1961 for leather and leather manufactures, bicycles, and non-ferrous metals (and, for only some measures, for automobiles, sewing machines, and electric lamps); and during 1962 for matches, bicycles, non-ferrous metals, and iron and steel (and, for only some measures, for leather and leather manufactures). While, in the Appendix, we discuss several ways in which such phenomena of 'negative value added' or 'value subtracted' can arise from economic reasons, we suspect that in Tables 17.1 and 17.2 they are to be attributed mainly to the statistical difficulties which we have enumerated earlier. This seems particularly to be the case with industries such as leather and leather manufactures and sewing machines, where India presumably is internationally competitive.[1]

On the whole, however, the results are indicative of the following major conclusions:

(1) the results can be sensitive to the treatment of non-traded goods;

(2) they also show sensitivity to the year chosen: reflecting both changes in (A.S.I.) input-coefficients used and the premium data;

(3) even if we take the average of the four measures, the chief conclusion relates to the enormously *wide* range of effective rates between the different industries; and

(4) some of the effective rates are enormously high in absolute value: we see no reason to suspect these estimates are widely unreliable; rather, our hunch is that Q.R. régimes of the Indian type do in fact throw up the possibilities of such bizarre results emerging.

---

[1] This would also seem to be the reason why, for example, between 1961 and 1962, matches, and iron and steel shift from positive to negative value added. We may also note, in this connection, that in each year we use different input-coefficients data, derived from the corresponding A.S.I. censuses.

TABLE 17.1
EFFECTIVE RATES OF PROTECTION IN DIFFERENT INDUSTRIES, 1961

Method of calculation	V_j	V_j'	V_j''	Effective rate of protection due to Q.R.s $\frac{(2)-(3)}{(4)} \times 100$	Effective rate of protection due to tariffs $\frac{(3)-(4)}{(4)} \times 100$	Effective rate of protection due to Q.R.s and tariffs $\frac{(2)-(4)}{(4)} \times 100$
(1)	(2)	(3)	(4)	(5)	(6)	(7)
(A) Consumer goods industries						
Soap and glycerine (nominal tariff rate = 100%)						
I(a)	15,16,21,990	11,51,80,210	3,21,19,089	113·46	258·60	372·06
I(b)	16,24,73,830	12,60,32,050	4,29,70,937	84·81	193·30	278·10
II(a)	15,16,21,990	11,52,41,580	3,21,14,459	113·28	258·85	372·13
II(b)	16,24,73,830	12,60,93,420	4,29,66,307	84·67	193·47	278·14
Matches (nominal tariff rate = 143%)						
I(a)	5,06,69,580	10,67,64,160	2,69,82,326	−207·89	295·68	87·79
I(b)	6,41,34,856	12,02,29,430	4,04,47,602	−138·69	197·25	58·56
II(a)	5,06,69,580	10,67,75,090	2,69,86,906	−207·90	295·66	87·76
II(b)	6,41,34,856	12,02,40,360	4,04,52,182	−138·70	197·24	58·54
Electric fans (nominal tariff rate = 54·6%)						
I(a)	4,06,02,660	1,25,75,134	62,09,210	451·39	102·42	553·91
I(b)	4,36,20,513	1,55,92,987	92,27,063	303·76	68·99	372·75
II(a)	4,06,02,660	1,51,10,813	60,54,520	421·04	149·58	570·62
II(b)	4,36,20,513	1,81,28,666	90,72,373	280·99	99·82	380·81
Glass and glassware (nominal tariff rate = 56·25%)						
I(a)	6,14,98,740	11,12,33,180	6,43,41,581	−77·30	72·88	−4·42
I(b)	7,14,89,786	12,12,24,220	7,43,32,627	−66·90	63·08	−3·82
II(a)	6,14,98,740	11,31,16,020	6,42,64,331	−80·32	76·02	−4·30
II(b)	7,14,89,786	13,31,07,360	7,43,55,277	−69·51	6?·76	−3·8?

I(a)	51,96,319	35,02,177	−5,33,906	−317·31	−755·95	−1,073·26
I(b)	55,85,182	38,91,040	−1,45,043	−1,168·03	−2,782·68	−3,950·71
II(a)	51,96,319	53,09,077	−5,45,155	20·69	−1,073·87	−1,053·18
II(b)	55,85,182	56,97,940	−1,56,292	72·14	−3,745·69	−3,673·55

Bicycles (nominal standard tariff = 75%; nominal preferential tariff = 65%)

I(a)	3,82,49,250	−7,52,25,015	−5,61,19,269	−202·20	34·04	−168·16
I(b)	4,49,91,113	−6,84,83,152	−4,93,77,406	−229·81	38·69	−191·12
II(a)	3,82,49,250	−7,22,21,706	−5,89,04,149	−187·54	22·61	−164·93
II(b)	4,49,91,113	−6,54,79,843	−5,21,62,286	−211·78	25·53	−186·25

Sewing machines (nominal standard tariff = 45%; nominal preferential tariff = 35%)

I(a)	1,58,86,566	−88,392	−2,65,098	−6,026·04	−66·66	−6,092·71
I(b)	1,73,32,491	13,57,533	11,80,827	1,352·87	14·96	1,367·83
II(a)	1,58,86,566	−9,86,579	−2,86,883	−5,881·55	243·90	−5,637·65
II(b)	1,73,32,491	4,59,346	11,59,042	1,455·79	−60·37	1,395·42

Electric lamps (nominal standard tariff = 85%)

I(a)	1,52,49,669	17,53,405	−21,57,479	625·56	−181·27	−806·83
I(b)	1,77,73,859	42,77,595	3,66,711	3,680·35	1,066·48	4,746·83
II(a)	1,52,49,669	19,58,401	−21,73,137	−611·62	−190·12	−801·74
II(b)	1,77,73,859	44,82,591	3,51,053	3,786·11	1,176·90	4,963·01

Rubber and rubber manufactures (nominal tariff rate = 50%)

I(a)	26,30,98,330	15,35,53,090		0·79	71·34	72·13
I(b)	28,09,93,730	17,14,48,490		0·71	63·89	64·60
II(a)	26,32,65,890	15,28,22,930		0·45	72·50	72·95
II(b)	28,15,21,290	17,07,18,330		0·41	64·90	65·31

(B) Intermediate goods and raw materials industries

Paper and paper board (nominal tariff rate = 74·7%)

I(a)	18,11,54,950	12,80,04,330	2,22,01,550	239·40	476·56	715·96
I(b)	22,05,44,510	16,73,93,890	6,15,91,110	86·30	171·78	258·08

TABLE 17.1—continued

Method of calculation	V_j	V_j'	V_j''	Effective rate of protection due to Q.R.s $\frac{(2)-(3)}{(4)} \times 100$	Effective rate of protection due to tariffs $\frac{(3)-(4)}{(4)} \times 100$	Effective rate of protection due to Q.R.s and tariffs $\frac{(2)-(4)}{(4)} \times 100$
(1)	(2)	(3)	(4)	(5)	(6)	(7)
Non-ferrous metals (nominal tariff rate = 44.9%)						
II(a)	18,11,54,950	12,90,40,400	2,21,99,250	234·76	481·28	716·04
II(b)	22,05,44,510	16,84,29,960	6,15,88,810	84·62	173·47	258·09
Iron and steel (nominal tariff rate = 21·25%; nominal preferential rate = 15·75%)						
I(a)	11,51,23,180	−4,05,39,931	−4,18,78,726	−371·70	−3·20	−374·90
I(b)	13,53,23,540	−2,03,39,563	−2,16,78,358	−718·05	−6·18	−724·23
II(a)	11,51,23,180	−3,93,99,749	−4,21,76,596	−366·36	−6·58	−372·96
II(b)	13,53,23,540	−1,91,99,381	−2,19,76,228	−703·13	−12·64	−715·77
I(a)	71,37,24,700	15,37,88,880	12,28,78,770	455·59	25·15	480·84
I(b)	82,95,98,990	26,96,63,170	23,87,53,060	234·52	12·95	247·47
II(a)	71,37,24,700	12,43,29,930	12,28,43,990	479·79	1·21	481·00
II(b)	82,95,98,990	24,02,04,220	23,87,18,280	246·90	0·62	247·52
Turpentine and rosin (nominal tariff rate = 29·50%)						
I(a)	73,38,261	45,29,947	33,77,626	83·14	34·12	117·26
I(b)	75,59,918	47,51,604	35,99,283	78·02	32·02	110·04
II(a)	73,38,261	45,30,881	33,77,626	83·12	34·14	117·26
II(b)	75,59,918	47,52,538	35,99,283	78·00	32·04	110·04
Plastics (nominal tariff rate = 20%)						
I(a)	2,12,15,749	1,14,76,533	1,21,66,106	80·05	−5·67	74·38
I(b)	2,42,88,449	1,45,49,233	1,52,38,806	63·92	−4·53	59·39

II(a)	2,12,15,749	1,23,95,496		72·79	2·30	75·09
II(b)	2,42,88,449	1,54,68,196		58·07	1·83	59·90

(C) Capital goods industries

Textile machinery (nominal tariff rate = 15%)

I(a)	7,30,15,300	37,62,386	88,88,896	779·09	57·67	721·42
I(b)	8,21,42,084	1,28,89,170	1,80,15,680	384·41	-28·46	355·95
II(a)	7,30,15,300	43,38,131	88,31,894	777·60	50·88	726·72
II(b)	8,21,42,084	1,34,64,915	1,79,58,678	382·41	-25·02	357·39

Automobiles (nominal tariff rate = 50·9%; nominal preferential tariff = 46·1%)

I(a)	35,08,36,500	-6,56,22,242	-9,78,09,772	-425·78	-32·91	-458·69
I(b)	43,70,30,610	2,05,71,870	1,16,15,660	-3,585·33	-277·10	-3,862·43
II(a)	35,08,36,500	-7,90,92,872	-9,83,09,242	-437·32	-19·55	-456·87
II(b)	43,70,30,610	71,01,240	-1,21,15,130	-3,548·70	-158·61	-3,707·31

Shipbuilding (nominal tariff rate = 20%)

I(a)	5,47,60,250	20,50,889	25,59,946	2,059·01	19·89	2,039·12
I(b)	6,07,27,240	80,17,879	85,26,936	618·15	-5·97	612·18
II(a)	5,47,60,250	24,16,180	25,20,714	2,076·56	4·15	2,072·41
II(b)	6,07,27,240	83,83,170	84,87,704	616·70	-1·23	615·47

Notes: I(a) = Case when non-traded inputs are considered as inputs with zero tariffs and standard tariff rates alone are applied to the inputs.

II(a) = Case when non-traded inputs are considered as inputs with zero tariffs and preferential tariff rates are applied to the inputs wherever relevant.

I(b) = Case when non-traded inputs are included in the value added and standard tariff rates alone are applied to the inputs.

II(b) = Case when non-traded inputs are included in the value added and preferential tariff rates are applied wherever relevant.

Column 5 refers to protection that *additionally* accrues from Q.R.s, *beyond* the level conferred by tariffs. Columns 5 and 6 thus add up to *total* protection. The value-added figures are in Rupees.

TABLE 17.2
EFFECTIVE RATES OF PROTECTION IN DIFFERENT INDUSTRIES, 1962

(1)	(2)	(3)	(4)	(5)	(6)	(7)
(A) Consumer goods industries						
Matches (nominal tariff rate = 143%)						
I(a)	5,32,50,780	4,78,92,091	−1,55,17,408	−34·54	−408·63	−443·17
I(b)	5,58,09,269	5,04,50,580	−1,29,58,919	−41·35	−489·31	−530·66
II(a)	5,32,50,780	4,78,97,091	−1,55,13,041	−34·51	−408·75	−443·26
II(b)	5,58,09,269	5,04,55,580	−1,29,54,552	−41·33	−489·48	−530·81
Bicycles (nominal tariff rate = 75%; nominal preferential tariff = 65%)						
I(a)	6,43,75,590	−3,86,09,520	−3,72,87,692	−276·19	3·54	−272·65
I(b)	7,98,48,899	−2,31,36,211	−2,18,14,383	−472·10	6·06	−466·04
II(a)	6,43,75,590	−4,12,84,860	−3,78,44,934	−279·19	9·09	−270·10
II(b)	7,98,48,899	−2,58,11,551	−2,23,71,625	−472·30	15·38	−456·92
Sewing machines (nominal tariff rate = 45%; nominal preferential rate = 35%)						
I(a)	2,21,21,253	90,76,862	59,10,038	220·72	53·58	274·30
I(b)	2,36,28,756	1,05,84,365	74,17,541	175·86	42·69	218·55
II(a)	2,21,21,253	73,10,284	59,98,725	246·91	21·86	268·77
II(b)	2,36,28,756	88,17,787	75,06,228	197·32	17·47	214·79
Electric fans (nominal tariff rate = 54·6%)						
I(a)	3,67,42,630	1,49,48,322	85,56,770	254·70	74·70	329·40
I(b)	3,89,48,825	1,80,54,517	1,16,62,965	186·87	54·80	241·67
II(a)	3,67,42,630	1,70,38,086	83,34,998	236·40	104·42	340·82
II(b)	3,98,48,825	2,01,44,281	1,14,41,193	172·20	76·09	248·29

Electric lamps (nominal tariff rate = 85%)

I(a)	1,84,30,628	21,44,634	371·23	288·15	759·38
I(b)	2,16,41,150	53,55,156	148·67	155·45	304·12
II(a)	1,84,30,628	1,06,74,965	362·87	399·46	762·33
II(b)	2,16,41,150	1,38,85,487	145·02	159·65	304·67

Leather and leather manufactures (nominal tariff rate = 100%)

I(a)	1,01,95,238	−7,96,209	43·47	−1,337·00	−1,380·47
I(b)	1,13,78,498	3,87,051	89·42	2,750·37	2,839·79
II(a)	1,01,95,238	−8,34,623	266·06	−1,587·60	−1,321·54
II(b)	1,13,78,498	3,48,637	−636·93	3,800·64	3,163·71

Glass and glassware (nominal tariff rate = 56·25%)

I(a)	12,10,76,030	6,88,93,629	−76·34	75·74	−0·60
I(b)	8,02,53,071	8,06,69,360	−65·21	64·69	−0·52
II(a)	6,84,77,340	6,88,34,349	−79·56	79·04	−0·52
II(b)	8,02,53,071	8,06,11,090	−67·93	67·49	−0·44

Rubber and rubber manufactures (nominal tariff rate = 50%)

I(a)	25,08,19,220	12,75,22,350	28·89	96·69	125·58
I(b)	31,52,60,460	15,51,21,700	13·75	79·48	103·23
II(a)	28,76,61,110	12,66,83,450	28·22	98·85	127·07
II(b)	31,52,60,460	15,42,82,800	23·17	81·17	104·34

(B) Intermediate goods and raw materials industries

Plastics (nominal tariff rate = 20%)

I(a)	4,13,01,320	40,80,526	398·23	−56·34	341·89
I(b)	4,70,68,777	98,47,983	246·26	−34·84	211·42

TABLE 17.2—continued

(1)	(2)	(3)	(4)	(5)	(6)	(7)
II(a)	4,13,01,320	50,95,943	87,47,241	413·90	−41·74	372·16
II(b)	4,70,68,777	1,08,63,400	1,45,14,698	249·44	−25·16	224·28
			Non-ferrous metals (nominal tariff rate = 44·9%)			
I(a)	16,89,94,100	−16,24,48,010	−13,10,49,410	−252·91	23·96	−228·95
I(b)	19,60,07,220	−13,54,34,890	−10,40,36,290	−318·58	30·18	−288·40
II(a)	16,89,94,100	−16,07,30,780	−13,13,50,360	−251·03	22·37	−228·66
II(b)	19,60,07,220	−13,37,17,660	−10,43,37,240	−316·02	28·16	−287·86
		Iron and steel (nominal tariff rate = 21·25%; nominal preferential tariff = 15·75%)				
I(a)	30,49,99,000	−34,00,79,000	−28,43,82,630	−226·84	19·59	−207·25
I(b)	44,99,50,660	−19,51,27,340	−13,94,30,970	−462·65	39·95	−422·70
II(a)	30,49,99,000	−35,33,52,990	−28,44,92,210	−231·41	24·20	−207·21
II(b)	44,99,50,660	−20,84,01,330	−13,95,40,550	−471·80	49·35	−422·45
			Turpentine and rosin (nominal tariff rate = 29·50%)			
I(a)	59,26,896	44,95,695	33,33,192	42·93	34·88	77·81
I(b)	62,57,797	48,26,596	36,64,093	39·06	31·73	70·79
II(a)	59,26,896	44,96,144	33,33,192	42·92	34·89	77·81
II(b)	62,57,797	48,27,045	36,64,093	39·05	31·74	70·79
			Paper and paper board (nominal tariff rate = 74·7%)			
I(a)	21,66,00,690	19,66,29,180	5,38,20,720	37·11	265·34	302·45

I(b)	26,29,65,700	24,29,94,190	10,01,85,730	19·94	142·54	162·48
II(a)	21,66,00,690	19,77,48,820	5,38,16,300	35·03	267·45	302·48
II(b)	26,29,65,700	24,41,13,830	10,01,81,310	18·82	143·67	162·49

(C) Capital goods industries

Textile machinery (nominal tariff rate = 15%)

I(a)	8,50,93,910	−19,75,659	1,24,52,309	699·22	−115·86	583·36
I(b)	9,63,24,633	92,55,064	2,36,83,032	367·64	−60·92	306·72
II(a)	8,50,93,910	−15,45,180	1,24,22,951	697·41	−112·44	584·97
II(b)	9,63,24,633	96,85,543	23,65,374	366·28	−59·05	307·23

Automobiles (nominal standard tariff = 50·9%; nominal preferential tariff = 46·1%)

I(a)	49,95,28,900	11,61,70,380	1,84,20,110	2,081·20	530·67	2,611·87
I(b)	60,49,26,010	22,15,67,490	12,38,17,220	309·61	78·95	388·56
II(a)	49,95,28,900	9,85,48,710	1,80,13,660	2,225·98	447·08	2,673·06
II(b)	60,49,26,010	20,39,45,820	12,34,10,770	324·91	65·26	390·17

Ship and boat building (nominal tariff rate = 20%)

I(a)	6,18,37,800	1,85,60,481	1,63,93,273	263·99	13·22	277·21
I(b)	6,85,75,313	2,52,97,994	2,31,30,786	187·10	9·37	196·47
II(a)	6,18,37,800	1,89,30,405	1,23,72,015	262·07	15·63	277·70
II(b)	6,85,75,313	2,56,67,918	2,31,09,528	185·67	11·07	196·74

Notes: I(a), I(b), II(a), and II(b) same as for Table 17.1.

Finally, in Table 17.3, we present the *average*, and dispersion, of the effective rates of protection during 1961 and 1962. For convenience, however, these are expressed now as the incremental value-added divided by value-added at *domestic* prices (whereas

TABLE 17.3

AVERAGE AND DISPERSION OF EFFECTIVE PROTECTION, 1961 AND 1962

Case considered		Protection due to Q.R.s	Protection due to tariffs	Protection due to all factors
(1)		(2)	(3)	(4)
I(a)	1961	64·57 (63·6)	22·64 (32·1)	87·99 (37·8)
	1962	86·51 (79·8)	20·71 (34·7)	107·25 (52·5)
I(b)	1961	56·71 (52·4)	19·10 (27·6)	75·80 (30·8)
	1962	70·62 (60·8)	17·05 (29·7)	88·31 (37·0)
II(a)	1961	67·19 (63·0)	15·91 (32·9)	88·19 (38·4)
	1962	87·15 (81·5)	20·57 (35·6)	106·83 (52·9)
II(b)	1961	57·87 (52·9)	18·08 (28·4)	75·97 (31·3)
	1962	72·33 (61·3)	16·24 (30·8)	38·62 (87·9)
III(a)	1961	7·70 (82·9)	72·93 (68·3)	80·63 (29·4)
	1962	74·76 (146·1)	19·43 (107·6)	93·89 (51·3)
III(b)	1961	7·35 (70·9)	63·57 (57·7)	69·91 (24·6)
	1962	61·32 (113·1)	16·08 (88·5)	77·40 (36·1)
IV(a)	1961	15·04 (90·2)	66·44 (73·8)	81·47 (31·3)
	1962	84·94 (148·6)	15·86 (133·1)	91·77 (56·5)
IV(b)	1961	11·91 (74·0)	56·77 (63·2)	70·14 (25·5)
	1962	64·91 (122·8)	13·16 (92·6)	78·08 (35·9)

Notes: 1. Column 2 is: $\dfrac{V_j - V'_j}{V_j}$

Column 3 is: $\dfrac{V_j' - V''_j}{V_j}$

Column 4 is: $\dfrac{V_j - V''_j}{V_j}$

2. The weights used, for getting the averages and standard deviations (in brackets), are the shares in domestic value added of each industry.

3. Cases III and IV relate to measures based on conversion of specific into *ad valorem* tariffs, using premium data to deflate A.S.I. unit values.

Source: Calculations based on data in columns 2–4 in Tables 17.1 and 17.2, for I(a)–II(b), and on unpublished estimates for III(a)–IV(b).

in Tables 17.1 and 17.2, the divisor was value-added at *international* prices). This table underlines the fact that, during these years (though less so when significant export subsidization in later years began to redress the situation), the net protective effect of the foreign trade régime might have been in the range of levels as high as 80–100 per cent (column 4), measured as the ratio of incremental value-added to value-added at domestic prices, and higher still when measured as the ratio of incremental value-added to value-added at international prices (as in Tables 17.1 and 17.2).

Appendix

THE PHENOMENON OF 'NEGATIVE VALUE-ADDED' OR 'VALUE-SUBTRACTED' INDUSTRIES

We have already mentioned cases where, at international prices, value added becomes negative. Similar cases where value is subtracted, rather than added, have been found also for other countries, such as the Philippines, Brazil, and Pakistan.[1] In this Appendix we consider several possible explanations of such cases of 'value subtracted': our analysis is fully general and not confined to the Indian cases.

Statistical explanations

Before we go on to discuss the various *economic* explanations of this phenomenon, we may consider some of the statistical difficulties which may account for these results, in which case there would be no economic implications concerning efficiency.

(1) We may first note that where, unlike our procedure for computing effective rates of protection (where we proceeded from data in *domestic* prices), the statistical calculations involve international valuations via *direct* estimates of c.i.f. and f.o.b. prices from recorded trade data, the reliability of such valuations may be limited. This is because customs valuation procedures tend to be discretionary and the exercise of such discretion may have differential incidence on inputs and outputs for specific industries. Also, the practice of under-invoicing and over-invoicing of trade declarations will affect the trade valuations. Since the tariffs on

---

[1] Such cases have been brought to our attention by Joel Bergsman for Brazil and by John Power for the Philippines. An earlier example is the thorough study of Soligo and Stern, 'Tariff Protection, Import Substitution, and Investment Efficiency', *Pakistan Development Review*, Summer, 1965. Their work, however, does not allow for the effects of quantitative restrictions. Stephen Lewis, in his companion study of Pakistan for the O.E.C.D. Project, has made new estimates which allow for Q.R.s.

finished items tend to exceed those on intermediates, in general, the incentive to under-invoice the former is, *ceteris paribus*, greater and thus could bias the estimates of value added (at international prices) downwards. Then again there are quality differences to be worried about, which could be serious. Domestic tractors may, for example, be quite different from imported ones: and if the domestically produced tractors are more expensive (c.i.f.) than the imported ones (c.i.f.), as may well be the case,[1] and if no offsetting statistical bias occurs with respect to inputs, then the bias would be to understate value added (at international prices).

(2) Where, instead, the statistical calculations proceed, as with our estimates, on the basis of *domestic* values which are then deflated by tariffs, premia, etc., to arrive at international values, there are again difficulties associated with a variety of factors. Thus, for example, the conversion of specific tariffs into 'equivalent' *ad valorem* tariffs may be inaccurate; or the tariffs actually applied may have been different from those specified—a result of discretion which is available under most, including the Indian, customs. Where premium information is used, it may be subject to error. The transport margins may have been wrongly estimated. Even the inputs, obtained from detailed censuses, are available frequently only in broad groups and the corresponding inference of tariffs and premia may result in errors which, in specific cases, lead to an underestimation of value added (in international prices).

But there are also a whole range of economic explanations which we may note here.

Economic explanations

(1) The simplest reason which occurs to the analyst who is looking for inefficient investment decisions in sheltered markets is that tariffs, quotas, exchange control, explicit subsidies to production, and/or implicit subsidization of public sector production enable investment to occur in such activities, at obvious cost to the economy. This is probably the most likely explanation.

(2) However, there are alternative explanations, whose implica-

---

[1] There is no reason to think that the less developed countries will produce the less sophisticated varieties first. In fact, our work with trade and domestic price data has thrown up several examples of such a 'paradox'.

tions are somewhat different. For example, the phenomenon, if observed at any point of time, may merely reflect short-run losses; it is well known that a firm may continue to produce, even if variable costs are not covered, for a variety of reasons. Thus, if input costs (c.i.f.) happen to exceed the output price (c.i.f.), owing to the two being on different cycles internationally for example, negative value added could well be *observed* during such a period without there being any legitimate inference as to the overall efficiency of such investments.

(3) Further, the phenomenon of negative value added (at international prices) could occur for the simple reason that quantitative restrictions combine with restricted domestic entry to confer monopoly power on firms. Two cases may be distinguished. (*a*) Where a foreign firm, importing its own components for assembly, is thus granted *de facto* a quota in the local market for the assembled product, the natural result is to enable it to earn this profit. Since odium may attach to earning this profit openly by showing 'abnormal' profits on the assembly, or price control may follow on such a practice, the foreign firm will prefer to raise its accounting price for *components* as well. Thus, the value added (at international prices), when observed from international values as charged, could perfectly well be negative owing merely to the creation of (possibly inadvertent) monopolies by governmental policies. If such were the case, it would be *wrong* to conclude that investment in the specific assembly process, with negative value added, is *necessarily* unproductive and shows lack of comparative advantage. Rather, the valid inference is that investment in this specific activity is wasteful owing to monopoly creating policies, and could show positive returns if these policies were not present (although these returns may be relatively low and thus the country may have no comparative advantage in the industry).

(*b*) The preceding argument applies, *mutatis mutandis*, also to independent *domestic* firms importing components from foreign firms under contractual agreements. The anticipated monopoly profit may well be imputed, by competition among the licensed domestic firms, to the foreign firm from whom collaboration and/or supply of components are sought—although the picture could get more complex, and less likely to produce the examined phenomenon, if initially there were competition among both

BB

foreign firms interested in the local market and the domestic firms.[1]

Instances which fit into these cases are not difficult to find in India: the example of the unassembled imports of a Fiat car, whose direct and indirect costs (c.i.f.) exceeded at one time the (c.i.f.) cost of a finished Fiat, is only one telling example.

(4) An alternative explanation of the phenomenon, however, might be the fact noted by Jack Baranson that components which add up to a very high value of the finished item *may* cost more to deliver c.i.f. when they have to be treated for labour-intensive handling abroad. According to him, a 100 per cent knocked-down Volvo may cost about 10 per cent more to deliver to Malaysia than an assembled one, owing to special handling and packing, additional shipping costs and increased production costs on truck panels to prepare them for labour-intensive welding. In so far as *this* leads to negative value added, the investment in assembling cannot be justified (except by reference to externalities) and is a result purely of inefficient investment decisions resulting from a protective framework. Tibor Scitovsky has come across cases of a similar type where the transportation of unassembled batteries is, for example, more hazardous and hence sufficiently more expensive than the transport of assembled batteries to make the unassembled parts more expensive c.i.f.

(5) Yet another explanation may be the fact that foreign firms, fearful of invoking hostile attention to repatriation of their profits, prefer to take them out by putting an artificially high 'accounting' price on the components they buy from 'parent' firms. In this case, except for the fact that repatriation of profits is possibly larger than otherwise and hence implies, *ceteris paribus*, a capital outflow, there is no other 'adverse' effect and the investment in the industry showing negative value added may be perfectly productive from the social point of view.

(6) Another way in which negative value added (at international prices) arises is owing to export subsidization policies which can lead to processing of inputs and subsequent export at (f.o.b.) returns which fall short of the cost of the inputs (evaluated at

---

[1] These cases merely amount to yet further illustration of the well-known dictum that quotas should not be allotted to *foreign* suppliers for *they* would then earn the monopoly revenue; in the present cases we are dealing with the possibility of an *indirect* conferment of such quotas on foreign firms.

international prices). We shall note cases of this kind for India in the chapter on Export Policy in Part III. We shall note there that the phenomenon of value subtracted can arise, thanks to export subsidization, when the effective export rate on output exceeds the effective import rate for inputs.

Note further that, in this instance, the phenomenon of negative value added (at international prices), arises *not* because investment in the industry is economically wasteful *per se*, but because (net) export subsidization makes it so. It is perfectly conceivable therefore that, with such incentives removed, the industry would show positive returns (at international prices) and might even have *comparative* advantage in production (though not for export).[1]

---

[1] Unless techniques are changed, resulting in a suitably altered relationship between inputs and output in the activity.

18
Export Policy—Part I[1]

INDIAN export policy has evolved over the period from indifference, pessimistic neglect, and, for several major items, even a constellation of measures adding up to positive discouragement, to growing encouragement via escalating subsidization (culminating in the 1966 devaluation) and promotional measures undertaken by the Government. These two periods *broadly* correspond to the first two Five-Year Plans (1951/6 and 1956/61) and the period thereafter.

These shifts in export policy are of interest in themselves. But they are also particularly important in any evaluation of the investment strategy that India deliberately adopted, beginning with the Second Five-Year Plan. The assumption of stagnant export earnings leads to the proposition that an increasing share of investment will require an increase in the *domestic production* of the capital goods which constitute the investment: this becomes a matter of simple arithmetic.

As we have argued earlier, it is not entirely clear whether the Second Five-Year Plan was formulated with an *explicit* view that India's export earnings would be stagnant; or whether, as seems plausible, the influential planner at the time, Professor Mahalanobis, who was not an economist but a physicist by training, *implicitly* assumed a closed economy or a situation of stagnant export earnings through inelasticity of export demand, and planned on the assumption that an increasing supply of

[1] Our analysis in this chapter has profited immensely from the brilliant and careful study of Professor Manmohan Singh, *India's Export Trends*. This was the first, systematic and intensive examination of Indian export performance which challenged successfully the complacent view, then widely held and expounded in S. J. Patel, 'Export Prospects and Economic Growth—India', *Economic Journal*, September 1959, that Indian exports were stagnant, since the Korean War boom's collapse, entirely owing to stagnant world demand. Benjamin Cohen's 'The Stagnation of Indian Exports, 1951–1961', *Quarterly Journal of Economics*, November 1964, is also a useful reference.

investment goods, implicit in the rising share of investment in growing income, would require a growing capital goods sector in production. That the latter explanation is more plausible seems to follow, not merely from the fact of Professor Mahalanobis being not an economist and hence not clearly seeing the possibility of transformation through foreign trade as a way of procuring capital goods but also from three other considerations. The argument that significant export expansion was unlikely was not spelled out at all in the early draft documents but is certainly an *ex-post* rationalization of the adopted investment strategy, without any detailed exploration of the export possibilities. Further, the balance of payments position during the First Plan (1951/6) was fairly comfortable and the export performance was reasonably impressive, so that export pessimism cannot be read into the situation at the time of the formulation of the Second Plan. Finally, the influence of Soviet thinking on Professor Mahalanobis at the time seems to have been considerable.

In any case, regardless of whether export pessimism led to the considerable shift in the Second Plan towards investments in capital goods industries or whether the export pessimism was invented *post facto* to rationalize this shift in investment strategy, there is little doubt that Indian economic policy towards export earnings was shaped through the Second Plan period on the assumption that they could not be raised, thus accentuating the indifference and even negative interference of the First Plan period (when a modest level of Plan expenditure and the Korean War combined to make export performance satisfactory). Remedying this policy started only towards the beginning of the Third Plan (1961/6), and then with insufficient attention until the later part of the Third Plan period.

In this chapter we shall focus primarily on export performance and policies during the decade of stagnation ending with the Second Five-Year Plan in 1961. Performance and policies during the Third Plan period and later, when there was a break from the previous period's record, will be analysed in the next chapter.

EXPORT PERFORMANCE

Before we analyse export policies in detail, it is useful to examine India's export performance during the period of our study.

Table 18.1 highlights the most significant feature of India's export performance: the precipitous decline in the share of Indian exports in world exports since 1947–9, continuing for practically the entire decade ending in 1961/2. Undoubtedly, the

TABLE 18.1

INDIA'S EXPORTS AND SHARE OF TOTAL VALUE OF WORLD EXPORTS, 1947–66

Calendar year	World exports (U.S. $ million)	Indian exports (U.S. $ million)	Indian exports as percentage of world exports (col. 3; col. 2)
(1)	(2)	(3)	(4)
1947	48,549	1,234	2·5
1948	54,058	1,371	2·5
1949	55,102	1,288	2·3
1950	57,110	1,146	2·0
1951	77,140	1,611	2·1
1952	74,170	1,295	1·7
1953	74,930	1,116	1·5
1954	77,670	1,182	1·5
1955	84,550	1,276	1·5
1956	93,880	1,300	1·4
1957	100,880	1,379	1·4
1958	96,080	1,221	1·3
1959	101,780	1,304	1·3
1960	113,200	1,333	1·2
1961	118,700	1,396	1·2
1962	124,700	1,403	1·1
1963	136,000	1,631	1·2
1964	152,600	1,749	1·1
1965	165,500	1,686	1·0
1966	181,300	1,606	0·9

Sources: 1947–49—*International Financial Statistics* (*I.F.S.*), February 1952 (International Monetary Fund), pp. xvii–xviii.
1950–60—*I.F.S.*, ibid., May 1961, pp. 36, 38.
1961—*I.F.S.*, December 1962, pp. 38, 40.
1962–6—*I.F.S.*, October 1967 (I.M.F.), pp. 34, 36.
  The table is adapted from Benjamin Cohen, 'The Stagnation of Indian Exports, 1951–1961', *Quarterly Journal of Economics*, 78, November 1964, p. 605.

significance of this decline is somewhat exaggerated by the fact that the war-devastated countries, especially Japan and Western Europe, recovered to their pre-war trade levels through the period when the Indian share declined steeply—a factor which was masked by the Korean War's effect on primary export performances. Yet, the fact of the decline in India's share, and the stagnation of her export earnings, are incontrovertible.

This picture is only filled out, rather than substantially altered, if we examine the behaviour of export volumes and prices separ-

TABLE 18.2
EXPORT EARNINGS, VOLUME AND PRICE INDICES 1948–66

Year	Value of Indian exports (U.S. $ million)	Export value index (1958 = 100)	Export price index (1958 = 100)	Export volume index (1958 = 100)
	(1)	(2)	(3)	(4)
1948	1,363	111·63	130	85·87
1949	n.a.	n.a.	n.a.	n.a.
1950	1,146	93·86	98	95·78
1951	1,611	131·94	143	92·27
1952	1,295	106·06	117	90·65
1953	1,116	91·40	100	91·40
1954	1,182	96·81	102	94·91
1955	1,276	104·50	100	104·50
1956	1,300	106·47	101	105·42
1957	1,379	112·94	101	111·82
1958	1,221	100·00	100	100·00
1959	1,304	106·80	100	106·80
1960	1,333	109·17	109	100·16
1961	1,396	114·33	111	103·00
1962	1,403	114·91	106	108·41
1963	1,631	133·58	106	126·02
1964	1,749	143·24	106	135·13
1965	1,686	138·08	112	123·29
1966	1,606	131·53	111	118·50

Notes: 1. *The Yearbook of International Trade Statistics (1965)*, United Nations, 1967, also gives price and volume index numbers for India, referring to *financial* rather than calendar years, except for 1956–9 when the I.M.F. series taken here tally with the U.N. series, for price (though not entirely for volume, while giving a very similar picture).

2. The export price index is in dollar values, so that the 1949 and 1966 devaluations of the rupee do not affect the picture.

Sources: Column 1 is taken from I.M.F., *International Financial Statistics*, December 1957, and December 1960; so also is column 3. Columns 2 and 4 are estimated from these two columns.

ately over the period. Table 18.2 contains these estimates. These indicate strongly that the First Plan period, while it showed *on the average* an improvement over the previous three years' average export performance, largely achieved this thanks to the enormous price-gain during the two Korean War boom years:

TABLE 18.3
INDIA'S EXPORT EARNINGS FROM PRINCIPAL COMMODITIES, 1951-60
(In Rs. million)

	1951/2	1952/3	1953/4	1954/5	1955/6	1956/7	1957/8	1958/9	1959/60	1960/1
1. Total exports	7,288·9	5,723·0	5,261·6	5,884·7	6,038·5	6,130·3	5,845·2	5,531·9	6,299·0	6,329·4
Commodity composition										
2. Jute manufactures	2,697·3	1,289·2	1,137·6	1,237·8	1,182·5	1,188·1	1,109·2	1,011·5	1,090·0	1,317·2
3. Tea	939·4	808·6	1,021·6	1,477·4	1,091·4	1,451·4	1,136·5	1,206·9	1,290·9	1,235·9
4. Cotton fabrics	521·5	620·6	636·4	633·1	566·3	629·6	584·7	454·8	641·5	576·5
5. Vegetable oils	236·1	255·4	48·9	200·2	343·5	155·9	105·9	63·7	148·1	85·4
6. Iron ore	10·0	37·0	58·2	42·1	62·7	93·1	118·6	96·5	145·9	170·3
7. Manganese ore	156·9	217·6	242·7	129·2	107·2	258·1	207·0	136·4	119·9	140·6
8. Mica	132·1	90·1	79·9	67·2	83·7	87·7	86·6	95·8	100·4	101·5
9. Unmanufactured tobacco	161·4	130·3	110·2	117·6	106·5	124·8	146·3	146·8	135·3	146·1
10. Coffee	5·5	13·9	14·6	76·4	14·9	66·9	67·3	78·9	63·3	72·2
11. Cashew kernels	90·5	129·8	109·9	107·0	129·2	145·3	151·6	158·5	160·5	189·1
12. Manufactured leather	250·2	201·1	249·7	205·8	225·2	209·7	209·2	188·6	304·5	248·5
13. Spices	291·7	205·9	162·0	104·3	93·1	78·0	80·1	80·1	144·6	166·4
14. Coir yarn and manufactures	102·8	71·6	81·5	84·5	89·4	96·9	82·8	82·1	88·6	90·0
15. Raw cotton	136·7	193·3	94·0	101·9	296·9	134·6	90·8	166·2	100·6	70·0
16. Lac	148·7	74·4	67·6	105·5	117·1	94·6	68·5	57·0	62·9	63·2
17. Raw wool	49·0	84·1	58·7	86·1	97·3	104·0	110·8	96·6	122·1	77·2
18. *Sub Total (2-17)*	5,929·8	4,422·9	4,173·5	4,776·1	4,606·9	4,918·7	4,445·9	4,210·4	4,719·1	4,750·1

Note: Statistics relate to Indian fiscal years beginning 1 April.

Source: Statistics published by the Director-General of Commercial Intelligence and Statistics, Calcutta. Reproduced from M. Singh, op. cit., p. 15.

TABLE 18·4
LINEAR REGRESSION EQUATIONS FOR EXPORT VOLUME AND PRICE
INDICES AND SELECTED EXPORT EARNINGS, 1948–61

Item regressed on time (Equation: $x = a + bt$)	Period	Unit	Estimated coefficients and their standard errors Constant term (a)	Regression coefficient (b)
(1)	(2)	(3)	(4)	(5)
1. Value of Indian exports	1948–61	Million Rs.	1,289·11 (78·33)	1·80* (9·87)
2. Value of Indian exports	1951–61	,,	1,319·98 (87·94)	−1·62* (12·97)
3. Value of Indian exports	1953–61	,,	1,149·39 (45·10)	25·83 (8·01)
4. Export price index	1948–61	1958 = 100	119·42 (7·63)	−1·54* (0·96)
5. Export price index	1951–61	,,	118·27 (7·95)	−1·77* (1·17)
6. Export price index	1953–61	,,	97·33 (2·39)	1·07 (0·42)
7. Export volume index	1948–61	,,	88·58 (3·11)	1·44 (0·39)
8. Export volume index	1951–61	,,	91·61 (3·56)	1·41 (0·52)
9. Export volume index	1953–61	1958 = 100	98·89 (4·30)	1·02* (0·76)
10. Jute manufactures	1952–3/ 1960–1	Million Rs.	1,220·07 (73·65)	−9·28* (13·09)
11. Tea	,,	,,	1,017·74 (145·08)	36·69* (25·78)
12. Cotton fabrics	,,	,,	635·33 (42·48)	−8·32* (7·55)
13. Vegetable oils	,,	,,	230·75 (67·95)	−14·88* (12·08)
14. Iron ore	,,	,,	11·51 (11·93)	16·02 (2·12)
15. Manganese ore	,,	,,	222·54 (52·29)	−7·87* (9·29)
16. Mica	,,	,,	74·17 (5·85)	2·79 (1·04)
17. Unmanufactured tobacco	,,	,,	109·60 (8·78)	3·94 (1·56)
18. Coffee	1952–3/ 1960–1	,,	15·65 (15·91)	7·28 (2·83)
19. Cashew kernels	1952–3/ 1960–1	Million Rs.	99·46 (9·08)	8·57 (1·61)
20. Manufactured leather	,,	,,	201·62 (25·56)	5·06* (4·54)
21. Spices	,,	,,	146·47 (35·23)	−4·53* (6·26)
22. Coir yarn and manufactures	,,	,,	78·31 (4·65)	1·39* (0·83)
23. Raw cotton	,,	,,	184·61 (51·77)	−9·18* (9·20)
24. Lac	,,	,,	96·02 (14·92)	−3·41* (2·65)
25. Raw wool	,,	,,	76·56 (12·94)	3·28* (2·30)
26. Sub-total (10–25)	,,	,,	4,420·41 (193·55)	27·55* (34·39)

Note: Values of the regression coefficient marked with an asterisk are not significant at the 5 per cent level of significance.

Source: Rows 1–9 calculated from Table 18.2; rows 10–26 calculated from Table 18.3.

1951/2 and 1952/3. On the other hand, there is a continuous though mild improvement in the average export *volume* through these years, which is masked in the value figures because of the post-Korean War decline in prices. As against this, the Second Plan period shows stagnation in both average prices and volume. For the decade, as a whole, leaving the Korean War boom out, the stagnation in both average price and volume is quite striking.[1]

TABLE 18.5
INDIAN AND WORLD EXPORTS OF JUTE MANUFACTURES, 1937, 1948–60
(Volume in 'ooo metric tons and value in million Rs.)

Year	Indian exports		Volume of world exports	India's share of world exports (%)
	(A) Value	(B) Volume		
1937	290·8	1,048·0	1,181·1	88·7
1948–50 (average)	1,289·4	825·7	849·3	97·2
1951	2,402·8	789·2	921·1	85·7
1952	1,632·5	746·0	840·2	88·8
1953	1,106·4	759·3	901·2	84·3
1954	1,213·9	855·7	987·5	86·7
1955	1,237·6	891·1	1,044·4	85·3
1956	1,125·1	876·8	1,068·7	82·0
1957	1,148·8	873·5	1,056·7	82·7
1958	1,038·1	806·2	1,023·4	78·8
1959	1,107·5	874·0	1,166·7	74·9
1960	1,255·4	810·4	1,105·2	73·3

Note: Figures for India relate to calendar years. Figures for India are those published by the Director-General of Commercial Intelligence and Statistics and have been converted into metric weights.
Source: M. Singh, op. cit., p. 38.

The picture that emerges from the aggregate behaviour of export values, volumes, and prices is reflected in the performance of individual commodities. Table 18.3 shows the breakdown of Indian exports by principal commodities through this decade. Table 18.4, containing estimates of the linear regression equation $x = a + bt$ (with x as the export value and t as time) fitted to the data on each item for 1952/3 through to 1960/1, shows that,

[1] The regression equation $x = a + bt$, fitted to the price and volume indices, for the periods 1947–61, 1951–61, and 1953–61, confirms the statistical significance of this stagnation. The estimated equations are reproduced in Table 18.4.

except for cashew kernels, iron ore, and coffee, there is no upward trend of statistical significance to be found in the export performance of any of the commodities.

Further, if we examine the principal export commodities, many of them exhibit not merely a dismal rate of growth of earnings; they are also characterized by a falling share in the world market. We shall shortly proceed to examine the implication of these falling shares for the thesis that India could not have expanded

TABLE 18.6
EXPORTS OF TEA: WORLD, INDIA, CEYLON, INDONESIA, AND AFRICA
(Annual averages in 'ooo metric tons)

	1934–8	1948–50	1955–7	1958–60
World exports	360·1	387·8	464·4	496·2
India	156·7	191·6	201·9	212·5
Ceylon	99·6	134·8	163·2	182·1
Indonesia	67·6	19·2	33·0	33·1
Africa	6·9	13·3	27·2	37·2
Relative shares: percentages				
India	43·5	49·4	43·5	42·8
Ceylon	27·7	34·8	35·1	36·7
Indonesia	18·8	5·0	7·1	6·7
Africa	1·9	3·4	5·9	7·5

Source: M. Singh, op. cit., p. 58.

her export earnings because of a demand bottleneck. We merely note here that, in five major export items adding up to over 50 per cent of total export earnings—jute manufactures, tea, cotton textiles, vegetable oilseeds and oils, and unmanufactured tobacco—there was a discernible, and at times considerable, reduction in India's share in world trade.

Thus, for jute textiles, Table 18.5 shows that there was a practically continuous decline from the 1948–50 average share of 97·2 per cent to under 75 per cent by 1959–60. For tea, Table 18.6 shows that the share declined from 49·4 per cent on the average for 1948–50 to 42·8 per cent for 1958–60. For cotton textiles, Table 18.7 shows again that the share was 11·3 per cent in 1948–50 but remained below that for the bulk of the subsequent years, the average for 1958–60 being 10·0 per cent. For vegetable oilseeds and oils, Table 18.8 shows that the Indian share of groundnuts trade fell drastically from 11·9 per cent in 1948–50 to as low as 3·0 per cent during 1958–60, whereas for linseed the

TABLE 18.7

EXPORTS OF COTTON TEXTILES FROM INDIA, JAPAN, THE UNITED KINGDOM, THE UNITED STATES, AND WORLD TOTALS ('000 METRIC TONS) WITH RELATIVE SHARES OF THESE COUNTRIES, 1948–1960

	1948–50 (annual average)	1951	1952	1953	1954	1955	1956	1957	1958	1959	1960	1958–60 (annual average)
Value of Indian exports (mil. Rs.)	837·7	943·7	741·1	638·4	723·2	637·2	622·8	749·4	575·8	716·8	689·7	660·8
Volume												
World	839·7	989·8	800·3	795·8	876·3	832·2	876·7	946·3	852·7	983·8	1,132·3	989·6
India	94·8	103·5	81·0	86·4	116·7	97·0	93·5	113·0	89·8	113·9	93·5	99·1
Japan	94·7	131·1	101·4	114·5	151·8	141·2	149·8	176·6	153·0	160·4	204·9	172·8
United Kingdom	148·7	154·5	114·9	118·7	115·0	101·8	92·9	92·9	77·8	72·3	66·9	72·3
United States	125·9	133·3	110·2	95·8	95·0	84·3	81·2	90·0	78·7	73·2	70·2	74·0
Relative shares (per cent)												
India	11·3	10·5	10·1	10·8	13·4	10·4	10·7	11·9	10·5	11·6	8·3	10·0
Japan	11·3	13·2	12·6	14·4	17·3	16·9	17·1	18·7	17·9	16·3	18·1	17·5
United Kingdom	17·7	15·7	14·4	15·0	13·1	12·3	10·6	9·8	9·1	7·3	5·0	7·3
United States	15·0	13·4	13·7	12·1	10·8	10·1	9·2	9·5	9·2	7·4	6·2	7·5

Source: Reproduced from M. Singh, op. cit., p. 74.

TABLE 18.8
WORLD TRADE IN VEGETABLE OILSEEDS AND OILS (OIL EQUIVALENT)
AND INDIA'S SHARE OF WORLD EXPORTS
(Volume in '000 metric tons)

(A) Volume of world exports (annual average)

	1934–8	1948–50	1955–7	1958–60
Groundnuts	770	570	753·3	798·7
Linseed	780	350	511·7	453·7
Castor	105	115	135·3	138·0
Twelve major oilseeds and oils	4,725	3,610	5,141·0	5,372·0

(B) India's share of world exports (%)

	1934–8	1948–50	1955–7	1958–60
Groundnuts	44·5	11·9	9·8	3·0
Linseed	10·9	8·0	8·8	3·5
Castor	26·5	22·1	31·9	23·7

Note: The pre-war figures of world exports are not strictly comparable with the post-war figures. The latter underestimate the volume of world trade because exports of some non-reporting countries (mostly the Sino-Soviet areas) are excluded.

Source: Reproduced from M. Singh, op. cit., p. 102.

decline was from 8·0 to 3·5 per cent. For unmanufactured tobacco, Table 18.9 shows again, except for two early years, a sizeable reduction from the 1948–50 average share of 7·2 per cent to figures continuously close to 5·0 per cent.

TABLE 18.9
INDIA'S SHARE IN EXPORTS OF UNMANUFACTURED TOBACCO
(Volume in '000 metric tons)

Year	World exports	Indian exports	India's share (%)
1948–50 (average)	529	37·9	7·2
1951	617	56·5	9·2
1952	545	42·1	7·7
1953	606	31·5	5·2
1954	632	33·6	5·3
1955	667	35·3	5·3
1956	688	42·3	6·1
1957	732	36·4	5·0
1958	708	48·1	6·8
1959	707	37·7	5·3
1960	764	40·7	5·3
1958–60 (average)	726	42·2	5·8

Note: The figures of world exports exclude exports of some non-reporting countries, mostly members of the Sino-Soviet area.

Sources: F.A.O. Trade Year Books. Reproduced from M. Singh, op. cit., p. 130.

EXPORT POLICIES

The pertinent question, therefore, is whether the undoubted stagnation in India's export earnings during this decade, spanning the first two Five-Year Plans, was beyond India's control, to be attributed to 'demand conditions', or whether domestic Indian policies contributed to this phenomenon. If, as we shall argue,[1] the domestic policies of the Indian Government, *via* export controls and quotas, export duties, inflationary pressures, and other policies aimed at promoting domestic consumption, were responsible for inhibiting the expansion of export earnings, then the immediate question is whether the potential expansion of export earnings which was lost was large enough to have made a significant difference to the Mahalanobis-type investment strategy underlying the Second and Third Five-Year Plans. We now proceed to examine these two questions.

There is an unmistakable impact of domestic policies on the export performance of the vast bulk of India's traditional exports. While we shall establish this contention *via* an analysis of the main commodities, taken in turn, we may note here that there was indeed a sluggishness in world exports of many of these items but that India evidently failed to make the best use of whatever trade possibilities were available. This is reflected in the evidence that we have already presented on the declining shares of India's exports in world trade in tea, jute manufactures, cotton textiles, tobacco, and vegetable oils and oilseeds (Tables 18.5–18.9). The general factors that explain these developments are to be found in:

(1) export controls, which were started during the second world war and carried over, for much of the early part of our decade, for jute manufactures (until 1958), tea (throughout), cotton textiles (until 1953), vegetable oilseeds and oils (exports of which remained banned, in many cases, from 1952), as also other items such as raw cotton (through the period), raw wool (from 1953), coffee, manganese ore, and hides and skins;

(2) export duties, which affected several export commodities through most of the decade, and which are listed in Table 18.10; and

---

[1] In this, we agree with Manmohan Singh, op. cit.; and also Cohen, op. cit.

TABLE 18.10
EXPORT DUTIES IN INDIA, 1950–60
(As on 1 January of every year)

	1950	1951	1952	1953	1954	1955	1956	1957	1958	1959	1960
1. Jute manufactures (Rs. per long ton)											
(a) Hessian	350	1,500	1,500	275	120	10					
(b) Sacking	50	150	150	175	80	80					
(c) Other	350	80	80								
2. Tea (Rs. per 100 lb.)	25	25	25	25	25	43	37	50	38	26	24
3. Raw cotton (Rs. per bale of 400 lb.) Bengal Deshi	100	400	400	125	125	150	50	100	100	25	25
4. Coffee (Rs. per cwt.)					62·5	62·5					
5. Raw wool	30% (ad valorem)	30% (ad valorem)									
6. Black pepper (Rs. per cwt.)	30% (ad valorem)	120	150	150	65 or 30%[a]						
7. Cotton cloth	15% (ad valorem)	15%	25% (ad valorem)[b]	25%	10%	10% (ad valorem)[c]	6·25%[d]				
8. Manganese ore (Rs. per long ton)	15% (ad valorem)	15%	15%	15%	15%			10–30[f]	10–30		
9. Groundnut oil (Rs. per long ton)	160	160	300		50	100	150	150	150		
10. Linseed oil (Rs. per long ton)	160	160	200	200							
11. Castor oil (Rs. per long ton)			300	300	300	200	125	175	175		

a Whichever is less.

b Excluding cloth of 35s and above and also handloom cloth.

c This duty related only to cloth of 17 counts or below.

d Only on coarse cloth.

e Up to 38 per cent m.n. content—nil; 38–40 per cent—Rs. 10; 40–44 per cent—Rs. 20; over 44 per cent m.n. content—Rs.30.

f Up to 42 per cent m.n. content—nil; 42–44 per cent—Rs. 10; over 44 per cent—Rs. 30. The blanks in the table mean zero duties.

Source: Indian Customs Tariffs. Reproduced from M. Singh, op. cit, p. 163.

(3) the growing strength of domestic demand, accentuated in some cases by governmental excise and promotional activities: e.g., the excise duties on tea were lower than the total export levy throughout the decade, and the Coffee Board actively encouraged the domestic consumption of coffee through promotional campaigns.

We shall now examine these factors by focusing on some of the major export items taken individually.

Jute manufactures

We have already noted the decline in India's share of world trade in jute manufactures, through our period (Table 18.5). This decline was further accompanied by a generally stagnant world trade, world exports of jute manufactures for 1937, 1948–50, 1955–7, and 1958–60 being 1,181·1, 849·3, 1,056·6, and 1,098·4 thousand metric tons respectively. This stagnation in world trade appears quite significant in relation to pre-war performance, although there is a mild growth over the 1948–50 level primarily in the first half of our decade.

The world trend in exports of jute manufactures has been demonstrated by Manmohan Singh to be essentially a result of exogenous factors other than rises in their price. The growth of bulk deliveries and modern marketing techniques have made traditional jute burlap containers increasingly obsolete and only considerable reductions in the export price of jute manufactures might have helped to mitigate this adverse trend, resulting from the changing structure and economic organization of the importing countries.[1]

However, India's declining share is to be explained largely by her own failure to maintain competitiveness in foreign markets. Pakistan has become an important rival supplier since 1954:

---

[1] Singh is careful to add: 'However, in the post war-years until 1951, the competitive position of jute was further weakened by a steep rise in its prices while the prices of paper bags remained relatively stable. This must have done lasting damage to the use of jute goods in the importing countries and, although there were extraordinary difficulties on the supply side, this was a development whose rigour could have been moderated by more far-sighted [subsidization] policies in India and Pakistan. It is only in this last respect that policies pursued by the exporting countries did contribute to a stagnation in the consumption of jute goods in the importing countries. However, their influence can easily be exaggerated.' Op cit., p. 50.

especially since 1959, the export subsidy provided by the Pakistani Bonus Voucher Scheme[1] led to an effective subsidization in the range of 25 per cent *ad valorem*, which helped Pakistan offset her cost disadvantage and emerge as a sizeable exporter of jute manufactures.[2] While the Indian authorities did eliminate most of the jute duties by 1956 (cf. Table 18.10) and export controls had been lifted since 1952, no attempt was made, with the emergence from 1954 of Pakistan as an active rival supplier, to enable the Indian jute industry to compete more aggressively in order to contain the new entrant.

How far the Indian authorities could have done this, however, depends on the assumption we make with respect to Pakistani behaviour. In so far as India had the vast bulk of the market, it is possible that Pakistan might have matched all price-cutting by India, in the certain hope that the immediate loss inflicted by such a price-war on India would be very much greater than on herself. If so, a policy of aggressive competition by India to prevent the emergence of Pakistan as a major supplier of jute manufactures could have been expensive rather than productive in the short run. On the other hand, the possibility of such aggressive competition would probably have led to a more concerted and mutually beneficial arrangement among the two countries that would have permitted India to retain a larger share of the world market than it managed to keep. On balance, therefore, the probability is high that India's passive acquiescence in Pakistan's emergence as a major supplier led to a significant reduction in her export earnings.[3]

Tea

If we examine Table 18.6 carefully, we find that India's share at the end of our decade was close to her 1934-8 share. However, it had fallen by over 10 per cent of the share in 1948-50. It is clear that the loss of Indonesia's share from its 1934-8 level was

[1] This scheme corresponds to the Indian Import Entitlement Schemes, under which eligible exporters receive premium-fetching import licenses *pro rata* to the f.o.b. value of exports. We discuss these schemes in the next two chapters.

[2] Pakistani exports of jute manufactures rose steadily from 90·4 to 190·7 thousand metric tons between 1957 and 1960, thus amounting to over a quarter of Indian exports by 1960 from a share of around 10 per cent in 1957 and yet lower earlier.

[3] We present quantitative estimates of this loss of earnings later in this chapter.

CC

picked up not by India but by Ceylon and Africa during the decade.

In addition to the shortfall in Indian tea exports as a share of world exports, world tea imports were not characterized by rapid growth. Total imports of tea by the developed countries were 309·1, 307·7, 358·0, and 369·7 thousand metric tons during 1934–8, 1948–50, 1954–6, and 1958–60 respectively.[1] Obviously, the rate of growth of consumption of tea had decelerated towards the latter half of our decade. This was primarily due to the low income inelasticity of demand for tea—estimated to be as low as 0·04 in the United Kingdom[2]—which asserted itself as soon as *per capita* consumption of tea had been restored to pre-war levels. Moreover, there is no reason to expect that the price policies of the supplying countries *in toto* played a significant role in preventing the quantity demanded from growing more rapidly. Not merely are all the estimated price-elasticities of demand for tea strikingly low, but even the relative price of tea, as compared with coffee and cocoa which constitute its close substitutes, actually fell rather than rose through our decade.[3]

But, while the stagnation of world demand, reflecting itself in a growth of export volume by a mere 28 per cent between 1948–50 and 1958–60, must be attributed to factors beyond the control of the supplying countries, including India, the falling share of Indian exports is to be explained by domestic policies.

(1) The Indian Government did not spend anything remotely comparable with what Ceylon spent, by way of promotional expenditures through this decade.

(2) While the emergent African supplies were of common teas and hence competed directly with Indian rather than Ceylonese exports—Ceylonese exports consisting more of high-grade teas—the Indian supplies were allowed to become generally uncompetitive. Not merely were labour costs rising more rapidly in India; there were also export levies and quotas which made supplies to foreign markets more expensive.

We have thus seen, in Table 18.10, that the export duties and cess amounted to between 10 and 15 per cent of the f.o.b. price of Indian tea. Moreover, there were regulatory export quotas through

---

[1] M. Singh, op. cit., p. 61 (Table IV.3).
[2] The estimate is by Richard Stone; quoted in M. Singh, op. cit., p. 61.
[3] M. Singh, op. cit., pp. 62–3.

the period. Designed with a view to ensuring domestic availability and restraining domestic prices within desired limits, the quotas were inevitably handed out on an administrative, 'fair share' basis. The effect was that, while in each year actual exports were below the aggregate quota, there was still a premium put on quotas which were clearly bought by those who wanted to export in excess of their quotas. It appears (Table 18.11) that, from 1954

TABLE 18.11
AVERAGE ANNUAL PRICES OF QUOTA RIGHTS AND EXPORT PRICES OF
TEA AT CALCUTTA AUCTIONS
(Rs. per lb.)

	1954	1955	1956	1957	1958	1959	1960
Average quota price	0·54	0·39	0·16	0·21	0·08	0·02	0·05
Average export price	2·86	2·55	2·15	2·23	2·14	2·17	2·38

Source: M. Singh, op. cit., p. 68 (Table IV.9).

to 1960, the average quota price was positive and, at times, even around 15 per cent of the average export price of tea.[1] The net effect was clearly to raise the marginal cost of supply above what it would have been if the export market were unfettered by quotas.

How far was the price factor really important? On this issue, we also have the evidence provided by Benjamin Cohen,[2] which indicates that there was, in fact, an inverse relationship between India's relative share in volume, as also (for some estimates) in value, of tea exports *vis-à-vis* other competitors and India's relative export price.

Using the symbols:

q_1 = quantity of commodity 1 imported by a specific importer (country or 'rest of the world') from India;

---

[1] It might appear odd that, when quotas were not exhausted, there should still be a positive price for them. This apparent paradox obviously arises from the possibility that, in an uncertain world, quotas may be purchased (or retained) in expectation of a favourable return and then left unexploited when the expectations prove false. Also, if one compares the discrepancy between quotas and their utilization, on the one hand, with the average quota price on the other, there seems to be an inverse relationship, which is naturally what one would expect. For evidence on the extent of under-utilization of quotas, see M. Singh, op. cit., p. 67 (Table IV.8).

[2] *Quarterly Journal of Economics*, op. cit.

$q_2 =$ quantity of commodity 2 imported by a specific importer from India;

$p_1 =$ delivered price of commodity 1 to the specific importer; and

$p_2 =$ delivered price of commodity 2 to the specific importer,

and postulating that the exports of Ceylonese, Indian, and other teas can be treated as non-homogeneous and hence 'different' commodites, Cohen hypothesises that

$$\left(\frac{q_1}{q_2}\right) = \left(\frac{p_1}{p_2}\right)^k$$

and k will be negative. If k is negative *and* less than -1, there will also be an inverse relationship between *value* shares and relative prices, as can be seen by rewriting the above relation as:

$$\left(\frac{p_1 q_1}{p_2 q_2}\right) = \left(\frac{p_1}{p_2}\right)^{k+1}$$

On estimating the least-squares regression of $\log \left(\frac{q_1}{q_2}\right) = i + k$ $\log \left(\frac{p_1}{p_2}\right)$, Cohen finds that:

(1) For the United Kingdom tea imports from Ceylon and India, taking the period 1952–62, the estimated k is[1] $-1\cdot057$ [$0\cdot550$] with $R = 0\cdot56$ (significant at $0\cdot90$).

(2) For India and Ceylon again, but taking their total exports instead of exports to the United Kingdom alone, and the period 1952–61, the estimated k is $-0\cdot811$ [$\cdot0498$] with $R = 0\cdot50$.

(3) For India and 'rest of world' tea exports, for 1952–60, the estimated k is $-0\cdot736$ [$0\cdot500$] with $R = 0\cdot49$.[2]

Thus, while the best result is for the United Kingdom market, the estimates uniformly imply that market volume shares are responsive to relative prices and, for the United Kingdom market, that the value shares are as well.

(4) Finally, we may note here that the relatively buoyant domestic market was not restrained, in the interest of exports,

---

[1] The standard error of k is given in brackets after the estimate, both here and below.

[2] For details, see Cohen, op. cit., pp. 609–10. Cohen is also careful to note that the statistical limitions of the analysis are quite serious—e.g. serial correlation and simultaneous determination of q_1/q_2 and p_1/p_2. However, the estimates are quite suggestive and, for well-known reasons, the elasticities are likely to be underestimates.

but on the contrary the sizeable export levies compared most unfavourably with the insignificant central excise duty on tea throughout the period 1950–60.[1]

Cotton textiles

While India's share of the world market in both jute manufactures and tea declined quite conspicuously during 1950–60, the decline in her share in cotton textiles exports was relatively mild. Indeed, for two years, 1954 and 1959, it even recovered beyond the 1948–50 average level (Table 18.7).

But the true picture is obscured if we look only at the Indian share. It is quite evident that, over the decade, the shares of the United Kingdom and the United States fell considerably and this loss appears to have been exploited by Japan almost to double her relative share, whereas India not merely failed to seize this opportunity but, in fact, registered even a decline in her share. This decline was particularly acute in yarn exports (Table 18.12). And, in terms of absolute value, as Table 18.3 shows, in each year except 1961 Indian exports of cotton textiles were below the average 1948–50 level. In fact, as Manmohan Singh pointedly notes, 'The average annual value of exports during the three-year period 1958–60 was 21 per cent lower than the corresponding value during 1948–50.'[2]

World export performance during the decade was also dismal. As Table 18.12 shows, the volume of world exports of cotton textiles increased by only 17·9 per cent from 1948–50 to 1958–60. The sluggishness was particularly concentrated on tissues and yarn, which accounted for about 90 per cent of the cotton textiles trade.

Was this sluggishness in world trade attributable to the policies of the supplying countries or was it beyond their control (as we have seen with jute textiles and tea)? A breakdown of world imports into imports by net-importing countries and net-exporting countries shows that the former fell by 2·2 per cent between 1948–50 and 1958–60,[3] and that this primarily determined the

---

[1] Cf. M. Singh, op. cit., pp. 70–1.   [2] Op. cit., p. 73.

[3] This decline is accentuated to 7·4 per cent if Western European net-importers and Canada are excluded. On the other hand, the net exporters, the United States and the United Kingdom, permitted a rapid expansion of imports into themselves from the Asian net-exporting countries, thus leading to the recorded moderate expansion of world exports. Cf. M. Singh, op. cit., pp. 79–80.

TABLE 18.12
EXPORTS OF COTTON TEXTILES: INDIA AND WORLD
(Annual averages, volume in '000 metric tons)

	1948–50	1955–7	1958–60	Per cent change, 1948–50 to 1958–60
1. India's exports				
Value (million Rs.)	837·7	669·8	600·8	−21·1
Volume:				
All cotton textiles	94·8	101·2	99·1	4·5
Tissues	71·1	88·7	82·5	16·0
Yarn	18·7	7·1	10·6	−43·3
Other	5·1	5·4	5·9	15·7
2. World export volume				
All cotton textiles	839·7	885·1	989·6	17·9
Tissues	589·5	633·3	686·1	16·4
Yarn	173·0	146·6	188·3	8·8
Other	77·2	105·2	115·1	49·1
3. India's relative share (%)				
All cotton textiles	11·3	11·4	10·0	
Tissues	12·1	14·0	12·0	
Yarn	10·8	4·8	5·6	
Other	6·6	5·1	5·1	

Note: As a result of rounding, the parts do not exactly add up to the totals.
Source: M. Singh, op. cit., p. 76 (Table V.2).

relative stagnation in world exports. In turn, this has been shown by Manmohan Singh to have been caused, partly by the substitution of synthetics and other textiles for cotton textiles, but largely by the growth of import-substituting, cotton textile industries in these net-importing countries. As Singh has cogently pointed out:

Cotton textiles is an industry which lends itself most easily to import substitution. Its requirements of capital are much more modest than those of many other modern industries. Its demands for expensive technical skills are also not very rigorous, and in any case many countries have a tradition of hand-loom weaving, so that the learning of new techniques is not too difficult to process. . . . It is an industry whose development is often not contingent on the creation of fresh demand. It can readily draw upon the existing demand by simply replacing imports. . . . No wonder that cotton textiles are an early favourite in programmes of industrial development in most underdeveloped countries. . . . In the post-war years, countries like Egypt, Turkey, and Pakistan have not only become self-sufficient but have also started exporting textiles in a short period of less than a decade. This is a process which is now under way in other Asian and African countries. As a result international trade in cotton textiles shows no strong upward trends. Since the development of textile industries in underdeveloped countries is often part of a wider process of industrialization it is extremely doubtful if the speed or the rigour of import substitution could be significantly modified by price-output policies of major exporters of cotton textiles. Therefore the stagnation of world trade in cotton textiles cannot be attributed in any simple manner to the policies of the exporting countries.[1]

The decline in India's relative share, and particularly her inability to expand this share as Japan strikingly did during the decade, are to be explained with reference to internal policies. There were indeed exceptional factors, such as the post-war dislocation of the Japanese and West European industry, supply bottlenecks in textile machinery which held up capacity expansion in the newly emergent countries, and sterling area discrimination against dollar-source imports, which pushed the Indian share to its high levels in the early years up to 1951, which produced advantages of inevitably short duration. It is nonetheless correct to argue that India managed to lose its share and failed to gain from increasing imports by the United Kingdom and the United States, while Japan, Pakistan, and Hong Kong in particular managed to do quite well.

Among the factors responsible for this performance were: (1) the rising relative costs of production, labour, and raw cotton, *vis-à-vis* foreign competitors; and (2) explicit governmental policies which hampered the expansion and modernization of machinery and led to the poor and stagnant quality of textiles in a market where improving quality from rival suppliers was a major competitive force.

The rise in the relative costs of Indian production, as also the growing profitability of the home market, have been well-documented by Manmohan Singh.[2] In addition, Cohen[3] has provided suggestive evidence that the market shares of rival suppliers were

[1] Op. cit., p. 83.
[2] Ibid., pp. 87–90 and 93–6. See, in particular, Table V.10, which compares the indices of the wholesale prices of textiles in India and Japan.
[3] Op. cit., p. 609.

responsive to relative prices. His least-squares regression equation, of the form fitted to tea exports, shows that, for United Kingdom imports of cotton cloth imports from India and Hong Kong between 1951 and 1962, k takes the value $-3\cdot214$ [$1\cdot578$] with $R = 0\cdot54$, thus indicating that both value and volume shares vary inversely with relative prices.

In particular, while the Japanese Government and industry took meticulous steps to improve quality, even ruling in March 1958 that only cloth of washable colour or better could be exported, and widely adopting automatic screen printing, Indian exports remained primarily centred on coarse and medium cloth where the impact of import-substitution abroad was naturally the greatest. A major contributory factor to this situation was the Government's hostility to the installation of automatic looms which alone could help India compete successfully with rivals as the preference for 'flawless' cloth increased. The reasons for the stringent restrictions imposed on the installation of automatic looms were that (1) retrenchment of current employees would become necessary, and (2) protection of labour-intensive methods was considered more economical to a labour-surplus economy. Retrenchment could have been eased if total production were growing rapidly; however, even this was restrained because the mill-sector's expansion was controlled in the interests of handloom-weavers. Neither of the economic arguments in favour of labour-intensive processes, however, was decisive, especially if foreign exchange availability was a serious bottleneck to India's investment and development goals. Nor, for that matter, was this form of argument used to eliminate the investments in heavily capital-intensive investment goods industries beginning with the Second Five-Year Plan, so that the argument seems very much like special pleading for a politically determined decision to prevent the growth of the mill-sector and its rationalization via installation of automatic looms.

Vegetable oilseeds and oils

The impact of India's domestic policies in reducing India's share in world exports emerges most strikingly in the case of the vegetable oilseeds and oils, groundnuts and linseed.

As Table 18.8 shows, India's share in the groundnut trade collapsed from 44·5 per cent in 1934–8 to 11·9 per cent in 1948–50 and yet further to 3·0 per cent by 1958–60. For linseed, the corresponding figures are 10·9, 8·0, and 3·5 per cent. Clearly, therefore, it is impossible to regard the shortfalls in Indian performance (Table 18.3, item 5) as anything but a result of domestic policies.

In groundnuts, government policies were designed explicitly with a view to ensuring domestic availability and preventing undue rises in domestic prices. Until 1958, there were

rigorous controls on the export of vegetable oilseeds and oils, and groundnut and groundnut oil were subject to the severest restrictions of all. In many years the Government went so far as to ban altogether the export of groundnut oil from India. . . . The policy of the Government was to allow the export of groundnut oil only if prices in the home market threatened, as they occasionally did, to fall in the face of a bumper crop. Thus an exceptionally good crop in 1955 led to liberal export quotas but soon the policy was reversed and exports of groundnut oil remained banned for the greater part of 1956, 1957, and 1958. In this way export markets were deliberately sacrificed in the interests of domestic consumption.[1]

In addition, the overall production of oils was hampered by governmental policies which, aimed at protecting the village-industry sector, resulted in inefficiency in extracting oils from the oilseeds. The policy was opposed even to extracting mills operating beyond approved capacity, so that the old village 'ghanis' would be protected.

While the impact of domestic policies on India's export performance was most striking in the four major exports we have just discussed, and which constituted 50–58 per cent of India's total export earnings on the average through 1948–60, it was not absent from other items.

Tobacco

With tobacco, for example, we noted in Table 18.9 the fall in India's share in world trade, from 7·2 per cent during 1948–50 to around 5·0 per cent during the ensuing decade. While the possibilities of India maintaining her share in the world market for her Virginia flue-cured tobacco cannot have been easy, in view of U.S. surplus disposals and long-term agreements entered into by the other major rival, Rhodesia, with importing countries, there

[1] M. Singh, op. cit., p. 106.

is no evidence that the Indian Government made any attempts at bolstering exports.

Coffee

With coffee, the responsibility of domestic policies in holding back a major expansion of export earnings appears to have been more obvious. Unlike the preceding five commodities, India remained virtually an atomistic supplier in the world market and could have easily expanded her exports if only foreign sales had been made relatively more attractive. On the contrary,

until 1957 the whole emphasis of the Coffee Board, the official agency charged with the collection of the entire produce from producers and arranging for its internal and external distribution, was on satisfying the home market, regardless of its effect on exports. As early as 1952 the Government had sanctioned this policy of the Board, even if it meant a total suspension of exports. No wonder that the Coffee Board was busier in encouraging the growth of a 'coffee habit' in India than in promoting exports. . . . In addition the export proceeds were used to subsidize deliberately the domestic consumption of coffee. . . . To ensure that domestic consumers were kept supplied with the needed quantities exports were severely controlled, even when they were more profitable than the home sales. . . . Besides, the whole system of marketing the quantities made available for export showed an extremely short-sighted view. The quantities earmarked for export by the Coffee Board are sold in auctions to the registered exporters. At first they are provided with the samples. These they send abroad and then submit their tenders for coffee on the basis of the offers they receive. The tenders are tabulated by the Board and the highest tender for each lot is accepted. The whole system, therefore, rests on the assumption that India has only to offer more coffee to the world for it to be readily absorbed. The registered exporters cannot enter into any firm commitment with foreign buyers because they are not sure whether their tender will be accepted by the Coffee Board. On their part the foreign buyers cannot be sure that supplies will be readily forthcoming from India. Indian coffees are mainly used for the purpose of blending with other varieties, and unless blenders can be sure of their supplies from India they are unlikely to use Indian coffee in their blends. Thus the marketing procedure adopted by the Board has helped in making Indian coffee 'a very uncertain commodity' in the eyes of foreign customers. Surprisingly, there has been no provision of forward sales for export purposes which could have helped exporters and importers to plan their sales and purchases well in advance.[1]

[1] M. Singh, op. cit., pp. 137–8.

Manganese ore

Indian exports of manganese ore have done well in relation to 1948–50. However, when we look at India's relative share in the two principal markets, the United States and the United Kingdom, there is a distinct decline through the decade. The major explanation of this decline, especially in the U.S. market, seems to be the emergence of Brazil as a supplier, whose main attraction was that it enabled the United States to reduce her strategic dependence on more distant sources. The growth of the U.S.S.R. as a supplier also made an important difference, which aggressive price competition by India might not have contained.

However, Indian policy also made its inevitable contribution to this state of affairs. Occasional export duties, whose yield along with royalty and freight has been estimated[1] to have been around 29 per cent of the f.o.b. value of exports between 1956–7 and 1959–60, were imposed despite growing competition from Brazil and the U.S.S.R. That this factor may have been of considerable importance is indicated by Cohen's estimated linear regression equation, which gives $k = 1.878$ [2.612] with $R = 0.25$ for the United Kingdom manganese ore imports from India and the U.S.S.R. for 1953–62. Further, export quotas were occasionally in operation (as in 1953), the ostensible reasons being to conserve deposits and/or to 'co-ordinate' exports in order to 'facilitate transport arrangements'. Moreover, from 1956, manganese ore exports tended to be assigned to the State Trading Corporation, with its quota rising to 50 per cent of the total in 1957. Not merely has there been some criticism of the S.T.C'.s handling of its own quotas,[2] but official policy with respect to the allocation of quotas to private exporters also led to avoidable uncertainties. Further, occasionally the S.T.C. quotas were transferred to private exporters for a charge, thereby raising the marginal cost of exports financed under such quotas.

Leather

In the case of leather exports, India's share in the value of world trade actually fell, from 29 per cent in 1951 to 19 per cent in 1960.

---

[1] Cohen, op. cit., p. 616.
[2] *The State Trading Corporation and India's Export Trade*, The Economist Intelligence Unit, Ltd., London, 1961. Cited in M. Singh, op. cit.

TABLE 18.13
ESTIMATION OF EXPANSION OF EXPORT SALES IF VOLUME SHARES WERE MAINTAINED AT 1948–50 LEVELS

Commodity (1)	1951 (2)	1952 (3)	1953 (4)	1954 (5)	1955 (6)	1956 (7)	1957 (8)	1958 (9)	1959 (10)	1960 (11)	1951–60 Total (12)
(A) Jute manufactures											
A.1: Hypothetical incremental export earnings (in million Rs.)	323·06	154·66	170·00	147·75	172·29	207·85	202·03	242·78	329·50	408·74	2,358·66
A.2: A.1 as a percentage of actual export earnings	13·44	9·47	15·36	12·17	13·92	18·47	17·58	23·58	29·75	32·55	
(B) Tea											
B.1: Hypothetical incremental export earnings (in million Rs.)	58·53	62·29	0·40	275·49	265·21	47·43	192·47	138·68	167·22	290·12	1,497·84
B.2: B.1 as a percentage of actual export earnings	6·23	7·70	0·03	18·64	24·29	3·26	16·93	10·69	12·95	23·47	
(C) Cotton textiles											
C.1: Hypothetical incremental export earnings (in million Rs.)	76·11	86·31	26·05	Negative	Negative	37·08	Negative	42·05	Negative	254·12	521·72
C.2: C.1 as a percentage of actual export earnings	8·06	11·64	4·08			5·95		7·29		36·84	
(D) Unmanufactured tobacco											
D.1: Hypothetical incremental export earnings (in million Rs.)	Negative	Negative	Negative	41·66	38·39	21·35	65·53	8·78	47·39	51·36	274·46
D.2: D.1 as a percentage of actual export earnings				35·42	36·04	17·10	44·79	5·97	47·39	35·02	35·15

(E) Groundnuts and oil	
E.1: Hypothetical incremental export earnings (in million Rs.)	Negative, Negative, 40·07, 164·60, 70·57, Negative, 153·50, 138·89, 59·87, 94·85, 722·35
E.2: Hypothetical incremental export volume as a percentage of actual export volume	Negative, 228·08, 152·12, 163·93, 10,762·50, 445·00, 82·39, 438·18
(F) Linseed and oil	
F.1: Hypothetical incremental export earnings (in million Rs.)	26·94, Negative, 16·96, 179·76, Negative, 57·58, 17·02, 26·98, 39·62, 364·86
F.2: Hypothetical incremental export volume as a percentage of actual export volume	66·40, 257·89, 1,700·00, 208·39, 54·30, 102·62, 437·68
Total of A–F	
Total hypothetical incremental export earnings (in million Rs.)	484·64, 303·26, 253·48, 809·26, 475·89, 384·28, 671·11, 588·20, 630·96, 1,138·81, 5,739·89
Total hypothetical incremental export earnings (in million Rs.) as a percentage of total actual export earnings from these commodities	10·65, 9·76, 8·56, 22·06, 14·47, 10·82, 21·76, 19·77, 18·78, 31·21, 16·45

Source: Calculated on the basis of average volume shares in 1948–50, from pp. 15, 38, 57, 74, 75, 99, 101, and 130, of M. Singh, op. cit. The hypothetical incremental export earnings for jute manufactures, tea, cotton textiles, and unmanufactured tobacco are derived by first multiplying the 1948–50 volume shares with the volume of world trade and then multiplying the result with the unit price of exports $\left(\text{i.e. } \dfrac{\text{Indian export earnings}}{\text{Indian export volume}}\right)$. For groundnut and linseed oil, the hypothetical incremental export *volume* is first derived on the basis of 1948–50 shares; the hypothetical incremental export earnings are then derived by multiplying this incremental volume with the unit price of all oil and oilseed exports. The export value figures of tea, unmanufactured tobacco, groundnut and oil, and linseed and oil are on a financial year basis.

The decline was more drastic in her principal market, the United Kingdom, from 82 to 58 per cent over the same period.[1]

The quality of the leather has been a problem—the major difficulty being the local cow slaughter legislation which leads to deterioration in the quality of the hides and skins. In addition, the relative price factor appears to indicate that the relative profitability of the domestic market must have played an important role as well. Cohen's estimated equations give $k = 2 \cdot 182$ [$0 \cdot 474$] with $R = 0 \cdot 85$ for the United Kingdom imports of goat skins from India and the 'rest of the world' for 1951–60, and $k = -1 \cdot 565$ [$1 \cdot 456$] with $R = 0 \cdot 77$ for the United Kingdom imports of cattle hides from India and the 'rest of the world' for 1951–60.

Thus, except for a limited number of bright spots, such as iron ore (Table 18.3, item 6) the decade 1951–60 reveals a stagnation of export earnings whose proximate causes are to be found, for the most part, in domestic policies within India. This conclusion holds for anything up to 75–80 per cent of India's total export earnings, for which we have presented detailed analysis here.

The next question to which we now turn is whether we can quantify the 'loss' of export earnings that these policies 'cost' India. Economists are invariably on tricky ground when they speculate in this way. And yet such speculation is called for, as we have already argued, since the order of magnitude that we emerge with would have a significant bearing on our evaluation of India's key investment decisions.

The preceding analysis suggests that we may not be too far out if we assume the 1948–50 shares for the major commodities—jute manufactures, tea, cotton textiles, groundnut, linseed oils and oilseeds, and tobacco—and, assuming that unit values and world volumes would not have changed from the observed levels each year, we work out the hypothetical earnings that would have accrued to India. We treat these as somewhat optimistic estimates, as it is probable that attempts by India at maintaining her share would, in many cases, have tended to depress the unit values.[2]

The resulting estimates are reproduced in Table 18.13. They

---

[1] Cohen, op. cit., p. 615.

[2] On the other hand, the 'negative' entries in Table 18.13 show that the 1948–50 average was by no means the highest feasible share even in the ensuing decade, for cotton textiles, tobacco, groundnut, and linseed oilseeds and oils.

are quite striking. The overall improvement in feasible export earnings, over the ten years 1951–60, comes for these five commodities to around 16·5 per cent of the actual performance. If we add, to the estimated improvement of Rs. 5,740 million, a rough estimate of the potential improvement in three other items— coffee, manganese ore, and leather—we get close to an overall figure of about Rs. 6,200 million.[1]

Indeed, if we examine the entire range of exports, including spices, raw wool, coir manufactures, and newer manufactures involving light engineering goods, over the decade 1951–60, the figure of potential improvement in export earnings could reasonably be put close to Rs. 8,200 million, estimated at 10 per cent on the items other than the commodities separately estimated in Table 18.13.[2]

That this estimate is large enough to have made a significant impact on the investment allocations to heavy industry, without reversing altogether the shift to them with the Second Five-Year Plan, is clear.[3] We treat this issue at greater length in the chapters where we discuss the industrial policies of the Indian planning authorities. Immediately, however, we proceed to a description and evaluation of the shift to more energetic export policy in India with the Third Five-Year Plan.

---

[1] We merely add an approximate 10 per cent of the actual earnings on these three items to the estimate in Table 18.13.

[2] That Indian export policies on most of the *other* commodities also served to inhibit exports is evident from Singh's excellent analysis, op. cit.

[3] It might be argued that a more energetic export policy resulting in these higher export earnings would have led to a reduced level of aid flow to India. However, this view presupposes that the aid givers would have ignored the savings-implications of such a decision. We find no evidence to support such a view.

19

Export Policy—Part II[1]

THE average export performance during the Third Plan appears (from Table 18.2) to have picked up significantly above the average Second Plan performance, not merely in value but in volume as well, even though, as a percentage of world trade, there was no improvement and, if anything, some deterioration (Table 18.1).

This improvement, however, seems to have been confined to the first three years (1961/2, 1962/3, and 1963/4) of the Third Plan and thereafter the export performance seems to have tapered off again to a stagnant level, through the remaining two years.[2] But this picture of *sharp* early improvements and later stagnation needs to be modified. The improvement through the Third Plan appears somewhat steadier if we note, in particular, the improvement in the export figures which extended statistical coverage brought about since 1961/2. Thus, the inclusion of Goa's foreign trade improved the export value by Rs. 180 million; there have also been additions of overland exports to Nepal and parcel post exports, which are estimated to have increased export estimates by another Rs. 150–170 million. Adjustments for these factors would deflate the earlier sharp improvements, though they would not change the picture of later relapse into stagnation.

There are essentially two major explanations of the improvement in India's export performance, both of which are to be traced to a more energetic attempt at promoting exports.

---

[1] Much of this chapter is based on the work done earlier by Bhagwati in his study, prepared in the course of 1965 and completed in 1966, on *Import Entitlement Schemes for Export Promotion*. Only such material has been utilized which was derived from already-published sources such as *Export Promotion Handbooks* and *Annual Reports* of the Ministry of International Trade, and which was obtained from private trade in personal interviews.

[2] The 1966/7 figure of export performance was even less than the previous year's.

(1) The first factor was the major improvement in exports to the Soviet-bloc countries, beginning around 1960/1: this accounted for an improvement by nearly Rs. 1 billion[1] between 1964/5 levels and 1960/1 levels. As Table 19.1 shows, 50 per cent of the improve-

TABLE 19.1
EXPORTS BY MAJOR DESTINATIONS: 1956/7–1960/1, AND 1961/2 1965/6
(In Rs. 00,000)

| Destination | Average | | | % change on Second Plan total | % of total change |
	Second Plan	Third Plan	Change		
Socialist countries	3,571	11,329	+7,758	217	49·11
(U.S.S.R. therein)	(2,345)	(3,524)	(+3,524)		
W. Europe	23,233	23,832	(+599)	17	3·79
(E.E.C. therein)	(4,662)	(5,743)	(+1,081)		
(E.F.T.A. therein)	(17,587)	(17,022)	(−565)		
Asia and Oceania	15,962	19,003	+3,041	19	19·25
(Japan therein)	(3,033)	(5,535)	(+2,502)		
Africa	4,749	5,215	+466	9	2·95
(U.A.R. therein)	(1,090)	(1,596)	(+506)		
Americas	12,857	16,791	+3,934	31	24·90
(United States therein)	(9,276)	(13,114)	(+3,838)		
TOTAL	60,372	76,170	15,798	26	100·00

Source: *Basic Statistical Material Relating to Foreign Trade, Production and Prices*, Volume XIII—Part II, Government of India, 1967.

ment in average Third Plan export performance over the Second Plan came from the trade with socialist countries. As we shall see later, not all of this increment in trade is to be put down to energetic export promotion by the authorities; a fraction of it reflects merely the Soviet-bloc policy of securing aid repayments in kind. Also, how far these export earnings reflected genuine expansion, and did not in turn adversely affect exports to normal commercial markets in the 'rest of the world', is a point of some interest.

(2) The second factor behind the improvement in export performance was a shift towards export subsidization on a major scale. While subsidization undoubtedly has earlier origins, the scale was never large enough to merit description as a programme until 1961/2. Furthermore, subsidies increased through the Third Plan.

Before we proceed to discuss these two aspects of India's export policies in detail, we may briefly examine export performance in

[1] By billion, we mean 1,000 million, throughout this work.

TABLE 19.2
EXPORTS OF SELECTED ITEMS FROM INDIA, 1957/8–1959/60 AND 1961/2–1965/6, BY MAJOR DESTINATIONS

Commodity	Annual average: 1957/58–1959/60		Annual average: 1961/2–1965/6		Change in annual average value between two periods
	Quantity ('000 tons)	Value (million Rs.)	Quantity ('000 tons)	Value (million Rs.)	
(1)	(2)	(3)	(4)	(5)	(6)
1. *Oil cakes and meal*					
Socialist countries	34·8	13·1	390·4	150·1	+137·0
Rest	291·8	99·9	483·2	166·3	+66·4
2. *Iron ore*					
Socialist countries	789·3	39·8	1,844·2	84·2	+44·4
Rest	1,231·8	90·2	8,418·0	288·7	+198·5
3. *Cashew Kernels*					
Socialist Countries	4·7	20·4	12·8	59·2	+38·8
Rest	34·3	139·0	36·9	171·4	+32·4
4. *Coffee*					
Socialist Countries	4·1	19·2	14·0	58·5	+39·3
Rest	10·8	50·5	12·2	44·1	−6·4
5. *Mica*					
Socialist countries	1·32	11·7	2·78	28·8	+17·1
Rest	22·57	84·3	30·54	73·3	−11·0
6. *Footwear*					
Socialist countries	0·5 million	12·4	0·8 million	16·1	+3·7
Rest	4·1 pairs	15·0	6·0 pairs	20·3	+5·3
7. *Tea*					
Socialist countries	10·8	80·3	20·4	136·5	+56·2
Rest	190·2	182·0	188·8		+2·6

8. Jute manufactures					
Socialist countries	20·0	29·6	105·0	191·8	+162·2
Rest	822·0	1,102·2	788·4	1,421·7	+319·5
9. Unmanufactured tobacco					
Socialist countries	3·9	6·4	28·2	64·6	+58·2
Rest	38·7	140·4	32·4	129·6	−10·8
10. Groundnuts					
Socialist countries	1·1	9·0	11·6	12·6	+3·6
Rest	17·4	15·6	14·7	14·9	−0·7
11. Castor oil					
Socialist countries	6·9	11·2	15·6	24·1	+12·9
Rest	32·6	50·1	8·5	12·4	−37·7
12. Raw wool					
Socialist countries	32·9	20·4	53·9	33·5	+13·1
Rest	130·4	78·1	60·6	35·1	−43·0
13. Manganese ore					
Socialist countries	45·8	7·3	138·2	17·0	+9·7
Rest	1,169·5	178·3	989·2	85·6	−92·7
14. Lac					
Socialist countries	15·5	4·0	31·2	8·1	+4·1
Rest	253·3	59·7	153·8	36·3	−23·4
15. Pepper					
Socialist countries	64·8	20·0	91·2	34·3	+14·3
Rest	95·5	31·3	119·2	42·6	+11·3
16. Goat skins					
Socialist countries	57·1	49·3	78·4	58·2	+8·9
Rest	61·0	33·9	37·6	25·4	−8·5
17. Total of 1–16					
Socialist countries	—	354·1	—	977·6	+623·5
Rest	—	3,351·5	—	3,660·1	+308·6

Source: Dharm Narain, *Aid Through Trade*, UNCTAD Secretariat, December 1967. Based on primary data from Directorate General of Commercial Intelligence and Services, Calcutta.

terms of commodities. Table 19.2 contains the pertinent information on selected commodities for 1961/2 to 1965/6, further broken
broken down by socialist countries and 'the rest'.[1] It is clear from
this table that the major improvement in Indian performance was
to be attributed to expansion of trade in oil cakes and meal, iron
ore, cashew kernels, coffee, but most dramatically in jute manufactures.[2] In addition, the Indian economy emerged, during this
period, as an exporter of engineering goods, chemicals and allied
products, and art silk fabrics: this was largely thanks to the gener-
ous import entitlement schemes granted to these industries, as we
shall soon see.

A. POLICIES OF EXPORT SUBSIDIZATION

Export subsidization policies took essentially two major forms: (1)
fiscal measures; and (2) import entitlement schemes (which entitled
exporters to premium-carrying import licences). In addition to
these measures, which improved the direct profitability of export
sales, there were also some promotional activities, in the form, for
example, of budgetary appropriations for market development,
which indirectly raised the profitability of foreign sales to domestic
producers and traders.

(1) Fiscal Measures

Among the fiscal measures which the export drive was based on
were: (i) exemptions from sales taxes on final sales and refunds of
indirect taxes, domestic and customs, on inputs; (ii) direct-tax
concessions; (iii) outright subsidies; and (iv) rail freight concessions.

(i) Exemptions and refunds from indirect taxes (sales, customs,
and excise) were generally made available to Indian exporters although their incidence was not always as intended owing to

---

[1] To facilitate the drawing of conclusions, we have included the average performance in the preceding three years as well. Remember that Table 19.1
gives the destinations in greater detail.

[2] The export performance of cotton textiles, not covered in Table 19.2, remained relatively dismal through the Third Plan period, if anything actually
declining in value. Thus, the average Second Plan exports of mill-made
cotton piecegoods were Rs. 517·4 million as against the average Third Plan
figure of Rs. 455·4 million. Cf. *Basic Statistics* . . ., op. cit., p. 49.

dilatory procedures and inefficiencies. These exemptions, refunds, and rebates applied to both imported components and to exported outputs.[1]

Drawbacks of import duties were introduced for raw materials used in finished articles exported (including art silk fabrics, cars, dry radio batteries, electric fans, and cigarettes) in 1954.[2] Rebates of excise duty were announced in 1956, with immediate applicability to the raw materials used in exported ready-made apparel, tents, and sugar products and to direct exports of cotton and silk fabrics produced on powerlooms.[3] The scope of both these measures was considerably enlarged later on, though several inefficiencies of procedure and insufficient accessibility to the drawbacks and rebates persisted through the ensuing years. Thus, for example, reporting in 1963, the Chanda Committee on Central Excise Reorganisation made the following comment:

Industry and official witnesses both complain that the existence of these differing procedures, each with its own special provisions which are again in many cases deliberalised by executive instructions, renders it difficult to understand or to apply the rules correctly. In the result, the exporter runs the risk inadvertently of committing a breach of the rules which may entail refusal of the refund. Representatives of manufacturers and exporters complain that the details of these schemes are based on a distrust of their *bona-fides*; the procedures and restrictions are designed to prevent fraudulent claims being made rather than to facilitate exports or to ensure full and prompt repayment of duty paid on finished goods and/or on the materials used in their production.[4]

Even the process of devising rates and procedures for such claims, and announcing them in advance so that the export benefits would become reasonably forecastable, was not undertaken with alacrity and speed. By 1960 the procedures and rates for granting drawbacks on import duties had been worked out only for eighty-nine commodities, and for refunds of excise duty on twenty-seven

[1] In addition, export production 'under bond' has also been possible, in some cases; but its incidence is minimal.

[2] Cf. Notification No. 51/F. No. 5/I-32/5/53-Cus—I, Ministry of Finance (Revenue Division), Government of India, New Delhi, 28 May 1954.

[3] Cf. Notification, No. 18-CER/56, Ministry of Finance (Department of Revenue), Government of India, New Delhi, 27 November 1956.

[4] Report of the *Central Excise Reorganisation Committee*, Government of India Press, Delhi, 1963, pp. 81–2. More details on the difficulties can be found on pp. 80–5.

items; the remainder, which constituted the overwhelming bulk of potential and actual exports, still had to go through detailed procedures.[1]

The exemptions from *sales* taxes raised even more difficulties in practice. As the Mudaliar Committee pointed out:

At present the last sale, constituting the actual transaction between Indian exporters and foreign importers is exempt, within the meaning of Article 286 of the Constitution, from the payment of sales tax. However, it is not easy to get the remission of sales tax in many cases, as the expression 'in the cause of export' in the Central Sales Tax Act is rather ambiguous. Besides, sales tax falls at more than one point. There is also an inter-State sales tax; and these inflate the export costs in varying degrees. But the difficulty is that sales tax is a State subject; and its rate varies from State to State. So the question arises: at what point to give the rebate and at what rate? Also, as sales tax is one of the most important sources of revenue to the State governments, they have been extremely averse to parting with any ingredient of it. Indeed, Assam levies an export tax on Tea, whereas West Bengal levies an entry tax.[2]

While no breakdown of the refunds, rebates, and drawbacks actually earned on different export items is available it is estimated that the refund of excise duties in 1963/4 was around Rs. 5·80 crores.

(ii) More important have been the *direct* tax concessions, which have been made in three successive budgets. The first, and somewhat hesitant, step was taken with the 1962 budget which gave a non-discriminatory tax concession to exporters. Apart from its non-selectivity, the subsidy was characterized by its being calculated on profits from exports (with the tax rate being fixed thereon at 45 per cent instead of the standard 50 per cent).[3]

The 1963 budget added a different kind of tax incentive. It was both selective (the eligible industries, listed in Appendix I, Table 19.8, being essentially the newer manufacturing industries) and related, not to profits, but directly to the f.o.b. value of exports—at 2 per cent thereof.

---

[1] *Handbook of Export Trade Control*, Ministry of Commerce and Industry, Government of India, New Delhi, 1960, pp. 34–6 and 263–5.

[2] Report of the *Import and Export Policy Committee*, Ministry of Commerce and Industry, Government of India, New Delhi, 1962, pp. 36–7.

[3] In view of the difficulty of breaking down overall profits into home and export profits, the operational rule was to split profits into these two categories in the same proportion as sales in the two markets.

The 1965 budget took the further striking step of giving selective concessions, described as tax credits, at *different* rates to different industries. Besides, the rates went up to as far as 15 per cent and were extended to a larger number of industries (Table 19.8). Yet, in relation to the import entitlement schemes which are discussed in section 2 below, the incentives were relatively small and confined to a small range of exports.[1]

(iii) In addition to the tax-concessions granted through the budget, which therefore must be classified as subsidy-equivalents, there were also two other major forms of subsidization in the system: (*a*) open, cash subsidy by budgetary appropriation, for sugar; and (*b*) disguised cash subsidy, in the shape of losses incurred by the State Trading Corporation (S.T.C.) on exports of certain commodities, which were 'financed' by profits on other (essentially import) trade.[2]

Exports of sugar were openly subsidized, the magnitude of the subsidy running at Rs. 142 and Rs. 35 million in 1962/3 and 1963/4 respectively.[3] Exports of sugar, during the same periods, ran at Rs. 169·2 and Rs. 260·3 million respectively,[4] thus indicating an export subsidy which could, as needs arose, rise up to over 80 per cent of the f.o.b. value of exports.

The operations of the S.T.C. which were tantamount to export subsidization are readily inferred from its Annual Reports. Describing its activities, the S.T.C. had the following to say:

Only such commodities were entrusted to the Corporation where bulk contracting and bulk handling were considered advantageous or which

[1] Of the twenty-five items listed in Table 19.9 as eligible for the entitlement schemes, only fifteen items (adding up to less than 10 per cent of Indian exports) were eligible for 10 and 15 per cent tax credits, for example: these were mostly minerals, ores, fresh fruits, and beverages.

[2] How far losses should be considered 'commercial' and how far as subsidy-equivalents, when the trading organization is in the public-sector, is a delicate question. However, where sale at a loss is a policy-determined phenomenon, occurring at the instruction of the Ministry in charge of international trade, it would be meaningful to classify the value of the losses as approximately measuring the implicit subsidy in these exports. Among the commodities on which the S.T.C. took continuing losses were cement, sodium bichromate, groundnut oil, lemongrass oil, and de-oiled linseed cakes.

[3] Estimates from the Department of Economic Affairs, Ministry of Finance, Government of India. These estimates are directly available from published sources as well.

[4] The estimates are from: *Basic Statistical Material Relating to Foreign Trade, Production and Prices*, Annual Volume XIII, Part II, Government of India, 1967 and are available from other printed sources as well.

were in short supply and presented peculiar problems of fair distribution. Government also entrusted to the Corporation, to a limited extent, some highly speculative commodities, trading in which yields a high margin of profit. *Further, Government required the Corporation to handle some commodities the export of which was becoming increasingly difficult due to high internal costs.*[1]

In addition, the S.T.C. Reports stated:

The demand for cement in the country continued to be far in excess of actual availability. But, in order to maintain and develop markets . . . and to earn the much needed foreign exchange, the Corporation continued to effect exports . . . to Ceylon, Afghanistan, East Pakistan and the countries of Persian Gulf. . . . The terms of trade, however, improved substantially, and the loss, therefore, was reduced from Rs. 17·05 lakhs during the previous year to Rs. 2·41 lakhs during the year under report.[2]

During the year under review Government desired that the Corporation should, in order to earn foreign exchange, undertake the export of groundnut oil, for which there was a large export market. The internal cost of this oil being out of line with the international prices, the Corporation had *necessarily* to suffer losses, which it had to meet from its Trade Development Reserve and other business profits. . . . A loss of Rs. 50·21 lakhs is . . . reflected in the accounts. . . .[3]

Exports of [Manioc Meal] to West Germany which was taken up in 1962–63 . . . in order to earn foreign exchange. . . . Since there is a disparity in the internal and international prices the loss resulting from these exports has been met from the Trade Development Centre.[4]

(iv) With respect to rail freight concessions, as early as 1960 the Ministry of Railways had agreed to grant reductions in freight to selected commodities for transportation between specified destinations. The commodities covered ranged from motor vehicle batteries and oil pressure lamps to textile machinery and bicycles: they were essentially non-agriculture-based manufactures whose exports were a recent phenomenon.[5]

An examination of the eligible routes and corresponding con-

---

[1] *Annual Report, 1961–62*, S.T.C. Ltd., New Delhi, p. 4 [the italics are inserted by us].
[2] Ibid., p. 7.
[3] Ibid., p. 7 [the italics are inserted by us].
[4] Ibid., *1963–64*, p. 7.
[5] Fruit and Vegetable Processes were included. For detail, see *Handbook of Export Trade Control*, Ministry of Commerce and Industry, Government of India, 1960, pp. 298–305.

cessions indicates that the intention was to offset the transport cost 'disadvantage' to exporters, even sometimes to the point of providing progressively concessional rates as distance increased (as with manganese ore)! As the export drive intensified, this aspect of rail freight concessions was to have more appeal for the authorities in charge of export promotion, despite its obvious contradiction to economic logic.[1] The notion that transport costs may reflect real costs to the economy and the fact that, if anything, the 'shadow' freight rates were almost certainly higher than those charged on a non-concessional basis,[2] seem to have concerned none of the authorities in charge of the export drive.[3]

In addition to these direct, fiscal measures, involving explicit or implicit subsidization of exports, at budgetary expense,[4] there were also (i) budgetary grants for promotional activities, such as the Market Development Fund under which the activities of the numerous Export Promotion Councils were financed along with research exhibitions and market surveys geared to export expansion, and (ii) special allocations of scarce items at controlled prices, including priority access to rail space[5] and allocations of domestic materials, such as iron and steel, which constituted effective subsidization in so far as these facilities and materials, if purchased at (black) market prices, would have been otherwise more expensive.

---

[1] Demands for such 'perverse' concessions were frequently made and can be found in many unpublished Board of Trade proceedings and memoranda by business groups. A typical example is the following statement by the Secretary of the Engineering Export Promotion Council: 'There are many items which are produced in inland centres but they cannot be exported, among others, because of the high freight. [Therefore] concessions (normally equal to 50% of freight chargeable) have been given on movements of certain goods to ports and also, in some cases, on the movement of raw materials for the manufacture of export products.' R. K. Singh. *Prosperity through Exports*, p. 113.

[2] L. Lefeber and M. Datta-Chaudhuri, 'Transportation Policy in India', in P. N. Rosenstein-Rodan (ed.), *Pricing and Fiscal Policies*. While these authors raise pertinent questions relating to the underpricing of transport in India, their methods for 'correcting' to 'true, social' values have been critically reviewed by K. Sundaram, 'The "True" Social Freight Rates on Land Transportation in India: A Note', *Indian Economic Review*, III (New Series), April 1968.

[3] Secondary welfare-considerations, such as the consequent shifting of the incentive to transport, between rail and road, were also not raised.

[4] Rail freight concessions and S.T.C. losses were also drains on the budget since the profits on Railways and S.T.C. directly constituted revenue for the budget.

[5] Cf. *Handbook of Export Trade Control*, op. cit., pp. 306–16.

(2) Import entitlement schemes

While the export promotion measures deployed by the Indian Government had, therefore, numerous aspects (including outright subsidies and tax concessions), the principal instrument of export promotion soon became the import entitlement schemes, under which eligible exporters received import licences, fetching high import premia, *pro rata* to the value of exports effected. The importance of these schemes is apparent from the steady increase in the value of import licences issued against them through the period (Table 19.3) and the fact that, with the average premium

TABLE 19.3
ISSUANCE OF EXPORT PROMOTION IMPORT LICENCES[a]
(In Rs. crores)

Period	Value
1961/2	
April–September	14·74
October–March	12·13
1962/3	
April–September	13·95
October–March	19·01
1963/4	
April–September	23·54
October–March	41·31
1964/5	
April–September	42·21
October–November	11·38

[a] These estimates were prepared in February, 1965. They tend to be revised frequently. They are to be treated as giving broad orders of magnitude only.

Source: Bhagwati, op. cit., p. 8, based on published materials.

on these licences running at anywhere around 70–80 per cent, the effective subsidization implied ran up to around Rs. 50 crores in 1963/4 itself and thus significantly exceeded the effective subsidy flowing from any or all of the other measures of export promotion.

We thus consider the import entitlement schemes at considerable length, examining their main features and their economic characteristics. Here again there were major changes with the devaluation in June 1966 when the schemes were discontinued, to be revived later in a different form. Again, we have considered these changes separately, later in this volume, along with the other changes in import and industrial policies that came with the devaluation. Our present analysis, therefore, refers essentially to the pre-devaluation, Third Plan period.

Evolution of the import entitlement schemes[1]

By early 1965 the import entitlement schemes already had a very considerable coverage. Table 19.9 in Appendix I lists all the schemes then in force, with the corresponding, values of exports in 1963 and 1964 entered against each scheme.

The vast majority of these schemes were being administered by statutory bodies, the Export Promotion Councils (E.P.C.s). There were still a few items which were handled by the C.C.I. & E.'s offices at the Ports; but these had over the years been gradually reduced and merged into the more regular schemes operated through the E.P.C.s.

In fact, the continuing (though dwindling) operation by the C.C.I. & E.'s Port Offices of some entitlement schemes reflected a historical evolution which transformed the original entitlement schemes, dating back to at least as far as 1950 in some cases, from an attempt at supplying otherwise prohibited imports of raw materials to industries aiming at export—most of the items being precious stones for jewellery and such others—to full-blooded schemes designed to make exports *attractive* in relation to home sales.

Table 19.10 in Appendix I summarizes neatly this transition, showing all the administrative changes in agencies and the nomenclature which brought the original schemes into their ultimate form. Up to and excluding the April–September 1958 period, entitlements were designed merely to break the production bottlenecks caused by import prohibitions in export industries and had been applied to a limited, though varying, number of specified commodities; and the scheme appeared as Appendix 23 in the Redbooks.

From April–September 1958 up to, but excluding the April–September 1960 period, the major change concerned the intro-

---

[1] We give a brief account here of the main administrative changes, as it throws light on the manner in which the schemes were gradually enlarged and reshaped to become the principal instrument of export promotion.

duction of a new entitlements scheme, to be operated by the Development Wing of the Ministry of Commerce and Industry, covering several 'new' industries listed in the Redbook. This scheme followed the foreign exchange crisis which came with the Second Five-Year Plan. The shortage of foreign exchange for maintenance imports, and the resulting excess capacity in several of the newly established industries, led apparently to the view that these industries should 'earn the foreign exchange they needed'. The notion that these industries formed the core of an export drive had not yet appeared on the scene. There was, however, a small recognition of the need to boost exports and a very limited number of *ad hoc* schemes were provided for under a Directorate of Export Promotion.

During the period from April to September 1960 up to, but excluding, April 1963 to March 1964, there was a policy shift in favour of the export-promotion view of these entitlement schemes. The Port Authorities (Appendix 23) schemes, reduced in relative importance, continued as Scheme No. 3 and the Development Wing schemes as Scheme No. 1. However, increasingly, several industries were taken out of the Development Wing and assigned to be administered by the growing number of Export Promotion Councils, as Scheme No. 2.

By April 1963 to March 1964, the Development Wing Scheme No. 2 had been eliminated and the entitlement schemes, now fully regarded as export promotion measures aimed at boosting exports, were administratively under two heads: Part I Schemes, being the ones administered by the E.P.C.s; and Part II Schemes, being the remnants of the schemes operated hitherto by the (C.C.I. & E.) Port Authorities. Since then, the Part II Schemes were shifted gradually to the relevant E.P.C.s, so that nearly all of the entitlements, with relatively unimportant exceptions (except for films, jewellery, and oils) were under the Part I Scheme administered by E.P.C.s by early 1965.

The rates of import entitlements.

Even a cursory examination of recent rates-schedules for import entitlements under the export promotion schemes (as, for example, for engineering and chemicals in Tables 19.11 and 19.12 in Appendix I) shows that wide variations existed in these rates for different products. When we sought the criterion used for fixing these rates, governmental declarations seemed to yield definitive answers. Take, for example, a typical statement:

The most important feature of these schemes is that a specified percentage of the f.o.b. value of exports is allowed to be used for importing raw materials and components required in the production of the export products or a group of allied products. The import entitlement is generally determined on the basis of twice the import content subject to a maximum of 75 per cent of the f.o.b. value of exports.[1]

Two central principles seemed to emerge from these and other declarations: (1) the import entitlement would not exceed 75 per cent of f.o.b. export value; and (2) the import entitlement would, subject to the preceding constraint, equal only twice the value of import content.

As it turned out, however, neither of these principles appears to have been taken seriously since the intensification of the export drive began during 1963.

(A) The '*not-greater-than-75-per-cent-of-f.o.b.-value*' rule was often violated quite seriously. The export promotion schemes, as from February 1964,[2] for example, offered the following entitlements in excess of 75 per cent:

(1) *Engineering goods:* 100 per cent for non-ferrous items, alloys and fully processed manufactures and stainless steel products (with twenty-nine listed items).

(2) *Chemicals and allied products:* 95 per cent for zinc oxide.

(3) *Pearls, precious stones and diamonds:* 80 per cent for all items.

(4) *Vegetable oils:* 80 per cent for vanaspati/hydrogenated oil (including crude hardened oil) and refined vegetable oils (including salad oil), viz. refined groundnut oil, refined cottonseed oil and refined rice gram oil etc.

(5) *Cotton textiles:*

(i) *Cotton cloth and yarn:* Three different additive schemes of entitlement operated, leading to *total* entitlements in *excess* of 75 per cent:

---

[1] *Annual Report, 1963–64*, Ministry of International Trade, New Delhi, 1965, p. 14.
[2] Bhagwati, op. cit. The information presented in the text is also readily available from published brochures of the corresponding Export Promotion Councils.

(a) *Entitlement for coal-tar dyes and textiles chemicals*

	Cloth			Yarn	
Category	Grey, %	Bleached, %	Dyed, painted or processed, %	Grey, %	Processed, %
Mills whose cloth/yarn exported	2	2	2	2	—
Registered processors' processing cloth/yarn	—	4	8	—	2
Exporters	2	2	5	2	5
TOTAL	4	8	15	4	7

(b) *Entitlement of raw cotton*

Category	Cotton entitlement, %
Fine and superfine cloth and yarn of 60s and above	$66\frac{2}{3}$
Coarse and medium cloth and yarn below 60s	$66\frac{2}{3}$[a]

[a] Part of this was exchangeable into cash.

(c) *Entitlement for machinery:* 20 per cent of f.o.b. export value was also available for import of textile machinery.

(ii) *Ready-made garments:* $91\frac{2}{3}$ per cent: of which 25 per cent for coal tar dyes, textiles chemicals, embellishments and trimmings and industrial sewing machines; and $66\frac{2}{3}$ per cent for cotton (to be surrendered to the Textile Commissioner at premium prices).

(iii) *Cotton hosiery:* $81\frac{2}{3}$ per cent: of which 15 per cent for coal-tar dyes, textiles chemicals, trimmings, knitting machines etc.; and $66\frac{2}{3}$ per cent for cotton (to be surrendered at premium prices).

(iv) *Mixed fabrics with cotton yarn input in excess of 75 per cent of total raw material cost:* Same as for cotton textile fabrics.

(v) *Non-fabric cotton manufactures:* $81\frac{2}{3}$ per cent: of which 15 per cent for coal-tar dyes and textiles chemicals; and $66\frac{2}{3}$ per cent for cotton (to be surrendered at premium prices).

(vi) *Embroidered cloth:* 81⅔ per cent: same as for non-fabric cotton manufactures.

(6) *Art silk goods:* 100 per cent for import of art silk yarn.

(7) *Woollen goods:* 100 per cent for several imports for example, dyes and chemicals (as permitted under the Redbook) not exceeding 5 per cent and so on.

These schemes covered near to half of the export earnings acknowledged officially to be receiving assistance via import entitlement schemes during 1963/4 and 1964/5, so that it was somewhat disingenuous to suggest that 'generally' the entitlement had been kept within 75 per cent of the f.o.b. value. Even as late as the April 1965 to March 1966 period, at least pearls, cut diamonds, precious and semi-precious stones, different hydrogenated oils, and jewellery carried an 80 per cent entitlement.

(B) Similarly, the rule that *the import entitlement would equal twice the import-content* (while keeping within 75 per cent of f.o.b. value) *and no more,* was not so obviously followed. The very fact that large numbers of (production-wise) diverse commodities were grouped into a single rate—as in Appendix I, Tables 19.9, 19.11, and 19.12—itself implies that no such rule could have been valid with any exactitude. More significantly, it became gradually customary to have minimum entitlements, quite obviously because the 'twice-the-import-content' rule did not give enough incentive to export, for several commodities.

For example, during the period July–December 1964 the already existing *minimum* rate of import entitlement of 20 per cent was raised to 40 per cent of the f.o.b. value of exports (following upon representations from several exporters keen to export items with less than 20 per cent import content), for the whole range of 'chemicals and allied products'. An identical minimum, at 40 per cent was also made available for 'paper and allied products'. The importance of this shift to higher minima can be partially gauged from the fact that several chemicals and allied products, at least as from 1 February 1964, were below the 40 per cent bracket: sodium chloride, sodium bichromate, ferric alumina, alums, manufactures of ceramics, sanitary-ware and fittings, pottery, refractory, washed and processed china clay, deadburnt magnesite, fireclay, wood turpentine, naptha, calcium, lactate ethyl acetate, alcoholic perfumes, processed talc, blended rosa oil, red oxide and yellow oxide pigments of iron, caoutachoucine, and several other items. Yet other examples are provided by the 20 per cent minimum for several natural essential oils and the 20 per cent minimum for sports goods which became a uniform $32\frac{1}{2}$ per cent by July–December 1964.

The operation of *supplementary* entitlements, where the normal entitlements were inadequate as export incentives, was also practised. Several interviewees admitted the existence, at the time, of a clandestine, unlisted scheme of this kind, which consisted of entitlements for high-premium dryfruit, given apparently to exporters (from any scheme) on an *ad hoc* basis. Exporters from engineering and chemicals admitted this during interviews; and several junior officers of E.P.C.s also corroborated this (pointing out that this lent an unsavoury touch to the export promotion efforts, often causing bickering from exporters who had suddenly heard about some rivals benefiting from this scheme while, from ignorance, they had not).[1]

Why were these principles, that the entitlement would equal twice the value of import content while not exceeding 75 per cent of f.o.b. value, so clearly flouted? It appears as though the authorities initially thought that some uniform incentive should be provided and this uniformity was thought to be present in the rule of twice-the-import-content on the ground that each exporter could thus earn one extra import-content to produce one more unit for domestic sale. Of course, this does not at all mean a uniform *ad valorem* incentive to export for all commodities covered by such a scheme; but that does not appear to have been appreciated. At the same time, the ceiling of 75 per cent of f.o.b. value appears to have been imposed for any or all of the following reasons: (i) the schemes were supposed to yield net foreign exchange for non-exporting industries and hence entitlements in excess of 100 per cent seemed ruled out; (ii) an excessive entitlement might encourage over-invoicing of exports; and perhaps (iii) larger entitlements would result in 'throw-away' exports. None of these reasons is, in itself, logically tenable; however, they indicate the kinds of considerations behind the 75 per cent ceiling.

---

[1] We may also legitimately ask what 'import content' really meant in cases, no doubt numerous, where 'import substitutes' were available within India. This inherent administrative ambiguity itself left considerable scope for 'flexibility' in rate fixation.

The general flouting of the 75 per cent ceiling and the twice-the-import-content rule appears to have been a reflection of the shift in practice to the notion that the value of exports must generally be maximized and that uniformity of the kind implicit in the twice-the-import-content rule, as also any ceiling on the entitlements, must not be taken so seriously as to impede the export drive.[1] These attitudes were evident also in the growing number of concessions granted for rail transport and the accelerating clamour even for (economically) perverse rules under which the concessional rates would be linked directly with the distance over which the goods must be carried.[2] We shall revert to this point later, when we evaluate the economic effects of the entitlement schemes.

Permissible imports.

Unlike some exchange retention schemes, the import entitlement schemes did not permit free use of the entitlements. Invariably, a list of authorized imports was issued. An analysis of these lists and accompanying official declarations shows several features.

(1) The imports allowed were claimed to be direct inputs into the industries covered by the exports promotion scheme in question. This was generally correct; but there were important qualifications.

(a) Since different industries were frequently grouped together into a single scheme, the directness of the importable inputs, as far as any *one* industry was concerned, could not be considered to be really maintained by the scheme.

(b) Similarly, from the viewpoint of the exporting manufacturer, if he was a multi-product manufacturer and the different products had interchangeable materials, the directness of the imported inputs into the exported product surely did not rule out in practice their use for manufacture of the other unexported products within the same firm.

(c) Moreover, as many materials (especially chemicals) go into a large range of industries, thus straddling different export promotion schemes, and as the legal transferability of entitlements

[1] The Reports of the E.P.C.'s, Board of Trade Reports, interviewees in the export sector, participants in the Institute of Foreign Trade Seminars on different export items and officials overwhelmingly support the above conclusion as to the then current views on export policy.
[2] We have already commented on this earlier in the present chapter.

EE

frequently occurred via traders, it is only natural that *illegal*, inter-scheme transfers also occurred from time to time.

(*d*) Finally, the 'directness' principle was openly flouted eventually by the introduction of the special dryfruits scheme under which *ad hoc* licences were given to exporters of diverse items (including chemicals and engineering products) to import high-premium-yielding dryfruit. This scheme amounted of course to nothing but an indirect method of cash subsidization and no pretence could be made of dryfruit being a direct input into the exported items.

Why was there this insistence (expressed in several policy declarations to that effect) on the direct usability of the imports within the scheme? There seem to have been three major reasons for this.

(i) The entitlement schemes evolved, as we have seen, from schemes whose principal objective was to make available imported materials otherwise unobtainable in the domestic markets owing to import prohibitions. Even the later, Development Wing-administered schemes had a similar conception of the role of entitlements and the (associated) export-subsidization aspect was not appreciated. There was undoubtedly a hangover of these notions even after the initiation of the more intensive schemes, beginning with 1963/4. This continued to affect, until the elimination of the schemes, official thinking at different levels.

(ii) Another motive was to restrict the use of the allotted foreign exchange to only the exporting industries. Of course this does not require that only 'direct inputs' be allowed; but this appears to have been the intention of the policy-makers in any case.

(iii) The most important motive, however, seems to have been the desire to be on the right side of the GATT and the I.M.F. The persistent, official stand about the 'directness' of imports appears to have prevented the GATT from denouncing the schemes as export subsidies and the I.M.F. from condemning them as multiple exchange practices although, of course, they do constitute, *de facto*, export subsidies *and* multiple exchange practices. It is not at all clear where these institutions draw their (economically nonsensical) lines between the acceptable and the nonacceptable (though, in essentials, equivalent) practices with respect to trade and exchange policies; but, in this instance, the entitlement schemes appear to have been successfully defended as consistent with I.M.F. and GATT conventions in view of their (apparent) 'direct-inputs-only' feature.

(2) There were, further, occasional changes of items in permissible imports of materials and components. There appears to have been a conflict between the interests of the exporters and those of the domestic producers of materials competing with imports. Exporters sought to include high-premia materials, whereas domestic producers of these materials opposed this because inclusion in the permissible imports list would reduce their profits. In a sheltered market these conflicts assumed economic significance, and the occasional shifts in items on the import list seemed often to reflect the relative bargaining positions of the pressure groups involved rather than significant changes in objective economic conditions.[1]

(3) In the beginning, the use of entitlements was further restricted to the import of materials, spares, and components, while the import of capital goods for replacing or extending capacity was excluded. This restriction was probably prompted by a desire not to disrupt Capital Goods (Import) control (C.G.C.) although of course there was no reason why permission to import equipment could not be allowed, subject to prior approval by C.G.C. Yet another reason may have been that the influential policy-makers really regarded the entitlement schemes as more or less breaking the bottlenecks to exports arising from inability to use *current* capacity because of scarcity of imported materials and did not fully appreciate the subsidy-aspect of the schemes or the possibility that expansion of capacity in the export industries itself might be desirable from the viewpoint of export promotion. These restrictions, however, were gradually reduced and, in some cases, altogether eliminated, so that it became customary eventually to have large proportions of the entitlement specified as expendable on imports of equipment.

Transferability of import entitlements

While import entitlements had earlier been for long time subjected to extremely stringent restrictions concerning transferability and

[1] Thus, for example, the occasional argument, when an item was taken off the lists, that 'there is now enough domestic capacity' for producing the item, was often a reflection of significant pressure by these producers. When is domestic production 'adequate'; and at what price is this adequacy being considered? There is surely a great looseness in the use of these concepts.

sale, they eventually became more readily saleable although several restrictions continued. Several variants of transferability were employed in the different schemes.

A typical formula, widely used, permitted the entitlement to be transferred by the exporter, who might be a trader or a manufacturer–exporter, to other manufacturers covered by the *same entitlement scheme*. Among other variants the engineering scheme, for example, had transferability which was restricted within each of *three* groups: (i) general engineering and electrical manufactures; (ii) machinery and transport equipment; and (iii) non-ferrous semis, alloys, and fully processed manufactures. In fish products, handicrafts, processed goods, leather and leather manufactures, silk fabrics and ready-made silk garments, again the transferability of imports was confined to other *exporters* within the scheme and does not appear to have been extended to all manufacturers. For dyes and chemicals entitlements in art silk exports, on the other hand, transferability extended even to units in cotton and woollen textiles.

Oddly enough, however, *imports* against entitlements were not so lightly treated by the administration; they could not generally be transferred. Thus, import entitlements, but not imports against them, were generally transferable, but only to other manufacturers under the same (administrative) scheme.

Why was transferability of entitlements restricted within the different schemes? Two advantages were clearly supposed to follow from it.

(i) On the one hand, the notion of priority in allocation of foreign exchange was considered to have been preserved: the free market, fed by the transferred entitlements, was accessible, in schemewise segments, only to exporting industries. It is not at all clear, however, that this 'internalization' of free market supplies and demands, *by each scheme*, was necessary from this viewpoint. It was surely possible to merge the exporting industries together and to operate the free market on a unified basis which still excluded from itself demands from non-priority users. There was further no significance, other than that of self-justifying assertion, in attaching these *implicit* priorities on a segmented basis among the different exporting industries. Since entitlement rates varied and differing supply situations and import scarcities combined to yield different premia on entitlements, there was no clear economic significance that could be attached to the resulting discrimination in the profitabilities of different (subsidized) exports. Indeed, one may well ask what was the justification, other than purely administrative demands, for allowing transferability within a scheme, which often comprised several diverse commodities as in the case of the Chemicals and Allied Products Scheme.

(ii) On the other hand, it was argued that the 'internalization' of the free exchange market, by segmented schemes, was easier to put across to the I.M.F. and the GATT on the ground that this made it, not an (explicit) subsidy scheme, but a scheme aimed at 'allocating scarce foreign exchange for production to export industries'. It is difficult to consider this argument seriously, however, as the Pakistani Export Bonus Voucher Scheme appears to have survived any such difficulties from these international institutions, despite its unification of the entitlement market.

Premium on entitlements.

Thus import entitlements were generally transferable within a scheme, and could earn whatever premium cleared the market at any point of time. However, before we go on to discuss the level of the premia earned, we must mention certain restrictions that were occasionally imposed on the premium chargeable.

Occasionally, indeed not infrequently, ceilings were imposed on the chargeable premium. These seem to have been attributable to a number of diverse factors. Partly they seem to have reflected a confusion with respect to the aims of these schemes. Thus, certain responsible officials apparently continued to believe that the schemes were intended to 'replace import content' or, where additional entitlements were given, merely to reward manufacturer– exporters by enabling them to 'produce more than other rivals who did not export'. Alternatively, these restrictions reflected a desire to keep the premium within bounds so as to prevent the scheme from being abused by short-sighted traders in search of quick profits. The intention may also have been to have an orderly sale of the entitlements, at a regulated premium, so as to prevent 'undesirable fluctuations'; or indeed it may have been a policy to ensure (by implicit income transfer) that the profitability of the domestic producers of import-substitutes was not too badly hit— as when 65 per cent of the coal-tar dyes entitlement for exporters of cotton piecegoods had to be surrendered at a fixed premium to coal-tar dyes manufacturers, or four-fifths of the machinery entitlement had to be handed over at a fixed premium to textile machinery manufacturers. At times, bigger manufacturers, who wished to pay a lower premium for their purchase of the entitlements, appear to have used their organized influence on E.P.C.s to purchase the entitlement compulsorily at regulated prices, ostensibly to prevent fluctuations but actually to increase their own profits—a charge sometimes levelled by exporters against pools such as that operated by the Cotton Textiles Export Promotion Council. In yet another variant, the fixed premia, when the entitlement was compulsorily sold to the Government, amounted merely to an indirect method of cash subsidization by the Government. This was the case, at one time, with 30 per cent of import entitlements in the art silk export scheme: these were compulsorily surrendered and, against every rupee worth of entitlement so surrendered, the manufacturer–exporter was allocated 75 lb. of indigenous yarn at concessional prices.

In all other cases, which constituted the bulk of the entitlements issued, the effective subsidization to any exporter depended on the premium on the entitlements (in addition, of course, to the entitlement rate itself).[1] In practice, the segmentation of the different entitlement markets meant that the level of the premium varied from commodity to commodity. Besides, the premium varied over time, within each market. The factors which must have determined the premium included: the restrictiveness of the permissible imports list, the entitlement rate, the leakage into prohibited sales, and expectations about the current and future inflow of entitlements into the market.[2]

It is interesting to examine the level at which the premium could be, and the export incentives that it thus constituted. Our investigations indicated that the average premium in most of the schemes (including engineering, chemicals, and plastics) stayed around 70–80 per cent, whereas in cotton textiles it tended to be less and

[1] Here, as elsewhere, we are referring only to the incentive being provided to an individual atomistic exporter under the entitlement schemes. It would be incorrect to generalize the argument to the proposition that, therefore, the replacement of such a scheme by an identical *ad valorem* export subsidy would produce equivalent real effects.

[2] For example, the premia rose severely, for these licences, during May–June 1965 when the import policy announcement was delayed and the removal of the entitlement schemes was widely expected. This happened again in the months prior to devaluation in June 1966.

TABLE 19.4
EXPORT INCENTIVE (I.E. PERCENTAGE PREMIUM ON F.O.B. VALUE) FOR COTTON PIECEGOODS

Destination and type of process	U.K.			Australia and New Zealand			Rest of world: Asia, Africa, E. Europe, Canada, S. America, W. Indies			U.S.A. and West Europe		
	Grey	Bleached	Processed	Grey	Bleached	Processed	Grey	Bleached	Processed	Grey	Bleached	Processed
	(1)	(2)	(3)	(4)	(5)	(6)	(7)	(8)	(9)	(10)	(11)	(12)
(A) Coarse/medium below Rs. 1/10 per square metre including towels and Furnishing (i.e. Np. 91–97 per square yard)												
as on 1.5.65	28/30	31/33	34/40	35/37	33/40	41/47	39/42	42/45	45/52	43/46	46/49	50/56
as on 1.9.65	26/28	29/30	31/36	33/35	36/38	38/43	37/39	40/42	42/47	42/44	44/46	46/51
as on 1.10.65 to 31.3.66	31/34	34/36	36/42	38/41	41/43	43/49	43/45	45/48	48/53	47/49	49/52	52/58
(B) Coarse/medium between Rs. 1/10 to 1/49 per square metre												
as on 1.5.65	33/36	36/39	40/46	39/42	43/45	46/62	43/46	47/49	50/56	47/50	50/53	53/60
as on 1.9.65	31/33	34/35	36/41	37/39	40/42	42/47	41/43	44/46	46/51	45/47	47/49	50/55
as on 1.10.65 to 31.3.66	36/39	39/41	41/47	43/45	45/47	48/53	47/49	49/51	52/57	50/52	53/55	55/61
(C) Coarse/medium of Rs. 1/50 and above per square metre (i.e. Rs. 125·42 per square yard)												
as on 1.5.65	39/44	42/44	45/51	43/46	46/49	50/56	46/49	49/52	53/59	49/52	52/55	55/62
as on 1.9.65	36/38	39/40	41/46	41/43	43/45	46/50	44/46	46/48	49/53	47/49	49/51	51/56
as on 1.10.65 to 31.3.66	41/44	44/46	46/52	46/48	49/51	51/57	49/51	52/54	54/60	52/54	54/57	57/63
(D) Fine												
as on 1.5.65	39/41	42/44	45/51	47/50	51/50	54/60	53/55	56/59	59/66	58/61	61/64	65/71
from 1.9.65	36/38	38/40	41/46	45/47	47/49	50/54	50/52	53/55	55/60	55/57	58/60	60/65
from 1.10.65 to 31.3.66	41/43	44/46	46/52	50/52	52/55	55/61	55/58	58/60	61/66	60/63	63/65	66/71
(E) Superfine												
as on 1.5.65	51/54	54/57	58/64	51/54	54/57	58/64	51/54	54/57	58/64	51/54	54/57	58/64
as on 1.9.65	47/49	50/52	52/57	47/49	50/52	52/57	47/49	50/52	52/57	47/49	50/52	52/57
from 1.10.65 to 31.3.66	52/55	55/57	57/63	52/55	55/57	57/63	52/55	55/57	57/63	52/55	55/57	57/63

Note: Indirect/Direct estimates are given. The direct estimate is the *sum* of incentives given to manufacturers and exporters; if exports were through other traders, they would get the incentive for exporters and the mill would get therefore a reduced entitlement.

Source: An exporting mill in Ahmedabad.

TABLE 19.5
ENTITLEMENTS ARISING OUT OF EXPORTS OF CLOTH AND MONETARY VALUE THEREOF, AS AT 11.2.65

Category	Coarse medium A			Coarse medium B			Coarse medium C			Fine D			Superfine F		
	G	B	P	G	B	P	G	B	P	G	B	P	G	B	P
	(1)	(2)	(3)	(4)	(5)	(6)	(7)	(8)	(9)	(10)	(11)	(12)	(13)	(14)	(15)
1. F.O.B. value of exports	100	100	100	100	100	100	100	100	100	100	100	100	100	100	100
2. Entitlements															
(a) Cotton	40·00	40·00	40·00	56·00	56·00	56·00	72·00	72·00	72·00	66·6	66·6	66·6	100	100	100
(b) Dyes intermediates	1·30	3·90	6·50	1·30	3·90	6·50	1·30	3·90	6·50	1·30	3·90	6·50	1·30	3·30	6·50
(c) Coal-tar dyes	0·50	1·50	2·50	0·50	1·50	2·50	0·50	1·50	2·50	0·50	1·50	2·50	0·50	1·50	2·5
(d) Caustic soda	0·20	0·60	1·00	0·20	0·60	1·00	0·20	0·60	1·00	0·20	0·60	1·00	0·20	0·60	1·00
(e) Machinery 'A'	20·00	20·00	20·00	20·00	20·00	20·00	20·00	20·00	20·00	20·00	20·00	20·00	20·00	20·00	20·00
(f) Machinery 'B'	5·00	5·00	5·00	5·00	5·00	5·00	5·00	5·00	5·00	5·00	5·00	5·00	5·00	5·00	5·00
(g) Distance	3·00	3·00	3·00	3·00	3·00	3·00	3·00	3·00	3·00	3·00	3·00	3·00	Nil	Nil	Nil
3. Premia on entitlements															
(a) Cotton	34·00	34·00	34·00	34·00	34·00	34·00	34·00	34·00	34·00	37·60	37·60	37·60	37·60	37·60	37·60
(b) Dyes intermediates	60·00	60·00	60·00	60·00	60·00	60·00	60·00	60·00	60·00	60·00	60·00	60·00	60·00	60·00	60·00
(c) Coal-tar dyes	150·00	150·00	150·00	150·00	150·00	150·00	150·00	150·00	150·00	150·00	150·00	150·00	150·00	150·00	150·00
(d) Caustic soda	100·00	100·00	100·00	100·00	100·00	100·00	100·00	100·00	100·00	100·00	100·00	100·00	100·00	100·00	100·00
(e) Machinery 'A'	40·00	40·00	40·00	40·00	40·00	40·00	40·00	40·00	40·00	40·00	40·00	40·00	40·00	40·00	40·00
(f) Machinery 'B'	30·00	30·00	30·00	30·00	30·00	30·00	30·00	30·00	30·00	30·00	30·00	30·00	30·00	30·00	30·00
(g) Distance	26·60	26·60	26·60	24·00	24·00	24·00	18·00	18·00	18·00	33·30	33·30	33·30	—	—	—
4. Cash value of entitlements on premium															
(a) Cotton	13·60	13·60	13·60	19·04	19·04	19·04	24·48	24·48	24·48	25·06	25·06	25·06	37·60	37·60	37·60
(b) Dyes intermediates	0·78	2·34	3·90	0·78	2·34	3·90	0·78	2·34	3·90	0·78	2·34	3·90	0·78	2·34	3·90

	G	B	P	G	B	P	G	B	P	G	B	P	G	B	P
(c) Coal-tar dyes	0·75	2·25	3·75	0·75	2·25	3·75	0·75	2·25	3·75	0·75	2·25	3·75	0·75	2·25	3·75
(d) Caustic soda	0·20	0·60	1·00	0·20	0·60	1·00	0·20	0·60	1·00	0·20	0·60	1·00	0·20	0·60	1·00
(e) Machinery 'A'	8·00	8·00	8·00	8·00	8·00	8·00	8·00	8·00	8·00	8·00	8·00	8·00	8·00	8·00	8·00
(f) Machinery 'B'	1·50	1·50	1·50	1·50	1·50	1·50	1·50	1·50	1·50	1·50	1·50	1·50	1·50	1·50	1·50
(g) Distance	0·80	0·80	0·80	0·72	0·72	0·72	0·54	0·54	0·54	1·00	1·00	1·00	—	—	—
TOTAL	25·63	29·09	32·55	30·99	34·45	37·91	36·25	39·71	43·17	37·29	40·75	44·21	48·83	52·29	55·75
5. Cash Premiums for															
(a) United Kingdom	Nil	Nil	Nil	Nil	Nil	Nil	Nil	Nil	Nil	Nil	Nil	Nil	Nil	Nil	Nil
(b) Australia–New Zealand	5·59	5·59	5·59	5·04	5·04	5·04	3·78	3·78	3·78	7·00	7·00	7·00	Nil	Nil	Nil
(c) United States, West Europe	13·30	13·30	13·30	12·00	12·00	12·00	9·00	9·00	9·00	16·66	16·66	16·66	Nil	Nil	Nil
(d) Rest of World	9·58	9·58	9·58	8·64	8·64	8·64	—	—	—	—	—	—	Nil	Nil	Nil
6. Mode of exports															
If through exporter add*	3·00	3·00	7·50	3·00	3·00	7·50	3·00	3·00	3·00	3·00	3·00	3·00	3·00	3·00	3·00
7. If exported by exporter*															
(a) United Kingdom	25·63	29·09	32·55	30·99	34·40	37·90	36·25	39·71	43·17	37·29	40·75	44·21	48·83	52·29	55·75
(b) Australia–New Zealand	31·22	34·68	38·14	36·03	51·10	59·30	40·03	43·48	46·95	44·29	47·75	51·21	48·83	52·29	55·75
(c) United States–West Europe	38·93	42·39	45·85	42·99	46·40	49·91	45·23	48·71	52·17	53·95	57·41	60·87	48·83	52·29	55·75
(d) Rest of World	35·21	38·67	42·13	39·63	43·00	46·65	42·73	46·19	49·65	49·29	52·75	56·21	48·83	52·29	55·75
8. If exported directly															
(a) United Kingdom	28·63	32·09	40·05	33·99	37·45	45·41	39·25	42·71	50·67	40·29	43·75	51·71	51·83	55·29	63·25
(b) Australia–West Europe	34·12	37·68	45·64	39·09	42·49	50·45	48·03	46·49	54·45	47·29	50·75	58·71	51·83	55·29	63·25
(c) United States–West Europe	41·93	45·39	53·35	45·99	48·45	57·41	48·25	51·71	59·67	56·85	60·41	68·37	51·83	55·29	63·25
(d) Rest of World	38·21	41·67	49·63	42·63	43·05	54·05	45·73	49·09	57·15	52·29	55·75	63·71	51·83	55·29	63·25

Notes: G, B, and P in the column headings stand for Grey, Bleached, and Processed cloth.

The above calculations are based on current market premia as under:

(1) Global cotton, 40 per cent; (2) P.L. 480, 16 per cent; (3) Coal-tar dyes, 150 per cent; (4) Caustic soda, 100 per cent; (5) Machinery 'A' 40 per cent.

* There is an additional entitlement for the exporter for dyes and chemicals.

Source: An exporter in Ahmedabad.

in rayon and art silks it was significantly more.[1] It is instructive to consider, for a few items, the precise way in which the premia on different entitlements combined to yield the effective export subsidy. We consider two cases, cotton textiles and rayon piece-goods, for which we managed to get reliable information on these schemes: the rayon data are also of further interest in so far as they indicate the importance of rebates and drawbacks for exports.

For cotton piecegoods, Table 19.4 shows at three different recent dates the total export incentive (i.e. premium on f.o.b. value) that was available, as calculated by a mill-exporter, under the Cotton Textiles Export Promotion Scheme. Note that the effective subsidy on export value amounted, in May 1965, to as little as 28·30 per cent and as much as 65·71 per cent, and varied according to category and destination. Besides, the effective incentives changed somewhat, under each category of cloth, over time.[2]

Table 19.5 indicates, for cotton cloth, how the calculations of *ad valorem* subsidy were arrived at. The following features are of interest. (1) The entitlements took numerous forms: there were entitlements for coal-tar dyes, for cotton, for soda ash, for machinery, and for dyes intermediates. (2) Nor were all these entitlements fully transferable at *any* premium: the calculation of the cotton premium involved an assumption concerning how much cotton was 'surrenderable' and at what rate; the machinery entitlement was divided into Entitlement 'A' (20 per cent) which was transferable and Entitlement 'B' (5 per cent) which had to be surrendered to the Textile Commissioner at a fixed premium of 30 per cent; coal-tar dyes entitlements also were partly surrenderable to coal-tar dyes and chemicals manufacturers at a cash premium of 60 per cent; and so on. (3) There was a varying cash premium on surrenderable cotton, depending on destination (shown in item 5). (4) There was a 'distance' premium allowed on the surrenderable value of the cotton entitlement (shown in items 3

---

[1] We refer here to the premia during 1964 and 1965, excluding the periods when expectations had sharply changed to raise the premia upwards (as when the rayon entitlements fetched a premium in the range of 400 per cent during the months preceding devaluation).

[2] Data that we do not reproduce here show that (1) the effective subsidy varied rather more than is suggested by Table 19.4, and (2) the variations in the effective subsidy in this scheme, as distinct from many others, were due to changes in premium values rather than changes in the entitlement rates.

and 4), which was applicable to mills situated over a distance of 322 kilometres from the ports of Bombay, Madras, and Calcutta. (5) Finally, the premia assumed on the entitlements were often quite high: as much as 150 per cent for coal-tar dyes and 100 per cent for caustic soda.

For rayon textiles, covered in Table 19.6, the premia were even higher and, taking also into account drawbacks and rebates of excise duty and the current entitlement rate, the effective *ad valorem* subsidy on exports worked out to as high as 300 per cent on several items during 1965. Table 19·6 shows these calculations for six different items in rayon textiles: for each, the 50 per cent entitlement of yarn carried the then current 400 per cent premium thus yielding an immediate subsidy of 200 per cent on f.o.b. export value, whereas the overall subsidy (taking into account *other* incentives such as rebates and drawbacks) works out to around 250–300 per cent on f.o.b. export value.[1]

We may also note that examination of the differentials between f.o.b. export and domestic sale prices of many chemical, engineering, and other items indicated differentials in the range of 80–120 per cent on domestic sale price during this period. This would, however, reflect the effective export subsidy available for such exports by atomistic exporters only in a purely competitive situation, not otherwise (see Appendix II). As a *general* proposition, it is incorrect to deduce, if a product is priced at Rs. x per unit in India and at Rs. y ($<x$) f.o.b. for export, that the degree of effective 'devaluation' or the effective, *ad valorem* export subsidy rate involved is $\dfrac{x-y}{y}$. This is a valid argument only when there is perfect competition in domestic sales *and* the firm is able to sell varying amounts in foreign markets without affecting the international price.[2] For example, it is well known that manufacturing firms often charge a higher price at home than abroad (as Milton Gilbert documented over twenty-five years ago for U.S. firms)[3] the

---

[1] Even this astonishing subsidy left exports only marginally profitable in relation to home sales.

[2] For elaboration of this argument, see Appendix II.

[3] Cf. M. Gilbert, 'A Sample Study of Differences Between Domestic and Export Pricing Policy of United States Corporations', *Temporary National Economic Committee Monograph* No. 6, Part I. Washington, D.C., Government Printing Office, 1940, pp. 3–93. Forty-five of seventy-six interviewee corporations or groups were found charging lower export than domestic prices.

TABLE 19.6

EXPORT INCENTIVES FOR RAYON PIECEGOODS AS AT JUNE 1965: SOME SAMPLE SORTS

(1) Sort No.	(2) Warp	(3) Weft	(4) Width, inches	(5) Drawback of duty for yarn used in making cloth	(6) Rebate of excise duty	(7) F.O.B. value	(8) Entitlem't at international price	(9) 50% entitlem't value at market rate	(10) Entitlem't for import of dyes and chemicals	(11) Value at market rate of (10)	(12) Total realization due to export 5+6+7+9+11	(13) Market rate in local market
2100 viscose crapee dyed	100D viscose 110 ends per inch	100D viscose 68 picks	36	0·42	0·09	0·70	0·72	0·35 (1·40)a	n.p. 0·013	0·002	2·63	2·50
1532 viscose satin	150D Br viscose 220 ends per inch	150D Br viscose 52 pick per inch	36	0·72	0·09	0·80	0·96	0·40 (1·60)a	0·016	0·024	3·23	2·80
15244	150D Br viscose 220 ends per inch	150D Br viscose 52 pick per inch	42	0·84	0·11	0·96	1·20	0·48 (1·92)a	0·02	0·030	3·86	3·12
50942 nylon Georgette	15D nylon 168/inch	40D nylon 92/inch	45	0·52	0·12	1·40	1·40	0·70 (2·80)a	0·028	0·04	5·92	4·70
			(All above-mentioned four varieties are dyed and bleached varieties)									
50942 nylon Georgette print	15D nylon 168/inch	40D nylon 92/inch	45	0·52	0·12	1·60	1·60	0·60 (3·20)a	0·028	0·04	5·48	5·20
2100 viscose crepe print	100 viscose 110 ends per inch	100D viscose 68 picks	36	0·42	0·09	0·90	0·94	0·45 (1·90)a	0·013	0·02	3·33	3·00

a The figure given is 400 per cent of the above-mentioned item, i.e. the market value of entitlement in June 1965.

Source: An exporting mill in Bombay.

most-cited reason being the differences in their 'monopoly power' between the two markets.

Changes and variability in the export incentive offered by the entitlements schemes

So far we have considered the questions of the fixation of entitlement rates, the transferability of the entitlements and the average level which the premium on transferable entitlements seemed to reach in the markets during 1964 and 1965. From this, it is easy to infer, as in fact we did for certain rayon items and cotton piecegoods in detail, the effective subsidy which was available, at a single point of time, on export sales to an atomistic exporter. But the question remains whether this export incentive tended to be variable, with the effective subsidy on exports changing from time to time.[1]

There is little doubt that the export incentives were variable under the entitlement schemes, although it is difficult to quantify this variability accurately in view of the paucity of reliable information for many schemes. There were three major reasons why such variability arose:

(1) changes in the *coverage* of the schemes

(i) products were included and/or excluded from period to period; and

(ii) exports to certain areas were excluded and/or their entitlements were changed from time to time;

(2) changes in entitlement for *given* products, arising from changes in formula used or revised notions about the incentives, from time to time; and

(3) changes in the premium on the entitlements, arising from—

(i) revisions in rules governing the transferability of entitlements; or

(ii) changes in the coverage of the items for whose import the entitlements could be used; or

(iii) inevitable, periodic shifts in the premium which entitlement licences (with given coverage and transferability) enjoyed in the market; or any combination of all these factors.

We will examine each of these factors in turn.

---

[1] How far this instability was a result of the special characteristics of the entitlement schemes, and how far it would have afflicted alternative forms of export subsidization, is a matter we discuss later.

(1) Changes in the *product and area coverage* of the entitlement schemes have already been shown by us to have occurred occasionally. The reasons for such changes were rarely made explicit; but they must have reflected policy reaction to short-run changes in the balance of payments position with certain currency blocs (involving area restrictions on eligibility for import entitlements) and short-run changes in domestic availabilites (involving product exclusion from, or inclusion in, the entitlement schemes).

Instances of such changes in both upward and downward directions were not at all difficult to find in the period up to 1961/2. Subsequently, however, the changes were overwhelmingly in the direction of 'liberalization'. This reflected the growing pressure to make exports more profitable, on the part of the exporters, combined with an accommodating Ministry whose objective was to maximize export earnings.[1] Even the few 'restrictive' clauses with respect to product coverage, which lingered on, were most probably prompted by user–producer lobbies whose power outweighed that of the producers of the product.

(2) Changes in entitlements for individual products, arising from *variations in the rates of entitlement* available, were also a feature of the operation of these schemes. Once again, however, the post-1962 trend (except for certain notorious items such as rayon and art silks) was by and large in favour of increasing entitlements. Thus, as we noted earlier while discussing minimum entitlements, the period July–December 1964 marked a shift in the entitlements for 'chemicals and allied products' from a minimum of 20 per cent of f.o.b. export value to 40 per cent, thereby resulting in an upward shift in the entitlement rate of several products. This was also the case for 'paper and allied products' where the minimum entitlement rate was again raised to 40 per cent during the same period. Upward revisions for *individual* products also were common.

Most of these upward revisions, of course, took place in the face of 'rules' such as that the entitlements would be at twice the value

[1] For example, the Government decided in 1964 to allow import entitlement against exports of drugs and pharmaceuticals (excluding sera, vaccines, and alcoholoids and their derivatives) to Afghanistan. Similarly, during the same period (July–December 1964), several new products were made eligible for entitlements under the Paper and Allied Products export promotion scheme. Again, the entitlements under the scheme were extended to several new items during 1963–4.

of import content. Moreover, explicit changes in these rules themselves had also occurred in earlier years. For example, in the late 1950s when several manufacturing industries were first given export incentives under the Development Wing (Ministry of Commerce) schemes, the general rule was that the entitlement would be at 75 per cent of the value of the goods exported (by a producer) *in excess of* exports in 1956, or twice the value of imported raw materials used in the manufacture of the goods exported, whichever was less, so that there was a concept of entitlement being available only for incremental exports which disappeared completely from the scene. The introduction of the dryfruit entitlements schemes, to provide additional incentives for many exporters who merely had to plead a case of heavy losses from exports to secure this benefit in addition to their normal entitlements, was another telling example of this liberalization of benefits.

(3) While, however, changes in the area, coverage, and rates were generally in an upward direction from 1961/2, so that instability (in the sense of rise and fall in effective subsidy) could not be attributed, generally speaking, to such changes, this does not appear to have been the case with *changes in the premium* earned on the entitlements.

Changes in the premium were, of course, inherent in the scheme. However, they arose also from policy changes in the coverage of permissible imports or in the transferability of entitlements or in the permissible source of imports.

(i) We have noted already that the transferability of entitlements was, in the vast majority of export promotion schemes, eventually made possible in the sense that the entitlement could be assigned to, and issued in the name of, any producer *within* the industries covered by the same export promotion scheme. (This was a liberalization away from the original rules which required that imports be used only within the exporters' own plant.) No changes were made in this regard and therefore changes in the premium cannot be explained in this fashion.

(ii) Changes in the list of permissible imports, on the other hand, continued to be quite frequent. These changes, when restrictive, not merely took the form of excluding certain items; frequently the entitlements were even split up into specified percentage maxima for different groups of materials and these maxima were changed from time to time, resulting in changes in the importability of the affected items.[1]

We may recall that entitlements eventually came to be expendable on imports of capital goods, equipment, and spares. In this respect the trend was definitely in the direction of liberalization. The earlier rules had frequently excluded such imports altogether or permitted them up to only very limited amounts such as 5–10 per cent of f.o.b. export value. The liberalization, as in the case of chemicals and allied products for example, was at times complete, with *entire* entitlements available for such imports. However, it would be a mistake to forget that, despite such overall liberalization, the permissible imports of specific capital goods and spares continued to be controlled and hence changes in permissible imports and thus in the value of the entitlements continued. The D.G.T.D. generally controlled these imports. And here, as with materials and components, the domestic supply position affected what was allowed to be imported. Instability, therefore, continued to afflict this area in much the same way as with raw materials and components.

(iii) Periodic changes in the rules governing the use of entitlements occurred also in their currency-area coverage. However in this respect the trend was in favour of liberalization. Thus the standard rule that exports to rupee-payment-agreement countries would get entitlements usable only on imports from those countries (as a group) was steadily liberalized in some cases: for example, the percentage of 'revalidation' of such entitlements, for non-rupee-payment countries, was increased from 25 to 40 per cent, as of July–December 1964, for chemicals and allied products.

Thus, the general *trend* with respect to product and area coverage, rates, and sources open for imports was upward and towards a greater range and size of effective export subsidization. Further, there were factors such as changes in the permissible basket of imports which, quite apart from 'normal' fluctuations that might characterize the premium in view of factors such as a changing balance of payments situation, imparted a degree of

[1] If it can be assumed that the importability of items was excluded or cut only when the premium on their import was reduced, then obviously the change was immaterial from the point of view of the profitability of the entitlement. But this argument does raise the natural retort that, if indeed the restriction did not reduce profitability, it was not necessary either, since the entitlement could not then have been used for importing the excluded item anyway. Hence, we cannot escape the conclusion that instability in the *de facto* profitability of entitlements was undoubtedly introduced by the frequent changes in permissible imports.

instability to the effective subsidy earned by individual exporters under the entitlement schemes.

Indian export promotion policies were thus based essentially on the entitlement schemes described at length by us and had extended by 1965/6 in one form or another, to nearly 80 per cent of Indian export earnings, although the magnitude of export-subsidization they involved was unforeseeably discriminatory in incidence among the different items.[1]

While we analyse in the next chapter the economic efficiency of these schemes as instruments of export promotion, as compared with alternative instruments such as direct *ad valorem* subsidies or devaluation, we merely note here that these schemes were undoubtedly instrumental in sustaining the spurt in Indian export performance during the Third Plan. In fact, while these schemes suffered from numerous defects, they managed to underline one important lesson for Indian planners: that export earnings *could* be increased by making exports profitable. They served thus to remove, from the Indian scene, the widespread 'elasticity pessimism' which had characterized earlier thinking and policies. By bringing whole new ranges of products into the field of export, quite apart from offsetting the increasing cost disadvantage of even traditional exports such as cotton textiles, the entitlement schemes (and associated fiscal measures) managed to get export performance off the hook which an overvalued exchange rate constituted.[2]

B. EXPANSION OF EXPORTS TO SOCIALIST COUNTRIES[3]

In addition to these policies of export subsidization, the promotional measures extended to an active exploration and use of the

---

[1] It is remarkable, however, that the Ministry of International Trade continued, for long, to understate seriously the coverage of the entitlement schemes. On this issue, see Bhagwati, op. cit. (sub-section on *Coverage*).

[2] The resulting diversification of exports can be seen, *within* the group 'engineering', by computing the well-known commodity concentration index

$$100\sqrt{\sum \frac{X_{ij}^2}{X_j}}$$

where X_{ij} = India's exports of engineering goods for sub-group i and X_j = India's total exports of engineering goods. When this index is computed by eighty commodity sub-groups for 1956–8 and 1962–4, the value of the index shows a decline from 27·2 to 17·8. The corresponding *geographical* concentration index, by 92 countries, shows a similar decline from 26·4 to 21·6. Cf. Bhagwati, op. cit., p. 72.

[3] These are the Soviet Union, Poland, Czechoslovakia, Bulgaria, Rumania, East Germany, and Yugoslavia.

possibilities of trade with socialist countries. As we have already noted (Table 19.1), nearly half of the improvement in Third Plan performance was via exports to socialist countries. This trade occurred within the context of trade agreements.[1] The important aspects of this trade may be commented upon.

(1) A part of this trade merely reflected the repayments (in kind) of Soviet-bloc aid. This aid was almost exclusively of a twelve-year maturity, with a 2 per cent interest rate, and repayable in kind. During the Second Plan, amortization and interest payments came to 11·9 per cent of exports to socialist countries and, despite striking growth in exports, was still at 9·6 per cent of total exports during the Third Plan.[2]

(2) The trade was conducted via the State Trading Corporation, although this was not a necessary condition for trade with socialist countries (as evidenced by their trade with other 'capitalist' countries).

(3) The prices at which exports were effected do not appear to have been unduly low, in relation to sales to 'traditional', non-socialist markets. Dharm Narain, on comparing unit values in the two markets, after carefully rejecting as many non-comparable items as possible, found that, if anything, the unit values for exports to the socialist countries were generally more favourable to India, rather than less, thus conforming to the opinion of 'knowledgeable business circles [that] the prices paid by some of the socialist countries have been 5–10 per cent higher for India's internationally traded commodities'.[3]

(4) How far was the expansion of exports to the socialist bloc a net expansion? And how much did it cut into sales to traditional markets? This question has two facets. (i) On the one hand, we could argue that the socialist countries, having (for political reasons) decided to import more from India, disposed of the commodities in *other* markets, thereby offsetting the apparent gain in India's export performance. This could happen through direct shunting of the goods to third markets (without prior importation and re-

---

[1] Such trade agreements have been signed with several other countries as well. These agreements range from simple expressions of willingness to increase trade, and attached lists of possible commodities, to more specific and contractual obligations with clearing arrangements. The agreements with the socialist countries belonged generally to the latter variety.

[2] For the figures, cf. Dharm Narain, op. cit., Table 17.

[3] Ibid., pp. 44–5.

export) or through re-export or, what is yet more difficult to as-
certain, through exportation or reduced importation of *substitut-
able* items of export interest to India. (ii) On the other hand, we
could argue from the supply side and, in view of the analysis of
supply difficulties for different commodities in the preceding
chapter, suspect that expansion of exports to socialist countries,
under trade agreements, might have cut into the hesitant expansion
of Indian exports to traditional markets.

The former question has been ably analysed by Dharm Narain
who, on comparing the partner-country trade data for socialist
countries and India, as also the import data of India's traditional
customers (with respect to *their* import from socialist countries of
items exported by India *to* socialist countries), finds little concrete
evidence for the re-routing or re-export phenomenon, despite the
prevalence of considerable criticism of such a practice among
Indian business circles.[1] On the more intractable question of supply
difficulties, Dharm Narain's conclusions are again favourable to
the thesis that the trade with socialist countries represented largely
a net addition.[2]

Having described, at length, the principal features of India's
export performance and policies through the Third Plan period,
we now proceed to a systematic analysis of the *economic* efficiency
of these policies of export promotion: for there are important
and interesting lessons to learn here. This analysis will also provide
a useful backdrop to our description and evaluation of the entire
pattern of effective exchange rates that the Indian economy had
come to acquire prior to the devaluation of the rupee in June 1966
and the attempts thereafter at altering this precise pattern.

---

[1] However, his excellent analysis does not extend to the more difficult empirical
problem of the effect on 'substitutes', already referred to by us in the text.

[2] 'Even though the quantification of actual displacement has not been possible,
[our analysis seems] to suggest that something like three-fourths, at least, of
India's exports to socialist countries have not been at the expense of her
exports to other markets,' op. cit., p. 29. However, Dharm Narain's analysis
is not always fully satisfactory on this issue and may have under-estimated
the extent to which exports to traditional markets would *otherwise* have
increased. For example, while he carefully notes that the decline in India's
share in the London tea market continued at almost the same pace during
the Third Plan as before, he is not necessarily correct in inferring that,
therefore, the expansion of tea exports to socialist countries was wholly a
net gain: particularly so, when (as we have already noted) supply difficulties
were a major explanatory factor in this declining share through the earlier
decade.

APPENDIX I

Six Tables Relating to Tax Concessions and Credits for Exports and Export Promotion Schemes

The Tables and statements relating to tax concessions and credits for exports, as also to details of the import entitlement schemes (including engineering goods and chemicals), have been brought together in this Appendix.

TABLE 19.7
THE PROVISIONS OF FINANCE ACTS, 1963, AND 1964, FOR REBATES ON
INCOME TAX FOR EXPORTS

The Finance Act, 1963, introduced a concession in the form of a rebate of income tax on 2 per cent of exports (or sales in India for exports) of articles manufactured by specified industries; it was contained in Sub-section (5) of Section 2 of the Finance Act. The industries covered by this rebate were those specified in the First Schedule to the Industries (Development and Regulation) Act of 1951 with certain exceptions including fuels, certain textiles, sugar, vegetable oils and vanaspati, cement, gypsum products, and cigarettes. The Finance Act, 1964, slightly modified the list of eligible industries, (with non-applicability extended to newsprint, pulp, arms, and ammunition), while maintaining the form of the tax incentive intact. The concession was to be withdrawn along with that granted by the Finance Act, 1962, through the Finance (No. 2) Act, 1967, with effect from 6 June 1966 when the rupee was devalued.

The industries covered in the First Schedule of the Industries (Development and Regulation) Act, 1951, included the following broad groups of industries:

1. Metallurgical industries: ferrous, non-ferrous
2. Fuels
3. Boilers and steam generating plants
4. Prime movers (other than electrical generators)
5. Electrical equipment
6. Telecommunications
7. Transportation
8. Industrial machinery (specialized equipment, general items of machinery used in several industries and other items of industrial machinery)
9. Machine tools
10. Agricultural machinery
11. Earth-moving machinery
12. Miscellaneous mechanical and engineering industries
13. Commercial, office, and household equipment
14. Medical and surgical appliances
15. Industrial instruments
16. Scientific instruments
17. Mathematical, surveying, and drawing instruments
18. Fertilizers
19. Chemicals (other than fertilizers)
20. Photographic raw film and paper
21. Dye-stuffs
22. Drugs and pharmaceuticals
23. Textiles (including those dyed, printed, or otherwise processed)

TABLE 19.7—*continued*

24. Paper and pulp, including paper products
25. Sugar
26. Fermentation industries
27. Food-processing industries
28. Vegetable oils and vanaspati
29. Soaps, cosmetics, and toilet preparations
30. Rubber goods
31. Leather, leather goods, and pickers
32. Glue and gelatin
33. Glass
34. Ceramics
35. Cement and gypsum products
36. Timber products
37. Defence industries (arms and ammunition)
38. Miscellaneous industries (cigarettes)

Source: *Finance Acts*, 1963 and 1964, Government of India, New Delhi; and *Industries (Development and Regulation) Act*, 1951, Government of India, New Delhi.

TABLE 19.8

SCHEDULE OF TAX CREDITS UNDER THE FINANCE ACT, 1965
(per cent of f.o.b. value)

(A) *2 per cent tax credit*
 1. Jute manufactures
 2. Tea (loose), other than green tea
 3. Cashew kernels in consumer packing of 2 kg. and less
 4. De-oiled rice bran

(B) *5 per cent tax credit*
 1. Tea in consumer packs of 1 kg. and less
 2. Green tea
 3. Calcined magnesite

(C) *10 per cent tax credit*
 1. Iron ore fines (raw, washed or pelletized)
 2. Lumpy iron ore originating from points (mines) whose nearest loading point is not less than 200 kilometres away from the port of loading, irrespective of the mode of transport between such loading point and such port.
 3. Coal
 4. Fresh fruits
 5. Surgical cotton and dressings
 6. Guar gum refined, pulverized or treated
 7. Myrobalan fruit extract
 8. Crushed bones
 9. Refractories
 10. Tiles and earthenware

(D) *15 per cent tax credit*
 1. Manganese ore containing 48 per cent or less of manganese (Mn.)
 2. All mineral ores other than iron and manganese ores
 3. Ferro-manganese
 4. Alcoholic beverages
 5. Processed mica powder

Source: *Finance Act*, 1965, Government of India, New Delhi.

TABLE 19.9

THE TOTAL NUMBER OF EXPORT PROMOTION SCHEMES WITH IMPORT ENTITLEMENTS IN FORCE IN EARLY 1965[a] WITH CORRESPONDING DESCRIPTION OF ENTITLEMENTS AND VALUES OF EXPORTS IN 1963 AND 1964

Export promotion scheme	Broad magnitude and some salient features of import entitlements	Value of exports in 1963 (Rs. lakh)	Value of exports in 1964 (Rs. lakh)
(1)	(2)	(3)	(4)
(A) Schemes where import entitlements are generous and incentive-oriented and/or explicitly admitted by government to be such.			
1. Engineering goods	(i) High entitlements, ranging up to 100 per cent of export value for several items (ii) Varying entitlements for different products[b] (iii) Entitlements usable for specified but numerous components, raw materials and also for capital goods and spare parts up to a specified percentage of the entitlement	1,264	1,322
2. Chemicals and allied products	(i) High entitlements, ranging up to 90 per cent of export value for one item (ii) Varying entitlements for different products[b] (iii) Entitlements usable for specified but numerous components and raw materials or alternatively for capital goods and spare parts	436	834
3. Plastics and linoleum goods	(i) High and varying entitlements, ranging up to 75 per cent for most products (ii) Entitlements usable for specified raw materials (plus unlisted items, on application if approved) and also for capital goods and spare parts in some cases	29	37
4. Certain natural essential oils	High entitlements fixed generally at twice the value of import content with minimum of 20 per cent	304	299
5. Handicrafts	(i) Fairly high and varying entitlements, ranging up to 30, 50, and even 80 per cent (ii) Entitlements usable for specified materials	2,900	2,469
6. Finished leather and leather products	(i) Fairly high entitlements: starting at 10–20 per cent, and 35 per cent for leather manufactures and travel goods, and 50 per cent for leather washers (ii) Entitlements usable for specified materials (plus unlisted items, on successful application) and also, in some cases, capital goods up to a limited percentage of entitlement	448	573
7. Woollen carpets, rugs, and druggets	(i) Fairly large entitlements, ranging between 25 and 45 per cent of export value (ii) Entitlements available for permissible raw materials	516 (included in handicrafts)	542 (included in handicrafts)

Item	Entitlement	Total: 5,532	Total: 7,247
9. Cotton textiles	(i) Large and varying entitlements, going over 100 per cent for certain items		
	(ii) Entitlements available, in various specified percentages, for raw cotton, machinery, and		
	of which		
	(i) Cotton fabrics	4,887	5,834
	(ii) Cotton yarn and thread (estimated)	645	614
	(iii) Other cotton textiles	795	799
10. Books, journals, paper, and paper products	(i) High and varying entitlements, ranging up to 75 per cent in several cases	160	208
	(ii) Entitlements available for specified materials or alternatively entirely for capital goods and spare parts		
11. Fish and fish products	(i) Entitlements up to 15 per cent for fish and fish products/preparations	559	653
	(ii) Entitlements available for various specified raw materials, within different limits; and also within specified limits, for consumable stores, machinery and spare parts		
12. Processed foods	(i) Entitlements ranging principally over 10–20 per cent	30	58
	(ii) Entitlements available for specified materials, and also, within 10 per cent of f.o.b. value limit, for machinery and spare parts		
13. Coir yarn and coir products[e]	(i) Entitlements very limited in value, ranging only between 2 and 10 per cent of f.o.b. value	1,191	1,144
	(ii) Entitlements available only for specified raw materials and spares		
14. Tanned hide and skins[d]	Entitlements up to 9 per cent for specified raw materials and additional 10 per cent for capital goods and spares		1,200 (estimated)
15. Cashew kernels[d]	Domestic entitlements for tinplates (used in containers) are significantly in excess of the quantity used in exports; for box strappings, they equal the actual use; and varying cashew entitlements are available on application	2,144	2,659
16. Pearls, precious stones, diamonds, imitation jewellery, etc.	(i) High entitlements, up to 80 per cent of f.o.b. value	1,508	1,869
	(ii) Entitlements available for specified materials and also within the limited percentages of entitlements, for machinery and tools, and chemicals		
17. Gold jewellery and gold articles (Parts III and IV, for 14 carat gold or less)	(i) Entitlement at 50 per cent of f.o.b. value	(included in handicrafts)	(included in handicrafts)
	(ii) Entitlement to be available for specified materials such as diamonds, pearls, unset, and even for chemicals and varnishes as also machinery up to limited amounts		
18. Wooden manufactures and timber products	(i) High and varying entitlements, ranging up to 75 per cent in some cases	n.a.	79 (estimated)
	(ii) Entitlements generally to be used for specified materials and sometimes within specified limits for capital goods		
19. Fabrics of synthetic fibre and spunglass (including art silk fabrics)			

TABLE 19.9—continued

Export promotion scheme	Broad magnitude and some salient features of import entitlements	Value of exports in 1963 (Rs. lakh)	Value of exports in 1964 (Rs. lakh)
(1)	(2)	(3)	(4)
20. Vanaspati/hydrogenated oils and refined vegetable oils; refined castor oil, groundnut oil, cotton seed oil, etc.	(i) Entitlements range principally between 60 and 80 per cent of export value (ii) Entitlements generally available for specified raw materials, as also, within specified limits, for capital goods and spare parts	1,819	1,465
21. Cinematographic films and other films	(i) Entitlements range from 37½ per cent on unexposed to 75 per cent on exposed films (ii) Entitlements available for specified but wide range of materials, accessories, and, within specified limits, for equipment also	198	218
22. Agarbattis (and Chandan Dhoop)	(i) Entitlements at 25 per cent of f.o.b. value (ii) Entitlements available for specified raw materials and accessories only	28	29
23. Ink tablets*d*	(i) Entitlements from 35 to 50 per cent of f.o.b. value (ii) Entitlements available for specified raw materials only	n.a.	n.a.
24. Breakfast cocoa*d*	(i) Entitlements claimed to be up to twice the import content, subject to a maximum of 75 per cent of f.o.b. value (ii) Entitlements available only for cocoa beans	n.a.	n.a.
TOTAL		(Approximately) 19,270	22,384
(B) Schemes where import entitlements are claimed to be very limited, and/or are often restricted to imports of only balancing equipment, spare parts, etc., to the exclusion of raw materials and components; *and also* where the inherent export incentive aspect of such entitlements is explicitly ignored in governmental, public documents.			
1. Salt	Limited entitlement, at 10 per cent of f.o.b. value, available only for machinery, equipment, spares, tools, testing apparatus, chemicals, caustic soda, etc.	43	86
2. Unmanufactured tobacco	Ostensibly only replacement and minimum import entitlements allowed	2,283	2,239
3. Cigars	(i) Entitlements vary and can go up to 50 per cent for cigars using imported tobacco (ii) Available only for importing tobacco, etc. (iii) There does not appear to be any explicit incentive in the form of larger entitlement than import content	n.a.	n.a.
4. Minerals and mineral ores (covering	Entitlements available for 'approved' varieties of machinery,	*Total:* 6,911	*Total:* 7,070

Item	Description	(iii) Kyanite / (iv) Other minerals / (v) Ferro-manganese	(iii) Kyanite / (iv) Other / (v) Ferro-manganese
(iii) Kyanite		72	35
(iv) Other minerals	the f.o.b. value of exports'. 2½ per cent on special chemicals also permitted, within overall entitlement	143	65
(v) Ferro-manganese		41	
5. Walnut kernels	Entitlement at 2 per cent of f.o.b. value, available only for importing specified raw materials (butter or parchment paper)	148 (walnuts)	179 (walnuts)
6. Ship-repairing	Only replacement imports ostensibly granted as entitlements	n.a.	n.a.
7. Tea	1 per cent of f.o.b. value available as entitlement, to be placed at the disposal of Tea Board for final allocation among planters, for machinery. equipment, apparatus, appliances, etc.	13,500	12,537
8. Coffee	(i) 1 per cent of f.o.b. value available as entitlement to be placed at disposal of Coffee Board for final allocation among planters, for machinery, equipment, etc. (ii) 3 per cent of f.o.b. value available for chicory powder	778	1,371
9. Bones (crushed, grist, dust, etc.)	Entitlements at 10 per cent of f.o.b. value of exports, available for permissible items of equipment, spares, tools, and partly for certain chemicals	244	271
10. Oil cakes	3 per cent entitlement for de-oiled cakes, available for permissible raw materials; 10 per cent for de-oiled linseed cake and 75 per cent for copra oilcake, for importing copra and/or palm oil	3,462	3,766
11. Bristles	Entitlement up to 2½ per cent of f.o.b. value of exports, available for specified materials only	167	132
12. Dressed horse and cow tail hair	Entitlement up to 2½ per cent of f.o.b. value of exports, available for specified materials only	n.a.	n.a.
TOTAL		(Approximately) 27,538	27,653

a The dates vary, but almost never prior to February 1964. The information is claimed to be valid as of May 1965. Some minor schemes have been aggregated (as in (A) 17) and a very tiny number ignored as too trivial in importance.

b For both engineering goods and chemicals, separate lists of the varying rates of entitlement at 1 February 1964, have been reproduced in the Appendix, to illustrate the vast variations within each Scheme.

c Coir yarn and coir products, alone among the schemes in Table (A), had a rather limited entitlement. But they were explicitly treated as an Incentive Scheme by the Ministry of Commerce.

d (1) Although cashew kernels have been included in List (A) here, the Ministry of Commerce listed them, in its *Annual Report, 1964–5*, as exported 'without special assistance' and by implication, without any *import* entitlement of significance. However, the import entitlement both *de jure* and *de facto*, for box strappings and raw cashew, seemed to work on an openly incentive basis. The entitlement for (domestic) tinplate was even more candidly on an incentive (i.e. greater-than-replacement) basis.

(2) Wooden manufactures and timber products also were omitted by the Ministry of Commerce from the list of exports with special assistance; and here also, this seemed wrong.

(3) Ink tablets and breakfast cocoa also belong legitimately to List (A).

(4) So also do tanned hides and skins.

Source: Bhagwati, op. cit.; the primary source being: *Report on Export Promotion* (for July–December 1964).

TABLE 19.10
MAJOR CHANGES IN THE EXPORT PROMOTION SCHEMES (WITH RESPECT TO ENTITLEMENTS)

Up to and excluding April–September 1958	*From April–September 1958 to, but excluding, April–September 1960*	*From April–September 1960 to, but excluding, April 1963–March 1964*	*From April 1963 to March 1964 onwards until elimination in June 1966*
(1) Single scheme, with commodities specified in schedule to Appendix 23, existed. Individual import entitlements were listed	(1) The scheme, hitherto operated under schedule to Appendix 23, continued, with virtually similar coverage and intentions	(1) The old, 'schedule' scheme now became *Scheme No. 3*. The commodities covered continued to be similar and they were listed in Annexure III to Appendix 23. The licensing continued to be done by the Port Authorities (C.C.I. & E.'s branches)	(1) Part I and II schemes were in vogue; both listed commodities. *Part II* corresponded to the preceding period's scheme No. 3. They were administered by the C.C.I. & E.'s Port Authorities
	(2) A new scheme, to be operated by the Development Wing of the Ministry of C. & I., was introduced covering many new manufacturing industries, listed in the *Redbook*	(2) The Development Wing Scheme now became Scheme No. 1, with Annexure I to Appendix 23 listing the eligible items. Over time, the commodities as covered dwindled as they were increasingly transferred to Scheme No. 2 below	(2) Part I Schemes, corresponded to the preceding period's schemes Nos. 1 and 2 or rather to the Scheme No. 2 because the coverage of Scheme No. 1 had practically reduced to nullity by April 1963. These schemes were administered by the Export Promotion Councils
(i) Additional features:		(3) There was also Scheme No. 2 which was run by Export Promotion Councils and which increasingly cut into the Development Wing Schemes. Annexure II to App. 23 contained the list of eligible items	
(a) Advance entitlement, against bond, was possible			
(b) Commodities, not listed, could be considered for inclusion on application to C.C. & I., New Delhi		(i) Priority among schemes was laid down	
(ii) This scheme had been operated, *de facto*, for a varying number of commodities from practically 1950 onwards	(3) Certain *ad hoc* schemes were also introduced explicitly, to be operated by the Directorate of Export Promotion. No information given		
	(i) Multiple entitlement, to more than one scheme above, was allowed on application and consideration, until April–September 1959		
	(ii) A special, and separately listed, scheme was in operation for art silk yarn		

Source: *Redbooks* on Import Control Policy, Government of India, New Delhi.

TABLE 19.11

IMPORT ENTITLEMENT FOR PRODUCTS COVERED BY THE ENGINEERING
EXPORT PROMOTION SCHEME, AS A PERCENTAGE OF THE F.O.B. VALUE
OF EXPORT, AS IN EARLY 1964

Part I. General engineering and electrical manufactures

(A) *20 per cent*

1. Wooden furniture
2. Gramophone records and sundries
3. Bicycle components and accessories:
    (i)   Bells made of steel sheets and strips
    (ii)   Stands
    (iii) Gear cover
    (iv)   Mudgear
    (v)   Crank cotter pins
    (vi)   Lamp brackets
    (vii) Saddles
    (viii) Fork
    (ix)   Handle bars
    (x)   Brake parts and brake shoes
    (xi)   Any other items not specified elsewhere
4. Electric motor horns d.c. 12 volts

(B) *30 per cent*

1. R.C.A. re-recording system
2. Copper coated mica-elements

(C) *40 per cent*

1. Fabricated steel structurals including transmission line towers (made of
   mild steel) and poles, pressed steel tanks, bridge and roof sections, sub-
   station structures and railway wagons.
Note. In the case of towers (incorporating high tensile steel), import entitlement
would be twice the imported content subject to the maximum of 75 per cent
f.o.b. value of exports.
2. Steel pipes and tubes and tubular poles, plain or galvanized and fittings
   thereof
3. Mild steel arc-welding electrodes
4. Bolts, nuts, rivets, wire nails, screws, split and cotton pins
5. Ferrous builders' hardware
6. Conduit pipes
7. Steel drums and containers
8. Tinplate containers
9. Steel expanded metal
10. Steel weld-mash
11. Steel furniture for home, office, and security purposes (other than tubular)
12. Railway track fasteners fittings and accessories
13. Steel doors and windows
14. Steel trunks
15. Electric fans, all types
16. Electric motors, all types
17. Electric transformers
18. Electric control gear and switchgear
19. Electric lighting fittings (other than plastic)

TABLE 19.11—*continued*

20. Sewing machines
21. Weighing machines and scales
22. Mathematical instruments
23. Industrial and scientific instruments
24. Hurricane lanterns
25. Steel and tinplate trays and advertisement novelties
26. Agricultural implements and tools
27. Barbed wires
28. Coated abrasives
29. Cutlery other than stainless steel cutlery
30. Calendar rims and hangers
31. Duplicators
32. Earth augers
33. G.I. buckets (made of G.P. sheets)
34. Gaffer grips with steel studs
35. Handpumps and components
36. Ice cans
37. Rolling shutters
38. Sluice valves
39. Stove cleaning needles
40. Stay assembly rods
41. Thermit portions
42. Watering cans
43. W.I. split pulleys
44. Steel and tinplate washers
45. Paint brushes
46. Bicycle components and accessories:

(i) B.B. axle	(iv) Cones	(vii) Gear and cranks
(ii) B.B. shells	(v) Cups	(viii) Handle
(iii) Hubs	(vi) Seat and chain stay	(ix) Pedals

47. Jigs and fixtures
48. Trainlighting dynamos
49. Iron and steel castings

Note. Notwithstanding anything contained in this scheme, it is open to persons exporting iron and steel castings to make a declaration to the Council that, in view of the fact that he is a merchant–exporter, or that no imported materials are required for use in his factory or factories, he is unable to utilize the aforesaid import entitlement and thereupon the Council may give him any other facilities which have been approved by the Department of International Trade, in lieu of his not claiming the aforesaid import entitlement.

50. Umbrella sticks, and metallic fittings of all types excluding umbrella ribs.
51. Hair belting
52. R.C.C. pipes
53. Burners for hurricane lanterns
54.

(D)

Complete bicycles: Rs. 30 per complete bicycle. Of this not more than Rs. 4 per bicycle may be utilized for import of components, namely, chains, three-speed hubs, and freewheels and the balance for the import of permissible raw materials and consumable stores.

TABLE 19.11—*continued*

Note. I. In the case of exporters who are members of the Cycle Manufacturers' Association of India, Calcutta, the application to the Engineering Export Promotion Council, Calcutta, should be accompanied by a certificate from the Export Committee of the Cycle Manufacturers' Association of India, Calcutta, certifying the actual exports, both in quantity of complete bicycles and value, made by the exporter concerned and the amount of cash subsidy paid to him from out of the Cycle Export Pool.

Note II. A bicycle fitted with saddle, tyres, and tubes would be considered to be a complete bicycle for the purpose of claiming an import entitlement of Rs. 30. Other accessories will qualify for extra entitlement.

(E) *50 per cent*

1. G.I. buckets
2. Tubular steel furniture
3. Paper pins and clips
4. Umbrellas (see notes 1 and 2 below)

   (i) *Umbrella exporters*
       $32\frac{1}{2}$%—*to be utilized for import of:*

       (*a*) Coloured or printed umbrella cloth made of nylon art silk or other synthetic fibres, excluding cotton umbrella cloth
       (*b*) Components for folding umbrella frames
       (*c*) Automatic devices for opening and closing of umbrellas
       (*d*) Elastic tapes
       (*e*) Permissible dyes and chemicals, for a value not exceeding 15 per cent of the face value of the licence

The permissible dyes chemicals, import of which may be allowed shall be those mentioned in the Annexure to public Notice No. 87—ITC(PN)/58, dated 31 October 1958, as modified from time to time.

   (ii) *Umbrella ribs manufacturers who have supplied ribs to umbrella exporters:*
        $17\frac{1}{2}$ *per cent to be utilized for the import of:*

        (*a*) Mild steel wire rods or wire
        (*b*) High carbon steel wire rods or wire
        (*c*) High carbon steel strips
        (*d*) Non-ferrous tubes: brass, aluminium and aluminium alloy, copper and copper alloy tubes
        (*e*) Mild steel strips
        (*f*) Plastic and nylon moulding powder (thermo-setting and thermo-plastic) excluding banned items viz: UF, PF, PVC, Polyethylene (low density) and polystyrene) and
        (*g*) tool and alloy steels.

Note. Dyes and chemicals (item 4(i)(*e*)), coloured or printed umbrella cloth made of nylon art silk or other synthetic fibres, excluding cotton umbrella cloth (item 4(i)(*a*)) and elastic tapes (item 4(i)(*d*)), allowed to be imported against export of umbrellas can be sold by exporters of umbrellas to any unit in the textile industry.

5. Staple pins
6. Hair grips
7. Venetian blinds and auto-blinds
8. Meat mincers
9. Domestic grinders

TABLE 19.11—*continued*

10. Ice cream freezers
11. Fruit juice machines

(F) *60 per cent*

1. Electric lamps, G.L.S. miniature and fluorescen
2. Dry batteries
3. Storage batteries
4. Radio receivers (valve based)
5. Public address equipment
6. Typewriters
7. Water filters
8. Cigarette tin-cutters

(G) *75 per cent*

1. Ghamellas
2. Enamelware
3. Crowncork
4. R.S. and pilfer proof closures
5. Aluminium capsules
6. Razor blades
7. Airconditioning and refrigeration equipment including water coolers (domestic as well as commercial)
8. Electrical wiring accessories (other than plastic)
9. Pressure lamps and stoves.
10. Zip fasteners
11. Snap fasteners
12. E.P.N.S. and German silver ware
13. Tyre inflators
14. Hand rotary dusters and sprayers
15. Arc welding electrodes (other than mild steel) and gas welding rods (other than mild steel)
16. Telephone and exchange equipment
17. Radio receivers (transistorized)
18. Steel wire gauze, mesh, and nettings
19. Panel pins
20. Steel bright bars and shaftings
21. Engineers' steel files
22. Hacksaw blades and bandsaw blades
23. Twist drills
24. Milling cutters
25. Cameras, all sorts
26. L.P. gas cylinders
27. Drop forged hand tools
28. Electricity meters (single phase and poly phase)
29. Umbrella ribs
30. Bicycle components and accessories:

(i) Spokes	(iii) Bells made of brass	(v) Free wheels
(ii) Rims	(iv) Oil-bath gear-case	(vi) Bicycle chains

31. Pressure cookers
32. Dyes—all types
33. Metal moulds and patterns—all types
34. Upholstery springs

TABLE 19.11—*continued*

35. Pencil sharpeners
36. Shoe tacks
37. Studio light
38. Flexible conduit tubes
39. Steel balls
40. Electronic instruments including multimeters
41. Plastic line testers
42. Gas burners hot plates
43. Wood working screws
44. Tungsten metal
45. Ammonium para tungsten
46. To 58 hand tools
59. Sink and drain cleaners
60. Hexagon brake tools
61. Electric laundry irons
62. Diamond cutting tools and diamond powder
63. Hand sewing needles
64 and 64A. Drum closures
64B and 64C. Die cast zinc plugs with gaskets
65. Steel wire ropes

Part II. Machinery and transport equipment

(A) *40 per cent*

1. Diesel engines (stationary)
2. Industrial shunters
3. Power driven pumps
4. Lathes, all types
5. Milling machines
6. Drilling machines (including radial drilling machines)
7. Shaping machines
8. Planing machines
9. Hacksaw machines
10. Power presses
11. Machine tools, not elsewhere specified
12. Textile machinery
13. Sugar mill machinery
14. Tea processing machinery (other than Mactear Rotorvane Continuous Tea Roller)
15. Jute mill machinery
16. Oil mill machinery
17. Rice, dal, and flour mill machinery
18. Industrial machinery not otherwise specified
19. Bus body kits
20. Belt sanders and polishers
21. Metre gauge and steam locomotives
22. Chaff cutters
23. Construction machinery like concrete mixers, concrete vibrators, tar boilers, etc.

(B) *60 per cent*

1. Gas plants
2. Mactear Rotorvane Continuous Tea Rollers

TABLE 19.11—*continued*

(C) *75 per cent*

1. Passenger cars, trucks, jeeps, station wagons, and other motor vehicles
2. Motor-cycles, scooters, and three-wheelers
3. Diesel engines (vehicular)
4. Petrol engines
5. Automobile ancillaries and accessories
6. Air compressors
7. Earth-moving equipment, all types
8. Agricultural tractors
9. Fork lift trucks
10. Components, spare parts, ancillaries and accessories for serials (A), (1 to 18, 20, 21, and 23), (C) (3, 3, 6 to 9).
11. Trailers

Part III. Non-ferrous semis, alloys and fully processed manufactures and stainless steel products

100 per cent

1. Copper utensils
2. Brass utensils
3. Aluminium utensils
4. Non-ferrous expanded metal
5. Non-ferrous wire gauze, mesh, and netting, and other water and steam fittings
6. Non-ferrous bib cocks, stop cocks, valves, and other water and steam fittings
7. Non-ferrous castings and forgings, all sorts
8. Bare copper conductors
9. All aluminium and A.C.S.R. conductors
10. Aluminium architectural specialities
11. Aluminium doors and windows
12. Flash light and torch light cases
13. Nickel anodes
14. Non-ferrous builders' hardware
15. Safety razors
16. Aluminium chains, plain or anodized
17. Non-ferrous alloys (all types)
18. Non-ferrous semis (e.g. plates, sheets, strips, tubes, rods) whether rolled or extruded or drawn
19. All types, grades and sizes of insulated electric cables
20. All articles and manufactures of stainless steel, including stainless steel utensils, stainless steel watch straps, stainless steel surgical instruments, stainless steel cutlery and tableware and industrial equipments, components, ancillaries, and accessories made of stainless steel.
21. Brass buckets
22. Brass tubular household light fittings
23. Brass and aluminium eyelets
24. Penholder nibs
25. Aluminium tubular furniture
26. Flash light components
27. Fountain pen parts (brass and aluminium)
28. Printing types
29. Scales, weight, and jewellery tools

Source: Ministry of International Trade, from published sources.

TABLE 19.12

IMPORT ENTITLEMENT FOR CHEMICALS AND ALLIED PRODUCTS IN EARLY 1964

GG

Import entitlement as a per cent of the f.o.b. value of exports	Items of export	Items permitted to be imported against the import entitlement for the corresponding sub-groups
(1)	(2)	(3)
	Group I	
	(a)	
20	Sodium chloride (vacuum and pure), sodium carbonate monohydrate, sodium sulphate, sodium thiosulphate, ammonium chloride, calcium carbonate (pptd.), calcium chloride, calcium oxide (lime), magnesium chloride, magnesium sulphate (B.P. and tech.), magnesium carbonate (pptd.) magnesium oxychloride, carbon dioxide gas hydrogen peroxide, liquid chloride, ferrous sulphate, hydrochloric acid, activated bleaching earth, bentonite sodium base, synthetic floor hardening compound, sodium bicarbonate (B.P. and tech.)	Inorganic chemicals, chemicals raw materials, etc., covered under V/22–31 of the I.T.C. schedule (other than those banned and restricted) and all permitted items in Appendix 28 of the *Redbook*
30	Sodium bichromate, ferric alumina, alums	Caustic soda (fused), caustic potash, potassium carbonate, hard coke, anthracite coal, petroleum coke, gum arabic, potassium chloride (technical), sodium and potassium cyanide, sodium and potassium ferrocyanide, graphite electrodes, ammonium nitrate (tech. grade), potassium permanganate (up to 10 per cent of face value of licence), bromine, non-rusting chromium steel in slabs, bars, and powder, ammonium carbonate and bicarbonate, ammonium sulphate (electrolythic grade), ammonium sulphocyanide, sodium sulphate, sodium nitrate, etc.
40	Sodium perborate, potassium chromate, chromic acid battery grade sulphuric acid, sodium and potassium bromide, water treatment chemicals (e.g. Alfloc compounds, sodium aluminate, sodium hexametaphosphate), case hardening compounds, heat treatment salts, nitrous oxide gas	
60	Potassium bichromate, bleaching powder	Import of zinc, copper, lead nickel, cadmium, selenium, cobalt, tin, mercury, will be permitted for full entitlement against export of items containing the particular metal
75	Potassium chlorate, calcium carbide, copper sulphate, lead acetate and nitrate; mercury chloride and oxide, nickel sulphate, nickel chloride and carbonate, sodium stannate, zinc chloride, zinc sulphate, tin chloride, tin oxide, copper oxychloride (tech.)	Carborundum powder (not more than 10 per cent of f.o.b. value) yellow petroleum jelly (not more than 5 per cent of f.o.b. value)
	(b)	
20	Manufactures of ceramics, sanitaryware and fittings, pottery, refractory, washed and processed china clay, deadbUrnt magnesite, fireclay	Heavy soda ash (up to 50 per cent of the f.o.b. export value of glass and glassware only), sheet glass (up to 35 per cent of f.o.b. value export of laminated safety glass only) arsenic oxide, ball and china clay, flake graphite, plate glass, ceramic colours and transfers, raw asbestos, magnesium carbonate light. Salenium, cadmium metal, interlayer lacquer for manufacture of safety glass, asbestos cloth, etc. Carborundum powder (not more than 10 per cent of f.o.b. export value)
40	Glazed tiles	
50	Artificial teeth (porcelain type)	

TABLE 19.12—continued

Import entitlement as a per cent of the f.o.b. value of exports (1)	Items of export (2)	Items permitted to be imported against the import entitlement for the corresponding sub-groups (3)
70	Glass and glassware, mirrors, laminated safety glass. Clinical thermometers (see note 8)	Yellow petroleum jelly (not more than 5 per cent of f.o.b. export value)
	Asbestos jointings; packings and other asbestos products, asbestos cement products	a Gold-coated pins, shells and allay, solders, Feldspar, calcium carbonate, ceramic colours.
	Group II	
	(a)	
20	Wood turpentine, benzene, toluene, xylene, napthalen, (including anthracene), solvent, naptha, liquid glucose, ethyl alcohol, other organic alcohols, acetic acid, ethyl acetate, calcium lactate, sodium and potassium acetate, benzene hexachloride (tech.)	2. All organic chemicals, solvents, etc. covered in Appendix 28 of the *Redbook* and V/22–31 of the I.T.C. Schedule. All dye intermediates listed in Appendix 40 of the *Redbook*. All drugs raw materials, intermediates etc. as covered under Appendix 19 of the *Redbook* and also tartaric acid, citric acid, acetic anhydride, dichloroquinoline, maminophenol, di-chloracetic acid ester of aminophenol, diethyl-aminophenol, hydrazine hydrate, nitroacetophenon, anthraquinone, phenol, aniline, Bnapthol, phenylacetamide, ethyl methyl pyridine, gama picoline, piperazine hydrate, 8-hydroxy quiniline, iodine, acetone, methanol, triethanolamine etc., gum arabic (up to 5 per cent of f.o.b. value) against export of drugs and pharmaceuticals. All chemical raw materials, etc., covered under V/22–31 of the I.T.C. schedule, required in the manufacture of insecticides, pesticides, etc.
40	Other organic solvents	
50	Hydroquinone, sodium and potassium citrate, sodium salychlate, saccharine, drugs and pharmaceuticals, intermediates for drugs	Bismuth, mercury (against export of items containing mercury), diacetone alcohol, mercury, iodine
60	Insecticides, pesticides, weedicides, rodenticides (formulations only)	All aromatic chemicals covered in list 5 in Appendix 28 of the *Redbook*
75	Synthetic coal-tar dyes, intermediates for dyes organic colouring matters, flourescent, bleaching agents, bismuth based drugs, mercury based drugs. Hydraulic brake fluid, cotton-seed dressing mixture	
	(b)	
20	Processed talc (cosmetic and pharmaceutical grade), blended rosa oil, sulphonated castor oil	Essential oils and perfumery materials covered under IV/127–129 and IV/132 of the I.T.C. Schedule and; copra, palm, oil, palmkernel oil (tallow by specific recommendation in each case) glassine paper and natural pine oil (up to 5 per cent face value of import licence)
30	Alcoholic perfumes	
40	Refined glycerine, textile auxiliaries, emulsifiers, demulsifiers	

50	Cosmetics, toiletries, dentifrice, fatty acids	dicalcium phosphate (cosmetic and pharmaceutical grade), calcium carbonate (cosmetic and pharmaceutical grade), alkyl benzenes, alkyl phenols, isopropyl alcohol, methyl ethyl ketone, alkylomine, sodium benzoate, dental detergent chips, Irish moss extract, methyl para-hydrony benzoate, methyl salicylate, zinc sulphocarbolate, palm kernel monoethanolamine, layryl sulphate, ethylone diamine tetracetic acid salts and esters
60	Toilet soaps, laundry soaps, industrial soaps, non-alcoholic perfumery compounds	
70	Hair-dye	Cedarwood oil (against toilet soaps and cosmetics), hexachlorophene, [paraphenyline diamine; borium peroxide against export of hair-dye. Spindle oils and petroleum jelly (up to 5 per cent of f.o.b. export value against export of cosmetics and toiletries (including hair oils, hair pomade, brilliantine)
75	Synthetic detergents	
	(c)	
20	Red oxide and yellow oxide pigments of iron, distempers, refined and processed baryte powder and blanefixe, ultramarine blue	Raw materials for paints, pigments, etc., covered under Appendix 29 of the *Redbook*. Also the following: Gilsonite raw Tripoli, Gopla gum, synthetic resins, nitrocellulose, naphthenic acid, Persian Gulf red oxide, meleicanhydride, maleic acid, phthalic anhydride, normalbutyl alcohol, chlorinated rubber compounds, carbon black (ink grade). In the case of lead pigments only, exporters can use their full entitlement for import of unwrought lead
70	Paints, varnishes, enamels, lacquers and other pigments, white lead, lead chromate: (i) Lemon chrome (ii) Mid-chrome (iii) Primrose chrome (iv) Orange chrome	
75	Printers' inks, synthetic resin adhesive	Gum arabic (up to 5 per cent f.o.b. value) against printer's ink, paints, varnishes, and distempers: (i) Araldite (ii) Hardens
95	Zinc oxide	Import of zinc is permitted for full entitlement against export of zinc oxide only
	(d)	
20	Cauotachoucine	(i) Natural rubber
75	Tyres, tubes, hoses, beltings, rubber, footwear, surgical and medical appliances of rubber. Foam and sponge rubber, industrial appliances of rubber, other miscellaneous articles of rubber	(ii) Not more than 20 per cent of the f.o.b. value of export can be utilized for the import of each of the following: Carbon black, S.B.R. synthetic rubber, rayon tyre cord, and anti-oxidants (iii) For the present, there will be no restriction on the import of the following within the import entitlement: rubber accelerators, rubber softeners, rubber chemicals and colours, reclaimed rubber, bead wire, bead wire rings, plasticisers and peptisers (iv) Import of tube valves will be allowed to only exporters of rubber tyres to the extent of 10 per cent than more the actual number of tyres exported

Source: Ministry of International Trade, from published sources.

APPENDIX II

On the inference of equivalent ad valorem
export subsidies from price differentials

It is frequently asserted that the extent of *ad valorem* export subsidy provided and hence also the degree of effective devaluation with respect to any export can be inferred directly by observing the excess of domestic unit price over f.o.b. (subsidy-excluded) foreign unit price of the exported commodity. This view is incorrect except in the restrictive case where the commodity is domestically produced *and* sold abroad within a competitive framework.

Take the case of such universal competitiveness. In Figure 1,

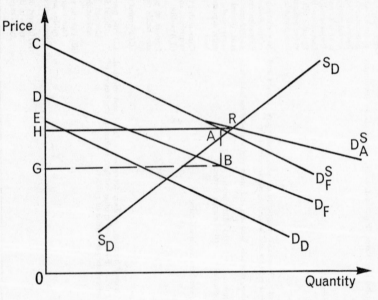

Figure 1

D_D and D_F represent the domestic and foreign demand curves for the commodity, and S_D is the domestic supply curve. With the export subsidy CD/OD, the effective foreign demand curve becomes $D_F{}^S$ and the aggregate demand curve then is $D_A{}^S$. The equilibrium, intersection point then is R, the domestic price is OH and the f.o.b. foreign price (*exclusive of subsidy*) is OG. HG/OG

($=AB/OG$) is *both* the subsidy rate on export price *and* the price differential ($OH - OG = HG$) divided by the export price (OG). Thus, the observed price differential reflects the export subsidy in this case.

However, consider for example the case where the domestic situation is that of monopoly. In Figure 2, AR_D is the domestic

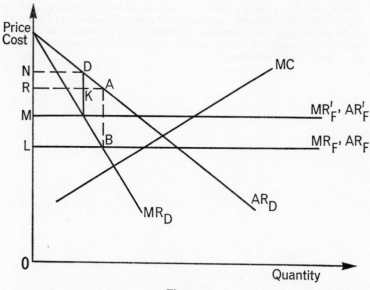

Figure 2

demand curve, AR_F is the foreign demand curve, MC the marginal cost curve, MR_D the marginal domestic revenue curve of the monopolist and $MR_F(= AR_F)$ the marginal, foreign revenue curve. $MR'_F(= AR'_F)$ represents the marginal, foreign revenue curve *after* the grant of an export subsidy at the rate ML/OL.

Taking the situation *before* subsidy, we see that the equilibrium domestic price at OR *exceeds* the foreign price at OL by $RL(= AB)$, even though no export subsidy is being granted.

Note also that, even after the grant of export subsidy at rate ML/OL, the differential increases by DK to NL ($>RL$), but by less than the subsidy (ML) so that it is not even possible to claim that the subsidy will result in an equal *increment* in the differential between domestic and foreign (subsidy-exclusive) unit prices.

A similar conclusion, with respect to the possibility of inferring the degree of *ad valorem* subsidy from the price differentials on subsidy-assisted exports of commodities holds analogously for the opposite situation when a firm sells within a competitive domestic framework but is faced with a less than infinitely elastic demand curve for its sales abroad.[1]

[1] This *is* a possible situation, although not analysed in the literature. While it seems to have been generally assumed that a domestic competitive framework necessarily implies competitiveness in foreign sales, unevenness in the incidence of information on foreign markets among different firms, for example, may disrupt this assumption.

20

Export Policy—Part III

In this chapter we attempt to evaluate the economic efficiency of the export promotion measures we have described in the preceding chapter, focusing essentially on the import entitlement schemes which were the major plank of this shift in the Indian Government's export policies during the Third Plan. Before we attempt this evaluation, however, it will be useful to highlight the special features, of economic significance, which characterized the Indian entitlement schemes.

SPECIAL FEATURES OF THE ENTITLEMENT SCHEMES

Of course the Indian entitlement schemes were not entirely novel. A large number of countries had, in fact, resorted to them during the post-war period of dollar shortage, the general practice then being to allow their exporters to retain a portion of their dollar earnings for their own use, or transfer them at a premium in the market, under what were described as 'retention quota' schemes.

Japan has also occasionally resorted to similar schemes. For example, under the so-called 'link' scheme, the export of Japanese woollen products was stimulated from 1950 onwards by linking raw wool imports with exports of woollen products.[1] More

---

[1] 'When a manufacturer exported a woollen article, he received an import entitlement which permitted the holder to import a certain quantity of wool, the amount depending upon the total allocation of woollen imports to holders of such rights ... Although the permit was issued in the first instance to the actual exporter, it was in fact shared by all the manufacturers and dealers through whose hands the product in question passed; thus all along the line there was some incentive to divert sales to export, or likely export, outlets. The link system was important during the nineteen-fifties ...' S. J. Wells, *British Export Performance*, pp. 94–5.

important, there have been 'retention certificate' schemes under which certificates were issued entitling the exporter (or his transferee) to import specified commodities (including high-premium luxury goods) up to around 3 per cent of the export value.

Closer home has been the Pakistan *export bonus* scheme, started in 1959 and occasionally modified thereafter. Noteworthy are the following features: (i) the value of exports covered by this scheme is very considerable, amounting to nearly 40 per cent of Pakistan's exports in 1960 and 1961; (ii) the range of imports permitted does not exclude consumer goods; (iii) the market for export bonus vouchers is unified;[1] and (iv) over time, the entitlement rates have been reduced to a very limited number.[2]

Largely, though not entirely, in contrast to the foregoing schemes, the Indian import entitlement schemes were distinguished by the following features of economic significance:

(1) the number of entitlement rates was very large and subject to occasional change;

(2) by and large, the entitlement rates were below 100 per cent export value;

(3) the market for the (transferable) entitlements was segmented by export promotion schemes;[3]

(4) the premium on entitlements showed fluctuations in the different, segmented markets;

(5) the list of permissible imports throughout excluded consumer goods;[4]

(6) the value of exports covered by the scheme, on the most liberal interpretation which would include tea and coffee exports, came to only around 60 per cent of the total Indian exports and to around 30 per cent on more restricted assumptions (which would confine the list to only Group A in Table 19.9); and

(7) the value of imports coming under entitlements was

---

[1] Moreover, it is claimed that, insofar as aid-inflow and reserve position allow, 'open-market' type operations are undertaken by liberalization or deliberalization of import policy so as to reduce the fluctuations of the premium in this market.

[2] For details, a useful reference is H. J. Bruton and S. R. Bose, *The Pakistan Export Bonus Scheme* (No. 11, Monographs in the Economics of Development, April 1963), Institute of Development Economics, Karachi, Pakistan.

[3] except for trivial exceptions.

[4] The only exception was the 'dryfruit scheme' which was later to be suspended.

throughout less than 5 per cent of the *total* value of imports (including aid-financed imports).[1]

The import entitlement schemes, set in the framework of an over-valued exchange rate, were undoubtedly a useful improvement on a situation where otherwise exports were being seriously discriminated against. But the essential question is whether these were an *efficient* way of countering the effect of the over-valuation of the exchange rate on exports. The analysis that follows in this chapter is addressed to this question and seeks to establish the inefficiency of such schemes.

As the Indian import entitlement schemes were characterized by considerable segmentation, differential rates and non-transferability resulting in differential premia, we shall analyse the efficiency of these schemes, (*a*) on the hypothetical assumption that these markets and rates were unified, and (*b*) on the more realistic assumption that the markets and rates were differentiated. We will, in fact, be arguing that these schemes were basically an inefficient way of simulating the working of a flexible exchange-rate system; and that these inefficiencies were compounded by the differential nature of the effective subsidization granted under the Indian régime.

(a) Subsidy aspects *per se*

Among the several, significant aspects of the Indian import entitlement schemes, omitting (as we have noted) the aspect of differential rates and selectivity in general, we shall note the following main features: over-invoicing of exports; revenue effect; self-limiting export promotion; instability of the incentive offered; utilization of foreign exchange allocations for creating incentives; and welfare effects.

Over-invoicing of exports.

In so far as the import entitlement schemes constituted subsidy measures, they gave rise to an incentive, *ceteris paribus*, to over-invoice exports: an incentive that would be eliminated under a straightforward, direct adjustment of the exchange rate (which

[1] This last characteristic, namely, the low proportion of total imports going through the entitlement system was shared by the Pakistan scheme. So was characteristic (2).

would obviate the need to subsidize exports to counter the disincentive offered to exports by the over-valuation of the exchange rate).

As Bhagwati has argued elsewhere,[1] the incentive to over-invoice exports will arise when the effective export subsidy exceeds the black market premium charged for illegal foreign exchange: when this condition is satisfied, it will pay the exporter to over-invoice the value of his exports as the gain he makes by getting extra subsidy on the over-invoiced part of his export declaration will outweigh the premium-cost of buying foreign exchange in the black market to the magnitude of the over-invoiced part of his declared value of exports.

We have secured empirical evidence for arguing that the Indian entitlement schemes did, in fact, lead to significant over-invoicing of exports. In arriving at this conclusion, however, we could not employ the technique of comparing partner-country statistics to check whether the Indian export declarations exceeded the partner-country import data. Since over-invoicing was supposed to occur (according to our informants) largely with the free ports such as Aden, Hong Kong, and Panama, there was unfortunately little possibility of getting 'objective' evidence by partner-country comparisons of identical transactions—such data were just not available for these areas. Moreover, some of the over-invoicing was alleged to occur at *both* ends—the importer over-invoicing his imports as well—because the importing 'Indian' traders in Malaysia and East Africa were alleged to be pulling out capital from these countries and repatriating it to India in contravention of capital transfer controls; this also eliminated the possibility of using successfully the partner-country data-comparison technique to get statistical evidence in support of the over-invoiced exports hypothesis.

Hence we were compelled to rely on the somewhat slender method of securing testimonies from traders who admitted to the prevalence of over-invoicing in art silks, plastics, ores, chemicals, and engineering goods, and, indeed, over a very wide range of exports. But we could do a little better than this. We examined

---

[1] 'On the Underinvoicing of Imports', *Bulletin of the Oxford University Institute of Economics and Statistics*, 26, November 1964, and 'Fiscal Policies, the Faking of Foreign Trade Declarations, and the Balance of Payments', ibid., 29, February 1967.

also whether the incentives offered to exports were high enough, in relation to the black market premia on foreign exchange, to yield significant incentive to over-invoice exports.

For this purpose, it was adequate to compare the black market discounts on the Indian rupee with the subsidy rates implied by the entitlement rates and premia. We found that there had indeed been a considerable incentive, since 1961/2, to over-invoice exports. In Chapter 19 we examined both the entitlement rates (Tables 19.11 and 19.12) and the occasional levels of premia (Tables 19.4 to 19.6) around 1964–6. If we contrast these with the discounts at which the Indian rupee seems to have been transacted in the black market during this period,[1] e.g. centres such as Aden, Nairobi, Mombassa, and Hong Kong, it appears quite reasonable to conclude that over-invoicing must have occurred especially in areas such as art silks, plastics, several engineering products and chemicals. These are precisely the areas where over-invoicing was also alleged by our informants to have occurred; it was apparently notoriously heavy in art silks and plastics whereas its incidence, though not considered to be equally intensive, had been somewhat facilitated by the ease with which prices can be faked in engineering and chemical products.

Is such over-invoicing of exports necessarily harmful? Bhagwati has argued elsewhere,[2] at length, that the effects on the balance of payments position will not necessarily be disadvantageous and may, in fact, be beneficial if the effect is to bring into legal channels the foreign exchange that might otherwise have been in the illegal market and used for illegal and hence non-priority areas (such as capital flight). Hence, contrary to the general view which would regard such practices as detrimental to economic welfare, it is possible that over-invoicing may not have been harmful for the Indian economy.[3]

---

[1] Note that this market is imperfect and hence we have differences in the rates. Moreover, there are different rates for *currency* exchange, which usually show somewhat higher discounts and are not as relevant to our analysis as the rates for transfer. Finally, it should be remarked that these rates should be regarded as more or less *approximate* estimates, unlike official statistics.

[2] *Bulletin of the Oxford University Institute of Economics and Statistics*, 1967, op. cit.

[3] Bhagwati, ibid., has also examined the possible impact on aid inflow when the official entries in the balance of payments records change as a result of such over-invoicing and hence the external performance of the economy may be favourably assessed by aid givers who wish to see better export performance before they extend aid.

Bhagwati has also pointed to an interesting short-term implication of such over-invoicing, which may have actually been of some empirical significance in the Indian context during 1964/5. All countries which have exchange control on capital movements impose a time-limit on the (possible) lag between exports and the surrender of the exchange earned therefrom: for example, with insignificant exceptions for certain capital goods, the permitted lag in India has been six months. Within this permissible limit, exporters have the choice of either keeping their earnings abroad or remitting them home. The former will usually take the shape of a trade credit or may even be an explicit short-term investment. In either case, the basic choice will be determined by the factors governing the rates of return on either option. These rates of return are supposed to be a reflection largely of respective short-term interest rates and it seems sensible to argue, at the least, that a widening of the difference between foreign and domestic short-term interest rates, in favour of the former, will tend to lengthen the average lag between exports and export receipts.

And so will over-invoicing of exports generally lengthen this lag. The over-invoiced part of the declared value has to be secured from illegal sources; this is likely to take time if the exporter wishes to find out the cheapest source for illegal purchase of foreign exchange. More important, the exporter can avoid altogether any interest charge on the cost (equivalent to the premium on illegal foreign exchange) incurred by the purchase of illegal foreign exchange by putting it off till the very end of the permissible period. Hence, he has a definite incentive, as long as the interest rate is positive, to defer (as long as possible) the return of the over-invoiced part of the export earnings. This will, therefore, increase, *ceteris paribus*, the average lag on total export earnings, to the extent that such over-invoicing is a new, or an increasing phenomenon.[1] In so far as this happens, further, the time-profile of receipts of foreign exchange will undoubtedly be affected—and

[1] This is precisely what is likely to have happened in the case of India during the fiscal year 1964/5 when a very large excess of recorded exports over export earnings developed along with an intensification of the export promotion drive. For details, see Bhagwati, 'Why Export Receipts Lag Behind Exports', *Economic Weekly*, 27, 24 July 1965. For an illuminating theoretical analysis of the effect of an extended lag, between exports and receipts, on the time-profile of the difference between the two, Bent Hansen's *Foreign Trade Credits and Exchange Reserves*, Amsterdam, North-Holland Publishing Co., 1961, remains the standard work so far.

the result may well be, after taking into account the source from which the illegal exchange comes to 'finance' the over-invoicing, a net deterioration in the *immediate* availability of foreign exchange to the country.

Finally, we must also note here that the incentive to over-invoice led some exporters, especially (though not exclusively) in sectors such as plastics and art silks, to send out shoddy goods with faked, higher-price declarations, which were cleared in foreign markets at 'what they could fetch'. At a time when India's immediate and long-term export drive had to rest increasingly on the export of manufactures (and, for that matter, quality and complex manufactures by and large), the building up of goodwill was quite important: this was precisely what was jeopardized by the practitioners of over-invoicing. We shall soon see that the instability of the incentive offered by the entitlement schemes, combined with the differential incidence of the benefits on the numerous, different items, accentuated this phenomenon by encouraging the entry into the export trade of roving traders, in search of quick profits, whose primary objective was short-run, immediate profit maximization.[1]

Revenue effects

An argument frequently advanced in India in favour of the import entitlement schemes, as a method of export subsidization, as against direct subsidization, is that these schemes finance themselves: the subsidy is paid by the users of the import licences. However, in so far as this is the case, it would be equally open for the authorities to levy such a tax directly on imports and to finance therewith a direct subsidy on exports. Hence, the argument in favour of the entitlement schemes must rest on an illusion; taxation of imports may be feasible if disguised but not otherwise. Such an illusion may well exist; but we doubt its plausibility and have seen no evidence in support thereof.

Besides, we may note that if we were to compare a régime with an over-valued exchange rate combined with entitlement schemes for export, with an adjusted exchange rate, the revenue effect would

---

[1] It is perhaps worth noting here the complaints which were made to us by some interviewees, who seemed quite genuinely concerned at the time, about the occasional rise of such traders in influence both in some Export Promotion Councils and sometimes with the Ministry of Commerce, entirely due to their ability (thanks to over-invoicing) to deliver more impressive, even though fictitious, results.

have been against the former régime for the simple reason that imports exceeded exports approximately by the amount of the net aid inflow which was quite considerable.

Self-limiting nature of the subsidy.

Further, the entitlement schemes contrasted unfavourably with direct, *ad valorem*, subsidies in another respect. Whereas *ad valorem* subsidies apply the incentive equally at all levels of export (and concomitant prices), the entitlement schemes build into their structure an important feature which reduces the incentive with the value of exports achieved.

This self-limiting aspect, implying that the more successful the scheme is in increasing exports, the less the incentive to export *at the margin*, arises from the fact that the incentive rests crucially on the entitlement premium (once the entitlement rate is fixed). If export value increases, thanks to the entitlement schemes, import entitlements entering the market will proportionately increase, thus tending to push the premium down. But the lower the premium the lower also the incentive, at the margin, on exports.

An *ad valorem* subsidy instead would maintain the incentive. A flexible exchange rate or suitable devaluation, on the other hand, would have similar effects to an *ad valorem* subsidy, except for the incremental cost of imported and import-competing inputs which would operate with respect to the import side.

Instability of the incentive.

A related feature of such export subsidization schemes is the additional source of instability that they constitute, in view of the fact that the premium on entitlements will vary, in contrast to an *ad valorem* export subsidy. Moreover, as we have already noted, the frequent changes in the premia brought about by changing rules concerning permissible imports and transferability, for example, as also frequent changes in the entitlement rates themselves, constituted further elements of instability in the operation of the entitlement schemes in India.

Utilization of foreign exchange allocations for creating export incentives.

The economic consequences and inefficiencies that we have just discussed arose primarily from the fact that the entitlement schemes operated by diverting the allocations of premium-fetching imports, by way of economic reward and incentive, to exporters. Among the other effects of such a policy, we may now note two in particular.

(1) The system may have resulted in foreign exchange being allocated to industries (which albeit were induced thereby to export) for non-priority uses.[1]

Thus, for example, if imports of luxury goods were permitted under the entitlements schemes, and this was merely to provide a high-premium incentive for export, and the import of luxury goods was otherwise intended to be prohibited, this could well be regarded as a *minus* factor in the evaluation of the entitlement schemes (from the point of view of this policy). On the other hand, if the Government did not seek to prohibit imports of these luxury goods or if they were merely diverted from established importers to import entitlements, the foreign exchange used (via the entitlements) on importing these luxury goods could not be properly regarded as 'misallocation' from the viewpoint of socially-declared objectives. Thus, for example, the Pakistan bonus scheme has permitted imports of consumer goods (including luxury goods) but so has their general, import licensing policy.[2]

On the other hand, the Indian entitlement schemes, as we have noted, followed exclusively the principle of exclusion of consumer goods (with the temporary aberration provided by the dryfruit scheme).[3] Where, however, the leakage into non-priority allocations may be alleged to have occurred is in industries such as art silk where the *total* foreign exchange allocations (A.U. plus import entitlement licences), as a result of the export incentive taking the form of import entitlements rather than *ad valorem* subsidies, may have been greater than otherwise. In the absence of any statistical evidence being available on A.U. licences by sector-of-use (for any length of time, for this industry), it is impossible to arrive at any reasonably firm conclusion on this question. It is worth noting, in this connection, the following official statement:

[1] The reader may recall that we have already noted in other chapters, for example on Import Policy, that the notion of 'priorities' has been tenuous in India.

[2] Bruton and Bose, op. cit., point out that, in fact, the proportion of consumer goods imports in *total export bonus* imports does not compare at all unfavourably with the corresponding proportion in *overall* imports.

[3] Even with dryfruit, it is not clear whether the Established Importer licences for their 'normal' import were cut to 'compensate' for this phenomenon.

In many cases, the traditional imports of some of the raw materials of these [export] industries which were being licenced on actual users basis, viz., rayon and man made fibres, copra, palm oil and tallow, raw silk have been stopped, and these imports have been linked up as import entitlements under the export promotion schemes.[1]

The official statement, however, does not necessarily mean that no net diversion of foreign exchange to these industries had occurred as a result of the entitlement schemes: it is quite possible that the issuance of A.U. licences would have been reduced for these industries *even if* there had been no entitlement schemes.

At the same time, we may note that a policy of export promotion which aims at reducing the normal allocation of A.U. imports to an industry and forcing it to earn its imports via exports (at lower prices than on domestic sales), will also reduce, *ceteris paribus*, the profitability of such industries and hence investments therein and its export performance in the long run. Thus, while such a policy may make sense if the intention is to regard an industry as essentially non-priority and to exploit it primarily with a view to maximizing its immediate exports, it would be a self-frustrating policy if the aim was to sustain a long-run export drive on the basis of such policies.

(2) Another effect of the use of foreign exchange allocations for promoting exports, in the Indian context, was quite favourable (although it would have ceased to be so under an adjusted exchange rate which could obviate the reliance on strict import controls and the resulting inflexibility). When these entitlement schemes were operating, there was practically no legal way of getting hold of foreign exchange in order to break expensive bottlenecks and unforeseen demands. The entitlement markets thus served to introduce a much-needed flexibility in an otherwise excessively inflexible system.

While this basic advantage to the economy, arising from the introduction of legal accessibility to scarce imports (albeit with restrictions, but still significant), was considerable, many exporters whom we interviewed argued that the entitlement schemes, in view of their granting such access to imports, were also a superior, more effective way of sustaining an export drive than *ad valorem* financial subsidies. (1) It was argued that *flexibility* of access to foreign exchange was a considerable advantage, which would not

[1] *Annual Report*, 1964–1965, Ministry of Commerce, New Delhi, p. 15.

be available if the subsidy was a financial one; and that their export performance would have been affected adversely by the replacement of these schemes by financial subsidies. (2) It was further argued that the vast majority of exporting producers exported just enough to get the amount of foreign exchange for maintaining full capacity utilization in their plants and that their motivation in exporting was *not* to increase overall profits but to expand capacity utilization; and hence the export drive would suffer by the replacement of entitlement schemes by purely financial incentives. (3) Finally, it was also claimed that, with foreign exchange not otherwise available in a free market, it was possible that firms which might find it attractive to export on being given a financial incentive to do so, might not be in a position to produce at all for export (the assumption, of course, being that their A.U. allocations were meagre).

While these beliefs were strongly held, only the last argument has some element of logic in it. The first argument is fallacious because any advantage following from flexibility can be quantified and the corresponding incentive always provided through fiscal subsidies. As for the second argument, there is little evidence of Indian firms following a policy of output, rather than profit, expansion: the very fact that many firms were known to sell, at least at the margin, their entitlement licences, indicates that the force of this argument is not considerable. The last argument, based on the fact that firms restricting themselves to legal purchases would not be able to produce for export, but would have to confine themselves to diverting existing production to exports, has some plausibility. Even in this case, however, we have to allow for the fact that incremental export earnings would be released into the economy and hence could be used eventually for augmenting production for exports. We are thus left essentially with the argument that the entitlement schemes introduced flexibility into the import régime, undoubtedly resulting in sizeable gains via the breaking of costly bottlenecks.

Other welfare effects

We may now consider other more direct welfare effects associated with the fact that the entitlement schemes involved a departure from unified exchange rates.

We may note that an *ad valorem* subsidy on exports would help,

HH

in an over-valued exchange-rate situation, to reduce the discrimination against exports. On the other hand, a system under which export subsidization is combined with an over-valued exchange rate involving import controls differs significantly from a system where the exchange rate is altered to equilibrium levels and thus implies a unified exchange-rate policy.

Thus, in the Indian-type import régime, we have already noted that imports were partly allocated on an A.U. basis and hence the effective rate on these imports was the parity plus the relevant tariff. On the other hand, in so far as other inputs were purchased from the market, the effective import rate on these included the import premium as well. Thus, as we have already indicated in the chapter on effective rates of protection, there followed non-unified exchange rates and unpredictably different and bizarre incentives for resource allocation.

In this situation, the introduction of even a unified export subsidy would have perpetuated the continuation of non-unified exchange rates, while helping to reduce the overall disincentive to exports.[1] But, in fact, such a subsidy would give rise to the possibility of losses arising from the effective export rate for a commodity *exceeding* the effective average import rate on its inputs: such a situation could lead to the possibility mentioned by us earlier, of the process yielding 'value subtracted' at international prices.

This possibility can be demonstrated readily, in the framework of a slightly idealized model where we assume that *all* imports are bought at premium-inclusive prices (thus omitting the A.U. imports). In fact, as we shall soon demonstrate, the possibility of negative value added increases if we admit non-transferable A.U. imports.

In our idealized model, then, let e be the entitlement rate on f.o.b. export value and y the premium rate on entitlements. Then ey is the full premium rate on export value. Let P_x stand for unit export price (which is, for simplicity, assumed to be constant), P_m for unit (average) price of the 'import content' of exportables, m_x for the import content per unit exportable[2] and P_D for the domestic unit price of the exportable commodity.

---

[1] In point of fact, as we have already noted, even the effective export subsidy rates varied widely. We analyse this later in the chapter.

[2] From the viewpoint of the present analysis, 'import content' must be defined as inclusive of 'tradable' content, even though the inputs may be locally produced.

Then, two conditions must be satisfied before export can be effected:

$$P_x(1 + ey) \geqq P_D \qquad (1)$$

and

$$P_x > P_m \cdot m_x \cdot \frac{(1 + y)}{(1 + ey)} \qquad (2)$$

The former condition merely states that the return from unit export must be at least equal to the return from unit sale in the domestic market. This is necessary because otherwise domestic sale will be preferred to foreign sale. The second condition further states that the revenue from unit export must exceed *at least* the value of the import content, at the premium y, in the domestic market. If this is not so, the unit will not be produced at all and the producer will find it more profitable to sell away the import content.

Now, consistent with these two conditions, we *can* have $P_x < P_m \cdot m_x$ if $e > 1$, i.e. if the entitlement rate is more than 100 per cent. But $P_x < P_m \cdot m_x$ means that the f.o.b. export value falls *below* the foreign exchange value of the import content involved in this exportation, so that there is a net loss of foreign exchange and value subtraction.[1]

Note, however, that if over-invoicing is practised, the possibility of this phenomenon occurring increases further significantly; and we can have value subtraction even when $e < 1$ (which was substantially the Indian case). In this case, condition (2) becomes:

$$P_x > P_m \cdot m_x \frac{1 + y}{1 + ey + k(ey - \rho)} \qquad (2a)$$

where k is the proportion of f.o.b. export value by which export value is raised by over-invoicing and ρ is the black market premium on foreign exchange. It will be noted that, even if $e < 1$, it will now be possible to have $P_x < P_m \cdot m_x$ consistent with conditions (1) and (2a) being satisfied. Since over-invoicing was a widespread phenomenon, as we have already noted, in view of the undue reliance on heavy export subsidization (and tariff levies) in lieu of an official exchange rate alteration, the prospect of net losses of value subtraction arising in India despite the entitlement rate generally being less than unity for this reason could not be dismissed as negligible.

---

[1] Note that this phenomenon would be ruled out if the exchange rate were unified, which would be the case if $e = 1$.

If, further, we were to introduce into this model the possibility of non-transferable A.U. import allocations, then it is possible that the implicit, opportunity-cost premium r on these A.U. imports may be less than y. In this case, condition (2) modifies to:

$$P_x > P_m \cdot m_x \frac{(1 + r)}{(1 + ey)} \tag{2b}$$

and the possibility of value subtraction (i.e. $P_x < P_m \cdot m_x$) can arise again even if $e < 1$. Under the Indian-type régime, therefore, the possibility of value subtraction arising was very real indeed.

Value subtraction, in a different sense, could arise under the Indian trade régime in yet another way, with identical items being exported and imported—the loss then being proportional to the excess of the unit import price over the unit export price.[1] This phenomenon could, and in fact did, arise in India occasionally (e.g. with PVC exports). Logically, this could happen as a result merely of the differential rates on exports and imports, provided there was a differential between unit import and export prices. This is seen readily as follows.

If $P_m{}^x$ stands for the unit f.o.b. export price of an input and $P_m{}^m$ for its unit c.i.f. import price, it is possible that output of this input from existing productive capacity will be diverted to foreign exports, domestic price becoming $P_m{}^x(1 + ey)$. On the other hand, the import price (inclusive of the premium y) will be $P_m{}^m(1 + y)$. It follows that it will pay both the domestic producers to export this input and the users of this input to import it (and earn the extra premium) if $e > 1$ and hence $P_m{}^x(1 + ey) = P_m{}^m(1 + y)$, as required by the market. Once again, phenomena such as over-invoicing of exports would make this form of value subtraction possible even if $e < 1$.

(b) Selectivity of the subsidization

In point of fact, many of the inefficiencies resulting from the entitlement schemes were compounded by the selectivity with which

[1] For India, the unit export price was below the unit import price for two reasons: (i) owing to insurance and freight; and (ii) markets being not always perfect, the common practical experience seemed to be that price 'reductions' were often necessary for a *newly* emerging exporter (of manufactures) like India whereas import prices were relatively inflexible.

they were administered and from which we have so far been abstracting.

Undoubtedly, in an ideal world, we should want to make rational departures from unified exchange rates. There are, in fact, a vast number of grounds on which we can argue for optimal intervention in the shape of trade tariffs and subsidies and tax-cum-subsidies on production, consumption, and factor-use.[1]

However, the Indian export subsidization schemes involved policy intervention in a selective manner, without any economic rationale. As we have already shown in the preceding chapter, the principle apparently aimed at in the beginning was the supply of one more unit of 'import-content', in addition to 'replacement', as the economic incentive for export promotion. The equivalent *ad valorem* subsidy, therefore, would have varied between different export commodities and, converted into different *ad valorem* rates of import entitlements for different commodities, it did. The effective export subsidy further varied between commodities because, for administrative reasons and as a result of notions about priorities in some undefined sense, the entitlement licences could be marketed, as we have already seen, only within segmented markets and hence carried differential premia.[2]

In point of fact, towards 1965/6, the principle of export subsidization had clearly begun to veer around to the proposition that exports should be maximized—although, we should not forget that, on many *traditional* exports which were outside the range of such export subsidization, domestic absorption continued to create difficulties in the way of more successful export promotion.

The principle of maximizing exports, which became fairly widespread among the newer manufactures, was practised via a continuous tendency towards raising the effective subsidization. Also, we have already noted how it became generally possible to ask the Ministry of International Trade for *ad hoc* entitlements, for chemical and engineering exports, to make up for any ostensible difference between the domestic sale price of a product and

[1] For an exhaustive discussion of these arguments, see Bhagwati, *The Theory and Practice of Commercial Policy: Departures from Unified Exchange Rates*, International Finance Section, Princeton University, 1968.

[2] The considerable segmentation of the entitlement markets may also have contributed to instability in the premia which prevailed in these markets. However, theoretically we cannot establish this as a necessary consequence of market segmentation whereby both supply and demand are fragmented.

its supposed f.o.b. export price plus the subsidy normally available through drawbacks, fiscal tax concessions, and entitlements.[1] In addition, we have also noted how transport freight concessions were sought, and sometimes granted, to compensate for 'transport cost disadvantage' to products manufactured in the hinterland.[2] The fact that transport involves a real cost to the economy and hence must be accounted for, instead of being compensated for, was apparently forgotten in the general strategy of pushing out any and all of the new exports in particular.

Thus, the policy of export promotion generally adopted during the Third Plan period, ending in the devaluation of 6 June 1966, can best be described as having ultimately become one of indiscriminate export promotion, with even a perverse bias towards fixing the subsidy inversely to the competitive strength of the exportable commodity. This system had its counterpart in the indiscriminate protection that import policy furnished to domestic industries. Thus, the twin principles governing production and trade could be summed up, cynically but realistically: India should produce whatever it can, and India should export whatever it produces.

Commenting on this system elsewhere, Bhagwati[3] has argued that a policy of export maximization is politically inevitable, except when constrained by domestic-absorption problems (as on India's traditional exports, many of which directly enter the consumption of articulate groups), as soon as the Government has set up an independent Ministry in charge of export promotion:

Often the Minister's political reputation depends on his producing a sizeable increase in export earnings, *no matter how*. Thus, for example, when Goa was taken over by India and the Indian statistics thereafter showed a sizeable increment in export earnings, the Minister's reputation went up: Indian exports were beginning to move! Changes in the terms of trade, brought about by external factors, have a similar effect. Michael Michaely tells me that the Israeli Minister responsible for exports once refused to release export figures until somehow the figure was pushed up above the preceding year's level! Perhaps the answer is to abolish all separate Ministries for exports, and to educate politicians

---

[1] This was done via the so-called 'dryfruit' entitlement scheme, noted by us in the preceding chapter.
[2] This principle also underlay the working of the cotton textiles scheme, as is seen from the preceding chapter.
[3] *The Theory and Practice of Commercial Policy* . . . , op. cit., pp. 58–9.

and international institutions that exports *in themselves* are a poor index of efficiency in economic performance.

It is thus difficult to escape the conclusion that, while the Third Plan witnessed a major shift towards export subsidization, export promotion policies were inefficiently designed and implemented.[1] These policies were to change, fairly significantly, in the direction of greater efficiency with devaluation in June 1966. We discuss these changes later in the volume. For the present, we proceed to describe now the major outlines of the effective exchange-rate system as it operated prior to this devaluation, in the light of our description and analysis of import and export policies.

---

[1] We may note, in this connection, the widespread notion in India, which has found its way even into responsible Ministerial speeches, that each industry should 'earn its own imports' by effecting suitable exports. There have also been influential attempts at making exports obligatory for every industry. A related governmental policy has been to permit the expansion or creation of industrial capacity under contractual obligation to export a certain proportion of the output (as with PVC powder from Kotah), which can, and did, lead often to inefficient and 'throw-away' exports.

21

The Effective Exchange-Rate System

In the light of the preceding six chapters on import and export policies, we can now describe the major features of the effective exchange-rate system, as defined by the interaction of exchange rate and trade policies which India had acquired during the period preceding the June 1966 devaluation. But first we must note two major respects in which Indian economic policy in this area had already changed somewhat before devaluation: (1) remittances had been subsidized; and (2) tariffs were increasingly resorted to, in order to mop up part of the large premia on imports.

National defence remittance scheme

Immediately after the termination of the Indo-Pakistan war, when the foreign exchange situation had deteriorated as a consequence of the conflict and the concurrent moratorium on Western aid, the Indian Government introduced, in October 1965, the National Defence Remittance Scheme. In principle, this scheme involved an extension of the import entitlement principle to remittances, so that invisibles were brought within the purview of subsidization for the first time.

Under this scheme, which was eventually to be abolished along with the import entitlement schemes for exports when the rupee was devalued, Indian nationals resident abroad were given import licences to the value of 60 per cent of their remittances to India. Since these licences were marketable at a premium, in effect the remittances were being subsidized by the full amount of the price at which the licences could be sold. The effective subsidy enjoyed on such remittances, which totalled Rs. 70 crores during the period of the operation of the scheme, is reproduced in Table 21.1. Both the rise in the value of remittances during this period over their earlier levels and the fact that the premium on

TABLE 21.1
PERCENTAGE PREMIUM ON NATIONAL DEFENCE REMITTANCE CERTIFICATES

Date	Premium %	Date	Premium %
28.10.65	207	29.12.65	220
29.10.65	207	3.1.66	220–222
3.11.65	210	4.1.66	220–222
4.11.65	209	5.1.66	221
5.11.65	203	6.1.66	220
7.11.65	200	7.1.66	219
8.11.65	202	8.1.66	218–219
10.11.65	202½	10.1.66	218
12.11.65	203	11.1.66	217
15.11.65	205	13.1.66	217–218
18.11.65	203	15.1.66	217
20.11.65	200	17.1.66	214
22.11.65	198	18.1.66	211–214
25.11.65	195	19.1.66	207–209
28.11.65	198–200	20 to	
29.11.65	205–207	24.1.66	200–205
30.11.65	207–212	25.1.66	195
2.12.65	212–213	26.1.66	190
4.12.65	210–212	27.1.66	188
6.12.65	212–214	28.1.66	181
8.12.65	215–216	3.2.66	178
10.12.65	216	7.2.66	182
11.12.65	218	8.2.66	181
14.12.65	222–225	11.2.66	185–187
16.12.65	225–226	16.2.66	190–191
20.12.65	223	18.2.66	191
21.12.65	225	19.2.66	191
23.12.65	220	22.2.66	186
25.12.65	220–221	23.2.66	184
27.12.65	222–224	24.2.66	190–192
26.2.66	188	20.4.66	142–147
3.3.66	180	21.4.66	121
4.3.66	177	28.4.66	136
5.3.66	182	29.4.66	138–141
6.3.66	180	30.4.66	140
7.3.66	180	3.5.66	141–142
8.3.66	178	4.5.66	141
9.3.66	174	6.5.66	140
10.3.66	172	10.5.66	141
11.3.66	170	12.5.66	148–150
12.3.66	168	16.5.66	146–147
16.3.66	164	19.5.66	148–149
17.3.66	164	23.5.66	144
18.3.66	160	31.5.66	147
22 to		1.6.66	143
25.3.66	160–162	2.6.66	139

TABLE 21.1—*continued*

	%		%
25 to		8.6.66	110
28.3.66	158–160	14.6.66	118
28 to		15.6.66	120
4.4.66	155–156	16.6.66	78–80
5.4.66	150	30.6.66	92–93
6.4.66	145–146	2.7.66	91
7.4.66	140	6.7.66	88
13.4.66	115	7.7.66	92
14.4.66	111	11.7.66	80
16.4.66	122	12.7.66	80
19.4.66	149	15 to	
		16.7.66	81–82
		17.7.66	85–88
		19.7.66	85
		20.7.66	84
		21.7.66	82
		22.7.66	79
		27.7.66	82
		28.7.66	
		to	81–84
		2.8.66	

Note: The percentage premium represents the full value of the profit to be made on Rs. 100 worth of remittance.

Source: A trading firm in Bombay.

entitlements fell as remittances came in, suggest that remittances responded to the price incentive.

We may note, however, that, in consonance with the bureaucratic restrictions on entitlements for exports, numerous restrictions were built into this scheme as well. The N.D.R. import licences could, in general, be sold only to producers ('actual users') for certain permissible imports or to general traders who, in turn, were permitted to import, for resale, only those commodities which were specified in Public Notices published from time to time. Again, the N.D.R. licences once issued to actual users could not be retransferred to other actual users. Furthermore, the list of commodities, once opted for by the actual user in getting his licence issued to him against his N.D.R. purchase could not be changed even if this change was sought within the *overall* list of permissible imports. The bureaucratic nature of such inflexibility, and its economic irrationale, were strikingly highlighted when, with the introduction of liberal import licensing along with the June 1966 devaluation, many actual users who had got sulphur specified on their N.D.R. licences, in view of its high premium, found sulphur prices tumbling and wished to shift to other imports. The Government eventually permitted this to be done, but again with considerable reluctance and restrictions: for example, the sulphur licences could be converted only into mutton tallow licences. Bureaucratic notions about 'priority', without any demonstrable rationale, obviously had carried over into the operation of the N.D.R. scheme as well.

Increasing use of tariffs

From 1962/3 onwards, import duties were also used more frequently to mop up the import premia and add to national revenue. Table 21.2 summarizes this trend, showing that the average import duty (collected on dutiable imports) rose steadily up to the devaluation when, concurrently with the parity change, many duties were revised downwards.[1]

The vast majority of these tariff increases were selective and differential, although some reliance was placed on across-the-board duties later in the period. In 1962/3, for example, import duties were raised on some iron and steel items, silk yarn, copra, cars, and machine tools. In 1963/4 the budget was used to raise import duties further on machinery, raw cotton, rubber, palm oil, iron and steel manufactures, mineral oils and dyes, among other commodities.

Beginning with the 1963/4 budget, however, the principle of across-the-board rate revisions was introduced. For 1963/4 a *surcharge* was levied on all dutiable articles at a flat rate of 10 per cent of the existing import duty. In addition, a genuine across-the-board 'regulatory duty' was levied at 10 per cent *ad valorem* (unless the rate at 25 per cent of the existing duty worked out higher, in which case this higher rate was applicable).[2]

While the later budgets continued to raise average tariffs, the only major change introduced was through the supplementary budget in 1965/6, when the principle of across-the-board tariffs was further underlined by a major revision in the tariff rates which aimed at reducing the wide range of selectivity and reducing the

---

[1] Needless to say, we are aware of the well-known difficulties associated with our measure of the average tariff level (as also with other, alternative measures). We do think, however, that it is an adequate method of underlining the fact that the Government increasingly resorted to tariff increases through the period.

[2] This regulatory duty came into effect only on 17 February 1965.

TABLE 21.2
AVERAGE INCIDENCE OF IMPORT DUTIES, 1962-7
(Rs. crores)

Item	1962/3	1963/4	1964/5	1965/6	1966/7 (April–May 1966)	June 1966 to March 1967
Total imports	1,131·47	1,222·85	1,349·03	1,394·04	227·14	1,674·61
Deduct non-dutiable imports, viz.,						
(i) Food	144·26	179·60	282·14	309·11	64·41	507·98
(ii) Fertilizers	29·71	37·64	32·86	44·82	9·19	87·50
(iii) Crude petroleum	30·15	46·17	27·23	34·87	2·85	33·49
(iv) Hides and skins—raw and salted	2·77	3·36	3·14	2·37	0·18	1·51
(v) Newsprints	6·93	6·93	7·40	6·18	1·03	10·75
(vi) Books	3·00	3·38	4·13	3·21	0·47	3·60
	216·82	277·08	356·90	400·56	78·13	644·83
Dutiable imports (estimates)	914·65	945·77	992·13	993·48	149·01	1,029·78
						(post-devaluation rupees)
Total net import duty revenue	234·69	326·06	403·04	547·30	92·39	392·64
Average import duty on dutiable imports, %	25·7	34·5	40·0	55	62	38

Source: Department of Economic Affairs, Ministry of Finance; at request.

rates to a smaller number. The broad structure of the nominal tariffs that emerged from these changes is reproduced in Table 21.3. Thus, while import duties were being raised in lieu of the devaluation which was to come only in 1966, attempts were clearly

TABLE 21.3
AVERAGE RATES OF NOMINAL IMPORT DUTY ON BROAD CLASSES OF COMMODITIES, AFTER THE SUPPLEMENTARY BUDGET, 1965–6

Item	Percentage rate of import duty[a]
Plant and machinery	35
Agricultural machinery	15
Basic industrial raw materials	40
Processed industrial materials	60
Consumer goods	100

[a] To these rates we must add the regulatory duty of 10 per cent.
Source: Department of Economic Affairs, Ministry of Finance.

made to introduce more uniformity in the tariff rates, this providing the backdrop to the move towards a formal rate change and greater unification of the exchange rates for different activities, which was to begin with the devaluation.

The effective exchange rates

During the few months preceding devaluation in June 1966, therefore, the effective exchange-rate system could be described as having reached a stage of *de facto* though *ad hoc* and partial devaluation, with significant elements of a flexible exchange-rate policy. These elements are easily summarized.

(1) On the *export* side, a varying degree of effective changes in the parity had occurred, thanks to the subsidization measures. This improvement differed between commodities. Besides, its incidence varied, depending on the entitlement premia as also the frequent changes in the entitlement rates.

(2) At the same time, the subsidization of remittances through the N.D.R. scheme had extended the improvement in the effective exchange rate to this area of *invisibles*. However, other important invisibles such as tourist earnings remained effectively at the I.M.F. parity.

(3) On the *import* side, increased use by the Government of

tariffs, some on an across-the-board basis and others on a differential basis, had systematically, though inadequately, begun to cut into import premia on several commodities, again simulating the effects of a devaluation, albeit unevenly. The taxation of invisible imports, however, had not been attempted: for example, foreign travel (when permitted) could be undertaken at the parity rate.

(4) Thus, there was effective, but partial and uneven, *devaluation* of the exchange rate on a vast number of items of visible trade and on remittances among invisibles. The average degree of such *de facto* lowering of the exchange rate is extremely difficult to quantify, in view of the differential and changing character of export subsidization. But it could be put at around 80–100 per cent subsidization on many new manufactures (e.g. chemicals, engineering products, plastics, and art silks) with the average import duty at around 50 per cent.

(5) Moreover, the system had significant elements of a *flexible exchange rate* policy embedded in it. The effective exchange rate on all exports and remittances enjoying the benefit of import entitlement schemes thus varied with the import premia on entitlement licences, which were totally free to change with changing foreign exchange supplies and demands. Since up to 60 per cent of the total value of exports was covered by these schemes, the prevalence of a *de facto*, fluctuating rate system on the export side was by no means an insignificant phenomenon. Moreover, while tariffs were fixed for greater lengths of time, they *did* change annually—and, via supplementary budgets, even at lesser intervals—so that even on the import side the effective exchange-rate system could not be described as that of an unadulterated pegged exchange rate.

It was against this background, with partial shifts towards a more rational trade and exchange rate policy but with a still considerable carry-over of the inefficient package of import and export policies which we have described in the preceding six chapters, that the devaluation of 6 June 1966, was announced. This was to underline dramatically the growing shift to what we may call aptly the new economic policy of economic liberalism and increased reliance on the market mechanism as distinct from detailed and comprehensive controls.

PART VIII

Towards a New Economic Policy

22

Experiments with Economic Liberalism

THE devaluation of the rupee in June 1966, quite apart from the contemporaneous measures taken to liberalize import and industrial licensing, was perhaps the most dramatic episode in the shift of Indian economic policies towards a greater and more sophisticated reliance on the market mechanism. On the other hand, this shift had begun before devaluation and had been ushered in via measures such as the decontrol (however limited) of steel distribution and exemption of a number of industries from industrial licensing. We briefly review these policy shifts in this chapter and draw some important conclusions relating to India's prospects of continuing with its new economic policies, and development policy in general.

Industrial licensing

The Swaminathan Committee on Industries Development Procedures (1965), to whose Report we have referred in the chapters on industrial licensing and strategy, had argued for de-licensing a number of industries, mainly with a view to reducing delays through a reduction in the work-load of the Licensing Committee. The Swaminathan Committee's proposed criterion for exemption of industries from licensing was surprising:[1]

... generally speaking, industries which do not involve the import of capital goods or raw materials should be exempted from the licensing provisions of the Act by the issue of an exemption notification under Section 29-B of the Industries (Development and Regulation) Act. It should, by and large, be left to the economic judgement of the entrepreneur to decide whether or not he will enter these fields and make an investment and to what extent. In these fields the targets laid down by the Planning Commission would serve as indicative targets and as a

[1] Quoted in Estimates Committee Report, 1967–68, op. cit., p. 177.

II

factor to be considered by the prospective investor in his assessment of demand and other economic data.

From an economic viewpoint, this criterion made no sense. Even if the sole purpose of industrial licensing were to consist in preserving foreign exchange, the rule of thumb proposed was naïve in so far as it took into account only the direct foreign exchange requirements and ignored other foreign exchange repercussions. We might add further that the Committee qualified this intention, arguing that exemption should be withheld in the interest of the development of the small-scale and co-operative sectors, whenever necessary.

In any event, on the strength of the direct foreign-exchange-use criterion, the Swaminathan Committee proposed illustratively the de-licensing of the following industries: (1) cotton textile; (2) sugar; (3) cement; (4) toilet preparations; (5) paper and newsprint; (6) fire bricks; (7) hand tools; (8) furniture components; (9) plywood; and (10) milk foods.

Concrete policy action was to follow in May 1966, when eleven industries were formally delicensed: (1) iron and steel castings and forgings; (2) iron and steel structurals; (3) electric motors up to 10 h.p.; (4) pulp; (5) glue and gelatin; (6) glass; (7) power alcohol; (8) solvent extracted oils; (9) fire bricks and furnace linings; (10) cement, gypsum, and insulating boards; and (11) timber products. Announcing this policy shift in the Rajya Sabha on 9 May 1966, the Minister of Industrial Development and Company Affairs stated:[1]

Two basic considerations which have been kept in view in the preparation of this list are:

(i) The items are those in respect of which there is no substantial import of components or raw materials.

(ii) Industries in respect of which protection to the small and cottage industries is of importance have been left out.

The above list is by no means exhaustive. It is proposed to examine the schedule to the Industries (Development and Regulation) Act with a view to announcing further additions to this list from time to time. Apart from the two considerations mentioned . . . above, an additional factor which will be taken into account in preparing further lists will be the need for the accelerated development of industries with export potential.

[1] Estimates Committee Report, op. cit.

The Government, therefore, appeared to have accepted the Swaminathan Committee's criteria. However, on explaining to the Estimates Committee, 1967–68, the reasons for the divergence between the list of de-licensed industries and the list suggested by the Swaminathan Committee, the governmental spokesman produced yet other considerations as relevant to de-licensing of industries. For example, toilet preparations had not been de-licensed because they were not 'particularly a priority item and it was thought that there was no purpose in allowing decontrol in a field in which we may not want substantial quantity to be added'. On the other hand, furniture components were not de-licensed for the curious reason that 'they are minor items and it was not thought important enough for being de-licensed'. Milk food was kept on licensing 'in view of the importance of proper quality standards,'[1] with no regard to the fact that free licensing combined with statutory quality requirements would have been preferable. In brief, therefore, the criteria applied for de-licensing tended to be a curious amalgam of bad economics (e.g. the direct foreign exchange criterion) and inherited acceptance of earlier practices (e.g. refusal to de-license 'minor' industries such as furniture components).

In November 1966 twenty-nine additional industries were de-licensed.[2] In addition to these, two other industries, paper and newsprint and hand tools, had already been de-licensed during July 1966.

These moves towards industrial de-licensing were preceded by a raising of the exemption limit for licensing to units with investment above Rs. 25 lakhs (with a few exceptions). In addition, while

[1] Estimates Committee Report, op. cit., pp. 178–180.
[2] These were: (1) cast iron spun pipes; (2) steel ingots/billets by electric furnace; (3) non-vehicular internal/combustion engines below 50 h.p.; (4) electric motors up to 50 h.p.; (5) electric furnaces without import of switchgear and transformer; (6) bicycles and components; (7) tea machinery; (8) power-driven pumps; (9) agricultural sprayers (except manual) (conventional and knapsack type with indigenous engines); (10) air and gas compressors up to 6 C.M.C.; (11) fire-fighting equipment; (12) coated abrasives; (13) sewing machines and components; (14) weighing machines; (15) mathematical, surveying, and drawing instruments; (16) mixed fertilizers; (17) calcium carbonate; (18) barium carbonate; (19) barium chloride; (20) barium nitrate; (21) barium sulphate; (22) *blanc fixe*; (23) activated bleaching earth; (24) activated carbon; (25) metallic stearates; (26) sodium aluminate; (27) paperboard/strawboard; (28) paper for packaging; (29) hardboard, including fibre board, chip board, and particle boards.

licensing had generally been necessary for 'substantial expansion' involving expansion by more than 10 per cent of the registered capacity, this limit was generally raised to 25 per cent.

Another significant relaxation related to the diversification of production by units licensed for specific products. Subject to qualifications (such as the exclusion of products mainly made in the small-scale sector), 1966 witnessed the grant of permission to diversify production up to 25 per cent of the existing capacity.[1]

While all the measures which we have reviewed so far represented significant shifts towards economic liberalism, they fell short of a restructuring of the system on the basis of clear and hard analysis. Such an analysis would have led to a radically different pattern of industrial planning and policy.

Recognizing that India is in a 'structural' situation where capital is not malleable, and that she does not trade atomistically in world markets, we must admit that fairly detailed 'looking-ahead' of the industrial structure cannot be avoided. Given perfect foresight and total accuracy of information, combined with full specification of the utility function, time horizon, and other relevant variables, one could in principle generate the optimum time path of all industrial investments in detail. However, we live in a world of imperfect information (on technological coefficients, substitution possibilities, etc.) and imperfect foresight (concerning technological progress, changes in world market conditions, foreign aid availability, vagaries in the natural elements determining agricultural harvest, etc.). It is therefore impossible, in practice, to draw up a detailed investment plan which is truly optimal; and even the task of drawing up a reasonably consistent, realistic, and detailed investment plan would seem to require more sophisticated tools of analysis,

---

[1] Note that this measure of liberalization also represented a halting and ill-defined move towards a more efficient system: the decision to stop diversification at 25 per cent of the originally licensed capacity was based on (1) choice of 25 per cent without any clear rationale as to the relevant number; (2) a failure to think the problem through and ask why further diversification should not be permitted; and (3) the consequent inability to see that a system under which full diversification was automatically permitted except for a small list of priority outputs (whose production might be required on schedule) and with a small, banned list of prohibited, non-priority items of manufacture, would have made much greater sense, both administratively and in terms of economic efficiency. We take up this question later in the chapter at greater length.

and sharper data-gathering systems, than are available at the moment. These complexities have become particularly acute for India where the vastly increased detail and interdependence of the developing industrial structure today accentuates further the difficulties inherent in the administration of a detailed control system by means of a few officials.

These considerations suggest that planning in depth, which cannot be avoided in a structural situation, should be restricted to a few, well-chosen industries. The choice of such industries could be made with reference to the criterion that any industry in which gestation lags (including those in decision-making) are too long to permit fairly easy, rapid, and relatively inexpensive correction of any shortfalls, should be carefully planned and implemented. Investment in industries whose development is socially advantageous but cannot be confidently expected to come about as a result of market forces, mainly because of incorrect appreciation in the market of the growth in demand for their products, must be planned. In the former category for India some examples are steel, machine-building, and fertilizers. As a good instance of the latter may be mentioned the opposition to the expansion of investment in steel in the early years of the Second Plan. It must be mentioned, however, that investment licensing is *not* the instrument which would bring about investment in these areas. What is required, besides careful planning, is the appropriate machinery to get the projects implemented. The Indian situation (even after the liberalization measures just reviewed) was that while licensing prevented some from entering certain fields either because these were reserved for the public sector or because enough capacity was licensed already, there was no way to ensure that the licensed capacity in fact was installed. The shortfalls in the Third Plan in steel and fertilizers were symptomatic of this.

At the other end of the spectrum, one should be able to specify industries which are of very low priority from a social point of view. In these cases outright prohibition of capacity creation could be an alternative. Given that these are low priority items already being produced in the economy, one may alternatively impose sufficiently high excise duties to curb the demand for such products thereby making expansion of these industries relatively unprofitable. Logically this would also mean that one should announce a set of excise duties in advance of production for such commodities which are not currently being produced and which may get produced if outright prohibitions are not used. Since the range of low priority industrial production can be fairly wide and this range is by no means beyond India's present industrial achievement, it would be difficult to announce a comprehensive set of advance excises; it would, therefore, be necessary to add a statement of broad categories of products where prospective investors should expect stiff excise duties if production is undertaken.

Once the two categories of 'high' and 'low' priority industries in the above sense are determined, there does not seem to be any overriding consideration for investment licensing of the others.

What about the supplementary goals served by investment licensing which have been sought, even if unsuccessfully, by the Indian licensing system, namely: reduction in concentration of ownership; reduction in geographical concentration; and protection of the small producer?

As we have already seen, since there was no effective control on resale of enterprises once they were licensed, the first objective could hardly be considered as being served by investment licensing. Further, even if there were re-sale control or anti-merger regulations, there would be nothing to prevent an entrepreneurial group getting licences through *benami* (i.e., via use of another name) transactions. The same objectives could, therefore, be more efficiently, though perhaps less dramatically, served by more positive action through easier access to credit and 'know-how' to potential newcomers.

Regarding the second objective, we must say that regional concentration might have been a serious problem when investment in social overheads and infrastructure was very unevenly distributed. The past fifteen years of planning have reduced disparities of this sort in India and also created some infrastructure in all the states If experience shows that industrialization without licensing tends to gravitate towards certain areas, the other areas could be subsidized so as to offer inducements to attract industry. Moreover, public sector investment in the so-called 'footloose' industries or in building infrastructure could be used towards this objective.

Regarding the third objective of promoting and protecting the small entrepreneur there is little reason to believe that the existing system of investment licensing achieves it. In fact, as we have already seen in the earlier chapters on import and industrial licensing, the very procedure of taking out an investment licence is one which is understood and overcome more easily by the relatively well-established and more affluent producers. Even if one sought to protect the small producer through prevention of growth of capacity in the competing large-scale sector, this could be done without licensing through the levy of appropriately stiff excise on the output of the large-scale sector.

Thus, a full-scale evaluation of the working of the existing controls over industrial investment in the light of the objectives to be fulfilled by industrial planning would have led to a much more significant shift towards delicensing, with explicit emergence of reliance on other policies to fulfil objectives such as the promotion of new and small-scale entrepreneurs.

Import liberalization and devaluation

Alongside the devaluation of June 1966, the Government also radically changed its import licensing policies, in terms of both A.U. imports and the import entitlements granted to exporters. An analysis of the devaluation and the accompanying reduction in tariffs and elimination of the import entitlement schemes will be given later in this section. First, we review the import liberalization measures for A.U. licensing.

The import liberalization measures extended to fifty-nine priority industries, covering almost 80 per cent of the organized sector's output. Listed in the Press Note of 21 June 1966, these industries were given almost total freedom to import their raw materials and components, although restrictions on sources and the necessity to secure licences were continued:

For the 59 priority industries raw materials, components and spares required for production up to full capacity for six months will be provided. The priority industries include many important export industries, industries meeting the common requirements of people and above all capital building industries. In the case of other industries, allocations will be made according to the resources available and the essentiality of the product. For all industries, licensing will naturally conform to the availability of foreign exchange from different sources.

Small scale industrial units making the same products as the priority industries will be given the same liberal facilities. Assessment of their requirements by sponsoring authorities may cause delay. It is, therefore, proposed to grant them licenses immediately to the extent of thrice the rupee value of the licenses given in 1964–65. In the case of other small scale units import licenses will be issued for twice the rupee value of licenses issued in 1964–65. . . .

In recent years there has been a large increase in the output of spare parts for various industries. Many of these have, therefore, been banned for import. All the same there is a considerable volume of industrial, earthmoving, construction and other equipment which may not be fully utilised because of lack of adequate spare parts, which are not made in the country. It is, therefore, proposed to license freely both to actual users and traders the import from the U.S.A. of a wide range of spare parts other than those whose import is banned. The quotas for established importers from other sources are also being raised.[1]

The import 'liberalization' implied in this policy shift reflected the planned increment in the availability of maintenance aid (at nearly $900 million) which was promised at the time the policy package involving both devaluation and import liberalization was being urged upon the Indian Government by the World Bank and donor countries. It was assumed that the incremental supply of maintenance aid plus the net increase in the effective cost of imports thanks to devaluation (even after adjusting for the reduction in tariffs) would be adequate to meet any conceivable demands for raw materials and components. In the event, as we shall presently see, the full aid could not be utilized, largely because of the recession in industrial production that was to characterize most of the period following upon June 1966.

In any case, the import liberalization was extremely limited in scope, with the cardinal principle of 'indigenous availability' continuing to plague the administration of the licensing system. Thus, for example, the *Import Trade Control Handbook of Rules and Procedures* (1967) had the following pertinent guidelines for licence applicants:

(ii) Full details of the items applied for and justification for their import *vis-à-vis* use of indigenous substitutes, the value/quantity in respect of each item and the ITC classification of the items should be invariably indicated in the application for license;

(iii) Detailed end-use of the raw materials/components applied for should be mentioned in the application; . . .

(vi) The efforts made for procuring the goods applied for or substitutes thereof from the internal market or indigenous manufacturers and the result of such efforts should also be indicated in the applica-

[1] Quoted in Estimates Committee Report, op. cit., p. 166.

tion (the indigenous manufacturers published in the Hand Book of Indigenous Manufacturers should be contacted for the supply of articles manufactured by them); . . .[1]

The Ministry was soon to come under fire for having (inadvertently) issued licences to import items where there was domestic capacity. Speaking in the Rajya Sabha on 10 August 1967, the Minister for Industrial Development was constrained to reassure the House that if any of the items for which import licences had been issued were being indigenously manufactured, the continuation of such licences would be reconsidered as per 'strict order' issued to that effect.[2]

The lapse into the chaotic principle of indigenous availability was epitomized in the Press Note issued by the Ministry of Commerce on April 1968, stating the import policy for April 1968–March 1969 and containing this policy statement:

(vii) Account has been taken of the development of indigenous production. Consequently as many as 260 items which are now produced in the country in sufficient quantity and reasonable quality, have been taken off the permissible list. These include certain items of drugs, medicines, chemicals, machine tools, etc.

(viii) 197 items will be allowed to actual users only on restricted basis . . .

(xi) Industrial units wanting to import plant and equipment of a value exceeding Rs. 7·5 lakhs will have to advertise their requirements before they apply for import licenses, so that the indigenous manufacturers get an opportunity of offering to meet the whole or part of the demand from domestic production. The procedure will also apply in the case of import of steel castings and forgings of a value of Rs. 50,000 or or more.[3]

The continuance of the principle of 'indigenous availability' was partly to be attributed to the recession in industrial investment and output that happened to occur contemporaneously with import liberalization and devaluation. At a time when there was lack of effective demand for output in several industries, it proved impossible to argue for the dismantling of automatic protection of all industries through import controls. In a very real sense, therefore, the timing of import liberalization was not ideal, in retrospect: a

---

[1] Ministry of Commerce, Government of India, Chapter IV.
[2] Cf. report in *The Times of India*, 11 August 1967.
[3] Ministry of Commerce, Government of India, New Delhi.

burgeoning economy would have increased the chance of making an effective dent in the practice of granting automatic protection to every activity. On the other hand, it was clear that it was quite naïve to expect the industrialists, who had been conditioned over a long period to the comfortable situation of a totally sheltered market, to agree to a switchover to an efficient system involving international competition and competitiveness as a price of survival. In this, the pressure groups were often in the company of disinterested politicians (such as the Finance Minister, Morarji Desai) whose thinking also had been conditioned by the planning philosophy of the earlier period: that anything which could be produced and supplied from domestic capacity must automatically be precluded from imports. It was thus obvious that getting away from the backlog of the earlier economic philosophy was a Herculean task.

It is often thought that the optimal strategy for development in the less developed countries would be to get investment going behind quota and tariff walls, the primary requirement being the creation of the inducement to invest in the quickest fashion.[1] At the *next* stage, when the inducement to invest has been taken care of, the neo-classical concern with efficiency should become the focal point of economic policy. Unfortunately, this two-stage theory of development is impractical. It is just too difficult, and at best an extremely slow process, to get away from the first stage *unless* the growth of grossly inefficient industries has been ruthlessly suppressed from the beginning and the second stage has been explicitly kept in view and made an essential ingredient of the economic policies pursued in the first stage.

The devaluation

While the import liberalization programme was ill-timed, in the sense that (i) the industrial recession prevented the already difficult process of dislodging the principle of 'indigenous availability' from getting anywhere, and (ii) the line of credit, in the shape of the significant step-up of maintenance aid to $900 million, could not be exploited in view of lack of effective demand, the devalu-

---

[1] Albert Hirschman somewhat misleadingly describes this kind of growth as 'hothouse industrialization'. The indiscriminate growth of industries which occurs under such a strategy is indeed the opposite of the orderly arrangements of flowers and plants to be found in hothouses.

ation of the rupee in June 1966 also appears in retrospect to have been ill-timed, but from a *political* point of view. This was largely due to political considerations emerging from the advocacy of the measure by the World Bank, and other factors linked mainly with the second big agricultural drought during 1966–7 (following upon that in 1965–6) which was a principal factor leading to a general price rise and, paradoxically, an industrial recession.[1]

The devaluation came under heavy political fire because the Government clearly gave the impression of being forced into it by the World Bank which serviced the Aid-India Club. That the measure was adopted under heavy pressure from this source is indisputable: it would have been difficult to expect a Government on the threshold of a General Election to be enthusiastic about devaluation, no matter how justified it was on economic grounds. The result was that many people, certainly among the articulate groups, felt strongly that India had capitulated to foreigners, that this would whet their appetite only further to shift Indian economic policies towards what the U.S. ideological position demanded, and that India had been forced to adopt a measure which was almost certainly inspired by a foreign ideological position and was detrimental to her economic interests. The fact that devaluations are announced necessarily without prior consultation was also a contributory factor to the general resentment among influential party bosses (such as the Congress President, Kamaraj) who felt that such an important decision, affecting the electoral prospects of the Congress Party, should have been taken after consultation with the Party. The hesitation of the bulk of the bureaucracy, who only haltingly were coming around to the new economic philosophy, and the general feeling that devaluation was a national disgrace—an Anglo-Saxon sentiment with really no place in a country with hardly any claim to a prestigious currency, in any sense at all—were also factors which augured ill for the devaluation. Apart from these, however, there was an important economic

---

[1] For a description and analysis of the industrial recession, refer to the Economic Survey, 1967–68, op. cit., Chapter III. Put briefly, the growth of industrial output fell from 5·6 per cent in 1965 to 2·6 per cent in 1966 and around 1·4 per cent in the first three-quarters of 1967. A major, though not the only, cause was the shortfall in agricultural inputs and the deceleration in government expenditures, in a tight food supply situation, which directly affected the demand for many investment industries dependent on governmental orders. The second drought was thus a major factor in the industrial recession we refer to in the text.

aspect of the devaluation which made the decision to devalue in June 1966 somewhat hazardous.

And this was that the devaluation of the rupee from Rs. 4·76 per dollar to Rs. 7·50, by 36·5 per cent, was accompanied by a significant reduction in import duties, the levy of off-setting export duties on traditional, primary exports (such as jute and tea), and the elimination of the import entitlement schemes. The net devaluation, when we consider the effect of the removal and/or reduction in export subsidies and import duties, was, therefore, considerably less than was imagined by unsophisticated critics at the time. Thus, in an important sense the devaluation that was announced was a measure to rationalize the system of *ad hoc* export subsidies (and import duties) which had grown up in lieu of a formal devaluation and should have been judged *as such*.

The fact that the *net* devaluation was much smaller than the gross parity change compromised the possibility that a significant rise in exports would ensue. And yet this was how the devaluation was partly to be judged in public evaluations later. Furthermore, three other factors impeded any major improvement in export performance:

(i) The removal of the lucrative export subsidies must have reduced the over-invoicing of exports which we described in Part VII. Clearly this incentive was lost under the new régime. On the other hand, the effect of the elimination of over-invoicing of exports must have been to reduce *apparent* export performance in industries which had earlier qualified for the lucrative import entitlement schemes. Unless, therefore, allowance was made for this factor, an analyst of devaluation was certain to underrate the effect, if any, of the devaluation on export performance—as in fact did happen. The loss of apparent export earnings on this count might well have been as high as 10–20 per cent of the value of exports covered by the earlier import entitlement schemes.

(ii) Secondly, the removal of the entitlement schemes, and the rationalization that the devaluation implied, also meant that *some* exports which were harmful and represented national loss, must have been eliminated by the new régime. As we noted earlier, the main purpose of the devaluation (as conceived by its principal domestic proponents at the time) was to replace the notion of *maximization* of exports with the notion of *efficient* exports. The loss in export earnings, insofar as it represented the elimination or reduction of wasteful exports, was thus *desirable* rather than an ill-effect of the devaluation and the new régime. But, as might well be expected, the public discussion of the issue did not allow for this element of sophistication either.

(iii) Thirdly, the very fact that export subsidies had been eliminated (although they were to be revived shortly, albeit in an improved form) underlined that devaluation had been the outcome of an *internal* tussle between the Ministry of International Trade and the Ministry of Finance. The latter was in favour of the new régime; but the elimination of export subsidies implied, for the Ministry of International Trade, a considerable loss of patronage via total freedom to raise export incentives indiscriminately. For quite some time after devaluation, therefore, the Minister for International Trade was known to go around assuring businessmen that he would start the subsidies again, very soon. The effect of such assurances, combined with pressures from the new exporting pressure groups on the Government to revive the subsidies, must have been to deter immediate exports until the expected revival of subsidies occurred. An important reason why devaluation was deemed widely to be unsuccessful was the fact that most critics tended to compare export performance during the year *immediately* after the devaluation with that during the twelve months immediately prior to it, without any allowance for long-term effects. This *naïveté* also led to more unfavourable comparisons and misleading conclusions; the Minister of International Trade was merely helping to stack the cards even more against a favourable, immediate outcome regarding export performance.

Finally, we may note that devaluation was misguidedly criticized by those who made the typical error of not asking what would have happened if there had been no devaluation instead of arguing, on a *post hoc ergo propter hoc* basis, that what followed upon devaluation must have been caused by it. The second major drought of 1966-7, which succeeded that in 1965-6, led to an inevitable rise in the price-level of agriculture-based and agricultural products which had nothing to do with devaluation as such. However, the general price rise was attributed uncritically to devaluation, much to the detriment of the measure, and hardly any critic made allowance for the effect that two successive droughts would have exercised on export performance even if there had been no devaluation.

Thus devaluation, however desirable it was on strictly economic grounds, came at a time, and in a form, which reduced critically its chance of being accepted and judged discriminatingly by the public (who resented the price rise following the drought), the pressure groups (of exporters deprived of lucrative subsidies), the radical groups (who assumed that the move must be decried because it was being forced upon India by the World Bank and donor agencies such as USAID) and the politicians (who resented the loss of patronage following upon the elimination of the entitlement schemes and/or failure to be consulted on the decision). These difficulties were compounded by governmental diffidence in putting across the devaluation, and the import liberalization scheme, in a positive way: in particular, the feeling that the Government had been forced into a policy it did not wish to adopt, by aid agencies, was enhanced by the generally apologetic tone of government spokesmen. Also, the facts that the net devaluation was considerably less than the parity change, and that the devaluation must accordingly be judged as essentially a move to clean up the existing system which had grown up largely in lieu of a formal parity change, were not put across forcefully although this might have helped to educated public opinion into looking at the move in a more discriminating fashion.

Export subsidies

But, even if devaluation did not prove to be a political success, and was probably discredited as an effective policy instrument for the reasons which we have discussed at some length, we may still ask whether, from an objective point of view, its primary purpose of replacing the inefficient system of *ad hoc* and *variable* export subsidies (matched by increasing tariffs to mop up the import premia) was achieved. On this issue, we feel that success was moderate rather than total. We have already noted that the Minister for International Trade was extremely keen to revive the subsidies, and the political tussle led to a limited revival. While the import entitlement schemes, as originally operated (see Part V), disappeared, these industries continued to be given 'pure replacement' licences for imports. However, this was hardly a matter of significance any longer, in view of import liberalization which gave almost total access to imports to the fifty-nine priority industries covering nearly 80 per cent of organized industrial sector output.[1] On the other hand, the major concession was the grant of cash assistance, on a selective and limited basis, to a whole range of new manufactures. But the major departure from earlier practices was that there were only three rates: 10, 15, and 20 per cent. Further, the product coverage was mainly limited to engineering chemicals. While it seemed that this might lead to revived pressures for the variable subsidies of the earlier period, and that hence this revival of subsidies in an explicit form was probably a tactical mistake, the lesson that such a subsidy system would be wasteful seemed to have been learned. While, therefore, the cash assistance schemes were later extended to sports goods, processed foods, etc., the subsidy levels were pegged fairly firmly.

Attempts at promoting exports were to take a variety of other forms. For example, the Import Policy notices drew exporters' attention to the fact that their applications for expansion of industrial capacity would be treated very favourably and that they would be given licences to import their raw materials from 'sources of their own choice'.[2] An innovation was the so-called 'green form' allotment of indigenous raw materials to exporting units. Under this scheme, the Government sought to ensure 'prompt supplies of certain indigenous raw materials to manufacturing units in the engineering, chemicals (including drugs, dyes, paints, glass, ceramics and rubber industries), plastics, processed foods, and garments industry'.[3] More interesting was the policy innovation of supplying prime iron and steel, at *international* prices, to exporters of engineering goods. In addition, attempts at simplifying procedures for expeditious dispensation of cash assistance, drawbacks, and tax credits were intensified. Finally, the provision of export credits (at effectively subsidized rates of interest) was enlarged: for example, the Reserve Bank of India decided during 1967 to charge a concessional rate of $4\frac{1}{2}$ per cent to commercial banks for refinancing

---

[1] However, there was some advantage in securing licences for imports from *any* source, as against a tied source, which was possible when the licence was earned through entitlement for replacement.

[2] Cf. *Press Note* of the Ministry of Commerce, on Import Policy for April 1968 to March 1969, dated 1 April 1968, Government of India, New Delhi.

[3] *Handbook of Export Promotion*, Directorate of Commercial Publicity, Ministry of Commerce, New Delhi, 1967; p. 75.

facilities relating to the pre-shipment and post-shipment advances made by banks to exporters.[1]

Other industrial controls

The experiments with economic liberalism, which we have been discussing so far, also included a gradual exemption of industrial items, including cement and steel, from price and distribution controls.

The control of prices and distribution of steel, in all forms, was total until March 1964. However, the celebrated Report of the Raj Committee led to a decontrol of steel price and distribution except with respect to pig iron, ingot items and bottom plate, billets and tin bars, sheets and wide strip, tin plates, and a few other items. Although, however, the decontrolled items accounted for nearly two-thirds of total steel output, it is interesting that decontrol was withheld largely from those items where the Raj Committee had indicated the grossest abuses. Gradually, however, decontrol was extended to other items until, by May 1967, it was fully comprehensive.

The other major decontrolled item was to be cement. Decontrol of price and distribution became effective in January 1966. While it was apparently complete, and the market price was allowed to rise to more remunerative levels, the Government had partially offset it by binding the industry, as part of the decontrol arrangements, to supply at least 50 per cent of its output to the Government's enterprises at controlled prices. However, this particular experiment was to prove short-lived and the Government was to revert to retail price fixation and distribution by a government-controlled agency (the Cement Corporation of India) from January 1968.

Apart from these two major attempts at decontrol, of price and distribution, the success of which was less than total, the Government also proceeded during this period to loosen its hold on other manufactures. Many commercial vehicles, for example, were exempted from the informal price control which had been exercised from 1963, and also from distributional controls, during 1967. Again, while statutory control on mills (imposed in October 1964) to produce certain varieties of cloth, in certain minimum

---

[1] *Report* of the Ministry of Commerce, 1967–68, Government of India, New Delhi, Chapter III.

amounts, was continued, the scope of such control was reduced considerably by dropping several varieties of cloth from this scheme in May 1968.

All these experiments indicated a growing awareness at the governmental level that effective control of price and distribution could affect long-term growth of supply (e.g. cement) or that, in case of considerable shortages, controls were just ineffective and the final consumers ended up paying scarcity prices in any case (e.g. steel). Governmental intervention thus had to be continually reviewed. Further, it had to be confined to areas where: (i) either for equity reasons or for 'priority-use' considerations, a certain pattern of distribution had to be achieved and no alternative method of distribution (such as outright subsidies to the individuals or firms in whose favour the distribution was desired) was superior or feasible; or (ii) monopoly regulation required it, and superior alternative policies, such as trust-busting, were unavailable. Furthermore, in the former case, the price accruing to the producer was to reflect the incentive needed for long-term growth of supply, instead of being reduced in the interest of the consumer on grounds of 'equity': such an implicit subsidy was better provided from more general sources of revenue if the shortage (leading to the 'equity' problem) was not to be accentuated.

Future prospects

Ideally, the régime to which India would have moved, if the shifts towards economic liberalism had been fully thought out *and* had not run into the second drought and the recession, would have been somewhat as follows:[1]

(1) Industrial licensing would have been removed from the pivotal place assigned to it. Instead, we would have had a concentration of industrial planning in depth for a limited number of 'priority' industries chosen largely on the criteria of imperfect foresight by market participants and relative difficulty of rapid and inexpensive correction of shortfalls. A few non-priority industries might have been either prohibited outright or subjected to stiff excise duties. The rest would then have been left to market forces.

(2) Regional dispersion of industrial activity, in so far as it was

[1] What we describe below represents the substance of what, for example, was recommended by J. Bhagwati and T. N. Srinivasan, op. cit., in early 1966.

KK

inescapable, would have been undertaken by incentives granted for attracting 'footloose' industries, thus reducing the costs of meeting such an objective to a minimum. New and small-scale entrepreneurs would have been encouraged by direct action such as institutions designed to make credit and finance available to them.

(3) Consistent with this system, the method of import allocations would have had to be re-cast. Ideally, we could have had a flexible exchange-rate policy, with the few priority sectors assured of their capital goods and maintenance imports by subsidies to enable them to outbid their rivals. Alternatively, consistent with a pegged exchange rate system, the import régime could have been adapted as follows.

With respect to the allocation of foreign exchange for capital goods imports, an appropriate method would have been to pre-empt exchange for the high priority projects for their capital goods requirements, while leaving the remaining exchange to be freely bid for by other entrepreneurs, private and public.[1] The reason for pre-emption would have been *not* to subsidize the high priority sectors but instead to make sure that they *definitely* secured their capital goods requirements. Since, however, a significant premium on imports in the remaining sector could continue, especially if the exchange rate were changed only haltingly, there would have been an effective subsidy on the use of foreign exchange by the high priority users under this scheme. Since such a system of dual rates is inefficient, and may even generate illegal sales of exchange to other users, thereby frustrating the very purpose of pre-emption, it would have been necessary to use tariff policy from time to time to make the effective exchange rates applicable to the two sectors come fairly close to one another.[2]

With respect to maintenance imports and A.U. licensing, the system for allocation of foreign exchange among industrial users could have been broadly similar. The high priority sectors could

---

[1] High priority sectors obviously must include high priority non-industrial sectors as well.

[2] It may be feared that aid-tying arrangements might have made the adoption of such a system impossible. However, all that would have been entailed by tying would have been a reduction in the economic efficiency of the system advocated in the text: the symptom of this inefficiency being the *de facto* emergence of multiple rates, by source, that would have arisen from aid-tying by source for example. On this issue, see Bhagwati, *The Tying of Aid*, op. cit.

again have got their imports on a pre-emption basis whereas the remaining entrepreneurs would have had to bid for the rest of the exchange. Alternatively, if for some reason such an action were found unacceptable the present system of A.U. licensing could have been continued purely as a convenient method of *initial* allocation to the remaining entrepreneurs and free, legal resale, allowed. It is worth considering whether even in the high priority sectors pre-emption might have covered something less than their entire requirement of maintenance imports, the remaining requirements being procured from the free market. This might have had a salutary efficiency effect on their use of imported materials.

These arrangements would have been consistent with protection of domestic industries, where necessary, since it would always have been open to use tariff policy for this purpose. In fact, such a revival of the Tariff Commission would have been quite useful in preventing the excessive feather-bedding which total reliance on quantitative restriction had generated.

(4) In the absence of willingness to adjust the exchange rate freely, the new régime would also have had to resort more readily to tariffs and export subsidies, noting that selectivity (unless ruthlessly and discriminatingly exercised) could be extremely irrational and might even be impractical (at a detailed level) *and* that the burden of exchange-rate adjustment could not, in practice, be transferred to an equivalent trade tariffs and subsidies mechanism without, at some stage, leading to inefficiencies.[1]

(5) Finally, such a régime would have relied on fiscal policies to continue raising the rate of domestic savings to higher levels, while relying upon the new framework of efficient economic policies relating to industrial planning and foreign trade, which would have facilitated the securing of higher rates of return to the resources thus secured by fiscal policy.

Perhaps, despite the fumbling nature of their experiments in this direction, the policy-makers might have ended up with such a pattern of trade and industrial policies, marking a radical departure from the policies of the earlier period. However, the drought of 1966–7 and the industrial recession which accompanied it were, as we have already argued, among the factors that compromised this possibility fairly seriously during the two years after devaluation.

[1] On the last point, see J. Bhagwati's *The Theory and Practice of Commercial Policy*, op. cit., pp. 63–4.

The excellent harvest during the latter half of 1967–8 altered these dim prospects. However, the sudden prospect of grossly diminished foreign aid, even for maintenance imports, during 1968 made the foreign exchange situation look extremely difficult, and at the end of that year India was threatened with a possible relapse into earlier policies: for one thing, when crises develop it is extremely difficult to resist the temptation to control all allocations; for another, a major shortfall in aid is likely to provoke political resentments against donor countries, and hence against the new economic policies associated in the public mind with donor-country and World Bank pressures. From this point of view, the prospects of India holding on to her newly emerging shift in economic policies seemed less certain than was hoped for in 1966.[1]

---

[1] We have not reviewed here the other important shift in Indian economic policy which began during the same period as the major moves to economic liberalism: namely, the shift in investments and policy interest to the agricultural sector. This was largely prompted by the two droughts of 1965–6 and 1966–7 which underlined the precarious margin between domestic supplies and need; it was also a shift which was actively promoted by the donor countries and the World Bank. For details, the *Economic Survey* 1967–8, op. cit., is again a good source. Also see Max Millikan, op. cit.

PART IX

Conclusions

23
Lessons[1]

WHAT general lessons can we draw from our analysis of India's experiment with planned industrialization since its Independence? It seems to us manifest, even though policy analysis in economic questions can rarely be as definitive as in the natural sciences, that Indian planning for industrialization suffered from excessive attention to targets down to product level, and a wasteful physical approach to setting and implementation thereof, along with a generally inefficient framework of economic policies designed to regulate the growth of industrialization. Towards the end of the period we have studied, India did begin to pull away from this type of planning, in the direction of greater flexibility and concern for the more important decisions (combined with a greater area of decision-making left outside the Government). India was beginning to learn the basic lesson that costs mattered, cost–benefit calculations had to be increasingly made, alternative projects needed to be weighed against one another, and the framework of trade, exchange rate, and investment policies had to be carefully designed to exploit India's advantages in the availability of enterprise, efficient administration, education, and a tradition of growing industrialization (over a century).

India did not plan too much; in certain important ways it just planned inadequately. Physical, cost–benefit ignoring and choice-negligent planning, combined with detailed regulation of such inefficiently determined targets, really proved to be a negation of rational planning. This, in itself, is a major lesson: and India's experience is of relevance to other developing countries which are at the stage of development and industrialization where enough economic agents and opportunities exist for there to be rational

[1] This chapter is *not* a summary. Nor does it seek to comment on the big question of the prospects for the Indian economy. It is a brief statement of the broad conclusions to which we are led by the study concerning the kind of planning that would be suitable for countries endowed, like India, with a fair mix of education, efficient civil service, and entrepreneurship with industrial experience.

choices amongst alternative projects and industries within a framework of incentives provided by economic policies.

Having said this, we would re-emphasize two things: (1) the inefficiencies in planning which we have highlighted in this volume were probably inevitable: there is no escape from 'learning by doing' and it is pertinent to remember that few, if any, critics, and least of all the *laissez-faire* advocates, grasped the full dimensions of the planning and developmental problems faced by India around 1950; and (2) none of the improvements in the planning of trade, industrialization and related economic policies which we have advocated in this volume are incompatible with the basic objectives of a socialist society which stresses distributive justice, equality and the eradication of material poverty; indeed, these socialist objectives, which we fully share, have been frustrated in many instances by the existing policies and would be better served by the policy changes which we have suggested.

India's experience has also a direct bearing on the strategy of development which consists in the generation of booming industrial investments by cutting off imports and offering sheltered markets indiscriminately. Offered as a description, this is what has happened in some developing countries, especially in Latin America. On the other hand, offered as a prescription, such an approach negates the very meaning of planning and leads to an indiscriminate growth of industries regardless of costs. And, once these industries have taken root, it is extremely difficult to revert to efficient policies.

You cannot have 'growth' first and 'efficiency' next; the two processes have to go hand in hand. Indian experience highlights these lessons dramatically. The growth of industrialization in India was far from being entirely in response to sheltered markets: on the contrary, as we have seen, the aim was to regulate it through detailed targeting and industrial licensing, with the Q.R. régime serving to buttress these decisions (through the elimination of foreign competition). Since the targeting failed to consider costs, the results *de facto* were similar to those which would have obtained in the 'cut-off-imports-and-industrialize' strategy. The nature and results of Indian experience, which we have detailed at length in this study, ought to disabuse economists and policy-makers of the attractiveness of such simplistic solutions to development: there are no short-cuts to sustained and efficient growth.

List of Works Cited

I. OFFICIAL PUBLICATIONS

(1) INTERNATIONAL

INTERNATIONAL BANK FOR RECONSTRUCTION AND DEVELOPMENT

Honavar, R. M., 'Industrial Efficiency and Aid Tying', *Economic Development Institute*, IBRD, Washington, D.C., mimeo, 1967.

INTERNATIONAL MONETARY FUND

International Financial Statistics, 1947 to 1966.

ORGANISATION FOR ECONOMIC CO-OPERATION AND DEVELOPMENT

National Accounts of Less Developed Countries, O.E.C.D., Paris, July 1968.
Population of Less Developed Countries, (Research Division), O.E.C.D. Development Centre, August 1967.

UNITED NATIONS

The Yearbook of International Trade Statistics (1965), U.N., 1967.

UNITED NATIONS CONFERENCE ON TRADE AND DEVELOPMENT

Bhagwati, J., 'The Tying of Aid', UNCTAD Secretariat, New York, TD/7/Supp. 4; Item 126 (ii) of the agenda of the *New Delhi 2nd UNCTAD Conference*, February 1968; reprinted in J. Bhagwati and R. S. Eckaus (ed.), *Foreign Aid*, Penguin, 1970.
Lal, D., 'The Cost of Aid Tying: A Study of India's Chemical Industry', *UNCTAD Secretariat*, New York, 1968 (unpublished).
Narain, D., 'Aid Through Trade', *UNCTAD Secretariat*, December 1967 (unpublished).

(2) NATIONAL

INDIA

Cabinet Secretariat

Estimates of National Income, Central Statistical Organization, October 1967.

National Income Statistics: Proposals for a Revised Series, Central Statistical Organization, 1961.

Public Administration in India: Report of a Survey, (by Paul Appleby), New Delhi, 1953.

Re-examination of India's Administrative System with Special Reference to Administration of the Government's Industrial and Commercial Enterprises, (by Paul Appleby), New Delhi, 1956.

Ten Years of Indian Manufactures (1946–1955), Directorate of Industrial Statistics, Calcutta.

Department of Commercial Intelligence and Statistics

Indian Customs Tariff (50th Issue), Calcutta, 30 June 1961.

Statistical Abstracts Relating to British India: No. 35, 1890–91 to 1899–1900, pub. 1901; No. 52, 1907–08 to 1916–17, pub. 1919; No. 56, 1911–12 to 1920–21, pub. 1924; No. 65, 1930–31, pub. 1933; No. 72, 1939–40, pub. 1943.

Indian Fiscal Commissions

(First) Indian Fiscal Commission, 1921–22, Report.

Report of the Indian Fiscal Commission (1949–50), Government of India, 1951.

Lok Sabha Secretariat

Eleventh Report, Fourth Lok Sabha, 1967–68, New Delhi.

Fifty-second Report on Personnel Policies of Public Undertakings, 1963–64, New Delhi, 1964.

Ninth Report of the Committee on Industrial Licensing, New Delhi, 1967.

Sixth Report of the Committee on Public Undertakings, New Delhi, 1965.

Ministry of Commerce

Annual Report, 1964–65, New Delhi.

Basic Statistical Material Relating to Foreign Trade, Production and Prices, Annual Volume XIII, Part II, 1967.

Handbook of Export Promotion, Directorate of Commercial Publicity, New Delhi, 1967.

Import Trade Control Handbook of Rules and Procedures, 1967.
Press Note of the Ministry of Commerce on Import Policy for April 1968 to March 1969, New Delhi, 1 April 1968.
Report of the Ministry of Commerce, 1967–68, New Delhi.
Report of Study Team on Import and Export Trade Control Organization, Part I, 1965; Part II, 1966.

Ministry of Commerce and Industry

Handbook of Export Trade Control, New Delhi, 1960.
Redbooks on Import Control Policy, New Delhi, numerous dates.
Report of the Import and Export Policy Committee, New Delhi, 1962.

Ministry of Education

Progress of Education in India, 1947–1952, New Delhi, 1953.

Ministry of Finance

Annual Reports of the Working of Industrial and Commercial Undertakings of the Central Government, 1960–61 to 1965–66, New Delhi.
Economic Survey: 1967: 68, New Delhi, 1968.
Finance Acts 1963 and 1964, New Delhi.
Indian Economic Statistics, Part II (Public Finance).
Notification No. S1/F/No. 5/I–32/5/53–Cus–I, (Revenue Division), New Delhi, 28 May 1954.
Notification No. 18–CER/56, (Dept. of Revenue), New Delhi, 27 November 1956.
Report of the Central Excise Reorganization Committee, Delhi, 1963.
Report of the Committee on Utilization of External Assistance, New Delhi, 1964.
Report of Enquiry on the Administration of Dalmia-Jain Companies, New Delhi, 1963.
Report on Import Entitlement Schemes for Export Promotion, (prepared by J. Bhagwati for Ministry of Finance), 1966.
Statistical Abstracts (India): New Series: starting 1949, Office of Economic Adviser to Government of India (Ministry of Finance), New Delhi.

Ministry of International Trade

Annual Report, New Delhi, several dates (including 1965).
Report on Export Promotion for July-December 1964, New Delhi, 1965.

Ministry of Labour

Indian Labour Gazette, No. 8, February 1956.

504   LIST OF WORKS CITED

Ministry of Labour, Employment and Rehabilitation
Indian Labour Statistics, 1968.

Ministry of Railways
Supplement to the *Report of the Railway Board on Indian Railways*, 1962–63, New Delhi, 1964.

Ministry of Steel and Heavy Industries
Report of the (Raj) Committee of Steel Control, New Delhi, October 1963.

Planning Commission
First Five Year Plan, New Delhi.
Second Five Year Plan, New Delhi.
Third Five Year Plan, New Delhi.
Third Five Year Plan Progress Report, 1961–62, New Delhi.
Third Five Year Plan—A Mid-Term appraisal, New Delhi.
Third Five Year Plan Progress Report: 1963–1965, New Delhi.
Fourth Five Year Plan (A Draft Outline), New Delhi, August 1966.
Notes on Perspective of Development: 1960–61 to 1975–76, Perspective Planning Division, 1964.
Heavy Electricals (India) Limited, Committee on Plan Projects, November 1964, New Delhi.
Industrial Planning and Licensing Policy, (by R. K. Hazari), Government of India, 1967.
Report on Indian and State Administrative Services and Problems of District Administration, (by V. T. Krishnamachari), New Delhi, August 1962.

Reserve Bank of India
'Foreign Collaboration in Indian Industry', *Reserve Bank of India Bulletin*, July 1969.
Reports on Currency and Finance of the Reserve Bank of India, Bombay.
Reserve Bank of India Bulletins, Bombay, 1960–65.
Shivamaggi, H. 'Trends in Money and Real Wages in India: 1951–1961', *Reserve Bank of India Bulletin*, April 1964.
Supplement to Monetary and Banking Statistics (1950–1960), Part II, Bombay.

The Royal Commission on Labour in India
Report of the Royal Commission on Labour in India, June 1931.

State Trading Corporation Ltd.
Annual Report, 1963–64, New Delhi.

UNITED STATES

United States Information Service
Fact Sheet on United States Economic Assistance to India, New Delhi,
22 July 1968.

II. OTHER PUBLICATIONS

Arthagnani, 'How Not to Set Up and Run a Project', *Economic Weekly*,
15 May 1965.
Bailey, F. G. 'Politics and Society in Contemporary Orissa', in C. H.
Philips (ed.), *Politics and Society in India*, Oxford, 1963.
Balassa, B. 'Tariff Protection in Industrial Countries: An Evaluation',
Journal of Political Economy, LXXIII, December 1965.
Barber, C. L. 'Canadian Tariff Policy', *Canadian Journal of Economics
and Political Science*, Vol. XXI, November 1955.
Basu, Aparna. *Indian Education and Politics, 1898–1920*, Unpublished
Ph.D. dissertation, Cambridge University, 1966.
Basu, S. K. *The Managing Agency System: In Prospect and Retrospect.*
World Press Ltd., Calcutta, 1958.
Bauer, P. T. *Indian Economic Policy and Development*, 1961.
Bhagwati, J. 'Uneasy Co-existence', *Seminar*, February 1960, New
Delhi.
  'Indian Balance of Payments Policy and Exchange Auctions',
  Oxford Economic Papers, February 1962.
  'Economies of Scale, Distribution of Industry and Programming',
  Economic Weekly, 1 September 1962.
  'More on Devaluation', *Economic Weekly*, 6 October 1962.
  'The Art and Science of Targetry', *Yojana* (Planning Commission
  Journal), 13 October 1963.
  'Monopoly in Public Enterprise', in V. V. Ramanadham (ed.),
  The Working of the Public Sector, Papers and Proceedings of the
  Third All-India Seminar on Public Enterprise at Osmania Uni-
  versity, Hyderabad, December 1963, Allied Publishers, 1963.
  'On the Underinvoicing of Imports', *Bulletin of the Oxford University
  Institute of Economics and Statistics*, Vol. 26, November 1964.
  'Fiscal Policies, the Faking of Foreign Trade Declarations and the
  Balance of Payments', *Bulletin of the Oxford University Institute
  of Economics and Statistics*, Vol. 29, February 1967.
  'Why Export Receipts Lag Behind Exports', *Economic Weekly*,
  Vol. 27, 24 July 1965.
  The Economics of Underdeveloped Countries, McGraw-Hill, 1966.
  'Review of Hanson, "The Process of Planning", Oxford University
  Press, 1966', *Public Administration*, Summer 1967.

'On the Equivalence of Tariffs and Quotas', in Caves, Kenen, and Johnson (eds.), *Trade, Growth and Balance of Payments (Essays in Honor of Gottfried Haberler)*, Rand McNally, 1965.

'More on the Equivalence of Tariffs and Quotas', *American Economic Review*, March 1968.

These two papers have been rewritten together and published in: *Trade, Tariffs and Growth: Essays in the Theory of International Trade*, Weidenfeld and Nicolson, and M.I.T. Press, 1969.

The Theory and Practice of Commercial Policy: Departures from Unified Exchange Rates, International Finance Section, Princeton University, 1968.

'Trade Liberalization Among LDC's, Trade Theory and GATT Rules', in J. N. Wolfe (ed.), *Value, Capital and Growth: Essays in Honour of J. R. Hicks*, Edinburgh University Press, 1968.

Bhagwati, J. and Chakravarty, S. *Contributions to Indian Economic Analysis: A Survey*, American Economic Association, *Supplement to American Economic Review*, September 1969.

Bhagwati, J. and Srinivasan, T. N. 'Licensing and Control of Industry', paper submitted to the Prime Minister's Conference for Young Industrialists, March 1966.

Brahmananda, P. R. and Vakil, C. N. *Planning for an Expanding Economy*, Bombay, 1955.

Brecher, M. *Succession in India: A Study in Decision-making*, Oxford University Press, London, 1966.

Brimmer, A. 'Some Aspects of the Rise and Behaviour of the Business Communities in Bombay', unpublished research paper, M.I.T., Center for International Studies, August 1953.

Brown, H. *Parry's of Madras. A Story of British Enterprise in India*, Parry, Madras, 1954.

Bruton, H. J. and Bose, S. R. *The Pakistan Export Bonus Scheme* (No. 11, Monograph in the Economics of Development, April 1963), Institute of Development Economics, Karachi, Pakistan.

Buchanan, D. H. *The Development of Capitalist Enterprise in India*, Frank Cass & Co., Ltd., 1966.

Chenery, H. 'Patterns of Industrial Growth', *American Economic Review*, September 1960.

Cohen, B. 'The Stagnation of Indian Exports, 1951–1961', *Quarterly Journal of Economics*, November 1964.

Cooper, C. A. and Massell, B. 'Toward a General Theory of Customs Unions for Developing Countries', *Journal of Political Economy*, October 1965.

Corden, W. M. 'The Tariff', in Alex Hunter (ed.), *The Economics of Australian Industry*, Melbourne, Melbourne University Press, 1963.

'The Structure of a Tariff System and the Effective Protective Rate', *Journal of Political Economy*, LXXIV, June 1966.

Dantwala, M. L. 'Incentives and Disincentives in Indian Agriculture', *Indian Journal of Agricultural Economics*, April-June 1967.

Datar, B. N. *Labour Economics*, Allied Publishers, Ltd., Delhi, 1966.

Datar, B. N. and Patel, I. G. 'Employment during the Second World War', *Indian Economic Review*, February 1956.

Dell, S. *A Latin American Common Market?* London: Oxford University Press, 1966.

Desai, Padma. 'The Development of the Indian Economy: An Exercise in Economic Planning', *Oxford Economic Papers*, November 1963.

Tariff Protection in India: 1947-1965, Delhi School of Economics Monograph, 1970.

'Alternative Measures of Import Substitution', *Oxford Economic Papers*, November 1969.

'Growth and Structural Change in the Indian Manufacturing Sector, 1951-1966', *Indian Economic Journal*, 1970, forthcoming.

An Analysis of Import Substitution: 1951-1964, Delhi School of Economics Monograph, 1970.

Domar, E. D. 'A Soviet Model of Growth', in E. D. Domar, *Essays in the Theory of Growth*, New York, 1957.

Eckaus, R. S. and Parikh, K. *Planning for Growth*, M.I.T. Press, 1968.

Economic Weekly, unsigned, 'Speeding up Industrial Licensing', 18 January 1964.

The Economist Intelligence Unit, Ltd., *The State Trading Corporation and India's Export Trade*, London, 1961.

Eddison, J. *Industrial Development in the Growth of the Pulp and Paper Industry in India*, Center for International Studies, M.I.T., February 1955.

Furber, H. *John Company at Law*, Harvard University Press, Cambridge, 1951.

Gadgil, D. R. *Industrial Evolution of India*. Madras: Oxford University Press, 1924.

'Planning and Administration', Barve Memorial Lecture, 6 March 1968, Delhi (forthcoming).

Gilbert, M. *A Sample Study of Differences between Domestic and Export Pricing Policy of United States Corporations*, Temporary National Economic Committee Monograph No. 6, Part I, Washington, D.C., Government Printing Office, 1940.

Gokhale Institute of Politics and Economics, *Notes on the Rise of the Business Communities in India*, 1951.

Guha, R. *A Rule of Property for Bengal: An Essay on the Idea of Permanent Settlement*, Paris: Mouton and Company, 1963.

Habib, I. 'Potentialities of Capitalistic Development in the Economy of Mughal India', *Journal of Economic History*, Vol. XXIX, March 1969.

Hansen, Bent. *Foreign Trade Credits and Exchange Reserves*. Amsterdam: North-Holland Publishing Co., 1961.

Long- and Short-term Planning in Underdeveloped Countries, de Vries Lectures, 1966, North-Holland Series, Amsterdam, 1967.

Hanson, A. H. *The Process of Planning*. London: Oxford University Press, 1966.

Haq, Mahbub ul. 'Tied Credits: A Quantitative Analysis', in John Adler and Paul Kuznets (eds.), *Capital Movements and Economic Growth*, Macmillan, 1968.

Hazari, B. R. 'The Import Intensity of Consumption in India', *Indian Economic Review*, October 1967.

Hazari, R. K. *Structure of the Corporate Private Sector*, Asia Publishing House, Bombay, 1966.

James, R. C. 'The Casual Labour Problem in Indian Manufacturing', *Quarterly Journal of Economics*, February 1960.

Johnson, H. G. 'The Theory of Tariff Structure with Special Reference to World Trade and Development', in H. G. Johnson and P. B. Kenen (eds.), *Trade and Development*. (Etudes et Travaux de l'Institut Universitaire de Hautes Etudes Internationales.) Geneva: Libraire, 1965.

Keenan, J. *A Steel Man in India*.

Kidron, M. *Foreign Investments in India*. London: Oxford University Press, 1965.

King, Blair. 'The Origin of the Managing Agency System', *Journal of Asian Studies*, Vol. 26, November 1966.

Komiya, R. 'A Note on Professor Mahalanobis' Model of Indian Economic Planning', *Review of Economics and Statistics*, February 1959, Vol. 41.

Krishnamachari, V. T. *Fundamentals of Planning in India*. Calcutta: Orient Longmans, 1962.

Krishnamurti, J. 'Secular Changes in Occupational Structure', *Indian Economic and Social History Review*, Vol. II, No. 2, June 1965.

'Changes in the Composition of the Working Force in Manufacturing, 1901–1951: A Theoretical and Empirical Analysis', *Indian Economic and Social History Review*, March 1967.

Krishnamurthy, K. and Sastry, D. U. *Inventories in the Organised Manufacturing Sector of the Indian Economy*, Institute of Economic Growth, Delhi, 1968.

Lambert, R. *Workers, Factories and Social Change in India*. New Jersey: Princeton University Press, 1963.

Lefeber, L. and Datta-Chaudhuri, M. 'Transportation Policy in

India', in P. N. Rosenstein-Rodan (ed.), *Pricing and Fiscal Policies.* London: George Allen and Unwin Ltd., 1964.

Lewis, J. P. *Quiet Crisis in India.* Washington D.C.: Brookings Institution, 1962.

Lewis, S. R. and Soligo, R. 'Growth and Structural Change in Pakistan Manufacturing Industry, 1954–1964', *Pakistan Development Review.*

Lindblom, C. *Indian Import Controls.* New Delhi: USAID, July 1965.

Little, I. M. D. and Clifford, J. M. *International Aid.* London: George Allen and Unwin, 1965.

Mahalanobis, P. C. 'Some Observations on the Process of Growth of National Income', *Sankhya,* September 1953.

'The Approach of Operational Research to Planning in India', *Sankhya,* Vol. 16, December 1955.

Malenbaum, W. 'India and China: Development Contrasts', *Journal of Political Economy,* Vol. 64, February 1956.

'India and China: Constrasts in Development Performance', *American Economic Review,* Vol. 49, June 1959.

Mathur, P. N., Kulkarni, A. R., Venkataramaiah, P. and Narain Das, 'Notes on 32 × 32 Input–Output Table: 1963', Paper presented at Second All-India Input–Output Seminar, Poona (India), 1967.

Mazumdar, H. and Solomon, M. J. 'Inventory Holding by Manufactures in India and the United States', Indian Statistical Institute, mimeo., 1960.

Millikan, M. 'India in Transition: Economic Development: Performance and Prospects', *Foreign Affairs,* April 1968.

Morris, M. D. 'Towards a Re-interpretation of Nineteenth Century Indian Economic History', *The Journal of Economic History,* Vol. XXIII, No. 4, December 1963.

The Emergence of an Industrial Labour Force in India. Berkeley and Los Angeles: University of California Press, 1965.

Morris-Jones, W. H. 'India's Political Idioms', in C. H. Philips (ed.), *Politics and Society in India.* London: George Allen and Unwin, 1963.

Mukerjee, D. 'India in Transition: Politics of Manoeuvre', *Foreign Affairs,* April 1968.

Mukerjee, D. 'Heavy Hand of Politics on Public Sector', *Statesman,* 3 May 1968.

Mukherji, K. *Levels of Economic Activity and Public Expenditure in India: A Historical and Quantitative Study.* Poona: Gokhale Institute Studies No. 45, 1965.

Myers, C. *Labour Problems in the Industrialization of India.* Bombay: Asia Publishing House, 1958.

Naipaul, V. S. *An Area of Darkness.* Andre Deutsch, 1964.

LL

Narain, D. and Rao, V. K. R. V. *Foreign Aid and India's Economic Development*, Asia Publishing House, 1963.

Nigam, R. K. 'Composition of Boards of Directors of Government Companies', in V. V. Ramanadham (ed.), *Efficacy of Public Enterprise*, Proceedings of the Second Seminar on Public Enterprises, 1962, Allied Publishers, 1963.

Panchamukhi, V. R. 'The Problem of Import Substitution', Mimeographed, University of Bombay, 1965.

Pandit, D. P. 'Creative Response in Indian Economy: A Regional Analysis', *Economic Weekly*, 23 February and 2 March 1957.

Paranjape, H. K. *The Industrial Management Pool, An Administrative Experiment*. New Delhi: Indian Institute of Public Administration, 1963.

The Flight of Technical Personnel in Public Undertakings. New Delhi: Institute of Public Administration, 1964.

Pardiwala, 'Exchange Banks in India', *Economic Weekly*, 10 February 1951.

Patel, S. J. 'Export Prospects and Economic Growth—India', *Economic Journal*, September 1959.

Raj, K. N. *Some Economic Aspects of the Bhakra–Nangal Project*. Delhi: Asia Publishing House, 1960.

Indian Economic Growth: Performance and Prospects. Delhi: Allied Publishers, 1965.

India, Pakistan and China: Economic Growth and Outlook. Allied Publishers, 1966.

Ramaswami, V. K. and Srinivasan, T. N. 'Theory of Effective Protection under Factor Substitution', in J. Bhagwati, R. W. Jones, R. A. Mundell, and J. Vanek (eds.), Festschrift volume for C. P. Kindleberger, M.I.T. Press, 1970 (forthcoming).

Rao, V. K. R. V. 'The Public Sector in India', *Applied Economic Papers*, Osmanio University, March 1961.

(ed.), *Agricultural Labour in India* (Studies in Economic Growth, No. 3), Institute of Economic Growth. New Delhi: Asia Publishing House, 1962.

Raychaudhuri, T. 'A Re-interpretation of Nineteenth Century Indian Economic History', *The Indian Economic and Social History Review*, Vol. V (No. 1), March 1968.

'Conditions Favourable to Growth in India's Pre-colonial Economy', Paper presented to the Fourth International Economic History Congress, Bloomington, Indiana, U.S.A., 1968.

Reddaway, W. B. *The Development of the Indian Economy*. London: George Allen and Unwin Ltd., 1962.

'The Development of the Indian Economy: The Objects of the Exercise Restated', *Oxford Economic Papers*, November 1963.

Reed, Stanley. (ed.), *Indian Year Book, 1921*, Bombay, Bennett Coleman & Co. Ltd., 1929.

Rosen, G. *Some Aspects of Industrial Finance in India*, Center for International Studies, M.I.T., The Free Press of Glencoe, 1962. *Industrial Change in India*. Illinois: Free Press, 1958.

Rosenstein-Rodan, P. N. (ed.), *Pricing and Fiscal Policies*. Cambridge: M.I.T. Press, 1964.

Seth, N. R. 'An Indian Factory—Aspects of its Social Framework', *Journal of M. S. University of Baroda*, Vol. 9, March 1960.

Shah, K. T. (ed.), *Report of the National Planning Committee*, Bombay, 1944.

Shenoy, B. R. *Indian Economic Policy*, Popular Prakashan, Bombay, 1968.

Shivamaggi, H., Rajagopalan, N., and Venkatachalam, T. R. 'Wages, Labour Productivity and Costs of Production, 1951–1961', *Economic and Political Weekly*, 4 May 1968.

Shourie, A. *Allocation of Foreign Exchange in India*, unpublished Ph.D. thesis for Syracuse University, September 1966.

Singh, Manmohan. *India's Export Trends*. Oxford: Clarendon Press, 1964.

Singh, R. K. *Prosperity through Exports*, World Trade Centre, Calcutta, 1965.

Sinha, N. K. *The Economic History of Bengal*, Vol. I, firma K. K. Mukhopadhyaya, Calcutta, 1961.

Sivasabramanian, S. *National Income of India 1900–01 – 1946–47*, unpublished Ph.D. thesis submitted to Delhi University, 1965.

Smith, V. *A History of India*. Oxford University Press, 1932.

Soligo, R. and Stern, R. 'Tariff Protection, Import Substitution and Investment Efficiency', *Pakistan Development Review*, Summer 1965.

Spencer, L. *India, Mixed Enterprise and Western Business*, Martimes Nijhoft, The Hague, 1959.

Srinivas, M. N. *Caste in Modern India and Other Essays*. Asia Publishing House, 1962.

Stock Exchange Official Directory (Bombay) Vol. I, The Stock Exchange, Bombay.

Streeten, P. and Lipton, M. (eds.), *The Crisis of Indian Planning*, R.I.I.A., Oxford University Press, 1968.

Index